The Psychology of Adjustment and Well-Being

STANLEY L. BRODSKY
UNIVERSITY OF ALABAMA

The Psychology of Adjustment and Well-Being

HOLT, RINEHART AND WINSTON

New York • Chicago • San Francisco •
Philadelphia • Montreal • Toronto •
London • Sydney • Tokyo

Dedicated with love and appreciation

to my mother, Selma Brodsky Kaplan
to my son, Michael Brodsky
and to my daughter, Rachel Brodsky

Publisher *Susan Meyers*
Acquisition Editor *Heidi Udell*
Developmental Editor *Carol Einhorn*
Production Manager *Stefania Taflinska*
Production Management *York Production Services*
Composition *York Production Services*
Cover and Interior Design *York Production Services*
Photo Researcher *Nicolette C. Harlan*
Permissions Editor *Valerie Eads*
Sales Representative *Charles Pensinger*

Photo and literary credits begin on page I-17.

Printed in the United States of America

8 9 0 1   032   9 8 7 6 5 4 3 2 1

ISBN 0-03-013368-8

Library of Congress Cataloging-in-Publication Data

Brodsky, Stanley L., 1939–
  The psychology of adjustment and well-being.

  Includes bibliographies and index.
  1. Adjustment (Psychology) I. Title. [DNLM:
1. Adaptation, Psychological. 2. Mental Health.
BF 335 B864p]
BF335.B72   1988   155.2′4   87-33541
ISBN 0-03-013368-8

*W*hen a large undertaking comes to fruition, one tends to think back to the project's beginnings. As this book went through the final stages of production, I found myself making just such reflections, remembering why I initially decided to write a text on the psychology of adjustment.

To begin with, I wanted to write a text that gave a balanced presentation of the principles of adjustment. Through my own teaching of the adjustment course, and my examination of the texts available for the course, I discovered that many books attempting to be comprehensive were burdened with lists of theories and research findings. These books lacked the personal touches, which I find effectively communicate the choices and changes we all face. Other texts were overly growth-oriented, at the expense of presenting a substantive body of knowledge from the psychology literature. In this book, my effort has been to combine the personal and the academic, presenting the research in a meaningful, accessible framework.

Beyond this, I had two major goals for this book. The first was to provide students with a text that focuses not only on adjustment problems but also on adjustment successes. My personal approach to adjustment is not pathology-oriented but health-oriented. Furthermore, I knew that the readers of this book would be a basically healthy population and I wanted to emphasize situations and aspects of adjustment that would relate to their experience. To this end, I have paid a great deal of attention to the concept of personal well-being, as the title suggests.

THE WELL-BEING THEME

The term "well-being" originally came from humanistic psychology. However, like many concepts that came from particular orientations, it has now become a general term that encompasses social competence, positive affect, global life satisfaction, self-efficacy, and other descriptors of successful functioning. An essential component of this text is to look not only at adjustment, but also at the varied forms of successful functioning that comprise well-being.

The idea of well-being is explored on four levels in the book:

- *Individual Chapter Coverage*   Several chapters are dedicated in substantial part to well-being issues. Chapter 1 outlines the concept of well-being, Chapter 5 considers physical illness and well-being, Chapter 10 is about sexual adjustment and well-being, and Chapter 14 presents psycho-therapy and well-being. Chapter 15 closes the book with a summary of three overall themes in well-being.

- *Organization of Subtopics within Each Chapter*   The well-being implications of subtopics within each chapter are discussed. Thus, in Chapter 4, which covers stress, a discussion of hardiness and exceptionally successful management of stress follows the sections on stressful events. Chapter 2 presents the well-being components of each personality theory immediately following the main elaboration of that theory. Similar well-being subtopics are developed about interpersonal relationships, assertiveness, and searching for jobs, among several others.

- *"Explorations in Well-Being"*   Each chapter includes boxed exercises for the student to gain a personal understanding of the wellness issues in the chapter. Thus, when we look at imagery and healing in the chapter on Physical Health and Illness (Chapter 5), the student is presented explorations in the use of imagery to understand health concerns. An exploration in the chapter on Stress and Coping (Chapter 4) provides an opportunity to assess daily stressors and rewards. In the chapter on Loving and Being Loved (Chapter 10), the student can examine feelings toward cherished companions with the Rubin "Liking and Loving" scales.

- *Appended Presentation of Psychological Disorders*   Psychological disorders are discussed in an appended optional chapter at the end of the text, for those instructors who wish to cover this material in their adjustment courses. It is placed separately to underscore the text's focus on wellness, while at the same time to ensure that this material is an available option for instruction that more broadly emphasizes adjustmental problems and disorders.

My second goal in writing *The Psychology of Adjustment and Well-Being* was to create a book that is both scholarly and fun. A basic core of material is common to all adjustment courses, and I have tried to present this material in a straightforward, readable manner. Beyond this core, I have included content within the broad scope of adjustment that fascinated me and was fun to write about. These broader reaches of the psychology of adjustment include:

- *Emphasis on Nonverbal Communication*   I have devoted an entire chapter (Chapter 9) to nonverbal behaviors. More emotion is communicated nonverbally than verbally, and emotions and feelings are critical to the understanding of the psychology of adjustment. Typically, however, nonverbal communication receives only minor coverage. In this chapter, I have incorporated units that involve the reader, asking students to observe others around them, to try out demonstration exercises, and to learn through photographs and drawings.

- *Emphasis on Cross-Cultural Differences*   Cross-cultural material on adjustment is, similarly, not usually included in adjustment texts. I have assumed that students will share my interest in the ways culture influences communication and adjustment. In Bangalore, India, when people shake their heads from side to side, it does not indicate disagreement, as we would assume, but agreement. The academic expectations for a high-school student in Japan are markedly more stressful than those held in this country. We can observe these cultural influences on behaviors that range from specific interactions with friends to our general values and societal pressures. Most of the chapters in the text discuss such cross-cultural observations.

- *"Focus on Development" Boxes*   All of us are interested in how we will change over the course of our lives. Adjustment translates into one set of demands for an 18 year old and quite another for a 50 year old. While some common issues will always be present, enough differences exist over the life cycle to call for particular attention. The "Focus on Development" boxes interspersed throughout the text discuss changes pertaining to such developmental issues as the self-concept, friendships, vocational choice, and different psychotherapies for different age groups. In addition, one chapter is devoted fully to adjustment over the life cycle.

A diversity of fascinating topics is only the foundation of what makes a text pleasurable, however. This also requires putting into written words the sense of excitement many of us feel in talking about psychological concepts.

It means tying in elements from daily life experiences, and from literature and poetry, with scientific knowledge. All of these are rich sources of information about human behavior, and drawing upon them helps present the psychology of adjustment in an accessible, meaningful way.

THE ORGANIZATION OF THE TEXT

Part I: Overview of Adjustment and Well-Being

The first three chapters introduce the study of adjustment through the major theories and issues in the field. Chapter 1 discusses the nature of adjustment from its emergence in the mental hygiene movement and then into its more contemporary meanings. These core definitions lead to the concept of well-being and the process of attaining well-being by exercising choice and control in one's life. Chapter 2 examines psychoanalytic, behavioral, and humanistic theories of personality. Each personality theory is related to the concepts of adjustment and well-being developed in the first chapter. Chapter 3 considers the self-concept and self-esteem as continuing components of personality that influence most adjustmental demands and successes.

Part II: The Individual

Some demands for adjustment arise more from within the individual's characteristics and some others arise more from situations and other people (although it is clear that all adjustment issues have some of both elements). Part II discusses those demands and adjustments that have strong individual components. Chapter 4 presents the nature of stress in daily events and in catastrophic events, and then examines healthy as well as problematic ways of coping with such stressors. Chapter 5 carries these issues forward into the particular kinds of stressful circumstances imposed by physical illness. The chapter concludes with the uses of imagery and other means of pursuing high-level wellness. Chapter 6 looks at nonassertive and aggressive individuals, and points the way toward effective assertiveness. Then, Chapter 7 reviews individual transitions throughout the life cycle, concluding with the problems and solutions in the last events in the life cycle: death and dying.

Part III: Adjustment and Well-Being with Others

These four chapters explore aspects of relationships with significant people in our lives. Chapter 8 looks at interpersonal relationships in general, and at friendships and the development of rewarding and positive relationships in particular. Chapter 9 offers an understanding of nonverbal communications, the means through which feelings are expressed both voluntarily and involuntarily. Awareness of nonverbal messages allows more personal mastery of oneself with others. Chapter 10 considers romantic love, in terms of both the giving and receiving involved. Infatuation and falling in love are distinguished from longer-lasting forms of loving. Chapter 11 focuses on sexual adjustment. First, problems in sexual adjustment are described, followed by discussion of sex therapies, and then of celibacy and sexual well-being resolutions.

Part IV: Competency and Achievement

While the prior sections have been concerned with the individual alone and with others, this part is concerned with mastery and completion of specific life tasks. Chapter 12 considers the nature of work, what kinds of work are least and most rewarding, and finally career choice and job searching. Chapter 13 attends to our interactions with the physical environment, such as places in which we work and live, and our subjective environments, such as the experience of time. Chapter 14 delves into the task of psychotherapy; what it is, how well it works, and ways in which one can benefit most and help others. Finally, Chapter 15 refocuses on the well-being theme that appears in other chapters. This concluding chapter considers the extent to which we may determine our own lives, and the nature of self-fulfillment and peak experiences in life.

PEDAGOGICAL AIDS

Several features of the book were included to aid the learning process. Each chapter opens with an outline of the major topics that will be discussed and closes with a point-by-point summary of the chapter contents. The key terms are listed at the end of the chapter for review purposes. These terms are again listed at the end of the book in a complete glossary.

SUPPLEMENTARY MATERIALS

This text is accompanied by a complete program of ancillaries designed to enhance learning and teaching.

Study Guide

The *Study Guide* is a manual of review materials for the student, organized into chapters that correspond to the text. Each chapter contains a chapter overview, learning objectives, a list of key terms, suggested related readings, and a self-test segment comprised of true/false, multiple-choice, and essay questions.

The *Study Guide* should help students develop good study habits and provide hints for preparing for exams. In addition, five of the multiple choice questions in each chapter are also included in the *Instructor's Test Item File;* this may further motivate students to use these materials for review.

Instructor's Manual and Test Bank

The *Instructor's Manual* is organized into chapters as well. Each chapter includes a chapter outline, teaching objectives, lecture suggestions, discussion questions, class projects, and annotated film suggestions. An introduction explains how best to make use of the manual, and appendices offer suggestions for how to construct a syllabus and a test.

Immediately following these teaching aids is a test item file containing 75 multiple choice questions for every chapter in the text. Each question is coded with the correct answer, the text page reference, and whether the item tests knowledge or application.

Computerized Test Banks

A computerized test item file is available for use on the Apple and IBM personal computers.

ACKNOWLEDGMENTS

There are many people I would like to recognize for their labors and contributions to this text. First, Carol Einhorn, my Developmental Editor at Holt, Rinehart and Winston, who joined me in the Herculean effort of editing and revising the manuscript. She extended kind humor and episodes of saintly forgiveness for my missed deadlines. Susan Meyers, Publisher at Holt, and Heidi Udell, Acquisitions Editor for Psychology, were also planners and conceptualizers for the project. Susan Bogle, Production Coordinator for York Production Services, extended extraordinary efforts in managing the production of the text. I am indebted, too, to Warren Abraham, who is now the Psychology Editor at John Wiley and Sons, for two years of constructive collaboration during the book's early stages, and for a continuing friendship.

Many students and colleagues have helped as well. Ann Freeman, Katherine Clausell, Carolyn Robinson, Kathy Ronan, Renee Hutto, Mike Brodsky, and David White have provided wonderful assistance in library research. Among the colleagues to whom I am grateful are Constance Fischer, Jill Bley, Allison Morris, Howard Miller, Ronald Rogers, Elizabeth McDonel, Madelaine Hill, Donald West and Richard Dana. The careful typing of the manuscripts was done by Ann Jones, Leona Johnson, Tammye

Herring, and Houston Lockett. Finally, many reviewers have been generous with their ideas and responses to the book. I particularly wish to acknowledge the contributions of Marsha Beauchamp, Mt. San Antonio Community College; Jack Bushey, Harrisburg Community College; Desmond Cartwright, University of Colorado; Kenneth Davidson, Wayne State University; Edwin Druding, Phoenix College; Jim Ferguson, Oregon State University; Bennie Gilbert, Stephens College; Knud Larsen, Oregon State University; Robert MacAleese, Spring Hill College; James Nevitt, Mid-Plains Community College; James Riley, Southeastern Massachusetts University; Mike Scheible, Gateway Technical Institute; Dale Schroer, Fresno City College; Adolph Streng, Eastfield College; and David Weight, Brigham Young University.

S.L.B.
Tuscaloosa, Alabama
December, 1987

BRIEF CONTENTS

 P A R T IV

COMPETENCY AND ACHIEVEMENT

PART I

OVERVIEW OF ADJUSTMENT AND WELL-BEING

2 _____

3 _____

P A R T II

THE INDIVIDUAL

4

7 —————————————————————————

P A R T III

ADJUSTMENT AND WELL-BEING WITH OTHERS

8

|| _____

P A R T IV

COMPETENCY AND ACHIEVEMENT

12

13

FEATURES

Overview of Adjustment and Well-Being

CHAPTER 1

Adjustment and Well-Being: An Introduction

Transformation

It is just possible that high school gym classes and locker rooms are the sources of more embarrassment and teasing than any other adolescent experience. That certainly was true for Jeffrey Bellingrath. It all started when one boy in his gym class said Jeffrey walked like a duck, with his feet pointed way out to the side. "You walk stupid, Jeffrey!" the boy yelled. "You waddle. Look at Jeffrey waddle, look at Jeffrey waddle."

At that point, another boy called out, "Quack, quack, quack," and soon a chorus of quacking noises followed Jeffrey throughout the class, into the locker room, and out of the school yard. As humiliating as these noises were to Jeffrey, what made it worse was that he thought they were right. Once the boys had teased him, he began to watch how he walked, and he did put the right foot pointing far to the right, and he did place his left foot pointing far to the left, and he did sort of sway and waddle.

Jeffrey fought back the tears and said nothing to the continued teasing and the continued quacking. However, from that day on, he did concentrate on how he walked. Keep from waddling like a duck, that's what he wanted. He carefully put his feet one in front of the other in a straight line. If he did not pay attention, his feet would go back to pointing to the side, so he had to watch them much of the time.

Teenage boys rarely can talk to their parents about being teased. So when Mr. and Mrs. Bellingrath asked him what was wrong, he shrugged and said, "Nothing." His parents were aware he often no longer looked them in the eye. They interpreted his looking down at his feet as a sign he had done something wrong. Late at night, Mr. and Mrs. Bellingrath would talk about what might have happened. Jeffrey had always been such a good boy. Could it be depression? Was he thinking of suicide? If not that, it must be guilt they were seeing. Drugs. Perhaps that was it. Drugs. So many teenagers are using drugs nowadays. All week long, they worried, they asked, they watched. Jeffrey said nothing.

The gym teacher called Jeffrey aside the next week. Mr. Hardy had seen the teasing and understood what was happening. He saw Jeffrey looking down, and he noticed the careful placement of feet north and south, never pointing east or west. And he saw how much this effort shut Jeffrey off from others. He told Jeffrey what he saw.

"Mr. Hardy, I just can't stand all those boys quacking at me. I feel so stupid, like such a jerk."

"Jeffrey, my grandfather used to tell me something that has to do with you. He would say 'Where there's muck, there's brass!'"

"What does that mean?"

"It means that in the most ugly, unpleasant things in life, there are really valuable things, too. Your walking to the side—you may think that's muck, but now that's something that ballet dancers—men and women—work for years to develop. They exercise, they practice, they train. You can tell a really great dancer because his feet point out when he walks. It gives him stability and grace and poise. And martial arts experts do this, too. They learn to keep their feet pointed out because then they can't be easily knocked down. It gives them balance. What you are trying to get rid of is what thousands of athletes are trying to achieve."

Mr. Hardy had Jeffrey stand feet pointing ahead, and then to the side, to show him how much better balanced he was the latter way.

Mr. and Mrs. Bellingrath were pleased to see that what had been happening was a passing phase. Jeffrey stopped looking down, except now and then. When the boys said "Quack quack, quack quack," Jeffrey came right back at them with "Quack quack, quack quack," and the quacking soon became a distant memory.

Let's consider what happened with Jeffrey. His looking down as he practiced walking straight was misinterpreted. The people closest to him thought he was acting differently. In fact, he *was* acting strangely. He was paying less attention to them and more attention to his feet. Jeffrey adjusted his walk because of his classmate's comment that he waddled like a duck.

Changes in people important to us produce changes in us. We often worry or wonder. Jeffrey's behaviors were a passing preoccupation, but they created feelings of neglect or isolation in his parents. While their interpretations were not on target, they were right that Jeffrey's behavior had changed. The behavior of some of Jeffrey's classmates had changed, too. He now had to deal with new and different demands in his gym class. Reacting to different life demands is what adjustment is about. This book looks at current psychological knowledge about the ways we adjust to the demands of our companions, our environments, our bodies, and our emotions.

Each chapter considers both adjustment deficiencies and well-being opportunities. Adjustment deficiencies are ways in which we are not able to cope successfully with life's demands, so that we feel unhappy and ineffective in attaining our goals.

Possibilities for resolving adjustment difficulties will be presented for each topic. No single grand insight can resolve the uncertainties in living or can master all adjustment challenges. Hardly. But pathways that we may *choose* to follow can sometimes be identified, and some of them are presented in this text.

THE BACKGROUND OF A PSYCHOLOGY OF ADJUSTMENT

Behind the psychology of adjustment lie a series of events that are like the foundation of a building. While not visible, they are the basic structure onto which the visible part has been constructed. The first event was the

Mental hygiene movement

development of the ***mental hygiene movement,*** the direct parent of the psychology of adjustment.

The Mental Hygiene Movement

When thirty-year-old Yale graduate Clifford Beers was released from his psychiatric hospitalization in 1904, he boiled with indignation at the way psychiatric patients were treated and how little knowledge existed about psychological problems. Beers wrote a best-selling book, *A Mind That Found Itself* (1907), and, in 1909, founded the National Committee for Mental Hygiene. Beers was a compelling speaker and a tireless campaigner on behalf of mental patients. As a result of his efforts, the pursuit of mental hygiene became a well-established movement in the first half of the twentieth century.

This movement compared psychological adjustment to physical adjustment, promoting an attitude best captured in the saying "a strong mind in a strong body." Mental hygiene was felt to be promoted by avoiding exposure to illness-causing environments, by understanding rather than blaming the sufferers, and by scientifically building strength and mental resistance. Heightened emotional flexibility was particularly valued.

In 1936, Laurance Shaffer wrote a widely used book titled *The Psychology of Adjustment: An Objective Approach to Mental Hygiene.* Shaffer criticized the practices of lecturing and punishing individuals with problems in living, pointing out that social ridicule only made the problems worse. He condemned the prevailing view that a self-application of common sense would straighten out any maladjustments. The mental hygiene movement sought to eliminate the negative judgments about maladjustment and instead to substitute a scientific understanding of human adjustment. Shaffer defined mental hygiene this way:

> Mental hygiene refers to the prevention of inadequate adjustments and to the processes by which maladjusted persons are restored to normal living. Mental hygiene is therefore a practical art. . .

> *(Shaffer, 1936, p. 435)*

The success of the mental hygiene movement can be seen by how widely its assertions have become part of general social beliefs. Typical statements of the mental hygienist were that people must like themselves in order to have sound mental health, that one should build up rather than tear down another's self-worth, that reality must be faced directly, that blaming people for their maladjustments is futile, and that we all struggle constantly to meet our basic needs (Carroll, 1947).

Adjustment

By 1950, the term *hygiene* had lost some of its original meaning as "healthful" and began to be used in the more limited sense of "cleanliness." The word **adjustment** quickly replaced mental hygiene in college courses as well as professional usage, and the meaning of adjustment expanded as well.

Five meanings emerged that have persisted to the present time. These are

Adjustment

Normality

1. *Adjustment as **normality**.*   Normality may be thought of statistically, so that adjustment would be like the arithmetic average, describing the typical person. It also may be defined as the absence of incapacitating

PART I.

Origin, Objects and Plans
OF
The National Committee for Mental Hygiene

PART II.
(Pages 6 and 7)

The Mental Hygiene Movement
State Societies for Mental Hygiene

PART III.
(Pages 8 to 13)

Information regarding the following topics:

1. Importance of the problem of mental health and the care of the insane.
2. The prevalence of insanity.
3. Present increase of our insane population in institutions.
4. Annual number of commitments.
5. Chances for recovery.
6. The cost of caring for the insane.
7. The economic loss through mental disease.
8. Is insanity increasing ?
9. The nature, causes and prevention of mental disorders.
10. Marriage of feeble-minded, and immigration, as prolific sources of insanity.

N. C. M.

PART IV
(Pages 14 and 15)

Description of Mental Hygiene Exhibit
List of Publications

PUBLISHED BY
THE NATIONAL COMMITTEE FOR MENTAL HYGIENE
50 UNION SQUARE, NEW YORK
1912

The psychology of adjustment is a direct descendant of the mental hygiene movement. This movement, started in the early 1900s, promoted the understanding rather than the condemnation of people with psychological problems. Many of the movement's assertions have become part of current social beliefs; for instance, the movement promoted the ideas that psychological adjustment is like physical adjustment and that, by avoiding exposure to illness-causing environments, people can expect better mental health (a strong mind in a strong body).

problems arising from internal or social conditions (Sawry & Telford, 1963). This view of adjustment will be elaborated as part of the well-being section.

Internal harmony

2. *Adjustment as **internal harmony**.*   This is the concept that adjustment is freedom from internal strife and comfort with personal needs and values.

Social competence

3. *Adjustment as **social competence**.*   Human beings live in environments made up of other individuals, of social groups, and of organized institutions. Adjustment means effectively dealing with these social environments so that one's goals are reasonably met.

Mastery of changing demands

4. *Adjustment as **mastery of changing demands**.*   Change is a basic characteristic of our society. Technological change is rapid and accelerating. People frequently change jobs, places of residence, and other immediate environments. Every year a new threat to drinking water or to the ozone layer or in the form of a new sexually transmitted disease appears. Managing such changing conditions in a successful manner is part of adjustment.

Self-fulfillment

5. *Adjustment as **self-fulfillment**.*   This definition includes meanings 2, 3, and 4—internal harmony, social competence, and mastery of changing demands. It goes beyond these as well to address the realization of potential, including emotional potential, intellectual potential, interpersonal potential, and general potential for satisfaction and happiness as a human being. Total fulfillment of potential is never expected, but movement toward that goal is important. This component of adjustment will be discussed shortly under the heading of well-being.

These five definitions of adjustment are used in this book. However, one concept related to adjustment as self-fulfillment will be developed, that of well-being. Well-being is not independent of adjustment, but instead presents its own particular emphasis.

WELL-BEING

Well-being

Maybe the best way to explain to you about the nature of ***well-being*** is to tell you about my friend Ann. Ann is not happy all the time. Nor is she secure all the time. At the moment I write this, a member of her family is ill, and she is worried. She has taken on more than she should have. She has less time than she chooses for pleasure. In spite of these pressures on her, she remains productive in her work and is usually cheerful with her friends and colleagues. Ann is a person who, at bad and good times in her life, is able to find friends, activities, and ways of thinking and feeling that positively influence her. If Ann were serenely comfortable in most aspects of her life, we might think about applying the label "self-actualized" to her, but that would not really be accurate. Rather, Ann is a person who has achieved a high level of well-being because she knows many pathways to well-being.

Well-being is a subjective emotional state that includes positive affect (feelings of happiness and pleasure), relatively little negative affect (feelings of unhappiness, depression, and anxiety), and general life satisfaction (one's overall weighing of gratification and contentment in one's life).

The Maladjustment to Well-Being Continuum

So what is well-being? Well-being is not simply the absence of problems. I can explain this by asking you to imagine a seesaw. The midpoint in the seesaw can be called adjustment. It is a time when everything is in balance, although sometimes this is only a momentary balance. Thus, the demands of life are in balance with our abilities to manage them. In psychological terms, this midpoint is the absence of maladjustment. Everything is neither great nor terrible at that moment. We have no sense of being overwhelmed, of being impossibly frustrated, of being unable to keep on with the pressing difficulty of the moment. Nor is there any feeling of profound satisfaction.

Maladjustment

At the left side of the seesaw midpoint is ***maladjustment.*** When this end of the seesaw is down, we are miserable, ineffective, and stuck. Some demand of life has presented us with a situation that is disastrous (or at least burdensome). Such a life situation can be something going wrong in our bodies, or some demands made by people around us, or some events in our physical environments. When such events seem to outweigh everything else, we may feel helpless or frustrated or without purpose in life, and that left end of the seesaw tilts way down. This is maladjustment.

EXPLORATION IN WELL-BEING

Maladjustments, Adjustments, and Well-Being

This exploration invites you to consider your own major areas of possible maladjustment, means of adjusting, and well-being in the critical areas in your life. Listed below are the topics covered in this text. For each one, indicate first what your possible personal maladjustment may have been. Since this is for your own use, it is not necessary to write out a description of the maladjustment—instead, put down a word, a name, or even a letter or a drawing that would indicate what it is. Consider that the possible maladjustment would have been a time of internal strife for you, you may have felt incompetent in some social situation, or you may have experienced some inability to handle a changing demand in your life. Then in the middle column—using the same method of signaling to yourself by giving a word or letter or name—indicate what you did to bring yourself back into balance. Finally, on the far right, indicate the events or means that helped you to achieve well-being—high positive feelings or satisfactions with this aspect of your life. It is not necessary to fill in each blank. Each of the listed topics are the subject of a chapter in this book. The tables at the end of Chapters 3 through 15 will present the nature of moving toward well-being and away from well-being for each of these challenges.

For some people, life is a matter of ups and downs between the two points of maladjustment and adjustment. Things are either truly worrisome or they are simply okay, and their feelings shift depending on many factors. These two points on our hypothetical seesaw will be the subject of the largest part of this book. We know a great deal about maladjustment and the process of getting adjusted and back in balance. However, one particular perspective will appear in this book—that of well-being, which is located on the far right side of the mental seesaw.

Well-Being Defined

Positive affect
Negative affect
General life satisfaction

Well-being is more than the simple absence of maladjustment or the holding of self in an equilibrium between discomfort and comfort. Well-being is a subjective emotional state of *positive affect* (affect means emotions or feelings), relatively low *negative affect*, and *general life satisfaction* (Diener, 1984). Positive affect includes the feelings of happiness, pleasure, enjoyment, joy, and fun. Negative affect sometimes coexists with positive affect. Negative affect includes the presence of substantial feelings of unhappiness, depression, anger, frustration, or anxiety. Life satisfaction,

	Possible Maladjustments	Adjustments	Well-Being
Self-concept: The total way you feel about yourself			
Physical health and illness			
Asserting yourself and handling anger			
Transitions from one phase in your life to another			
Friendships and other interpersonal relationships			
Communicating to others, especially nonverbally			
Loving and being loved			
Sexual adjustment			
Work and career			
Comfort and efficiency in your immediate environment			
Helping others and being helped			
Other issues personal just to you			

the third component of well-being, is a cognitive judgment. It refers to the overall assessment one makes of one's life. Life satisfaction goes beyond feelings about a single event; rather, it is the total weighing of gratification and contentment.

Well-being has the following four characteristics:

1. *It is subjective and emotional.*   It is what the individual feels and thinks about himself or herself. No right or wrong absolutes are present, because the imposition of right or wrong judgments are part of adjustment to society. Most psychologists write about well-being as subjective well-being (SWB) for that reason.

2. *It is a state.*   It is temporary in nature, and not a continuous part of who we are. Psychologically healthy and hardy people may have more frequent instances of well-being than other people, but, as with all of

A GUIDE TO EXPLORATIONS IN WELL-BEING

Close your mouth and gently press your finger against the *right* side of your nose so that the airflow in and out passes only through your *left* nostril.

If you keep this up for five minutes, a shift in brain wave activity is likely to occur. Studies of brain wave activity on the left and right hemispheres of the brain indicate that breathing through the left nostril yields more right hemisphere activity. That, in turn, is associated with more symbolic, intuitive thinking and feeling (Shannahoff-Khalsa, 1984). Why would left nostril breathing lead to more right hemisphere activity? Because there is a crossing over of cerebral nerve pathways, so that left-side functions tend to be seated in the right hemisphere, and vise-versa.

The boxes throughout this book fall into two categories: *explorations* of the kind that are usually labelled as right hemisphere, and more descriptive explanations of issues, the kind of activity that is usually labelled as left hemisphere. Note that the labels are oversimplifications of complex cerebral activities. Still, they allow us to discuss these brain functions.

Close your mouth and gently press your finger against the *left* side of your nose so that the airflow in and out passes only through your *right* nostril.

Now a person monitoring your brain waves would see a shift. More activity would be present in the left hemisphere. You may feel or think differently, having changed from left to right nostril breathing. Under normal circumstances (without breathing cycles of this sort), you would not be aware of shifts between right and left hemisphere activity. Yet this simple, not unpleasant method seems to

us, this state comes and goes. There is no one personality type that experiences well-being more often than others. An investigation of how much personality traits contribute to SWB found modest figures. Personality traits accounted for 8 percent, 20 percent, and 14 percent of the variance (a measure of relative contribution) of positive affect, negative affect, and life satisfaction, respectively (Emmons & Diener, 1985).

3. *It is the product of personal strivings.*   Personal strivings are the goals or purposes individuals characteristically seek to meet through their everyday behaviors. All three components of well-being—positive affect, negative affect, and life satisfaction—have been found to be significantly related to perceptions of accomplishment of personal strivings (Emmons, 1986).

promote a shift some people can feel—and use. The alternation of nasal passage breathing is part of Yoga exercises that is described as promoting a feeling of peace. Contemporary research suggests it may be a vehicle for learning about yourself.

> Certain cognitive functions, such as language skills, mathematics and other rational processes that are thought to be primarily localized in the left hemisphere, might possibly be augmented by breathing through the right nostril for 10 to 15 minutes. Forced breathing though the left nostril might accentuate the creativity that is thought to be characteristic of right-hemisphere intelligence.

> *(Shannahoff-Khalsa, 1984, p. 73)*

In this book, some boxes offer explorations in personal well-being; they are not intended to teach in the expected way that textbooks teach. Instead, they are invitations to try out personal possibilities related to the topics of the chapter. When the self-concept is discussed, you will be invited to learn more about your own self-concept. When stress and coping are presented, you will have the opportunity to examine your own stresses and coping styles.

Other boxes are small steps to the side of the main text. Sometimes they are too informal to be in the text proper—material that might produce a puzzled "huh?" had it not been identified as an aside. Other times information is in a box because it presents a small unit of knowledge complete in itself.

It isn't necessary to breathe through the left nostril while reading about and trying the personal explorations, nor breathing through the right nostril while reading the text itself. Like all such opportunities for personal explorations in this text, they are invitations to sample, at your convenience, many items from a large menu of personal possibilities.

4. *It is more than the absence of negative affect and personal conflicts.* While much relief and satisfaction can be felt from the simple escape from (or resolution of) personal conflict, this state falls short of well-being. A well-being experience comes from moving toward desired life goals and toward desired ways of being.

Well-being thus encompasses the deliberate movement toward, as well as the achievement of, positive emotional states. The right side of the mental seesaw is heaviest in well-being, but since it is a state, we can predict it will go up and down at times.

When pressures accumulate too much, individuals may be in a maladjusted state, with much distress. When a person is experiencing stress but managing it more or less okay, then the person is in a state of adjustment. If a person thrives on a particular problem, finds it challenging and within control, then he or she feels well-being. A person doesn't always have to be in a state of full-blown, shout-to-the-world well-being to be moving along that path. Rather, a person may be a little ways along the seesaw, tilting in the direction of well-being.

How is well-being attained? That is, how do we get that right-hand side of the imaginary seesaw to go down often? A heavy subject. And for the purposes of this text, a heady subject: heady, meaning both exhilarating and cognitive. Many of the solutions to be examined in this text are **cognitive,** explaining how to *think* about adjustment and well-being issues. Thus, in the chapter on loving, one pathway to well-being is concentration: to concentrate (at least part of the time) on the person with whom you are involved and not to try to listen to music, watch television, read, or eat at the same time. In the chapter on psychotherapy, the well-being suggestions are to consider self-therapy and to help others. In the chapter on the self-concept, information is given on how to reduce uncomfortable gaps between the private self and public self-presentation.

These possible solutions are called "cognitive" because as a student you are reading about them, not living them, not doing them, not necessarily acting on them. In a recent book about how people change, James Prochaska (1984) argued that **precontemplation** and then **contemplation** stages are necessary before people change. In precontemplation, you have to get ready to think about changing, to decide that something should be done. In the contemplation phase, you start thinking about what actually should be done, the actions that should be taken. That's why the suggested pathways to well-being are included in this text: to offer material for contemplation, and to provide information that you may wish to use as part of deciding whether you wish to be different as a person.

Remember my friend Ann? She moves often to states of well-being by several means. Her positive affect develops quietly and peacefully, as she allows happy feelings to flow into her mind. She talks to people she

Cognitive

*Precontemplation
Contemplation*

loves—to her husband, to her good friends—and is enlivened by them. Life satisfaction comes as she throws herself into her dancing, an activity that allows her to feel whole, and into her work as a therapist, because making others better helps keep her well. As Ann's mental seesaw moves up and down, she is able to lean enough to the right to carry a sense of well-being much of the time. When I ask her how much, she says at least half the time—not a bad proportion of well-being at all.

In this outline, I have described people as sitting sometimes on the left extreme of maladjustment: sometimes on the middle range of adjustment; and sometimes on the right side, the more rewarding and satisfying end, well-being. In discussing many of the topics in this book, I will follow the same order. First I will talk about some ways things have gone wrong—the problems or difficulties or criticisms. Then I will move to adjustment, and finally to well-being.

Surveys of Well-Being

Now that some basic assumptions about well-being have been presented, you may be wondering how extensive well-being is in Americans. The major source of information about well-being has been national surveys of happiness and life satisfaction. These surveys follow the familiar procedures of political pollsters. That is, the pollsters select a sample of one or two thousand people based on a recent census and generalize their answers on the survey to the American population.

In these national surveys, positive affect is measured in several ways, but one consistent measure has been the simple interview question: "Taking all things together, how would you say things are these days—would you say you are very happy, pretty happy, or not too happy?" Life satisfaction is assessed by an equally straightforward approach: the subjects are asked to rate on a seven-point scale how happy they are with their lives as a whole these days. While as many as sixty-eight measures of global well-being have been employed (Andrews & Withey, 1976), the answer to this one question is used to judge overall life satisfaction. Although it may seem a bit simplistic to depend on the answers to just one question, the answers are valuable. Almost everyone has thoughts about overall life satisfaction, and the majority of Americans do a running evaluation of personal life satisfaction. Although the findings were reported in the mid-1970s, there is a sound basis for believing that they apply equally to the current time (Diener, 1984).

Positive affect has been found to partly, but not totally, relate to overall life satisfaction. The relationship in a sample of 2,147 persons in a nationwide sample is shown in Figure 1–1. Of those individuals who indicated they were "completely satisfied" with their overall lives, 59 percent indicated they were very happy, 40 percent were pretty happy

FIGURE 1-1 Reports of Happiness by Degree of Overall Satisfaction with Life

From Campbell, Converse & Rodgers, 1976, p. 35.

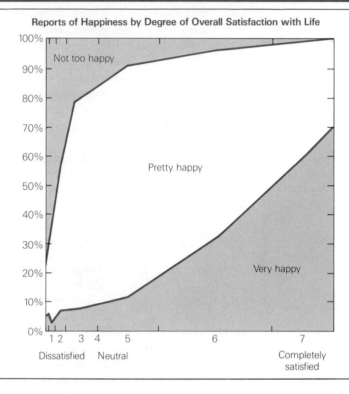

Reports of Happiness by Degree of Overall Satisfaction with Life

and 1 percent were not too happy these days (Campbell, Converse & Rodgers, 1976, p. 35). On the other end, of those who felt completely dissatisfied with their lives, 74 percent were not too happy, 21 percent were pretty happy, and only 5 percent were very happy.

Americans are generally high in life satisfaction. Thus, in the Campbell, Converse and Rodgers (1976) study, 65 percent of the respondents rated their lives (on a seven-point scale) as a six or seven—that is, highly enjoyable. Other ratings showed that 62 percent recorded a six or seven for rewarding lives, 70 percent for worthwhile, 70 percent for friendly and 68 percent for hopeful.

What in daily life accounts for a global sense of well-being? The most important items cited are listed in the table at the top of p. 15, "Factors Accounting for a Global Sense of Well-Being."

The best way of interpreting these findings is to simply count areas of satisfaction and assume the higher the number, the more satisfied a person will be. However, it may also be that some still-to-be-determined number of minimum satisfactions must be present before we have clear sense of personal well-being.

Factors Accounting for a Global Sense of Well-Being	
Satisfaction with life apart from working hours	29%*
Family life	28%
Standard of living	23%
Work	18%
Marriage	16%
Savings and investments	15%
Friendships	13%
City or county	11%
Housing	11%
Amount of education	9%

*Variance estimates

The other major survey of the American public appeared in the book by Frank Andrews and Stephen Withey, *Social Indicators of Well-Being* (1976). Their project studied all three aspects of well-being: positive affect, negative affect, and life satisfaction. They drew three separate samples, ranging from 1,072 to 1,433 individuals.

To find out about positive affect, the survey asked respondents how happy they were. The results on a seven-point scale are given in the table, "Respondents' Perceptions of Their Own Happiness."

Respondents' Perceptions of Their Own Happiness	
Delighted	13%
Pleased	40%
Mostly satisfied	33%
Mixed	9%
Mostly dissatisfied	3%
Unhappy	1%
Terrible	1%

From Andrews & Withey, 1976, p. 319.

More detailed information about positive affect is seen in Table 1–1. At least 50 percent of the individuals who responded had felt excited, proud, pleased, and that things were going their way at least several times in the prior few weeks. Similar high percents were found for respondents' feeling that things were interesting, enjoyable, worthwhile, full, and rewarding for them.

The results for negative affect are also seen in Table 1–1. Restlessness was the most frequently felt of these negative emotions, with 26 percent of the people having had several episodes of restlessness and 16 percent having had a lot of restless episodes. In contrast, 76 percent had not

TABLE 1-1   Positive and Negative Affects in Recent Weeks

	Never	Once	Several	A Lot
Positive affects				
Excited	36%	11%	40%	13%
Proud	30%	16%	47%	7%
Pleased	20%	13%	57%	10%
On top of the world	68%	6%	20%	6%
Things going your way	32%	7%	50%	11%
Negative affects				
Restless	50%	8%	26%	16%
Lonely	76%	7%	12%	5%
Bored	63%	7%	22%	8%
Depressed	69%	8%	18%	5%
Upset	81%	11%	7%	1%

From Andrews & Withey, 1976, p. 321.

experienced loneliness, 63 percent had no boredom, 69 percent had not been depressed, and 81 percent had not been upset in the prior few weeks.

Finally, satisfaction with life as a whole was investigated. Nineteen percent indicated they found life as a whole completely satisfying; 69 percent found it pretty satisfying; 12 percent found it not very satisfying. These results support the findings of the Campbell, Converse, and Rodgers (1976) study. Most Americans find life at least pretty satisfying, and they report much more positive affect than negative affect. Thus, research does not agree with the outlook of Henry David Thoreau, who wrote that "The mass of men lead lives of quiet desperation." Instead, Americans in general have predominantly positive affect and satisfaction with living. Only a minority lead lives of desperation, and there is no reason to believe they are quiet about it.

In these surveys, what individuals say about themselves is accepted. No opportunity exists to look into excessive self-criticism or overly optimistic self-presentation. Nevertheless, such obvious information of what people report is valuable by itself. The box, "In Praise of Obvious Solutions," explores that issue of valuing simple and straightforward sources of knowledge.

Less obvious sources of information will be explored later in this book. As the text moves through the topics of self-concept in Chapter 3, and then stress and coping in Chapter 4, we will examine self-presentation and defense mechanisms. After all, when individuals overstate or understate how they feel about themselves, we want to sort out their real feelings from their style of presentation. To paraphrase the poet Louis Simpson,

"You couldn't be nearly as desirable as you think you are for I heard you singing" (1983, p. 139). We will be taking a close look at the ways in which people unrealistically see themselves as desirable and as undesirable.

Conformity and Adjustment

Well-being and adjustment to life demands include a reconciliation of individual goals with societal needs. What others want for us does not necessarily coincide with what we want, or even with what is best, for ourselves. We are always confronted with the questions of forced conformity.

When I told a psychologist friend I was writing an adjustment text-book, she indignantly asked, "How could *you* write a book about *adjust-ment?*" She felt adjustment always means compromise. Certainly all of us are exposed to various pressures from people and institutions. Part of

Conformity, a goal of many cult groups, often requires people to surrender important aspects of their individuality. Here, Reverend Sun Myung Moon of the Unification Church blesses over two thousand couples at a mass marriage. Reverend Moon personally matched all the couples that wed. Do you think these couples would have chosen different spouses had they been given the choice? What other life choices do you think these people have sacrificed in order to conform to the conventions of this social group?

Conformity

the goals of the mental activities of most social groups are pressures to get along and to conform. That **conformity** in turn may require surrendering important aspects of ourselves as individuals. Therefore, to some observers the term *adjustment* suggests acceptance of psychology as a social tool to stamp out individuality and eccentricity. All nonconformity would be labeled "maladjustment."

Conformity is a genuine issue. Indeed, in some totalitarian governments, maladjustment *is* defined as failing to conform to required beliefs and behaviors. The Soviet Union has a well-documented history of using psychiatric hospitals to confine dissidents. Anti-state nonconformists are frequently diagnosed as suffering from "sluggish schizophrenia" (Brody, 1985). The United States has sometimes acted similarly. The poet Ezra Pound was psychiatrically hospitalized in 1946 to avoid the embarrassment of trying one of the nation's most noted writers for treason.

IN PRAISE OF OBVIOUS SOLUTIONS

Not all personal adjustments call for complex psychological solutions. Many personal challenges are easily met in direct ways. The excessive search for psychological complexities and issues can interfere with our effectiveness. The person who is always examining his or her motives and dynamics may find it difficult to buy a loaf of bread or hold hands on a date. To be overly self-conscious can be a disorder in its own right.

This principle is called *parsimony,* which means that the simplest explanation that works should be accepted. Thus, the answer to the question "Am I a nervous person?" has been found to be highly correlated with scores on the most used psychological test of anxiety.

Sometimes people pursue the complex because they do not see the obvious. It is possible to be blind to the simple because of a fixed set of psychological expectations. One set of riddles has been developed to test awareness of the obvious in solving problems (Raudsepp, 1980). Do you see the obvious? Try these problems. The answers are listed at the bottom of the box.

1. One month has 28 days. Of the remaining 11 months, how many have 30 days?

2. A woman gave a beggar 50 cents. The woman is the beggar's sister, but the beggar is not the woman's brother. What is their relationship?

3. Do they have a fourth of July in England?

4. A farmer has 4 7/9 haystacks in one corner of his field and 5 2/9 haystacks in another corner of his field. If he puts them all together, how many haystacks will he have?

5. If you stand on a hard marble floor, how can you drop a raw egg five feet without breaking its shell?

The forced conformity view does illuminate the roles of social and government pressures on adjustment. Current concepts of adjustment go well beyond this notion of forced conformity. After all, comfortable conformity can be healthy and productive in the attainment of overall life satisfaction. Furthermore, individually chosen ways of living can be more than reflections of group pressures. Individual choice and control in life are important to positive affect and to life satisfaction. Risks and responsibility for change come with choice and change, our next topics.

CONTROL AND CHANGE IN OUR LIVES

. . . Most men and women choose and successfully achieve beneficial changes. They do this largely on their own, with some help from friends and family. If through some magic telescope one could observe this ac-

---

6. Two fathers and two sons shot three deer. Yet each took home one deer. How is that possible?

7. Why can't a man living in New York City be buried west of the Mississippi?

8. You are sitting in a room with 12 friends. Can any of them seat themselves in any particular place in this room where it would be impossible for you to do so?

(Raudsepp, 1980, pp. 14–15)

These riddles don't necessarily mean one will or will not be able to resolve personal adjustments. They do reflect how the obvious sometimes calls for a careful look and how easy it can be to overlook obvious and easy answers to our daily problems.

Answers

1. All of them
2. Sisters
3. Yes
4. One
5. Hold it above your head in one hand and drop it into your other hand held above the floor.
6. They are grandfather, father, and son.
7. He is alive.
8. On your lap.

tivity, one would be struck by how common and widespread it is, by the amount of time and personal energy devoted to it, and by its positive impact on human happiness and well-being.

(Allen Tough, 1982, p. 158)

Some people see few choices available to them in life. It seems to them they are swept away by forces beyond their control. Other people seem to control their lives. They experience a sense of being stuck. When change occurs, they feel they have no opportunity available to influence the outcome. Such people have an ***external locus of control*** (Rotter, 1966). That is, the control of their lives seems outside them, or in an external locus, and other people or powerful forces determine what happens to them. One example can be seen in Manual, a character in the Oscar Lewis book, *Children of Sanchez* (1961), who thinks:

External locus of control

> To me, one's destiny is controlled by a mysterious hand that moves all things. Only for the select, do things turn out as planned; to those of us who are born to be tamale eaters, heaven sends only tamales.

(Lewis, 1961, p. 171)

EXPLORATION IN WELL-BEING

Control of Your Life

Do you see yourself as having substantial control over the important events in your life? If you do, there is a good chance that you will have more life satisfaction than individuals whose locus of control is external. First, see how much you agree with the following items:

People's misfortunes result from the mistakes they make.

Getting people to do the right thing depends upon ability; luck has little or nothing to do with it.

In the case of the well-prepared student, there is rarely if ever such a thing as an unfair test.

When people are mean to you, it is because you did something to make them mean.

Many times the reactions of people seem understandable to me. I always feel in control of what I am doing.

Agreement with these items indicates that you do see locus of control as lying within people. Now, using the same agree–disagree choices, respond to each of the following items, which reflect external locus of control:

The external locus of control has been studied using a number of questionnaires. Respondents to these various questionnaires have demonstrated the fatalism of externalizers. They feel they control little in life. In general, the less likely people are to be able to attain valued goals in society, the more likely they are to have an external locus of control. One researcher in this area has concluded that "Blacks, Spanish-Americans, Indians, and other minority groups who do not enjoy as much access to opportunity as do the predominant caucasian groups in North American society are found to hold fatalistic, external control beliefs" (Lefcourt, 1976, p. 25).

Internal locus of control

In contrast, many other people feel in charge of their lives and are said to have an ***internal locus of control*** (Rotter, 1966). By this we mean they feel they control their own destinies. Note we are talking only about the perception of being in control; no conclusions are drawn about true control over lives. Internal locus has been found to be related positively to well-being, except in the cases of grandiose people who feel they have control over all important events in their lives and in everyone else's.

When control is felt to be located inside us—that is, has an internal locus—we feel in a position to make deliberate changes in our lives out

Most people can't realize the extent to which their lives are controlled by accidental happenings.

It is not always wise to plan too far ahead because many things turn out to be a matter of good or bad fortune anyhow.

Many times, exam questions tend to be so unrelated to course work that studying is really useless.

When someone gets mad at you, you usually feel there is nothing you can do about it.

There's not much use in worrying about things—what will be, will be.

I think life is mostly a gamble.

These two sets of items are drawn from several scales that have been developed to measure locus of control. Check their accuracy for you. Do you feel your life is within your control? And do you also agree with most of the internal control items and disagree with most of the external control items? In the same sense, you can check your perspective if you feel that most important aspects of your life—and those in most people's lives—are not within individual control. This text aims to help you understand the key psychological aspects of living and what to do to make a difference so that more of your life can be the result of deliberate decision.

of choice. Most of us do not fall exclusively into a category of having internal or external locus of control, but rather lie somewhere between, usually leaning a little one way or the other. Thus, we see at least some important decisions in our lives as being within our intentional control.

Such intentional actions are part of what make us feel free and responsible. In this book, we examine the intentional changes toward well-being that we may wish to make. The idea of intentional changes suggests that large chunks of our lives are truly in our own hands. In the accompanying box, "A Decision to Change," M. Scott Peck (1978) describes one event that triggered a crucial intentional change in his life.

One research study supports the proposition that deliberate changes in our lives are widespread. Allen Tough (1982) interviewed 150 American, British, and Canadian men and women about the largest intentional changes they had made in the past two years of their lives. One-third of the respondents spoke about job or career changes, the most common of which was simply moving from one job to another. Another 21 percent had substantial changes in human relationships, emotions, and self-perceptions. Typically, they became either more or less involved with families, friends, or spouses.

Changes in enjoyable activities were reported by 11 percent of the respondents. These men and women talked about adding some activity,

A DECISION TO CHANGE

One night recently I decided to spend some free time building a happier and closer relationship with my fourteen-year-old daughter. For several weeks she had been urging me to play chess with her, so I suggested a game. She eagerly accepted and we settled down to a most even and challenging game. It was a school night, however, and at nine o'clock my daughter asked if I could hurry my moves, because she needed to get to bed; she had to get up at six in the morning. I knew her to be rigidly disciplined in her sleeping habits, and it seemed to me that she should be able to give up some of this rigidity. I told her, "Come on, you can go to bed a little later for once. You shouldn't start games that you can't finish. We're having fun." We played on for another fifteen minutes, during which time she became visibly discomfited. Finally, she pleaded, "Please, Daddy, please hurry your moves." "No. . ." I replied, "Chess is a serious game. If you're going to play it well, you're going to play it slowly. If you don't want to play it seriously, you might as well not play it at all." And so, with her feeling miserable, we continued for another ten minutes, until suddenly my daughter burst into tears, yelled that she conceded the stupid game, and ran weeping up the stairs.

including social activities, hobbies, or recreational activities. Change of residence was reported by another 10 percent. The rest of the answers were scattered. Only 4 percent reported no major intentional changes.

The respondents did not view these changes as small changes, either. In the Tough research, 31 percent said the changes were huge or enormous, and 40 percent more rated them as large and important. Furthermore, 51 percent felt that the changes had contributed to their happiness either a large or enormous amount.

This study affirms the potential we have for changing ourselves and aspects of our lives. Most of us are not helpless and without control; we only *perceive* ourselves as lacking control. Once we believe that we may intentionally reshape ourselves and our lives, then our reshaping may begin. The first step is the *belief.* When we do not see ourselves as able to make such choices, and have external locuses of control, we are without choice. The belief in choice permits choice.

Every change involves risk. After all, we move into an uncertain state. Even if we are unhappy, we at least know the psychological devils or annoyances with which we live. An unhappy but predictable present is more satisfactory to some than a prospectively better but risky future. We can count on clear personal risks involved in personal changes. Poet Shel Silverstein knows of such risks:

. . . What had gone wrong? The answer was obvious. But I did not want to see the answer, so it took me two hours to wade through the pain of accepting the fact that I had botched the evening by allowing my desire to win a chess game become more important than my desire to build a relationship with my daughter. I was depressed in earnest then. How had I gotten so out of balance? Gradually it dawned on me that my desire to win was too great and that I needed to give up some of this desire. Yet even this little giving up seemed impossible. All my life my desire to win had served me in good stead, for I had won many things. How was it possible to play chess without wanting to win?

. . . My depression is over now. I have given up part of my desire to win at games. That part of me is gone now. It died. It had to die. I killed it. I killed it with my desire to win at parenting. When I was a child my desire to win at games served me well. As a parent I recognized that it got in my way. So it had to go. The times have changed. To move with them I had to give it up. I do not miss it. I thought I would, but I don't.

(Peck, 1978, pp. 67–69).

Albert Einstein and Mother Theresa are probable examples of people with what psychologists would describe as an internal locus of control. Such people feel in control of their lives; they make deliberate changes in and decisions about their lives. People who have an internal locus of control often are capable of making monumental contributions to society. Albert Einstein's contributions to science and Mother Theresa's contributions to humanity and world peace support this proposition.

The fanciest dive that ever was dove
Was done by Melissa of Coconut Grove.
She bounced on the board and flew into the air
With a twist of her head and a twirl of her hair.
She did thirty-four jackknives, backflipped and spun,
Quadruple gainered, and reached for the sun,
And then somersaulted nine times and a quarter—
And looked down and saw that the pool had no water.

(Shel Silverstein, 1981, p. 30)

That's our fear—that leaping into new ways of being will find us landing hard and painfully. For some people, staying as they are represents a form of avoidance. They remain rooted in their present behaviors. When the fear of being hurt through new behaviors arises, they cope by studiously avoiding the new behaviors. The feeling of relief at having evaded the possible pain is itself reinforcing: The relief feels good. They don't change.

Risking Change

Who does change? People who are most accustomed to taking risks change. Furthermore, people who have had the most positive experiences with taking risks change. The key to giving up avoidance behaviors is to take risks. For some, dramatic risk taking makes the difference. For many others, modest and gradual ventures into changes works best. Consider the following examples of people who took risks and found their risk taking had a positive impact:

> *A young man who tried out for the boxing team, risking being beaten up in the ring:* "I lost the fight, but in spite of it I was glad I went through with it. I actually was a happier person and felt that I had accomplished something and would try other things."
>
> *A woman who traveled alone after separating from her husband:* "As a result of this experience I had a real feeling of my own power as a coping person—one who is able to take reasonable risks and deal successfully with new situations. . . . I still look back on that experience when my self-confidence starts to slip. Having done it once, I know I can achieve those feelings again."
>
> *A successful graduate student drops out for a year:* "For the first time in my life, I felt real. . . . Taking a year off to find where I wanted to go was like my saying, 'Sorry, Gentlemen, I have a date with life.'"

(Siegelman, 1983, pp. 83, 123)

If these people had taken the option of avoidance, not daring to fight, not risking a trip alone, not making a decision to live out of school for a while, they would never have been able to change toward more courageous and independent behaviors.

Each of these people made highly personal and individual decisions, yet it was not possible for them to know with certainty that their decisions were indeed the best choices. Such weighting of values, choices, and outcomes must be judgments within us. Thus, this book does not offer prescriptions for change, with mandates on how to become a better person. Such unrealistic notions are the province of newspaper advice columns and popular books about "psychology for everybody." Instead, my goal is to present multiple possibilities, based on contemporary psychological knowledge.

Should you try out some of these potential solutions? That question is best answered by answering other questions. Do the possible solutions fit your values and beliefs? Are you comfortable with them? Do they make sense for your goals? Consider the described solutions as a menu from which you may choose a few things that seem just right for you. Remember that these are possible pathways and are not designed to be absolute prescriptions for self-change.

THE "TOWARD WELL-BEING" TABLES

In each chapter in this text, the implications for well-being will be summarized. In this chapter, Table 1–2 presents just such a summary. The three topics of components of well-being, of conformity to group pressure, and of personal change are addressed. In each succeeding chapter, a list of directions "Toward Well-Being" and a parallel set, "Away from

TABLE I–2 The Nature of Well-Being	
Toward Well-Being	**Away from Well-Being**
Has strong positive affect along many dimensions	Has little positive affect
Has low or infrequent negative affect	Has high and frequent negative affect along several dimensions
Has substantial satisfaction with life as a whole	Has substantial dissatisfaction with life as a whole
Reconciles decisions and values with the realities of group and societal norms	Feels forced to conform to social norms
Makes deliberate individual choices	Makes few deliberate decisions; feels swept along
Perceives being in control of own life	Perceives life being out of control
Takes reasonable risks in interests of personal goals	Refuses to take risks or takes irrational risks

Well-Being," will close the discussion. These tables are not intended to be comprehensive summaries, but rather to identify the essence of well-being implications.

SUMMARY

Adjustment is the process of dealing with the origins of the demands of our bodies, our emotions, and our environments. The psychology of adjustment can be traced to 1907, when Clifford Beers founded the mental hygiene movement. By whatever title, "adjustment" includes responding to influences toward forced conformity. However, conformity can be a positive as well as a negative event and can be part of achievement of important personal aims.

This text is titled *The Psychology of Adjustment and Well-Being* to emphasize the continuum ranging from maladjustment at one extreme, to adjustment at a middle point, and then to well-being at the most positive end. Well-being is defined as a subjective emotional state composed of positive affect, relatively little negative affect, and global life satisfaction. Such well-being comes in part from the attainment of positive strivings, and it encompasses more than the simple absence of symptoms or conflicts. National surveys on well-being have found that most Americans are reasonably satisfied with their lives as a whole, and a majority characteristically report frequent happiness and pleasure and infrequent boredom and depression.

Change involves risk. The people who change the most are those who are most accustomed to taking risks and changing. While we never know with certainty the outcomes of risky decisions, the alternative of doing little or nothing out of fear of failure is a worse choice. This text sets forth a series of options, much like items on a menu, from which people may wish to choose.

Key Terms

Adjustment	Mastery of changing demands
Cognitive	Mental hygiene movement
Conformity	Negative affect
Contemplation	Normality
External locus of control	Positive affect
General life satisfaction	Precontemplation
Internal harmony	Self-fulfillment
Internal locus of control	Social competence
Maladjustment	Well-being

Recommended Reading

Campbell, A., Converse, P.E. & Rodgers, W.L. (1976). *The quality of American life: Perceptions, evaluations, and satisfactions.* New York: Russell Sage Foundation. Most Americans do experience fairly high levels of well-being.

This research volume looks at the methodologies of reaching this conclusion and at just who has positive feelings and overall life satisfaction and why.

Lefcourt, H.M. (1976). *Locus of control.* Hillsdale, NJ: Lawrence Erlbaum Associates. An extensive review of the literature and nine scales for measurement of internal and external locus of control are in this book. Written for researchers, this book is the best guide in one volume to what we know about locus of control.

Peck, M.S. (1978). *The road less traveled.* New York: Touchstone. A friend of mine went through a period of giving this book to all her friends. It's a personal book about problem solving. The author shares himself with the reader and takes us on a thoughtful psychological and spiritual journey.

Siegelman, E.Y. (1983). *Personal risk: Mastering change in love and work.* New York: Harper & Row. After discussing the kinds of risks people take and ways people change, this book offers a self-test of risk styles. You have a chance to judge whether you are a careless risk taker, an anxious and overcautious risk taker, or a balanced risk taker. Balanced is a nice word to describe this book, too. It is sensible and readable, and it offers many descriptions of risk takers and risks in life, while also being grounded in psychological perspectives.

2

CHAPTER

Theories of Personality

Zinz recording. Day five on planet three, so-lar system SO–1. No contacts with highest authorities. Fonf and I remain in room with vertical rows of metal rods at entrance/exit point. Continue to monitor natives. Recording completed.

"Fonf, you are still monitoring natives in adjoining life space?"

"Yes, Zinz. They discuss us. Join monitoring."

Six people sat around the table in the makeshift conference room of the Rockingham County jail. The Colonel was at the head of the table. The other men and women were psychologists brought here to assess the aliens. Dr. Scott Ellison was completing his report.

". . . our belief is that basic trust as humans know it comes from the security of the oral stage of development. With no mouth visible on either of the aliens, trust and love are less likely to develop. It's only a theory, because we know so little about generalizing to aliens."

"I guess it's my turn," the intense woman in the dark suit interjected. She was Dr. Betty Efron, who had been a pioneer in identifying culture conflict as Americans worked in other countries.

"Goodness knows, I must chime in that my ideas are only theories too. However, I conjecture that these creatures find part of their fundamental life satisfaction in adventure. From our tracking of their vessel, they have been on an intersolar voyage for at least twenty years. Persistence may be a key element of their psychological make-up. We need to realize that none of our assumptions about human nature necessarily hold."

The third psychologist was ready for his turn. He was Harrison Forrest, long recognized for his work with the apes of Malawi.

"This is the third day of the aliens being held in custody and five days since they appeared on the statehouse lawn. The potato shape of the body appears rigid while the thin appendages and stalks that cover the body are continuously in motion. The creatures show no response to changes in light, to food placed before them, to water in bowls or glasses, to television programs. Maps of the Milky Way and the solar system have elicited nothing as well. My operating hypothesis is that the stimuli to which they respond are not ones that occur within our natural Earth environment. However, that, like Dr. Ellison's and Dr. Efron's statements, is only a preliminary theory."

"Fonf?"

"Yes, Zinz."

"I have noted that the natives have a narrow range of artificially supported temperatures. Please monitor alone for a minute."

"Yes, Zinz. Monitoring."

A blinding flash of light filled the conference room. Chairs, tables, curtains, people, turned white then red. Finally only piles of ash were left on the floor.

"Zinz, I note little life existence tolerance to varying heat levels. Life functions have ceased. However, Zinz, I am unclear on the purpose of your raising adjacent room to present heat. What was your reason for ceasing natives' life existence?"

"I had not all of the facts about their fragile body structures. Thus, I was not at all certain what would happen, Fonf. It was only a theory."

THEORIES AND PERSONALITY

The psychologists looking at Zinz and Fonf were in search of a theory to account for these visiting Mr. Potatoheads that looked and acted like nothing on earth. A theory seemed important so that the few facts they had could be connected and informed guesses could made about as yet unknown aspects of the two visitors. Zinz had a modest theory, too: that humans could not tolerate heat. Although testing his theory did have the interesting side effect of cremating the humans, the theory itself might be lauded as clear and testable. That observation leads us to the first issue in considering theories of personality, which is, what makes a good theory? Then we move to, what is personality?

I won't go into the argument that nothing is as useful as a good theory—although I am tempted to make the case that reliable cars, abundant money, and pencil sharpeners are pretty darned useful. Our topic is what makes a *good theory*. First, a theory must be clear and explicit. All too often, theories in psychology can be murky, with the basic tenets not visibly stated. Second, a good theory should withstand empirical testing. In that way, the theory can generate research, so we can learn how accurate and comprehensive the theory is, and how it needs to be modified. However, when facts do not support a theory, the theory is not always discarded, especially if its followers believe in it strongly enough. Robert Frost understood that process when he wrote

> . . . why abandon a belief
> Merely because it ceases to be true.
> Cling to it long enough, and not a doubt
> It will turn true again, for so it goes.

(Frost, 1946, p. 12)

Theories of personality are not prized possessions; instead, they are ways of describing important aspects of human nature. Different definitions of personality come out of different theories. What is dogma to one theorist is heresy to another. For that reason, some psychologists argue against accepting any one general definition of personality (Hall & Lindzey, 1978). There are, nonetheless, ways in which personality can be understood.

Personality is the stable core of who a person is. The personality is a summary of the consistent ways a person thinks, feels, and behaves. The terms *stable* and *consistent* indicate that we are not talking about one-time or rare behaviors, but rather about long-term characteristics. The term *core* means significant character traits, and not trivial or incidental acts.

Three theories of personality have been dominant forces in the twentieth century. These are psychoanalysis, behaviorism, and humanistic psy-

Good theory (margin note)

Personality (margin note)

Personality, the stable core of who a person is, is the sum of the consistent ways the person thinks, feels, and behaves.

chology. In this chapter, we examine these theories in turn, and consider how each relates to adjustment and well-being. Our first theory is the most known, most discussed, and most criticized of all: psychoanalysis.

 ## PSYCHOANALYSIS

Psychoanalysis

Psychoanalysis is at once a theory of personality, an approach to treatment of disorders, and a way of thinking about humankind that has had a profound influence in this century. Developed by Sigmund Freud (1856–1939), this theoretical perspective has revolutionized our understanding of humanity. The central assertion of psychoanalysis is that humankind is not primarily conscious, but instead is primarily unconscious in thought and irrational in motive. This issue of consciousness and the unconscious will be our starting place in looking at psychoanalysis. Then we discuss the id, ego, and superego—the mental apparatus of Freudian theory—and, finally, we turn to the ways in which Freud saw psychosexual development advance through oral, anal, and phallic stages.

Consciousness

What are you aware of, right now? What can you bring into awareness, if you choose? What of your feelings and experiences can you not recall, even if you try?

Conscious

The answer to the first of these three questions is the *conscious,* what you are aware of at a given instant. The content you can think of, if you choose—such as what clothing you wore yesterday—is called the

Preconscious
Unconscious

preconscious. Instincts and unacceptable memories and experiences fall in the *unconscious,* which is defined as all of the mental processes and content not available to awareness. Even if the unacceptable events were once conscious, we no longer are able to think of them.

Consciousness is like a spotlight that lights up the subject at which it is directed. Preconsciousness is everything that is not being directly lit at the moment, but which is within the range of the spotlight. If we want to look at anything within this range, we can. However, there are always vast areas outside the range of any spotlight that cannot be illuminated: these are the areas of the unconscious (Stafford-Clark, 1965).

The unconscious plays a key role in psychoanalytic thinking. First, it encompasses all of our primitive drives. Second, the unconscious is the repository of repressed feelings and desires. Events and feelings from infancy and childhood are especially repressed and stored. Repressed desires insistently make small aspects of themselves known through dreams, slips of the tongue, and humor. For example, a secretary working with me found herself accidentally and repeatedly making typing errors that were related to some personal problems she had. In place of "San Francisco Bay Area," she typed "San Francisco Boy Area." When presented with the word "computate," she typed "copulate." Psychoanalytic theory surely would interpret these errors as a sign of important and repressed sexual conflicts. Figure 2–1 gives another example of how the unconscious manifests itself.

The conscious and unconscious underlie much of Freud's portrait of human functioning. Material in conscious awareness tends to be rational. Material in the unconscious is irrational and emotionally charged. This is seen in the Freudian concepts of id, ego, and superego, our next subjects. Together, these three components make up the mental structure: the unconscious functioning of the id, the conscious and preconscious functioning of the ego, and the mixed conscious and unconscious workings of the superego.

Sigmund Freud is best known for his development of the psychoanalytic perspective that asserts that human thought is primarily unconscious and human motive is primarily irrational.

The Mental Structure

The id

According to Freudian theory, each of us is born with continuing pressure to satisfy basic instinctive drives. These drives for gratification build in

FIGURE 2–1: Jokes and the Unconscious. Like dreams and slips of the tongue, jokes were described by Freud as a means for unconscious, repressed "animal" feelings to escape the steel-fisted control of the superego. For that reason, jokes use double meanings and allusions to aggression and sexuality. This Ralph Steadman drawing shows a possible reaction of a colleague of Freud's to the idea of a scholarly paper about jokes.

From Steadman, 1979, pp. 10–11.

intensity. When they are satisfied, the release of tension is the foundation for all pleasures. The drives compose the most primitive part of the mental apparatus, the **id.**

Id

The infant is born "all id." Every need, whether for hunger or to be changed, requires instant action or the infant responds with anger or rage. Thus, the infant (as well as adults dominated by the id) operate on a formula of "I want what I want when I want it and I will not take no for an answer" (Strupp, 1967).

The ego

Ego

If the id is the instinctive, irrational drives of the human, the **ego** is the rational aspect of human personality. It is the means by which one mediates between the demands of the id and the reality of a world in which other people live and to which attention must be directed. The ego develops as infants learn to delay gratification, to anticipate what will happen, and to internalize the attitudes of significant others around them. The ego has been called the "executive" of our functions. It directs, reconciles, compromises, negotiates, plans, and takes into account the internal balance sheet of drives and satisfactions. The ego is mostly, but not totally, conscious.

Note that the term *ego*, as we speak of it here, is unrelated to the popular usage, in which ego is used as a synonym for pride or narcissism.

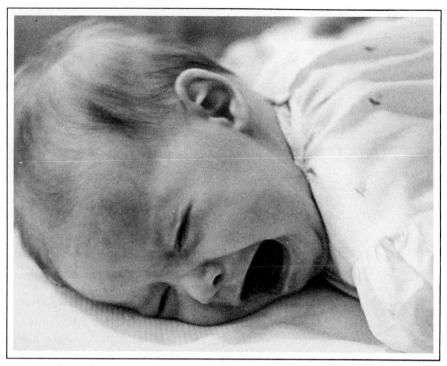

The newborn is "all id." If an infant's need, whether for food or clean diapers, is not immediately addressed, the infant responds with anger or rage.

The superego

The **superego** is often defined as the conscience, the moral authority of the person. Passing judgment on what is right and wrong, good and bad, allowed and forbidden is the function of the superego. Freud conceived of the individual as being engaged in continuous, internal warfare between the raw, primitive drives of the id and the efforts at iron-fisted control by the superego.

If the message of the id is yes, yes, yes, then the message of the superego is no, no, no. Such no's develop in people from their parents' saying no. The parental authority becomes internalized. The superego arises in one additional way. We will discuss shortly how childhood sexual desire for possession of the opposite sex parent is forbidden and impossible. Growing up includes the development of a strong superego to watch out for all such unacceptable feelings.

In these battles between desire and conscience, the ego is seen as the mediator. It is the part of the person that attends to proper behavior in particular situations and then deliberately gratifies or denies the instinctive need. (Figure 2–2 summarizes and illustrates the roles of the id, the

FIGURE 2–2: The Id, The
Ego, and the Superego

*From Appignanesi, 1979,
pp. 156–159.*

The Id   The ID (Latin for 'it') is the primitive, unconscious basis of the psyche dominated by primary urges. The psyche of a newborn child is primarily ID. But contact with the external world modifies part of the ID. Perception of this difference is what begins to differentiate the EGO. Ego development is imprinted by the instinctual structure of the libido (mouth, anus, genitals). In other words, self-awareness and bodily activity develop together.

The Ego   Freud gives the ego several important functions.

1. The ego is guide in reality. It can adapt or change.
2. Conscious perceptions belong to the ego. This is an aspect of the ego turned towards external reality.
3. But the ego also acts as an inhibiting agency. This is another aspect of the ego which is turned internally and functions unconsciously. For instance, the ego's **repression** of the id is unconscious. This is one of the ego's defense functions. These functions are all unconscious.

The Super-ego   The super-ego is not just 'conscience.' It is the heir to the Oedipus complex. Here's how it works.

FIGURE 2–2   (continued)   Here is one example of the ego's defense mechanism.

The infant feels deep hostility toward its parents, which it cannot
express . . .

So the infant projects its aggression on to them . . .

Which seems reflected back as exaggerated strictness . . .

FIGURE 2–2 (continued)

As the Oedipal impulses are repressed and disappear, their place is taken by the super-ego. The super-ego is introjected parental authority. It is the result of a defensive effort which prohibits the expression of Oedipal wishes.

ego, and the superego.) The balance of id, ego, and superego emerges from a developmental process. Greatly overactive superego actions, as well as fiercely repressed feelings and drives of the id, come from one's failure to pass through these developmental stages—our next topic.

Psychosexual Stages of Development

Everyone passes through five stages of development from birth through adolescence, according to Freud. The personality itself is for the most part formed within the first five years of life as the child progresses through the oral, anal, and phallic stages. These are called psychosexual stages, because all pleasure is described as being sexual. In fact, that is a working definition of sexuality: If it arises from the body and is a pleasurable physical sensation, psychoanalysis considers it sexual. The locus of pleasure begins at the mouth.

The first year of life: The oral stage

Oral stage

Freud held that human personality is shaped initially in infancy, a period during which the mouth is the major source of pleasurable and erotic sensations. The earliest pleasure seems to be sucking, and indeed sucking is a well-developed instinct in young infants. The infant begins life in the *oral stage* fully dependent, unable to survive without the care of others. At this early point in life, the individual will either come to know the world as a secure, loving, dependable environment or as an uncertain and rejecting one. If the oral needs of infants are met and they feel that the world is a place of predictable gratification, then they will have passed through this stage successfully. When there is a deprivation of nurturance and love and security in the earliest years, a person is then fixated at this point, always hungering for the satisfaction and pleasures never fulfilled.

The second and third years of life: The anal stage

Anal stage

The second psychosexual stage focuses on anal control. The infant has no conflict over anal functions. As soon as sufficient tension builds up in the bowels, the anal sphincter relaxes and the bowels evacuate. However, parents (and society) demand at some point that children learn how and when to release their bowels. What has been a pleasurable experience (the release of tension) now becomes a source of conflict. Freud saw children as wanting the pleasure of letting go whenever they please, but society demands control and insists on the relinquishing of this source of enjoyment. Society is usually so successful in demanding compliance that all aspects of bowel evacuation become labeled as dirty and vulgar. However, enjoyment of anal functions sometimes persists into adulthood.

> Even in our ultraclean society, many people still find it difficult to imagine that their anuses can be a source of sensual satisfaction. In the privacy of their own bathrooms, however, many people can admit to themselves that the releasing of the anus can be the real "pause that refreshes." As one of my constipated patients said, it is his most pleasurable time of the month.
>
> *(Prochaska, 1984, p. 25)*

The early childhood struggle for control of this enjoyable process also is manifested in subsequent personality development. Individuals who resolve the conflict with excessive control become controlled all their lives. They are stingy, obsessive, fastidiously clean, and precise. "Holding on" becomes primary in their daily living.

On the other hand, if children have been overindulged and allowed to train themselves when they feel like it, the opposite traits are said to emerge. These individuals are self-indulgent. They are sloppy and disorganized. After all, control was not forced on them during toilet training. They easily let go of their emotions, of their money, of their impulses.

FREUD AND SEXUALITY: THE PURITANICAL SCIENTIST

Freud's attitude to sexuality throws another light on his fundamental interests and the motives that urged him forward in his researches. On the one hand there is no doubt that he was greatly excited over his discovery that sexual factors play an *essential* part in the causation of neuroses—I repeat "essential," for they had often been admitted to be occasional factors—and that he made it one of his chief aims to carry through in minute detail his Libido theory of the neuroses. On the other hand, his descriptions of sexual activities are so matter-of-fact that many readers have found them almost dry and totally lacking in warmth. From all I know of him I should say that he displayed less than the average *personal* interest in what is often an absorbing topic. There was never any gusto or even savor in mentioning a sexual topic. He would have been out of place in the usual club room, for he seldom related sexual jokes and then only when they had a special point illustrating a general theme. He always gave the impression of being an unusually chaste person—the word "puritanical" would not be out of place—and all we know of his early development confirms this conception.

Indeed, this must be the explanation of his almost naive surprise when his announcement of discoveries in this field met with such a cold reception. [Freud wrote] "I did not at first perceive the peculiar nature of what I had discovered. Without thinking, I sacrificed at its inception

Phallic stage

Age four or five: The *phallic stage*

By age five, a child's experience of sexuality has localized in the genitals. While not ready for the sexual act, the genitals nonetheless are the source of pleasurable sensations. In the absence of parental discouragement (either in explicit or subtle ways), children often do touch themselves and masturbate.

Oedipus complex

Freud stated that the primary emotional attachment of children is toward the nurturing mother. The male child (even more than the female child) sees the father as a rival for the mother's affection. Thus, the child develops the **Oedipus complex,** which is a repressed (but nonetheless genuine) fear that his father will castrate him because of his desire for his mother. The fear is made more intense by parental threats designed to stop the child from touching his penis in play and pleasure. In turn, little girls are said to want their fathers exclusively and sexually and to compete with their mothers—a situation called the **Electra complex.** The feelings of incest are so unacceptable that virtually no older children are aware or able to recall their desires for their parents.

Electra complex

my popularity as a physician, and the growth of a large consulting practice among nervous patients, by enquiries relating to the sexual factors involved in the causation of their neuroses; this brought me a great many new facts which definitely confirmed my conviction of the practical importance of the sexual factor. Unsuspectingly, I spoke before the Vienna Neurological Society, then under the presidency of Krafft-Ebing, expecting to be compensated by the interest and recognition of my colleagues for the material losses I had willingly undergone. I treated my discoveries as ordinary contributions to science and hoped to be met in the same spirit. But the silence with which my addresses were received, the void which formed itself about me, the insinuations that found their way to me, caused me gradually to realize that one cannot count upon views about the part played by sexuality in the etiology of the neuroses meeting with the same reception as other communications. I understood that from now onwards I belonged to those who have 'troubled the sleep of the world,' as Hebbel says, and that I could not reckon upon objectivity and tolerance. Since, however, my conviction of the general accuracy of my observations and conclusions grew and grew, and as my confidence in my own judgment was by no means slight, any more than my moral courage, there could be no doubt about the outcome of the situation."

(Jones, 1953, pp. 270–271)

Latency stage

From age six until puberty: The latency stage

Between six years of age and the onset of puberty, childhood sexuality quietly falls into a lull. It does not appear, nor is it developed further. Freud described the signs of sexuality as vanishing until puberty and the genital stage. The impulses and conflicts of the oral, anal, and phallic stages are stored in the unconscious during this period.

Genital stage

Puberty: The genital stage

When early adolescents reach the genital stage, they are capable of the full sexual act, and full genital functioning is possible. At this time, the renewed sex drive brings out unresolved conflicts of the earlier stages. This beginning of adulthood sees the rebirth of the conflicts that are dilemmas of life's development.

Other Directions in Psychoanalysis

As Sigmund Freud's ideas became known and, in part, accepted, a group of energetic people gathered around him for informal discussions. Most of these followers eventually departed from their discipleship. The two most celebrated and influential dissidents were Alfred Adler and Carl Jung.

Alfred Adler

Adler's departure was early and bitter, because he rejected the basic Freudian precept that sexuality and seeking of pleasure were the dominant human motives. Instead, Adler developed three major themes.

1. *Social responsibility* is a fundamental aspect of well-being. People who are maladjusted are selfish. Psychological adjustment takes into account the needs and interests of others and society, and altruism is thus important in personal life.

2. *Striving for superiority* is the underlying human motive. By the term *striving,* Adler did not necessarily mean that individuals had to compete and win. Rather, he meant that a genuine sense of personal mastery and competence in life is crucial. Because of physical weaknesses and the helplessness everyone experiences as children, inferiority complexes are always developed. ***Striving for superiority*** and mastery is a universal way of compensating for feelings of inferiority.

Striving for superiority

Lifestyle analysis

3. The development of personality may be understood through a ***lifestyle analysis,*** in which position in the family birth order and relationship to siblings and parents lead to characteristic styles of seeking attention and superiority.

A few Adlerians are seen today, but Adlerian psychology has faded away because of its success. Adler's ideas have become so much a part of present-day personality theories that they no longer stand out on their own. Instead, other personality approaches include Adler's concepts of compensatory striving and social responsibility. Only the topics of lifestyle analysis and siblings' influences remain distinct and separate Adlerian concerns.

Carl Jung

Carl Jung was Freud's most favored disciple, a man Freud loved, the most talented of his followers, his handpicked successor. Thus, when Jung left the circle of Freud's disciples, it was a stinging blow to Freud. The most important of Jung's ideas that differed from those of Freud were the collective unconscious, extroversion–introversion, and the spiritual nature of humankind.

Collective unconscious

1. The ***collective unconscious*** is Jung's term for the part of the mind that goes beyond personal, individual awareness and experience. The collective unconscious is not available to us in obvious and clear forms. Rather, mythology, imagery, dreams, and mystical experiences are means for these common experiences of the human race to become known. Thus, we may define the collective unconscious as those inherited mental images and ideas that are common to all humanity and that are released from passive storage through repeatedly appearing images and myths.

Extroversion
Introversion

2. Jung also was known for his description of personality types. He wrote initially about ***extroversion***—being caught up in ideas and feelings outside oneself—and ***introversion***—which is the personal emphasis on internal, subjective thoughts and feelings. He later expanded his descriptions to include rational and irrational elements in both functions.

Jung formed the early foundation for humanistic psychology in his emphasis on the mystical, subjective, and spiritual within individuals. While Jungian psychologists are not numerous, they are visible, and several training centers prepare mental health professionals to apply Jungian principles to their practice of psychotherapy.

Changes to the theory of psychosexual development

In psychoanalysis after Freud, several healthy branches can be seen. The view of psychosexual development has changed. Under the influence of Erik Erikson, the sexual components were deemphasized, in favor of ***psychosocial development.*** That is, the oral, anal, and phallic stages were

Psychosocial development

replaced by the developmental crises of *trust versus mistrust, autonomy versus shame,* and *initiative versus guilt* in relationships with others. Furthermore, personality development was no longer seen as stopping at around age five or six; instead, personality was perceived as continuing to develop through the life cycle. Chapter 7 on transitions and the life cycle will examine such adult development.

An ego psychology emerged that values the self and conscious behavior in place of the id and instincts. That is, sexuality and aggression were no longer described as fundamental instinctive drives, unmanageable and unacceptable. Finally, under the initial influences of Alfred Adler, the social forces and responsibilities drew more attention. People were not seen as living in a vacuum; instead, duty and interpersonal processes were more valued.

Well-Being

Psychoanalysis has been accused of being a sickness-oriented theory because Freud described the development of illness much more than he described health and well-being. According to psychoanalytic theory, individuals are often disturbed in part because they become fixated at one of the stages of development. A sign of well-being is having progressed through the oral, anal, and phallic stages to function maturely at the genital stage of life.

Another aspect of psychoanalytic well-being is freedom from determinism. Freud believed that most people have their actions restricted by their childhood conflicts and fixations. To be free of such predetermined behaviors is a sign of well-being. Thus, one psychoanalyst writes of the well person "His principal characteristic would seem to be flexibility—the ability to react to a situation not in terms of past neurotic notions but by acting in a way that tends to reduce his tension in a realistic, socially desirable manner" (Levitas, 1965, p. 349).

Fundamental to Freud's ideas of well-being, however, was conscious resolution of the conflicts everyone feels about their basic instinctive drives of aggression and sexuality. People not only become fixated, but their expression of these drives becomes repressed. They are driven underground, into the unconscious. Well-being consists of increasing those times at which the unconscious is made conscious and then allowing an open, deliberate reconciliation of drives with reality and moral beliefs. Because so much of who we are is unconscious and repressed, we can't manage such resolutions unless we have been fully analyzed.

Freud stressed psychoanalysis to achieve well-being. Freud, in fact, analyzed himself. For him, this was a process both of self-discovery and discovery of the nature of personality. Although he was at times discou aged about his analysis, more often he felt hopeful, as he expressed in a letter to Wilhelm Fliess (October 10, 1897).

> Everything is still dark, including even the nature of the problems, but at the same time I have a reassuring feeling that one only has to put one's hand in one's own store-cupboard to be able to extract—in its own good time—what one needs.
>
> *(Bonaparte, Freud & Kris, 1954, p. 227)*

Once psychoanalysis is completed and important parts of the unconscious are brought to light, Freud felt that successful work and love would result. Working successfully and loving well were the products of the well-analyzed person and the indicators of genuine well-being. It should not be surprising that Freud valued work. He himself was dedicated to his patients and his writing, and he regularly worked eighteen-hour days until his death at age eighty-five. Freud so greatly esteemed the power of love that, in 1908, he proposed that an Academy of Love should be established to study what love is and how it affects people.

BEHAVIORAL APPROACHES

Origins

Behaviorism

While many sparks had appeared earlier to briefly ignite **behaviorism,** the glowing beacon was lit when John B. Watson wrote an article, "Psychology as the behaviorist views it" (1913), and a subsequent book, *Behavior: An Introduction to Comparative Psychology* (1914). The psychological community was electrified. The next year, Watson was elected president of the American Psychological Association. A new way of thinking about psychology seemed to illuminate all the dark shadows of psychological research. What Watson proposed at the time may seem tame to the reader nowadays, but seldom in the history of psychology have such strong statements been so rapidly embraced. After all, psychoanalysis was attacked or ignored in its first years. Humanistic psychology, which we shall soon cover, slowly evolved. But the behaviorist proposals of John B. Watson were unequivocal answers to the questions of the majority of American psychologists at the time and, in their modern forms, of many present psychologists.

Watson presented three principles. First, he insisted psychology must become genuinely scientific. It must study only what is observable, that is, the *behavior* of animals and humans. The observable is not what they feel—you can never know what they feel—and it's not what they think— you can't know what they think. It is what the subjects *do,* what you can systematically watch, record, study, and control.

John B. Watson

Behaviorists believed that psychology must be a genuinely scientific study. Research should focus only on behavior that is directly observable (what a person *does*). Speculation about a person's thoughts or feelings, which are not directly observable, is unscientific and not an appropriate basis for psychological research.

Stimulus–response

The second principle proposed by Watson was that of ***stimulus-response.*** The scientific study of behavior occurs by understanding the response (the behavior) of an organism to a stimulus (any object or event that makes a difference in behavior). Scientists vary stimuli to ascertain what responses will follow.

The third principle was that behavior is learned—and may be un-learned as well. Unlike the prior psychological theories, which drew on religion, philosophy, and heredity, behaviorism held that our environment makes us what we are. We learn by being conditioned—a concept we will discuss in detail later.

The **law of effect** stated by Edward Thorndike was central to Watson's third principle. This law states there is a connection between what organisms do and the consequences that follow. If the consequences are positive, the behavior is more likely to recur. If the consequences are negative, the behavior will be less likely to recur. Behavioral theory in the tradition of Watson is an influential force in psychology. It has been called (by nonpartisans in this struggle between legions of competing theorists) "most elegant, most economical, and shows the closest link to its natural science forebears" (Hall & Lindzey, 1978, p. 563). The foundations of behavioral theory are the two special kinds of conditioning: classical conditioning and operant conditioning.

Classical Conditioning

Does the name Pavlov ring a bell? In the nineteenth century, the Russian physiologist Ivan Pavlov found that if you make a noise, by clicking or ringing a bell, or flash a light at the same time dogs are served food, the dogs will develop the same salivating to the sounds or lights that they originally had to the sight of the food. **Classical conditioning** is the learning that occurs when a neutral stimulus (such as a light or a ringing bell) is paired with a stimulus that naturally produces some behavior.

Four terms are used in describing classical conditioning.

Unconditioned stimulus (UCS). In Pavlov's studies, the food presented to the dogs was the UCS. More generally, this is the stimulus that is powerful enough to produce behavior without any prior learning.

Unconditioned response (UR). The UR in Pavlov's study was the dogs' salivation at the sight of the food. This is the natural, often instinctive response that is part of a physiological reflex or untrained action.

Conditioned stimulus (CS). The CS is the neutral event or stimulus (like Pavlov's bell) that is paired with the unconditioned stimulus.

Conditioned response (CR). The dogs' salivating just to the sound of the bell was their CR. This is the learned response that was formerly made only to the UCS but that is now made to the CS.

This phenomenon is not limited to laboratory animals in simple studies. All of human development is seen as affected by conditioning. The emotional warmth of child toward parents begins with conditioning from satisfactions of feeding and changing and touching. Almost all basic gratifications are paired with human contacts. Therefore, bonds of love and affection, as well as the disruptions of anger, are conditioned responses. The personal contacts that presumably are initially neutral stimuli become associated with more basic, instinctive responses. In the debate between advocates of heredity and advocates of environmental influences on personality development, then, the behaviorists have traditionally lined up on the side of the environment. Conditioning and learning are what shape human personality, and the newborn infant is seen as a blank slate on which beliefs, typical emotions, and predictable behaviors are inscribed.

Operant Conditioning

When you buy eggs in a market in England, you often have a choice of regular white eggs or brown free-range eggs. The regular white eggs come from chickens that have been fed and confined in cages in henhouses. Free-range eggs come from hens that are allowed to forage freely about the yard or farm. (These more expensive free-range eggs are believed to be more nutritious). Subjects in classical conditioning studies are placed, in a way, in the situation like that of the confined chickens. The subjects are restrained in place and, for the duration of the experiment, are under the control of the researcher.

FOCUS ON DEVELOPMENT

The Earliest Behavioral View: John B. Watson Looks at Human Development

The behaviorist finds that the human being at birth is a very lowly piece of unformed protoplasm, ready to be shaped by any family in whose care it first placed. This piece of protoplasm breathes, makes babbling, gurgling, cooing sounds with its vocal mechanisms, slaps its arms and legs about, moves its arms and toes, cries, excretes through the skin and other organs the waste matter from its food.

. . . contrasted with what the human infant has to learn, (heredity) is all-unimportant. Take any newborn American youngster and transport him into the interior of China and give him over to the exclusive care of a Chinese family and he will develop flawless Chinese, wear a quenue, worship his ancestors, eat with a chopstick, sit on a mat.

I can take the squirmings of the throat muscles and weave them into those highly organized acts we call talking and singing (and, yes, even thinking). I can take the infantile squirmings of the gut—the unstriped muscular tissue of the alimentary tract, diaphragm, heart, respiration, etc., and actually organize them into complicated emotional responses we call fears, loves, and rages.

(Watson, 1928, pp. 28, 31–33)

Operant conditioning

Operant conditioning is defined as that process in which freely emitted behaviors are modified by their consequences or outcomes. During operant conditioning, experimental subjects are somewhat like those free-ranging chickens. The subjects do what they would naturally do, and selected aspects of their behaviors are valued. In operant conditioning, those aspects are reinforced.

The term *operant* was first used by B.F. Skinner, the father of operant conditioning. Even more than other behaviorists, Skinner absolutely rejected interpretations of what an experimental animal felt. His experiments drew on existing behaviors that were simple and repetitive, typically of pigeons pecking. His studies addressed the effects of reinforcers on the rate or frequency of responses. The schedules of reinforcers (that is, the patterns that were used) were studied, with particular attention to what schedules led to behaviors persisting long after all reinforcement ceased. Although Skinner's research was in the laboratory with experimental animals, operant conditioning may be viewed in many daily life experiences. Let's take an example in child rearing.

The first time an infant grabs the spoon with which mother is feeding him, he may attempt to feed himself, but he gets peach puree on the floor, his face, and mother's shirt. If mother coos and says, "Oh, aren't you getting strong and independent," the behavior will be positively reinforced and will have a greater likelihood of occurring again. If the mother stiffens and sharply says, "Naughty, messy boy," these acts may reduce the probability of the behavior recurring. Operant conditioning occurs when some spontaneous behaviors are rewarded. Frequently, a connection is consciously made between the reinforcers and subsequent actions. It is not unusual for parents to inadvertently reward a child's dependency with attention and then to be distressed at how dependent the infant has become.

Shaping

You may have seen trained animal shows in which pigeons play the piano, elephants balance on one leg, or domestic cats leap through hoops and retrieve thrown objects. Such feats are attained by the operant procedure of ***shaping***, in which particular freely occurring behaviors are positively reinforced. A process of successive approximations is followed, in which rewards are given only as the behavior more closely approximates the final desired goals.

Reinforcers are much more than pellets of food or words of encouragement. For most of us, doing something well can be itself a positive reinforcer. Grades and money are obvious reinforcers; subtle rewards, such as the desirable emotional state of excitement at a sporting event or increases in attention and approval from valued others, are less obvious reinforcers. Suppose you stop reading just now, look out the window, and say, "The sky is moody." Animated attention from a companion and an ensuing discussion of the moody qualities in nature may help reinforce your making such statements. On the other hand, a disinterested "uh-huh" from your companion may be part of a process that would discourage you from making such observations.

Modern Behaviorism

In the early years of behaviorism, it was a matter of "us versus them." Either you accepted observed behavior as the substance of psychology, or you were one of those nonscientific others that looked at feelings and experience. Then behaviorism changed.

Stimulus–organism–response

The stimulus–response (S–R) theory was supplemented by *stimulus-organism-response* (S–O–R) theory, in which the role of the organism in interpreting and reacting internally to the stimulus was valued. This in turn was followed by cognitive behavioral psychology. Whereas Watson

FOCUS ON DEVELOPMENT

The Contemporary Behavioral Perspective

While behavioral psychology in Watson's time stood alone and independent of much of existing psychology, a much closer relationship between the various branches is present today. In the case of treating developmental problems, behavioral approaches have become an integral part of theory and practices. Behaviors of children have been carefully specified; observation and recording is a central part of much work, and research is regularly applied. A clear example of how influential behavioral ideas have become may be seen in the clinical/experimental view of childhood developed by Steven Schwartz and James H. Johnson (1985). Here is what they have observed:

1. The majority of problems children have in growing up are not illnesses, but rather are temporary and common problems in development.

2. The most frequent of these developmental problems are the difficult temperament, bladder and bowel control, childhood fears, social avoidance, temper tantrums and aggressive behavior, noncompliance, thumb sucking, and nightmares.

3. Noncompliance, childhood fears, thumb sucking, and nightmares, in particular, are not unusual, and most incidents do not represent major psychological difficulties. Noncompliance describes children whose actions do not conform to their parents' wishes.

They may not do things that the parent asks them to do (e.g., cleaning their room), or they may not *stop* doing things that the parent asks them

had proclaimed that thoughts were inaccessible, modern behaviorists frequently incorporated them, giving them a label of cognitions, and using cognitions to reinterpret or rehearse behaviors.

An impetus for this change was the development of research on decision making. Models of thinking were developed. Decision-trees emerged. In turn, more subtle forms of conditioning followed, in which internal processes could be modified by directing individuals to imagine scenes and feelings and to reduce muscular tension. George Kelly (1955) developed a theory of personal constructs for looking at the basic dimensions about which people organized their thoughts and beliefs. These ***personal constructs*** are like binoculars through which we see other people and our environment. As a result, we respond to what (and only what) is in our field of vision. Consider, for example, a man who has suspicion–trust as his major construct. Every contact he has with acquaintances or friends

Personal constructs

not to do (e.g., picking on little brother). Further, they may not adhere to basic rules that the parents may have established (e.g., putting their feet on the sofa when they have been previously told not to).

(Schwartz & Johnson, 1985, p. 106)

Because noncompliance is the most frequent complaint of parents who bring their children to psychological clinics, I will next note the typical behavioral methods of dealing with it (Forehand & McMahon, 1981; Schwartz & Johnson, 1985).

1. Parents are aided in understanding which commands to their children produce low levels of compliance. They are discouraged from giving vague commands ("Be a good boy"), from using a series of commands all at once, from using commands that blur into requests, and from following commands with a rationale that distracts the child from the original instruction.

2. Parents are assisted in developing commands that increase compliance. Effective commands are direct and specific, firmly telling the child what to do, after getting the child's attention. These commands are presented one at a time. A wait of five seconds should follow each command, so that additional statements do not sidetrack the parent or child.

These uses of behavioral approaches can be found in every area of psychology. The specificity, the accountability for techniques in use, and incorporation of objective methods and scientific outlooks have become a part of all fields of psychology related to adjustment.

would involve him in an internal decision of whether to suspiciously question the other person's motives or to think of the other individual as loyal and trustworthy.

Kelly also held that people act like objective scientists. They develop constructs, which are essentially theories about their personal worlds. Then they form hypotheses, continually test these hypotheses through what they do and what happens as a consequence of their actions, and finally modify their theories as needed.

Some behaviorists remain strictly committed to stimulus–response models of conditioning, but others, like Kelly, have expanded their area of concern, considering all of human experience to be within their realm, provided the methodology of examining the experience is objective, standardized, and accountable.

Well-Being

In behavioral theory, well-being rests both in the environment and in the organism. Environments (which include the people around us) bring out adaptive or maladaptive or particularly effective responses. Thus, the presence of stimuli that elicit health and reinforcers that maintain it make up two components for well-being.

Well-being, however, is associated with long-established characteristics in the individual as well. Thus, a learned sense of competence in life's tasks is part of well-being. Repeated success experiences produce this felt ability to master whatever is before you. In the same sense, well-being means being able to extend positive reinforcers to others, to serve as a nurturing part of the environment.

Maladjusted people do not discern stimuli clearly. Instead, they react with responses that do not fit the nature of the situation. Better adjustment occurs with the more accurate perception of stimuli and well-differentiated responses.

Finally, behaviorism is sometimes associated with a philosophy of life that rejects the mystical and subjective. Behavioral approaches embrace the objective and the known. If something cannot be measured or watched or assessed, it is of less scholarly interest and, thus, less pertinent to the understanding of well-being.

HUMANISTIC PSYCHOLOGY

Origins

Humanistic psychology

While both psychoanalysis and behaviorism struggle to be scientific and objective, **humanistic psychology** takes quite an opposing position. It is an orientation that (1) values the subjective in human experiencing,

Carl R. Rogers

(2) concerns itself with the meaning of life, (3) assumes that humans strive to be the best and most complete people they can be, and (4) utilizes the unique human traits of will, responsibility, and spirituality. Its roots are found in the writings of the nineteenth-century existentialist Soren Kierkegaard, as well as the twentieth-century philosopher Paul Tillich. Both have emphasized how the perceived meaning of one's life is what shapes individual human existence. Maladjustment, from this view, comes from living lies—that is, from living inauthentically and denying intentional choices. Maladjusted people do not take responsibility for who they are, and they permit the artificial in society to block their natural tendencies toward personal improvement and fulfillment.

The nature of humanistic psychology today was shaped in part by Carl Rogers, who began as a psychotherapist and counselor for children and adults. Rogers has summed up his forty-six years of activity, and indeed humanistic psychology, by proclaiming

> by and large, I think I have been a painfully embarrassing phenomenon to the academic psychologist. *I do not fit* . . . I am seen . . . as softheaded, unscientific, cultish, too easy on students, full of strange and upsetting enthusiasms about ephemeral things like the self, therapist attitudes, and encounters groups.

(Rogers, 1980, p. 51)

To the behaviorist, humanistic psychology truly is wishy-washy and mystical. Humanistic psychologists, however, embrace their subjective methods as the primary ways to understand the essence of human experience and purpose. The tendency toward self-actualization is one such essential human purpose.

The Actualizing Tendency

Actualizing tendency

The *actualizing tendency,* which may be defined as the movement in organisms toward fulfilling their potential, is a central belief of humanistic psychology. What makes all humans "tick" is the movement to be the best we can, to be as close to perfection (whatever that may mean for the individual) as possible. The word *actualizing* was created from the same stem as the word *actual* and refers to making potential capabilities into actual functioning.

Carl Rogers (1980) believes that people have vast resources for actualizing their behaviors, attitudes, and self-concepts. Three conditions especially promote such growth: *congruence, unconditional positive regard,* and *empathic understanding.* These interpersonal conditions occur anywhere: between parent and child, between friends, between mates, between teachers and students, and between therapists and clients. Let's consider these three conditions.

Congruence

Unconditional positive regard

Congruence.   When people are genuine, so that what they feel is consistent with how they act, they are in a state of ***congruence***. There's no phoniness: What they feel, what they are aware of, and what they do are the same. Exposed to congruence in others, individuals can relinquish the lies and postures in their own lives, can let go of those artificial ways of acting that interfere with actualization.

Unconditional positive regard.   Most people accept us conditionally. If we say the right things, dress the right way, hold the correct beliefs, and behave in expected ways, then approval comes from others. Ac-

When a person cares for us and prizes us for who we are, regardless of what we are feeling or thinking or doing at that moment, that person has unconditional positive regard for us. Babies often receive this kind of unconditional and nonjudgmental affection. Can you think of any other examples of people or behavior that inspire this type of regard?

tualization comes, however, when we are regarded unconditionally, without such requirements. We are cared about and prized for who we are, whatever we are feeling or thinking or doing at that moment. Affection does not have to be won. It is simply there, without performance demands. The affection is unconditional, nonjudgmental.

Empathic understanding

Empathic understanding.   This condition occurs when another person ". . . senses accurately [our] feelings and personal meanings . . . and communicates this understanding" (Rogers, 1980, p. 116). Such listening with real understanding is rare, yet it is a potent condition for growth.

How do these three conditions allow people to become actualized? Rogers (1980) writes of how potatoes he used to store in the basement over the winter would occasionally sprout and send pale, spindly shoots up toward the far window. They would never mature and fulfill their potential. So it is with those people living in incongruent, nonempathic, and conditional environments. They remain emotionally stunted. Genuine caring, understanding, and acceptance are the bright lights under which personality thrives. Individuals incorporate within themselves the conditions of congruence, unconditional positive regard, and empathic understanding. They come to be more caring of themselves, to prize who they are. They are more understanding and empathic about their own needs, and they finally become more congruent. They let go of the need to act to please others (in which approval is conditional) and can pay attention to who they themselves are.

Maslow

Another of the primary writers on humanistic psychology has been Abraham Maslow (1954, 1968). Maslow not only held that the origin and goals of science come from human values, he went much further. He asserted that science itself is a value system. Every time a scientist classifies or abstracts or even attends to some event or phenomenon, the work is being done in relation to the scientist's own human needs. Maslow saw psychologists engaged in an exaggerated search for pure, untainted science, in which technique is overemphasized. Researchers into human nature thus become overly caught up in the means of studying, and quantification often becomes an end to itself. Scientists become trapped by their apparatus and methods, and they come to believe that truths about human functioning may only arise from instrumentation and their own scientific methods.

Maslow urged that psychologists should center their work on the problem, not on the artificial techniques for studying human problems. Out of his concern that human nature was reduced to small, meaning-

Abraham H. Maslow urged psychologists to center their work on the *problem,* not to become overly caught up in the *means* of studying and not to allow quantification to become an end in itself.

less elements in psychological research, Maslow described holistic theory as an alternative. *Holism* means that the whole person is studied, in the changing, dynamic context of his or her life, environment, and motivations. Healthy motivation is central to Maslow's thinking about the study of human beings; when it is present, we can understand what well-adjusted and high-functioning people are like. Scientists also should be healthier, Maslow argued. Scientists have subjective needs and interests, and, so they will be equipped to be open and constructive in investigating human experience, they should be emotionally healthy and receive psychotherapy.

The Subjective

Not only do Maslow and other humanistic psychologists value the *subjective* in both experience and in methods of study, but they see the subjective as *primary* in understanding all events. One leading humanistic psychologist captured this view when he wrote, ". . . any statement we make about the world (the 'out there') is inevitably, inescapably, a statement about our theory of ourselves (the 'in here')" (Bugental, 1967, p. 6). This emphasis leads to a discarding of the objective. Indeed, at one time, Sidney Jourard (1968) called for a redoing of all psychological research with humans, with the experimenters this time acting warm and human and open, instead of detached and scientific and objective. Jourard felt that the research findings in every area of human functioning would be altogether different.

This attention to the subjective means that humanistic psychology rejects research with other species. We cannot gain access to the experience of white rats, red hawks, or any other laboratory animal. Furthermore, normative findings and group patterns are unimportant. The individual and his or her idiosyncratic, personal, and unpredictable ways of being are the core of humanistic psychology.

Because the subjective is valued, poems, fiction, paintings, and fantasies are subjects for learning about humans. Standardized measures, such as intelligence tests, always do a disservice to the uniqueness of individuals. Instead, humanistic psychology uses all the personal forms through which we express ourselves.

Current Status

Humanistic psychologists see people in subjective terms and as governed by free will. Their current work continues to be seated in this philosophy of human nature. They believe there are no absolute truths or absolute realities, but only truths and realities as individuals personally see and understand them. If you and I agree something is real, we coauthor that reality.

At the same time that this philosophy of subjectivity was being developed, some humanistic psychologists engaged in the practice of psychology. The leading writer in the practice of humanistic psychology has been Constance Fischer, of Duquesne University in Pittsburgh. To Fischer (1985), a key to applied humanistic psychology is a respect for the perspectives of others. In her case, this respect came initially from attending seventeen schools in ten states and three countries before she finished college. Fischer has concluded that psychology (and sociology and education) were wrong when they modeled themselves after the physical sciences. The alternative is **human science psychology** (Giorgi, 1970), in which the traditional pursuits of physical science methods are discarded. In place of them, human science psychology emphasizes

Human science psychology

1. Qualitative, descriptive methods. These replace or at least supplement the statistics-oriented data that summarize rather than describe people.
2. Direct study of actual events and experiences, as they can be observed or as people report them. This contrasts with manipulation of variables in the laboratories of physical scientists.

These methods are used in psychological assessments and psychotherapy as well as in research. For example, consider this exchange between a psychologist and a client who is being given the Rorschach inkblot test:

Client: Jesus, you must be making something of all these insides I'm seeing

Assessor: I am a little surprised; what do you think is going on?

Client: Maybe you think I'm falling apart. (Long pause) Maybe you think I think women are just anatomy . . .

(Fischer, 1985, p. 95)

At this point, most psychologists would stay studiously neutral, saying little. In this particular situation, the psychologist was using the human science approach: the assessor next asked the client what experience in his life was related to what he saw on the inkblots. The client then described an incident in which his father chased his mother around the kitchen table with a butcher knife. In this example, the human science assessor did not treat the test results as ends in themselves, but rather related them back to the client's history and current emotional reactions (Fischer, 1985).

The current status of humanistic psychology is that it is an elaboration of uniqueness and meaning in human life. Equally prominent is its role in opposition to behaviorism and determinism. In his presidential address to the Division of Humanistic Psychology of the American Psychological Association, David Morganstern described humanistic psychology as

> . . . a third force reaction to the narrow mechanistic and deterministic views of man-as-controlled, held by both psychoanalysis and the behaviorists. . . . The thirty year groundswell of humanistic thought brought a renewed emphasis on the worth and capacities of men and women.

> *(Morganstern, 1982, pp. 5–6)*

Well-Being

Well-being is easier to define in humanistic psychology than in most other theories because it is so central to humanistic writers. Four elements of well-being can be identified within this school of thought.

1. *Natural growth.* In maladjusted people, their natural movement toward improvement is stunted. To attain well-being, people must be "unblocked," opening the ability to improve themselves, to move toward fulfillment of potential ways of feeling and being.

2. *Honesty and spontaneity.* Life is unfettered and unshackled by phoniness. Instead, people are honest with themselves and others. They act responsibly but freely. Their actions are consistent with their feelings and thoughts.

3. *Unconditional caring.* In well-being, we love others for who they truly are, not for some image in our minds. We accept people and care for them genuinely and without ulterior motives. Others are appreciated for who they are becoming and how they are developing.

4. *Actualized experiences.* Moments of deep serenity and fulfillment are experienced. At times, ordinary life is transcended, and we move toward spiritual or enlightened existence.

TABLE 2-1 Well-Being in the Major Personality Theories		
	Toward Well-Being	Away from Well-Being
Psychoanalysis	Is free from fixations	Becomes fixated at early oral, anal, or phallic stages
	Has helped the unconscious become conscious through analysis	Is unaware of unconscious influences
	Has an active and dominant ego	Is dominated or imbalanced by id or superego

TABLE 2–1 Well-Being in the Major Personality Theories (continued)		
	Toward Well-Being	**Away from Well-Being**
Psychoanalysis	Is able to love and work	Has neurotic barriers to loving and working well
Behaviorism	Has experienced health-producing environments	Has experienced distress-producing environments
	Has learned competence and self-efficacy	Has learned incompetence
	Acts to elicit positive reinforcers	Elicits negative reinforcers
	Seeks the verifiable and objective in personal life	Seeks the mystical and subjective in life
	Discerns different stimuli well	Discerns different stimuli poorly
Humanistic psychology	Has developed natural tendencies toward growth	Has had natural tendencies toward growth thwarted
	Is honest and spontaneous in daily life	Lies to self and others and is constricted in daily life
	Can unconditionally befriend and love	Can befriend and love only conditionally and judgmentally
	Has transcendental and actualized life experiences	Has humdrum and unenlightened life

SUMMARY

A good personality theory is defined as a clear and explicit set of statements that will withstand empirical testing. Personality itself is the stable core of the individual—who a person is and how he or she thinks, feels, and behaves.

Psychoanalysis is a theory of personality developed by Sigmund Freud. It states that the conscious is made up of awareness of current thoughts and feelings. Thoughts and feelings accessible to awareness are in the preconscious, and inaccessible material is in the unconscious. The unconscious is the reservoir for unacceptable instinctive drives and repressed feelings and experiences.

Mental structure as described by Freud is made up of the id, the ego, and the superego. The id is the unconscious repository of primitive drives and need for satisfaction. The ego mediates rationally and consciously between instinctive drives and the external world. The partly conscious superego censors and passes judgment of rightness or wrongness on actions and thoughts.

Personality develops in five stages. In the oral stage, pleasure and conflict center on the mouth, sucking, and oral gratification. Then comes the anal stage, in which the activity of learning control of the anal sphincter becomes a battleground for social and parental control versus instinctive self-satisfaction. The third key stage is the phallic stage, at which time the genitals become a source of gratification. At this time, attraction to the opposite sex parent leads to the universal incest taboo and fear of punishment. In boys, this conflict is the Oedipal complex, and in girls, the Electra complex. In the latency stage, a period of developmental inactivity occurs, followed by the confrontation with the capacity for full sexual functioning in the genital stage.

In psychoanalytic thinking, well-being is moving through the developmental stages without being fixated, bringing repressed unconscious content into consciousness through psychoanalytic treatment, and being able to live flexibly and to love and work well.

Behaviorism, shaped by John B. Watson and B.F. Skinner, scientifically observes behavior and disdains inaccessible internal events. This approach assumes that behavior is learned, not inborn, and that understanding stimulus–response connections provides the basis for understanding behavior.

In classical conditioning, a neutral stimulus is paired with a stimulus that produces a response without prior learning. Then a new, conditioned response to the formerly neutral stimulus occurs. In contrast, in operant conditioning, freely emitted behaviors are modified or shaped by their consequences. Modern behaviorism has taken into account the organism's internal processes, but there is a continued emphasis on scientific objectivity and control.

Well-being in behaviorist theory is exhibited in learned competencies, in clear differentiation of stimuli, in stimuli that elicit health, and in the ability to extend positive reinforcers to others.

Humanistic psychology contrasts with both behaviorism and psychoanalysis in that it values subjectivity, meaning of life, and people's tendencies to fulfill or actualize themselves. Actualization is promoted by congruence between how individuals feel and how they behave, by valuing others without conditions, and by empathically understanding other people.

The study of subjective human experience is an important part of this school. For that reason, objective and standardized tests in psychology are used in conjunction with unique creations such as poems and fantasies. Four elements make up well-being in humanistic psychology. They are attainment of natural growth as a person, honesty and spontaneity in living, unconditional caring for others, and actualized experiences.

Key Terms

Actualizing tendency	**Law of effect**
Anal stage	**Lifestyle analysis**
Behaviorism	**Oedipus complex**
Classical conditioning	**Operant conditioning**
Collective unconscious	**Oral stage**
Conditioned response	**Personal constructs**
Conditioned stimulus	**Personality**
Congruence	**Phallic stage**
Conscious	**Preconscious**
Ego	**Psychoanalysis**
Electra complex	**Psychosocial development**
Empathic understanding	**Shaping**
Extroversion	**Stimulus-organism-response**
Genital stage	**Stimulus-response**
Good theory	**Striving for superiority**
Holism	**Subjective**
Human science psychology	**Superego**
Humanistic psychology	**Unconditional positive regard**
Id	**Unconditioned response**
Introversion	**Unconditioned stimulus**
Latency stage	**Unconscious**

Recommended Reading

Appignanesi, R. (1979). *Freud for beginners* (Illustrations by Oscar Zarate). London: Writers and Readers Publishing Cooperative. Is it possible for a cartoon book to be all at once playful and serious? Can illustrations truly bring life to many of the abstract notions within Freudian theory? Is it possible to read something today that can shock and offend us as much as Viennese citizens were shocked and offended by Freud in the year 1900? Yes. Yes. Yes.

Mischel, W. (1986). *Introduction to personality* (4th ed.). New York: Holt, Rinehart & Winston. If you are interested in learning more about theories of personality, read Mischel's book. It is clear. It is comprehensive. Here is a book used for upper-level psychology courses that is actually readable. On that basis, it is radical, too.

Rogers, C.R. (1980). *A way of being.* Boston: Houghton Mifflin. This book explores both Rogers's way of being and humanistic psychology's way of being; it is personal, informal, chatty. Rogers looks back and looks forward at the meaning of his work and his beliefs.

3

CHAPTER

The Self-Concept

Squeal

The Mercedes 380 SEL limousine had loud brakes, and when Jonathan heard that ear-piercing squeal, he knew that the big black limousine was in front of Rosemary's house. Jonathan rushed out. The two goons in the double-breasted suits and wide-brim hats already had Rosemary in their arms, while the little beady-eyed man with the thin-lipped smile looked on.

Jonathan leaped, twisted in midair, and double kicked one of the goons to the ground. An elbow to the solar plexus left the second one gasping for air. Rosemary reached for Jonathan's arm as the smile faded from the face of the little man with the beady eyes. Jonathan stepped forward, an aura of power surrounding him with white light, and he would have destroyed all three of the men had his attention not been drawn once again to the other students taking notes. Blinking away Mercedes, thugs, and Rosemary on his arm, he resumed writing. The instructor droned on about the self-concept and about the ideal self each of us carries.

In one sense, Jonathan carried no more with him than he had to. He led what an observer might call a simple life. Jonathan lived quietly, never got in trouble, was always prompt. To the public eye, he was neither troublesome nor conspicuous. You could tell from his wardrobe.

He had two sets of clothes: the browns and the blues. On brown days, he would wear tan chinos, a light beige shirt (occasionally striped), and a brown sleeveless sweater. On blue days, he wore unwrinkled blue jeans, gray or blue shirts, and blue sleeveless sweaters. He liked V-necked T-shirts, too. They didn't show. Jonathan's hair was medium length, brown, straight. He was carefully shaven. He was minimally noticeable, and not by accident.

He wanted people to see him as dependable and trustworthy and unobtrusive. They did. He didn't want them to see him as flamboyant or showy or egotistical. They didn't.

As the class went on, Jonathan noticed Rosemary diagonally in front of him, taking few notes. She wasn't conscientious about keeping up her notebook. If there was anything Jonathan knew he was, it was conscientious. Oh, he knew he was other things too, sometimes sad and discouraged, and scared, and sometimes feeling a skinned-knee sensitivity to what others might think. As these ideas rolled on in his mind, his eyes glazed over a little. Then he stopped and lifted his ears (Jonathan was one of the few people who have prehensile or grasping ears, but his skill had been rarely seen by others after he was teased in the second grade about being a "Dumbo boy"). He thought he heard something. He did.

It was the sound of squealing brakes from the Mercedes 380 SEL limousine. He knew what he had to do. Jonathan rushed out. . .

In class and out, Jonathan had a consistent face he presented to other people—a cautious, conservative image that we know as the public self. How Jonathan really saw himself—ah, that was as a different person. Part of his most personal thoughts about himself were his fantasized ideals. Jonathan the brave hero, Jonathan the intrepid rescuer, Jonathan the suitor of Rosemary—these were all pieces of his ideal. There is more the story doesn't tell us, about how he actually saw himself, his beliefs, attitudes, thoughts, and feelings about himself as a man, a student, a person in transition. Our example of Jonathan's ways of thinking and feeling about himself is our introduction to the unification of all the ways we feel about and see ourselves: the self-concept. Despite Jonathan's seeming awareness of these elements of his self-concept, it is possible he had little real knowledge of himself. John Davies put such lack of awareness in verse, writing

> We that acquaint ourselves with every zone
> And pass both tropics and behold the poles,
> When we come home are to ourselves unknown,
> And unacquainted still with our own souls.

(Evans, 1968, p. 616)

This chapter looks at the ways we are to ourselves unknown and how these ways can become known.

Before we begin our discussion, it should be pointed out that the self-concept is not a physical entity that can be weighed or measured. However, people conceive of themselves as having certain qualities, as behaving in ways they recognize as "me." Such concepts make it seem *as if* there is a consistent, yet flexible, self-concept. The key words are "as if." Like many other concepts in psychology, including intelligence and personality, we create the notion of self-concept and then treat it as if it were real because it allows for the development of theory and research. However, we must not lose track of the fact that we are speaking of a theoretical construct. With this in mind, we now may define the ***self-concept.***

Self-concept

HOW WE SEE OURSELVES: THE SELF-CONCEPT

The *self-concept* is defined as the totality of beliefs, perceptions, and feelings people hold about themselves. It describes what a person is now, has been in the past, and the person's understandings of who he or she is becoming. This contemporary definition echoes William James's one-hundred-year-old description of the self-concept of the elegant gentry:

> . . . a man's Self is the sum total of all that he can call his own . . . not only his body and his psychic powers, but his clothes and his house, his wife and his children, his ancestors and friends, his reputation and works, his lands and horses, and yacht and bank account.

(James, 1890, p. 291)

Thus, the self includes not only all the things we think of as *me*, but also all of the things seen as *mine*. This material self is part of the self-concept, and it includes body, clothing, and possessions.

Self-descriptions include the fixed ways we "objectively" see our-selves. If you think to yourself of your shirt or blouse size and have a clear image of how your body fits that size, then you have an image of your objective self. It is stable, and a view of yourself as you are.

In contrast are the ways you see yourself psychologically dealing with the events in your life. This process is fluid; it is an adaptive aspect of the self that pays attention to personal reactions and changes. How you perceive yourself in the process of change is most related to your personal adjustment. We will now examine three aspects of the self-concept: the self-concept as a totality, the consistent nature of the self-concept, and the self-concept as it evolves and changes.

The Self-Concept Is a Totality

No *single* belief or perception about ourselves determines our self-concept. Rather, the self-concept is the sum of our perceptions, understandings, and beliefs about ourselves. We all have specific components of our self-views about which we feel especially good and others about which we feel particularly vulnerable. Our views about how desirable we are as family members may differ from our views of ourselves socially, and those in turn may be different from how we see ourselves as athletes, as academics, while speaking before groups, and in crises. Each of these aspects truly is us. Yet none describes us fully.

The self-concept is the sum of all of these aspects. It is our under-standing about who we are, how good we are at everything we do, how we appear, how effectively we achieve our aims, and how others see us.

Within the total self-concept there are subcategories. Studies have been made, for example, of the academic self-concept, of the social self-concept, and of the physical self-concept. The more narrowly the self-concept is studied, the better we can come to know it.

The Self-Concept Is Consistent

The major ways we come to think about ourselves do not usually arise from isolated instances. Rather, they grow from a series of experiences over years and decades. We then form a core of consistent perceptions about these experiences. People who see themselves primarily as effective achievers carry that self-concept into many settings. Persons who see themselves as unlikable often will be consistent in holding that view, even when information, such as people openly liking them, may be to the contrary.

A *consistency rule* has been observed (Noren-Hebeisen, 1981) that states the self-concept functions to maximize gain and minimize loss for the person. Many studies throw light on this phenomenon. For example,

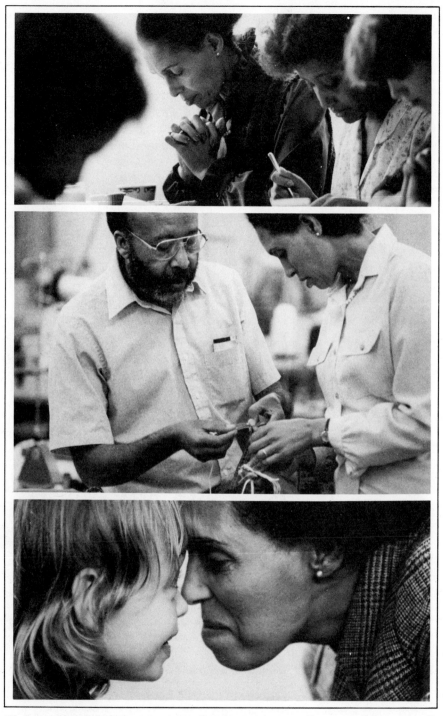

We have no single belief or perception that determines our self-concept. Rather, our self-concept is the totality of all of our understandings of ourselves.

people with high and low levels of self-esteem behave differently when placed in situations where they will be critically evaluated as opposed to situations where they will be subjected to a very easy evaluation. People with low self-esteem choose to put their effort into the easy evaluation: anticipating failure in the tough situation, they don't even attempt it. People with high self-esteem do just the opposite, putting their energies into the difficult evaluation situation, already assuming they will succeed in the easy evaluation (Sigall & Gould, 1977). Each type of person chooses

This man is a leper. He is poor, he has a negative self-concept, and his life is filled with despair. How can those of us with a terrible illness or affliction work toward having a positive self-concept?

the course of action consistent with his or her self-concept; each seeks the highest payoff and least investment of unnecessary effort.

The same responses can be seen in students with good and poor academic self-concepts. The students with high academic self-concepts put their efforts into their toughest courses. The students who see themselves as low achievers put more time into the easier courses, where they believe they will get the better grades. These outcomes are affected in part by different degrees of the development of and the consistency of the students' self-concepts.

Not everyone has self-concepts developed to the same extent. People who have unstable and vague self-concepts will be less consistent. More consistent self-concepts, those with similar features over time, tend to appear in persons who are more mature and perceive with greater clarity who they are.

Consistency allows us to maintain personal identities, so we may say we are the same persons today that we were yesterday and are likely to be tomorrow. In Steven Donaldson's (1977) epic novels about the adventures of Thomas Covenant, the hero is a leper. Despite being transported to a new world in which his leprosy has disappeared, Covenant continues to think of himself as a leper, and he carries with him as his constant companions the despair and alienation that come from his self-concept as a leper. As a leper, he knew himself to be useless, helpless, doomed.

While Thomas Covenant is an example of how self-concepts are consistent, he is also a model for how people can change as situations demand. His courage, born of despair, eventually allowed Covenant to become a hero in a new world. Self-images do change, and sometimes the spirit of the times, or *zeitgeist*, allows people to rise above their limitations and become extraordinary people in extraordinary times.

Despite these instances, research studies have found how vitally important it is to individuals to maintain stable and consistent self-concepts. Even under conditions that challenge their views of themselves, most people are firmly committed to confirming their sense of self (see, for example, Markus & Kunda, 1986). Although this long-term self-concept is highly stable, the self-concept at any given moment—what has been called the *working self-concept*—is more reactive to changes in situations. While people do strive to see themselves consistently, their self-concepts do change. We will examine such changes next.

The Self-Concept Evolves and Changes

The self-concept is not absolutely fixed in most people. As we experience new things, we compare the new data to our existing understanding of ourselves, and our self-concepts may be revised according to what we

Zeitgeist

learn. The more powerful our learning experiences, the more likely our self-concepts will change.

Even in the absence of dramatic events, a continued evolution of the self-concept occurs. People may grow intellectually and emotionally. They test out their desirability and effectiveness in hundreds of ways. Of course, we tend to filter events in ways consistent with our existing views. Such filtering, however, does not stop all new information. It only screens out some of it, and we can modify what we think about our worth and efficacy based on new experiences. Modifications and evolution toward well-being are part of what has been called the ***mutable self.***

Mutable self

The word *mutable* means changeability. The mutable self is one that changes, develops, and is able to assume whichever of the many components of the self a situation requires (Zurcher, 1977). Unlike a self-concept to which a person is bound and limited, a mutable self-concept is flexible and open.

> . . . the person who has developed a Mutable Self is open to the widest possible range of human experiences and is able to draw deeply upon personal capacities and potential. He or she is a *complete* self.
>
> *(Zurcher, 1977, p. 223)*

People who have their primary reference point in one narrow self-concept find that their greatest source of satisfaction. However, having a mutable self allows one a greater range of possible satisfactions. All of the options for being, thinking, and feeling about self and others are seen as the freeing agents.

Can anyone become mutable? It takes the deliberate process of moving nondefensively from one aspect of self-concept into another and beyond. Once one is mutable and change is already mastered inside, it becomes easy to extend it outside to others and to the social forces in our lives.

Let us note that the self-concept is both highly consistent and changeable. The changeable qualities of the self-concept arise in large part from social dynamics acting on the working self. Unlike the long-term self-concept, which is so resistant to change, the ***working self-concept*** shifts in temporary ways. These shifts are often subtle, not demanding major revisions in how individuals think or feel about themselves (Markus & Kunda, 1986). Consider a person in a conformity experiment who asserts which poster he likes best and then discovers all of his companions dislike it. He may feel a passing sense of discomfort about his self-worth. However, no lasting effects occur.

Working self-concept

Such social interchanges may affect self-concepts much in the way moods may be affected by daily events. Take simple instances of changes in physical self-perceptions. People who see themselves as quite tall may

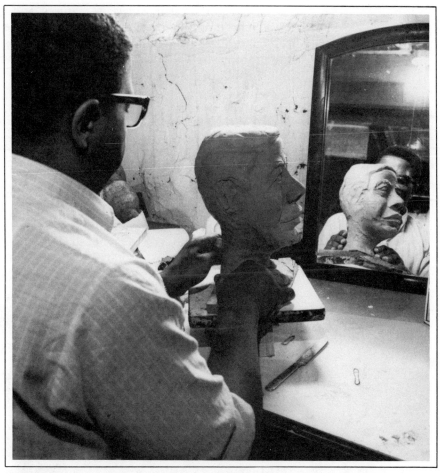

Our self-concept continually evolves and changes, much in the same way this man's skill and talent as a sculptor develops. The sculptor draws on his past experience and applies what he has learned to his art. He will test out the desirability of the finished product by showing it to other people, who will offer their opinions. Then he will modify his approach so that his next work of art will be based on this new information. This cycle will continue for each new piece of art.

have a jarring shift in that self-concept aspect when they walk between two basketball players. Persons who see themselves as very physically attractive may shift that judgment downward when in the company of exceptionally attractive companions. Conversely, people who perceive themselves as unattractive may shift their self-judgments upward, depending on their company (Gergen, 1981).

Factors other than physical features and social interactions influence our understanding of self-concepts. One factor that affects our self-concepts is the common beliefs held in our society. Let us now examine the ways in which such common beliefs and expectations affect our thinking about self-concepts.

COMMON BELIEFS ABOUT THE SELF-CONCEPT

Sayings and proverbs reflect widely held ideas about the self. When we say that the stingy man always sees himself as thrifty and that the cowardly person sees himself as cautious, we are stating beliefs about the self-concept. In the same manner, we speak about the basis for self-esteem, or regard for oneself, when we repeat the sayings that people have to love themselves before others can love them and that people truly have to believe they can accomplish their goals before the goals can be accomplished.

The pleasantness of this social interchange will support this man's positive sense of himself in social situations.

Many beliefs about self-concept turn out to be myths, unsupported by research. In the most comprehensive review of self-concept literature, Ruth C. Wylie (1979) has identified these beliefs and what is known about them. Let us consider some of them.

Socioeconomic Status and Self-Esteem

The belief: ". . . parents who feel that members of their [social] class are typically inferior or superior persons may, accordingly, convey a sense of inferiority or superiority to their children before, and apart from, the child's development of a sense of his own socioeconomic level" (Wylie, 1979, pp. 60–61). This belief also holds that society's disdain toward the lower classes becomes incorporated into the self-images and self-esteem of the children raised in those classes.

The facts support neither proposition. Studies of these issues have not been conclusive, and indeed one large investigation yielded the unexpected and paradoxical finding that the lower classes had higher self-esteem. However, the final assessment by this and four dozen other studies of social status and self-esteem was skeptical.

> . . . [the studies] have yielded contradictory, weak, mostly null results regarding the relationship of socioeconomic level and over-all self-regard. Certainly no support is given to the extreme, but typical, views quoted at the outset concerning the unfavorable impact of lower class status on self-regard.

(Wylie, 1979, p. 115)

Once, when writer Gertrude Stein went to Oakland, California, to see what was there, she wrote that "there is 'no there' there." In the same sense, when we go to the research literature to see what compelling links exist between socioeconomic levels and self-esteem, we find nothing there.

Family Influences on the Self-Concept

The belief: Our folk wisdom includes hundreds of observations about how loved children grow up to love themselves. If parents are accepting of their children, and hold them in high esteem, the children will subsequently have high self-esteem, because they have learned to value themselves. Those psychologists concerned with birth order and self-esteem have assumed that first borns will be most valued because they are most wanted and loved. Furthermore, it has been speculated that broken homes due to divorce and father absence would lead to children's low self-regard, because of their lessened opportunities for identification with a loved parent.

The facts are that no *cause and effect* relationships have been determined. However, children's self-esteem levels are generally positively related to the levels of regard and rapport that they report their parents have toward them. Children from broken homes and homes where the father is absent show no higher or lower self-esteem than children from homes in which both parents are present. Birth order seems to have little impact. However, male and only children were found to have especially high self-esteem.

We do know what parental behaviors promote self-esteem in their children. The basic requirement seems to be genuine acceptance of the children. Once that is present, children develop regard for themselves in homes that have clear rules and regulations that are enforced consistently. Harsh and rigid punishment does not help; however, the presence of reasonable limits and rules that have some flexibility and are appropriate to the age of the children is associated with the development of high self-esteem in children. Why? Stanley Coopersmith writes of it in the following terms: "Detailed definition of standards, and their consistent presentation and enforcement, presents the child with a wealth of information that he himself can employ to appraise and anticipate the consequences of his actions" (1967, p. 239).

More than just parents affect self-esteem. As children grow up, their self-regard is increasingly shaped by teachers and peers as well. Just as the number of valued people in a child's life expands, so do the sources of information that help to shape that child's self-image (Cotton, 1983).

A note is in order about youths with low self-esteem. They tend to feel unloved or rejected and uncertain and powerless in their lives. Coopersmith observes that they expect both rejection and failure, which become self-fulfilling prophecies for both parent and child. Later in this chapter we will examine such self-fulfilling prophecies.

Age and the Self-Concept

The belief: Children have an emerging sense of self as they grow up, with self-regard and identity increasing through childhood, preadolescence, and adolescence and adulthood. In contrast, Wylie (1979) has concluded that, although some researchers report self-regard increasing with age, about the same numbers of investigators report self-regard decreasing with age. Furthermore, many studies show little change as their subjects grow older. Whether or not self-esteem rises seems to depend on day-to-day personal relationships with parents, teachers, and peers.

When the elderly were investigated, some correlates of positive self-regard were found. In part as a function of higher education, positive self-concepts among the elderly were related to feeling bright and alert, being good at getting things done, and being physically active.

This woman is poor, but that doesn't mean her life and the life of her child are, or ever will be, unhappy or void of self-esteem. In fact, most investigations found that children from lower socioeconomic classes had neither lower nor *higher* self-esteem than did people with more wealth and greater status in society. In other studies, children's self-esteem was generally positively related to the regard they received from their parents. These latter studies suggest that this child's future could be bright indeed.

With some of the characteristics of self-concepts outlined, we now move to the first of our components of the self: the public, or social, self.

ASPECTS OF THE SELF-CONCEPT

The Public Self

> All clowns are masked and all *personae*
> Flow from choices; sad and gay, wise,
> Moody and humorous are chosen faces. . .

(Schwartz, 1982, p. 67)

Public self

The ***public self*** is the image we wish to present to others. It consists of all of the desirable characteristics we want to have attributed to us and the ways in which we behave to elicit these perceptions. For some people, the public self is clearly understood, a set of explicit, well-defined traits toward which their actions are oriented. James Thurber described one component of his public self as he would have liked it to be.

One afternoon almost two years ago, at a cocktail party (at least this is the way I have been telling the story), an eager middle-aged woman said to me, "Do you belong to the Lost Generation, Mr. T?" and I retorted, coldly and quick as a flash, "No, Madam, I belong to the Hiding Generation."

As a matter of fact, no woman ever asked me such a question at a cocktail party or anywhere else. I thought up the little dialogue one night when I couldn't sleep. At the time, my retort seemed pretty sharp and satirical to me, and I hoped that some day somebody *would* ask me if I belonged to the Lost Generation, so that I could say no, I belonged to the Hiding Generation. But nobody ever has.

(Thurber, 1935, p. 178)

The Thurber public self was witty, cool, and sharp. Most people share common public self-concepts; they are interested in being seen as competent, likable, and sincere. The trouble is that the ordinary situations of life are such that we often do not feel competent, likable, or sincere. In these situations, our public self becomes a false self, distant from our private self. Some of this role presentation is natural. However, when carried to an extreme, the public self can be felt and seen as artificial and uncomfortable. Then we become interpersonal chameleons, working overly hard to fit in.

The public self has been called the "looking glass" self. This refers to the process in which we come to see ourselves as we believe others see us. The looking glass or public self is most affected by persons on whose judgments we especially rely, such as parents, close friends, and others truly significant to us. Furthermore, whether the opinions held by others are positive or negative influences how much we respect their opinions. Rosenberg (1979) has pointed out that we often value the opinions of people who think highly of us and tend to be less concerned with the assessments of our detractors. Beyond the positive or negative nature of others' judgments, we also depend on whether the persons have reasonable bases for assessing us and on how much consensus exists among the people who judge us.

There is no question that the social judgments of others are powerful in affecting how we choose to present ourselves. With few exceptions, we truly, deeply want others' attention, recognition, and approval.

No more fiendish punishment could be devised, were such a thing physically possible, than that one should be turned loose in society and remain absolutely unnoticed by all the members thereof. If no one turned round when we entered, answered when we spoke, or minded what we did, but if every person we met "cut us dead," and acted as if we were nonexisting things, a kind of rage and impotent despair would ere long well up in us, from which the cruelest bodily tortures would be a relief.

(James, 1890, pp. 293–294)

William James went on to point out how many public selves there are. He observed, "*. . . a man has as many social selves as there are individuals who recognize him* and carry an image of him in their mind" (1890, p. 294).

Expedience has been described as one of the major characteristics of the public self (Jourard, 1974). By "expedience," we mean that people act in ways that are immediately advantageous to them to produce an effect. Sometimes we think sentences to ourselves to affirm a view. We may think something to the effect: "I am a worthless human being unless most of the people I meet like me and approve of me." Then our public self presentation will attempt to achieve that liking and approval. Sidney Jourard has written that such public self presentation is much like the art of sculpture:

> A sculptor manipulates clay and then steps back to see whether the statue he is creating resembles the image he has in mind. If it doesn't, he continues to work at it, until by successive approximations he has brought into reality something which hitherto existed only as a preferred idea or image.
>
> By the same token, a person may hold an image of his own person-

How others judge us socially powerfully affects how we choose to present ourselves. The majority of us profoundly want the attention, and approval of those around us.

ality that he wants to construct in the mind of another person. Instead of clay, he employs his own carefully selected behavior and conversation.

(Jourard, 1974, p. 163)

The Private Self

Apart from the ways we act to elicit liking and approval from others, we also accumulate inner views of ourselves. The private self is defined as those accumulated understandings of ourselves as we *really* are. The ***private self*** encompasses the fears, insecurities, and inadequacies we admit to almost no one. It includes the truly felt positive aspects as well

Private self

OUR PUBLIC FACES AND OUR PUBLIC SELVES

The public self is seen in a person's facial expressions, which often yield more emotional messages than do the person's words. With a superior in an organization, we often put on our *subordinate* face: the tension around the mouth and forehead shows our role. With uninvited strangers begging for money on the street, we attach a *distant* face, indicating unavailability and disinterest. In loving moments, we have our *affectionate* faces. When the dark house erupts with friends wishing us happy birthday, our *surprised/delighted* face appears. Have you noticed how some people are almost unrecognizable when they are asleep, because they have given up their public selves and allowed their faces to relax? They do not need their faces to present certain appearances to others during sleep.

The public self works best if we allow some of our true selves to be seen. Instead of seeming to be all appearance, we can be seen as having substance. Such personal visibility occurs when we stop making harsh critical judgments about personal feelings surfacing in these public selves. Virginia Satir offers a suggestion.

> Would it sound very bizarre to entertain the idea that each of your faces, no matter how you have judged them in the past, can be used to work for you? . . . Make a list for yourself, of all the different faces that you know about, dividing them into those which you label good and those you label bad. Each of your faces, regardless of whether you label it good or bad, holds the seed, the germ, so to speak, of new energy and new uses, something like finding a pretty face under a lot of dirt. I recommend just washing off the dirt and being careful not to destroy the whole face.

(Satir, 1978, pp. 63–65)

as negative aspects. In the absence of having to impress or please others, our private self emerges as the unfiltered core of our being. The private self, therefore, is often referred to as the *actual* self.

When people are nondefensive and secure in their private selves, they are more likely to share their true selves with others. Revealing our genuine personal characteristics and beliefs reduces the image-sustaining aspects of our public selves, so others see and accept us as we really are. However, people who are defensive and insecure in their private selves *increase* the image-sustaining aspects of their public selves because they are unable to reveal their underlying characteristics to others. In turn, they may become so caught up with the public presentation of their selves that they become alienated from their private selves. Such people are interpersonally limited by their public self presentation. They are recognized by others as being all façade and having little substance.

The Ideal Self

Ideal self

Each of us carries with us an idealized self-image. This ***ideal self*** is defined as the totality of the desired and fantasized selves we wish we could be. For some of us, the ideal self may be quite physical and clear; we may wish we were more attractive, thinner, more muscular, taller, or shorter. We often desire an ideal temperament, perhaps without moodiness or selfish moments. We may have an ideal image of being able to have sparkling conversations with people we value. We may carry an intellectually ideal self.

Ideals are important, because they give us a frame of reference for judging who we are and to what we aspire. Yet how far our ideal selves are from our actual self-concept tells us about some aspects of adjustment.

Consider the person whose ideal self is enormously elevated above the real self. Such a person is doomed to dissatisfaction because the ideal is so unreachable. British writer-physician-television personality-theater director Jonathan Miller is an example. Despite his considerable achievements, Miller was seriously dissatisfied. Growing up in the academic elite of Cambridge, England, he had always wanted much more for himself. Miller has said, "I've always had a sense that I've somehow let myself down or not done what I ought to have done" (Engstrom, 1983, p. 63), and he has admitted that his life has been "an endless rhapsody of self-doubt" (Blandford, 1982, p. 24). His marvelous accomplishments were always insufficient according to his idealized standards.

"Universal Should List"

The ideal self takes many forms, one of which is the unspoken standards one has for being a good person. When we continually say "I *should* be this way" and "I *should* do that," we set up an ideal self related to the ***"Universal Should List"***—that is, the universal pattern of telling ourselves what we should be doing. Satir describes such a list of idealized traits.

RULES FOR BEING A GOOD PERSON
I MUST ALWAYS BE
Right
Clean
Bright
Sane
Good
Healthy
Obedient
NO MATTER WHAT THE COST OR SITUATION

(Satir, 1978, p. 25)

The key words in this list are *always*, and *no matter what*, concepts that inevitably place our ideal selves at a great distance from what we realistically are.

Some people see their ideal and actual selves as quite close. These people may feel one of two different levels of security and contentment. One level is felt by the person who has attained great personal satisfaction. Approaching one's ideal means that the person can be content with having attained some of life's major objectives.

A much lower level of satisfaction with self may be felt, however, by persons who are not comfortable being self-critical. They artificially inflate their stated self-worth (or lower what they would consider as their ideal self) in order to be at ease. To some degree, this is normal. La Rochefoucauld, in his *Maxims*, observed that "we should have but little pleasure, were we never to flatter ourselves." Used to an extreme, this defensive maneuver is part of a pattern of denying or repressing thoughts that are disquieting. The ideal self remains elevated. People simply refuse to deal with how far they may be from that ideal and instead hunt for reasons for esteeming themselves. This defensive posture is a common process that has been long observed. In his nineteenth-century *Notebooks*, Samuel Butler wrote

> He is a poor creature who does not believe himself to be better than the whole world else. No matter how ill we may be, or how low we have fallen, we would not change identity with any other person. Hence our self-conceit sustains and always must sustain us . . .

(Evans, 1968, p. 615)

Now that we have discussed the private self, the public self, and the ideal self, we can consider the awareness of these elements of the overall self-concept. The extent to which we are aware of the private and public self has been labelled *self-consciousness* by Arnold Buss (1980). His theory of self-consciousness is limited to how we pay attention to and what we think about ourselves. His concerns with the enduring and persistent levels of heightened awareness of self may be divided into the categories of ***private self-consciousness*** and ***public self-consciousness.***

Private Self-Consciousness

Private awareness describes not only clearly felt states, such as the contractions of your stomach when you are hungry, but also feelings, such as depression, love, lust, anger, elation, loyalty, competitive striving, and personal fantasies. When you pay attention to these private aspects of yourself, two events occur: the emotions associated with self-awareness become more intense, and the events themselves become clearer and more distinct.

Daily writing in a diary illustrates these processes. The attention paid to private events, no matter what they are, makes the events more intense and clearer in the writer's mind. Table 3–1 lists five common private self-awareness actions and their influences on the person.

TABLE 3-1 Private and Public Self-Consciousness

Private Self-Consciousness

What you do	*What your attention is focused on*
Introspection	Bodily processes
Writing a diary	Moods
Daydreaming	Emotions
Meditation	Self-evaluation
Looking in a small hand mirror	

This leads to clearer knowledge of self or to feeling experiences more intensely.

Public Self-Consciousness

The situation	*What it leads to*
A. You are in front of An audience A camera A microphone or you are being shunned	The public self is emphasized; you feel uncomfortable, inhibited, and sometimes disorganized.
B. You are receiving Perceptual feedback An image of yourself in a three-sided mirror A photograph of yourself A videotape of yourself An audiotape of yourself	External perceptions of you are not as good as your self-image; seeing yourself in one of these ways leads to a drop in your self-esteem.

Adapted from Buss, 1980, pp. 22, 37.

Buss's studies of over two thousand University of Texas students suggest that the following ten items make up the basic factors in private self-consciousness:

I reflect about myself a lot.
I'm generally attentive to my inner feelings.
I'm always trying to figure myself out.
I'm constantly examining my motives.
I'm alert to changes in my mood.
I tend to scrutinize myself.
Generally, I'm aware of myself.
I'm aware of the way my mind works when I work through a problem.
I'm often the subject of my own fantasies.
I sometimes have the feeling that I'm off somewhere watching myself.

(Buss, 1980, pp. 43–44)

People who feel that most of these items are true describe themselves as warm, reflective, and complicated. They know themselves well. Buss also describes a typical study in which a group of college students with high private self-consciousness was given a peppermint flavored soft drink. They rated it on strength of flavor. They were then given an identical second drink and told it had a stronger flavor. They weren't fooled. Their ratings stayed just the same. People with high private self-consciousness know themselves and trust their judgments. They are clearly tuned into their feelings.

Public Self-Consciousness

Public self-consciousness

Public self-consciousness is the way in which we are uncertain of ourselves in public and our awareness that others are observing us. Both our *appearance* and our *style* are factors that can cause public self-consciousness. Appearance refers to our characteristics, such as facial acne or scars, haircuts, height, facial features, and body build. Style refers to our posture, our manners, our volume of speech, the social roles we play, and our other overt behaviors.

Public self-consciousness can arise from being stared at, performing on stage, standing in front of a large group, or being ignored at a time when we expect attention. To see the actual state of public self-awareness, observe someone who is about to be photographed or tape recorded. In such situations; most of us play with our hair or clothing, make faces, or act embarrassed. The feedback from a photograph or tape recording causes a temporary drop in our self-esteem. We usually think we look or sound better than we do in actuality. As I have already stated, people with high ideal self-concepts will be especially dissatisfied with their ordinary ways of talking and presenting themselves.

Sometimes, when we are in public, we may be aware that other people are observing and evaluating us. This awareness is public self-consciousness. Public self-consciousness may make some of us so uncomfortable that we change our appearance and style to conform to the expectations of others.

The same research that defined private self-consciousness yielded the following items that exemplify public self-consciousness. Most of these items relate to social anxiety and concerns.

I'm concerned about what other people think of me.
I usually worry about making a good impression.
I'm concerned about the way I present myself.
I'm self-conscious about the way I look.
I'm usually aware of my appearance.
One of the last things I do before leaving my house is look in the mirror.
I'm concerned about my style of doing things.

(Buss, 1980, p. 44)

People with high levels of public self-consciousness are very suscepti-ble to scrutiny and shunning. Concern about themselves as social objects influences them powerfully. When they think, for example, that they will have to discuss their views in public, they feel anxious, they anticipate possible criticism, and they may moderate their views to conform to those of others (Tunnell, 1984). Conforming behavior to the expectations of other people and to one's own expectations has a label of its own; it is called the ***self-fulfilling prophecy.***

Self-fulfilling prophecy

Self-Fulfilling Prophecies

Others' expectations do influence our self-concepts and expectancies in wide-ranging ways. In his play *Pygmalion,* Bernard Shaw wrote the following lines for Liza Doolittle (speaking to Colonel Pickering):

> Your calling me Miss Doolittle that day when I first came to Wimpole Street. That was the beginning of self-respect for me . . . You see, really and truly, apart from the things anyone can pick up (the dressing and the proper way of speaking, and so on), the difference between a lady and a flower girl is not how she behaves, but how she's treated. I shall always be a flower girl to Professor Higgens, because he always treats me as a flower girl, and always will; but I know I can be a lady to you, because you always treat me as a lady, and always will.

> *(Shaw, 1930, p. 278)*

The original Pygmalion was a king of Cyprus and a talented sculptor who fashioned a beautiful woman out of marble. He desperately wanted the statue to come to life. His hopes were realized by the goddess Aphrodite, who gave life to the statue, and the woman Galateas came into being. The Pygmalion principle is defined as the influence of other people's expectations upon our behaviors and self-concepts. When others think we are competent or attractive and desirable, we think of ourselves in those ways and act on those beliefs. Nowhere is the Pygmalion effect better illustrated than in the Jean Giraudoux play, *L'Appolon de Bellac.*

> Agnes, a timid girl, is nervously waiting to be called into a president's office for a job interview. Also in the waiting room is a young man who, on learning about her fears, tells her that the simplest way of dealing with people is to tell them that they are handsome. Although at first she is shocked by the apparent dishonesty of his suggestion, he manages to convince her that telling somebody that he is handsome makes him so, and thus there is no dishonesty involved. She follows his advice and is immediately successful with the grouchy clerk, then with the haughty vice-president, and with the directors. Eventually the president comes storming out of his office.
> "Miss Agnes, for fifteen years this organization has been steeped in melancholy, jealousy and suspicion. And now, suddenly this morning, everything is changed. My reception clerk, ordinarily a species of hyena—(the clerk smiles affably) has become so affable he even bows to his own shadow on the wall—(Clerk contemplates his silhouette in the

sunshine with a nod of approval. It nods back.) The first Vice-President, whose reputation for stuffiness and formality has never been seriously challenged, insists on sitting at the Directors' meeting in his shirt sleeves, God knows why. . .''

The president, too, becomes a changed man as soon as Agnes tells him that he is handsome. A little later, in the presence of his quarrelsome wife Therese, he arrives at the most significant conclusion, namely that saying to others that they are handsome makes oneself beautiful.

"Have you ever stopped to wonder, Therese, why the good Lord made women? Obviously they were not torn from our ribs in order to make life a torment for us. Women exist in order to tell men that they are handsome. And those who say it the most are those who are most beautiful. Agnes tells me I'm handsome. It's because she's beautiful. You tell me I'm ugly. Why?''

(Watzlawick, Weakland & Fisch, 1974, pp. 132–133)

The self-fulfilling prophecy can be negative or positive. One classic example of a negative self-fulfilling prophecy is a student's fear of a mathematics course. When a student believes that he or she is no good at math, every difficult problem seems to confirm that inability. Studying for tests is especially discouraging, because the student anticipates failure. As a result, the student daydreams or worries about the effect of the poor grades. Less time is put into studying, and more time is focused on the student's own fears. To avoid the discomfort of thoughts of failure, the student avoids studying math. Eventually, when tests are returned with poor grades, the student receives this information as further confirmation of how untalented he or she is in math. In other words, the student's belief that he or she will do poorly is a major force in the student's actually doing poorly.

Self-fulfilling prophecies are present in experimental psychology as well. For instance, it is possible for researchers inadvertently to structure an experiment in such a way that they elicit from their subjects the response that supports their hypotheses. This ***experimenter effect*** can be avoided in part by having studies conducted by collaborators who are unaware of the hypotheses.

Self-fulfilling prophecies have powerful applications for improving self-concepts and behaviors. Examples have been offered by Robert Rosenthal and Lenore Jacobson in their book, *Pygmalion in the Classroom* (1968). In one case, they describe a shy, socially awkward woman who was treated as popular, charming, and successful by a group of college men who were her friends. Not surprisingly, she became poised, confident, and socially graceful as a result.

In their own research, Rosenthal and Jacobson manipulated teacher expectations by falsely identifying children who were "spurters" in school.

Experimenter effect

At one meeting, the teachers were given completely false information about these children. The test scores given were not real scores. The teachers were told

> All children show hills, plateaus, and valleys in their scholarly progress. The study being conducted at Harvard with the support of the National Science Foundation is interested in those children who show an unusually forward spurt of academic progress. . . . We are further validating a test which predicts the likelihood that a child will show an inflection point or "spurt" within the near future . . . the top 20 percent of the children *will* show a more significant inflection or spurt in their learning within the next year or less than will the remaining 80 percent of the children.
>
> *(Rosenthal & Jacobson, 1968, p. 66)*

The students in the first and second grade who the teachers were led to believe would have imminent intellectual development tended to show such development. This pattern was not present in students in later grades, perhaps because of the accumulation of information that may have already molded student and teacher expectations.

The case of one boy who was identified as a spurter in the first grade illustrates the kinds of changes reported by Rosenthal and Jacobson. Jose was a Mexican-American boy, speaking with a slight Spanish accent, whose father worked in a foundry and whose mother worked as a meat packer. He had been assigned to a low-ability first grade group by his kindergarten teacher. He was tested, as were all of the children, four months before being identified as a spurter and then eight months after. His pretest IQ was 61 and his posttest IQ was 106; the major event between the two testings was the teachers' high expectations for him to be an intellectual spurter. While the Rosenthal and Jacobson studies do not yet have broad general application, they nevertheless give partial confirmation to the expectancy effect.

Can We Change Others' Self-Concepts?

The self-fulfilling prophecy suggests that the self-concepts of other people may be indeed be changed. However, changing expectations is a difficult task, and few of us are able to deliberately and consciously behave so differently as to change others.

According to one prominent researcher in the field, the potential for us to reshape others' self-concepts is limited. William Fitts (1981) asserts that the people with whom we are concerned must change themselves. In terms of changing others' negative self-concepts, Fitts points out

> You can't! There's no way you can reach into someone else's psyche and rearrange their self-perceptions. The real issues are what do *they* have to

do in order to perceive themselves differently, and how can you help them to define and implement those steps?

(Fitts, 1981, p. 262)

He goes on to suggest that an alternative is simply learning to accept and value these people as they are.

However, if change is indeed a goal, then one step to achieve it is changing behaviors—if people act differently toward someone, then that person's self-concept often changes. Many exhortive and behavioral approaches use this principle. The target person is cajoled into behaving a certain way in the belief that behavior can lead and self-concept can then fall into step.

For both significant others and ourselves, one way to improve poor self-concepts is by giving up the excessive commitment to presenting an image. In place of this strain to offer a forced public self can be substituted a more genuine real self. The end result will be higher self-esteem.

SELF-ESTEEM

We now examine those aspects of the self-concept that are "active, force-ful, and capable of change. It [the self-concept] interprets and organizes self-relevant actions and experiences; it has motivational consequences, providing the incentives, standards, plans, rules, and scripts for behav-ior" (Markus & Wurf, 1987). The dynamic, active self-concept is seen in functions such as self-evaluation maintenance.

Self-Evaluation Maintenance

Individuals may seek to maintain positive self-evaluation through the accomplishments of others. Self-evaluation maintenance (SEM) assumes that a basic human motive is to behave so that we feel we are competent and others see us as competent (Tesser & Campbell, 1983). That process does not have to come from our own lives, but may occur through reflection, in what has been termed the BIRG effect.

Basking in reflected glory

BIRG stands for ***Basking In Reflected Glory***, because the desired effect of bragging about the achievements of a relative or friend is to raise one's self-evaluations. Thus, when a neighbor tells us about a sister or son who is an Olympic gold medal winner, the neighbor may be considered, in part, to be trying to raise his or her self-worth. Abraham Tesser and Jennifer Campbell (1983) point out that the closer the relationship of the other person (who has the accomplishment) to the speaker, and the more outstanding the accomplishment, then the more pronounced will be the BIRG effect.

Why would *not* speaking of a friend's or relative's accomplishments make a speaker feel inferior by comparison? The answer lies in the *relevance* of the comparison. The winning performance of a young man who is a competitive swimmer might be relevant to another person of the same age who is also a competitive swimmer and whose self-evaluation might suffer by comparison. On the other hand, we can assume that a less relevant speaker, such as a person who is much older or younger or who is disinterested in athletics, would have an increased self-evaluation because of the BIRG effect.

FOCUS ON DEVELOPMENT

Self-Evaluation Through the Life Cycle

> The baby new to earth and sky,
>   What time his tender palm is pressed
>   Against the circle of the breast,
> Has never thought 'that this is I'.
>
> But as he grows he gathers much,
>   And learns the use of 'I' and 'me'
>   And finds 'I am not what I see,
> And other than the things I touch.
>
> So rounds he to a separate mind
>   From whence clear memory may begin,
>   As thro' the frame that binds him in
> His isolation grows defined.

(Tennyson, 1850, In Memoriam XLV)

How people evaluate themselves changes through the life span. For example, children under five years of age and adults over age sixty-five typically use their past performances as the bases for their self-concept evaluations, rather than looking to what others do for comparison. Once they are three to four years of age, children develop sufficient memory for them to look at what they have done before to judge their successes. However, they have yet to extend their social world enough to appreciate what others do. Children of this age are not affected in major ways by the performances of others (Suls & Mullen, 1982).

In old age as well, people do not judge themselves according to what others do, because they tend to withdraw (or be withdrawn) from social values and contacts. They lose friends and abilities. Their frequent physical isolation as well as their emotional detachment leave them less opportunity for social comparisons.

Cutting off reflected failure

A related form of SEM is the act of ***Cutting Off Reflected Failure,*** in which individuals distance themselves from unsuccessful people or institutions. This distancing is designed to cut connections with unattractive, negative, or unsuccessful things that would make the individual negative by association in the eyes of others (Snyder, Lassegard & Ford, 1986). An example of this cutting off is when many fewer students wear T-shirts or sweatshirts with the college's name after the school's team suffers a sports loss. BIRGing, of course, would be wearing the college insignia after a college athletic victory.

Instead, they tend to judge themselves on the basis of what they could do when they were younger.

In the times between early childhood and old age, social comparisons become a more potent force in self-evaluations. Children become concerned about competing with classmates. During adolescence and early adulthood, comparisons with peers become most important. Self-esteem is tied to social comparisons. Adolescents think, "I'm okay if I like Bruce Springsteen because my friends all like Bruce Springsteen."

In middle age, social comparisons with dissimilar groups seem to affect self-evaluation. As people approach forty years of age, they begin to take stock of themselves and look at others as a frame of reference. Competition in the workplace and social marketplace lead them to compare themselves with younger co-workers and with older, more established co-workers.

The following table summarizes people's bases for evaluating themselves throughout the life span.

Sources of Self-Evaluations at Different Ages

Age	Source
Under age five	Comparison with own prior performances
From age five through adolescence	Comparison with both own performances and how well peers do
In adolescence and early adulthood	Social comparison with others of same age
In middle adulthood	Social comparison with others of varying ages
In late adulthood (age sixty-five and older)	Comparison with own prior performances

Adapted from Suls & Mullen, 1982.

Negative Statements

Our self-esteem is affected by the examination of aspects of ourselves we dislike. These aspects are often hidden and part of the private self. We indicate some more publicly by making negative statements about ourselves. However, such negative statements cannot always be taken at face value.

When someone makes a negative statement about himself or herself, we should not automatically assume the statement to be a sign of a negative self-concept. Indeed, many factors lead people to make self-critical comments, including actions just completed that are truly inferior by some reasonable standard. A self-critical comment can be a statement of fact. A woman who customarily bowls 200 and who has just bowled a score of 120 may accurately observe that her game is off, that she is doing dreadfully, and she just can't seem to throw a ball right. Only *persistent* negative and critical self-statements may indicate a negative self-concept, but before a conclusion can be made, cultural and competence issues must be considered. Let us look at the research on cultural issues first.

In American society, people frequently follow their successes by making ***self-enhancing*** statements, such as "I did that well." However, this pattern does not necessarily hold for other cultures. Studying fifty-six students at the Chinese University of Hong Kong, Bond, Leung, and Wan (1982) presented videotapes of individuals completing a test and commenting on the outcomes. Students observed these individuals making both self-enhancing and self-effacing statements about their performances. The videotaped self-effacing individuals said: "I just made it by luck this time. If I have to do it again, I don't know what would turn out" (Bond, Leung & Wan, 1982, p. 160). The self-effacing individuals were judged more likable and less anxious than the self-enhancing subjects in ratings by the Hong Kong students.

Americans also value ***self-effacing*** behaviors in cooperative and group situations, such as team sports, in which modesty is more the rule. However, in competitive and individual performances, such as tennis and swimming matches, positive statements of self-achievement are frequent and accepted by Americans (Bond, Leung & Wan, 1982).

Men and women react differently to success and failure experiences. After successfully mastering intellectual tasks, female college students are more likely than male students to identify their achievements as due to good luck. In turn, failures lead women more than men to attribute the cause to bad luck. Males judge their successes and failures as due to higher ability or lower ability, respectively (Deaux & Farris, 1977). This tendency for men more than women to see ability as the cause of success extends to elementary school children, suggesting that it is an outlook that is socialized very early.

Self-enhancing

Self-effacing

Individuals also may make self-critical and self-effacing statements regarding their competence in an area that is part of their personal identities. Think of an award-winning biochemist who has published extensively on the structure of cells. Such a person would be more comfortable making self-critical statements about his or her work in this area than another scientist with far fewer achievements. The basic idea has been put this way: "To the extent that one's background allows the person to point to strong evidence of being complete in the area of pursuit, that person will more readily be publicly self-abasing" (Gollwitzer, Wicklund & Hilton, 1982, p. 359). In the absence of that sense of clear competence, people are reluctant to be self-critical, probably because such self-criticism strikes home to an aspect of personal insecurity.

EXPLORATIONS IN WELL-BEING

Measuring Your Self-Esteem

One of the most reliable and valid measures of global self-esteem is the New York State Self-Esteem Scale (Rosenberg, 1979). To determine self-esteem, the respondent indicates *strongly agree, agree, disagree,* or *strongly disagree* for each of the following items:

1. On the whole, I am satisfied with myself.
2. At times, I think I am no good at all.
3. I feel that I have a number of good qualities.
4. I am able to do things as well as most people.
5. I feel I do not have much to be proud of.
6. I certainly feel useless at times.
7. I feel that I'm a person of worth, at least on an equal plane with others.
8. I wish I could have more respect for myself.
9. All in all, I am inclined to feel that I am a failure.
10. I take a positive attitude toward myself.

Items 1, 3, 4, 7, and 10 are written so that strongly agree and agree answers indicate positive self-esteem. Items 2, 5, 6, 8, and 9 are written so that disagree and strongly disagree answers indicate positive self-esteem

This scales uses a typical approach. It uses straightforward, obvious items that depend on the willingness of the person to be honest. When most of the items are answered honestly and as noted, the person's responses indicate high self-esteem. The opposite answers indicate low self-esteem. A mixture of scores, with no pattern, indicates a mixed self-evaluation.

Discounting

Even when people receive positive information about their achievements, which potentially could improve their self-concepts, they sometimes use a *discounting* process. Discounting means giving a low value to positive information about self-worth. A boy who gets an excellent grade on a test and then explains that it was due to luck, and that he was not really prepared, is discounting his academic performance. A girl may minimize her first place in a competitive running event because she has more experience than the runners with whom she compares herself. Individuals may also discount low levels of performance by attributing the cause to factors other than themselves (Suls & Mullen, 1982).

Narcissism

To this point, we have generally considered self-esteem to be a positive aspect of adjustment. Those people who feel very good about themselves are seen as having achieved a desirable state. Yet there exist cases of exaggerated self-esteem, mixed with self-centeredness and braggadocio. This state has been called *narcissism,* a subject of attention from both psychoanalytic and social psychologists. In the novel *Mention My Name in Atlantis,* the lead character gives a good instance of narcissism:

> First, it has been said—by ignorant, cheating rascals!—that I, Hoptor the Vintner, am no more than a thief, panderer, and peddler of influence of the most dubious sort. This narrative shall, perforce, prove all that false, and paint a portrait of myself neither flattering nor distorted, but only truthful: revealing me as I am—brave, resourceful, compassionate, keenly intelligent; in short, a humanitarian of the first rank.

(Jakes, 1972, p. 1)

The term *narcissism* comes from the Greek myth of the boy Narcissus, who upon seeing his reflection in the water falls deeply in love with his own image and pines away in hopeless love, until he is transformed into the narcissus flower. Narcissism has been called *simple selfishness* (James, 1890), a term that describes bodily selfishness and putting one's own personal comforts, satisfactions, and impulses first. The term applies equally well to social pride and selfishness, in which individuals are constantly puffed up with pride about themselves.

Freud viewed narcissism as instinctive; he wrote that humans have only so much predetermined instinctive drive for pleasure and satisfaction. To the extent people regard themselves highly, they have less energy available for loving and valuing others. Like so many Freudian concepts, the definition of narcissism has undergone substantial revision. The major redefinition was made by Karen Horney, who asserted that narcissism is made up of two features: "appearing unduly significant to oneself and craving undue admiration from others" (Horney, 1939, p. 90). Self-esteem is fine, according to Horney. It is only self-inflation, which is directed at eliciting admiration from others, that is problematic.

According to this view, narcissism serves to silence the person's uneasiness and insecurity. Unfortunately, it also can lead to more showmanship than substance and to excessive expectations of success without sweat.

> He feels he should be recognized as a genius without having to give evidence of it by actual work. Women should single him out without his actively doing anything about it. . . . The characteristic feature of these attitudes is the expectation that devotion or glory can be obtained without effort and initiative of his own.
>
> *(Horney, 1939, p. 95)*

Have you ever paid someone a compliment on his or her appearance and then seen that person immediately gaze appreciatively into a mirror? (Maybe you have responded this way as well!) This pleased reaction is one example of momentary narcissistic behavior.

A narcissist has been defined by social psychologist Robert Wicklund (1982) as a person who dwells on personal success experiences. Wicklund described a study to illustrate this. Men who were sought after by attractive women confederates were compared to a control group. Both groups were asked to choose between listening to tape recordings of their own voices or of other men's voices. The sought-after men listened to their own voices significantly more than they listened to the voices of other men. Narcissism, then, was the men's choice to listen to their own voices after their positive experiences with attractive women. The pleasure of the sounds of themselves was defined as narcissistic. Think of people who have been paid compliments about their appearances and who then appreciatively look at themselves in a mirror. An exactly parallel psychological process was demonstrated in these studies of narcissism.

To this point, we have examined components of the self-concept and of self-esteem. These feelings about self occur in part during contact with other people, and the individual makes choices about sharing his or her self with others. That process of sharing of self is known as self-disclosure, our next issue.

Self-Disclosure

"Who really knows you?" "If I share who I truly am with you, will you share who you truly are with me?" These questions open up the area of **self-disclosure** in personal relationships.

Self-disclosure

THE MOST BEAUTIFUL WOMAN IN THE WORLD: A CASE STUDY OF NARCISSISM AND THE SELF-FULFILLING PROPHECY

Adela Terrell, of Sussex on the Thames, was easily the most beautiful creature. Adela was twenty, and so far did she out distance the world that it seemed certain she would be the most beautiful for many, many years. But then one day, one of her suitors (she had 104 of them) exclaimed that without question Adela must be the most ideal item yet spawned. Adela, flattered, began to ponder on the truth of the statement. That night, alone in her room, she examined herself pore by pore in her mirror. (This was after mirrors.) It took her close to dawn to finish her inspection, but by that time it was clear to her that the young man had been quite correct in his assessment: She was, through no real fault of her own, perfect.

As she strolled through the family rose gardens watching the sun rise, she felt happier than she had ever been. "Not only am I perfect," she said to herself, "I am probably the first perfect person in the whole long history of the universe. Not a part of me could stand improving, how lucky I am to be perfect and rich and sought after and sensitive and young and . . ."

All of us have ways of concealing who we genuinely are. Our public selves can be so formidable or fixed that no one sees past them and into the real us. We may become committed to sex roles, so that others around us see the independent, competent male role we play or the social and charming female role we play, and little more. We may be fearful of the social consequences of letting our real selves be seen and heard, apart from narrow ways that are convenient.

Self-disclosure is the revealing of information about oneself, including feelings, thoughts, and experiences. Self-disclosure has been further defined as any statement that begins with "I." Thus "I think that I . . ." or "I feel . . ." or "I plan next week to . . ." all begin self-disclosure statements.

The pioneer in the study of self-disclosure was Sidney Jourard, whose 1964 book *The Transparent Self* triggered a continuing flow of research and writing. Jourard held that when people disclose their real selves to each other, they learn of the extent to which they are both similar and different, and they learn of each other's needs. According to Jourard, only when you know another person by that person voluntarily revealing his or her real self can you be a friend or can you love that person. Otherwise, that person remains mysterious, with your understanding of him or her influenced as much by your preconceptions as by the reality. Jourard wrote

> It is a simple, patent fact that when a man discloses his self, his inner experience to another, fully, spontaneously, and honestly, then the mystery

Young?

The mist was rising around her as Adela began to think. Well of course I'll *always* be sensitive, she thought, and I'll always be rich, but I don't quite see how I'm going to manage to always be young. And when I'm not young, how am I going to stay perfect? And if I'm not perfect, well, what else is there? What indeed? Adela furrowed her brow in desperate thought. It was the first time in her life her brow had ever had to furrow, and Adela gasped when she realized what she had done, horrified that she had somehow damaged it, perhaps permanently. She rushed back to her mirror and spent the morning, and although she managed to convince herself that she was still quite as perfect as ever, there was no question that she was not quite as happy as she had been.

She had begun to fret.

The first worry lines appeared within a fortnight; the first wrinkles within a month, and before the year was out, creases abounded. She married soon thereafter, the self-same man who accused her of sublimity, and gave him merry hell for many years.

(Goldman, 1973, pp. 34–35)

that he was decreases enormously. When a man discloses himself to me,
I find all my preconceptions and beliefs about him becoming altered, one
after the other, by the facts as they come forth.

(Jourard, 1964, p. 3)

The correlates of this theory have been outlined by Jourard as well.
They are

You show your love of another person by letting that person know
you.

We only come to know ourselves through disclosing ourselves to other
people.

Healthy personal adjustment includes the ability to make yourself fully
known to at least one other human being.

The more we struggle to avoid being known by other people, the less
energy we have left to put into coping with stressors.

Most people don't accept or realize how little they know the others
with whom they have contact.

Self-disclosure always occurs in some context. For example, when
you are with someone who is very sharing and disclosing, it is likely you
will reveal much about yourself. This phenomenon of disclosure begetting
disclosure has been called the ***dyadic effect.*** When one person in a dyad
(or pair) discloses great or small amounts of personal information, the
other person is likely to do the same.

Dyadic effect

It has been easy for men in traditional male roles to engage minimally
in self-disclosure. They are caught up in striving, in achievement, in
action, rather than in talking and sharing themselves. When this happens,
they are not emotionally accessible—indeed, one characteristic of the
traditional male role is to not allow oneself to be vulnerable, and instead
to be tough and able to handle anything.

One option people have is to deliberately seek out a few others
whom they trust—and who trust them—to share increasingly personal
information. Some risk is always felt in the disclosing process. However,
the opportunity for moving closer to others is present as well, using the
sharing as a vehicle.

There is an apparent optimum level of self-disclosure. Little or no
self-disclosure is problematic. Then, adjustment increases with rising
self-disclosure. However, after a certain point, disclosing about oneself
becomes indiscriminate. The person overdiscloses inappropriately to people who have not earned the right to receive this information. Strangers
waiting in line to buy tickets to a movie are puzzled if the person next to

them talks about her fears about her husband's forthcoming surgery for lung cancer.

We cannot enter into social relationships without sharing something of ourselves. The question becomes not whether to self-disclose, but rather how much, to whom, and in what situations. We do know some straightforward facts. People disclose more to individuals they like. Single persons disclose most to best friends, and spouses disclose to each other. People do attempt to maximize their rewards and minimize negative costs in social situations, and self-disclosure is employed toward that end. Couples who disclose highly to each other report greater marital satisfaction in contrast to the low satisfaction reported by couples with little mutual disclosure.

CULTURAL MANDATES AGAINST SELF-DISCLOSURE: THE GUSII OF WESTERN KENYA

In the highlands east of Lake Victoria in Kenya reside the Gusii, a culture of about one million Bantu-speaking people. The Gusii are of particular interest because of their cultural attitude toward self-disclosure. Among the Gusii, powerful norms prohibit the revealing of experiences, emotions, or achievements. Robert LeVine, an anthropologist, writes

> Their norms prohibit the presentation of a self-aggrandizing appearance through any behavior remotely interpretable as boasting, gloating, or flaunting. . . . For example, women usually did not announce being pregnant, or men tell of having gained employment or passed an important examination, to anyone in the family or neighborhood . . . such self-disclosure would be considered boastful and would provoke malevolent jealousy in the hearer.
>
> *(LeVine, 1982, p. 49)*

LeVine goes on to observe that "our 'healthy self-esteem' is conceit and selfishness by their standards" (1982, p. 63). The Gusii standards are important reminders of the extent to which judgments about the desirability of self-disclosure and the nature of self-worth are rooted in cultural contexts. Even within a nation like the United States, with its homogenizing media, substantial cultural differences exist between geographical regions and ethnic groups. Thus, judgments about every area of human behavior, and conclusions about the extent to which self-disclosure is a sign of well-being or maladjustment must be made with caution, remembering the lesson of the Gusii.

Thus, the implications for psychological well-being are to disclose at comfortable, midrange levels in appropriate situations with appropriate partners.

Experimental evidence supports the view of self-disclosure as a possible facilitator of relationships. One study of 209 undergraduate students found an inverse relationship between reported self-disclosure and loneliness. That is, students who were least lonely had high levels of disclosure to others. The most lonely students were the lowest disclosers (Mahon, 1982).

Well-being also seems to be associated with self-disclosure flexibility, or the ability of a person to change levels of disclosing according to the social situation and the persons who are nearby and available. Some people are absolutely inflexible. They reveal the same aspects and amount of themselves to virtually everyone. This may mean that the person is unable to share selectively with anyone or it would describe a person who overdiscloses. Such was the case of a person with whom I had a passing contact who, uninvited, talked about the times he was psychiatrically hospitalized and the dreams and fantasies he had been having.

People who are flexible in self-disclosure feel control over their sharing. They are aware of the appropriateness of discussing personal feelings, and they reveal themselves to those people whom they trust and with whom they have a foundation for sharing (Chelune, 1979). The best use of disclosure is just such a flexible manner, assessing the receptivity and closeness of the audience and the situation.

TABLE 3-2 Aspects of Self-Concepts Toward and Away from Well-Being	
Toward Well-Being	Away from Well-Being
Public self is consistent with private self	Public self is in conflict with private self
Ideal self is realistically and comfortably above actual self	Ideal self is exaggerated or minimized
Self-disclosure is flexible and fits partner, situation	Self-disclosure is inflexible
Self-concept is mutable	Self-concept is rigid
Has high private self-consciousness	Has high public self-consciousness
Expectations of competence and success are associated with self-fulfilling prophecies	Expectations of incompetence and failure are associated with self-fulfilling prophecies

SUMMARY

The *self-concept* has three characteristics: (1) it is the *totality,* or sum, of our beliefs, perceptions, and feelings about ourselves; (2) it is *consistent* over time and operates to minimize negative views of the self and to maximize positive aspects of the self; and (3) it continues to *evolve* and *change* with new experiences, rather than being rigidly fixed. Constructive openness to change is a positive function of the person and is known as the mutable self.

Many common beliefs about the self-concept have not been supported by research. Socioeconomic status is not significantly related to self-esteem. Children from broken homes and homes where the father is absent do not necessarily think poorly of themselves. However, genuine acceptance of the child in a home with clear, consistently enforced rules does lead to the child's self-acceptance. Finally, growing older does not predictably affect self-esteem.

A number of different aspects of the self have been identified. The *public self* is the image we present to others to evoke socially approved views of us as competent, sincere, and likable. The *private self* is our understanding of ourselves as we truly are, including all our doubts and insecurities. The *ideal self* is our desired image of what we would like to be. It is the sum of all the ways we aspire to be.

Awareness of the self is important as well. Clear awareness of what is happening within us, such as emotional and physical feelings, is known as *private self-consciousness.* In contrast, *public self-consciousness* is the way in which we are aware and uncertain of ourselves in public. Public self-consciousness is the embarrassment and discomfort we may feel when we are being watched or when we are speaking in public.

Other people's expectations, and our own, shape our behaviors. Self-fulfilling prophecies relate to the extent to which we become the expected or prophecied individuals.

Self-esteem may be understood through several processes. *Self-evaluation maintenance,* for example, includes Basking in Reflected Glory (BIRG), which allows feelings of self-esteem to arise from the accomplishments of others. Although persistent negative and self-critical statements may indicate poor self-esteem, in our culture self-effacing statements are appropriate and accepted in cooperative tasks and team sports. *Discounting* is a form of negative statement that minimizes achievements out of modesty or low self-esteem.

Lastly is *self-disclosure,* which is the ability to share ourselves genuinely and spontaneously, when we want to, with significant others. Flexible, middle-level, appropriate self-disclosure is a sign of well-being.

Key Terms

Basking in reflected glory   **Discounting**
Cutting off reflected failure   **Dyadic effect**

Expedience

Self-concept

Experimenter effect

Self-disclosure

Ideal self

Self-effacing

Mutable self

Self-enhancing

Narcissism

Self-fulfilling prophecy

Private self

Universal should list

Private self-consciousness

Working self-concept

Public self

Zeitgeist

Public self-consciousness

Recommended Reading

Rosenthal, R. & Jacobson, L. (1968). *Pygmalion in the classroom: Teacher expectation and pupils' intellectual development.* New York: Holt, Rinehart & Winston. It doesn't make any difference that a dozen critiques have appeared about the statistical procedures used in this research. The fundamental finding in this pioneer book remains: Individuals are profoundly affected by what they and what others think they are going to do. The first five chapters examine self-fulfilling prophecies in everyday life, in the healing professions, and in the behavioral sciences. I was captivated the first time I read this. I still am.

Wylie, R.C. (1974). *The self-concept: Vol. 1. A review of methodological considerations and measuring instruments.* Lincoln: University of Nebraska Press. This is the scholar's handbook for the self-concept. Sometimes murky, sometimes puzzling, sometimes fascinating, the self-concept leads to a labyrinth of scientific questions and some answers. If your interest is in finding what we do know and don't know about the self-concept, and how we know it, this book by Ruth Wylie should be your first choice.

II

PART

The Individual

Stress and Coping

•

Physical Health and Illness

•

Assertiveness and Aggression

•

Transitions and the Life Cycle

4

Stress and Coping

THE NATURE OF STRESS

What Is Stress?
The Engineering Model
The General Adaptation Syndrome
Stress Mediators
Life Events and Stress
Rural and Urban Sources of Stress
The PERI Study of Life Events

TRAUMATIC STRESSORS

Natural Disasters
Man-Made Disasters
Post-traumatic Stress Disorder

DEFENDING AGAINST STRESS

The Nature of Defense Mechanisms
Types of Defense Mechanisms
When Defense Mechanisms Are Used

WELL-BEING WHEN CONFRONTED WITH STRESSFUL EVENTS

The Hardy Personality
Sensation Seeking
Stress Inoculation

Not My Favorite Year

It might not have been the worst year of my life if my dad had not found Keith and me on the couch. You see, Dad had forgotten the tickets, so he had driven back to the house, left the car running, with Mom in it, and hurried inside.

When he saw us, his mouth opened and closed a few times, without any sounds coming out. Kind of like a guppy. Then he said a rushed "sorry" and left real fast.

Mom and Dad never said anything about it.

Things did get pretty tense, but we carried on. The next day, we visited Grandma in the nursing home and later went to Aunt Jo's for dinner.

The calls started the next week, after this holiday break. I was back in the dorm at about eleven one night when my Mom called. She wanted to know what I was doing. Had I been out? Was I feeling okay? I didn't have any trouble with anything, did I? Was I eating well?

A couple of nights later, Mom called again at the same time. Before the winter was over, she was calling every night to see if I was in by ten. If I wasn't, she would call every fifteen minutes.

The morning calls started a few days later. Had I slept well? Was I prepared for classes? I was to be sure to eat a good breakfast. Did I

do anything after she talked to me last night? Never asked, but never far from the surface, were her questions about what I might have been doing sexually.

That was the year my allergies started. I had to give up chocolate, and milk, and wheat products, and I couldn't go outside without a respirator. Still I couldn't breathe. Much of the time, I felt as if I was suffocating.

Eventually, the allergies did stop for good, well, almost for good. I went two thousand miles away to another school, in a part of the country with better air. Also, my dorm room didn't have a telephone. Allergies are peculiar things.

Once, my allergies did come back a little. I had returned to the school for a conference and was staying in my old dormitory with friends. That first day I walked into the dorm, I found it harder and harder to breathe until I had a full-blown attack. When I went off to the meetings, it was easier to breathe. At the end of the day, when I went back to the dorm, I had another allergic reaction. The second day, I had fewer symptoms. The third day, there were hardly any at all. By the end of the week, the allergies were totally gone.

Maybe it was good the allergies came back. It helped me remember what was not my favorite year.

 THE NATURE OF STRESS

The narrator of "Not My Favorite Year" describes a terribly stressful period in her life. Her mother's checking up on her behavior became more pressing to her than the ordinary stresses of studies, boyfriend, money, and sleeping problems. Don't assume that these other issues were not troublesome. They were. Still, she had already been worried about them and had partly come to grips with them.

Her allergies were a reaction to her mother's phone calls and suspicions. Her body became more reactive, and she felt suffocated in more ways than one. Her moving away was an effort to cope. The number of her mother's calls diminished to a manageable few. She was able to resume more of a routine, normal life.

This chapter is about the stresses of everyday life as well as the serious stressors we encounter. We will look not only at common sources of stress but also at the kinds of people who can (and cannot) handle stress.

What Is Stress?

Stress would seem to be an easy concept to define. After all, I know that I am feeling stressed when, the night before I am to give an important talk, drunken men yell in the hotel room next door and keep me awake. I also know I am suffering stress when I take on more than I should, and I am unprepared to participate in a meeting. Yet stress has been an elusive concept to define. The problem is that to some people stress is an outside event and to other people it is an internal reaction to events. Furthermore, one person's stress is another person's exciting challenge (Taylor, 1986). The conclusion of one meeting of stress researchers was that "some definitions are so broad that they include essentially anything that might happen to anyone" (Hamburg, 1981, p. 7).

Despite these difficulties, a definition of stress has emerged. *Stress may be defined as the assessment of events as threatening or potentially harmful and the subsequent responses, psychological and physical, to these threats.* Let us consider the elements that make up this definition.

Assessment. Whether the event is a nuclear disaster or missing a plane, unless the person experiencing it has evaluated the event as tension producing, it is not considered stressful. Only when the individual judges that the event makes a demand on or creates a tension within that individual do we label the situation as stressful.

Events. We often think of stressful events as external to us, such as the neighbor playing loud rock music at a time we want quiet. However, events that cause stress include internal events, such as states of hunger, or specific desires, or sleep deprivation. To distinguish our assessment of events from our responses, we call the events **stressors**. Our reactions are called **strains**.

Threatening or potentially harmful. The judgment of threat or potential harm depends on the individual. Some stressors are so serious, frequent, intense, or long-lasting that they are judged as threatening by almost everybody. These stressors are discussed later in this chapter in the section on traumatic stressors. Other events, such as missing a bus, having a headache, or moving to a new community, may be as-

Stress *(margin note)*

Stressors
Strains *(margin notes)*

sessed as threats requiring adjustive demands or as routine and unimportant, depending on the person. Persons who are least likely to see such events as stressors are discussed later in the section on the hardy personality.

Subsequent responses.   Strains follow the initial time of the event that has been assessed as stressful. Sometimes a simple cause and effect relationship between an event and a response can be seen. A person starts a new job. Six months later, that person develops an ulcer. However, the time sequence is not always so obvious. Many stressors are combinations of various events in a lifetime, and it can be difficult to know what events caused particular reactions.

Psychological responses.   Within the category of psychological responses we include cognitive, emotional, and behavioral responses. The cognitive responses are the ways in which the individual thinks about and evaluates the events—reactions of thinking and critiquing. The emotional responses are the person's mood changes. The behavioral responses are the observable differences in how the person behaves, what the individual actually does.

With these basic definitions outlined, we now may consider the nature of stress. We begin with a popular way of thinking about stress: the engineering model.

EXAMINATION HELL

The single most severe stressor on Japanese students is examinations, a concern greater than the concerns they feel about health, family problems, or friends. University admission is dependent upon a single examination. Preparation for that examination begins in childhood, and endless hours are spent memorizing answers to long lists of questions. Admission to a desirable university takes on fanatical importance in Japan. Momoru Iga writes

> Since education is virtually the only means for achieving security in this highly status conscious society, the people's desire for educational success is obsessive.

(Iga, 1981, p. 22)

Most students enroll in seven-days-a-week neighborhood cram schools in addition to their regular classes. Iga's summary of how Japanese students spend time indicates that junior high school students spend an average of 9.5 hours per day studying on weekdays, 7.5 hours a day on Saturdays, and 3.3 hours a day

The Engineering Model

When a certain amount of pressure is placed on a metal, the metal will flex and be able to return to normal. Beyond that amount, the metal will develop a permanent bend or, if enough pressure is exerted, the metal will crack or break. The engineering model of human stress relates stress on a person to presssure on metal. Mild stressors on people should have no effect. People will bounce back to normal. Moderate stressors should cause some permanent changes. Severe stressors should lead to serious breaks (Cox, 1978). This engineering model is closest to commonsense thinking about stress. That is, we say, "The stresses on them got heavier and heavier, and finally everything just gave way. They couldn't take the pressure."

The engineering model is appealing because the description of metal under pressure seems very scientific and objective. However, this model has proved to be too simple to account for human stress. We have already noted that our *perception* of stress influences our reactions. Furthermore, according to the engineering model, zero stress should have no effect on people. Yet, too little challenge or stress is itself unpleasant and distressing to us. Stress yields different reactions in different people. An explanation that accounts for patterns and interpretations of stressful events is needed. Therefore, we move now to a psychological stress model that considers three different responses to stress: the general adaptation syndrome of Hans Selye.

on Sundays. Admission to the better universities not only means an opportunity for prestigeful employment, but it also reflects directly on the students' parents. Case histories of parents committing suicide when their children were refused admission to the better universities have been reported. Furthermore, because women have so little access to career achievements in Japanese society, mothers become completely identified with their children's academic successes or failures. As Iga puts it, "If a child fails at school it is due to his mother's lack of supervision" (1981, p. 24).

Ten years or more of preparation culminates in a single examination, and the students' fears and need for achievement are so concentrated by this time that the experience has been labelled examination hell. The pressures result in obsessive concerns about failing, anxiety, and an extremely high rate of suicidal thoughts and successful suicides. Even in Japan, where suicide is not dishonorable, the number of suicides is astonishing. The rate of suicides in the age range of fifteen to twenty-four years is 16.5 per 100,000 in Japan. Equally important, 38.6 percent of male junior high school students and 60.3 percent of male high school students have expressed suicidal wishes. For these students, examination time truly is a do-or-die situation.

The General Adaptation Syndrome

In 1936, young Hans Selye prepared an extract of cattle ovaries that he hoped would lead to the discovery of a new hormone. Working in the Department of Biochemistry of Montreal's McGill University, he injected the extract into rats. His initial satisfaction at seeing physiological changes soon was replaced by the excitement of discovering that any injected toxic substance yielded the same three stress effects: the adrenal cortex enlarged, the lymph structures shrunk and shriveled, and bleeding ulcers developed in the stomach and duodenum. As a result of this experiment, Selye's career of almost a half-century in stress research was launched (Selye, 1976).

General adaptation syndrome
Alarm reaction

Selye found a three-stage pattern of response to stress, which he called the ***general adaptation syndrome,*** or GAS. The GAS starts with an ***alarm reaction,*** the body's "call to arms" to mobilize its defensive forces against any threat or attack of stress. The alarm reaction can be purely physical, such as the fever that helps kill invading bacteria when we are ill. This emergency reaction works equally with psychological danger—at least with what we perceive as psychological danger. Our own interpretations of events trigger the alarm reaction.

You are in a strange community, walking by yourself in the evening, and you find yourself confronted by five large, ominous-looking men, one of whom is flipping a switchblade knife open and closed. They look at each other knowingly and start to move toward you. After a second's hesitation, you run for ten minutes until you see they are not following. During this time, an alarm reaction will have been in effect in your body. Your heart will have been beating furiously fast, your muscles will have been tensed, your mouth will have gone dry. After you are safe, these signs of the GAS alarm reaction stage may well continue for a few minutes. We have the same response following a near auto accident. The body continues to react because it has been put into high gear to respond to the crisis.

Resistance

The second adaptive stage is ***resistance,*** which is a long-term, more stable adjustment. Nobody can manage to sustain emergency defenses indefinitely, so a less taxing reaction pattern follows. In the case of people who have been mugged on public streets, their resistance stage consists of becoming highly vigilant and suspicious, watching all the time for possible attacks. They worry. They put extra locks on their doors. They avoid dark streets and do not walk alone at night. They may lie awake at night, listening for burglars (LeJune & Alex, 1974).

In the GAS, each stage does not necessarily lead to the next. The alarm reaction stage may appear by itself and vanish. If the *resistance* stage appears, it may continue for a long time, or it may fade away as the threat becomes more remote. If the threat is truly severe and long-lasting, the

Exhaustion

adaptation can eventually become so taxing that resistance runs out and the third stage, *exhaustion,* sets in. The constant wear and tear of great stress leads our bodies' defenses to exhaustion. Some people collapse emotionally or physically and can't keep going. Sometimes they need to be hospitalized. Some attempt suicide.

According to Selye's theory of *nonspecificity,* any stressor could set off the GAS responses. No one specific event triggers unique body responses. Rather, thousands of possibly distressing events, including burns, infections, and fractures, may be considered together as a trigger, because the same strain responses may arise after any one of these stimuli. The

Soldiers train to be able to respond to highly stressful situations in a fast, effective way.

Nonspecificity

Selye **nonspecificity** hypothesis has been modified over time; for stressors of varying intensity and for particular individuals, there *are* specific responses. More importantly, we do not know just what causes a particular stimulus to be stressful (Hamburg, 1981).

Stress Mediators

Mediators are the filters that shape the impact of any stressor. This personal shaping and screening system explains why the same threatening event terribly distresses one person and has mild effects on a second person. Think of the different responses people have to riding roller coasters, skydiving, researching term papers, and creating needlepoint rainbows. In management–labor negotiations, the mediator acts to reconcile the demands of labor and the responses of company management. So it is with **stress mediators.** When stressful demands are acknowledged, the person's own mediating patterns receive and interpret them. Let us consider an example.

Stress mediators

CASTANEDA IN THE WOODS: THE ASSESSMENT OF THREAT

The same individual in the very same situation may choose to assess an event as threatening or not, from moment to moment. The person may speculate about a noise being a burglar, or possible assailant, and react to that possibility. Then the individual may rule that out, attribute the sound to a reassuring source, such as a loved one sleeping in the next room, and feel comfort. Castenada (1971) presents in his book *A Separate Reality* an example of such changing interpretations.

In this book the narrator was sleeping and a loud, deafening crack awakened him. At first he thought it was a gunshot. Ideas rushed through his head of how he was being watched, how the owner of the land on which he was sleeping may have taken him for a trespasser, and was shooting at him. Then this tension in mind and body passed as he thought that Don Juan, his spiritual guide through these journeys, was playing with him. He laughed and relaxed.

The noises began again, many of them coming quickly, and his comfort left. Now he panicked. He felt nauseous. He wanted to throw up. Finally absolute silence settled on him. He didn't know what to make of it. He vomited. He wept. He felt lost. His interpretations of ordinary, and not so ordinary, events shifted. As his interpretations of these sounds changed, so did his emotional state from distress to pleasure and back to distress.

I had a related experience when I lived briefly in Jerusalem. I had read of the terrorist events in the city. My first day there I walked around the center of the old city, looking around with interest and mild apprehension, when a

A teacher listens carefully to a student's comments. Then the teacher exclaims, "You haven't prepared very well, have you? You have missed the whole point here!" The student might respond to this situation by feeling humiliated and anxious, dwelling on the exchange for days. Or the student might defend the comments, saying that he did indeed make the correct point, and feel good about the exchange. Finally, the student might agree with the criticism and take it well if there is a bond of positive attachment with the teacher (West, Lively, Reiffer & Sheldon, 1986). Most stressors produce a wide range of personal and emotional responses. Differences in the responses arise in part from the stress resistance of the people involved.

The thresholds that must be overcome to produce distress are higher in stress-resistant people than in more vulnerable people. What makes a person more stress resistant? How a person has handled and perceived stressors in the past and what is important to that person affects his or her level of stress resistance.

The way a person perceives an event influences whether the event

man who spoke Hebrew or Arabic—my ability to distinguish between them was limited at the time—rushed to me, stood close, and spoke insistently. When I did not immediately respond, he firmly grasped my wrist. I assumed at once I was being attacked—kidnapped perhaps. As I began to struggle, he lifted my wrist, turned it so he could see the face of my watch, looked at it, released me, smiled, and walked away. The next time, and many times after, when someone approached, I understood, smiled, and while unable to tell the person the time in his language, quickly and comfortably turned the face of my watch toward him. These frequent instances soon were a routine, and in fact pleasant, courtesy in my meanderings about the city.

The nature of objective reality in these instances seemed blurred, as it often is in our own lives. The instruction from these episodes is the importance of how we evaluate what is happening. In this case, is the cracking noise a sign of danger or fun? Is a stranger speaking to you in a foreign city a cause for panic? More than we usually realize, we define and interpret for ourselves the nature of stressors in our lives.

functions as a stressor on that person. This seemingly innocuous state-ment reflects some dramatic implications for theories of stress, because it summarizes the approach of Tom Cox (1978), who emphasizes the psy-chological interactions between people and their environments. Let us look at a common potential stressor: heat.

Increasing heat can be an ecstatically positive or a painfully stressssful experience, depending on the situation and how a person interprets it. Think for a moment of the similarities between sitting in a sauna and sitting in an experimental heat chamber. In both cases, you are sitting in a barren room with air temperature forty degrees fahrenheit above a comfortable temperature. You perspire continuously, sweat dripping freely. Your skin flushes as your capillaries swell with blood. Your heart rate and respiration rise. You feel little sense of energy. If this room you are sitting in is a research chamber, or a prison cell, or a nonairconditioned room during a heat wave, the heat you are experiencing would surely be a stressor. On the other hand, if you are sitting in a sauna or a steam-room, you are probably actively and pleasurably seeking out the heat and its environment.

In the same sense, illness may be devastating or not at all disturbing to a person. An illness may be interpreted as a challenge to be met and con-quered. We shall consider later in this chapter those hardy personalities who respond to stressors with such positive and successful mediation.

Life Events and Stress

Social readjustment rating scale (SRRS)

When Thomas Holmes and R.H. Rahe (1967) developed a *social readjust-ment rating scale (SRRS)* to assess stressful life events and physical illness, they achieved a major breakthrough in stress research. Until that time, everyone "knew" that tragic events in people's lives were severe stress-ors that interfered with well-being. Thousands of cases were recorded of long-married persons who died shortly after their spouses' deaths. Mar-riage counselors often talked about the difficult adjustments of newly di-vorced persons. Losing a job, going to jail, and the death of a child all had visible and powerful negative consequences. Yet this knowledge was not presented systematically; often it was reported in case histories and anec-dotal stories. Holmes and Rahe carefully studied the lives of five thousand patients, identified forty-three events that were associated with the onset of disease, and assigned weights to each event, based on its likely asso-ciation with the development of illness. Their working assumption was simple: the greater the life change or crisis, the greater the likelihood of the stressor negatively influencing health. The product of this effort was the SRRS, a forty-three-item checklist of events in people's lives.

However, the general application of the life events list turned out to be far from simple. To begin with, the list was based on the lives of people who were urban residents from the Northwest of the United States; their experiences were quite different from those of people living in rural areas or small towns. Let us now look at these urban–rural differences in more detail.

Rural and Urban Sources of Stress

To find out the major differences between rural and urban stressors, F.T. Miller and a team of other investigators from the University of North Carolina gave the Holmes-Rahe SRRS to ninety-six representative citizens in a rural North Carolina county (Miller, Bentz, Aponte & Brogan, 1974). These rural people were generally poor and educated at the high school level or lower. They were compared to the urban subjects from the Pacific Northwest on whose lives the SRRS was originally developed. The highest stress events for the Pacific Northwest citizens were also the highest stress events for the rural North Carolina subjects. All of the people rated the death of a spouse or family member, divorce or marital separation, jail detention, and major injury or illness as events with the most difficult readjustment periods.

The differences between the two sets of subjects, however, show what it means to live in rural versus urban America. The greatest differences were between the ratings of the effects of marriage, of taking out large mortgages, of changes in the number of arguments with spouse, and of minor violations of the law.

The rural sample rated marriage as twenty-first in the list of forty-three stressors. The urban citizens rated it number four. Miller and associates explain this difference in rating as follows:

> In rural North Carolina when one marries the expectation is to move only a few miles and to stay where you move—or at least to stay in the locale. In an urban area marriage may mean the uprooting of one or the other of the couple, a change in living abode for more space, and a change in recreation because of a change in expenses.

> *(Miller, Bentz, Aponte & Brogan, 1974, p. 271)*

The meaning of taking out a mortgage assumed very different meanings in rural and urban life in the early 1970s.

> Taking out a mortgage of greater than $10,000 is almost antithetical for the rural North Carolinian, whereas such a loan might be assumed with relative ease by the city dweller. In the rural South, a general pay-as-you-go philosophy still prevails. This is particularly true for families where the money base is small.

> *(Miller, Bentz, Aponte & Brogan, 1974, p. 271)*

EXPLORATION IN WELL-BEING

Hassles and Uplifts

Hassles

One area of research parallel to interest in major stresses has examined the minor daily stresses of life—the **hassles.** Richard Lazarus (1979) has been responsible for the seminal research into hassles, and he points out the importance of our reactions to the daily minor irritants we all face. Sometimes trivial events take on great significance to us, because they represent our inability to cope with small problems. Lazarus (1979) cites the Charles Bukowski poem, "The Shoelace."

> It's not the large things that
> send a man to the madhouse . . .
> not the death of his love
> but a shoelace that snaps
> with no time left.

Some people with extremely high scores on stress and hassle scales nonetheless manage well in everyday life. The clue that reveals whether they can manage day-to-day life well is how do they handle and interpret daily hassles. Here is one hassle:

> I have a senile mother who is very old and troubled. She constantly calls me up and bothers me about the most recent crisis she's having, or to complain I'm not spending enough time with her, or whatever. And I've got problems of my own. At the same time, I want to be helpful to her.

(Lazarus, 1979, p. 57)

This kind of day-in, day-out annoyance could be something the speaker could take in stride, while still being concerned about his mother. On the other hand, his feelings of guilt, duty, and conflict could make these constant phone calls a source of teeth-grinding, stomach-churning distress. The meaning and importance people attribute to daily hassles are what influence the impact of those hassles (Flannery, 1986).

Make a list of your own daily hassles. Identify the five that seem most annoying.

1. _____
2. _____
3. _____
4. _____
5. _____

To compare, look at the daily minor hassles reported by high school students. Their most frequently reported hassle was "Troublesome thoughts about your future" (Miller, Tobacyk & Wilcox, 1985). The next four most frequently reported hassles were

Concerns about weight

Misplacing or losing things

Social obligations

Fear of rejection

All of these hassles were reported by at least 70 percent of the students.

While minor daily upsets may accumulate to cause distress, minor daily positive experiences may accumulate and cause relief and pleasure. The minor positive experiences are called *uplifts*. Now make a list of your five most common daily uplifts.

Uplifts

1. _____

2. _____

3. _____

4. _____

5. _____

In comparison, the most frequent uplifts reported by the high school students in the Miller, Tobacyk, and Wilcox study (1985) were

Eating out

Laughing

Having fun

Hugging and/or kissing

Visiting, phoning, writing someone

Perceptions of hassles and uplifts depend on the situation and age of the people involved. Consider the contrast between the hassles and uplifts reported by the high school students and those reported by nursing home residents with an average age of eighty-four (Miller, Wilcox & Soper, 1984). Their main hassles were worries about illness, being lonely, and having too much time on their hands. Their primary uplifts were praying, thinking about the past, feeling safe, and visiting or writing someone. In both of the age groups, these daily events have enormous emotional consequences. When life is one hassle after another, it can seem discouraging. When life is one uplift after another, the sun always seems to be shining.

Changes in arguments with spouses appear to be viewed much more seriously by urban dwellers (who rated it seventeenth) than by rural people studied (who rated it thirty-third). The much higher frequency of urban divorce may be why increases in marital arguments are more serious for city dwellers. The rural dwellers rated minor violations of the law as twenty-fifth in the stressor list; urban dwellers rated it fortieth. The apparent reason is that in rural areas everyone knows when the law is broken, even in small ways. The anonymity of living in a city means that almost no one is aware of a citizen's minor violation. These basic findings have been supported by other rural–urban comparisons (for example, Marotz-Baden & Colvin, 1986).

Stressors also arise from the different life-styles of the two settings. The more mobile, transient urban living leads people to turn inward, emphasizing eating and sleeping habits and concerns about further up-rooting. On the other hand, rural residents suffer more from "fishbowl" stressors of being seen and criticized by neighbors. The continuity of family relationships also leads rural residents to have more in-law problems. Concerns about pregnancy and family health arise from the greater impact of illness and the perceived poor medical help in rural areas.

The PERI Study of Life Events

PERI life events scale

The idea of using life events lists to assess stress has so fascinated social scientists that over one thousand studies have been conducted on the Holmes-Rahe SRRS alone, and many other lists have been formulated. The most promising of the other lists is the **PERI life events scale** (Dohrenwend, Krasnoff & Askenasy, 1979). PERI stands for Psychiatric Epidemiology Research Interview. Dohrenwend and colleagues asked residents of the Washington Heights section of New York City the question, "What was the first major event in your life that, for better or worse, interrupted or changed your usual activities?" They incorporated the responses, together with other information, into the 102-item PERI life events scale. The scale itself was then given to several groups of people from different social classes, who were asked to rate the stressfulness of the events.

The PERI life events list is shown in Table 4–1. The relative stress positions are presented for each of the events: a rating of one signifies the most stressful; a rating of ten signifies the least stressful.

When the first life events lists were developed, it was hoped that particular events would be predictable stressors. However, subsequent research (Dohrenwend et al., 1979; Depue & Monroe, 1986) showed that the effects were far from universal for varying groups. For example, blacks and Puerto Ricans rated stressful items differently than did whites.

Rural stressors are very different from urban stressors. This small rural community offers its citizens security and the comfort of having lifelong friends and seeing familiar faces. At the same time, everyone in the community knows what everyone else is doing, and so people's lives are scrutinized by fellow citizens and are the subject of town gossip.

Events More Stressful to Minorities	Events More Stressful to Whites
Started work	Birth of later child
Reduced work load	Repossession
Foreclosure of loan	Jail

Sex differences appeared as well: Women experienced the events as more stressful overall than did men. Only the event of marital infidelity was rated as more stressful by men than by women. (We might speculate

TABLE 4-1   The PERI Life Events List*

Having Children	Health	Crime and Legal Matters	Love and Marriage	Social Activities
1 Child died 1 Birth of first child 3 Birth of second child 3 Became pregnant 4 Abortion 5 Menopause	1 Physical illness 1 Unable to get treatment for injury or illness 3 Physical health improved	1 Went to jail 1 Convicted of a crime 1 Released from jail 2 Didn't get out of jail when expected 4 Involved in lawsuit 5 Assaulted 6 Robbed 10 Lost driver's license	1 Spouse died 1 Divorce 2 Marital infidelity 2 Marriage 6 Engaged 7 Started love affair 8 Engagement broken	2 Close friend died 8 Broke up with friend 8 Took a vacation 9 Made new friends 10 Took up or dropped a hobby or sport 10 Pet died, or pet acquired

Work	Finances	Residence	Family	School
3 Suffered a business loss or failure 3 Retired 4 Fired 4 Started work for the first time 5 Promoted or demoted 6 Laid off	3 Went on welfare 4 Foreclosure of loan 5 Received cut in wage or salary 6 Went off welfare 8 Took out a mortgage 9 Purchase or repossession of car or furniture bought on installment plan	1 Lost home due to fire or other disaster 3 Built home 4 Moved to worse residence or neighborhood 7 Remodeled a home 9 Moved to residence or neighborhood no better nor worse than last one	2 Family member other than child or spouse dies 7 New person moves into household 10 Change in frequency of family get-togethers	6 Started school after not attending for a long time 7 Graduated 7 Failed school 9 Changed schools

Adapted from Dohrenwend, Krasnoff & Askenasy, 1979.

* 1 is the most severe category of stressors; 10 is least stressful.

that the double standard of morality leads men to think their wives will never be unfaithful, while women perhaps are better prepared for marital infidelity in their husbands.) Women more readily report stressors of all sorts; they may actually experience more stress than men when faced with serious life changes. Alternatively, women may be more comfortable acknowledging what bothers them. Compared to men, women rated the following items as more stressful:

Broken engagement

Miscarriage

Death of a family member

Assault

Reduction in wages

Death of a pet

Ending tour of duty in the armed services

   Note that three work-related items have been discussed: started work, reduced work load, and reduction in wages. The specific nature of work stress is discussed separately in Chapter 12, "Work and Careers."

Mugging is an example of a serious stressor. The victim of such a stressful event may suffer from effects lasting far beyond a few weeks or a couple of months. Sometimes, the strains resulting from exposure to a stressor are not evident for a long time after the occurrence of the stressful event. For example, a year from now, this woman may develop an ulcer and have no logical explanation for it.

Let us finally consider the worst stressors we can face. The PERI includes items making up a *pathogenic triad* of extreme situations and stressors. This triad is composed of physical exhaustion, loss of social support, and fateful negative events (such as the death of a loved one). Research does not endorse the position of E.H. Chapin, who wrote, "out of suffering have emerged the strongest souls: the most massive characters are seared with scars." Rather, research shows that these severe stressors frequently have catastrophic effects in situations such as combat, concentration camps, and natural disasters. Serious potential harm may be precipitated by extreme events.

 ## TRAUMATIC STRESSORS

In writing of the Australian Aborigines, Basedow described what happens when the natives have a bone pointed at them.

> The man who discovers that he is being boned by an enemy is, indeed,
> a pitiable sight. He stands aghast, with his eyes staring at the treacherous
> pointer, and with his hands lifted as though to ward off the lethal medium,
> which he imagines is pouring into his body. His cheeks blanch and his
> eyes become glassy and the expression of his face becomes horribly dis-
> torted . . . from this time onwards he sickens and frets, refusing to eat and
> keeping aloof from the daily affairs of the tribe. Unless help is forthcoming
> in the shape of a counter charm administered by the hands of the Nan-
> garri, or medicine-man, his death is only a matter of a comparatively
> short time.
>
> *(Basedow, 1925, pp. 178–179)*

Catastrophes can be both overwhelming situations for single individuals and natural disasters for large groups of people. Catastrophes represent the extreme of environmental stressors, and studying their effects allows us to understand people's reactions to stressors in daily life.

Natural Disasters

On February 26, 1972, a slag dam built by the Pittston Mining Company collapsed at the middle fork of Buffalo Creek, West Virginia. One hundred thirty-two million gallons of mud, water, and sludge roared through the seventeen-mile-long Buffalo Creek valley, killing 125 people, injuring hundreds more, and carrying homes, churches, cars, and bodies past the horrified and dazed onlookers (Gleser, Green & Winget, 1981).

The Buffalo Creek survivors provided information that is among the most extensive ever recorded on the effects of a disaster. Because a suit was filed by the survivors against the mining company for improperly maintaining the dam, the aftereffects on the 650 survivors were carefully evaluated by several teams of social scientists.

The mining company's lawyers engaged a physician to do a separate evaluation. This doctor held that any long-term aftereffects must have arisen from preexisting mental problems, rather than from the flood itself. However, the social scientist teams drew opposite conclusions. They asserted that the symptoms were relatively uniform, that they did not simply represent continuing illness, and that the survivors did not overstate their symptoms because they hoped to win their suit.

Indeed, being caught in the Buffalo Creek flood was devastating. The survivors were sluggish and disorganized. They became even more listless and disinterested as time passed. Grief and despair were intermingled with irrational emotional outbursts. Insomnia and nightmares were frequent. Many of the survivors became fearful of drowning and were preoccupied with water, rain, and storms.

About one-third of the survivors increased their alcohol consumption, and about half smoked more and used prescription drugs more. Gleser and her colleagues (1981) gathered many case studies of the flood survivors. One typical example is Mr. O, a thirty-six-year-old married white man who lived with his wife and six children in a small trailer for thirteen months after the disaster.

> The feelings of depression and despondency were present with varying intensity all of the time. Prevailingly, Mr. O felt ". . . like in a haze, tired, dragged out and half-dead. . . ." He also had developed irritability, impatience, and short temper, becoming highly angered at the slightest inconvenience and frustration . . . at home he had torn his clothing, broken dishes, hacked at things, and verbally abused his wife and children. He felt they got on his nerves to the point he could hardly stand them . . . in the past two years he had frequently had the impulse to do away with himself."

> *(Gleser, Green & Winget, 1981, p. 58)*

Two years after the flood, three out of four of the men and nine out of ten of the women had difficulty falling asleep. Only 8 percent said they never had trouble falling asleep, compared to 42 percent of most adults. The rate of nightmares reported by the survivors was 50 percent, a rate two and a half times that of the general population. The common nightmare was of rain and then rising flood waters, with the dreamer or his or her relatives engulfed, screaming for help or drowning; then the dreamer awoke in a panic.

The survivors who nearly died or who lost friends or relatives suffered the most emotional harm. The most serious harm was seen in adults between the ages of twenty-five and fifty-five. The older and younger adults were less affected, and the children were affected least of all. Women were more traumatized than men, and white men and women were more affected than black men and women.

The out-of-court settlement of 13.5 million dollars included eight million dollars for "psychic impairment," a judgment that resulted in part from the findings of the social scientists. The average individual settlement was between six thousand and ten thousand dollars for children and for adults between six thousand dollars and (for the estate of one victim) one hundred and seventeen thousand dollars. After the settlement, and perhaps because of it, the mental health of most of the survivors did improve. They went through a reorganization process in which they rebuilt their lives and learned to depend more on their own resources. The passing of time and religious and social support also helped. However, three- and four-year follow-up studies indicated that about one-third of the survivors were still suffering considerable emotional distress.

Not everyone suffered. About 20 percent of the subjects were relatively free of anxiety, depression, and other consequences, a percentage found to be common by other studies of disaster survivors (Weiner, 1985). Yet for the remainder, and particularly for those who suffered major effects, this disaster indicates that normal coping styles of most relatively well-adjusted adults can be overwhelmed by an extreme disruption.

Such traumatic effects are by no means restricted to natural disasters. They arise from man-created circumstances as well. Let us turn to two such instances: the Lake Volta resettlement and the USS *Pueblo* POWs.

Man-Made Disasters

The Lake Volta resettlement

In the early 1960s, the Volta River of Ghana was dammed, creating the world's largest man-made lake, Lake Volta. The Volta Resettlement Authority removed eighty thousand persons from 740 villages and, as the only payment for the loss of their homes, property, and animals, placed each family in a ten-by-eleven feet one-room house. The settlers felt many stressful life events at once. They were thrust into a society of strangers, sometimes enemies. They were severely overcrowded, and the lack of privacy substantially reduced their sexual activity. They usually lost their means of subsistence. They were separated from familiar villages and they lost their possessions. Few people were satisfied with their new economic situations (60 percent of the people in comparable neighboring villages were satisfied).

Anthropologist D. Paul Lumsden (1975) followed these resettled villagers and found that they clearly experienced major emotional strains. In one settlement, 61 percent of the male household heads described ill health, fighting, backbiting, and theft. The most prominent symptom was increased drinking, with about 95 percent of the respondents stating they were drinking more often than they did presettlement.

The Volta Project villagers are a special group in the consideration of responses to disasters. Their eviction from their ancestral homes came from a governmental policy decision, over which they had no control. No deaths occurred. Still, the suddenness of the eviction, the loss of property, the massive disruption of the social environment all contributed to make this a man-made disaster for them.

Prisoners of war

The experiences of prisoners of war have provided a source of information about coping with severe stressors. One well-documented case is the adaptation of the crew of the USS *Pueblo*. From January 23 through December 23, 1968, the eighty-two crew members of the United States intelligence ship *Pueblo* were held captive by North Koreans who had attacked and boarded the ship in international waters. The crew members were threatened, beaten, and given unsanitary and inadequate food and living· quarters. Under the pressure of force, involuntary confessions to criminal acts were obtained from all crew members (Ford, 1975).

Within forty-eight hours of their release; the crew members were psychiatrically evaluated. The interviewers assessed whether the men had been able to cope successfully with the stress of confinement. Successful coping was defined as the ability to

(a) defend against excessive anxiety or depression;

(b) contribute to group support and morale; and

(c) provide realistic resistance to demands of the captors.

(Ford, 1975, p. 232)

Twenty-four of the men were judged to be in an upper group that coped well; thirty-one fell in a middle group; twenty-seven fell in a lower group that coped poorly. While all of the crew members were initially very anxious after capture, forty continued to have significant anxiety, and sixteen were very depressed, attempting suicide. The poor adjustment of the men was associated with their guilt at having given the forced confessions. These men experienced sleep disturbances, and they developed neurotic defense mechanisms, such as obsessive thinking.

On the other hand, the upper group, which adapted well, was found to be psychologically healthier; these men used mechanisms of faith, reality testing, denial, rationalization, and humor to adapt. Charles Ford wrote

> . . . they frequently stated that they maintained a faith in their commanding officer, religion, and country. It became apparent that there was considerable group support provided by the natural leaders who emerged in each of the rooms in which they had been randomly billeted. . . . Many of the rooms apparently operated like leaderless group therapy; there was ample time for extended review of their individual lives, hopes, aspirations, and accomplishments. . . . Furthermore, there were statements reflecting a belief in increased maturity on the part of the individual, greater appreciation for the American way of life, and a firm resolve for meaningful application to a purposeful life in the future.

(Ford, 1975, pp. 235–236)

Victims of capture by terrorists go through adjustmental challenges similar to those of prisoners of war, with one exception. The POWs rarely accept the beliefs of their captors. The victims of terrorism tend to submit to persuasion efforts and come to identify with their captor's views more than do POWs (Weiner, 1985). Why? Apparently because survival is so uncertain: "All control over personal destiny is taken away. Passivity, capitulation, submission, identification, and massive denial . . . may be the only ways of coping with and surviving such a situation" (Weiner, 1985, p. 55). This pattern of joining the terrorist captors is known as the *Stockholm Syndrome,* named after a hostage in a bank robbery in Stockholm, Sweden, who became intimate with and then engaged to one of her captors (Kuleshnyk, 1984).

Stockholm Syndrome

Post-traumatic Stress Disorder

We have observed that survivors of disasters share several symptoms with the victims of severe stressors in general. These individuals feel overwhelmingly anxious, unhappy, ineffective, and often lethargic. They have nightmares, trouble sleeping, and frequent emotional outbursts. They may reexperience the traumatic event.

When the cause of the trauma has been a wartime experience, the syndrome has been given a specific label. In World War I, emotional casualties of the prolonged trench warfare and artillery exchanges were described as suffering from shell shock. In World War II, the same behaviors were identified as battle fatigue. The Vietnam War produced a pattern of delayed strain that has been called the *post-traumatic stress disorder* (PTSD).

Post-traumatic stress disorder

The Vietnam War had different troop rotations than did earlier wars. In World Wars I and II, troops were kept at the front lines for extended and indefinite periods of time. However, in Vietnam troops were kept in battle zones for short, predetermined periods, and they knew exactly when they would be rotated back to the United States. Furthermore, the times in battle were interspersed with recreational periods in congenial settings. The battle fatigue of the prior wars was not seen. Rather, the soldiers' emotional reaction to the stressors of war was denied at first and then experienced sometime after the battle traumas. Thus, this stress disorder is called post-traumatic (Horowitz & Solomon, 1975).

The speed of return from war had an influence on stress as well. In World War II, a decompression period existed for battle veterans. They usually rode a slow troop ship back to the States and then served post duty before being discharged. Vietnam troops were often home only forty-eight hours after leaving Saigon.

The first reaction returning Vietnam soldiers had was happiness.

> . . . he would experience a period of relief, a latency period in which there
> was a feeling of well-being and relative good . . . the isolation of the [Viet-
> nam] experience from everyday life would continue for a while.

(Horowitz & Solomon, 1975, p. 69)

But this initial relief passed. Many veterans began to be aware of Vietnam
battle experiences that they had denied or to which they had been
numb. Sometimes the PTSD was precipitated by a crisis in marriage or
employment. Many veterans appeared at Veteran Administration clinics
seeking medication. They had nightmares as well as angry and other
emotional outbursts. Some veterans felt shame as well as anger. They
felt depersonalized, uninvolved in their lives. Veterans experiencing PTSD

POST-TRAUMATIC STRESS: SURVIVING THE ATOMIC BOMB

The Japanese residents of Hiroshima and Nagasaki who survived the atomic
bomb attacks in 1945 acquired the identity of *hibakusha,* "one who has undergone the atomic bomb." Psychiatrist Robert Jay Lifton (1964) spent four and a
half months intensively interviewing seventy-five Hiroshima survivors seventeen
years after the experience. The survivors spoke of an overwhelming encounter
with death, followed by an attempted psychic closing off, a denial of the dreadful sights and feelings. They obsessively feared "A-bomb disease," or delayed
radiation effects. Being a *hibakusha* meant

> . . . others see one *only* as a *hibakusha* bearing the taint of death, and
> therefore, in the deepest sense, turn away . . . For survivors seem not
> only to have experienced the atomic disaster, but to have imbibed it and
> incorporated it into their beings, including all of its elements of horror,
> evil, and particularly of death.

(Lifton, 1964, pp. 175–177)

The *hibakusha* felt guilty because they had lived when others died, and
they were filled with hostility toward demonstrators, toward Americans, and
toward those who view them with fear or disgust. Physical aftereffects surely
were present and noxious, yet not all survivors suffered long-term cancers or
illnesses. However, all did suffer emotional consequences. Their memories of
the disaster and their identity as survivors influenced all they did and everyone
with whom they interacted. Being a *hibakusha* was the single most important part
of the survivors' identities, and all their life experiences had to be understood
from this viewpoint.

Many Vietnam veterans suffer from post-traumatic stress disorder (PTSD), a condition in which they reexperience severely stressful wartime events. After returning to society, these soldiers often suffer from nightmares, insomnia, and frequent emotional outbursts. For many Vietnam veterans, PTSD has been treatable. Peer counselling groups have been successful in diminishing the emotional aftereffects of battle.

were depressed, frustrated, and distrustful of others offering help. They found it difficult to relate to people.

For many veterans, the PTSD has been treatable. In particular, peer counselling groups with other veterans have been successful in building trust, rebuilding self-worth, and lessening the emotional aftereffects of battle traumas.

While PTSD has been identified especially in Vietnam veterans, post-traumatic stress may appear in other individuals as well. In a study of sixty deputy sheriffs involved in shootings, about 30 percent were greatly affected (Stratton, Parker & Snibbe, 1984). Their crying, depression, and anger persisted, although these effects were lessened by the emotional support offered by supervisors and other deputies.

PTSD may persist over long time periods. In 1979, the Three Mile Island (TMI) nuclear power plant in Pennsylvania accidentally released radioactive gases into the atmosphere. Five years after the accident, TMI area residents were found to have continuing stress effects manifested in a variety of emotional and physical responses (Davidson & Baum, 1986).

DEFENDING AGAINST STRESS

The Nature of Defense Mechanisms

Defense mechanisms

Like disaster survivors and prisoners of war, at times we all are faced with problems for which no ready solution is available. With external difficulties, the problems may seem to be beyond our control, and we may feel worthless or scared. One way we respond is to use psychological devices to make the threat more tolerable. Unlike action solutions that change the problem, coping styles change how we experience the problem (Hovanitz, 1986). One major category of coping styles is **defense mechanisms.** The word *defense* means that we are engaged in a process to protect ourselves from possible hurt, failure, or rejection. An essential aspect of defense is to remove or armor ourselves from threat. The word *mechanism* describes an organized and consistent pattern of responding. This concept of the defense mechanism has had a remarkable longevity; it has persisted and been successfully used, almost without modifications, since Sigmund Freud wrote of *The Neuro-Psychoses of Defense* (1894).

Most people occasionally employ defense mechanisms, but a person who relies heavily on them is hampering his or her own everyday satisfactions and efficiency. People who are continually engaged in protective actions are less available to enjoy companions and challenges. Instead, maintaining defense mechanisms drains and preoccupies the people. Their work to maintain the mechanisms can be considerable. Their very defensiveness can interfere with their objectivity. It becomes necessary for them to interpret what they see, hear, and feel according to their guarded but sensitive self-images. Now let us consider the mechanisms themselves.

Types of Defense Mechanisms

Suppression

Suppression

Suppression is the conscious, deliberate refusal to face threatening possibilities. Of all the defense mechanisms, suppression is the only one that is consciously controlled. An example of suppression is the woman who found a dent in the rear of her brand new car. Seeing the dent was so unpleasant that she approached the car only from the front and carefully looked at the car from undamaged views only. In the same sense, people who have newly found they are suffering from a serious disease may purposefully keep the disease out of their thoughts and discussions. In other words, suppression is the deliberate looking away from problems. Because a conscious choice is made to suppress an uncomfortable thought or feeling, suppression is the most adaptive of all defense mechanisms. A band member who has had a nasty conflict with the band director may choose to suppress this anger while studying for an important test. The other defense mechanisms we use are less obvious to us. For the most part, we are not aware of how much we use them and when we use them.

Repression and denial

Repression

Repression is the exclusion from consciousness of anxiety-arousing thoughts, feelings, or memories, particularly those involving anger or sexuality. Unlike suppression, which is conscious, repression is unconscious. The repressor is not clearly aware of the anxiety nor of the ways in which it is repressed. In traditional psychoanalytic interpretations, everybody has repressed childhood sexual experiences. Indeed, it is not unusual for clients in psychotherapy to all at once remember physical or sexual attacks they suffered as young children.

Of all the defense mechanisms, repression has been subjected to the most rigorous scientific scrutiny. Research on repression suggests that strong repression is an extreme point on a continuum. At one end,

DENIAL IN ACTION

One example of the denial of unexpected trauma is given in the Franz Kafka story, *Metamorphosis* (1936). The story begins as follows:

> As Gregor Samsa awoke one morning from uneasy dreams he found himself transformed in his bed into a gigantic insect. He was lying on his hard, as it were armor-plated, back and when he lifted his head a little he could see his dome-like brown belly divided into stiff arched segments on top of which the bed-quilt could hardly keep in position and was about to slide off completely. His numerous legs, which were pitifully thin compared to the rest of his bulk, waved helplessly before his eyes.
>
> *(Kafka, 1936, p. 1)*

How does Gregor cope with this inexplicable catastrophe? He does what many people do: he avoids thinking about his new self and relies on familiar thoughts and concerns. Once Gregor establishes that he is not dreaming, his first thoughts are not of his physical crisis but of his job. He thinks how exhausting his work is, he thinks of his arrogant employer. He worries about making train connections, the discomfort of irregular meals, and how much trouble it is to be traveling constantly. Because he cannot cope rationally with his apparently impossible transformation, his denial process puts out of his mind for the moment what it means to be an insect and how he got that way. Instead, he copes by worrying about the things about which he knows how to worry.

the extreme *repressor* screens all upsetting thoughts from awareness. At the other end, the extreme *sensitizer* is very alert for all possible unpleasant memories and feelings and gets upset by them. Most people fall somewhere in the midrange of the continuum.

Denial is like repression in that it involves the exclusion of threats or fears from awareness. However, denial describes the exclusion of *external* events from consciousness. The failure to recognize the threatening nature of acid rain, toxic waste dumps, and living near nuclear power plants are all contemporary examples of widespread denial.

Projection

Both repression and *projection* are defense mechanisms that keep anxiety-arousing feelings out of awareness. With repression, the person holds it in. With projection, the person attributes the unacceptable thoughts to other people. When we use projection, we blame those around us for our problems. Thus, the person whose sexual feelings and desires are unacceptable may project these desires onto others, seeing these acquaintances as full of distasteful lust. The defensive aspect of projection is that the person unconsciously tries to feel better by making other people appear worse.

Displacement

Displacement is a defense mechanism in which the anxieties and drives are channeled toward nonthreatening objects. In particular, when people are frustrated and cannot directly express their upset, they become aggressive toward some available target. Kicking furniture, hitting a pet, and yelling at a younger brother can all be signs of displaced anger.

Not all *displacement* is maladaptive. Many creative efforts in art, music, writing, and scientific experiments may represent quite adaptive ways of handling unacceptable thoughts and feelings. Such adaptive and constructive channeling is the distinct defense mechanism of *sublimation,* which is the well-being analog of displacement.

Intellectualization and rationalization

Emotional detachment is the essence of *intellectualization.* Instead of being personally involved in discomforting events, persons who intellectualize do not allow themselves to care. They are analytical, cool, distant, uninvolved.

Closely related to intellectualization is the defense of *rationalization,* or the attempt to explain away anxiety-arousing fears. Rationalization presents an apparently logical analysis of a failure or fear. Thus, if you don't get a job for which you had applied, you might rationalize this failure by saying to a friend (and to yourself) that you really didn't want to have to move to that city, that the opportunities for advancement weren't that good, and that you actually prefer working in much smaller organizations.

Consider the case of a young man who had cared deeply about a woman he briefly dated. She broke off the relationship, explaining it was best for both of them. He was cerebral and used intellectualization in explaining to his friends that research showed that most relationships don't last long. He spoke about the situation as if he were an observer. Had he emphatically exclaimed that he was never interested in her anyway, he would have been engaging in rationalization, using socially acceptable reasons to justify this rejection.

Like the other defense mechanisms, mild intellectualization and rationalization can be adaptive. At times, we do not want to share unpleasant thoughts or distressing feelings with others. Only when these defense mechanisms become a characteristic style of dealing with most negative situations do they become maladaptive.

Other defense mechanisms

Sometimes it seems there are almost as many defense mechanisms as there are people who use them. The ones already discussed are the most fundamental. Still, four other defense mechanisms are briefly noted here to give a sense of the range of possible ways to deal with disquieting feelings.

Fantasy

Fantasy is the excessive indulgence in daydreaming or in unrealistic fantasies. **Fantasy** is used to escape from unpleasant fears into wishful thinking about grand achievements, great prestige, or being a martyr.

Regression

Regression is behaving in ways that belong to earlier stages in one's development. Acting babyish or dependent and having temper tantrums are examples of **regression.**

Identification

Identification is the active acceptance of the point of view and position of those persons who are causing the anxiety. A person using **identification** gives up his or her own emotional stance to be like the person who is the stressor.

Reaction formation

Reaction formation is the adoption of a feeling opposite to that actually felt. It can be seen in chronically angry people who always behave excessively nicely. A person who "doth protest too much" about not feeling or thinking something may be revealing a **reaction formation.**

When Defense Mechanisms Are Used

Defense mechanisms are not used all the time. Rather, they appear to be utilized according to how threatened the person is, what else is happening, and the personality characteristics of the individual. The *degree of threat* has been suggested by Richard Lazarus (1969) to be one of the most significant influences. The more anxiety-arousing the situation, the more likely a person will use defense mechanisms rather than taking realistic actions. As Lazarus puts it, "extreme solutions are more likely with extreme threats" (Lazarus, 1969, pp. 238–239).

What else is happening refers to the *context* variable. If the anxiety-arousing agent is clear, external, and specific and some action to deal with it is available, then defense mechanisms are less likely to be used. On the other hand, if we are anxious about a vague feeling or drive, then the inaccessibility of action will cause us to use defense mechanisms more frequently.

The personality and well-being of the individual also determine whether a defense mechanism will be used and, if so, which one. In part, the emotional strength of the person is a determinant. The more the person demonstrates characteristics of openness and security, the less need that person will have for defense mechanisms.

Those people who are most inclined to utilize the mechanisms of repression, denial, and projection to protect themselves from distressing information have been identified as **narrow scanners** (Heilbrun, 1984). Their defenses limit the amount of incoming information the people digest. Instead of scanning or assessing a wide range of possible alternatives to handle stress, narrow scanners see only the safe and nonthreatening possibilities. Such defensive patterns allow these people to look at the world with blinders on.

The choice of defense mechanisms is itself the product of lifelong adjustments. People use patterns that they have used before. This consistency of thinking and reacting is illustrated in an Ambrose Bierce story, in which a young ostrich complains to its mother of severe stomach pains. Once the mother ostrich discovers the young one has swallowed a keg of nails, she exclaims

> What! A whole keg of nails at your age! Why you will kill yourself that way. Go quickly, my child, and swallow a claw hammer.

(Bierce, 1946, p. 604)

Just as the mother ostrich understands that claw hammers remove nails, we all understand that defense mechanisms remove anxieties. However, applying the hammer to the nails is inappropriate in this case. Like defense mechanisms, it reflects an immediate fix-it view. The anxieties (and the nails) often remain, and the defense mechanisms simply shield us from the discomfort resulting from fearful thoughts and unpleasant feelings.

Not everyone needs shielding from unpleasant or threatening feelings. Defense mechanisms are a protective solution. We now turn to those adjustmental patterns that directly confront and master personal threats. We begin looking at successful coping by examining the hardy personality.

Narrow scanners

WELL-BEING WHEN CONFRONTED WITH STRESSFUL EVENTS

What a wonderful life I've had! I only wish I'd realized it sooner.

(Colette)

The Hardy Personality

Hardy personality

Stressful events do not necessarily harm us. Indeed, by looking at people who seek, enjoy, and grow from stressful events, we find one useful explanation of how these people address their lives. Suzanne Kobasa (1982) has labelled this positive response to stressors *hardiness,* a product of the ***hardy personality.*** While stress resistance may emerge from relationships and situations, hardiness is a characteristic of people themselves (Hammen, Mayo, deMayo & Marks, 1986). The hardy personality responds to stressful events with ***commitment, control,*** and ***challenge.*** Let us consider these three components in turn.

Commitment
Control
Challenge

Commitment has been defined as "the ability to believe in the truth, importance, and interest value of who one is and what one is doing . . . and thereby the tendency to involve oneself fully in the many situations of life" (Kobasa, 1982, p. 6). In other words, committed people have a sense of purpose in life. Their values are sound and they know their lives are worthwhile and that they are contributing to the lives and welfare of others.

When the German physician Albert Schweitzer gave up a promising career in music and philosophy to establish a hospital in Africa's least accessible jungle region, his sense of commitment allowed him to cope with diseases, insects, isolation, and sanitary problems. The same kinds of belief and dedication help other people armor themselves against the stressors of family deaths, rapid life changes, and the effects of disasters.

Control refers to our understanding that we truly can influence what happens to us and others; we can act to change things. A feeling of control allows us to be responsible, to accept stressors because our actions have allowed them to occur, and to behave in ways to cope with the stressors.

Feelings of control in coping with stressors come about in part from how people assess their abilities to cope. The positive judgment of being able to cope well has been called *self-efficacy* by Stanford psychologist Albert Bandura (1977). The self-efficacy theory holds that how people see situations and their abilities to handle them is crucial. If you have many personal experiences of failing in difficult situations, you may anticipate failure again and prepare for failure. On the other hand, if you feel you have handled similar situations well, then you will prepare for success. How you personally judge your past experiences, along with the reality of success, will affect how you assess your ability to cope.

However, more than judgments of past experiences affect self-efficacy. What you have seen other people doing, what others say and think, and what you physically feel in such situations make a difference. The implications are striking. The more your sense of self-efficacy is positive, the more successfully you can cope with demanding situations. To feel self-efficacy, you need many mastery experiences in which you learn you truly can master stressors. As self-efficacy rises, coping skills soar as well.

Challenge is the third component of the hardy personality. Because of the challenge involved some people take chances that would be stressful for others. Such people see potentially stressful events as desirable incentives. Change and stimulation make the world interesting to hardy people. Too much stability is dull for these people who welcome the unexpected and the risky. This thriving on challenge has also been called stress seeking and stimulation seeking. Stress seekers have a high optimal level of stimulation. Leaping out of planes to skydive, regular competition, rappelling down a mountain, and running hazardous rapids are joyful and satisfying activities to the stress seeker.

For stress seekers, such excitement is necessary for desirable living. Delaware psychologist Marvin Zuckerman has called such need for challenge *sensation seeking* and has sought to investigate what constitutes **sensation seeking** (Zuckerman, Eysenck & Eysenck, 1978).

Sensation seeking

Sensation Seeking

Sensation seeking turns out to be more complex than one would anticipate. For the past twenty years, Zuckerman has refined a series of scales to measure this pattern. Typical items from the most recent version of the scale are presented in Table 4–2. Through factor analysis, Zuckerman and his research colleagues have found that four independent factors make up sensation seeking. They are

Thrill and Adventure Seeking: The desire to engage in risky and adventurous activities

Experience Seeking: The pursuit of stimulation through the mind and senses, through travel, and by means of a nonconforming life-style

Disinhibition: Uninhibited participation in sexual, social, and drug experiences

Boredom Susceptibility: Intolerance for repetitive, dull events and people

(Zuckerman, Eysenck & Eysenck, 1978, pp. 144–145)

Although not everyone has to climb mountains or risk financial disaster to feel fulfilled, everyone does need some stressful stimulation, some challenge, for life to seem worthwhile. Hans Selye (1976) has called this amount of desirable and necessary stressors **eustress,** or positive stress. If

Eustress

TABLE 4-2   Sensation Seeking Scale: Typical Items*

Thrill and Adventure Seeking

I often wish I could be a mountain climber.
I sometimes like to do things that are a little frightening.
I would like to take up the sport of water skiing.
I would like to try parachute jumping.
I would like to sail a long distance in a small but seaworthy sailing craft.

Experience Seeking

I like some of the earthy body smells.
I like to explore a strange city or section of town, even if it means getting lost.
I have tried marijuana or would like to.
I like to try foods I have never tasted before.
People should dress in individual ways, even if the effects are sometimes
   strange.

Disinhibition

I like wild, uninhibited parties.
I enjoy the company of real "swingers."
I often like to get high (drinking liquor or smoking marijuana).
I like to have new and exciting experiences and sensations, even if they are a
   little unconventional or even illegal.
I like to date members of the opposite sex who are physically exciting.

Boredom Susceptibility

I can't stand watching a movie that I've seen before.
I get bored seeing the same old faces.
When you can predict almost everything a person can do and say, she or he
   must be a bore.
I get very restless if I have to stay around home for any length of time.
I like people who are sharp and witty, even if they do sometimes insult others.

* Adapted from Zuckerman, Eysenck & Eysenck, 1978, pp. 144-145.

enough stress is not present in work, people look to recreation for challenges. If neither work nor play offer challenge, many people find their eustress in reexperiencing the adventures of others, through movies, books, and watching sports or artistic performances. Stressors do not have to be physical, either. Intellectual or emotional challenges through problem solving or dealing with important relationships may also serve to provide intense stimulation.

Challenge by itself does not lead to psychological hardiness. However, challenge in combination with personal commitment and a sense of control over one's life and environment is the hallmark of the hardy personality. Can people become hardier? It appears so, and one of the important methods is stress inoculation, our next topic.

Stress Inoculation

The notion that people could be prepared for stress was very much in the air during World War II. I was rather forcibly introduced to that notion shortly after I was drafted into the Army in the fall of 1943 [and] . . . put through what was called a battle inoculation course. It included not only films, pamphlets, and illustrated lectures about the realities of combat dangers but also gradual exposure to actual battle stimuli under reasonably safe conditions. The most impressive feature of the battle inocula-

Indiana Jones is a true sensation seeker, because of his desire to engage in risky and adventurous activities. If you answer yes to the following questions, it is quite possible that you, too, are a sensation seeker: Do you look for constant stimulation of the mind and senses? A nonconforming life-style? Uninhibited participation in sexual and social experiences? Do you get bored easily?

tion course was that each of us had to crawl about 80 yards under live machine-gun fire in a simulated setting that was all too realistic.

(Janis, 1983, p. 68)

Imagine that *you* are about to try hang gliding for the first time. Your friends who hang glide have spoken to you about the exhilaration of hang gliding, about how the feeling of freedom is unmatched. So you enroll in a course. Yet, as you think about your decision, you realize that you are going to have to leap into the air from a cliff almost a half-mile up. No ladder. And you will fall at first. The hang glider seems agonizingly flimsy. You can deal with this kind of impending danger and existing fear by the procedure called stress inoculation.

Stress inoculation begins by warning people about what they should expect so that the stressful event is predictable. In military training, as well as in classes on hang gliding and sport parachuting, stress inoculation promotes hardiness. People are given experiences that arouse their fears and defenses just enough so that they are able to handle the genuine attack or stressor when it arrives.

Just as medical inoculation introduces just enough of a disease agent into the bloodstream to produce antibodies, so does stress inoculation arouse enough fear, under sufficiently safe and controlled conditions, to produce a sense of subjective well-being. Donald Meichenbaum and his colleagues (1983) have used three phases in stress inoculation: education, rehearsal, and practice and implementation.

Education

In World War II, exposing a new draftee to simulated battle conditions and likely noises, commands, and requirements made the real battle events predictable for the draftee. People often have intense fear of events such as battles and other major threats. Specific information about what to anticipate from the threat helps people deal with that threat. The person with a fatal disease usually copes better if he or she knows exactly what to expect in the forthcoming stages.

Rehearsal

Under safe, supervised conditions, rehearsal makes the real event more open to mastery. When people are taught sport parachuting, they jump off a platform and out of an airplane in the hanger many dozens of times in preparation for the real jump.

Practice and implementation

Overlearning teaches what has to be done through repeated practice. One way that people implement stress inoculation is through the use of positive self-statements that make the problem and its stages and solutions clear and explicit. For example, one client generated the following list of self-statements to deal with the fear of pain:

Preparing for the Stressor

What is it I have to do?
I can develop a plan to deal with it.
Don't worry, worrying won't solve anything.

Stage of Confronting and Handling the Problem

One step at a time, I can handle the challenge.
Just relax, breathe deeply and use one of the strategies.
This tenseness can be an ally, a cue to cope.
This anxiety is what the trainer said I might feel.
That's right; it's the reminder to use my coping skills.

Stage of Coping with Problem at Critical Moments

When the pain comes, just pause; keep focusing on what I have to do.
Don't try to eliminate the problem entirely; just keep it manageable.
When the difficulty mounts, I can switch to a different strategy; I'm in control.

Reinforcing Self-Statements

Good, I did it.
I handled it pretty well.
Wait until I tell the trainer about which procedures worked best.

(Meichenbaum, 1985, pp. 72–73)

The client learned about the nature of the problem, then tried a number of strategies, and finally practiced the applications. Self-statements, said aloud or to oneself, allow a person to cope much better with stressors. Fears are restated in nonthreatening language. Indeed, physical pain, as well as fear, can be reduced by such stress inoculations (Miller & Bowers, 1986).

The increase in control and commitment through the techniques of education, rehearsal, and practice and implementation link stress inoculations with the components of the hardy personality. The techniques build self-confidence and feelings of responsibility so that people truly can affect what happens in their lives and can become invested in successful coping methods (Janis, 1983).

Table 4–3 summarizes that ways we deal with stress that are indicative of well-being and those ways of dealing with stress that move us away from well-being.

TABLE 4–3　Stress and Well-Being

Toward Well-Being	Away from Well-Being
Stress is internally mediated in realistic ways and with positive consequences	Stress is poorly mediated with harmful consequences
Has few hassles, disasters, or other stressful life events	Has overwhelming number or intensity of hassles, disasters, and other stressful life events
Consciously copes with emotional threats in realistic and open ways	Uses defense mechanisms excessively in coping with emotional threats
Uses broad scannning of distressing information	Uses narrow scanning of distressing information
Responds to stress with commitment, control, and appreciation of challenge	Responds to stress by feeling purposeless, helpless; feels overstimulated

SUMMARY

Stressful experiences may be viewed as having three components: *stressors,* or the outside demands for us to adjust; *strains,* or the personal responses and changes that follow stressors; and *mediators,* or the filtering processes that shape the impact of stressors. How people interpret and assess stressors accounts for their differential impact. Hans Selye's *general adaptation syndrome* (GAS) is a model that calls attention to three common response patterns to stressors. First comes the *alarm reaction,* the body's emergency call to arms in a crisis. Then comes the *resistance* stage of longer-term adaptation. Lastly, under prolonged stressors, *exhaustion* may set in, and serious illness or death may follow.

The Holmes and Rahe research into life events and stress suggests that change by itself is stressful. Their systematic studies provided compelling proof that loss of loved ones and other such powerful life changes have hazardous health implications. Changes are least stressful when they are desired, anticipated, and subject to the control of the person.

An even more comprehensive approach to research on stress was the development of the PERI 102-item scale by the Dohrenwends. Application of this scale indicated that women report many more items as stressful than do men. Differences between rural and urban perceptions of stress were also seen.

Natural disasters are among the most severe stressors, but man-made situations can also have severe traumatic effects. The survivors of the Buffalo Creek flood were listless, disorganized, and had substantial sleep problems. The massive resettlement of Ghana villagers when the Volta River was dammed led to their increased drinking and fighting. A minority of the USS *Pueblo* POWs maintained their emotional well-being during their capture, but the poorly adjusted showed sleep disturbances, anxiety, and depression.

When direct resolutions to problems are not available, people resort to defense mechanisms to deal with their threatening or unacceptable feelings. *Suppression* is the conscious effort not to think or feel. *Repression* is the unconscious process of keeping anxiety-arousing anger or sexuality from awareness. *Denial* pushes unacceptable external threats out of awareness. *Projection* assigns to others our own feelings or reactions. *Intellectualization* uses emotional detachment to convert threatening feelings into abstract "logical" thoughts. *Rationalization* attempts to explain away anxiety-arousing fears. *Displacement* uses substitute outlets and means for dealing with unacceptable concerns. *Fantasy* is escaping excessively into daydreams and wishful thinking. *Regression* is returning to an earlier stage of adjustment. *Identification* is overly accepting the position or nature of the person causing the anxiety. *Reaction formation* is adopting a compensatory feeling opposite to that being genuinely experienced.

The people who are least susceptible to stressors in life have been identified as *hardy personalities.* Their stress resistance is due to three factors: *commitment* to a purpose in life and belief in themselves; *control* in coping with such problems, or at least the feeling of control; and acceptance of the *challenge* to overcome risks and obstacles as a meaningful part of their lives. Challenges are welcomed by *sensation seekers,* who become bored easily and who seek out thrills, diverse experiences, and uninhibited social lives.

We can be prepared for stressful situations through *stress inoculation,* or a sequence of education, rehearsal, and practice that arouses fears and anxieties just enough to improve our ability to cope with the real threat.

Key Terms

Alarm reaction	Intellectualization
Challenge	Narrow scanners
Commitment	Nonspecificity
Control	PERI life events scale
Defense mechanisms	Post-traumatic stress disorder
Denial	Projection
Displacement	Rationalization
Eustress	Reaction formation
Exhaustion	Regression
Fantasy	Repression
General adaptation syndrome	Repressor
Hardy personality	Resistance
Hassles	Sensation seeking
Identification	Sensitizer

**Social readjustment rating
  scale (SRRS)**
Stockholm Syndrome
Strains
Stress

Stress mediators
Stressors
Sublimation
Suppression
Uplifts

**Recommended
Reading**

Girdano, Daniel A. and Everly, George S. (1979) *Controlling Stress and Tension: A Holistic Approach.* Englewood Cliffs, NJ: Prentice-Hall. Out of the hundreds of books on self-management of stress, this book seemed truly useful to me. A large unit within the book is devoted to assessing one's own stress levels, drawing on known rating scales. Then instruction is given in relaxation, in meditation, in biofeedback, and in better managing the social environment to lessen personal strain.

Meichenbaum, Donald and Jarenko, Matt E. (Eds.) (1983) *Stress Reduction and Prevention.* New York: Plenum. Donald Meichenbaum is the trailblazer in leading the way in research into the nature of stress and treatment of strain. This edited volume gathers together Meichenbaum's own stress inoculation writings with those of the most prominant other stress experts.

Shaffer, Martin (1982) *Life After Stress.* New York: Plenum. This little workbook leads the reader through clear and practical steps in coping with stress. The detailed discussion of relaxation methods is especially helpful and can be immediately and comfortably tried by the reader.

5
CHAPTER

Physical Health and Illness

Passing a Small Stone

When psychoanalysts joke with each other, they tease about psychological issues such as repressed desires and fantasies. It is an in-group joke, however. Those outside the profession are not welcome to join in playful accusations of abnormalities and maladjustments. Even more of an intrusion is felt when outsiders are serious in their psychodiagnostic finger pointing. That's why Martin Grotjahn (1963) was so annoyed.

Grotjahn is a Beverly Hills psychoanalyst who felt a sharp pain in his back one day. It was like being stabbed. Soon after, he discovered blood in his urine. He had a kidney stone, which was slowly grinding its way to his bladder, irritating the pathway, causing bleeding, and now and then causing excruciating pain. With the pain came waves of overwhelming anxiety. He found himself becoming hysterical and embarrassed at his hysteria.

The kidney specialists took X rays. The kidney stone was indeed moving. However, the specialists were unsympathetic to his experiences. Indeed, because he was a psychoanalyst, they seemed to take particularly sweet pleasure in looking for psychological causes for his anxiety attacks and hysterical reactions to his pain. They patronized him. When he complained, they made him feel childish and foolish. What were the other stresses in his life, they wanted to know. How was his marriage? What was happening at work? Grotjahn was annoyed.

Finally, Grotjahn went to a fourth urologist, a man who was calm and understanding. He empathized with Grotjahn's suffering and described each of the symptoms Grotjahn would experience next. This specialist reassuringly told Grotjahn of the physiological links between kidney stone attacks and anxiety attacks.

Grotjahn was deeply relieved and passed the stone within twenty-four hours. The symptoms diminished and then ceased. After his final checkup, Grotjahn asked this doctor how he had gained such a gentle and considerate understanding of patients who suffer from kidney stones.

> Touched by the sincerity of our conversation, pleased but not flattered, he opened almost shamefacedly a lower drawer of his desk, and took out a little glass tube containing two dried up kidney stones. He looked at them, made them rattle, and said, "I know what it means to have kidney stones. These two were taken out of myself. They taught me a lot."

> *(Grotjahn, 1963, p. 149)*

 ## UNDERSTANDINGS OF ILLNESS

Dualistic

The first three kidney specialists Martin Grotjahn consulted were **dualistic** thinkers about the mind and body. Psychological and physical health are seen as altogether different in such dualism. Kidney stones, like tissue damage and bacterial infections, are observable and therefore real. Pain and other effects from the mind are unreal. The alternative to dualism is **holistic** thinking, which considers the person as a unified whole, in which all such pain is both real and subject to psychological interpretation. In

Holistic

holism, emotional and physical health combine to regulate every area of human function.

Why did Grotjahn suddenly pass his kidney stone after eighteen months of suffering? Certainly his relief following his meeting with the compassionate physician promoted well-being that helped his whole body. Psychological elements are present in every physical ailment. Why does one person respond to stressors that make him more vulnerable to disease? Why does another person break out with cold sores on her mouth at one particular time, even though the virus is always present? Why does one person react to an injury with fright, crying, and slow recovery, while another remains calm, matter of fact, and perhaps recovers more quickly? The following answer has been offered:

> It is evident that in a broad sense all diseases are psychosomatic. Even in the most obvious organic illnesses, physicians have learned, as a practical matter, to take account of the role of psychological adjustment. The strength of desire for recovery, the capacity for sensible care of the body, the willingness to cooperate with the physicians—these and many other aspects of psychological functions affect the treatment of any illness.
>
> *(Holland & Ward, 1966, p. 345)*

The attitude toward the illness itself influences the meaning of the illness in a person's everyday life. One woman who had continued pain from an ongoing infection of the fallopian tubes and ovaries wrote to me how dirty and worthless it made her feel.

> The main psychological assault on my self-image of these medical problems is the feeling of inferiority, and dirtiness, and unworthiness. You know that no matter how hard you try to be clean and pretty, that it's not something you have control over.

Fritz Perls (1969), the founder of Gestalt psychology, had a similar attitude toward his own illnesses. Whenever he was sick, he felt ashamed. Even at the time he developed tonsillitis while serving as a soldier in the trenches during World War I, he concealed his high fever. To have admitted that he was ill would have been showing weakness, and that was intolerable to him. In the same sense, Martin Grotjahn was not comfortable with the thought that his anxiety attacks were possibly due to psychological causes.

While some individuals react to illness with shame or despair, others maintain a positive outlook, their psychological well-being much less affected by their diseases. In the face of uncertainty about their health, people with positive expectations assume that the disease will pass quickly. Much like Martin Grotjahn at his moment of reassurance, they act on that assumption. They are able to maintain relationships, to work efficiently, and show a sense of inner satisfaction throughout the illness. For some college students who have been bedridden or hospitalized for months or years, illness has provided a time-out from school or companions. The resulting isolation frequently has served as a maturing agent that helped the students develop constructive long-term perspectives.

In our exploration of the psychological meaning of illness and health, pain will be our first topic. We will look at how this experience is interpreted. From that point, we will move to three disorders that have distinct psychological components. First, obesity and eating disorders will be examined. Then we will consider aspects of some severe health problems, including Type A behaviors and coronary heart disease and psychologi-

BECOMING AN AIDS VICTIM

Acquired immune deficiency syndrome (AIDS) has become a national health concern, occurring most frequently in homosexual men and individuals who received blood transfusions. The eventual reduction in immunity to infections is sufficiently severe that a large proportion of AIDS victims eventually die.

Devastating psychological consequences accompany AIDS. Health professionals frequently avoid extensive contact with the victims. Friends and co-workers fearfully cut off contact. The victims are seen as potentially contagious, even in passing social situations.

The victims themselves become depressed and feel helpless. In one study, of thirteen AIDS inpatients at San Francisco General Hospital who were referred for psychiatric consultation, twelve were given psychiatric diagnoses. They felt overwhelming uncertainty and anxiety about their illness. They were isolated from their families and friends: "Many spoke of feeling 'unclean' as they watched their caretakers enter their rooms masked, gowned, and gloved" (Dilley, Ochitill, Perl & Volberding, 1985, p. 84). Some patients felt their illness was a retribution for having many sexual partners. Like most persons with fatal diseases, these men felt depressed, numbed, and angry at their shortened life spans and physical losses.

AIDS, like cancer, deals a double-barrelled blow to its victims. The physical effects of progressive deterioration are accompanied by a stigma that is usually poisonous to the victims' interpersonal lives.

cal knowledge about cancer. We shall conclude with an examination of wellness, discussing placebo effects, the role of imagery in healing, and procedures for listening carefully to our bodies. We begin with the common starting point for much illness: the experience of pain.

PAIN

Pain

Pain may be defined as a private, subjective experience of hurt that is a signal of current or impending tissue damage. It alerts us that something is

This child with AIDS is receiving much love and attention from a caring doctor. However, many AIDS victims are avoided by others, considered contagious even in brief social situations. Thus, AIDS patients are dealt a devastating blow as both their physical and interpersonal relationships progressively deteriorate.

wrong, and it has a communicative role: expressions of pain bring others to our assistance (Blackman, 1982). The experiences of touching a hot stove, pricking your finger with a pin, having a massive heart attack, and eating fiery jalapeno peppers are quite different. In fact, pain can be as much a psychological experience as a physical experience. We learn and understand the specific physiological stimulation of "hurt" through a complex set of emotional processes.

The variable ways in which social groups react to pain is revealing. Traditional Eskimo villagers understand pain differently than most people, which is why an Eskimo will laugh in response to pain, "even when the stimulus involves a painful situation like having his arm ripped off by a polar bear" (Fordyce & Steger, 1979, p. 126). Differences appear between other groups within the United States. Yankees from New England, for example, respond matter-of-factly to laboratory-administered electric shock. Italians and Jews have more emotional expressions of pain. Italians are highly vocal and sensitive to pain, apparently because they are more expressive in response to life in general. In some studies, Irish Catholics have reported less pain than other ethnic groups. Racial comparisons have

Pain is the subjective experience of hurt; it is a signal of current or impending physical or psychological damage. Many factors affect a person's reaction to pain, including social and ethnic background.

found differences, too. Caucasians have the greatest tolerance for pain, blacks have somewhat less, and orientals consistently have the least tolerance and most sensitivity to pain (Blackman, 1982).

Psychological reactions to pain may take the form of what people do—motor reactions—or what people think—cognitive reactions. Let us consider motor reactions. If you develop a severe headache and complain aloud about the pain, grimacing, crying, moaning, and taking aspirin, your actions are observable. Your words and actions are reactions to the pain. Current theorists (for example, Sanders, 1979) consider motor reactions to be central aspects of the pain.

The cognitive reactions to pain are what you *think* and *feel.* For example, your headache might cause you to talk silently to yourself about how much you hurt and how hopeless life is, or you might have mental images of lying in bed helpless. Another cognitive aspect of the pain is the subjective feeling of pain.

Psychogenic pain

When observable physical causes of pain cannot be found, the experience is labelled ***psychogenic pain.*** Of course, this label does not mean no physiological cause is present; it means only that no physiological cause is known. Whether or not a physical cause, such as tissue damage or disease, is present, the experience of pain is real. The person genuinely hurts. The idea that the pain is partially or fully in the person's mind captures a key notion of pain. Pain is always in our minds, just as other behaviors and emotions are directed by our brains.

The nature of pain teaches us something about all health and illness. No illness is purely physical. Every disease exists in both body and mind. The ways in which we come to understand our bodies and how they hurt depend upon our views of ourselves. Even in the case of broken bones, the experience of the pain and temporary handicap is subjective and personal.

It is important to remember that pain serves a useful purpose. Pain alerts a person to a problem and often indicates the beginning of healing of wounds. Gibran has observed

> Much of your pain is self-chosen.
> It is bitter potion by which the physician
> within you heals your sick self.
> Therefore trust the physician, and drink his
> remedy in silence and tranquillity.

(Gibran, 1951, p. 52)

Theories of Pain

Three theories have been proposed to account for the experience of pain: (1) specific receptors, (2) pattern theory, and (3) gate control.

Specific receptor theory

1. *Specific receptor theory* arose at the end of the nineteenth century, about the time specific nerve endings were found to convey cold, heat, and pressure. Free nerve endings were believed to yield only pain when they were stimulated. Pain was seen as a *sensation,* much like the sensation of warmth, that was felt at these particular pain nerve endings.

Pattern theory

2. *Pattern theory* disagreed, holding that no special nerve endings were responsible for pain. Rather, the shifting patterns of impulses that reached the brain were believed to cause pain. If the stimulation was such that the impulses were close together physically and had little time elapse between them, as when a sharp object is pressed against the skin, the pattern signaled pain. Neither the specific receptor theory nor the pattern theory fully accounted for the experience of pain. However, they did set the stage for the gate control theory.

Gate control theory

3. *Gate control theory* began to explain why pain might be a subjective experience. Mechanisms in the dorsal horns of the spine work like a gate, letting some impulses through and blocking others (Melzack & Wall, 1965). Whether the gate opens or closes depends in part on what types of impulses and how many impulses flow to it. However, this "gate" may also open or close according to the individual's emotional state, background, and appraisal of the current situation. Thus, pain can flow like floodwaters or be cut off at the dam, depending upon the individual. This emphasis on what the individual brings to the experience of pain provides an explanation of why surgical anesthesia doesn't work well for some people and why other people are analgesic and almost totally insensitive to pain (Turk, Meichenbaum & Genest, 1983).

Analgesia

Analgesia is defined as insensitivity to pain. Physiological factors in the central nervous system are associated with analgesia. For example, when the brain produces the opiatelike substances *endorphins,* the transmission and receipt of pain impulses can be diminished. These substances act like morphine, and they occur naturally, fluctuating according to what is happening in the person's experience. In other words, they provide the answer to the question of just what does happen to the neural input in people who are not experiencing pain at expected times (Olson, Kastin & Coy, 1980).

Acute and Chronic Pain

You burn your finger on a hot stove. Your finger hurts; after a while, the pain ceases. You have just experienced acute or short-term intense pain. *Acute pain* is usually perceived as due to some tissue damage or harm to the body. Note, however, it is a *perception.* The experience of pain lies

Acute pain

Chronic pain

in part in the brain's central processing of experiences. In the case of chronic or long-term pain, the psychological factors are clearer. People with **chronic pain** tend to be anxious and depressed, states that seem to be associated with more intense pain in general and with brief pain becoming chronic. Furthermore, people who are depressed, frustrated, and angry do not respond well to pain treatment.

Consider the following example, where an acute pain could become chronic:

> A careless person backs suddenly into an open cupboard door and sharply strikes the occipital area (back of the head). This may be followed immediately by a sharp pain, and gasping, grimacing, or moaning, as well as dizziness or visual blurring. These sensations slowly fade as the time passes.
>
> But suppose the person's spouse has observed the incident and quickly expresses much attention and concern. A series of questions concerning the physiological status and well-being [of the victim] follows and the victim receives the luxury of being driven to and from work on this particular day.
>
> *(Fordyce & Steger, 1979, pp. 132–133)*

The victim's pain may continue well after tissue damage has healed. Not only as a result of the injury, but also as a result of the consequences of the *expression* of pain, the pain could persist.

The careless person bumping into the cupboard door felt pain that arose directly from the bump. Fordyce has observed that the spouse's attention to the pain changed the victim's behaviors and encouraged the continuation of the pain experience.

People are rarely aware of such influences on their pain experiences. Rather, they are aware of the subjective feelings of hurt and discomfort, and they are aware of the positive (or minimal) support of spouses and friends. The suffering person typically sees the cause and effect relationship in one direction. That is, the pain is seen as causing the emotional support. The emotional support is not seen as causing or maintaining the pain. People with this kind of social reinforcement are by no means the only individuals with little awareness of the processes and meaning of pain.

In general, people in pain find it difficult to gain insight about their experience, because the pain distracts them from other thoughts and commands their attention so. When the pain is severe, it feels as if it has always been there. Emily Dickinson described such pain.

> Pain has an element of blank;
> It cannot recollect
> When it began, or if there were
> A day when it was not
>
> *(Dickinson, 1967, p. 33)*

OBESITY AND EATING DISORDERS

Everyone in the known world has an eating disorder nowadays. At least, that is the way it sometimes appears when one considers the media attention to and the professional fascination with problems of obesity, bulimia, and anorexia. In this section, we examine existing knowledge about these problems. Our beginning point is the heavy topic of **obesity.**

Obesity

Obesity

> There was an Old Man of Calcutta,
> Who perpetually ate bread and butter;
> Till a great bit of muffin,
> On which he was stuffing,
> Choked that horrid Old Man of Calcutta.

(Lear, 1978, p. 39)

We are prejudiced against fat people. From childhood on through old age, the obese among us receive disapproval, dislike, and disdain. Overweight children are often taunted relentlessly. Overweight adults may find themselves unpopular and excluded from social activities and occupational possibilities. The prejudice against fat people seems to extend through every racial, religious, occupational, and economic grouping.

What made the Old Man of Calcutta so horrid in the Edward Lear limerick? His lack of self-control and continuous eating were his faults, and such social ridicule is typical. In a society that values slenderness, an obese person is presented with adjustmental demands. Let us look at the nature of fat itself.

> Fat, one of the basic constituents of body tissue, is an admirable result
> of evolution. It allows for compact storage of energy reserves, cushions
> the body against bumps and blows, provides insulation, and in moderate
> amounts promotes sex appeal by providing attractive curves in the proper
> places. Fat molecules are well adapted to the energy needs of the body,
> for they help balance the input of food and the output of energy. The
> question is how that balance is broken to cause excessive fat storage.

(Rodin, 1978, p. 38)

Why are some people prone to fat? Part of the answer is hereditary. Fat parents generally have fat children. Indeed, the tendency to become obese can be seen by the age of two (Rodin, 1978). However, eating habits are learned, and psychological issues also are involved.

One major psychological perspective on obesity is stated by the **emotional arousal hypothesis.** According to this hypothesis, obese people have greater responsiveness to the sight, smell, and taste of food, and they are emotionally more aroused by other stimuli as well. Stanley Schacter and

Emotional arousal hypothesis

Why are some people prone to become fat? Heredity is a major factor, but complex psychological issues also play a part. Many studies have attempted to answer the question of why some people become fat, but all have failed to find a single personality type among obese people.

his colleagues (1964) developed the emotional arousal hypothesis in a book with the unlikely title of *Emotion, Obesity, and Crime.* In Schacter's research, overweight people were found to be more physically activated by thinking about food than were normal weight people. The cause of this activation was not limited to food either. Emotionally disturbing stories about effects of the Hiroshima bombing or the devastation of leukemia emotionally affected overweight people more than nonobese subjects.

The emotional arousal hypothesis for obesity has been partially confirmed by research. Although it has been demonstrated that the obese eat when emotionally aroused or stressed, it has not yet been shown that they actually confuse other arousal states with hunger, nor that they necessarily eat more than normal weight people (Ley, 1980). Indeed, a substantially large group of nonobese people also eat when bored, anxious, or depressed.

A second psychological approach in research on obesity has been to search for the obese personality type. For a minority of obese people, eating disorders signal abnormal personality problems. Lindner described one woman who engaged in periodic gorging.

> She was subject to episodes of depression during which she would be seized by an overwhelming compulsion to gorge herself, to eat almost continuously. A victim of forces beyond her ken or control, when this strange urge came upon her she was ravenous—insatiable. Until she reached a stage of utter exhaustion, until her strained senses succumbed to total intoxication, she would cram herself with every available kind of food and drink.

(Lindner, 1955, p. 81)

Prompted by such clinical observations, a futile search ensued for the common personality traits in obese people—in other words, a search for the obese personality. No single personality type was discovered, any more than one would expect to find one personality type associated with slim people.

One other major hypothesis about obesity has been put forth. This is *set point theory*, which holds that a biologically preset body weight, the set point, exists for the obese and for the nonobese, too. The number and distribution of fat cells are seen as determining weight and proportion of fat to total body weight. Although diet and exercise can counteract the set point of weight, most people will hover around this weight when they eat as they choose. Set-point theory is useful with particular populations, such as individuals who need to understand their predisposition toward fat as part of a treatment program.

Obesity, however, is a complex phenomenon, and does not have to be attributed to a single cause. One important contributor is disorders in eating, a category that also includes the exaggerated dieting of anorexia nervosa and the gorging on food of bulimia.

Anorexia and Bulimia

The eating disorders of anorexia and bulimia arise in part from our societal attitudes toward body fat. These attitudes affect women in particular. Women worry about their weight more than men do. Women are more likely to overestimate their weight, to try to lose weight, and to wish to be thinner. Four out of every five adolescent girls wish they were thinner,

Set point theory

while only one of five adolescent boys wishes he were thinner. All in all, these findings reflect the cultural pressures on women to be thin. These pressures are sufficiently strong that a majority of thin girls—averaging five feet, five inches tall and weighing 110 pounds—want to lose weight (Ley, 1980).

One consequence of the desire to be thinner is undereating. At its most extreme is **anorexia nervosa,** a neurotic dread of being overweight that causes adolescent women to eat so little that their physical and mental health are harmed. These young women will often diet on as little as two hundred calories a day. One of the common reasons for such severe dieting cited by anorexic women is the image as well as the fear of being fat (Bell, Kirkpatrick & Rinn, 1986). These shriveled, emaciated women will frequently grasp their skin between their fingers and explain that they still have fat to remove.

The same extreme motivation for thinness drives individuals who suffer from **bulimia,** a word that literally means "ox hunger." Bulimia is an involuntary pattern of frequent, inconspicuous binging on high-caloric food, followed by shame, depression, and sometimes self-induced vomiting. While some observers have suggested that anorexia and bulimia are essentially the same disorder, the present approach is to consider them as separate behavior patterns. Not all bulimics become emaciated and not all anorexics binge, and these facts have led to the different diagnostic categories. The binging starts when the person is anxious or lonely or bored. An hour or more later, when she is stuffed with ice cream or doughnuts or candy, she feels depressed about the binge and self-critical at the loss of control.

The theories about the obese personality have been extended to include the sufferers of bulimia; as researchers have sought to identify the bulimic personality and differences in emotional arousal. The results have been the same: mixed findings, with no clear emergence of one theory (Striegel-Moore, Silberstein & Rodin, 1986). However, two new hypotheses about bulimia have been generated. The more tentative of the two is the psychodynamic theory, which holds that problems in feminine identity and sex role conflict are lived out in the form of the binge eating (Davis & Marsh, 1986). The better developed of the two hypotheses is the cognitive behavioral assumption that prolonged dieting leads to intense hunger and feelings of deprivation, so the thought and sight of food at times of stress can set off a voracious binge. The immediate consequences are reinforcing, but the longer-term effects are negative. The same thing happens with purging: immediate reinforcement and longer-term negative impact. The negative feelings and depression lead to dieting and self-denial, which sets the person up for a binge in the future (Gandour, 1984). This cycle is like an addiction, with incessant cravings that are never satisfied by more than a short but sometimes exquisitely pleasurable orgy of eating.

Anorexia nervosa

Bulimia

Is binging typical of young women in general? The answer was yes in a study of 663 normal weight female college students and 86 female students who were on the average 40 percent overweight (Hawkins & Clement, 1984). Among these subjects, 86 percent of the normal weight women and 94 percent of the overweight women stated that they did binge eat. Twenty-nine percent of the normal weight women binged at

LOSING CONTROL OVER EATING

Part of binge eating is the feeling of being out of control: instead of choosing to eat, the binge eater feels compelled to eat and is distressed about this feeling. One of the ways to assess your fear of losing control is to go through the following scale (Hawkins & Clement, 1984, p. 253). For each statement, answer *yes* or *no* as it applies to you.

1. I become anxious prior to eating.
2. I find myself preoccupied with foods.
3. I have gone on eating binges where I have felt that I may not be able to stop.
4. I feel that food controls my life.
5. I display self-control around food. (*reverse scored*)
6. I give too much time and thought to food.
7. I have the impulse to vomit after meals.

Normal weight women without eating disorders answer yes to one or two of these items. Women with eating disorders answer yes to six or seven items.

Some characteristics of extreme binge eaters have also been identified. You are probably a compulsive, episodic overeater if you endorse most or all of the following items:

1. I binge eat almost every day.
2. I binge for more than an hour at a time.
3. I eat until my stomach is painfully full and I cannot eat any more.
4. I eat very rapidly when binging.
5. I feel completely out of control during a binge.
6. I am moderately upset or hate myself afterwards.
7. I am very depressed after a binge.

(Adapted from Hawkins & Clement, 1984, pp. 233–234)

Individuals who affirm all these behaviors and feelings are typically in need of a sense of personal restraint. Although many pathways toward such restraint are possible, professional help is one option often chosen.

least once a week, with 9 percent reporting that they felt completely out of control during a binge and 17 percent reporting that they hated themselves during a binge. The overweight women binged more often and were markedly more negative. Fifty-nine percent binged at least once a week, with 38 percent feeling completely out of control, and 57 percent hating themselves. In contrast, college men report less frequent binging,

A person who binges feels out of control: instead of *choosing* to eat, the binge eater feels *compelled* to eat.

and almost all reported feeling in control of their eating habits. Although a high incidence of binging is reported among college-age women, all binging is not necessarily disordered or bulimic. Only about 8 percent of young women are sufficiently distressed, with symptoms sufficiently severe, that they truly are bulimic.

Treatment of bulimia is still in its childhood, and the disorder has proven resistant to a variety of treatment approaches. Nevertheless, among the many efforts, the following treatments have had at least some reported success (Gandour, 1984):

Hospitalization. Bulimic patients are hospitalized for two or three weeks to break the cycle of starvation–binging–purging. During this time, careful supervision leads the patients back to more conventional eating patterns.

Cognitive behavioral approaches. Patients first are required to keep a food diary to monitor the levels of food eaten. Limited eating is achieved by making the individuals self-conscious about the therapist knowing how much they had consumed. In the same sense, the patients' own heightened awareness of just how much they eat reduces their binging (Polivy & Herman, 1985). Next, patients are involved in activities that are incompatible with binge overeating, such as extensive exercising and spending time with friends. Finally, patients learn how to develop dietary control.

Stimulus and thought control. If a person's watching TV or being in the kitchen are associated with problem eating, these stimuli are identified and the person is taught to never eat while the TV is on or while actually in the kitchen—or for that matter while doing anything else but attending to the food. In addition, the person's intrusive and maladaptive thoughts about eating and weight are targeted and replaced with rational thoughts.

Psychotherapy. Both individual and group psychotherapy have been employed in treating eating disorders. The focus of such treatment tends to be on general problems in effective living and in emotional development.

All undereating and overeating appear as part of a diet–weight loss–lack of control–weight gain cycle that occurs in millions of men and women. Almost everybody can lose weight for a short time. And almost everybody regains some or all of the weight they lost through dieting. This weight loss and regain cycle occurs because people's behaviors remain the same. People have poor understanding of their eating habits, and they usually do not sustain calorie-oriented analyses of their food intake for very long. The behaviors themselves—eating too much, especially when not hungry, getting insufficient exercise, and having little control over what triggers eating—lead to the characteristic result of dieting: a brief success followed by a long-term failure.

SEVERE HEALTH PROBLEMS

Type A Behavior and Coronary Heart Disease

Do you ever set deadlines or quotas for yourself at work or at home?

1. Yes, once a week or more often

2. No—or yes, but only occasionally

How would your closest friend or your spouse rate you?

1. Definitely hard driving and competitive

2. Definitely relaxed and easygoing

Do you interrupt or complete others' sentences for them?

1. Yes, frequently

2. No, not usually

Type A personalities

Type B personalities

These response choices are part of questionnaires and interviews designed to distinguish between Type A and Type B individuals. The first response to each item is characteristic of *Type A personalities.* Such people strive relentlessly for high achievement, they bind themselves with strict time deadlines, and they approach their worlds competitively and aggressively. The second responses are associated with the more relaxed, less competitive, and nonhostile *Type B personalities.*

To understand how behavior can affect coronary heart disease (CHD), we need to examine the causes of heart disease. The two most common kinds of heart disease are *angina* and *myocardial infarction.* Angina describes pain from lack of oxygen to the heart muscles, due to increased demand (say, from exercise) and insufficient supply (as arteries narrow with age). Myocardial infarction is a heart attack in the form of stoppage or death of the heart wall muscles. Some known risk factors associated with CHD are getting older, being male, having high blood pressure, having high cholesterol levels, smoking cigarettes heavily, being overweight, and having parental histories of CHD.

Coronary heart disease is a serious health problem, representing the major cause of death among American men in the age range of thirty-five to fifty. Until the mid-1970s, the search for psychological factors to accompany the growing confirmation of physical causes had yielded minimum returns. Then Friedman and Rosenman (1974) found that Type A behaviors were associated twice as frequently with CHD than were Type

B behaviors. Another study of over three thousand men aged thirty-nine to fifty-nine looked independently at medical and behavioral problems over a period of eight and one-half years. Again, greater than twice the rate of fatal heart attacks and five times the number of coronary problems were found in the Type A men compared to Type B men (Rosenman, Brand, Jenkins, Friedman, Straus & Wurm, 1975).

Type A behavior

Note that **Type A behavior** and Type A personalities are not necessarily the same. Type A behavior is temporary and situational, while Type A personalities exhibit long-term, well-established patterns of behavior. Type A behavior emerges in many people in uncontrollable, stressful situations. Type A personalities have a knack for making almost any situation demanding and stressful. The Type A personality strives increasingly harder to master and resolve a situation that does not lend itself to control and mastery. As time passes, the inability of Type A personalities to escape the stress of time deadlines and nonresolvable problems apparently leads to heart disease. The best evidence available suggests that their protracted contact with stressful situations is the likely cause of the higher CHD rates among Type A personalities (Dembroski, MacDougall, Eliot & Buell, 1983).

Other reviewers have suggested that Type A behavior is the *result* of excessive reaction to stressful environments—that is, it is a way of coping rather than being a preexisting behavior (for example, see Taylor, 1986).

Healthy charismatics
Hostile competitives

Type A behavior is not simple to analyze. Type A behavior is actually a result of the complex interaction between emotions and the demands of a stressful society. The more closely researchers have looked at Type A behavior, the more aspects they have discovered. There is evidence that suggests there are in fact *two* patterns of behavior within Type A personalities: the *"healthy charismatics"* and the *"hostile competitives"* (Friedman, Hall & Harris, 1985). The healthy charismatics are the more emotionally expressive of the two. The hostile, competitive Type A personalities are those most at risk for developing coronary disease. When these Type A people respond to something, they do so instantly, rapidly, and usually loudly. They are verbally competitive and potentially hostile, trying always to get in the last word, and finishing others' sentences for them. Competitive drive, hostility, and rapid activity are joined by one more crucial factor: impatience. Whatever they are doing, their competitive Type A behavior calls for them to do it faster. Delays of any sort infuriate them (Dembroski et al., 1983).

Some treatments for Type A personalities are available. In typical programs, people with Type A personalities learn to modify their traits through efforts to relinquish their hectic and pressured approaches to living. Participants in such programs are instructed to seek out the longest of several lines when they have to wait. They learn to stop and look around when going somewhere. Deliberately standing at the back of the longest of several lines and stopping on the way to an appointment requires extraor-

The Type A personality tries harder and harder to master and resolve situations that do not lend themselves to control or resolution. Over time, the inability of the Type A personality to escape the stress of deadlines and nonresolvable problems can lead to the onset of heart disease. In typical programs to help such people, participants are taught strategies that will help them let go of their driving, competitive life-styles and move toward more moderated and relaxed interactions with their environments and companions.

dinary motivation on the part of Type A personalities. Many such people cannot even comfortably think of such behaviors. Yet, if their commitment is sufficient, they do let go of the driving, competitive style and move toward a more moderated and relaxed interaction with their environments and companions. A comparison of this kind of cognitive behavioral stress management with both aerobic exercise and weight training found stress management far more effective in reducing Type A behavioral reactions (Roskies et al., 1986).

Epidemiology and the Cancer-Prone Personality

Epidemiology

In the nineteenth century, medical science bounded into a new era of understanding with the development of **epidemiology.** The word *epidemiology* is derived from the same root as epidemic, and it means the study of the incidence, distribution, and control of disease in an entire population. Instead of simply treating patients, investigators examine entire neighborhoods, towns, and regions.

The control of typhoid epidemics exemplifies this approach. When typhoid patients complained of high fevers, were racked by severe diarrhea, headaches, and intestinal pain, and were physically weakened, physicians had no recourse but to treat them one at a time and as well as current medical knowledge then permitted. The public health practitioners of the nineteenth century tracked down the poisoned wells that caused the typhoid epidemics and shut off the typhoid bacteria at their source.

Primary prevention

Primary prevention is the goal of epidemiology. *Primary prevention* seeks to stop illness before it develops. In contrast, *secondary prevention* treats illness at the time it appears, and *tertiary prevention* treats illness after it has developed. Primary prevention objectives have been applied to every disease, including cancer. The Cancer Prevention Clinic at the University of Wisconsin has developed a program for individuals from cancer-prone families that teaches personal responsibilities, instructs about the disease, and offers counseling (Josten, Evans & Love, 1986).

Cancer describes several quite different diseases, as opposed to a single, uniform illness. This multiplicity of symptoms, sites of the tumors, and causes has made the study and prevention of cancer difficult. Yet several psychological elements seem to be present. Grief, depression, anxiety, and hopelessness have been seen in many cancer patients. Research into public health and preventive approaches suggested the existence of the *cancer-prone personality,* or the hypothesized set of emotional characteristics that would make people especially susceptible to cancer.

Cancer-prone personality

Emotional makeup is never a sole cause of cancer. Environmental factors, smoking habits, eating patterns, and, in the case of selected cancers, heredity, all play a role. Thus, our discussion of cancer-proneness deals with only one set of potentially contributing factors that may predispose a person to cancer. Our examination of emotional cancer-proneness begins with the two dominant theories and then moves to the research on this issue.

The two main theories of cancer-prone personalities are the loss depression syndrome and the ego defense mechanism. The **loss depression syndrome** is the most common theory, and it holds that people develop cancer following the loss of a significant person or object (Dattore, Shontz & Coyne, 1980). After a loved one dies, or a career is lost, a person who is already susceptible to feeling hopeless develops malignant tumors. Normal body defenses against disease are said to be weakened at such times. In a process much like the exhaustion phase of the general adaptation syndrome (discussed in the previous chapter), the malignancies are triggered as the resistance to all diseases diminishes.

The **ego defense mechanism theory** declares that excessive emotional repression and inhibition lead to the cancer—an internal cry of emotional pain making itself physically heard. Indeed, repression as a primary emotional response to unacceptable feelings does seem to be an attribute of many cancer patients.

The difference between the two theories may be understood by comparison. The loss depression theory attributes initial causes of cancer to the weight of intolerable outside or external events. The ego defense theory sees the causes as internal psychological forces.

One way of investigating the possibility of cancer-prone personalities is through long-term studies of people before and after the onset of their cancers. Three researchers did just such a follow-up with two hundred patients at a Veteran's Administration domiciliary section (Dattore, Shontz & Coyne, 1980). Of these men, seventy-five eventually came down with cancer of various kinds. All subjects had initially been given the Minnesota Multiphasic Personality Inventory, an objective, true–false test that is the most researched personality test in psychology. Compared to the noncancer patients, the cancer patients rated higher on the repression of threatening thoughts and impulses and lower on depression. The results were consistent with the theory that "... repression is the hallmark of the premorbid cancer personality" (Dattore, Shontz & Coyne, 1980, p. 232).

In a study of 110 lung cancer patients, 61 percent of the malignant cancers were successfully predicted by five psychosocial indicators (Horn & Picard, 1979). These predictive factors were (1) childhood instability, (2) job instability, (3) marriage instability, (4) lack of plans for the future, and (5) recent significant loss. Taken together, these factors were between one and two times as important as smoking history in predicting malignant lung tumors (Horne & Picard, 1979).

Children's health appears to be affected by these same factors as well. Jacobs and Charles (1980) compared the life events of twenty-five children with cancer and a matched comparison group of children with

Loss depression syndrome

Ego defense mechanism theory

minor ailments. A parental separation occurred in 32 percent of the cancer patients' families and in 12 percent of the control group's families. Twenty percent of the children with cancer, compared to 4 percent of the control group, had experienced a death in the family. A member of 60 percent of the patients' families and 24 percent of the control group's families had a major change in health or behavior, and 72 percent of the patients and 24 percent of the control group had moved within two years of the onset of the illness.

Yet one more study looked at interpersonal relationships and emotion style as possible causes of cancer. Grossarth-Maticek, Schmidt, Vetter, and Arndt (1984) took random samples of two entire communities and found seven psychological determinants of cancer. Figure 5–1 shows

FIGURE 5–1
Determinants of Cancer Incidence and Survival Time

Adapted from Grossarth-Maticek et al., 1984, p. 29.

Determinants of Cancer Incidence

Number of traumatic life events evoking chronic hopelessness	0.43
*Number of traumatic life events evoking chronic excitement	−0.32
Rational and antiemotional behavior	0.41
Tendency toward self-denial for the sake of harmonious social relationships	0.18
Lack of hypochondriasis	0.17
Absence of psychopathological symptoms such as anxiety	0.08
Lack of positive emotional contact	0.13

0.67
Cancer incidence

*Associated with *lower* incidence

Determinants of Survival Time

Change in pathological social interactions	+0.49
Chemotherapy	+0.35
Will to live (change value)	+0.34
Anxiety (initial value)	+0.20
Anxiety (change value)	+0.21
Blocking of expression of feelings and needs (change value)	+0.38
**Acceptance of interpersonal repression (change value)	−0.33
**Acceptance of interpersonal repression (initial value)	−0.22

0.41
Survival time

**Associated with *lower* survival time

the results of this study. By far, the best predictors of cancer were traumatic life events that led to the patients' feeling chronically hopeless and being antiemotional in repressing their own problems and relationship difficulties. Although such people were seen as being well-adjusted on the surface, in actuality they had low self-esteem, strove excessively for harmonious relationships, and let no anger or anxiety come forth. Note that people who responded to traumatic events with excitement and energy were significantly *less* likely to develop cancer.

Can these cancer-prone behavior patterns be reversed? Yes, and reversal of the repression of feelings in particular has a dramatic effect. Survival rates for cancer victims are increased significantly. Figure 5–1 shows the behavior changes associated with longer survival. When the victims remedied their disturbed relationships with others and learned to express their feelings and needs, their survival time rose significantly. Chemotherapy and the increased will to live also were important contributors to survival time.

Three problems limit the application of the findings of these studies. First, the results do not prove cause and effect relationships. The relationships are largely correlational and thus only suggestive. Second, the studies usually match the cancer patients and control groups only on obvious factors, such as age and sex. The differences between cancer victims and control subjects may be due to some third factor, such as social class or psychiatric history. Third, cancer itself may create depressed patients and families, job changes, and household moves, and few studies have conclusively looked at the preexisting conditions in the history of the cancer patients.

These three problems mean that repression and loss depression as contributors to cancer-proneness should be accepted with caution. The existing research does point in both directions, and thus our affirmative conclusion about the role of such emotional influences should be tentative.

Effects of Cancer on Victims' Lives

While the hunt for the cancer-prone personality goes on, psychological study has yielded a series of useful principles about the impact of cancer. Mages and Mendelsohn (1979) focused on how the discovery of a malignant tumor affects a person's life, and they found that a decided transition occurs. The person's self-concept, goals, values, and future perspectives all change in marked ways.

Most cancer patients see themselves as having undergone major personal changes as a result of the disease. Their aggressiveness and striving for achievement and recognition decline, while their tolerance and understanding increase. Overall, Mages and Mendelsohn report, "the impression is of lowered intensity and engagement in the external world coupled with a more benign focus on the small world of home, family and friends" (1979, p. 260). Many of these patients show withdrawal and disinterest, including less concern with sexual matters. The lessened emphasis on career achievement has different effects on men and women. Women tend to maintain about the same level of self-esteem after the disease, while men feel less worthwhile and desirable.

People seem to cope with cancer in three different ways. First, they

EXPLORATION IN WELL-BEING

You Are Told You Have Cancer

You are told you have cancer. A malignant tumor has been discovered in your body. Your future is uncertain. A program of radiation treatments and chemotherapy is about to begin immediately, a program that may make your hair fall out, make you sterile, and leave you violently nauseated—and may or may not succeed.

Think for a minute about what it would be like to be in this situation. Now, in your mind, decide

1. *Who should and should not be told?* Do you fear that people will feel sorry for you, and therefore you want nobody to know? In contrast, do you want to prove to yourself and everyone else that cancer is not so terrible, and so you want to tell everyone who might have a reason to be interested? Are there differences between your decision to tell family members and your decision to tell nonfamily members? The dimension here is whether you will be secretive or you will be disclosing about a deeply sensitive subject.

2. *How would you want your closest friends to act?* Do you want them to be the way they always have been with you? That is, do you prefer that they be no different? Or do you wish them to actively assist you and be concerned about your discomfort? Because they are your closest friends, they will notice when you look ill. Would you prefer they say nothing and be matter-of-fact? Or would you feel better if they asked about your health? For many people, the issues to consider are whether cancer would somehow harm a friendship and what role friendship would play in the disease experience.

3. *What would this mean for your career plans?* Some people throw themselves energetically into their studies or work after they learn they have cancer. Others diminish their work involvement. Would you rededicate yourself to school and career plans, and work harder than ever? In other words, would school and career become more important? Alternatively, would you put less effort into your studies and work, because it would have less meaning for you? The answer to this question reflects the role of school and work in your life priorities.

use techniques that serve to minimize their distress. People numb themselves to uncomfortable thoughts and fears, a coping pattern that occurs a little at a time and that often works well. Patients consciously avoid thinking about the cancer and its effects, a suppression that must be present to some degree for normal functioning to occur. Note that this avoidance is quite different from the severe repression of all feelings associated with imminent death.

4. *What changes in your attitudes and values would you expect?* Cancer typically promotes change. Think about your attitudes toward yourself, your activities, your ways of living. Would these be likely to change? Would you value some beliefs more and others less? Would your religious outlook change?

Two individuals have described their emotional reactions to being told they have cancer. Writer Andrew Silk (1981) was a nonsmoker, suddenly diagnosed as having a malignant lung tumor, who underwent chemical and radiation therapy. Psychotherapist Sheldon Kopp (1972) underwent surgery for a cancerous brain tumor; part of the tumor could not be removed.

Silk's initial reaction was weeping with his family members. Kopp called his cancer and surgery "growth experiences," and threw himself into his work with a buoyant happiness, until he suddenly was overwhelmed with self-pity and depression.

They both sought help from people they trusted. Andrew Silk gathered his closest friends and relatives around him, flying them to Norfolk, Virginia, where he lived. Silk explained: "I wanted to shout the words 'cancer' and 'tumor' both to convince myself I had the disease and to remove some of the terror from those words" (1981, p. 35). His doctor was important to him, because she spoke with a quiet authority and won his complete trust.

Kopp sought out an older psychotherapist, who listened and gave the wry response, "How come a big tough guy like you is thrown by a little thing like a brain tumor?" Kopp found that comment ". . . helped me to laugh at myself for thinking that I would be able to handle anything" (1972, p. 158).

In their own ways, Andrew Silk and Sheldon Kopp were able to handle their initial despair. Silk found what he called a surprising serenity as a cancer survivor. He observed that "This is not because I believe that I or the doctors have 'licked' cancer. On the contrary, I am acutely aware of my vulnerability" (1981, p. 95). Andrew Silk died of his cancer a few months after he wrote this statement.

Kopp's resolution was to accept the seriousness of his illness and to no longer deny it. He concluded, "I was in some ways helpless, and perhaps still in danger, but I was alive, and could have what I wanted if only I would surrender to things as they were" (1972, p. 158). Kopp has continued to practice and write about psychotherapy.

Second, patients actively attempt to deal with the disease, seeking out information and assuming responsibility for choosing between possible treatments, confronting physicians, and helping other patients.

The last of the three coping methods is turning to others. These patients allow others to help them emotionally. Some become highly religious or turn to family or friends for support and reassurance.

The reality of the illness, the medication, and the course of the disease always influence individuals' reactions. Furthermore, people have their own lifelong ways of dealing with crises, and they inevitably use these ways to deal with cancer, too. The social context of the cancer is crucial as well. If people are stigmatized, then they will have negative, depressed reactions. A supportive network of friends, family, work associates, and medical personnel will allow the patients to draw on a broader range of coping methods (Vess, Moreland & Schwebel, 1985).

WELLNESS AND THE RECOVERY FROM ILLNESS

Wellness

Wellness may be defined as the positive functioning of the whole physical person. Our concern so far in this chapter has been with pain, illness, and problem areas in people's lives. As we discussed in the sections on the self-fulfilling prophecy in Chapter 3 and on handling stress in Chapter 4, everybody has the potential for interpreting life events in ways that produce healthy outcomes. So it is for physical illness, too. Wellness activities encourage physical well-being through positive interpretations.

Placebo effect

When recovery from illness is the goal, the treatment component of positive interpretations is known as the ***placebo effect***, and this is our first wellness topic.

Placebo Effects

Placebos are inert medications, such as sugar pills, used as an alternative to active drugs in medical research and treatment. A placebo effect was seen in the novel *Catch-22* (Heller, 1955); all of the patients showing up at sick call for treatment were treated with the same regime. If the patients' temperatures were under 102 degrees, the medical technicians would paint their gums and toes with Gentian Violet—a relatively inert substance—and give them a laxative. If their temperatures were above 102, they were sent to the hospital. Men with temperatures exactly at 102 had to come back in an hour and have their temperatures taken again.

The patients often were dissatisfied, because their complaints were neglected. However, the physician was acting on a well-verified principle in medicine. Placebos *can* promote healing in many ailments, physical and mental, if the patients are convinced they will heal. The Catch-22 sick call

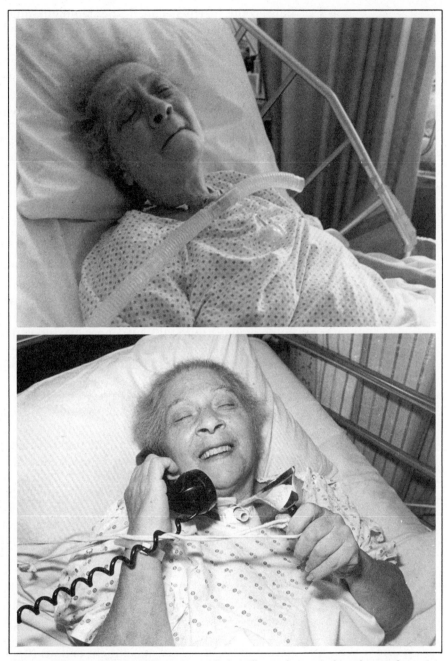

When cancer patients are ready to cope with their illness, they actively seek out information about their disease, confront their physicians, and assume responsibility for their chosen treatments. Many patients then turn to others for emotional support and reassurance. A supportive network of friends, family, and medical personnel will allow a cancer patient to draw upon a broader range of coping methods.

utilized the inert substances, but simply omitted the aspect common to every effective placebo: the reassurance that the treatment truly will work.

Jerome Frank (1961) pointed out that the history of medical treatment reflects placebo effectiveness. When experiments are conducted using the "double-blind method"—that is, an active medication and a placebo are tested and the identity of both is concealed from patient and doctor alike—placebos have been found to be effective in combating nausea and vomiting, eliminating warts, healing peptic ulcers, and improving the behavior of hospitalized psychiatric patients. By themselves, placebos succeed about 33 percent of the time across many experiments and for a broad range of symptoms and illnesses.

Hope is a component of placebo effects and is clearly helpful in the healing process. When patients are given placebo treatments, they do acquire hope for their future well-being. Hope is a vital factor in health, just as hopelessness and despair are associated with health decline and illness. Religious healing, for example, has been considered by psychological observers as a reflection of the basic effects of hope. From native witch doctors in primitive tribes to contemporary healers, belief in the worth of the treatment and hope in the outcome seem to lead to patient improvement.

Religious healing and placebos alike serve to remove the roadblocks to healing and release the power of the human body to heal itself. The same is true of medicine. Physicians who are both knowledgeable and humble know that they do not cure patients. Rather, they set mechanisms into motion through which patients cure themselves. Of course, the cure of many illnesses occurs naturally, without any medical aid. Consider, for example, the common cold.

At the turn of the century, one popular folk medicine remedy for the common cold was called Aunt Jane's Cold Remedy (Zimring & Hawkins, 1973). This mixture of whiskey, hot water, and sugar molasses was guaranteed to cure colds within ten days. This cure was quite predictable: most colds disappear by themselves in less than ten days, healed naturally by the body, without Aunt Jane's intoxicating assistance. But how can people, on their own, realize their potential for healing?

Wellness

The contemporary American medical system is technological and disease-oriented. Sometimes, individuals feel that the health orientations they seek are not present in organized medical care. For that reason, people have pursued a variety of self-help options (Cockerman, Leuschen, Kunz & Spaeth, 1986). Medical self-help is not exclusively a phenomenon of this era. In fact, Thomas Jefferson taught medical self-help courses at the University of Virginia. However, Americans have been increasingly interested in what they personally can do to promote their physical well-being.

Having a wellness view means paying attention to the positive functioning of your body, rather than only attending to it when a problem arises. This definition includes maintaining and improving physical health through exercise, health knowledge, and good diet. Individuals in organized wellness programs are regularly advised of ways to promote good health and to assume responsibility for maintaining good health.

As Figure 5–2 illustrates, physical health falls along a continuum much like the continuum of well-being discussed in Chapter 1. At the middle or neutral point of the continuum is no discernible illness or wellness. To the left of this neutral point are signs of physical problems,

LAUGHTER IS GOOD MEDICINE

Norman Cousins, the former editor of the *Saturday Review* was hospitalized when he came down with a serious illness. The connective tissues of his body were coming unstuck and his doctors hold him that his chance of survival was one in five hundred. Suffering miserably from hives and other side effects of the pain killers, Cousins discontinued all his medication, took massive doses of vitamin C, moved from the hospital to a luxurious hotel room (at much cheaper rates than his barren hospital room), and began to laugh. Believing that affirmative emotions were necessary to mobilize the healing abilities of his body, he ordered copies of "Candid Camera" television shows and Marx Brothers' movies, and had his nurse read to him from humorous books.

"It worked," Cousins wrote.

I made the joyous discovery that ten minutes of genuine belly laughter had an anesthetic effect and would give me at least two hours of pain-free sleep. When the pain killing effect of the laughter wore off, we would switch on the projector again, and not infrequently, it would lead to another pain-free sleep interval.

(Cousins, 1979, pp. 39–40)

Tests showed his body's ability to fight the inflammation of disease gradually but permanently improved. With glee, Cousins bubbled, "I was greatly elated by the discovery that there is a physiologic basis for the ancient theory that laughter is good medicine" (1979, p. 40).

Cousins's own experience has since been confirmed by a series of studies. Laughter has been found to aid the cardiovascular system and to increase the production of endorphins—the body's own painkilling chemicals—in the brain. The funny bone apparently does help us heal (University of California, Berkeley, Wellness Letter, 1985).

FIGURE 5–2   The Health
Continuum

Adapted from Travis, 1981.

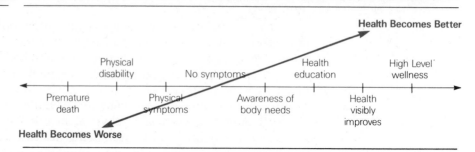

followed by actual symptoms, then disability, and finally premature death. Most health services have traditionally treated patients who fall within this area.

To the right of the neutral point are four stages of physical wellness: (1) awareness of body needs; (2) health education for oneself; (3) visible improvement in health and well-being; and (4) high-level wellness, or the lifelong process of actively preventing illness and improving physical fitness and potential (Travis, 1981).

The differences between wellness and illness can be understood by thinking in terms of automobile maintenance. If you only bring your car in for service when something is severely wrong with it, then the car is not likely to have a long, trouble-free life. On the other hand, if you ensure that your automobile receives regular preventive maintenance, by changing its oil, oil filters, tires, hoses, and other predictable wear parts, and you knowledgeably watch the functioning of this car, looking at what driving habits promote or interfere with the auto's running well, you are taking the wellness approach toward your car (Travis, 1981).

High-level wellness

With ***high-level wellness,*** self-responsibility is a core ingredient. As Ashleigh Brilliant stated, "Due to circumstances beyond my control, I am master of my fate and captain of my soul (1971, p. 90). Thus, disease is not seen simply as an unfortunate event about which we must do our best. Rather, disease is understood as a message that some changes must be made in life-style or self-care. A heart attack may dramatically illustrate this process if the victim subsequently stops smoking, gets regular exercise, changes diets, and modifies a rushed and tense life.

Inner doctor
Healing visualizations

Yet one does not have to suffer a heart attack or other severe health problem to begin maintaining wellness. The capacity for having a wellness outlook already exists within us all—we simply have to look at ourselves in resourceful and healthy ways. Such "looking" is called imagery, which uses imagination to simulate real-life experiences. We will consider two wellness applications of imagery: the ***inner doctor*** and ***healing visualizations.***

Imagery and Wellness

The inner doctor

In medieval days, barbers (as physicians were then called) applied leeches to suffering patients to cure them of every ill. In today's medicine, many patients still believe that all answers to their health concerns lie outside

Meditation is one first step in getting in touch with your inner doctor. Can you think of any other methods that will allow you to relax and listen to what your body is trying to tell you about your health and how to deal with stress?

them, in the form of drugs or the hands of physicians. Of course, for some situations, physicians and medications are the necessary and preferred choices. However, self-responsibility can supplement this common dependence. Guided imagery is one of many techniques that can help us deal with our everyday physical concerns, and it includes developing our own inner, imaginary doctors or advisors.

The inner doctor principle holds that you often do not listen to your body's messages, which tell you how to stay healthy and how to deal with stress. Your body sends tension, sleep disturbance, and other signals to you all the time. However, if you believe only physicians are qualified to interpret illnesses, you listen poorly to the messages of headaches or aching joints.

Think of a doctor within yourself who is knowledgeable and respected. A transformation may occur. Now you may pay attention to communications from your body, and once you have made such listening legitimate, you may come to listen to yourself very well. Then you will have access to suggestions, desires, and insights normally outside your awareness. You can utilize your intuitive inner resources (Bresler, 1984).

One path toward such listening has been mapped (Samuels & Bennett, 1973; Bresler, 1984). To create and meet your own inner doctor, first you slowly and gradually relax, and then you imagine a comfortable room in which you meet your doctor. You visualize what he or she looks like. Then think of your inner doctor as having the following traits:

Calm.   Your inner doctor is soothing and comforting.

Humane.   Your inner doctor fully understands your concerns and fears.

Firm and honest.   Your inner doctor gives you information and advice that may be difficult for you to accept.

Sense of humor.   Your inner doctor knows this is a game but, with goodwill and in the spirit of the consultation, is very attentive to your needs.

You may have one or several inner doctors. Once inner doctors exist for you, in your first meeting discuss what prompted you to seek them out.

> Tell them that you want them to be close at hand whenever you feel anxiety, confusion, or doubt about anything concerning your health, and to help you work out solutions.
> Tell them that you want them to act as a focal point toward which you will direct all knowledge for making and keeping your body well.
>
> *(Samuels & Bennett, 1973, p. 13)*

When you have created an inner doctor, you may take additional responsibility for your health. You should still call on physicians, but your health is more dependent on you. Your own natural healing forces and energies will emerge, as they do in many wellness promoting efforts.

At the Inner Health Program of the California Primary Physician Health Center, the inner doctor gives behavior prescriptions. For example, your inner doctor might prescribe: "Get at least twenty minutes of vigorous exercise three times a week. Eat only when hungry. Study every weeknight for two hours before watching television or going out." A quote from Albert Schweitzer appears in the notebook that Inner Health patients use.

> Each patient carries his own doctor inside him. They come to us not knowing the truth. We are at our best when we give the doctor who resides within each patient a chance to go to work.
>
> *(Beyette, 1981, p. 2)*

Healing visualizations

The ability to make an image in your mind has been with psychology since the 1880s, when Galton believed that imaging was a core aspect of intelligence. In the Galton (1883) studies of imaging, people were asked to picture themselves biting into an apple or jumping across a stream. People who visualize such experiences will actually feel the sensation in their bodies.

Imaging has come into many applications in contemporary psychology, including *systematic desensitization,* a procedure for gradually eliminating intense fears or phobias. Systematic desensitization will be discussed in Chapter 14, but we can note here that it often draws on the use of imagery. For example, people with snake phobias are asked to visualize a snake crawling toward them, or a snake behind a glass window in a zoo, or friends talking about a snake they have seen. When the image is clear in their minds, then body relaxation is induced simultaneously with the snake imagery, and their distress is reduced.

The imaging process appears again in sports psychology. Athletes are instructed to rehearse in their minds the physical motions and feelings of their specific sports activity. If the athletes see themselves from the outside, watching themselves perform the activity, little happens. However, if as they visualize the athletes feel they are actually engaged in the activity and experiencing it from within, then an unexpected bonus occurs. Their ability to perform the activity in reality improves.

The health psychology application for imaging is primarily teaching patients to visualize themselves fighting disease in specific and understandable ways. The application of the imaging process may be directed particularly to those patients who are feeling helpless. Cancer patients are taught to develop clear mental images of white cells destroying the cancer cells of their bodies. Patients begin with conventional procedures to become fully relaxed. Then, patients picture events such as the following in their minds:

> The (chemotherapy) drug transforms her leukocytes [white blood cells] into voracious sharks and the cancer cells into "frightened, grayish little fish." The sharks/leukocytes pursue the grayish fish/cancer cells which are envisioned as disorganized and disoriented, and then pounce upon them, rending them to bits with their long, jagged teeth and destroying them. At last, when the cancerous areas have been cleared out completely, the sharks are transformed into ordinary white blood cells once again and continue to course through her bloodstream. The chemotherapeutic agents, together with any "fish/cancer" refuse that remains, are visualized as being flushed out with her body fluids. All is peaceful, all is clean, and healthy within.

(Scarf, 1980, p. 40)

Guided imagery also has been employed for pain control. In one technique known as *glove anesthesia*, a patient is first taught to feel numbness in his or her hand, picturing the hand encased in a glove that is an anesthetic. Once the patient masters inducing hand numbness, he or she transfers the numbness to the painful area in the body by putting the hand on the place that hurts. For patients who feel helpless, this technique gives them a dramatic sense of control over their discomfort (Bresler, 1984). Imagery often promotes within patients the feelings of power and control over their illnesses. Those feelings of power and control may themselves be therapeutic.

Listening to the Body

Can you wiggle your ears? Only about one person in twenty can wiggle his or her ears, and if you ask an ear wiggler how that talent was acquired, the person will probably describe long periods of practice before a mirror, exploring the muscle movements of the face and head that move the ears.

One distinguished psychologist, Neal Miller, undertook an experiment. For six months, he spent fifteen minutes every day in front of his hall mirror attempting to wiggle his ears. At first nothing seemed to happen. Then, a little at a time, he was able to make small movements, until eventually he mastered full-blown ear wiggling. The principle that Miller demonstrated was that apparently unreachable realms of our physical functioning can be mastered once we pay attention to what we are doing. Indeed, as long ago as 1901, J.H. Bair was able to teach everybody who tried to wiggle their ears by use of an ingenious device that displayed the results of even tiny ear movements (Brown, 1974).

This process of paying attention to what we are doing extends body mastery. Physical changes occur once we envision ourselves as reaching further. Ear wiggling is probably of no intrinsic importance, beyond the entertainment value of a room full of people simultaneously wiggling and waving their ears—a sight that has to be seen to be appreciated. However, the mastery of an otherwise unavailable body skill has implications for the control of physical well-being.

Skin temperature is a case example. Most of us have either cold hands, with skin temperature in the range of seventy degrees Fahrenheit, or in the low to middle ninety-degree range. About 40 percent of all people fall in the lower range, and 60 percent fall in the higher range. Residents of colder climates and women have overall lower skin temperatures.

Both physical and emotional factors influence skin temperature. High skin temperatures serve some of the same functions as perspiration. The capillaries enlarge, more blood nears the surface, and heat is dissipated into the air.

EXPLORATION IN WELL-BEING

Raising Your Skin Temperature

Most people can raise their hand temperatures through voluntary control. The art of warming your hands is to be relaxed, quiet, and receptive. Sit comfortably and allow your hands to rest loosely in front of you. Use these relaxation techniques: Breathe slowly, allowing the breath to go through your body to tense areas, and then relax, allowing your breathing to soothe the tense areas. Then picture warmth flowing down into your hands. Feel the warmth developing in your hands. You are in the warm sun, and you feel the sun's rays heating your hands, the gentle heat making your hands feel good and relaxed and wonderful. Say to yourself

My hands feel warm and good. My hands feel so good. My right hand is sitting in the warm sun and it feels heavy and warm and wonderful. The warm feeling is moving down down down my arm and wrist into my hand. My left hand feels full and relaxed and so, so good. It feels wonderful. The sun is warming my hand and the warmth is filling my hand with soft warm good feelings. My hands are warm and heavy and relaxed and feel so, so good.

(Adapted from Surwit, 1978)

This exercise will raise hand temperature, and so will other relaxation methods. Tension cools hands. Comfort warms them, and any regular mental process you use to relax will be likely to warm your hands as a consequence. It has been observed that sexual stimulation, which generates body warmth in general, causes hand and foot temperature to rise, often close to body temperature (Surwit, 1978).

Just as surely as walking out of a well-heated house into a Northern Minnesota winter day, emotional factors will cool our hands and feet. Stress and anxiety produce cold, sweaty hands and feet. The surface blood vessels constrict, and nervousness produces perspiration (Surwit, 1978).

Biofeedback techniques can aid in the control of body processes, including skin temperature. We may warm or cool hands and feet with the aid of sensors that precisely display temperature readings, often to one-tenth of a degree change. The visual display of a slight success in hand warming provides immediate information to the person that his or her efforts are working, much like the mirror showed Neal Miller slight changes in his ear positions.

Physical health may be enhanced by awareness in many ways. In their book *Listening to the Body,* Masters and Houston (1978) described the extraordinary malleability of the human body. They hold that the motor cortex of the brain itself must be reorganized and that the most direct and accessible path to the cortex is through the muscles. The method is called *psychophysical reeducation,* and it applies emotions, thoughts, and movements to alter the habitual organization of the brain and body.

The method has been described by a variety of practitioners. The overall process involves communicating more knowledgeably with the brain. Masters and Houston point out

> The brain can produce small or quite extensive changes in the body, instantaneously or over long periods, and is in fact doing so all the time, whether consciously or unconsciously, in response to experiences originating inside or outside the body. These transforming experiences include our emotions, words, and images; if we can use these to communicate directly with the brain, then the mind will truly control the body. Otherwise, the body will be directed only by the brain-computer according to its inherited and acquired programs.
>
> *(Masters & Houston, 1978, pp. 62–63)*

The exercises to attain the goals of psychophysical reeducation consist of several steps.

1. Become aware of general body functioning. For example, pay attention now to the tension around your shoulders and neck as you read this. Then relax these muscles.

2. Feel the ways in which simply thinking about moving produces changes in muscle areas. Think about leaping across a small stream in the woods, one leg stretched far out to land on the bank. See if you can feel the stretching sensation.

3. Learn about the movement of limbs in reality and then reexperience the same movements through imagery. Slowly lift your right arm from resting to straight above your head. Let it down very slowly. Repeat.

Now do it in your mind, just as slowly, without actually moving your arm.

4. Exercise the eyes, mouth, shoulders, head, tongue, and whole body in ways that simultaneously increase body awareness and enhance mobility. For example, slowly run your tongue over the inside and outside of your teeth fifteen times. Pay attention to what you feel. Then, alternate pressing your tongue as hard as you can against the floor and roof of your mouth. Yawn several times. Tilt your head right and left. Finally, dart your tongue in and out rapidly and see how flexible it feels.

5. Use imagination to stimulate changes. You can achieve flexibility by imagining that you can reach far forward with your hands, or you can be more relaxed by imaging a masseuse massaging your body with oil over and over, deeper and deeper. The feelings among people who are able to image an experience are parallel to the feelings arising from the actual experience, and self-control increases as relaxation and control over muscle functions increase.

Table 5–1 summarizes how physical health relates to well-being. Practicing wellness techniques is one way to move toward overall well-being.

SUMMARY

Traditional *dualistic thinking* sees body and mind as separate human functions. In contrast, current views indicate that physical problems usually have some psychological process preceding them or resulting from them.

TABLE 5–1 Physical Health and Well-Being	
Toward Well-Being	**Away from Well-Being**
Has satisfying eating patterns	Has disordered eating patterns
Is comfortable coping with time deadlines and stressors	Has Type A (hostile and relentless) behavior when coping with time deadlines and stressors
Handles emotional losses and tensions without physical consequences	Has a cancer-prone personality
Reacts with hope to own physical illness	Responds to illness with despair
Maintains wellness beliefs and practices	Maintains illness beliefs and practices
Mobilizes healing through imagery	Cannot utilize natural healing resources

Pain is as much an emotional as a physical experience. Culture affects the pain experience, as does the amount of positive or negative reinforcement one receives upon expressing pain. *Gate control theory* suggests ways in which pain is physically stimulated by both internal psychological factors and external reactions. When a person in pain feels anxiety and depression, the pain is more likely to be long-lasting. Chronic pain often is accompanied (and prolonged) by the continuing reinforcement of emotional support.

The relationship between mind and body is shown by the studies of eating disorders. Overweight people may receive much social disapproval, and their subsequent anxiety may prompt them to continue to overeat. Furthermore, a psychological overresponsiveness may exist in obese people (and in the binge eaters known as bulimics). They react to the sight and taste of food, as well as to other people and emotional situations, with more intensity than do the nonobese. Although as many as 90 percent of young women binge eat, only about 8 percent suffer symptoms intense enough to merit the diagnosis of bulimia. When extreme dieting combines with extreme dread of body fat, young women may develop *anorexia nervosa,* a neurotic wasting away through minimal food intake.

Characteristic life-styles are associated with health and illness patterns. A *Type A personality* has a hard-driving, competitive, achievement- and deadline-oriented life-style that is a significant risk factor in the development of coronary heart disease. Type A behaviors can be alleviated through programmatic efforts to give up the self-imposed stress of relentless deadlines.

The field of *epidemiology* examines the distribution of diseases in order to find public health preventive measures. Epidemiology has pointed to depression from loss of valued others and repressive ego defenses as contributors to *cancer-proneness.* When people find they have cancer, a psychosocial transition occurs, in which their values, goals, and self-concepts become altered. Common adjustments are minimizing the distress, actively dealing with the disease, and turning to others for emotional help.

Wellness is defined as high-level well-being or health, well beyond the simple absence of symptoms of illness. The deeply held expectation of improvement frequently leads to health improvement or wellness. This is known as the *placebo effect.* Placebo cures arise from inert medications, from physicians' attitudes, and from hope on the part of the sufferer. To acquire high-level wellness, one must have body awareness, self-education, growth and improvement, and must actively prevent illness. Thus, wellness results from a broad range of human activities, including sleep, relaxation, and honest expression of emotions.

One method of organizing wellness and health-coping mechanisms is through *self-responsibility,* or an understanding of how we heal ourselves of physical symptoms. Each of us may carry an *inner doctor* to whom we can turn for advice and help. *Healing visualizations* are one way of serving as our own healers. Visualizing the healing of the body mobilizes natural healing abilities. This method particularly helps people who are feeling helpless about their health problems. Most people can visualize their hands warming up, their muscles relaxing, and the effects of medication.

Key Terms

Acute pain	**Hostile competitives**
Analgesia	**Inner doctor**
Anorexia nervosa	**Loss depression syndrome**
Bulimia	**Obesity**
Cancer-prone personality	**Pain**
Chronic pain	**Pattern theory**
Dualistic	**Placebo effect**
Ego defense mechanism theory	**Primary prevention**
Emotional arousal hypothesis	**Psychogenic pain**
Epidemiology	**Set point theory**
Gate control theory	**Specific receptor theory**
Healing visualizations	**Type A behavior**
Healthy charismatics	**Type A personalities**
High-level wellness	**Type B personalities**
Holistic	**Wellness**

Recommended Reading

Hawkins, R.C., II, Fremouw, W.J. & Clement, P.F. (Eds.). (1984). *The binge–purge syndrome: Diagnosis, treatment, and research.* New York: Springer. In the rush of new writings about bulimia, this edited book puts together the best of what we know. It's not comprehensive, but what it does cover is described with high-quality reporting. The writing is not intended for a lay audience, but nevertheless the content is accessible.

Masters, R. & Houston, J. (1978). *Listening to the body: The psychophysical way to health and awareness.* New York: Delta. Within the first two pages of reading this book, Masters and Houston have you examining how you change your posture and body simply to read. The book is brimming over with do-it-yourself exercises that make each point personal and relevant.

Samuels, M. & Bennett, H. (1973). *The well body book.* New York: Random House & Bookworks. *The Well Body Book* combines medical information for personal use with a self-responsibility philosophy about health care, drawing clear lines about when professional attention is needed. I love this book. It is human, involving, and thorough. The information you discover is just what a good friend who is also a physician would tell you.

Sheikh, A.A. (Ed.). (1984). *Imagination and healing: Vol. 1. Imagery and human development series.* Farmingdale, NY: Baywood. Vague concepts are translated into hard science in this edited book of eleven chapters on imagery. It starts with MacBeth and King Lear, closes with a case study of focused imagery in a cancerous area, and in between draws on the knowledge of thoughtful and distinguished practitioners of imagery and health.

6

CHAPTER

Assertiveness and Aggression

Carmi's hand froze with the fourth slice of almond cheesecake poised near his mouth. He saw Glenda looking at him hard, in that tense, disapproving way he knew too well. She made the best almond cheesecake he had ever tasted—actually it was the only almond cheesecake he had ever tasted, but he could eat and eat it. That's why she had warned him to let the guests have some cheesecake and not to hog it all himself.

It wasn't just his eating the cheesecake that prompted that look though. Carmi loaded a large rectangular slice on his napkin, gulped deeply from his drink, and went to her. He held out the cheesecake.

"Have some of your own cheesecake. It is the tastiest cheesecake in the world. It is wonderful cheesecake," he offered.

"No, thank you anyway," Glenda answered.

"Can I get you another drink? A little blush wine, babe?"

"I'm not thirsty," she replied stiffly. "Please do see to our guests."

Carmi moved to mingle and talk and laugh, and so did Glenda. He watched her. When they were together in any small grouping of friends, she was polite, as always, charming, as always, but the tension between them was tangible.

The guests thinned out. The last stragglers thanked their hosts and began to leave. Carmi and Glenda saw the final cluster of people to the door, each person not wanting to be the last one left after everyone else had departed.

Glenda and Carmi were finally alone. Glenda sat on the edge of a hard chair. She sat straight, hands clasped together. As Carmi moved toward her, her body visibly stiffened. She looked directly ahead of her, not acknowledging his approach.

Carmi crouched by her side, looking intently at her. His mind raced over the evening's events.

"Are you okay?" he asked.

"Yes," she snapped. But at the same time her eyes misted.

"Are you sure?"

"Yes. I'm fine."

"Listen," Carmi said, "If it's something I did after I had been drinking . . ."

"I said I'm fine!"

"Okay."

Carmi went to the doorway and paused, looked back, then went on through.

After he was gone, Glenda turned and looked at the empty doorway. Her heart was beating fast. How could he leave just like that, she wondered. He knows I'm not okay. He knows I'm so upset I can hardly keep from crying. Fine, my elbow! What's the matter with that man? Doesn't he ever listen to me?

THE ASSERTIVENESS CONTINUUM

When Glenda withheld her anger from Carmi, she did neither him nor herself a favor. Glenda felt unheard and ignored. Carmi knew something was wrong and felt uncertain and tense. Yet Glenda's actions, and inactions, seemed to be beyond her control. She did not think, "I shall say nothing." Rather, she acted the only way she knew how to act at the moment, containing her dissatisfaction under a neutral façade. Her behavior is an example of nonassertiveness. Carmi also was not assertive; after a couple of tentative efforts, he sat on his feelings, too. Their interaction of the moment passed, but their discomfort did not. They were unable to express their feelings in effective and considerate ways—one of the issues in this chapter on ***assertiveness.***

Assertiveness

In the realm of psychological concerns, assertiveness is a relative newcomer. In almost the brief twinkling of an eye, Joseph Wolpe's (1958) assertive training for passive and inhibited individuals has gone from a simple treatment to a broad-ranging approach for understanding social skills, personality traits, and situations. Assertiveness training now flowers in the form of assertion courses on almost every college campus and for many executives. Assertiveness training is an established ingredient as well in many behavior therapies for both inpatient schizophrenics and normal outpatients, and research has extended into the natures of nonassertive and assertive people.

Assertive behavior has three components.

1. Assertive behavior is interpersonal behavior involving the honest and relatively straightforward expression of thoughts and feelings.
2. Assertive behavior is socially appropriate.
3. When a person is behaving assertively, the feelings and welfare of others are taken into account. (*Rimm & Masters, 1979, p. 63*)

The extent to which feelings are honestly expressed can be understood as falling on a continuum. At one end of the continuum is nonassertive behavior; the nonassertive person is fearful of being foolish or rejected and, as a result, acts timid, cautious, and passive. Nonassertive persons typically feel bad about themselves and have little confidence in their actions.

In contrast to nonassertiveness, aggression and assertiveness are active behaviors. Instead of passively reacting to a situation, aggressive and assertive people are openly responsive. However, aggression carries with it the potential for harming or coercing others or being insensitive to others' rights and well-being. Part of aggressive behavior is actually being unpleasant in observable ways, either verbally or physically. Assertiveness, on the other hand, is socially aware and considerate behavior.

Note that not everybody fits into one category. Many of us are nonassertive in some situations, assertive in others, and aggressive in yet others. The high school principal may be domineering and aggressive with her secretary, assertive and open with her children, and yet passive and nonassertive with her mother. Furthermore, some people do not have one pattern that seems to predominate and so can be called neither assertive, nonassertive, nor aggressive. Keeping in mind that situations are important and that not everyone falls readily into a single category, we now may examine, in turn, nonassertiveness, assertiveness, and aggression. Our first topic will be nonassertiveness and the broader trait in which it is found, shyness.

NONASSERTIVENESS

Nonassertiveness and Shyness

Shyness
Nonassertiveness

Shyness and *nonassertiveness* are often grouped together. But shyness is different from nonassertiveness, at least in theory. The term *shyness* typically is used to describe a global personality characteristic. One analysis of thirteen articles about shyness concluded that the following features are the most commonly observed: silence, inhibition of behavior, stammering, physical awkwardness, little eye contact, and speaking with a voice that is quieter than usual (Harris, 1984a). A basic self-description definition has appeared as well. People are defined as shy if they think they are shy. Thinking you are so is part of what makes you so. On the other hand, the term *assertiveness* describes a skill, the ability (or in the case of nonassertiveness, the inability) to openly express feelings.

Despite these apparent differences in definition, shyness and nonassertiveness have much in common. Tucker, Weaver, and Redden (1983) had 30 instructors rate 419 college freshmen on a variety of characteristics, including assertiveness and shyness. In an analysis of the underlying factors, shyness and assertiveness were found to be opposite extremes of the same dimension. Shy people were never rated as assertive, and assertive people were never rated as shy.

Students as well as instructors recognize shy and nonassertive people. Members of two social fraternities identified their fellow members as unassertive, assertive, or aggressive. The members were then given the California Psychological Inventory, a standardized questionnaire used to assess personality patterns in normal populations (Paterson, Dickson, Layne & Anderson, 1984). The nonassertive students were, as expected, lower on measures of dominance, sociability, and social presence than were the other two groups. The assertive students were higher than the aggressive students on self-control and the ability to achieve through conventional and conforming means.

The overall results of various studies show a pattern. Nonassertive individuals are more shy and ineffective in social situations. Because nonassertiveness and shyness refer to essentially the same behaviors, we may discuss them at the same time. We begin by examining how widespread is shyness.

The Extent of the Problem

We have noted that to be shy means to be excessively cautious, timid, and reserved with others. Because of their discomfort with other people,

Most shy people are unhappy about their shyness and feel self-conscious rather than at ease with it. They blush excessively, feel butterflies in their stomachs, and are awkward and embarrassed in public situations. Shy people often have low self-images and feel out of control.

shy persons typically do not assert themselves. Rather, they quietly and passively allow events to unfold. Not only do they not speak up for themselves, but, as we will see, they self-consciously feel bad about themselves.

Philip Zimbardo (1977), the shyness czar of American psychology, has administered the Stanford Shyness Survey to five thousand people around the world. If a person completing the survey indicates that he or she is or has been shy, the person is then asked to answer questions such as the following:

How shy are you when you feel shy?

How often do you experience the feelings of shyness?

Is your shyness ever a personal problem for you?

When you are feeling shy, can you conceal it, and have others believe you are not feeling shy?

The survey goes on to explore causes and perceptions of shyness, situations that prompt shyness, and the feelings, thoughts, and sensations associated with shyness. The results of the survey have indicated that shyness is not an isolated feeling. About one-fourth of the five thousand subjects indicated they were shy now and always. Within this group was a subgroup of the intensely shy. Zimbardo describes them as follows:

> A lonely 4 percent—*true-blue shys*—told us that their self-definition of shyness was based on the fact that they were shy *all* of the time, in *all* situations, and with virtually *all* people.

(Zimbardo, 1977, p. 25)

EXPLORATION IN WELL-BEING

A Measure of Your Shyness

If someone were to ask you, "Are you shy?", the chances are you would be able to give a ready answer. Some people answer such a question with an immediate yes or no, while others will specify just when they are shy. They might say they are shy at first with new acquaintances, but not later. Some individuals will respond that they are shy with people much older than themselves, but not with their peers, or perhaps they are shy with their peers, but not with older people.

One element that muddies the self-image of being shy or not is sociability, or the preference for being with other people. Sociability is independent of shyness. It's possible to be not at all shy, but not sociable. That is, you would not be uncomfortable being with others, you would simply prefer not to be with others. On the other hand, one can be sociable and shy, wanting to be with other people but not feeling comfortable with them (Cheek & Buss, 1981). Because shyness is separate from sociability, one of the best ways to check out your degree of shyness is to use the following nine-item measure in which sociability is not included.

Answer each item by rating it from 0 (extremely uncharacteristic) to 4 (extremely characteristic). Afterwards, you can compare your scores to those of other students.

To people who are not shy, shyness is rarely seen as a serious problem. However, for the deeply shy, it can be a serious emotional and social concern. In one collection of 634 letters written in response to a television program on shyness, the following descriptions were given:

> Having suffered from this affliction [shyness] all my life, I don't think unless one has, people do not realize how painful it can be.

> I often make my parents think I'm going out to socialize, either meeting a girl or friends, but I usually end up walking the streets or sitting down in the pictures, to avoid questions.

> I am certain that to my colleagues at work I appear cold and aloof because I do not mix socially with them—not that I mix socially with anyone.

> *(Harris, 1984b, pp. 1083–1085).*

Peter Harris (1984b) holds that the minimizing of shyness by other people helps keep shy persons to themselves. Their timidity combines with these social attitudes to maintain, and sometimes worsen, their frequent isolation.

Experiencing shyness at some times and in some situations in one's

---

The Shyness Scale

0	1	2	3	4	I am socially somewhat awkward.
4	3	2	1	0	I don't find it hard to talk to strangers.*
0	1	2	3	4	I feel tense when I'm with people I don't know well.
0	1	2	3	4	When conversing I worry about saying something dumb.
0	1	2	3	4	I feel nervous when speaking to someone in authority.
0	1	2	3	4	I am often uncomfortable at parties and other social functions.
0	1	2	3	4	I feel inhibited in social situations.
0	1	2	3	4	I have trouble looking someone right in the eye.
0	1	2	3	4	I am more shy with members of the opposite sex.

_____ *Total*

From Cheeks & Buss, 1981, p. 332.
*Scoring reversed

Scoring key   Add up your total score, making certain to reverse the scoring for the second item. The average score for 340 University of Texas men was 14.8, and the average score for 572 University of Texas women was 14.4. Scores below 8 are low on shyness, and scores above 21 are high on shyness. The highest possible score is 36.

life is the norm. Only 7 percent of American students in the Zimbardo survey said they had never felt shy. Naturally, shyness has to do with where you are; shyness is more commonly experienced in Oriental than in Western cultures. In America, 60 percent of junior high school girls report shyness, but overall, women are no more or no less shy than men.

Shyness is not always unpleasant. Between 10 and 20 percent of all shy people like it and enjoy being anonymous and modest. The opportunities to be cautious and to avoid being obnoxious and intrusive feel good to these shy but satisfied individuals.

However, the majority of shy people report feeling discomfort rather than ease, unhappiness rather than pleasure, and self-consciousness rather than naturalness with their shyness. They describe suffering from excessive blushing and butterflies in their stomachs. Feeling their faces turn red and hot, they feel awkward and embarrassed and are unlikely to volunteer ideas or participate in a group activity. In these moments, their self-esteem plunges. Shy persons often are self-conscious about what others are thinking, and, if they are publicly embarrassed or distressed, they think even worse of themselves. They feel as if they are not in control of themselves (Zimbardo, 1977).

Not in Control and Anxious about It

When we discussed internal and external loci of control in Chapter 1, we observed that individuals with an external locus of control felt that they were carried along by events over which they had little control. Such a description fits the typical shy person. Shy people say that their problems in life seem uncontrollable. In one study of over two hundred Rice University students, shyness was significantly associated with loneliness and depression as well, but the sense of uncontrollability was the most common association (Anderson & Arnoult, 1985). One additional element came out: When shy people fail, they see the causes of the failure not as uncontrollable outside events, such as unfair tests, but rather as uncontrollable internal factors, such as an inability to concentrate. It is not the world that is beyond their control. It is that they cannot control how they themselves think and feel (Teglasi & Hoffman, 1982). When Glenda withdrew from Carmi after she was upset, her action was not fully within her control. She was aware that she needed to express herself, but doing so was beyond her reach at the moment.

Even when Glenda and other shy and nonassertive individuals do well and are briefly assertive, they tend to devalue what they have done. In one assertiveness study, the call went out for students who were either "quite assertive" or "quite nonassertive." Once fifty students had appeared, they were shown videotapes requiring assertive responses. The students were told to respond as assertively as possible; responses included refusing an unreasonable request and expressing a differing opinion (Alden & Cappe, 1981).

What followed cast new light on the nature of nonassertive persons. The nonassertive students were just as effective as the assertive students in this role-playing. No differences were found in the experimenters' ratings. For the nonassertive students themselves, however, it was another story. They felt less effective, less assertive, and more anxious than did the assertive students.

Certainly role-playing is not the same as being yourself. Nevertheless, this study's finding suggests that assertive social skills may be present in many self-identified nonassertive persons. Other studies confirm this theory. Nonassertive individuals think of themselves in different, often self-critical ways that interfere with their being assertive. For example, compared to assertive persons, they are much more vulnerable to peer pressure in conformity situations (Williams, 1984), apparently out of anxious concern for what the others would think of them. Such anticipatory anxiety may be considered maladaptive; it interferes with the people's acting in ways they might otherwise choose.

Passive-Aggressiveness: When Hostility Accompanies Nonassertiveness

"Hurry up, and get your report to me. I can't wait any longer," the supervisor insists. For three days, he has been trying to get a report from his assistant, and the assistant has made excuses, forgotten that it has to be done, apologized, and promised that it is on the way. For one reason after another, the report has been put off, and it is clear that the assistant has been stalling. Such intentional resistance to occupational and social demands is known as passive-aggressiveness.

Passive-aggressiveness

Like other forms of nonassertion, **passive-aggressiveness** conceals the person's actual feelings and thoughts. What surfaces is usually a string of ineffective acts. The person forgets he has to be somewhere. An employee repeatedly puts off an obligation, perhaps dawdling and wasting time. Another person may be superficially pleasant, but is persistently stubborn. Nobody can get him to do what he does not want to do. Passive-aggressive people carry much anger and resentment with them, but they are unable to express these feelings openly. Because they see anger as unjustified and unhealthy, their anger comes out in indirect ways that infuriate others. This resistant passivity may cause so many problems that friendships, romantic relationships, and occupational prospects all suffer (Stricker, 1983).

Considerable disagreement exists about exactly why individuals develop this pattern of behavior. One of the more accepted outlooks is that a person's passivity allows his or her anxiety about a difficult situation to diminish (Prout & Platt, 1983). The person is not being evaluated, at least for a while. In the long run, the strategy frequently backfires, and the involved companions or employers become exasperated.

Treatment of Nonassertiveness

Shyness and nonassertiveness are treatable problems. Zimbardo established a Shyness Clinic at Stanford University, and he has written a how-to book to aid shy people in overcoming their uncomfortable shyness (Zimbardo, 1977). Participants in the Zimbardo clinic follow these guidelines for treatment of shyness: First, they are taught that they can change. Then they are taught to understand and explore themselves before they move to the next stage, understanding their shyness. They study the development of shyness and conduct a cost and benefits analysis, because some

EXPLORATION IN WELL-BEING

Assertive Behavior on the Job

Assertiveness is important for effective behavior on the job as well as in personal events. Employees who are willing to speak up honestly for what they think and feel are respected, provided that they do so in a responsible way. In the same sense, supervisors who are comfortably assertive—not overbearing—are liked and respected by employees. Alberti and Emmons (1975) have used the following case to teach employees how to be appropriately assertive:

Working Late

You and your spouse have an evening engagement which has been planned for several weeks. Today is the date and you plan to leave immediately after work. During the day, however, your supervisor indicates that she/he would like you to stay late this evening to work on a special assignment.

Alternative Responses: (Pick the one you would most likely use)

1. You say nothing about your important plans and simply agree to stay until the work is finished.

2. In a nervous, abrupt voice you say, "No, I will not work late tonight." Then you criticize the boss for not planning the work schedule better. You then turn back to the work you were doing.

shyness works well for selected people. After that, their treatment follows the path of many other treatments for social problems. They are taught how to increase their self-esteem and how to be more socially successful and assertive.

Assertiveness training

Assertiveness training also is one of the frequent treatments for passive-aggressiveness. Individuals learn how to be more open with the expression of their feelings and how to give up the indirect sabotaging of their relationships and work. Therapists use role-playing to examine clients' underlying thoughts and eliminate their passive-aggressive behavior patterns.

The one unifying objective in all the treatments for nonassertiveness and passive-aggressiveness is the acquisition of assertive behaviors. To achieve this goal, subjects must understand the components of assertiveness, be able to identify situations that call for varying levels of assertive-

---

3. Talking to the supervisor in a firm but pleasant voice, you tell of your important plans and say you will not be able to stay this evening to work on the special assignments.

Commentary:

1. If you chose this approach you are in double trouble, first with yourself, second with your spouse. Your spouse has a perfect right to be upset at your nonassertiveness, your inability to speak for yourself and what is important to you. So often we hear complaints like "Oh, if I say anything to the boss I'll get fired, I just know I will" or "The boss is just not capable of understanding my viewpoint." Don't be a mind reader or a fortune-teller, be assertive.

2. This response is giving yourself away on several counts. First, if your voice is nervous and abrupt it signals the other person to beef up their defenses. Then, if you criticize the boss by making a value judgement on how the schedules are made out, there will be more bristling on his/her part. Stick with the fact that you have already made plans and that they are important. Don't allow yourself to get sidetracked by criticizing. Even if your claim is legitimate it is better to go in some other time and discuss that matter specifically.

3. The choice here is a good assertive response. Your voice is firm without calling for the other person to retaliate. You clearly state your case and don't hedge by asking, "Do you think I should work anyway?"

(Alberti & Emmons, 1975, pp. 116–118)

ness, and actually practice behaving assertively. We now shift our attention to the positive and responsible managing of feelings and thoughts: assertiveness.

ASSERTIVENESS

The Responsible Expression of Feelings

To this point, we have examined the nature of inhibition and nonassertiveness. Responsible behaviors in the expression of feelings are critical to assertiveness. Assertive persons are honest and confident about letting their feelings be known. They do not trample on the rights and feelings of other people. Rather, they are caring while being open about their feelings. When angered, they show anger. When saddened, they show sadness. When joyful, they show joy and often make others around them joyful.

Acting in assertive ways is believed to promote a sense of well-being and satisfaction from social situations (Rimm & Masters, 1979). These payoffs occur particularly when assertiveness behaviors are socially responsible. When some people speak out and let their feelings be known, they may be acting destructively. You are not responsibly assertive if you tell a person who accidentally bumps into you in the street that "clumsiness like that really annoys me" or if you instruct an employer to "stop being so stupid and picking on all of us." A responsible assertion, however, shows sensitivity to others' feelings. When assertive people take into consideration the effects of their assertiveness on others, they are being socially responsible.

Positive and Negative Assertions

Positive and negative assertions are quite different creatures. A positive assertion expresses good feelings. Telling a person how well he or she completed a task or letting someone know how much he or she is appreciated are examples of positive assertions. Negative assertion consists of criticizing or saying "no" in a situation that calls for criticism or calls for refusal of a request. Few unpleasant consequences will be likely to follow a positive assertion. Indeed, the effects are often encouraging. In contrast, making a negative assertion can be risky. The other person may react with anger or unhappiness.

Positive assertions are responsible expressions of liking and approval, showing a respect for the feelings and rights of others. Positive assertions are not flattery; rather they directly reflect what another person has done or a real aspect of that person. They tell a person how good you feel about him or her, give accurate feedback on good performance, or let the person know about your positive judgments in other ways. Positive

Positive assertions

Refusing to listen to a salesperson is an example of making a negative assertion. There will always be instances where someone asks something of us that we prefer to refuse. To effectively deal with these situations, we need to learn how to take a stand and say no in a responsible manner.

assertions may be mild, such as telling a child playing with a toy that "you lined up the pieces in a nice straight line," or they may be more emotional, such as saying to a close companion, "you are terrific and make me warm all over when you do that."

People who are generally assertive do well at being assertive in both positive and negative situations. That's not so for individuals with low assertiveness. They are more inhibited in the statements they make in negative situations (Pitcher & Meikle, 1980). In considering assertiveness levels, then, it is important to take into account the particular circumstances in which the subjects find themselves and how they judge those situations.

Not everyone is good at positive assertions. Some nonassertive people

Negative assertions

are guarded with both their positive and their negative feelings. In addition, people often have more difficulty making **negative assertions** than making positive assertions. Let us examine some situations requiring negative assertions.

In Figure 6–1, four cartoons present situations that call for negative assertions. Situations 1 and 2 deal with the need to assert rights, and situations 3 and 4 deal with the need to handle hostile attitudes by others. Consider how you would respond in these situations. Examples of successful assertive responses to the four situations are on pages 216–217.

We have noted that negative assertions criticize another's actions or refuse another's request. A negative assertion *says no* to an unacceptable request (Cooley & Hollandsworth, 1977). Making a negative assertion means taking a stand and saying no when you truly wish to say no. Situations always arise in which others will ask things of us that we prefer to decline. People will ask to borrow valued possessions, make social or sexual requests, or otherwise ask us to join in activities that we dislike doing or don't value. Giving a reasoned explanation of our refusal helps us decline responsibly, as does indicating an understanding of what the other person is feeling.

A negative assertion may also *assert rights.* It is inevitable that, in our organized, industrial society, people's differing interests will compete. Smokers and nonsmokers have different interests, as do people who play loud music and those who prefer quiet. The list goes on to cover almost every area of human activity. A basic principle in our society is to assert one's rights when others are interfering with reasonable expectations of freedom—from smoke, excessive noise, crowding, or any other infringement.

Minimal effective response

One way to assert your rights is to use the **minimal effective response.** As the term suggests, a minimal effective response is a behavior that effectively accomplishes one's objective with minimal effort and minimal negative emotion or consequences (Rimm & Masters, 1979). Take the example of a loud, talkative couple near you in a movie theater. What would you say to them? A passive, nonassertive response would be to simply sit, not say anything, and be unhappy. A minimal effective response would be to whisper, "I wonder if you'd mind being a little more quiet? I'm having trouble hearing" (Rimm & Masters, 1979, p. 76). If that does not work, you could then escalate to, "Look, would you please be a bit more quiet? I simply can't hear the movie." Then, if the couple continued their loud talking, your minimal assertion could be, "If you people don't quiet down, I'm going to call the manager."

The minimal effective response ensures that the other person's feelings are respected—you are not being pushy—and usually attains your goals. Many newly assertive persons discover that they are able to cope with most situations by using the minimal effective response.

FIGURE 6–1 Negative
Assertions: Four Situations

Some of these people can't see because of the hats people in front of them are wearing. How would *you* assert yourself in this situation?

Examples of Research on Assertiveness

Whenever an assertion is made, two people are involved: the assertive person and the individual to whom the assertion is addressed. To this point, our attention has been on the assertive person. However, research has looked at the impact of assertions on the recipients as well.

Consider the following situation:

You and a friend find a lecture quite boring, so rather than pay attention to it, you discuss what you did on the weekend. The female [or male, depending on experimental conditions] student sitting in front of you, who is also a good friend of yours [or whom you don't know, depending on the situation], turns around, looks you straight in the eye and says, "I can't hear what the lecturer is saying because you are talking and that really annoys me."

(Lewis & Gallois, 1984, p. 356)

How would you categorize this situation? A study of psychology freshmen found that most students saw this (and nine other situations) as both aggressive and assertive. However, the students were much more accepting of the remark when it came from a friend rather than from a stranger. They liked their friends more, and viewed them as less aggressive and more deserving of respect. Most of the differences between male and female responses were not significant. However, negative assertions made by the opposite sex were rated as more serious than same sex assertions. Men speaking to men and women speaking to women this way was not viewed as trivial, but was seen as decidedly less aggressive than opposite sex assertions.

Assertiveness research has often investigated behaviors in highly specific situations. Consider this example:

> The telephone rings, and when you answer it the woman speaking explains that she represents a company selling craft kits. No matter what you say, she goes on, explaining what a good value the kits are and how they would make good gifts. She will not stop talking. When you state that you have to leave or cannot talk any longer, she requests that you stay on the line and continues her pitch. What would you do?

In exactly this situation, the saleswoman on the phone was a researcher and persisted, until the listener said goodbye or hung up (Richins, 1983). The intent was to study the degree of assertiveness, nonassertiveness, and aggression displayed by the subjects, all of whom had participated in research on consumer assertiveness a few months earlier. What happened was that the people lowest on both assertiveness and aggression took the longest to get off the phone. On the average, they listened to the sales pitch for almost a full minute, while the most assertive subjects were off the phone in just over twenty seconds. Why did the nonassertive people take longer to end the conversation? They were making excuses and apologies, rather than giving straightforward expressions of disinterest.

You can check out how assertive you are as a consumer by answering three sample items from this particular study with either yes or no.

1. "If a salesperson has gone to a lot of trouble to find an item for me, I would be embarrassed not to buy it even if it isn't exactly right."

2. "In signing a sales contract or credit agreement, I am reluctant to ask for an explanation of everything I don't understand."

3. "I'd rather do almost anything than return a product to the store."

(Richins, 1983, p. 81)

All of these items indicate nonassertiveness when the answer is yes. By contrast, assertive consumers indicate they do not mind ending conversations with salespersons or notifying store management when service is particularly bad. Aggressive consumers feel that making a scene or being a little nasty sometimes is the best way to get a complaint handled or to deal with a rude salesperson.

AGGRESSION

Aggressive behavior

The first two patterns of behavior considered here have been nonassertiveness and assertiveness. Now we move to the third pattern: aggressiveness. **Aggressive behavior** reveals one's thoughts and feelings to others, but without the responsible and appropriate consideration of the others' rights and feelings. Often overbearing and abrasive, aggressive persons vent emotions without thinking about their impact. Their typical desire is to win, to come out on top. When faced with uncertainty, aggressive persons talk too much, too fast, and too loud. They explain how important it is to set others straight, to make others do things their way. Even in situations that call for quiet, they overwhelm others with their intrusive comments. Other people tend to respond to aggressiveness by withdrawing and backing away, frequently in anger or frustration (Alberti, 1977, pp. 24–25).

An example is the behavior of a young physician who joined the staff of a clinic at which I worked. He dominated every discussion with his thoughts about what should be done and with what he was feeling at the moment. He would fill the pauses in his criticisms and instructions with descriptions of his recent dreams. He had no inhibitions about telling everyone what to do, and how, with no appreciation of the feelings and possible contributions of the rest of us. His overbearing and inconsiderate style—characteristic of aggressive behavior—continued until a senior staff member gave him some gentle but candid feedback.

Recall Figure 6–1, which depicted four negative situations. The person being addressed in each cartoon could respond aggressively.

Possible Aggressive Responses to the Situations in Figure 6–1	
Other Person's Comment	**Aggressive Response**
1. "I cut in line ahead of you because I'm in a hurry."	"You will not. Now get back to the end of the line before I drag you there myself."
2. "The doctor sees no one without an appointment. You should know better."	"Don't you talk to *me* that way! I'm going to see that the doctor hears about this, and I'm going to do everything I can to get you fired."

Possible Aggressive Responses to the Situations in Figure 6–1 (continued)	
Other Person's Comment	Aggressive Response
3. "I had the right of way."	"You don't have the right to call yourself a driver. What did you do, learn how to drive from correspondence school?"
4. "It's dishonest of you to advertise a product you sell out in the first few hours."	"It is rude and ugly of you to call me dishonest. You are a nasty woman. Get out of this store this minute."

The nature of aggression extends well beyond the expression of thoughts and feelings. We now look at aggressive behavior more broadly, considering the related states of anger and hostility.

Anger, Hostility, and Aggression

The words *anger, hostility,* and *aggression* are sometimes used interchangeably in references to feelings and behavior. A person might say "I feel angry," "I feel hostile," or "I feel aggressive" to indicate the same state. However, the words do have different meanings and should be considered separately.

Anger *Anger* is an emotion, felt within us, that may or may not arise because of what other people do or because of the situation. Anger is a frequent emotion; most people report becoming angry at a frequency of from several times a day to several times a week (Averill, 1983). Even though most people may feel like acting aggressively when they are angry, they typically engage in a calming activity or talk the situation over with someone else.

Hostility *Hostility* is an attitude, in which negative judgments are made toward a person or object. While hostility may come from anger, it is not the same feeling. Typically, hostility follows unpleasant experiences or thoughts. A student may be angry because a mix-up during registration has ruined her planned course schedule. However, if she then develops a persistently negative attitude, perhaps thinking of the personnel in the registrar's office as "stupid blunderers," she may be considered hostile.

Aggression *Aggression* describes behavior. Unlike the internal emotion of anger and the attitude of hostility, aggression is an observable action. One does not have to be angry or hostile to be aggressive. Aggression can be a response to insecurity or impatience, or it can be part of ingrained personality traits. The child pushing another child who reaches for his rubber elephant is being aggressive by our definition. The child who allows the rubber elephant to be taken away and sits and stews as a result certainly is angry, and may become hostile, but is not aggressive, because the child does not act (or behave) unpleasantly or negatively.

"You don't have the right to call yourself a driver. What did you do, learn how to drive from correspondence school?" Aggression is an observable action, which in this case appears to overlap with anger (an emotion) and hostility (an attitude).

It is more usual than unusual for anger and hostility to be contained and not expressed. For most individuals, temporarily containing anger is not a problem, because they can dissipate it or release it with trusted companions or as part of responsible assertions. For a few people, the prolonged containment of anger is a serious problem, because it may erupt into violence. Let us look at violence, which is one person's imposition of physical harm upon another.

 ## VIOLENCE

Under particular circumstances, nonassertiveness can lead to aggressive and sometimes violent behavior. The three topics we examine now—overcontrol, spouse abuse, and child abuse—all show how ineffectual assertions can be associated with violence.

Overcontrol of Anger and Hostility

When a man who has a ten-year record of assaults kills another person, we understand the consistency of his life. History does help to predict the future. Thus, social scientists expect the past of a murderer to be filled with examples of uncontrolled violence.

However, no such immediate understanding of the action arises when we hear of a sudden, violent assault by a conforming, law-obedient person. The scenario is familiar. A well-respected person in a community kills one or several people, apparently without reason. When his neighbors are interviewed, they all agree that he was a meek, harmless, soft-spoken man, who attended church, acted politely, and never raised his voice in anger. Why does such a person kill? The study of violent men offers part of the answer to this question.

In his investigation of imprisoned murderers and assaulters, Edwin Megargee found problems with the belief that "... the violent person is invariably someone with 'all id and no lid'" (1971, p. 132), that is, someone totally impulsive and with no controls on himself. Megargee's early efforts to predict assaultive behavior led to a dead end because two kinds of people were in his prison samples: aggressive, uncontrolled men, and excessively inhibited, overcontrolled men. When the overcontrolled men engaged in an aggressive act, it was more likely to be an *extreme* act of violence.

The extremely assaultive prisoners were found to be overcontrolled, and the moderately assaultive prisoners were found to be chronically undercontrolled. Megargee wrote, "I had another of those infrequent lapses from stupidity. . . . Lo and behold I found that the extremely assaultive subjects got high scores on the scale [of *overcontrolled hostility*]" (1971, p. 142). The violent actions of a chronically overcontrolled person reflect the idea of the straw that broke the camel's back. That is, most overcontrolled people rigidly deny feelings of resentment that accumulate over time. Occasionally, a person simply cannot stand the burden one second longer, and when another weight or pressure is added to the burden, the overcontrolled person explodes with anger or aggression. Such radically nonassertive individuals suffer brief but violent explosions.

The dimensions of overcontrol and nonassertiveness extend beyond violence to other behaviors. This typology may help us to understand suicide patterns. Lester and Wright (1978) propose that most suicides are committed by overcontrolled persons who let strains build while tightly controlling their emotions. Finally, they kill themselves, apparently unable to stand the stress any longer. On the other hand, an unsuccessful suicide attempt may be viewed as part of the pattern of an undercontrolled personality—that is, a person impulsively harms himself or herself when faced with a serious problem. This pattern is supported by the ex-

Overcontrolled hostility

amination of sex differences in suicide. Women are more expressive of their emotions and are more likely to attempt suicide than are men, but they are less likely to be successful. Men, frequently with greater emotional overcontrol, are more likely to have successful suicide attempts. The extent to which men are unable to express their feelings in responsible, assertive ways is related to the next social problem we examine: spouse abuse.

Spouse Abuse

The combination of verbal nonassertiveness and periodic outbursts of physical aggression is frequently seen in the behaviors of husbands who beat their wives. The popular notion that persistently aggressive men are wife beaters is untrue. Rather, it is clear that men who physically abuse their wives are extremely controlling and dominating (Goolkasian, 1986), but at the same time are less verbally assertive and less articulate than are nonabusing husbands.

In a study conducted in Suffolk County, New York, Alan Rosenbaum and K. Daniel O'Leary (1981) studied twenty couples in marital therapy because the wives had been abused. These couples were compared to twenty other couples in therapy who were maritally unhappy, but nonvi-

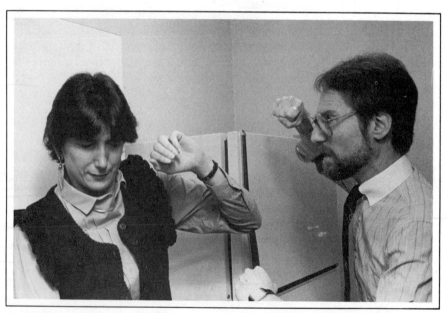

In the United States, about 1.8 million wives are seriously beaten by their husbands. Men who physically abuse their wives are extremely controlling and dominating. However, compared to nonabusing husbands, these men are also less verbally assertive and articulate.

olent, and to twenty couples who were satisfactorily married. The abusive husbands were found to be the least able to assert their rights and express their thoughts and feelings responsibly, as well being less assertive in dealing with their wives. The abusive husbands also were more likely to have been abused as children and to have witnessed parental violence in their own homes—a pattern that appears in the life histories of child abusers, too.

Family violence researcher Murray Straus (1977) directed interviews of 2,143 couples that asked about the occurrence of physical violence between husbands and wives. Straus developed a wife beating index composed of a list of acts that carried the risk of serious physical injury. These acts included hitting with the fist, beating, and threatening with or using a gun or knife. The rate of wife beating was 3.8 percent, which suggests that, of 47 million couples in the United States, about 1.8 million wives are seriously beaten by their husbands. Straus points out that, historically, a marriage license has amounted to a hitting license; the evidence of this is present not only from research, but from everyday expressions and jokes. Straus cites the old ditty

A woman, a horse, and a hickory tree
The more you beat 'em the better they be

(Straus, 1977, p. 455)

Wife beating is not the only type of marital violence. The percent of wives physically punishing their husbands is comparable, with 4.6 percent of wives reporting that they hit their husbands. However, husbands use more dangerous forms of violence. Wives are more likely to feel trapped, to be physically weaker, and to be more in need of outside help.

The Straus statistics may represent a low estimate of wife abuse. Irene Frieze (1980) reported that 34 percent of her sample of 137 Pittsburgh area women stated that their husbands had used force on them. Threats of violence were included in Frieze's definition of force.

In extensive interviews of 930 San Francisco women, drawn from a systematic randomized sample, Diana Russell (1982) used a strict criterion of *wife abuse*. She asked only about actual physical violence and rape within marriage. Of the women who had ever been married, 12 percent said they had been beaten and 14 percent said they had been raped by their husbands. Note that these are not daily occurrences. Nevertheless, it seems convincing that such assaults within marriages are not rare events and represent a serious, widespread social problem.

Child Abuse

Child abuse

Patterns of violence similar to those reported in incidents of spouse abuse are found in studies of **child abuse.** No one knows with even reasonable certainty how many children are abused. Richard Gelles (1979) summarized many studies and found that yearly estimates of serious child abuse ranged from approximately thirty thousand cases up to one and a half million cases. About seven hundred children die every year from child abuse.

Gelles (1979) had joined Straus in the 2,143 family interviews described earlier. Parents were asked if they had used any of several categories of violence toward their children (1) during the past year and (2) ever. The results are given in Table 6–1.

TABLE 6–1 Abuse of Children		
The Incident	Occurrence in the Past Year (%)	Occurrence Ever (%)
Slapped or spanked child	58.2	71.0
Pushed, grabbed, or shoved child	31.8	46.4
Hit child with something	13.4	20.0
Threw something at child	5.4	9.6
Kicked, bit, or hit child with fist	3.2	7.7
Beat child up	1.3	4.2
Threatened child with gun or knife	0.1	2.8
Used knife or gun on child	0.1	2.9

Adapted from Gelles, 1979, p. 81.

As expected, the milder punishments were more frequently reported than the severe punishments. However, Gelles stated that "an astoundingly large number of children . . . were kicked, punched, beat up, threatened with a gun or knife, or had a gun or knife actually used on them" (1979, p. 81). Apparently, between 1.4 and 2.3 million American children are beaten at some time while growing up.

But *why* do parents abuse their children? One explanation comes from the research of Joel Milner. Milner and Wimberly (1979) developed an inventory of child abuse potential, a list of 160 agree–disagree questions that they administered to groups of child-abusing parents and to matched groups of nonabusing parents. They found that parents who abused their children were emotionally distressed and rigid, lonely and unhappy, reported problems in their families and with their children, and had negative concepts of their children and themselves. Parents who abused tended to agree with the following items:

Distress:
I am often easily upset.
I am often angry inside.

Rigidity in expectations of a child's behavior:
A good child keeps his toys and clothes neat and orderly.
Children should never cause trouble.

Unhappiness:
I do not have a good sex life.
You cannot depend on others.

Problems from family and others:
My family fights a lot.
Other people have made my life unhappy.

Loneliness:
I am often lonely inside.
I sometimes feel worthless.

Child with problems:
I have a child who gets into trouble a lot.
I have a child who is slow.

Concept of child and of self:
I have a child who is bad.
Children should have play clothes and good clothes.

(Milner & Wimberly, 1980, pp. 879–880)

Milner and Wimberly (1980) have employed this instrument to distinguish child-abusing parents from nonabusing parents. When 65 parents in each group were studied, the most effective items on the Child Abuse Potential Scale accurately classified 125 of the 130 parents, or 96 percent, as either child abusers or nonabusers.

Despite the findings of these various studies, the prevention of spouse and child abuse remains minimal. Most abuses are concealed within the families. The victims typically feel embarrassed or unable to report the assaults, and they see themselves as helpless, unable to change the situation. Cases come to our attention primarily because the victims appear at emergency rooms for treatment or they resolutely gather their courage to leave their domestic situations.

PREVENTION AND CONTROL OF AGGRESSION AND VIOLENCE

Having identified three major instances of violence, we move to the questions of prevention and control. The inability to express feelings appropriately and responsibly substantially contributes to the violent behaviors that we have examined. Assertiveness training is one of the preferred treatments in these situations, and we will report one particular assertiveness solution that is used in marital quarrels. However, the first prevention strategy discussed here is the self-control of aggression. We then turn to assertiveness and empathy. The individuals able to express their feelings well, with empathic consideration for others, are more likely to be in control of their potential for violent acts. Finally, we consider tactics for coping with potential violence in general. No effort is made to offer a comprehensive guidebook to violence prevention and control methods. The three topics that follow are representative ways in which behavioral scientists think about violence prevention.

Self-Control

Controlling aggression was extremely difficult for the thirty-four men and women of Bloomington, Indiana, who participated in an experimental treatment program. According to Raymond Novaco's (1975) descriptions, these people regularly destroyed their possessions, assaulted others, and lost their tempers. Prior to treatment, these men and women reacted with disruptive and poorly controlled aggression to provocative situations. Among the situations they role-played before and after the program was the following:

> You have bought a pair of slacks that were on sale at a newly opened clothing store, and you soon discover that they have a hole in them that you didn't notice when you bought them. The next day, you return the

This customer is returning defective merchandise. How would you react if you were the customer? If you were the salesperson? Would you feel provoked to the point of making an angry outburst? Or would your reaction reflect a peaceful feeling of well-being and control?

slacks to the store hoping to exchange them for a pair that isn't defective. You enter the store holding the pants with your receipt, but it takes a while before someone comes to wait on you. Finally, a salesperson comes along.

A [Assistant]: "Can I show you something today, sir (ms.)?"

S [Subject]: "Yes, I want to exchange these pants I bought yesterday."

A: "Hum, that was one of our sale items. I'm very sorry, sir (ms.), but all sales were final on those items,"

S: "But these have a hole in them."

A: "That's ridiculous! We don't sell defective merchandise, sir (ms.)"

S: "Well, they were like this when I got them."

A: "Then what did you buy them for?"

S: "Because I didn't know they had a hole in them."

A: "Don't you look at what you are buying? Most people know what they are getting when they buy something. For all we know you could have put the hole in them yourself. You got them at a cheap price, and maybe decided that you didn't want them anymore and now you are trying to exchange them for a better pair. You know, some people try this sort of thing all the time."

(Novaco, 1975, p. 99)

Before their training, the men and women would react aggressively and excessively to this situation. After the program, the subjects handled such provocations calmly, effectively, and assertively. Their attitudes had changed from agitation to peaceful well-being.

This study showed that a training program that combined techniques worked best in promoting the subjects' self-control of aggression. The individuals were taught relaxation techniques and ways of controlling their thoughts and unstated sentences. Compared to a control group, which only paid attention to their patterns of anger for three weeks, the subjects' self-reported anger diminished, their blood pressure dropped, and the intensity of their angry responses to hypothetical and role-played situations lessened.

Anger management

Using **anger management** principles, Novaco gave his subjects the following instructions, which are good guidelines for all people who need to control their angry and aggressive outbursts:

1. Because getting angry is part of being unsure about yourself, remember your good and competent features.

2. Even when provoked, don't get personally involved. Do what has to be done to get the outcome you want.

3. Use alternative ways of dealing with anger.

4. Recognize the earliest signs of developing anger. Relax.

5. Once you feel agitated, instruct yourself to take care of the necessary task at hand. Don't get distracted.

6. If things seem to be getting out of hand, take charge by not getting angry when most other people would.

7. Look at the stages or pieces of the situations that otherwise would anger you.

8. Be sure to congratulate yourself for your successes in anger control.

(Novaco, 1975, pp. 93–94)

Self-control of anger is not the only path to experiencing well-being in otherwise difficult situations. We return now to the subject of assertiveness, only this time we consider it in the context of marital conflicts.

Assertiveness and Empathy

Believing that assertive verbal conflicts between husband and wife can be desirable, George Bach and Peter Wyden (1968) described a course of ***fight training*** for couples. To start, a couple must be truly interested in

Fight training

THE INSULT: VERBAL AGGRESSION AND RITUAL

One ritualized expression of aggression is the *insult booth,* which can be found at British country fairs. A dividing wall separates the speaker and the listener, with an open face-high window between them. The listener, who says nothing, can be either a companion of the speaker or the booth operator. For a small admission fee, the speaker is given five minutes to unleash the full force of verbal insults toward the listener. Because five minutes is a long time to be generating insults, the wall facing the speaker is covered with suggested accusations. The speaker may choose to call the listener an unwashed, underhanded, cockroach-infested wharf rat, for example. Insults made in this safe context are accompanied by great bursts of laughter and enjoyment—signs that otherwise personally unacceptable expressions are acceptable. The insults are shouted with pleasant relief.

Some people use insults automatically, as part of their everyday language. For other people, the mildest profanity is alien to them. Still others use fierce insults for almost magical purposes; they speak obscenities to dispel unpleasant events. When people curse after spilling hot coffee on themselves, their language can be interpreted both as an expression of distress and an incantation to reverse the accident.

Thinking of obscenities as potentially powerful words that can influence the world is more common in primitive cultures. An excerpt from a story by Oliver

working to improve their relationship and be willing to attend a thirteen-week course on marital conflict. There, the couple is taught how to fight fairly; like all assertive acts, respect for the other person's feelings and rights is a central ingredient. Why instruction in fair fighting, or for that matter, in fighting at all? Bach and Wyden explained it this way:

> Fighting is inevitable between mature intimates. Quarreling and making up are hallmarks of true intimacy. However earnestly a mature partner tries to live in harmony with a partner, he will have to fight for his very notions of harmony itself and come to terms with competing notions—and there are always competing interests.
>
> *(Bach & Wyden, 1968, p. 26)*

Couples that never quarrel at all are fight-phobic and suffer "loneliness a deux." Because so many people use controlling or passive-aggressive devices to gain their ends, a fight can be a welcome relief. Unstated topics rise to the surface. The potential then exists for the couple to clarify and extinguish the accumulated tensions they each carry around.

One key concern in the training is, How does the fight end? If a fight

---

LaFarge describes this process in one of the most vivid obscene insult passages in contemporary literature.

> Spud spoke sharply. He had been scared, he was mad, and he aimed to be madder. He began swearing, soft and mild at first, as his custom was, then as his wrath stood up in him, he got into the swing of his language and the air before his face changed color. He used the deep cussing of seamen, the low, venomous cussing of cattlemen, the freighters' whiplike oaths, and what he heard from the Mississippi roustabouts when he was a kid at home. He cussed the cussing of Mexican muleteers when they're feeling fine and want to tell the world, and when, at the end of a long, desert day, a mule steps on their feet. He used the dreadful, whining cussing with which Finn sailors can stop or start a storm, and his father's terrible Irish wrath, and Navajo and Apache and Ute words of shriveling strength, and coureur de bois talk, and Kit Carson's main oath on top of the lot, and all along through it he wove in and out the ideas that came to him, the voice of his anger pouring itself out full. The warriors ducked, raised their shields and touched their medicine bags. Cochise put his fan before his face, and twice he half raised his hand to ask Spud to stop. As the cowpuncher's voice died away at last, there was a thump on the ground between them, and the buzzard which had been sailing high above fell to earth, scorched clean of feathers.
>
> *(LaFarge, 1978, pp. 74–75)*

closes with withdrawal and anger, then the fight has not been successful. On the other hand, a positive making up promotes intimacy.

> For intimate partners, perhaps the richest payoff of well-managed conflict comes with yielding after a fight. Any intimate relationship implies some readiness to yield one's own self-interest when it clashes with that of the partner. . . .
>
> The final benefit of yielding is the tremendous feeling of well-being that comes from making a beloved person happy.
>
> *(Bach & Wyden, 1968, p. 33)*

One important technique in such fighting and indeed in all interpersonal relationships is the ability to put yourself in your partner's position and see the disagreement through your partner's eyes. Such empathy is important to well-being, and children as well as adults can be taught empathy.

With children, one starting point in developing their empathy is to ask them some questions.

> What would the world look like to you if you were as tall as Wilt Chamberlain—or as small as a cat? What birthday present would make each member of your family happier?
>
> *(Feshbach, 1979, p. 240)*

Empathy

These questions were part of a thirty-hour empathy training program that Norma Deitch Feshbach organized in selected Los Angeles elementary schools. She defined **empathy** as the ability to identify and experience the emotions another feels. Training in empathy for these third, fourth, and fifth graders included role-playing that involved pretending they were other people, discussions of stories, and games such as charades.

The most important changes in the children as a result of the training were a decrease in their aggressive acts and an increase in their positive social behaviors (Feshbach, 1983). How does empathy work to reduce aggression? Apparently, vicariously experiencing the pain and suffering of other people has an impact, as does learning how to see the world through the eyes of other people. Empathy training is not a panacea. However, children who complete empathy training do learn to care more about and become more attached to others. As a result, they are less disruptive in the classroom and less aggressive with other children, which are promising outcomes indeed.

Empathy and assertiveness training programs are no answers for the person who could be on the other side of a hostile interaction, the potential victim. Our final topic for this chapter is how to cope with potential violence, looking at what individuals should know about the probability of being a victim of violence and likely successful means of responding.

Coping with Potential Violence

If you are threatened by a possible assailant, two tongue-in-cheek responses have been suggested:

> Signify by a thunderously glowering look that just another hair's breadth hint of his aggression will incite to toupee ripping or in the case of a fellow with a full head of hair, the imminent need of a toupee . . .

> . . . If your adversary stands there in his splashily cut garments shouting that he is an expert in one of the arts of self-defense and has qualified to the high entitlement of a pink, black, blue, or green belt or other glorified gladitorial status, and that you had better watch out, jeeringly protrude your tongue at him. This has a way of defusing your opponent's killer instinct by delighting him with your seeming vulnerability.

> *(J.P. Donleavy, 1975, pp. 79–80)*

What should you actually do when faced with a potentially violent person or situation? It is clear that no single answer applies to all situations. Nevertheless, increasing research and clinical observations on violence suggest possible actions to avoid troublesome situations.

The National Crime Surveys commissioned by the U.S. Department of Justice (1983) described how victims of violent crime attempted to protect themselves. By far the most common response was taking no protective action whatever. Among victims of robbery and assault, such inaction was typical. Table 6–2 presents the patterns of other victim responses. As the table shows, victims most frequently used or tried to use physical force in self-protection. About one-third of rape victims tried physical force. Rape

TABLE 6-2 How Victims of Crime Protect Themselves

Victim Response	Percent of Victims Who Used Response by Type of Crime		
	Rape	Robbery	Assault
Used weapon (gun or knife)	1%	2%	2%
Used physical force	33%	23%	23%
Responded verbally (threatened, argued, reasoned)	17%	8%	13%
Attracted attention and tried to get help	15%	7%	6%
Used nonviolent evasion (resisted without force, used evasive action)	10%	11%	19%
Other	5%	4%	7%
Total %	100%	100%	100%
Total in each sample	873	5,868	24,876

Adapted from U.S. Department of Justice, 1983, p. 23.

victims also tried to attract attention and tried verbal responses more often than did the other types of victims.

The successes of the victims' responses may be judged by what proportion of them led to serious injury. A victim who tried physical force to resist had a 16 percent chance of serious injury. Trying to attract attention or doing nothing to protect oneself also had high percentages of injury (14 percent and 12 percent, respectively). On the other hand, the lowest likelihood of the victim being injured was associated with trying to talk one's way out of the situation (6 percent) and taking nonviolent evasive action (also 6 percent).

For potential victims, other preventive steps are to size up situations before entering them and then to move out of transactions or places upon becoming aware that something dangerous may be developing.

In a commentary on the prevention of rape, Ann Burgess and I likened preventive efforts to flight education principles (Burgess & Brodsky, 1981). Pilots avoid trouble in the air by carefully anticipating the possibility of danger and taking active steps to prevent it. In the same way, potential assaults may be avoided by the victim's recognizing in advance possible troublesome events, knowing his or her own resources for dealing with a threat, and staying calm enough to consider and act on alternatives. The following strategies are ways of coping with potential violence, including rape attempts:

Interrupt violence-prone sequences.   Many episodes of violence arise from a process of escalation, in which small disagreements or difficulties grow until they are so intense that violence erupts. Stay alert for the process of rapid escalation and interrupt the process by getting out or stopping your part of the escalation.

Seek specific help.   If danger seems to be developing, seek assistance from specific individuals around you. Don't issue a general call if many people are nearby. You are more likely to get help if your request is directed at one person.

Know your history.   Be aware of your abilities and the ways in which you have dealt with similar situations before. Utilize strategies that worked in the past.

Winning by losing.   Many people feel they must save face and not do something that may sound or look foolish. Allow yourself to lose face and take the risk that you may appear dumb or frightened when you seek help. Permit yourself to not be a "winner" in an argument.

Don't stop trying.   Some people say "Please don't harm me; I'll do whatever you say" when confronted by an assailant. Although this may help sometimes, often your fear and vulnerability will spur the assailant further, particularly if the assailant is a rapist. If the potential

TABLE 6-3 Assertiveness, Aggression, and Well-Being	
Toward Well-Being	**Away from Well-Being**
Comfortably passive and shy by choice	Uncomfortably shy, not by choice
Seeks assistance about problematic shyness or aggression	Accepts problematic shyness or aggression; feels helpless about it
Assertively expresses own feelings while respecting rights and feelings of others	Doesn't express own feelings or doesn't respect others' rights and feelings
Anger and hostility that is appropriate to the situation is expressed in assertive ways	Overly minimizes and overly controls chronic anger or hostility
Tempers aggression with empathy	Uncontrolled, untempered aggression
Evades or talks way out of threatened violence; keeps trying to prevent violent act	Passive, ineffectual in the face of threatened violence

assailant is tentative, act aloof and strong. In any case, escape if you can. Otherwise, buy time and then look for an opportunity to get aid, resist effectively, or leave.

In summary, Table 6–3 lists behaviors that appropriately utilize assertiveness in the interest of well-being, and those behaviors that use aggression or are nonassertive and that impair well-being.

SUMMARY

On the assertiveness continuum are three major points. At one far end is nonassertiveness, or the withholding of feelings and thoughts in passive and inhibited ways. In the center is assertiveness, or the expression of feelings and thoughts in ways considerate of others. Finally, at the other end there is aggression, in which feelings and thoughts are expressed without consideration of the rights and feelings of other people.

Shyness and nonassertiveness are closely related, and research indicates that most people see these two characteristics as the same. Zimbardo's (1977) research indicated that about one-fourth of shy people see themselves as chronically shy, and about 4 percent see themselves as shy with all people in all situations. Such shyness is a serious concern for the sufferers. However, among the less severely shy, between 10 and 20 percent like being shy. Nonassertive, shy people tend to attribute their behavior to internal factors not within their control. Even when they role-play assertiveness, these shy persons do not feel good about it.

When hostility comes through in the forms of obstinacy and ineffectiveness, the behavior is called passive-aggressiveness.

Being assertive means expressing feelings in responsible ways. Positive assertions are the responsible expressions of liking and approval, which come more easily than do negative assertions. Negative assertions typically refuse unreasonable requests or assert one's own rights. The most desirable negative assertion is the minimal effective response, or saying or doing the least necessary to accomplish one's aims.

Aggressive behavior is distinguished from healthy assertiveness by the lack of responsibility and consideration. Feelings are expressed readily, but without an appreciation of others' rights. Aggression always implies some action, while anger is an emotional, internal state, and hostility is an attitude of negative judgment. Overcontrolled hostility is the accumulation of negative attitudes and anger that, in some cases, explodes into severe violence.

Spouse abuse is an instance of severe violence that frequently is associated with nonassertive verbal behavior. Approximately 4 percent of all couples in the United States report physical violence between spouses, and 3.2 percent of parents report kicking, biting, or hitting their children with fists within the prior one year. Child-abusing parents tend to be distressed, rigid, lonely, and unhappy, to see problems in their own families and in their children, and to have negative concepts of their children and of themselves.

In looking toward solutions to handling aggressive behavior, one promising avenue is the self-control training by Novaco (1975), in which persons are taught relaxation techniques, control of their hostile thoughts, and detached and alternate ways to handle their anger. Other avenues include teaching couples how to fight fairly and assertively and training people to increase their personal empathy.

When actually confronted by a potentially violent person, doing nothing, generally seeking help, and resisting with physical force have the highest probability of injury. Talking one's way out of it, continuing to try to prevent the violence, and interrupting the sequence of events are all efforts that promise more effective resistance.

ASSERTIVE RESPONSES: CARTOONS IN FIGURE 6-1

1. "I have waited in line, and I expect you to do the same. Please go to the back of the line."

2. "I wouldn't have come now if it wasn't important. Please let the doctor know I'd appreciate his seeing me. I'll wait."

3. "I don't want to argue about who's right or wrong. We have to report this accident and exchange registration and license information."

4. "I know it's upsetting to find that we are out of the product after you have made a trip here. We wish we could help you, and if you had been here earlier we would have been happy to sell you one."

Key Terms

Aggression	**Hostility**
Aggressive behavior	**Minimal effective response**
Anger	**Negative assertions**
Anger management	**Nonassertiveness**
Assertiveness	**Overcontrolled hostility**
Assertiveness training	**Passive-aggressiveness**
Child abuse	**Positive assertions**
Empathy	**Shyness**
Fight training	**Spouse abuse**

Recommended Reading

Aberti R.E. & Emmons, M. (1975). *Stand up, speak out, talk back!* New York: Pocket Books. This how-to book tells how to become assertive. It offers useful advice for nonassertive individuals, presenting the ideas in an entertaining way.

Monahan, J. (1981). *The clinical prediction of violence.* Beverly Hills, CA: Sage. This award-winning volume describes what mental health professionals know and don't know about the prediction of violence. Although intended for psychologists and psychiatrists, it offers a state-of-the-art analysis of what is actually known about this subject.

Zimbardo, P.G. (1977). *Shyness.* New York: Jove/HBJ. The first part of this book on shyness is entitled, "What It Is," and the second part is entitled, "What to Do about It." Zimbardo has written a thoughtful guide to the nature of shyness. The first part informs, drawing heavily on case histories. The second part has dozens of exercises for and detailed information about overcoming shyness.

7

CHAPTER

Transitions and the Life Cycle

The Return

As he approached the statue of Abraham Lincoln, Peter was excited. The one-third-size replica of the Lincoln Memorial was directly in front of the main door of Lincoln High School. During his four years at Lincoln, Peter had leaned against, sat by, sprawled under, crouched by, and played next to the base of the statue. Coming back once again, he felt excited and good about being at Lincoln and seeing the statue. Some of his friends from high school had turned out to be not such good friends as time had passed, but Lincoln was always there, silent and understanding.

At first, Peter had gone back every month, and then less frequently. Now it had been a year since he'd been back. He was at the statue now because that's where Cindi had asked him to meet her after school. Peter liked Cindi. A lot. She had been busy all the times he had called, but he could understand that. She was something special.

The usual signs were taped to the statue. A group called the Concord Grapes was playing. Were they serious? The Concord Grapes? It's hard to believe what they are calling groups nowadays. Various program announcements around the school were taped to Lincoln, too. Thursday after school the meeting for the singing impaired was being held. Hmmph! Next thing there will be classes for the height impaired.

Cindi came out bubbling, but she slowed down when she saw Peter. Her walk became deliberate. She looked down. Then she told him what she had to tell him. He was too old. She didn't want to spend time with a man who was twenty-five years old. Many girls would. He was nice, and she didn't want to hurt him. He just wasn't one of the gang. He belonged to another generation. It was great that he had his own apartment, that he'd been to New York. She was impressed that he could talk about wines. Still, good luck. Keep in touch.

Then Peter was alone. Well, almost alone. Lincoln was there. Peter looked around. It was just a high school. It wasn't his high school any more. A person with all the things he had to do couldn't waste his time with these teenagers. They're so young. What a sad expression on your face, Mr. Lincoln, Peter thought. I never really noticed. You must have had a hard life.

THE NATURE OF TRANSITIONS

Transitions

. . . we proceed through the apparently small, meaningless, insignificant decisions and happenings of our daily lives and often decry how boring this can be or that nothing exciting or important ever happens to us. And then unexpectedly we can find ourselves in a larger-than-life climax and wonder how and why it happened . . . we find that the sudden, powerful event is really not of a single piece, but rather is a large puzzle that we have been slowly building out of the small decision-pieces of our daily "insignificant" lives.

(Gerber, 1982, p. 3)

The transition Peter was experiencing is common. He was learning about letting go of one era in his life and allowing himself to move into another. Despite having left high school some years earlier, he had retained more

The seemingly small, insignificant happenings and interactions of daily life actually build slowly, over time, to contribute to a climactic life event. When we experience such an event, we realize the importance of these "insignificant" happenings.

than fond memories. He still wanted to be part of that time and place, and he acted as if he were. As a consequence, he had not allowed himself to move fully into adulthood. He felt isolated from people his own age and sought out Cindi and others much younger.

Cindi did what many (but by no means all) girls her age would do. She accepted the judgments of her friends as vitally important and saw Peter as out of phase with her group.

The transition Peter was finally making was to surrender his commitment to adolescence and high school and become committed to the present instead. It is representative of many of the transitions through which we pass. Peter will have to adjust to a role associated with being and growing older.

When change occurs in our lives, we usually make some adjustments.

The ways in which we acted last year may no longer be appropriate. We may have become different, people's expectations of us may have changed, or some real change in the environment may have occurred, perhaps due to a death, graduation, or retirement. With more changes and new roles, we have greater adjustments to make. Getting settled in any new situation takes time and effort. In the same sense, letting go and becoming unsettled and then resettled in an existing situation requires renewed time and effort. Think of it in terms of equilibrium. In most situations, we become balanced—in equilibrium—after time. The balance is disrupted when a major transition occurrs, and then a new equilibrium has to be established.

This balancing process occurs in our ongoing adjustments, as well. When people are teetering precariously on a fine wire in their lives, they may feel that even a mild new breeze is catastrophic. When people are solidly settled, feet on the ground, small changes have little impact on them.

Life events

In this chapter, we will be looking at a variety of adult *life events.* Notice the term used is *life events,* rather than simply *events.* After all, opening a door, saying hello, or crossing the street can be considered events. A life event describes a *noteworthy* happening that has some effect on the person (Reese & Smyer, 1983). Winning a million dollars in a state lottery is noteworthy. Winning a free Coke at a fast food restaurant is not.

Two kinds of life events influence us: the *predictable* transitions of life, and the *unexpected* events of life. Each kind presents its own particular challenges for adjustment.

Unexpected Events

In contrast to your reactions to predictable events that are common throughout your life span, your responses to unexpected events are affected by a range of idiosyncratic factors. Unpredictable events catch you unaware. You react differently to different events. You live near a nuclear energy generating plant that suddenly leaks radioactivity into the air; your city is wrecked by an earthquake; your sister moves in with you; you win two million dollars in a state lottery; someone breaks into your house while you are out and steals your most valuable possessions; a long-divorced parent remarries—all these events are unexpected and would affect you differently.

Some researchers maintain that unexpected and nonnormative events shape our adult development more than do the life span experiences (Schlossberg, 1984). After all, the nature of predictable events is that we can prepare for them. We know years in advance about retirement, graduations, and turning forty. We know months in advance that we will be getting married or having children. The time lapse allows us an opportunity to think about what we will do and who we will be once we are retired, married, graduates, or parents. No such lead time is available with unexpected events.

Unexpected events include all significant life happenings for which it is not possible to plan. Some are obvious, such as flood, earthquakes, and auto accidents. Others are less obvious, such as an unplanned shift in our religious or other group affiliations. The effects of unexpected life events have been discussed in the chapters on stress and coping and physical health and illness. In this chapter, we look at **predictable** **transitions** throughout the span of our lives.

Unexpected events

Predictable transitions

Life Span Transitions

In the 1970s a flowering of interest in adult development appeared. Until that time, much interest had been directed toward child and adolescent development, and adulthood was seen as a stable time of continuity. One of the only dissenting voices was psychoanalyst Erik Erikson (1950, 1968, 1982), who postulated eight stages of life, in which basic conflicts were faced (see Figure 7–1). These stages included three adult periods

FIGURE 7–1 Erik Erikson's Eight Stages of Development

Adapted from Erickson, 1950 p. 273.

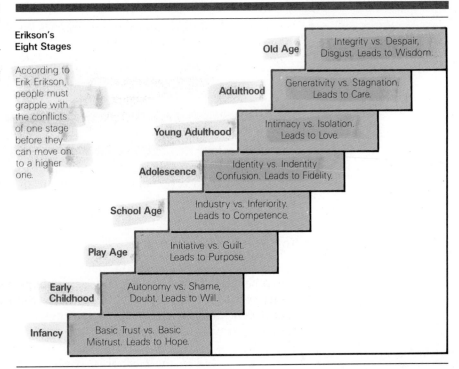

Erikson's Eight Stages

According to Erik Erikson, people must grapple with the conflicts of one stage before they can move on to a higher one.

Old Age — Integrity vs. Despair, Disgust. Leads to Wisdom.

Adulthood — Generativity vs. Stagnation. Leads to Care.

Young Adulthood — Intimacy vs. Isolation. Leads to Love.

Adolescence — Identity vs. Indentity Confusion. Leads to Fidelity.

School Age — Industry vs. Inferiority. Leads to Competence.

Play Age — Initiative vs. Guilt. Leads to Purpose.

Early Childhood — Autonomy vs. Shame, Doubt. Leads to Will.

Infancy — Basic Trust vs. Basic Mistrust. Leads to Hope.

Intimacy
Isolation
Generativity
Stagnation
Ego integrity
Despair

of development. According to this model, in young adulthood, the basic conflict to be resolved is to move toward **intimacy** with others or to move away from others toward **isolation.** Adulthood itself is characterized by either **generativity** (renewing oneself and helping the next generation) versus **stagnation** (being stuck in one's ideas and rules). Old age leads to the conflict between **ego integrity,** which is looking over one's life and accomplishments with satisfaction, versus **despair** about one's life.

The seeds planted by Erikson bore fruit when Daniel Levinson and his colleagues (1978) produced a professionally influential book, *The Seasons of a Man's Life,* and Gail Sheehy (1976) wrote *Passages,* her best-selling account of life's crises and transitions. At the same time, West Virginia University initiated a series of annual conferences on life span development. A new field was born! Sheehy wrote

> Studies of child development have plotted every nuance of growth and given us comforting labels such as the Terrible Twos and the Noisy Nines. Adolescence has been so carefully deciphered, most of the fun of being impossible has been taken out of it. But after meticulously documenting our periods of personality development up to the age of 18 or 20 . . . we are left to fend for ourselves on the way downstream to senescence, at which point we are picked up again by gerontologists.

(Sheehy, 1976, p. 10)

Life span psychology holds that certain predictable stages and stressors face us in adulthood (see Figure 7–2). Rather than being a time that smooths over adolescent turmoil, adulthood has its own unique transition points. The transition to early adulthood happens to most people in their late teens and early twenties. Particularly pressing among the next transition points is the midlife crisis. Levinson and Sheehy assert that between the ages of thirty-five and forty we all go through an inner struggle that focuses on coming to grips with the meaning of the middle years of our lives. Finally, later adulthood presents us with the challenges of aging and dying. All three of these transitions will be considered in detail shortly. However, first we look at the overall picture of transitions in the life cycle.

Infancy and toddlerhood

The period of first socialization spans from birth through two years of age, and it begins with the earliest contacts with the mother and father. These contacts lead to the affectionate bond known as attachment, which the infant indicates through a number of behaviors, such as social smiling, laughing, and showing anxiety at times of separation. Erik Erikson (1950) has described two psychosocial stages of development during this time. In the first year of life, the **basic trust versus distrust** stage occurs, in which

Basic trust versus distrust

FIGURE 7–2 Daniel Levinson's Stages of Development

Adapted from Levinson et al., 1978, p. 57.

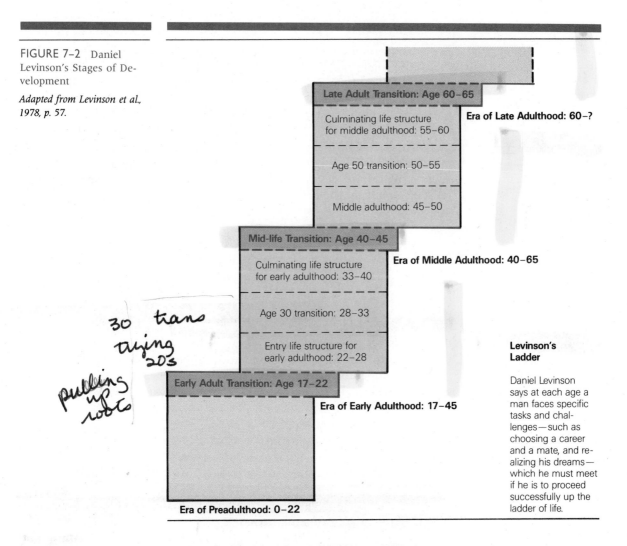

Late Adult Transition: Age 60–65

Culminating life structure for middle adulthood: 55–60

Era of Late Adulthood: 60–?

Age 50 transition: 50–55

Middle adulthood: 45–50

Mid-life Transition: Age 40–45

Culminating life structure for early adulthood: 33–40

Era of Middle Adulthood: 40–65

Age 30 transition: 28–33

Entry life structure for early adulthood: 22–28

Levinson's Ladder

Daniel Levinson says at each age a man faces specific tasks and challenges—such as choosing a career and a mate, and realizing his dreams—which he must meet if he is to proceed successfully up the ladder of life.

Early Adult Transition: Age 17–22

Era of Early Adulthood: 17–45

Era of Preadulthood: 0–22

the infant learns that the world is either a secure, nurturing, dependable place or is an undependable place. The infant has learned distrust if he or she reacts with anger, fear, distress, or apathy to the uncertainties of existence. In the period from one to three years of age, the second of the Erikson development stages occurs: the stage of ***autonomy versus shame and doubt.*** Successful transition through this stage leaves a child comfortable in his or her independence, having managed the oppositional period in which the response to many parental activities is saying no. Incomplete passage through this stage leaves the child feeling ashamed and uncertain about his or her independence.

Autonomy versus shame and doubt

Early childhood

Ages two through five are the early childhood years. During this time, children learn male and female behaviors and roles through self-awareness, from their parents' and peers' behaviors, and from television, books, teachers, sitters, and neighbors. In these preschool years, play is an important part of the children's learning mastery of their bodies, cooperation, creativity, and identification with adults. Erikson wrote of this time as the ***initiative versus guilt*** stage—that time at which children attempt to move out freely on their own to explore their worlds and their capabilities. If such activities are devalued as wrong or useless, then this developmental stage results in the children's feeling guilty about themselves and their activities.

Initiative versus guilt

Middle childhood

From six years of age to the onset of adolescence, children go beyond family activities into school activities, close friendships, and more of the adult environment. Their moral values emerge both within friendships and with respect to broader social concerns. The Erikson stage faced at this time is ***industry versus inferiority.*** Children who succeed at this stage develop a sense of accomplishment and competence. They work at school tasks, at competitive play, and derive self-worth from their activities. The children who do not resolve the crisis of this stage feel worthless and inept. That felt inferiority becomes part of their expectation that they will be unsuccessful at major life tasks.

Industry versus inferiority

Adolescence

Adolescence is the period from the onset of the physical and emotional changes of puberty to the time at which youths leave their family homes to live, work, or go to school on their own. The physical changes are often dramatic as children develop the bodies of adults. Children acquire new identities as they assume male or female sex roles, begin more mature relationships with other boys and girls, and often struggle within the family for independence of parental control. Erikson calls the crisis of this developing time in children's lives ***identity versus role diffusion.*** At this stage, adolescents search for their personal identities, seeking to answer the questions, "Who am I?" and "What do I hope to accomplish in life?" Finding a meaningful identity may take the form of a commitment to a career or to guiding personal principles. In the absence of a successful search for identity, youths feel vaguely lost, without purpose or meaning to their lives.

Identity versus role diffusion

PREDICTABLE CRISES OF ADULTHOOD

Looking at the four stages of childhood and adolescent development—infancy and toddlerhood, early childhood, middle childhood, and adolescence—has set the stage for us to move into the major focus of this chapter: adjustment and development throughout adulthood.

Early Adulthood Transitions

Three predictable crises of early adulthood have been identified by Sheehy (1976), Levinson and his colleagues (1978), and various other observers. These are the crises of pulling up roots, the trying twenties, and the age thirty transition; together they compose the phase of early adulthood.

In the early adult transition, youths move out of their parents' homes to live on their own and encounter true independence for the first time. They go to college, enter military service, or begin jobs.

Pulling up roots: The early adult transition

In the late teenage years through the early twenties, roughly between the ages of seventeen and twenty-two, leaving family and home are common early adult experiences and challenges. Charged with the peaks of their intellectual and physical vigor, youths go to college, into military service, or begin their first jobs. They move out of their family homes and are on their own for the first time. They have to maintain work or class schedules. They have to pay bills. They must master all the tasks of managing an independent life without the aid and sometimes interference of their parents. They encounter the first true experience of independence. They frequently feel a conflict between being independent and being dependent. This is the time at which they enter adulthood.

The trying twenties: Entering the adult world

In the early adulthood stage that covers the age range of approximately twenty-two to twenty-eight years, two competing goals are pursued. While trying to develop a stable and structured adult life, people experiment and take risks. For them, adulthood is somewhat tentative. In this phase, ". . . tasks are as enormous as they are exhilarating: To shape a Dream . . . To prepare for a lifework . . . And to form the capacity for intimacy" (Sheehy, 1976, p. 27). A life pattern is set in motion. We make enough decisions about what we should do with our lives to form a provisional framework.

The age thirty transition

During the age thirty transition, which extends through approximately age thirty-three, people often feel uneasy and constricted by the choices they made in their twenties. Established intimate commitments are either deepened or diminished. The discontent of this stage leads people to look afresh at their earlier life choices. People either change their employment or marital partner or they reaffirm their commitment to their existing job or spouse. At around age thirty-three comes a settling down period. During this time, people work persistently at advancement, at improving their lives, and at establishing their niche in society with pride and competence. With the completion of the age thirty transition, the early adulthood phase is over. Next comes the transition between early and late adulthood: the midlife crisis.

The Midlife to Late Adult Transitions

In their late thirties and early forties, people begin to realize the limits of mortality. They see this time as the beginning of the second half of

Toward the end of the age thirty transition, people work persistently to advance themselves and to establish their niche in society.

their lives. Most individuals realize that they are no longer young. People may ask themselves if they are doing what they truly wish to do with their lives. They may reexamine what they have done so far, their values and desires, and the suitability of their lives. This "deadline decade" makes them aware of life's time limits. The crisis is resolved with an examination and acceptance of who they are as people and what they choose to be. Levinson explains this period as follows:

> As he attempts to reappraise his life, a man discovers how much it has been based on illusions and he is faced with the task of *de-illusionment.* By this expression I mean a reduction of illusions, a recognition that long-held assumptions and beliefs about self and world are not true.

De-illusionment

(Levinson, Darrow, Klein, Levinson & Braxton, 1978, p. 192)

Three aspects of self and the world particularly call for the making of midlife resolutions. The first is the young–old focus. When it is clear that a person is no longer a youth, he or she must face moving toward middle age. The person is in between, neither young nor old.

Masculinity-femininity is a second transitional issue. As men's body strength and prowess diminish, they may express their masculinity through control over others and through other compensatory actions. At the same time, men may explore the feminine aspects of their feelings, or their gentler side. Women's fears of losing their desirability are accompanied sometimes by a redefining of the nature of their femininity. Roles are changed, or family tasks modified. Think of women who, upon becoming grandmothers, become strong and assertive.

The third transitional aspect is renewal versus resignation, which signals the beginning of middle adulthood.

Renewal or resignation

Renewal or resignation

Renewal is recognized by its other names: revitalization, emotional rebirth. Does a new purpose to life emerge? If not, the earlier goals of marriage, family, employment, and so on may not have been met. Without renewal, people may become depressed and resigned as their children leave home and as their intimate relationships come to seem stale (Miller, Denton & Tobacyk, 1986). Some realize that career promise has peaked. Sometimes people make negative choices carelessly, perhaps terminating a long marriage or employment or rashly moving from one city to another. Alternatively, people may discover renewed meaning and commitment to their life activities. Some people become *mentors* at this time, serving to guide younger friends or colleagues from their perspective as older and wiser.

Mentors

The stages after this point in middle adulthood have been less well-documented. Levinson and colleagues (1978) hold that new transitions occur about every five years. Three more stages, beginning at age fifty, have been described.

Age fifty transition

From ages fifty to fifty-five, early midlife transitions are stabilized. If no crisis appeared in the forties, it arises here.

Second middle adult phase

Ages fifty through sixty may see the completion of middle adulthood and the substantial achievements of life. Feelings of great fulfillment often appear at this time. In the absence of feeling such attainments, people may focus on the worth of their life efforts.

Late adult transition

A major turning point in the life cycle is thought to occur between ages sixty and sixty-five. The middle adulthood tasks are completed, and preparation for retirement and late adulthood is undertaken (Levinson et al., 1978).

DOES EVERYONE GO THROUGH THE SAME TRANSITIONS?

Are life transitions universal? If they are expected for everybody, then we all need to prepare for the next step or crisis; mental health agencies, as well, should help people deal with these problems. On the other hand, if many people don't go through such crises, we may misinterpret their other problems. Individuals who gear their lives around expected changes may judge themselves negatively if they have not met each anticipated step. So, we need to ask, does everyone go through the same transitions?

Daniel Levinson and colleagues (1978) delivered a resounding "yes!" in answer to this question. They acknowledged that every life is different and that the differences between people's lives are much greater than the similarities. However, they emphasized that even the most varied lives show the same developmental stages in the same order.

Let us look at the basis for their conclusion. Forty men between the ages of thirty-five and forty-five who lived in Boston, New York, or in between were extensively interviewed over a period of two to three months. The men interviewed were equally representative of four occupations: ten were hourly workers, ten were executives, ten were academic biologists, and ten were novelists. In addition, Levinson and coworkers examined writings by and about men in public life or about fictional characters, including Dante, Shakespeare, Abraham, Martin Luther, Bertrand Russell, King Lear, and Willy Loman. Levinson and colleagues drew the following conclusion:

> This sequence of eras and periods exists in all societies, throughout the human species, at the present stage in human evolution. . . . They represent the life cycle of the species. Individuals go through the periods in infinitely varied ways, but the periods themselves are universal.
>
> *(Levinson et al., 1978, p. 322)*

To support this view, they presented descriptive summaries of the forty interviewees.

However, there are possible problems with this study—problems with the small numbers, with only men being used, and with the limitation of one geographical region. Levinson has attempted to rectify at least one of these shortcomings in his companion study, "The Seasons of a Woman's Life," but he is the first to admit that more research must be done (Levinson, 1986, 1987). And some central problems remain. It is not always clear how a person's stage is determined. A researcher confronted with a person who appears not to be in an expected stage can always respond that the person is in another of the infinite individual patterns.

Furthermore, Levinson adds that some people may be delayed in going through some stages. Thus, scientifically verifying the theory that life transitions are universal becomes difficult.

One alternate attempt at verification was asking people themselves about their life stages. Marjorie Fiske Lowenthal and her colleagues (1975) asked 216 middle- and lower-class men and women who were about to enter a significant life transition about their aspirations, self-concepts, values, and coping patterns. All the preretirement subjects and the newly-weds related a substantial life stage transition, as expected. However, 4 percent of the high school graduates and 11 percent of the middle-aged subjects reported no transition. This study concluded that passing through stages and life phases is widespread, but perhaps not universal.

The Case Against Predictable Life Transitions

Some reviewers suggest that age is just one marker along the road in life transitions and is by no means the whole eight-lane highway (for example, see Lerner & Ryff, 1978). Much development in adults, they declare, comes from important experiences that vary greatly from person to person. That is why some individuals fit perfectly into the life cycle model and others are not moving at all in the predicted directions. To paraphrase a famous saying, you can predict all of the people some of the time, and some of the people all of the time, but you cannot predict all of the people all of the time. Because there are a substantial number of people whose development cannot be predicted (at least some of the time), qualifications must accompany the sometimes sweeping conclusions psychologists make about age stages and transitions.

There is still one more reason for caution. People from different historical periods have different adult development phases. People who grew up in the Great Depression had adult experiences and transitions unlike those of Americans born later in the twentieth century. Our values, personalities, outlooks, and adulthood are all influenced by the times we live in (Gergen, 1980). Simply put, age is not destiny.

The case against the existence of predictable life transitions has been especially developed by Leonard Pearlin (1982), a research sociologist at the National Institute of Mental Health. Pearlin interviewed twenty-three hundred Chicago residents between the ages of eighteen and sixty-five in 1972 and conducted follow-up interviews four years later. He asked about the strains people felt in their daily lives, in transitional periods, and in unexpected life happenings. His findings suggested that transitions by no means involve predictable emotional difficulties.

To begin with, Pearlin discovered that most life transitions have little emotional effects that are consistent across different individuals. Thus, giving birth, entering or leaving school, moving away from home, and becoming a grandparent all have no specific predictable effects. The only exception was becoming widowed, which consistently (and hardly surprisingly) led to depression.

The Pearlin study of middle-age transitions did not support the claims of Daniel Levinson, Gail Sheehy, and others that midlife is a distressing and disturbing time. Quite to the contrary, Pearlin described this as an especially peaceful time.

> There is no doubt that there are particular types of crises experienced by people who are in the midrange of their lives. What is doubtful are suggestions that crises are especially likely to surface in the middle part of the life span or that they are somehow more severe than those arising at other times in adult life . . . middle age simply does not emerge as the age at which people are outstandingly exposed or vulnerable to problems and crises . . . it is actually less demanding than other periods of adulthood.
>
> *(Pearlin, 1982, p. 62)*

This outlook sees multiple paths of aging and coping with transitions. Pearlin has indicated that it is easy to overstate the harmful effects of adult transitions. However, he saw most people he interviewed as coping successfully and with relative ease, a stark contrast to the stress and trauma oriented outlooks of other researchers. One way in which these sometimes contradictory results can be reconciled is to look at longitudinal research, or how the same people change over time.

Longitudinal Research

The study of adult transitions is particularly useful when it is related to people's entire lives. The most important and long-term studies over time have been conducted in the San Francisco bay area, beginning between 1923 and 1931. These studies are the Jean Walker MacFarlane Guidance Study, begun with 248 newborns in Berkeley, the Nancy Bayley Berkeley Growth Study of 61 infants, and the Oakland Growth Study, initiated with 212 fifth and six graders. These studies had extraordinary ranges of repeated assessments, including detailed follow-ups when the subjects were in the age range of thirty-six to fifty (Eichorn, Clausen, Haan, Honzik & Mussen, 1981).

This longitudinal research asked whether our adult transitions are strongly molded by our adolescent and earlier experiences. On the one hand is the childcentric view, which sees childhood and adolescence as so influential that they are like concrete molds that shape adult lives. The opposing view is the adultcentric, which sees the continuous development of the adult as not bound by earlier formative events. Like so many black-and-white issues, the truth seems to fall between the two poles.

Consider psychological health. When the Guidance Study subjects from the Berkeley infant group were followed for up to fifty years, major differences between men and women were found. For women, high correlations between adolescent and adult psychological health were found at age thirty. For men, they were found at age forty. At age thirty, women were more into fixed roles and were using the strengths they had developed during adolescence to master mothering and careers without burning out. By the time they were forty, they were found to be decidedly more poised and independent, no longer drawing on earlier adjustments. For men, age thirty was reported to be more a time of exploration and defining new roles, while age forty showed a settling into established patterns of responsibility and self-reliance (Peskin & Livson, 1981).

Nevertheless, much consistency was found over adulthood. Correlations of approximately 0.75, which are high and positive, were reported between psychological health at ages thirty-seven and forty-seven. When men and women act in traditional ways in their adolescence, their adult development is affected (Livson, 1973). The traditional adolescent boy who is socially conforming tends to become a productive and balanced person by the time he is forty. On the other hand, although rebellious and nontraditional adolescent males move in the mainstream direction and become more controlled, at forty they nevertheless maintain a power-oriented, often macho, assertiveness.

Traditional teenage girls move into adult roles based on caring for others; as mothers they embrace domestic values and life-styles, even after their children leave home. Nontraditional girls become individualistic and achievement-oriented, although when they have children at home they do not reject the mothering role. When not engaged in mothering, nontraditional women have more life conflicts but also are more goal-oriented and better able to free themselves of socially rigid roles as adults (Livson, 1973).

Implications

What does all this research mean to the understanding of the nature of life transitions? The first implication is that scientific foundations do underlie the theory that people go through life transitions at particular ages. However, the research does not support such transitions as absolute. Instead, people appear to show considerable variability. Some go through the midlife transition right at midlife. Others will pass through the transition at later or earlier times in their lives. A few souls seem to live their lives without going through the stages that most of their contemporaries experience.

Furthermore, transitions do not occur in isolation from the person's life. Instead, at some ages in particular, transitions have clear roots in the adolescent lives and coping styles of the people involved.

Not everyone manages their life transitions well. In the face of both expected transitions and unexpected events, some people are overwhelmed and unable to adapt. Others sail through easily. Let us turn now to the successful passing through of the three adult transitions: (1) early adulthood (especially leaving home and entering college), (2) the midlife transition, and (3) late adulthood and dying. Successful transitions of all three stages offer common opportunities for personal gains through what have been termed "teachable moments."

SUCCESSFUL TRANSITIONS

The Teachable Moment

Teachable moment

Life transitions may be opportunities as well as traumas. In normal and stable times, we tend to be stable. When nothing around us changes, we are unlikely to change. However, during transitions in our lives, our normal routines are disrupted. Because we are changing roles or behaviors or environments, we are exceptionally open to changing ourselves in other ways as well. This time of openness has been called "the teachable moment" (Havighurst, 1953). It is an openness that allows us to take on new ways of living and to be ready to change in deeper ways. When our change is a negative one, with lasting effects, it may be labeled as traumatic. When the change is positive, it reflects personal growth and improvement in response to the transition's opportunity.

What is it that changes? And how do we go about shaping our changes so that they are constructive? According to one review of these questions (Golan, 1981), the first change can be made in *life space,* or the parts of the environment and world with which we interact. Our plans for living and ways of interacting with the physical world around us may be adjusted. For example, moving to a new city may allow us more physically or socially active ways of living. Even with a simple event, such as moving across the street, or being promoted at work, there is the potential for experiencing different environments and activities.

Life space

The second change can be made in the *assumptive world.* Our assumptive world view describes the sum of our expectations and interpretations of what happens around us. A sudden transition allows us to gain new information and to rethink our working assumptions. Is the world dangerous? Are people likely to take advantage of us if we are not cautious? Should we take risks in personal situations about which we are uncertain?

Assumptive world

Let's assume that you are in transition from one stage or way of living to another. You are open to changing your life space and your assumptive world. To begin with, think of this as an opportunity. Utilize a self-fulfilling prophecy—if you believe that you can change positively at this time, you

Anticipating Life Crises

Growing older involves continuous change. We don't reach a plateau of maturity and satisfaction and settle at that point. Rather, we continue to change what we do, who we are, and what is expected of us. These changes are the bases of adult transitions. Yet few young adults actually anticipate the nature of such changes. Typically they have the following outlook:

> Most Americans expect to live until their 70s, to marry and have children, to possess good health, to work at a rewarding job, to retire, and even to die in due time. However, few anticipate joining the considerable number of adults who never marry, or have sexual problems, or confront divorce and the possible loss of their children, or find themselves unable to control the behavior of their children, or experience disability, or endure physical illness, or see a spouse die prematurely, or lose jobs, or undergo the functional limitations of advancing age.

(Albrecht & Gift, 1975, p. 241)

It is possible to anticipate life transitions and problems. Lowenthal and her colleagues (1975) asked their subjects to rate how much life satisfaction they have experienced and how much they anticipate they will experience each year of their lives. No right or wrong answers emerge from such a procedure. Instead, this process allows people to think about and rate life transitions and events. You may follow a similar procedure.

Instructions: Look at the sample life evaluations in Figure 7–3. On the blank life evaluation chart at the bottom of the figure, enter your present age. Then write in the age at which you expect to do (or already have done) the following events:

Graduate—mark with a capital *G*	Be most ill—mark with a capital *I*
Be married—mark with a capital *M*	Retire—mark with a capital *R*
Have children—mark with a capital *C*	Die—mark with a capital *D*
Have your most permanent job—mark with a capital *J*	

Now rate how satisfied you expect you will be, or you have been, above each age, using a nine-point scale. Extremely satisfied gets a rating of 9. Extremely dissatisfied gets a rating of 1. The middle point, or average satisfaction, should be rated 5. Connect the marks at each age, so that you have a single line that either rises or falls over time. This is *your* life evaluation chart. It can be used as a basis for change as well as evaluation. If there is a low point that worries you, pencil in a higher level as a goal to change what you anticipate.

Your life evaluation chart is not a fixed plan. It allows you a chance to put on paper and look at the expectations and judgments you already have about your life. With such expectations made visible, you have more opportunity to think about them and change them.

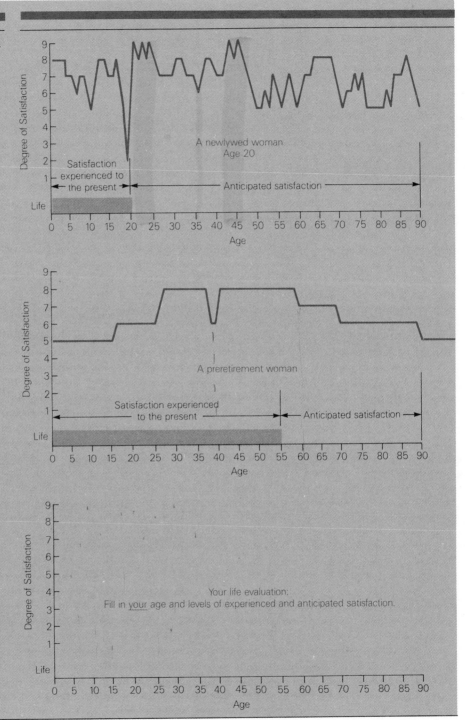

Top chart:

Degree of Satisfaction (y-axis, 1–9)

Satisfaction experienced to the present

A newlywed woman
Age 20

Anticipated satisfaction

Life

Age (x-axis, 0–90)

Middle chart:

Degree of Satisfaction (y-axis, 1–9)

A preretirement woman

Satisfaction experienced to the present

Anticipated satisfaction

Life

Age (x-axis, 0–90)

Bottom chart:

Degree of Satisfaction (y-axis, 1–9)

Your life evaluation:
Fill in your age and levels of experienced and anticipated satisfaction.

Life

Age (x-axis, 0–90)

will be more likely to change positively. However, all opportunities do not necessarily work out well. That means taking risks. If you are excessively cautious, you will not try out new beliefs and ways of acting.

In the opening vignette, Peter had been excessively tied to his high school identity and less able to change to fit his new situation. His trying out of new behaviors arose from Cindi's feedback. The more we can elicit feedback from others we value, the more likely we will be to adapt and to put our ideas into action. It is not enough to just think about how to be or what the world is like. It is necessary to try out new ways of behaving and to test newly forming ideas about our personal worlds.

Into Early Adulthood

You are only young once, but once is enough if you work it right.

(Nixon, 1962, p. xiii)

For most people, the transitions from one phase in their lives to another are vitally important. Ask individuals to look back on their pasts and describe significant events. They do not talk about the stable periods. Rather, they describe as most meaningful the points at which they were leaving one life stage and entering a new one. They talk about dating their first girlfriend or boyfriend, moving to a new school, leaving home, entering college, getting married, beginning the first job. The periods of time spent engaged in these activities typically are less memorable than the time of transition into them.

One intriguing element of transitions is the attitude of the persons involved. Consider the transition from adolescence to young adulthood. Extolling the virtues of being a teenager, and looking with disgust and rejection at both childhood and adulthood, the typical adolescent (even the unhappy adolescent) feels there is no better age to be. Transition to adulthood? Necessary? Yes. Desirable? Hardly! Adults see their current lives this way, too. They say they would never want to live through childhood and adolescence again (Rogers, 1979). A cartoon by Kliban (1976) captures this view. It shows an elderly, wrinkled man on a cane saying of childhood, "It was hell." Hell or not, we all pass through it, and one of the clearest breaks we make from childhood and adolescence is going out of the family and into the world.

Why is moving out of the parental home a key point in the individual's life? Although many other acts of independence are possible, this one offers a major opportunity for freedom and growing up (Nixon, 1962). The physical separation helps. Being out of the house means less chance for both parental surveillance and parental nurturance. For some, going back home after living away brings a sudden, unexpected rush of past dependence and prior ways of relating. When I was staying at my mother's house to attend my twentieth high school reunion and came home late, my mother was waiting angry and worried. She loudly explained that she had been worried to death, ready to call the police and hospitals, and she asked why hadn't I been considerate enough to phone and tell her I would be late. The scene was exactly the same as ones we had gone through twenty years earlier. Well, almost. In this case, I suggested we have a cup of tea and that I tell her about the evening. She accepted.

The stage of leaving the parental home calls for a new relationship with parents, coming to see them as they actually are—not just as *they* think they are or seem to be. At its best, it involves feeling warmth toward parents while moving to be independent of them. As Nixon has observed, "It is not a simple, quick and relatively painless cutting of the silver cord" (1962, p. 17). Instead, it is a complex and drawn out process, perhaps calling for painful trial and error efforts to achieve separation with goodwill. And it starts in adolescence.

Identity conflict

Erikson (1982) holds that the task of the adolescence stage is to master one's identity. The familiar term **identity conflict** grew out of Erikson's work, for he described the fundamental concern at this stage as being the clearing up of the confusion of identity. Adolescents struggle to understand who and what they are, apart from being their parents' children. They learn to have a personal, distinct identity. The identity comes from being part of a group and forming close friendships. Every Erikson-identified stage leads to a strength, and the identity conflict stage leaves the adolescent with a sense of *fidelity*, the loyal and free commitment to important peers.

Faithfulness and loyalty are seen in the cohesive and sometimes joyous social groups formed during this age. Backbiting or violating confidences within the social group are among the most negative possible acts for the adolescent.

Young adulthood follows adolescence, and the individual's basic task at this stage is to resolve the need for intimacy. Commitment and deep attachment are sought, and ideas about marriage are formulated. The hazard of this stage is that of isolation, in which fear or bad experiences promote a hands-off attitude and others are kept at a distance. When the early adulthood stage is successfully resolved, the strength that is gained is *love*, the ability to truly move to intimate connections and partnerships.

The beginning aspects of young adulthood have been noted to include *pulling up roots*. Part of sending down new roots is adapting to a new living environment: finding a place to live and making it a comfortable and personal place to be. For many people between the ages of seventeen and twenty-two, this new place is college.

A classic study of the effects of college on emotional growth is Douglas Heath's book, *Growing Up in College* (1968). Heath asked, does college actually change people? He made comprehensive investigations of students at Haverford, a small liberal arts college, beginning with their first term of school. By the end of their freshman year and again by the end of their senior year, clear effects had appeared in twenty areas of personality change. The greatest change was in the students' ability to reflect on their experiences and to represent experiences symbolically. One student commented about his reflections on himself.

> I think I've changed quite a bit here. I can truthfully say I wasn't aware. This is one of the things I can say that Haverford has done for me the most. It made me look beyond the ways things are, to look behind them.

(Heath, 1968, p. 124)

The second most common change was more personal. The students developed more awareness and understanding of themselves, especially in relation to others. This personal insight was accompanied by less self-centeredness and more attention to others. Two students indicated this change as follows:

> I don't think I was aware before of the different levels you can take people on, you must take people on: how serious you have to be with them, how much of yourself you divulge to them; how much you go out of your way to adjust to them . . .

(Heath, 1968, p. 128)

> Haverford has had a broadening effect. I can see people's points of view. I can see things in the light of what I feel; I can analyze them both ways.

(Heath, 1968, p. 129)

The seniors were emotionally more stable than the freshmen. Of course, the college experience itself was occurring simultaneously with growing older and growing up, so that assuming college caused the stability is risky. Nevertheless, at this time in their lives, the students did develop better symbolic ways of looking at experience, did understand themselves better, and did grow more stable. These occurrences are not unique to Haverford students. Good reasons exist to believe that such growth and stability are frequent outcomes of all students' college years.

Into the Middle Years

Why do some men at age forty buy convertibles, wear gold chains, chase teenage girls, and fanatically exercise, while other men at age forty smoothly and uneventfully continue their existing lives? Why do some forty-year-old women despair or grow restless, and, yes, buy convertibles, wear clothing suited to eighteen-year-olds, chase teenage boys, and fanatically exercise, while other forty-year-old women show no such dramatic transformations? The answer appears to be that, for some adults passing

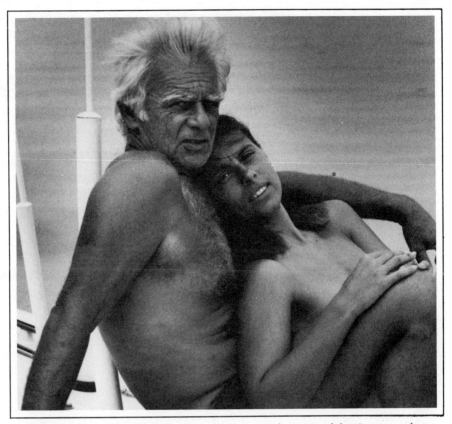

Being identified as a middle-aged person can be scary for some adults. Some people pass through this critical life phase smoothly. Others may try to cope by dressing like a teenager, fanatically exercising, or dating people much younger than themselves.

through critical life phases, the transition is threatening and problematic. The newly acquired identity, as a middle-aged person or as a preretirement adult or a parent without children at home, can be scary.

Potentially unpleasant though they may be, such transitions are not always difficult. Indeed, some people hardly know they occur. No earthquake has shaken their lives. Perhaps they have felt a passing shiver, and not much more. People with secure inner strength and warm support from others pass through such transitions most easily (Golan, 1981). That's not surprising, after all, since secure people with healthy support systems weather all crises best.

Four influences seem to help us pass successfully through these, and indeed all, adult transitions. Let us examine these influences.

1. *Gradual changes.*   The successful transition moves smoothly and barely perceptibly from one phase to another. The abrupt feeling of being jarred loose from a stage is disruptive and less likely to be associated with a positive and successful transition.

Expectations and actual physical changes are key elements in a transition. When changes are expected to be major, the expectation makes them so. Thinking that it is catastrophic to be forty (or fifty or sixty) years old helps make it so. Thinking little of it means little comes of it.

Actual physical changes influence continuity. If a person looks and feels at fifty much as he or she felt and looked at forty-five, he or she may feel the change into a new decade is minor. However, if the person's joints ache badly, his or her endurance has clearly diminished, and, in the morning mirror, his or her jowls appear to hang suddenly to the collarbone, then the transition may be harder for that person.

2. *Anticipation.*   The opportunity to think about oneself at a different stage often helps. Preparing for retirement, for example, by starting to

THE EMPTY NEST

Empty nest

During the past one hundred years, people have begun to live longer, and grown children rarely live in their parents' home. These changes have created the **empty nest** in American homes. The empty nest describes the home in which the last child has married or otherwise left home, and where the mother is alone with the father, without the task of child rearing. Such empty nests shared by a couple were rare in the 1880s, when, on the average, widowhood occurred within two years of the last child's leaving to work or to get married. In contrast, at least an eleven-year gap presently exists. The wife is usually portrayed as suffering loneliness and depression from the empty nest syndrome. However, this life transition is not always negative. The last child leaving may either be a "demoralizing reminder that their mothering role is no longer needed" or be "an elating liberation" (Treas & Bengtson, 1982).

Some mothers anticipate and handle the transition from parenthood to postparenthood in a matter-of-fact way, so that it makes little difference in their lives. For the women who are primarily invested in being a mother, the empty nest can be powerfully depressing (Golan, 1981). However, the majority of women are emotionally invested in husbands, community activities, friends, or work as well as their children, and their emotional lives are far from empty when the last child leaves. Indeed, the average mother does not show significant psychological problems when that youngest child departs. While they feel some pain, it typically is mixed with a decided sense of relief. "At last," many mothers exclaim, "I can live my own life again!"

think about travel and hobbies three years in advance makes retirement more comfortable. Anticipation of negative events is destructive. The man turning forty-five who feels he will be undesirable without his prior endurance and his prior full head of hair will have a difficult time. A positive anticipation of continuing (or developing) satisfaction aids the transition.

3. *Inner resources.* People who are good at relying on themselves in most stressful challenges tend to be good at handling transitions as well. A general factor of coping competence seems to exist, in which good coping skills master most of life's challenges.

4. *Assistance from others.* For those who cannot cope easily, successful transitions can be achieved with the help of others. Family members, friends, and professional help can aid in the transitional adjustment. Such aid can take the form of reassurance or assistance with the specific tasks and problems that are being faced (Golan, 1981). When a friend or relative is undergoing a transition, reassurance is almost always in order. Everyone needs comfort and needs to know that caring friends and family are there and still value them. Furthermore, when desired job opportunities fade out of reach, or when children move away, friends and family can help to combat the person's feelings of worthlessness and loneliness.

Into Later Adulthood: Adventure and Growth in the Later Years

My memory is failing.

It takes me all day to do what I used to do all day.

There's not much to live for.

When I was young, I was really something!

Sad and nostalgic statements by older men and women produce an image of the later years as a depressing period of diminishing abilities and wistful envying of the young. This time has been described as a disengagement process, in which there is an increasing isolation from friends and social interchanges (Cumming & Henry, 1979). Participation in work and family roles lessens due to retirement and deaths. Fewer people are available with whom the older person can interact, and the person disengages from others. For some older people, this scenario accurately describes their feelings about their lives. Yet millions of older adults lead lives full of satisfactions and adventure. Let us look now at the process of making successful transitions in later years and the paths that lead to happy and engaging resolutions.

For John McLeish (1976), the means of a successful transition into

Growing older doesn't have to be a depressing time of mourning lost abilities and envying the young. Millions of adults make a successful transition into this later life phase, filling their lives with excitement and adventure.

Ulyssean

the later years is to take a *Ulyssean* approach. The term is taken from Ulysses, the searcher-hero of Greek literature who confronted fate with grand adventures well into his seventies. Tennyson described Ulysses' call to adventure.

> Come, my friends,
> 'Tis not too late to seek a newer world.
> Push off, and sitting well in order smite
> The sounding furrows; for my purpose holds
> To sail beyond the sunset, and the baths
> Of all the western stars, until I die.

(Tennyson, 1872, p. 82)

Not all older adults have to venture forth on new and creative adventures to enliven their existence. The other choice is to remain productive and creative within the familiar arenas of work, home, and friendships. What is called for is "Openness of mind, sensitivity to the need for new ways and new experiences; resourcefulness; courage, curiosity and a continuing sense of wonder at the kaleidoscopic beauty and mystery of the world" (McLeish, 1976, p. 31). In order to pursue these goals, some specific actions may be taken.

1. Instead of fretting about how little time is left, appreciate the great amount of available relaxed time. Appointments and deadlines no longer need to direct your life. Free time means freedom to choose the most enjoyable ways to spend a day.

2. Look to sharpen your senses, and see, hear, feel, enjoy the array of fascinating things all around you. When artists and writers have trouble painting or writing, they often are instructed to look carefully at the world and people around them. Amazement and delight frequently follow their discovery of previously unseen aspects of daily life.

3. Stimulate creativity, ruling nothing out, and accept the fanciful, capricious, and impulsive in yourself. An adult life of social conformity may be relaxed in the later years, and the childlike, playful parts of yourself may be allowed to reemerge.

4. Adventure into new spiritual and occupational possibilities. Excitement and new meaning may be found in new careers as well as in spiritual journeys.

5. Use a personal journal to develop your insight and creativity. The daily diary has long been a traditional way to record emotions and personal events. Consider it useful as a source of stimulation, self-discipline, and self-awareness.

6. Become passionately committed to social causes. Create change. Believing deeply in and working for a purpose is rejuvenating.

7. Study a new language and visit a new culture. Exposure to new surroundings and new ways of learning contradict the thought that later life is a dead end and instead invest it with a sense of growth and wisdom. Elder hostels, which are short-term residential college programs for adults over age fifty-five, offer one way to experience this positive feeling.

8. Use a dictionary to build your vocabulary and break out of the confines of the vocabulary of the developmental years. Considerable satisfaction arises from mastering new words and expressing yourself more articulately.

Taking all of these actions may not be possible for every peson. Yet the suggestions show the range of creative options available. The difference between an unsuccessful transition and a successful transition into later adulthood is the difference between slowly disengaging into an isolated and sad life and actively making later life an adventure.

DEATH AND DYING: THE FINAL TRANSITION

Down, down, down, into the darkness of the grave,
Gently they go, the beautiful, the tender, the kind;
Quietly they go, the intelligent, the witty, the brave.
I know. But I do not approve. And I am not resigned.

(Edna St. Vincent Millay, 1968, p. 148)

TIME PERSPECTIVES

The old man's eyes gleam as he leans a little too close and begins to reminisce. "Let me tell you, youngster," he starts, "when I grew up things were very, very, very different. We had values! We believed in things. Important things. Bread cost five cents. And that was real bread, not cardboard. No one ever drove me to school. I walked. Then I worked after school. You don't know how easy you have it."

The popular image of older people living in the past has been studied and found to be at least partially true. Older people whose lives are wrapped up in thoughts about their past experiences tend to be those with less meaningful present and future activities. It is discouraging to have little to look forward to. Thus, older men and women who feel glum and without interesting future prospects tend especially to think and talk about past life events. For them, the present time passes slowly (Hendricks & Hendricks, 1977).

However, some reminiscing helps people to adjust to their current circumstances, allowing individuals to feel better, to cope with their anxieties about aging and death, and to see their lives in perspective. Some centers for senior citizens conduct regular programs of *reminiscence therapy*, which goes beyond simple restatement of the past. This therapy seeks to allow individuals to view the triumphs and tragedies of their lives from some overall perspective, so that they can reach Erickson's stage of ego integrity. If people can see a worthwhile pattern in their lives, then they are less susceptible to despair, to feeling that they have wasted their lives.

One additional reason older adults spend time looking back is that their present day activities often seem trivial. Younger people have many more turning points, important events, and frustrations in their lives than do older people. Of the 216 adults in the Lowenthal and colleagues (1975) study, almost all the high school students reported having had major turning points and frustrations in the

Reminiscence therapy

Awareness of our mortality is at the core of the midlife and later life crises. The body doesn't work quite as well as it used to. Minor ailments become prominent. Endurance diminishes. Friends become ill. Parents die. We pay attention to the knowledge that we will die and that we are moving closer to death. Sheehy puts it well: "The thought of death is too terrifying to confront head on, and so it keeps coming back in disguise: as pitching airplanes, swaying floors, precarious balconies, lovers' quarrels, mysterious backfires in our physical equipment" (1976, p. 9).

Today, death concerns are predictable crises and anticipated as part of the life cycle. However, it has not always been so. Our study of death and dying begins with a look back in time.

last five years. Under one-third of the preretirement men and women reported such events.

Percentage Reporting Turning Points in the Previous Five Years		
High school:	Men	96
	Women	77
Newlyweds:	Men	72
	Women	92
Middle-aged:	Men	27
	Women	35
Preretirement:	Men	25
	Women	14

Adapted from Lowenthal, Thurnher, Chiribuga & Associates, 1975.

These results were part of a wider pattern. Older adults were less involved with the important and interesting things they saw occurring in their lives. Younger and older adults alike felt that young adulthood was the most changeable and busiest time of their lives. Young adults, and particularly those in their twenties, saw their current period of life as the happiest. More young adults feel this way than do middle-aged and older adults. Approximately 60 percent of young adults reported holding this viewpoint; in contrast, only about a third of middle-aged and preretirement adults reported it. Almost everyone agreed that adolescence and old age were the unhappiest times. One more interesting finding reported an agecentric effect, in which the present age was viewed as especially favorable. Adjustment, then, is related to time perspectives. The more older people have a future orientation and plan ahead in their lives, the more satisfaction and happiness they feel (Lowenthal et al., 1975).

Dying Then and Now

For those of us who think of most natural deaths as occurring in hospital rooms, with hushed atmospheres, fearful anticipation, and whispered condolences, it may be startling to look back a few hundred years and see earlier attitudes toward death. Attitudes toward death were almost matter-

DEATH AND THE CELEBRATION OF LIFE

The occasion of the death of a family member can be handled in many ways. The family of teacher-musician Hugh Gunderson of Toledo, Ohio, made the Memorial Service following his death in April, 1983, into a celebration of his life. His wife wrote about it to family and friends.

> As you probably know, Hugh passed away at home during the night last Friday. While this past week has been difficult in many ways for all of us, we have also spent many hours talking about the richness of his life and of the family life we have shared together . . .

The death of a loved one often is followed by a very difficult time of grieving. This grief is usually mixed with happy memories of the person and his or her life accomplishments. Reminiscing in this way enables us to celebrate life.

of-fact. One historian has described it as ". . . the familiar resignation to the collective destiny of the species," the acceptance that "we shall all die" (Aries, 1974, p. 55). Most people tended to die calmly, simply, comprehending that their time had come.

By the fourteenth century, ritual and ceremony had developed and consisted of gatherings of family, children, and friends, as well as clergy

The memorial service on Monday was beautiful and inspiring. The children planned and participated in the service, and the mood was one of celebration of life. It was a gorgeous sunny day, and through the glass wall we could view beds of brilliant red tulips and hyacinths. In the room, the children displayed some of Hugh's favorite art works, flower arrangements, family photographs and his poetry.

The room was packed, with people standing around the sides, back, and crowding into the lobby—several times more people than we had expected. Once again, we felt the marvelous bond of love that Hugh had established with such a rich cross-section of people. Hugh's life was devoted to the discovery and preservation of beauty in all of nature and the arts: by enlivening those sensitivities in each of us, he lives on forever.

(Lorene Gunderson, personal communication, 1983)

The death itself often is kept antiseptic, quiet, dehumanized, and impersonal, the dead body whisked out of sight (Aries, 1974). Yet a trend is reemerging today, allowing people to die out of hospitals, sometimes at home and sometimes in hospice care, programs designed to support and deal with death and dying.

Humor serves to demystify death and release tensions. The "Mary Tyler Moore" television show about the funeral service for Chuckles the Clown has become an often-viewed classic because of Mary Tyler Moore's uncontrollable laughter during the memorial service, while Chuckles was being eulogized.

One person who did not know what he would want said about himself at a memorial service considered the message he would want left on his answering machine.

Hello. This is Don Becker speaking to you on tape. I can't come to the phone just now because I am dead. I do want to leave some messages. To my friends [naming some of them] I owe so much of the happiness of life. If you were one of my students, you provided me with much of the meaning of my life. If you're a member of the Suzuki Association of Massachusetts, please renew your membership without waiting for several notices from the person who takes over my position. And if you're a creditor, I want you to know the check's in the mail.

(Kari Gunderson, personal communication, 1983)

to bring the dying person to peace with the church. The dying person was the center of all activity. Still, the end of life was accepted and that helped the survivors to accept the loss of a loved one.

Anticipatory mourning

In the past two centuries, an increasingly dramatic view of death has arisen. **_Anticipatory mourning_** has evolved (Paul, 1986). People no longer die in the home, as they had for centuries. It is inconvenient. Instead, they go to die in a hospital, where they have a minor role in the domain of physicians and nurses. The dying person often is seen as a sign of failure, because the medical staff, trained and taught to heal, cannot save him or her. Increasingly advanced technology, which extends life beyond consciousness or desire, also reinforces the denial of death.

Reactions to Dying

Elisabeth Kubler-Ross has been one of the pioneers in writing about the psychological reactions to dying. In her 1969 book, *On Death and Dying,* she described five stages that two hundred dying patients went through. Later, she observed that these stages could occur in any order. Let us look at these reactions to dying.

Denial and isolation

Almost all of the patients, when told they had a terminal ailment, reacted with disbelief and unwillingness to accept the medical findings. This denial took the form of "No, not me," and was often followed by requests for more tests, shopping around for other doctors, and an avoidance of facing the prognosis. Denial is a normal reaction, particularly when the illness is first discovered. Later on, patients tend to isolate their feelings from the ongoing events, essentially engaging in a more sophisticated form of denial. One patient actively engaged in denial was "inappropriately cheerful, laughed and giggled, and reassured us that she was completely well" (Kubler-Ross, 1969, p. 39).

Anger

A patient may angrily demand "Why me?" Rage and fury appear at fate, at family and physicians, and at other people. The anger is usually (but not always) irrational. Other people are blamed for minor problems, and episodes of pouting may alternate with temper outbursts and expressions of resentment. The anger may be mixed with indignation as the person fumes "it's wrong this should happen to me, and it's especially wrong that it should happen at this time in my life."

Bargaining

In the movie *The End*, Burt Reynolds plays a dying man who swims out into the ocean as far as he can to speed up his forthcoming death. After he changes his mind, Reynolds, exhausted, swims back to shore making a promise to God about the extent to which he will contribute a share of his income to charity if he is permitted to live. Such bargaining typically offers God various kinds of good behaviors in exchange for living longer or without illness. These "negotiations" are rarely public, usually made either alone or with a minister.

Depression

Two kinds of depression appear. The first is a reactive sadness to the loss of abilities, appearance, and capacity to work or function. A second form of depression comes in preparation for death. This depression anticipates the children without their parent, considers the hopeless future for the ill person, and expresses sorrow about the progression of the illness.

Acceptance

When patients truly realize they are dying and have coped with some or all of the other stages of dying, they may be able to accept their present state and impending death. In order to reach such acceptance, patients need to have time to prepare and to receive considerable support from those around them. The anger will have been expressed. The denial will have dissipated. The mourning and depression and bargaining will have been exhausted. "Acceptance should not be mistaken for a happy stage. It is almost void of feelings. It is as if the pain had gone, the struggle is over, and there comes a time for 'the final rest before the long journey' as one patient phrased it" (Kubler-Ross, 1969, p. 100).

Phases, not stages

Although Kubler-Ross at first considered these reactions to dying as orderly, universal stages, she later revised her theory. Now Kubler-Ross and most other observers see these reactions to dying as phases that patients drift into and out of, in no certain order. Several phases may coexist at the same time, some being mild and others intense. Rather than passing systematically through stages, people experience most of these reactions at some time or other. Understanding the phases is useful, however, for it helps to explain behaviors that seem otherwise inexplicable to friends and family members.

Is Death a Life Crisis?

The provocative question, "Is death a life crisis?," was posed by Robert Kastenbaum (1975), who answered, "not necessarily." Kastenbaum is a **thanatologist,** a term that arises from the Greek words *thanos,* meaning death, and *logos,* meaning the study of something. He declares that individuals attribute many meanings to death and that it is by no means an automatic life crisis. After all, death is a certainty, and some deaths hardly produce a shudder. Some people approach death with serenity and without fear. Others see death as a preferred solution to intolerable problems.

The same forces that shape personality and adjustment throughout life are at work as death nears. People die the way they have lived. Dying may be traumatic and a crisis, if, for example, a terminal illness is mismanaged or important tasks are left undone. However, Kastenbaum believes this is not the characteristic pattern: "Most people do not just fall apart as death approaches" (1975, p. 48).

One more answer can be given to the question of why death should be awaited with peaceful acceptance by some and with fierce despair by others. It is because death has so many different meanings. To some,

Thanatologist

EXPLORATION IN WELL-BEING

Practice Dying

Have the room comfortable dark or dimly lighted.

Lie down on your bed or sofa or on the floor.

Let your body go. Imagine that the life is out of it. Do not speak or move.

Imagine that you have died: Your body is passive, lifeless, useless. Your body is discarded. Your funeral is about to take place.

Let go of your body. Let it be there as something which is no longer yours. Follow to the limit this feeling of being completely alone, abandoned, not loved—not in life, not in death. Cry, scream, curse, if this is what you feel. Go to the limit of your feeling. And after you have cried and screamed and cursed, when you are empty and exhausted, stop and listen.

This is your last party. Speak to everyone there, tell them all about yourself, about your mistakes and your suffering, about your love and your longings. No longer do you need to protect yourself, no longer do you need to hide behind a wall or a suit of armor. It is your last party: you can explode, you can be miserable or pitiful, insignificant or despicable. At your funeral you can be yourself.

death is a trigger, a stimulus that produces predictable responses. Death may be understood as an event, a process that may be a dramatic display or the quiet eye closing of beautiful actresses in movies. How the state of death is approached affects the actual process of dying.

Toward a Better Death

Some ways of dying are better than others. At some time, all of us have to adjust to the deaths of others and to our own approaching deaths (Calhoun, Abernathy & Selby, 1986). We know the characteristics of people who are capable of better deaths. These people appear to have a sense of a life well lived, of having accomplished much of what they wanted to do during their lives. They have become the kinds of persons they wished to become. They are able to look back on their lives with satisfaction. A sense of peace is with them; they are in the Kubler-Ross stage of acceptance. When faced with a life-threatening illness, they can die in many ways.

> One can rage into the night (as the poet Dylan Thomas would have it); go like a good child to bed; view the entire process as a new experience as

This is your chance: do what others have failed to do. Look at the unloved one, the miserable one. This is your chance to do an act of love toward one who has had no love. This is your chance to do justice where intentional or unintentional injustice has been committed. This is your chance to give warmth and courage to one who feels only coldness, loneliness and death.

Let your tears flow from the very depth of you. Let your bitterness flow out with them. And when the bitterness is out, your tears will be gentle and sweet. Then take the hand of this lifeless body of yours, take it in your hands and with respect and love bring it to your lips and kiss it.

Now gently come back to your living body.

With this feeling of respect and love, come back to your living body, and let this feeling remain with you, inside of you. Let it spread to each nerve, to each muscle, along every vein and artery. Let this feeling of respect and love spread out around you in everything, object or animal or human, that is part of your life. Feel this feeling of love and respect circulating inside you with the force of life itself; let it be in your blood, in the air you breathe. Feel it—accept it—give it.

(Huxley, 1963, p. 131)

though one were an interested observer—after all, you have never died before; be fearful and quake in uncontrollable ways that exasperate one; be regretful and rueful, almost nostalgic; be contemplative and somewhat resigned. There is sweet surrender ("Come sweet death") and resignation, and there is terrorized capitulation.

(Shneidman, 1980, p. 184)

No such thing as a best death exists for everybody. We all bring different backgrounds and beliefs to dying, as we do to all other experiences (McDonald & Hilgendorf, 1986). However, some elements do help. Warmth and emotional support from loved ones help. Meditation may aid people to achieve serenity about dying (Boerstler, 1986). Having opportunities to talk openly about their terminal illnesses, as opposed to considering it (or having it considered) a source of shame to be concealed, helps people. Dying at home or with hospice care, as opposed to dying in a hospital, may help. Having the opportunity to put business and personal affairs in order helps, because it allows people to feel a sense of closure to and accomplishment in their lives.

These aids may not make dying a positive event. Pain and fears usually are present. Nevertheless, their attitudes toward dying do profoundly influence the experience of the dying persons and their families. If a good death cannot always be achieved, at least a better death can sometimes be sought.

Well-being in death, dying and other transitions is listed in Table 7–1 along with those behaviors that reflect movement away from well-being in transitions.

A SWEET DEATH

As Roshi Taji, a contemporary Zen master, approached death, his senior disciples assembled at his bedside. One of them, remembering the Roshi was fond of a certain kind of cake, had spent half a day searching the pastry shops of Tokyo for this confection, which he now presented to Roshi Taji. With a wan smile the dying Roshi accepted a piece of the cake and slowly began munching it. As the Roshi grew weaker, his disciples leaned close and inquired whether he had any final words for them.

"Yes," the Roshi replied.

The disciples leaned forward eagerly. Please tell us!

"My, but this cake is delicious!" And with that he died.

(Kapleau, 1971, p. 67)

TABLE 7-1 Well-Being in Transitions and the Life Cycle	
Toward Well-Being	**Away from Well-Being**
Anticipates adult life transitions	Adult transitions are surprises
Common adult transitions pass gradually in a supportive environment	Abrupt, solitary transitions
Autonomy and commitments in early adult life transitions	Dependence and alienation in early adult transitions
Midlife renewal	Midlife resignation
Transitions experience as teachable moments	Experiences transitions as retrenching
Excitement about life in the later years	Despair in the later years
Acceptance in approaching death	Bitterness in approaching death

SUMMARY

Peter Pan aside (he proclaimed he would never grow up), the rest of us are faced with transitions in our life. Erik Erikson (1950, 1968, 1982) was the first person to present a systematic ordering of life's stages and transitions. The Erikson stages of adulthood and the works of Daniel Levinson (1978, 1986, 1987) and others investigated the stages of life.

In early adulthood, people pull up roots and leave their families and homes in a move toward independence. In the "trying twenties," people experiment with life and take risks, while searching for real intimacy. An age thirty transition follows, in which people experience some uneasiness and reconsider their life choices.

In the midlife transition to the second half of life, people either renew themselves or become resigned to being stuck where they are. In transitions at age fifty, at ages fifty to sixty, and finally into late adulthood, people optimally experience some stabilization of life, feel a sense of achievement, and wrap up midlife tasks.

There exists a teeth-bared disagreement about whether these life stages are universally experienced. Although Levinson's data support this view, Marjorie Fiske Lowenthal (1975) concludes that the stages are widespread but not universal. Leonard Pearlin (1982) concluded that the life stages existed more in the minds of researchers than in the lives of people in general. Longitudinal research studies support a midway point; such things exist, but not clearly for everyone.

There are constructive means for dealing with life transitions. To begin with, we should consider transitions to be teachable moments, opportunities to grow from life space changes and to reexamine assumptions about our world. In early adulthood, a constructive approach to transition may help us to become independent, while still maintaining a warm relationship with our parents. In the middle years, making gradual changes, anticipating what will happen, and drawing on our inner resources and others' assistance all help smooth transitional periods. In the later years, a Ulyssean approach—a journey of creativity, adventure, new learning, and appreciation of what is positive—is constructive.

Dying is the final transition of life. Kubler-Ross has suggested that five phases of dying can be identified: Denial and isolation, anger, bargaining, depression, and acceptance. Yet impending death is not always a life crisis. While some people approach despair, others approach it with a serene peace. The dying person can be helped to a better death with social support and warmth and by having the opportunity to get his or her life's business in order.

Key Terms

Anticipatory mourning	**Isolation**
Assumptive world	**Life events**
Autonomy versus shame and doubt	**Life space**
Basic trust versus distrust	**Mentors**
De-illusionment	**Predictable transitions**
Despair	**Reminiscence therapy**
Ego integrity	**Renewal or resignation**
Empty nest	**Stagnation**
Generativity	**Teachable moment**
Identity conflict	**Thanatologist**
Identity versus role diffusion	**Transitions**
Industry versus inferiority	**Ulyssean**
Initiative versus guilt	**Unexpected events**
Intimacy	

Recommended Reading

Erikson, E. (1950). *Childhood and society*. New York: Norton. This is the book that started the motor of professional attention racing toward adulthood stages. It's an oldie but goodie, and it is still a basic source book.

Levinson, D.J., Darrow, C.N., Klein, E.B., Levinson, M.H. & McKee, B. (1978). *The seasons of a man's life*. New York: Alfred A. Knopf. *Also* Sheehy, G. (1976). *Passages: Predictable crises of adult life*. New York: E.P. Dutton. My friends tell me that I shouldn't recommend Gail Sheehy's book *Passages* because she stole all her ideas from Levinson and made a fortune from them. Sounds like a soap opera, doesn't it? In any case, I'm not privy to any such inside information and cannot vouch for who did what. The Sheehy book is more chatty, emotional, and informal. The Levinson book is more scholarly, dispassionate, and formal. Both are recommended.

PART III

Adjustment and Well-Being with Others

Interpersonal Relationships

•

Nonverbal Communication

•

Loving and Being Loved

•

Sexual Adjustment

8

CHAPTER

Interpersonal Relationships

"I've got to confess something before we go ahead with this," she told me uncomfortably. "I hadn't thought I would say anything, but you are entitled to know."

Oh, dear. Drat. What's going to be coming out? Has she been seeing someone else all this time? Disease? Oh, Lord, please don't let it be herpes. Has she gotten it on with lots of other men? Is there something about me that is terrible? I can't stand confessions. I steeled myself and, appearing fully composed, told her, "No, love. You don't have to tell me anything. It isn't necessary. Really. Truly."

She squeezed her hands together, like she was wringing water out of them.

"I have to. Please," she pleaded.

Sometimes you don't have any choice; you have to let things happen. I told her to go ahead. I moved a little closer.

"You remember our first date?" she asked. Sure I did.

She explained that she had been unhappy at that time. It seemed hardly anyone asked her out twice. She didn't know why for certain, but she said it just hadn't felt good to be with guys on dates. Then, when I asked her out, she was in the sales workshop.

She said, "The teacher had just told us that no one actually listens much to anyone else. They are too busy trying to think of what they are going to say next. Or they are trying to impress the other person. Or they listen only to be beginning of what the person says."

The hesitancy in her voice had passed now and in its place was urgency.

"For four hours that day, we had been taught how to listen to our clients. We had been taught especially how to shut up and say just enough to make the client think and feel that we were totally interested in him, that he was the most important person in the

world to us. We had class demonstrations. We practiced with partners. Then, that night, you and I went out."

I told her I remembered. It was a wonderful time.

She hesitated again, and looked down at her lap. She finally went on.

"You were my practice subject that night. I mean, I was trying out all the sales listening stuff. I was feeding you all the smiles, nods, laughs, and listening techniques I had just learned. You were my guinea pig.

"At the end of the evening, when you told me what a great conversationalist I was, I was embarrassed and full of remorse. I hardly said two dozen things all night. Instead, I kept pretending you were the most important person in the whole world to me and that everything you said was fascinating and that I wanted to know much more about it. Since then, I have come to love you and enjoy you. But I had to tell you what I had done. Are you mad?"

"Am I mad, you want to know? Am I mad to find that the evening that changed my life was a sham? I'm not mad. I'm furious! You liar! You cheat! You phony! One thing I know for sure is I don't want to marry anyone like you. Let's call the whole thing off. I can't believe it. I just cannot believe it."

It's a good thing she did tell me. Otherwise I might have messed up my whole life.

Ending two.

"Am I mad, you want to know? Am I mad to find out that the evening that changed my life was an experiment? I'm not mad. How could I be? You were you that night, and I have come to know you better than anyone in my life. Thanks for telling me. Now let's get over to the rehearsal. We don't want to keep the minister waiting."

Ending three.
"Am I mad? How could I be? You see, I had attended a course that same day. . ."

Ending four.
"Am I mad? How could I be? Still, I would like to ask you about taking back that set of encyclopedias . . ."

Listening to each other is vital in good relationships. The good listener in our story established a caring contact with the other person and came to truly understand him in the nicest ways. The four endings to the interchange reflect possible ways the person could react in the given situation. Depending on the person, he could be outraged, delighted, indifferent, or saddened. This chapter explores the variety and nature of human relationships in general; love, sexual, work, and psychotherapy relationships will be considered in separate chapters.

The desire for human companionship is universal. Even crusty Henry David Thoreau, who went to live alone by Walden Pond, away from the quiet desperations and hindrances of others, acknowledged this need.

> I think that I love society as much as most, and am ready enough to fasten myself like a bloodsucker for the time to any full-blooded man that comes in my way.
>
> *(Thoreau, 1942, p. 97)*

We begin by discussing friendship relationships, by asking questions such as, Who becomes friends with whom? How do friendships among men and women vary? From there, we turn to the problems that arise in friendships and other relationships. The difficulties of loneliness and the deceits of Machiavellianism are explored. Finally, we look at the ways in which better listening, communicating, and cooperation can improve our relations with others. (The "great conversationalist" in our opening story used these latter techniques.)

FRIENDSHIPS

> There is an electricity about friendship relationships; they are like no other. Though we might not be able to choose our neighbors, relatives or the people with whom we work, friendships are an act of pure intention. Very few associations allow for such a free exchange of loyalty, trust, affection and, sometimes, doubt, hurt, and anger.
>
> *(Block, 1980, p. 5)*

Friendships

A real friend is a person central to our lives. Of all our relationships, ***friendships,*** family relationships, and love relationships have the deepest bonds of caring. Defining friendship may seem like an exercise in the obvious. Everyone knows or at least has an opinion on what a true friend is. There seem to be three identifiable characteristics that most people associate with friendships: they are very close, they are voluntary, and they are relatively enduring (Bell, 1981).

Friendships are very close.   A friend is invited to know us as we genuinely are, to see our private selves without the guises and pretenses of the public self. We feel close to friends and attached to them. We trust them.

Friendships are voluntary.   No social, family, or occupational rules dictate who we select or who selects us as friends. We freely choose friends. We freely choose when to terminate a friendship.

Some of our friendships last for much of our lives. These long-term attachments involve a combination of mutual trust, caring, honesty, and shared intimacies.

Friendships are relatively enduring. Some friendships last for much of our lives. By definition, friendship is the acceptance of a long-term caring and personal attachment, which goes beyond any particular situation in which we may temporarily find ourselves.

Friendship is based on trust and a valuing of the other's basic worth. Robert Bell has observed of friends, "they are never treated as instrumental means for achieving some private end by either party. One does not 'use' a friend" (1981, p. 13).

Not everyone is a suitable choice for a friend. We choose friends who are much like ourselves. Our friends tend to be about the same as us in terms of socioeconomic and demographic characteristics, to be of similar marital status, and to be of the same sex. Although not all friendships fit into this typical pattern, many do. Most people, but not everyone, have from one to five close friends. Approximately 25 percent of respondents in a *Psychology Today* survey reported having no friends (Parlee, 1979).

Being a friend is more than being open with another person and trusting that person. The mutual opening up about sensitive, personal matters leaves each friend potentially vulnerable. Tender aspects of one's feelings become exposed, and that requires a friend to be protective and to guard against irritating the sensitive area. Thus, in every friendship a balance must be achieved between candor, honest expression, and sharing on the one hand, and restraint from using such personal information to hurt a friend on the other. The process of **selective protectiveness** identifies and avoids overly touchy subjects, except by invitation. This protectiveness fosters the development of more sharing and closeness (Rawlins, 1983).

Selective protectiveness

Much of what we know about friendships derives from two major studies. In one investigation, Bell (1981) interviewed 101 women and 65 men for an average of two hours, asking about their views on and

LIKING AND FRIENDSHIP: SEVEN PRINCIPLES

1. We like those who like us.

2. We like those whose attitudes are similar to our own.

3. We like individuals whose personalities are similar to our own.

4. We like physically attractive people.

5. We like people who live near us.

6. We like people of approximately our own age.

7. We are friends with people of the same sex.

(Dickens & Perlman, 1981, p. 92)

experiences with friendship. In a separate investigation, Block (1980) used a fifty-two-item questionnaire completed by 2,063 people at shopping centers, vacation resorts, and through the mail. We will be referring to these two studies as we continue our discussion of friendship patterns.

Friendships between Women

One popular belief is that women are wary of each other, critical of each other, and consider friendships with other women as secondary, behind love relationships with men. A minority of women responding to the Block questionnaire did feel this way.

> To attach too much importance to friendships with women is adolescent.

> Interesting women choose the company of men; they do not seek out or open up to other women.

(Block, 1980, pp. 33–34)

The majority of women studied, however, indicated that they did have close friendships with other women, usually involving much intimacy and self-revelation. Block states that 53 percent of the women surveyed have such friendships. Furthermore, close female friendships are not a function of the twentieth-century women's movement; they have been present throughout the history of the United States. In a study of the diaries and correspondence of thirty-five American families between 1760 and 1880, close emotional ties were found between women (Smith-Rosenberg, 1975). Women were isolated from the primarily male working world and typically restricted to family roles and sex-segregated activities. Therefore, they became closely attached to each other and developed deep, meaningful friendships.

Bell's interviews suggested that women are able to trust each other and share with each other more than men are in friendships. "The evidence clearly indicates that the friendships of women are more frequent, more significant, and more interpersonally involved than those commonly found among men" (Bell, 1981, p. 60). Some women's descriptions of their friendships illustrate this point.

> I love my women friends for their warmth and compassion. I can share anything about my life with them and they never pass judgment or condemn.

> I have four close women friends . . . I can talk about all kinds of personal things. I think that friendships are more important than marriage.

(Bell, 1981, pp. 63–64)

> Last year my father died. For months I was besieged with despair. . . . The men in my life really didn't appreciate how I felt about the loss. . . . It was my women friends who really came through.

(Block, 1980, p. 34)

There have been close female friendships throughout history. A study of the diaries and correspondence of thirty-five American families living between 1760 and 1880 documented the deep emotional ties between women of this era. Because the women were isolated from the working world and restricted to family roles and sex-segregated activities, their attachments to each other became all the more meaningful.

When disruptions occur in women's friendships, the elements of competition and betrayal often do appear. In addition, the Block survey did report a number of instances of women lessening investments in a friendship when they became involved with a man.

Female friendships may also change through the life cycle. In preadolescence and adolescence, females spend a lot of time with other girls and develop close friendships. This pattern may diminish somewhat during late teenage years and the twenties, when most women marry, only to appear again in the thirties and later. As women go through middle age and become elderly, fewer men are around for companionship, because of the substantially briefer male life span and because many divorced men marry younger wives. Women find themselves once again in a sex-segregated life, and they again form close female friendships.

Friendships between Men

If women's friendships have been overly portrayed as fickle and shallow, men's friendships have been overly portrayed as deep, devoted, and loyal. The media images of male devotion and camaraderie are powerful: Hawkeye and B.J., the Lone Ranger and Tonto, Bert and Ernie, Luke Skywalker and Hans Solo. Indeed, many men do prefer the company of other men

FOCUS ON DEVELOPMENT

Friendship Over the Life Cycle

Momentary playmate stage

In their earliest years, children form superficial relationships. Before they enter school, children become friends with others primarily because they are near the others—a pattern, incidentally, that continues throughout adult life in modified versions. This preschool pattern is the ***momentary playmate stage***, in which the child is still quite self-centered and interested in others chiefly as they relate to possessions. From this point forward, friendships may be understood developmentally, with later patterns and expectations based upon earlier friendship stages (Dickens & Perlman, 1981).

Self-interest stage
Mutual responsibility stage

As friendships stabilize in the early school years, the important consideration for the individual often is what the other children can do for him or her; that is, *friendships serve **self-interests***. When children enter the age range of eight to fourteen, close relationships with friends, sharing, and ***mutual responsibility*** emerge. John La Gaipa (1981) collected five hundred essays about friendship by children in this age range, and he developed an inventory of children's conceptions of their friendships. Four factors were found to influence friendship. They are listed in order of importance.

Conventional morality.   Children judge each other as possible friends on the basis of honesty and character.

Mutual activities.   Having fun together, for example in games and sports, contributes to the forming of friendships.

Empathic understanding.   Children feel natural, secure, and relaxed with friends, and they count on their friends' trust and help.

Loyalty and commitment.   Children identify friends as those who will stand by them and be loyal.

Autonomous interdependence stage

Only when adolescence is reached does the stage of ***autonomous interdependence*** begin. As its name suggests, this stage allows friends to be both autonomous and dependent. The individual does not expect the friend's entire world to revolve around him or her. At the same time, friends seek and maintain a mutual depento women, and a majority of men do spend their work and leisure time primarily with other men. One man explained this as follows:

> There is a special quality to being friends with men and it wouldn't be the same with women. With my male friends there is something special—I don't know what but it isn't there with women.

(Bell, 1981, p. 63)

dence for meeting needs. The earlier friendship expectations are still present; loyalty and trust remain important. Of course, ties to parents and home loosen as adolescents become more independent. In turn, this makes adolescents more reliant on peers as sources of support and friendship.

Around the age of eight, children begin to form close friendships based on sharing and mutual responsibility. The qualities of friendship that have been found to be most important to children include honesty; having fun together; loyalty; and feeling natural, secure, and relaxed in each other's presence.

Men associate with each other primarily in nonfamily groups, often gathering at bars after work, or attending sporting events or games as a means to socialize. These gatherings are part of fairly large male social groups. However, men have fewer one-to-one friendships. Men have an average of 3.2 close friends, whereas women have an average of 4.7 close friends (Bell, 1981).

Only a minority of men feel they can fully trust and share their most personal feelings with their male friends—about one-third of the men in the Bell study said they could; about one-sixth of those in the Block research said they could. Men reported feeling that it is important to be seen as confident and secure and, therefore, many are reluctant to disclose personal weaknesses.

> I have a lot of acquaintances but no real close friends. . . . There are guys at work I'm friendly with. . . . But it doesn't go any further than that. We know little about each other nor is there any desire to know more.
>
> *(Block, 1980, p. 58)*

Many male relationships arise in the workplace, but sometimes men maintain distance from coworkers because of their feelings of competition and status differences. The competitiveness is commonly believed to come from men's assessing of each other to see who measures up. The status difference is present because of men's difficulty in befriending other males above or below their own positions in the business or social hierarchy. Time also is an issue. Some men are so involved in work-related activities that they have little time to develop and maintain friendships.

These pessimistic findings do not paint the whole picture of male friendships. When the patterns of close male friendships are considered, middle-class men, men who do not work together, and men approaching midlife are found to have the deepest friendships. Working-class men have more interchangeable, convenience-based friendships. Fewer friendships appear among men who work together. As men move toward midlife, they often are able to set aside machismo feelings that interfere with their moving toward closeness with other men, and they tend to accept themselves and others. Furthermore, with the increasing openness to breaking out of rigid sex roles that has emerged since the 1960s, men have further allowed themselves to move emotionally closer to other men.

> There are enriching male friendships, relationships of mutual trust, respect and protectiveness. Some men are tender with each other; they are capable of putting aside rivalry . . . they related feelings of relaxation; finding it less important to censor their thoughts and feelings, they felt more spontaneous in each other's presence, felt freer to ask favors and to do favors. They trusted each other.
>
> *(Block, 1980, p. 77)*

Only a minority of men feel they can fully trust and share their most personal feelings with their male friends. Those found to have the deepest friendships are middle-class men, men approaching midlife, and men who do not work together.

Friendship between Men and Women

"Male–female ties—not bound by lover status or marriage—are rare and precarious; neither men nor women, for the most part, find them comfortable" (Block, 1980, p. 91). This observation by Block reflected the fact that only 18 percent of his survey respondents reported close opposite sex friendships. Indeed, 40 percent of his subjects did not desire close friendships with members of the opposite sex. Bell's findings were similar. Even when such friendships are formed, most people find they feel closer and able to reveal more to same sex friends. One of the major reasons that appears to limit male–female friendships is the possibility of sexual relations.

Women surveyed reported

If it [sex] is not center stage, you can bet it's lurking in the wings.

(Block, 1980, p. 92)

I have no close male friends because my husband won't allow it. In our relationships with other couples if I talk to the man alone he really gets angry.

(Bell, 1981, p. 99)

The interference of sexual issues is equally present for many men. Consider the following typical comments:

When I meet a good-looking woman and I don't come on to her sexually, I feel empty. It's not just that I missed an opportunity, it's more than that. I experience a sense of failure.

I would like to have friendships with women; there's a whole range of emotions that can be tapped in these relationships, but it never works out. Either I'm sexually attracted and do not want "just" friendship or I'm not really attracted and she's offended or suspicious of me. One way or another, though, the sexual issues take precedence over everything else.

(Block, 1980, pp. 95–96)

Close friendships may develop between men and women who are not sexually attracted to each other or who are engaged in committed relationships with others.

The uncertainty and ambivalence about sexual issues with opposite sex friends acts in several ways. Women may be afraid that friendship with a male is an initiation of a sexual relationship. They also may be concerned about others' believing that the friendship is sexual. From men's point of view, the impediment to friendship with women is the development of their sexual feelings as part of being close to the women. For example, when women confide personal and intimate matters, some men understand—and sometimes misunderstand—these confidences as invitations to sexual relationships. Men are clearly able to understand the roles of men and women as lovers and mates, but not all men are able to understand the roles of the sexes in friendships.

Despite these obstacles, close friendships do appear between men and women. They develop when the friends are not sexually attracted to each other or are engaged in committed relationships to others. Friendships develop when men and women are not living sex-segregated lives at work or at leisure. If at work all the women are clerks and all the men supervisors, cross-sex friendships are unlikely to develop. If men and women are at the same status levels and are noncompetitive, such as in educational and professional occupations, friendships are more probable. When close male–female friendships are formed, the bond seems as deep or, in the case of men, deeper than the bond formed in same sex friendships.

> I have always felt I could be much closer to a woman as a friend than to any man. It is a real gut feeling I have. I feel that in general women care more about their friends than men do.

> My female friends are far more important to me than my male friends. . . . It gets down to the bottom line of there being trust with the women that is often not there with the man.

> *(Bell, 1981, p. 111)*

A trend seems to be developing; younger and better educated men are turning to women as their only close friends. Disillusioned with the barriers against men revealing weaknesses to each other, these men find openness and comfort with emotions in their friendships with women.

OTHER RELATIONSHIPS

Transient Relationships

Transient relationships

The general principles of friendship apply to relatively any enduring relationship. However, we have many fleeting relationships in our lives—relationships with waiters, clerks, receptionists, cashiers, telephone operators, flight attendants, and many others. In each of these contacts, more transpires than a simple exchange of money for goods and services. Even though the relationship is brief, nonrecurring, and more or less random, it involves a wide range of expectations, ways of relating, and patterns of behavior. Fred Davis (1959), drawing on his own six-month employment as a Chicago cab driver, examined these patterns. Davis observed four possible behavior patterns in transient business relationships (Davis, 1959, pp. 160–161, 163).

HOW RELATIONSHIPS DEVELOP

Interpersonal relations occur at different levels of the participants' personalities. Like onions, personalities have successive layers, with top layers being matter-of-fact elements about the person, and lower layers being characteristics increasingly more central to the person. The core or inner layers include vulnerable and socially sensitive characteristics, while biographical aspects such as gender and age are readily visible in the outer layer. As interpersonal relationships progress, the deeper layers are increasingly made accessible and penetrated, a process known as *social penetration* (Altman & Taylor, 1973).

Interactions with others may be examined by *breadth* as well as *depth*. Depth indicates how much the core self is tapped in a relationship—that is, the intensity of an interaction. Breadth is the *amount* of interaction on different topics. Thus, a broad-ranging relationship might touch on family, sports, reading interests, religion, and work. Breadth aspects are more easily achieved with the outer layers of personality than with the layers closer to personal core.

Altman and Taylor describe four basic principles underlying relationships (1973, pp. 39–44).

1. *"Social penetration processes proceed from superficial to intimate levels of exchange* [italics added]" (1973, p. 39). Because the superficial levels are the most accessible, they are the starting point for most relationships. A relationship can be seen as a wedge that slowly pries open the personality to expose deeper and deeper levels.

2. *Interactions continue at established and accessible levels of intimacy.* Once an area has been opened for exploration, both parties can return to it. Whatever depth has been achieved may be maintained as long as interactions occur at this depth.

3. *The speed at which a relationship progresses and how deep it goes depend upon the interpersonal rewards and costs.* If the interaction has more satisfying aspects than costs (unsatisfying aspects), then the relationship will grow and will reach deeper levels. The more satisfaction it produces, the faster it grows.

4. *Relationships develop faster in early and middle stages.* Because the initial barriers to relationships are near the surface and are more easily pierced, the beginnings

1. *The nonperson relationship.*   The client acts as if the driver (or waiter or stewardess) does not exist, paying minimal attention to the driver's presence, seeing the other person as an object. People who rudely argue or openly discuss questionable business deals in a taxi or restaurant demonstrate this pattern. Every person who has worked in a service position has stories of being treated as a nonperson.

---

of relationships develop more rapidly. However, as relationships deepen more armored barriers, which are harder to dissipate, are encountered. People protect the more vulnerable underlying areas of themselves.

Social penetration theory offers a useful explanation of the deterioration of social relationships. When conflicts at deeper personal levels are unresolved, relationships move away, back to more superficial levels and aspects. The more intimate and unresolved the conflict, the more likely this retreat to safer ground will occur. In most cases in which such relationships continue, the individuals move back and forth between excessive intimacy and withdrawal, until they achieve a reasonable midpoint or balance. This accommodation has been called the *porcupine dilemma.*

> One wintry day a couple of chilled porcupines huddled together for warmth. They found that they pricked each other with their quills; they moved apart and were again cold. After much experimentation, the porcupines found the distance at which they gave each other some warmth without too much sting.
>
> *(Bellak, 1971, p. 3)*

The porcupine dilemma describes a problem many people have in their relationships. For each of us, there is a comfort level of emotional nearness, a point at which our maximum comfort is reached. Beyond that point, the inevitable "quills" of being too close are felt sharply. The porcupine dilemma extends to social situations broader than one-to-one relationships. In cities and closed communities, too much crowding makes citizens feel uncomfortable. At the same time, life in the desert or in isolation is satisfactory for few of us. We need some contact and closeness, even if it is with strangers.

The range of individual differences for optimal closeness is great. Some people seek many intimate relationships and feel few intimacy pains, except during prolonged closeness. Others choose to be more distant, their sensitivity to excessive closeness being greater. An adjustment problem arises when a person has substantial dissatisfaction with his or her characteristic level of closeness. In such cases, ways of moving closer or gaining distance need to be explored and mastered.

The person who wants to make a successful pickup must project the image of a self that will interest the other enough to want to continue the present encounter and seek future ones.

2. *Focusing on the goal of the relationship.*   This pattern sharply focuses on how well and in what manner the narrow aims of the relationship—such as driving from the airport to town or bringing plates of food to the table—has been achieved. Workers and customers alike develop ways of acting that fit closely with the demands of their roles.

3. *Behavior-eliciting strategies.*   Planned tactics are concocted to control crucial outcomes of the relationship. Sometimes a worker's obvious politeness and attention are designed to get a tip or get the client to be quiet. Flight attendants and bartenders, for example, actively and skillfully encourage nondisruptive behaviors.

4. *The sounding board.* The transient nature of the relationship means that no long-term accountability for opinions is involved. Thus, either the worker or the client may engage in impassive monologues, using the anonymity of the taxi (or other situation) to pour out personal agonies, as if to clergy or psychotherapists.

Not all fleeting relationships involve a person offering service and a customer. Many social relationships are short-lived and uninvolving. Consider the case of strangers seeking to meet other strangers, a process that in particular social settings has been labelled the *pickup*. Most pickup attempts are not successful. Six tasks must be accomplished for a pickup to be successful.

(1) determine whether a particular other possesses the *qualifiers* that make it worth his while to bother to begin;

(2) determine whether the other is *cleared* (likely to be available) for an encounter and a relationship;

(3) find an *opener* that engages the other's attention;

(4) discover an *integrating topic* that interests the other as well as himself;

(5) project a *come-on self* that will induce the other to want to continue the present encounter and seek future ones;

(6) finally, schedule a *second encounter.*

(Davis, 1973, p. 4)

A person may well facilitate being picked up by having an unusual characteristic. Carrying a controversial book such as *Lady Chatterly's Lover* or *Mein Kampf* serves this purpose. Wearing clothing that identifies oneself as a skier, as a scuba diver, or as being associated with a country (a T-shirt with a Mexican logo) or institution (a Dartmouth sweatshirt) also gives strangers hints about possible openings they could use.

We tend to regard transient relationships as minor pieces of our lives, and so they are in the long run. Yet we broaden the scope of our examination of interpersonal relationships when we include a look at such transient relationships.

Pets: Relationships with Companion Animals

Companion animals

For many people, their relationships with their pets are central to their lives, sometimes even more important than their relationships with most other people. The importance of these contacts has been shown in emerging areas of psychological study and in the coining of the term **companion animals** to emphasize the companionship element in the pet–owner bond. Pets and animals play significant roles in our lives, as the following familiar lines from The Rime of the Ancient Mariner remind us:

He prayeth well, who loveth well
Both man and bird and beast.
He prayeth best, who loveth best
All things both great and small.

(Coleridge, 1935, p. 275)

In some special cases, the person's relationship with a companion animal is vital. For example, the blind owner's needs mandate a close involvement with his or her guide dog. Typically, blind people and their guide dogs are deeply involved with each other. In addition, their dogs serve as an impetus for blind people's growth and interaction with other people. Blind owners have written of their close relationships with their guide dogs.

> My dog has the basic values I believe in—health, activity, positive outlook, and trust. I feel so proud when I'm with him, in control and able to conquer my environment. I sense that people around me are admiring and awesome, and I like that respect.

> Tali is the only one I can turn to for comfort. She can't get too much love; just stroking her soft fur and thinking how grateful I am to her for all her dedication cheers me up.

> I can't explain this fully, but it's like my self-image is more flexible; I'm more spontaneous, more open to experience. Now I'm not in therapy or encounter groups or anything like that, and I believe the explanation is my dog. He's so outgoing, tuned in, and full of life.

> *(Zee, 1983, p. 478)*

Beyond, and perhaps a cause of, the psychological payoffs are the physical realities. Guide dogs do decrease the vulnerability of their blind owners, they do provide many forms of physical security, and, of course, they help their owners negotiate the daily difficulties in getting around.

Animal companionship may play a crucial role in the lives of other people as well. Older men with health impairments who lived with a pet were found to have improved general morale and slightly better mental and physical health than similar older men who lived without pets (Robb, 1983). Indeed, the placement of pets with the elderly has been described as therapeutic (Bustad & Hines, 1983). The owners gain not only exercise and companionship but also a sense of play, comfort, and the loving feelings of being needed. One example of an older woman in a nursing home illustrates the process.

> Marie was chosen because she had no family or friends, would not communicate, and remained curled in the fetal position with no interest in living. She also had sores on her legs from continual scratching. When other measures failed, she was moved in with Handsome [the Persian cat]. Whenever she began to scratch her legs, the cat played with her hands and distracted her. Within a month the sores were healed. She began to watch the cat and to talk to the staff about him. Gradually she invited other residents in to visit with him. Now she converses with strangers as well as the nursing home staff about the cat and other subjects.

> *(Bustad & Hines, 1983, p. 302)*

Owning an animal can be therapeutic for many elderly people. Their pets give them not only companionship and a reason to exercise but also comfort, a sense of playfulness, and the feeling of being needed.

Research has looked at the effects of interaction between people and other animals, too. For instance, Aaron Katcher and his colleagues (1983) examined how hypertensive (high blood pressure) subjects and individuals with normal blood pressure were affected by looking at about fifteen tropical fish in a fish tank for a twenty-minute period. The subjects' blood pressure was taken initially, and then under four other conditions: while the subjects read for two minutes, while they looked at a blank wall for twenty minutes, while they looked at the fish for twenty minutes, and once again while they read. In both groups, subjects' blood pressure dropped significantly from the initial levels and the levels taken during the reading period when the subjects were looking at the walls, and it dropped significantly further when the subjects were looking at the fish. The authors interpreted these results as suggesting that when we look at the living world around us we are changed in positive ways, we relax, and stressors affects us less.

Not all pets rescue owners from depression or high blood pressure, and much of the positive evidence to that effect is anecdotal or preliminary. However, a new and exuberant field of study is examining the benefits of owning companion animals. Half of all American homes have pets, and there are compelling reasons to believe that, for some owners, pets play important and positive roles in their owners' adjustments.

WHEN SOCIAL RELATIONSHIPS ARE DEFICIENT

Loneliness

When individuals want and need more social contact than they are experiencing, we may say they are *lonely*. Notice that the criterion is the *personal need* of the individual involved. For some people, a modest and occasional amount of social contact is satisfying; for others, more extensive and intense relationships are needed. Thus, no objective standard of social need applies to everyone. At the same time, being alone is different than being lonely. Being alone can either be satisfying or lonely, just as people may feel lonely in the frequent company of others.

Loneliness

Recent research and writing on **loneliness** have come from Daniel Perlman and Letitia Peplau (Peplau & Perlman, 1982; Perlman & Peplau, 1982), who have observed that lonely people tend to feel dissatisfied, unhappy, and restless and, furthermore, become oversensitive about the possibility of others rejecting them. They have identified three fundamental dimensions of loneliness (Perlman & Peplau, 1982, p. 4).

Negativity.   Negative feelings are associated with the sense of alienation from other people.

Social versus emotional loneliness.   Social loneliness, or the absence of a sense of attachment to community or others, leads to a feeling of being unacceptable. Being the "new kid on the block" may produce social loneliness. Even more serious is emotional loneliness, which is the absence of an intimate, close bond to another. Emotionally lonely people feel uncared for and empty.

Duration.   Chronic loneliness occurs when two or three years pass without satisfactory relationships. This may be contrasted with situational loneliness, which arises when one is newly widowed, living in a new community, or in a new job. Least problematic is transient loneliness, which is the everyday, brief, and passing moods of loneliness.

What are the effects of loneliness in terms of personal adjustment? One well-documented effect is *depression,* which occurs when the loneliness lasts over long periods of time and the experience is severe. Studies of chronically lonely people reveal patterns of compelling psychological distress and high scores on measures of anxiety and neuroticism. Such people believe that they personally are at fault for being unable to develop and keep rewarding social contacts; they believe quite accurately that they have fewer friends than their contemporaries; and they feel little control over their situation.

Contrary to popular views, the elderly are not the most lonely people. Surprisingly, *adolescents* are the age group most prone to loneliness. In one survey (Perlman & Peplau, 1982), 79 percent of respondents under the age of eighteen said they were sometimes or often lonely. In contrast, 53 percent of respondents between forty-five and fifty-four years of age and just 37 percent of respondents over fifty-four years old reported feelings of loneliness. A higher incidence of loneliness is also reported by those in lower socioeconomic groups and by widowed and divorced persons. Married persons reported the least loneliness.

Four ways of coping with loneliness have been described (Rubenstein & Shaver, 1982).

Sad passivity   (thinking, crying, doing nothing)

Active solitude   (running, reading, working)

Spending money   (this filled the lives of some people)

Social contact   (seeking out friends or acquaintances)

The lonely tend not to go to psychotherapists for help. Instead, they seek out friends, siblings, or other people in their social environment for company and assistance. Doing things on their own or passive behaviors seem not to help. Those most likely to overcome their isolation from others are people with positive self-images and for whom the loneliness is a situational event. Those people who see themselves as undesirable, unchangeable, and permanently caught in a lonely life find it difficult to overcome their felt lack of social relationships.

Embarrassment

You have just been told that you will be asked to dance to recorded music for sixty seconds, then sing the "Star Spangled Banner," laugh for thirty seconds, and finally imitate a five-year-old having a temper tantrum—all before a live audience. Imagine your reaction. Most people would feel embarrassment at the prospect. By embarrassment, we mean the public state of awkward mortification or chagrin. An audience of at least one other person must be present for embarrassment to appear.

Adolescents are most prone to loneliness. However, no matter how old you are, cultivating a positive self-image and recognizing that your loneliness is a situational event can help you overcome your feelings of isolation from others.

Rowland Miller (1982) used the preceding instructions in his investigation of the phenomenon of interpersonal embarrassment. The subjects were not actually asked to perform the acts; they were asked just to anticipate having to do them. Compared to people in a control nonembarrassment condition, the embarrassed people described themselves more critically, felt more grouchy and defensive, and became more shy.

Embarrassment is an almost universal phenomenon. There are several ways in which we can deal with this condition. For instance, "losing face" is typically followed by a compensatory act. We try to look better, to remedy the situation, so that other people do not think negatively of us. One common example of compensation is when you reach out to shake hands, the other person does not notice, and you then use the extended hand to adjust your clothing or hair. Another way of coping is to work

Empathic embarrassment

toward *empathic embarrassment.* When we confess our nervousness, on-lookers tend to share our feelings of discomfort and emotionally come to our rescue.

Machiavellianism

Machiavellianism

In 1532, Niccolo Machiavelli of Florence wrote a book titled *The Prince* that had an effect he could hardly have anticipated. It made his name synonymous with opportunism, deceit, and using other people for one's own gain. The development of the psychological notion of ***Machiavellianism*** arose when social psychologist Richard Christie (1970) was investigating interpersonal power and control strategies. When Christie first read Machiavelli's book, he thought the deceit and manipulations it described were bizarre, immoral, and despicable. However, after observing administrators in many organizations, he came to believe that Machiavelli's methods and those of contemporary administrators have much in common. This led to the identification of Machiavellianism, which is described as having the following characteristics:

1. A relative lack of emotional involvement in interpersonal relationships.
2. A lack of concern with conventional morality.

Machiavellian people are not emotionally disturbed, nor are they pursuing long-range ideological aims. Rather, they dispense favors and privileges and control others through a variety of guises to maintain day-to-day control.

Christie's study of the Machiavellian personality included a historical perspective of the Machiavellians of history. Two common themes emerged.

> One was the assumption that man is basically weak, fallible, and gullible. This unflattering view of human nature was intertwined with a second theme: if people are so weak, a rational man should take advantage of the situation to maximize his gains.
>
> *(Christie, 1970, p. 7)*

Christie and his colleagues believed that Machiavellianism was neither totally present nor absent in an individual, but that it existed in varying degrees. He constructed a scale to capture the essence of the Machiavellian personality. The items with a (+) are scored as Machiavellianism when the respondent agrees; (−) items are scored as Machiavellianism when the respondent disagrees.

+ The best way to handle people is to tell them what they want to hear.

- When you ask someone to do something for you, it is best to give the real reasons for wanting it rather than giving reasons which might carry more weight.
+ Anyone who completely trusts anyone else is asking for trouble.
+ It is hard to get ahead without cutting corners here and there.
- Honesty is the best policy in all cases.
+ It is safest to assume that all people have a vicious streak and it will come out when they are given a chance.
+ Never tell anyone the real reason you did something unless it is useful to do so.
- One should take action only when sure it is morally right.
+ It is wise to flatter important people.
- All in all, it is better to be humble and honest than important and dishonest.
- Barnum was very wrong when he said there's a sucker born every minute.
+ People suffering from incurable diseases should have the choice of being put painlessly to death.
- It is possible to be good in all respects.

TEASING

Positive Teasing

Negative Teasing

Teasing uses humor to annoy or ridicule another person. From early childhood, when children call each other "do-do," to adulthood, when social or work acquaintances humorously insult each other, teasing is a common experience. Jane Kessler (1982) has observed that, curiously, teasing is little studied, although it often is a source of serious frustration and unhappiness to the recipients.

There are differences between positive and negative teasing. **Positive teasing** involves good-intentioned jesting and kidding. Joking relationships exist in many work settings, providing acceptable outlets for hostility and reducing tension levels. Among some subcultures, the trading of ritualized insults, or "doing the dozens," is a valued part of expected social interaction. The exchanges place a premium on wit, quick thinking, and the more deft "putting down" of the other person. Unless the exchange becomes too personal and accurate, it is a routine and relatively comfortable interaction. However, if a person is teased about an obvious physical deformity or genuine discomfort, the teasing then falls within the boundaries of insult or negative teasing.

Negative teasing may include badgering and tormenting, and it is indicated by the aggressive aims of the teaser and the degree to which the teased feels insulted and attacked. In work settings, negative teasing can be a form of

— Most people are basically good and kind.

— There is no excuse for lying to someone else.

+ Most men forget the death of their father more easily than the loss of their property.

— Most people who get ahead in the world lead clean, normal lives.

+ Generally speaking, men won't work hard unless they're forced to do so.

+ The biggest difference between most criminals and other people is that criminals are stupid enough to get caught.

— Most men are brave.

(Christie, 1970, pp. 17–18)

Ingratiation

Ingratiation

Closely related to Machiavellianism is ***ingratiation,*** which is the use of strategies to increase feelings of interpersonal obligation and attraction for some ulterior motive. Machiavellianism and ingratiation both employ manipulative techniques to influence other people. However, Machiavellianism describes deceit, power, and influencing techniques in all settings,

harassment. In social relationships, negative teasing is felt as intimidation and attack.

Teasing develops from childhood in predictable patterns (Kessler, 1982). It begins with tricking, such as a child offering a candy or toy to another child and then pulling it away. Early teasing includes tricks such as, "I can spell Mississippi. Can you spell it?" Children also imitate the speech or behavior faults of others. Name play, such as calling someone named Mary, "Mary, Mary, quite contrary," and taunting about a physical characteristic, such as calling someone "big ears," are also forms of teasing. More elaborate insults and clever remarks are developed as people grow older.

What should a person do if he or she is the victim of teasing? There may be no single effective response. However, when working with handicapped children who were regularly teased by nonhandicapped children, Kessler (1982) found that her advice to ignore the teasing so it would go away was not fruitful. As a result, she adopted the "last word" strategy. In this strategy, what you say is less important than ensuring that you make some retort as quickly as possible. Whatever your teaser says, you need to reply, to assert something back in kind, and to get in the last word. This process moves the teased person out of the position of being a victim in a negative teasing relationship and into being more an equal in a social interaction.

particularly work and administration. Ingratiation refers only to the interpersonal process in which one person attempts to manage the relationship with another person so that he or she can use the personal bond for some individual goal. Ingratiation includes falsely praising and making other conciliatory statements to another person in order to gain that person's favor.

Ingratiation has many names. It has been called brownnosing, applepolishing, bootlicking, and sweet-talking. The perception of an ingratiating person is negative; such people are labelled teacher's pets, yes-men, or fair-weather friends. These labels demonstrate that ingratiation is most effective when it is subtle and not clearly visible. In his discussion of ingratiation, Edward E. Jones (1964) described how hypocrisy in general is frequently present in interpersonal relationships and how ingratiation in particular masks our feelings and distorts our judgments.

There are four primary tactics of ingratiation: *complimentary other enhancement, opinion conformity, self-presentation,* and *giving gifts and rendering favors* (Jones, 1964). **Complimentary other enhancement** refers to the use of flattery. We engage in this process when we ignore negative aspects of a person and exaggerate existing positive aspects. An example would be a student who is seeking high grades telling instructors that they are the most interesting, stimulating, and thoughtful teachers in the whole college—that they are just wonderful! The more basically believable the compliment, the more likely it is to be effective. Notice that the intention of the flatterer is what separates this process from ordinary efforts to be liked. The ingratiator has an ulterior motive.

Opinion conformity describes the process by which we attempt to present our beliefs as similar to the other person's. As we have already noted, people like others who are similar to them. Opinion conformity is most effective when occasional disagreements are deliberately allowed to appear, and when the ingratiator's strategy involves stating an opinion before the target person offers his or her opinion. For example, a successful ingratiator will know the other's political opinions and be able to anticipate what the target person might say before criticizing or praising a certain politician.

The **self-presentation** aspect of ingratiation calls for presenting oneself in a favorable light so that friendship becomes more valued. The contradictory tactics of self-enhancement and self-depreciation can both be used to achieve this goal. For example, an ingratiator might comment on how many people have been inviting him or her to go to one big game and then say that it's difficult to comprehend why so many people would want his or her company.

Finally, *giving gifts and offering favors* appear to be part of ingratiation. As a way of ingratiating oneself to another, the process of doing favors does more than simply produce an obligation. It seeks to obtain attraction

Complimentary other enhancement

Opinion conformity

Self-Presentation

and desirable social attitudes through the illicit means of favors and gifts rather than by earning them.

Although ingratiation has been presented as a maladaptive tactic that does not allow the straightforward development of relationships for intrinsic purposes, it may have positive values as well. Jones (1964) has pointed out that ingratiation between leaders and followers in an organization may have the positive effect of masking otherwise disruptive feelings of hostility, thereby allowing the organization to get on with its work.

EMOTIONAL NEGATIVISM AND OPTIMISM IN RELATIONSHIPS

Interpersonal Negativism

> . . . there's the example of a friend of ours who was trying to get his children to eat leafy green vegetables. Appeals to "it's good for you," starving children in China, and even Popeye having all failed dismally, our friend finally discovered a tactic that would work: He would bring to the dinner table elaborate dishes of spinach, et al., which he and his wife would eat with great enjoyment and firmly forbid the children to have. At first, the children watched with amused interest. Soon, however, they asked if they could have some. Showing great reluctance, our friend eventually "gave in."
>
> When the press predicted that Mr. [President] Johnson would get rid of all the Kennedy men in the White House, he invited them all to stay, and when he was later praised for doing so, he gradually let almost all of them resign. (James Reston)

> *(Brehm & Brehm, 1981, pp. 1–2)*

When a friend reacts negatively to something you say or do, just for the sake of being negative, it is frustrating. If you make a suggestion and the other person resists or disagrees for no good reason, you may be puzzled and annoyed by the negativism. There are two explanations of negativism: traits and situations. We begin this section by looking at negativistic traits.

According to the trait explanation of negativism, some individuals have ***negativistic personalities.*** Either immaturity or suspiciousness leads them to be reluctant to accept others' ideas and suggestions. When two-year-olds automatically say no to their parents and siblings, we understand that they are exploring autonomy and their right to say no. In an adult, however, such resistant behavior is seen as an immature response and an indication that the person is still struggling to define his or her independence from others. As a result, the person does not identify well with the needs and feelings of others. When suspiciousness causes negativism, the person resists because of his or her unwarranted concerns

Negativistic personalities

about ulterior motives. Distrust of others can be a long-standing trait, and a person's suspicion often is obvious.

Yet negativism is not limited to an immature few; most of us act negatively at times. When resistance is due to a situation and is not a characteristic trait, it is called *psychological reactance.* Psychologists Sharon Brehm and Jack Brehm (1981) of the University of Kansas have organized and articulated this theory.

Psychological reactance

Psychological reactance theory states that reactance may be expected to occur whenever a freedom to act or choose is threatened. The purpose of the reactance is to restore the free choice. The examples given at the beginning of this section illustrate the process: The children wanted to have the option of either eating or not eating green vegetables. President Johnson wanted the option of keeping or not keeping the Kennedy appointees. The first ending to the chapter's opening story was an example as well: The man saw his freedom to enter the relationship restricted by the woman's use of listening techniques.

The motivation to restore choice is increased when the threatened freedom is important. Threats to trivial freedoms do not incite a strong reaction. For example, if the sale of one brand of chewing gum were to be forbidden in your community, it is likely that little resistance would arise. If worship at a particular church were forbidden, however, a great uproar would predictably occur.

Freedom must exist for free choice to be threatened. The child who has never been given a choice as to whether or not to clean his or her bedroom is less likely to react negatively to instructions to clean up the room. Furthermore, implied threats to freedom may increase reactance. As Brehm and Brehm wrote, "When a newly married woman is told by her husband that he wants to spend a night out with his male friends, she may experience reactance not so much in regard to losing the company of her husband for the one night but rather in response to the implied threat that he will be leaving her alone many nights in the future" (1981, p. 5).

At some middle ground, both trait and situational theories of reactance come together. People who have a great sense of control over the outcome of events in their lives are likely to be very psychologically reactive. On the other hand, people who have an external locus of control—that is, who feel that environmental and outside factors influence their behaviors—would be less negativistic and reactive. Such people already assume they have little freedom and choice and are not prone to perceive attempts at persuasion as threats.

Interpersonal Optimism: The Pollyanna Principle

In the long-running public radio show "A Prairie Home Companion," the host ended the segment about Lake Woebegon by describing the

Pollyanna principle

mythical town as a place "where all the women are smart, all the men are good-looking, and all the children are above average." This appraisal of Lake Woebegon captures the idea of the *Pollyanna principle*: pleasant events and information are sought, remembered, and used far more than unpleasant events. This optimistic outlook is widespread in American society. In any given situation, our inclination is to react with positive thoughts and feelings.

Pollyanna herself was the youthful heroine of an Eleanor Porter novel and, later, a Walt Disney movie. She was so optimistic in the face of discouraging circumstances that in our language the word *Pollyanna* has come to mean "optimistic delight in the world." In their book, *The Pollyanna Principle* (1978), Matlin and Stang have concluded that being Pollyannaish is a core and predictable aspect of the human condition. We remember pleasant events more accurately than unpleasant events; there are more pleasant words than unpleasant words in the English language; and we assume that pleasant events are more likely to happen than unpleasant events, even when the probabilities of both are the same.

The Pollyanna principle also applies to how people judge each other, including how students and instructors evaluate each other. Here are the Matlin and Stang findings.

The average student is better than average. Grades given to students are distributed so that the average student—the arithmetic average student—actually has better than average grades. If the average grade is stated to be C (or 75 out of 100), the calculated mean grade will typically be higher than C (and higher than 75).

The average instructor is better than average. When students rate instructors as being below average, average, or better than average, at least three-fourths of the instructors receive better than average ratings.

Strangers are judged likeable. The general tendency is to give positive evaluations of unknown people. Even if the person to be rated has been identified in advance as one about whom no positive or negative feelings are held, the ratings are positive.

People in general are liked. Ratings of people in general are positive; people are generally viewed as good and likeable. The last line of *The Diary of Anne Frank*, written before Anne Frank and her family were taken to a Nazi death camp after two years of hiding, reads, "In spite of everything, I still believe that people are really good at heart" (Goodrich, 1956, p. 174).

Not everyone acts like Pollyanna, of course. There are those in the world who see discouragement at every step. Furthermore, people's positive views of others are influenced by what they feel they ought to say and their hopes that seeing others as good and desirable will elicit similar responses. Nevertheless, the Pollyanna principle reflects a general approach, in which an optimistic understanding of other people is a predictable conclusion.

DEVELOPING AND MAINTAINING FRIENDSHIPS

The desire to have friends is sufficiently widespread that hundreds of books have been published with formulas for friendship. We will begin our examination of some of the major formulas by looking at *exhortive* techniques. By exhortive techniques, we mean those methods that urge a person to assume socially pleasing ways of acting, in contrast to the psychological techniques that focus on developing the person's listening abilities and empathy. The best known of all the literature on exhortive approaches are the 1952 book by Norman Vincent Peale, *The Power of Positive Thinking,* and the 1936 book by Dale Carnegie, *How to Win Friends and Influence People.*

> . . . there are certain formulas and procedures which, if followed faithfully, can make you a person whom other people like. You can enjoy satisfactory personal relationships even if you are a "difficult" person or by nature shy and retiring, even unsocial . . . I cannot urge you too strongly to consider the importance of this subject and to give time and attention to its mastery, for you will never be fully happy or successful until you do.
>
> *(Peale, 1952, p. 191)*

Peale's theory of self-improvement centers on ten positive suggestions. Among these suggestions are two specific procedures to get others to like you. You are urged to (1) learn to remember names, and (2) never miss an opportunity to congratulate a person for an achievement. Other suggestions prescribe ways to be—the reader is told to become a comfortable person, to develop a relaxed easygoingness, to be humble, and to be an interesting person.

The problem with the specific suggestions is that they are not compelling influences on whether others like us and want to be friends with us. Although research has indicated that we like people who flatter us, despite our awareness that it is flattery rather than genuine compliments, such flattery does not stand alone as a basis for our making those people our friends. The broader personal suggestions are problematic, too. There is no doubt that people who are comfortable, easygoing, and interesting are better liked than tense, hard-driving, and dull people. However, the simple urging to become comfortable and interesting is unlikely to change uncomfortable or dull people. The alternative is to find the means to let others know that we truly are interested in them, that we hear them well, and that we speak with them in ways that promote friendships. Indeed, close friendships are characterized by attentive listening and by comfortable self-disclosure (McAdams, Healy & Krause, 1984).

Listening

Few people listen well. Many factors interfere with our ability to listen well to what others say. We sometimes become so concerned with what we are about to say that we do not really listen to what others are saying. Because it is difficult to pay attention to two simultaneous sources, we involuntarily screen out others to prepare better for our own turn to speak.

We often mistake partial messages for the full communication. Once another person has begun a message, we may complete that message in our minds. Much like a person completing a sentence for a stutterer, we act as if we have received the full message.

We carry our own needs into conversations so forcefully that they sometimes blur the themes of others' messages. No one can fit our needs perfectly, and as a result we may filter communications so that we hear only selected pieces.

Relationships of all sorts suffer seriously from such communication problems. Inevitably, both we and the other individuals involved realize that we are not being heard well, and our reactions may endanger the positive qualities that exist in our relationship. It's easy to tell how little most of us expect to be truly heard. Simply observe the language usages that emphasize our expectations of poor communication. We intersperse our statements with requests for confirmation. We ask: "Do you understand?" "Are you with me?" "You know?" "Do you hear what I'm telling you?" "You follow?" What we are communicating, of course, is that we believe our partners do not know at all what we are saying.

As a basic relationship improvement method, listening techniques are effective and simple. Three techniques to improve your listening skills are (1) ensuring that the other person has finished, (2) checking out the accuracy of what you have heard, and (3) listening to feelings as well as words.

Let the other person finish. We interrupt others because we are in a rush to express our opinions and "take the floor" in a conversation. The alternative is to let the other person truly be heard. By paying attention and waiting until the other person actually finishes what he or she is saying, we are more likely to listen well. Furthermore, listening well gives us more information on which to base our responses. Part of letting the other person finish is not to switch topics. Topic jumping is common among young children, who make comments only remotely related to what another child has said. Adult conversations are also subject to similar versions of topic jumping. By staying with the same topic and not anxiously leaping to something else on our minds, we may truly finish a topic in a conversation.

Checking accuracy.   The loss of accuracy in communication is so great that we need to use devices to determine whether we are listening

SUPPORT FROM FRIENDS: A SELF-RATING SCALE

No matter the number of friends a person seemingly has, it is how the person experiences these friendships that may be most important. If a person feels his or her needs for emotional support and attachment are fulfilled by friends, then the subjective experience of friendship may be satisfied. One way of measuring this subjective experience of friendship is with a rating scale developed by Procidano and Heller (1983). This scale is called the *Perceived Social Support from Friends.* Each time an underlined answer is chosen, one point is added to the overall score. The average score on this scale, based on three studies of 222 Indiana University undergraduates with a mean age of nineteen, is 15.5. Thus, according to these studies, most college students report good friendships. Scores of less than 5 indicate little felt support in friendships. Scores around 10 suggest the subjects feel medium support from friends. People who feel their friendships are highly supportive score 15 or higher.

Perceived Social Support from Friends

Directions: The following statements refer to the feelings and experiences that most people have at one time or another in their relationship with *friends.*
For each statement there are three possible answers: Yes, No, Don't know.
Please circle the answer you choose for each item.

<u>Yes</u>	No	Don't know	**1.**	My friends give me the moral support I need.
Yes	<u>No</u>	Don't know	**2.**	Most other people are closer to their friends than I am.
<u>Yes</u>	No	Don't know	**3.**	My friends enjoy hearing about what I think.
<u>Yes</u>	No	Don't know	**4.**	Certain friends come to me when they have problems or need advice.
<u>Yes</u>	No	Don't know	**5.**	I rely on my friends for emotional support.

well. Checking with the other person on what he or she said serves
that purpose. Typical statements that allow such checking of accuracy
are as follows: "Let me see if I heard you correctly. . . ," or "What you
seem to be saying is . . . ," or "So the basic thing that is concerning
you is . . ." (each of these would be followed by a restatement of the

Yes	<u>No</u>	Don't know	**6.**	If I felt that one or more of my friends were upset with me, I'd just keep it to myself.
Yes	<u>No</u>	Don't know	**7.**	I feel that I'm on the fringe in my circle of friends.
<u>Yes</u>	No	Don't know	**8.**	There is a friend I could go to if I were just feeling down, without feeling funny about it later.
<u>Yes</u>	No	Don't know	**9.**	My friends and I are very open about what we think about things.
<u>Yes</u>	No	Don't know	**10.**	My friends are sensitive to my personal needs.
<u>Yes</u>	No	Don't know	**11.**	My friends come to me for emotional support.
<u>Yes</u>	No	Don't know	**12.**	My friends are good at helping me solve problems.
<u>Yes</u>	No	Don't know	**13.**	I have a deep sharing relationship with a number of friends.
<u>Yes</u>	No	Don't know	**14.**	My friends get good ideas about how to do things or make things from me.
<u>Yes,</u>	No	Don't know	**15.**	When I confide in friends, it makes me feel uncomfortable.
<u>Yes</u>	No	Don't know	**16.**	My friends seek me out for companionship.
<u>Yes</u>	No	Don't know	**17.**	I think that my friends feel that I'm good at helping them solve problems.
Yes	<u>No</u>	Don't know	**18.**	I don't have a relationship with a friend that is as intimate as other people's relationships with friends.
<u>Yes</u>	No	Don't know	**19.**	I've recently gotten a good idea about how to do something from a friend.
Yes	<u>No</u>	Don't know	**20.**	I wish my friends were much different.

Adapted from Procidano & Heller, 1983, pp. 21-22.

Few people listen well. You can improve your listening skills by waiting for the other person to finish speaking, checking out the accuracy of what you have heard, and paying attention to the speaker's feelings and nonverbal communications as well as his or her words.

essence of the other person's message). Such statements elicit from the other person a confirmation that you have heard accurately, or, more often, a correction because you don't have the entire communication quite right and you have missed something.

Emotional accuracy.   When the other person has strong feelings, his or her tone of voice, facial expressions, or body postures may be the means of communication. The next chapter considers in detail the nature of such nonverbal communications. For the purposes of good listening, however, we should identify the speaker's central emotion as clearly as possible. Reflections such as "You're feeling terribly frustrated" or "The whole situation seems to have left you worn and hopeless" are examples of responses made to confirm the emotional content of a message.

All listening techniques need to be employed naturally and comfortably in the user's own language. If they are seen as techniques, they become impersonal barriers to good communication. However, most people are so receptive to others' attempts to careful listening that they will consider even the beginner's use of such techniques not as intrusive but instead as welcome and positive.

Communicating

Once we have heard the other person, then it is our turn to communicate. When we have listened well, our behavior often serves as a model. The other person frequently follows the patterns of waiting, listening, checking out our messages, and confirming the essence of our feelings. When we choose to speak, several principles should be kept in mind (Garner, 1981).

Don't talk too much. Sometimes from habit or insecurity, we say much more than we intend. Furthermore, much of what we say is repetitive, because we assume that we will not be heard well. A useful guideline for avoiding talking too much is to keep track informally of the extent to which each person speaks. If you find you are speaking much more than your partner, saying less may be in order.

Be concrete when talking about yourself. When we are vague and unclear, we erect a barrier that reduces the content of our communication. Instead of saying general truths, be specific. A vague statement might be, "I feel kind of funny at times like this." A specific statement might be, "I find myself becoming defensive and wanting to impress you with my achievements when you talk about your good grades."

Own your feelings. Many people respond to a conflict situation by placing blame on the other person. Thus, we say, "You are thoughtless and irresponsible when you keep me waiting." If you owned your feelings, you would say, "I find myself getting increasingly restless and upset when I am waiting for you." Making a clear statement of our own feelings gives us the opportunity to be responsible. We identify and accept our feelings, without blaming the other person. With our feelings openly expressed, the other person can react without the hurt that comes from having been attacked. Beginning every communication with the simple statement, "I feel . . . ," lubricates the path to conflict resolution—unless of course we use it as a means to attack, by saying, "I feel you have been thoughtless and irresponsible."

Stay in the present. Dwelling on what has happened in the past and what might happen in the future never allows a good resolution of what is happening in the present. Poor responses to others begin with historical views and anticipation of the future. When the subject of discussion is emotional and the context is a long-standing relationship, the speakers may need to make deliberate efforts to keep comments in the present tense. We tend to drag old skeletons out of the closet and worry about what will happen. However, the past cannot be changed, except in our minds, and the future is rarely predictable. It is the present moment that can be most easily reshaped to allow positive feelings and resolutions.

Observe the effects. Use the other person's reactions as a gauge of how well you are communicating. Think of the times you have a MEGO—my eyes glaze over—reaction when someone is talking but not really caring about what you think. When your listener's eyes become unfocused or body becomes restless, reconsider what you are doing. If the person is attending well, take it as a sign that what you are saying and how you are saying it are on target.

Confront with empathy.   Sometimes the other person makes a statement that calls for a challenging response. The resulting confrontation can turn into an attack if it is done insensitively. Effective confrontations are extended with empathy, so the other person knows you understand and emotionally appreciate what he or she is feeling. Be involved in the consequences of what you say. Try to confront tentatively. This gentle approach allows you both the opportunity to discuss the issues comfortably.

Stay with your style.   If we try to play negotiator, psychologist, or lawyer, we conceal our own natural selves. We need to act in the context of our own real selves. If you do play a role, play it as closely to who you are as possible and use your normal communication patterns. Don't try to change your whole self, because being unnatural and phony will interfere with other communication goals.

Use honest positives.   We noted earlier that *The Power of Positive Thinking* encouraged readers to use compliments and congratulations. A related but different way to develop good feelings in relationships is to use **honest positives,** which are truly felt statements about other persons' likeable and desirable behaviors. By encouraging others, our interactions feel better—and people are more likely to behave in ways consistent with what we encourage as well. It is important that such encouragement be genuine and not said for the purpose of achieving an effect. Almost any negative message can be rephrased as a positive message. Honest positives will provoke skepticism and suspicion if they are overly strong. For that reason, honest positives are best developed slowly, stated conservatively, and used only when you don't want something. Furthermore, making some occasional negative comments—honest but about minor issues—helps give honest positives more impact when they are stated (Garner, 1981).

Honest positives

Toward Cooperation

Cooperation

The process of ***cooperation*** in developing and maintaining relationships is the next issue we consider. *Cooperation* may be defined as the coordinated, joint behavior of two or more people aimed toward some end that results in desirable consequences for the involved individuals. Such working together for a common purpose is *not* the direct opposite of competition. While many choices may be between working together or competitively trying to outdo each other, in some situations a third choice exists— that of *individualistic actions.* Individuals who are pursuing some objective independently of the influences or participation of others are acting individualistically. Such people march to the beat of their own drummer and are not frequently concerned with competition or cooperation.

For many situations, cooperation is essential. These situations range from relatively simple tasks, such as moving pianos, to complex challenges, such as assembling airplanes and designing computers. The athletic team that cannot cooperate smoothly has a major obstacle in the path to its success. International negotiations can be viewed as exercises related to the development of cooperation.

The sphere of international relations, like most other group situations, is too broad to allow psychological study of what factors truly affect cooperation. For this reason, researchers have gone to the laboratory, using controlled conditions and restricted responses. In a series of studies on the nature of cooperation, Gerald Marwell and David Schmitt (1975) placed subjects in separate rooms and presented them with a choice to work alone or with another person to earn money. An electronic control panel signaled subjects as to whether other people chose to work with them and counted the money each subject earned in the experiment. The findings supported five general principles in cooperation (Marwell & Schmitt, 1985, pp. 4, 78, 91, 127, 146).

1. Most people do cooperate when they have the opportunity.
2. The greater the unfairness in the money paid, the more likely people will *not* cooperate. If the difference in pay is great enough, a substantial minority of people will withdraw from all cooperation and work on their own, even at a financial sacrifice. However, the majority will work together anyway.
3. The presence of interpersonal risk—in the form that one subject may take away or destroy the earnings of the other subject—almost totally interferes with cooperation.
4. Opportunities to talk and develop trust promote cooperation even under conditions of high risk.
5. Individuals cooperate much more with best friends than with strangers.

Cooperation is not necessarily a personality trait. Indeed, the situation itself can substantially mold how cooperation emerges between us and the people we value. To begin with, the issue of fairness is important. When we or our friends feel that the payoffs are unfair, the motives to cooperate plummet fast. We cooperate best when the outcomes and benefits seem just and equitable.

When sensitive issues such as the possibility of being slighted and receiving fewer benefits come up, good communication makes a difference. People who keep feelings of inequity bottled up are less likely to work readily with others. Talking about these concerns and using listening skills help to dissipate the fear of being used. Furthermore, with less risky work and more comfortable relationships, cooperation becomes better and more efficient.

Part of cooperation comes from individuation, or the process of feeling personally treated like a special, worthwhile human being. When we feel anonymous and deindividuated, we are not motivated to work closely with anyone else. When we are recognized and feel important, making cooperative efforts seems right and natural.

Cooperation is not a phenomenon separate from the other elements in interpersonal relationships. It is part of being in friendships and feeling free to make choices, and it both contributes to and results from having positive expectations and listening well. When all of these elements of interpersonal relationships are present, people cooperate with each other in mutually beneficial ways.

A list of behaviors that lead us toward and away from well-being in our interpersonal relationships appears in Table 8–1.

TABLE 8–1 Toward and Away from Well-Being in Interpersonal Relationships	
Toward Well-Being	Away from Well-Being
Close, enduring, voluntary relationships	Distant, transient, involuntary relationships
Loyal empathic friendships	Superficial friendships with ulterior motives
Sexual roles and issues not concerns	Sexual roles and issues strong concerns
Transient relationships that accomplish the purpose of the encounter	Transient relationships that are ineffective in achieving their objectives
Honesty in relationships	Dishonest and manipulative in relationships
Listens well and empathically	Poor listening as part of self-focus
Cooperation	Competition

SUMMARY

Friendships have three characteristics: they are relationships that are close, that are voluntary, and that are relatively enduring. No ulterior motive is involved in friendship. Friends allow themselves to be vulnerable and at the same time protect each other's vulnerabilities.

It has been found that the majority of women are able to trust and share with other women. Indeed, friendships between women are closer than those between men. Women's friendships are strongest when they arise in sex-segregated conditions and least strong during the teen years up to the thirties. The two major problems that arise in women's friendships are betrayal and competition.

The reality of men's friendships is very different from the myth of male devotion. Only about one-third to one-sixth of men feel they can disclose their most personal feelings to their male friends. Competitiveness and status differences interfere with such trust. The closest male friendships are found among middle-aged, middle-class men who don't work together and among men who are free of rigid sex roles.

Friendships between men and women are relatively uncommon. The possibility of sexual involvement makes many men and women wary about male–female friendships. Such friendships develop when sexual attraction is not present, when each person is in a committed relationship, or when the parties are not living sex-segregated lives.

The ways in which people form relationships may be understood through social penetration theory, which considers the levels or layers of personality and relationships. Interactions that go to core layers of personality are considered to have depth. Relationships that deal with many aspects of a person are considered to have breadth. People begin a relationship at a superficial level. As the relationship progresses, deeper levels of each individual's personality are revealed until a comfortable level of intimacy is reached. The growth of the relationship depends on how rewarding it is compared to its costs.

Not all relationships are close, voluntary, or enduring. Transient relationships between customers and persons offering services often fall into one of four patterns: it may be a nonperson relationship, it may focus attention on the instrumental aspect of the relationship, it may involve behavior-eliciting strategies, or it may involve one party acting as a sounding board. Another transient relationship is the pickup, an encounter between strangers that has its own prerequisites for success.

Having a pet—sometimes more elegantly labelled a companion animal by psychologists—offers a relationship as well. Particularly deep, intense, positive relationships are found between blind persons and their guide dogs. In many other settings, there have been observable therapeutic results of improved morale and health from people's contact with companion animals.

Loneliness occurs when people have insufficient social contact. Each of us has our own required level of social contact. Thus, loneliness is different from being alone. Loneliness means feeling negative and alienated, feeling no attachment to community or others, and having time pass without satisfactory relationships. Lonely people tend to become depressed, anxious, and self-blaming. They try to cope through sad passivity, active solitude, spending money, or seeking social contact. Adolescents are the loneliest of all age groups.

Embarrassment means social chagrin, awkwardness, or mortification. Embarrassed people feel self-critical, defensive, or shy. Embarrassment can be dealt with by developing empathy in the onlooker.

Machiavellianism describes people who use deceit and manipulation to control others. Moral issues seem to be of minimal concern to such individuals.

Some people are negative by nature and almost automatically resist or disagree with others. Sometimes people become negativistic because their freedom to act or choose is threatened. This phenomenon is known as psychological reactance. In contrast, interpersonal optimism is the seeking, remembering, and use of pleasant events and information; this is described as the Pollyanna Principle.

Many how-to books present methods for making friends. However, listening, communicating, and cooperating with others are primary ways to develop and maintain relationships. To listen well, one must let the other person finish speaking completely before responding, check out the accuracy of what one heard, both in content and in the emotional message, and stay with one's own conversational style.

To communicate well, one should not talk too much, should be specific, should own one's feelings, should keep the conversation in the present, should observe the effects of one's communications on others, and should confront with empathy. Stating honest positives, such as encouragement, helps in the communication process.

Part of building a good relationship is to look for situations that foster cooperation and then to work positively with others for common goals.

Key Terms

Autonomous interdependence stage	Mutual responsibility stage
Companion animals	Negative teasing
Complimentary other enhancement	Negativistic personalities
Cooperation	Opinion conformity
Empathic embarrassment	Pollyanna principle
Friendships	Positive teasing
Honest positives	Psychological reactance
Ingratiation	Selective protectiveness
Loneliness	Self-interest stage
Machiavellianism	Self-presentation
Momentary playmate stage	Transient relationships

Recommended Reading

Katcher, A.H. & Beck, A.M. (Eds.). (1983). *New perspectives on our lives with companion animals.* Philadelphia: University of Pennsylvania Press. This book is *the* primary resource for reading about pet–human interactions. Its fifty-one chapters discuss how companion animals influence human health (including therapeutic uses of pet ownership), the effects of losses of pets, predators as companions, and understandings of the ties between humans and animals.

Garner, A. (1981). *Conversationally speaking: Tested new ways to increase your personal and social effectiveness.* New York: McGraw-Hill Paperbacks. This little paperback offers advice for social skills and relationships. The suggestions come from psychological research and are accompanied by extensive examples.

Golde, R.A. (1979). *What you say is what you get.* New York: Hawthorne Books. This book is a Golde mine of techniques and information for developing social skills. Particularly useful chapters discuss how to listen well, how to be tolerably critical, and how to speak for yourself.

9

CHAPTER

Nonverbal Communication

The Understanding

Be kind, be polite. Be kind, be polite. Be nice, be kind, be polite. Remember, be very kind, be very nice, be very polite. Henry Hendrickson's thoughts centered on his instructions to himself. Be sure to be nice. Be certain to be polite. He knew he did not have the knack for working with people, and he would have quit on his own anyway, but he was determined not to be fired. Miss Walker had warned him that this was his last chance, and she would be joining him when he oriented the new girl this morning. Remember. Be nice. Be polite. Don't upset the new girl.

Miss Walker sat to the side as Henry began the orientation. In a controlled monotone, Hendrickson told the girl that they were looking forward to her being part of the company family. (Be kind, he thought.) His eyebrows and forehead furrowed as he explained that they were all one happy family. (Polite. Be polite.) His hands tightly closed into themselves, and he held his arms closely against his sides. He informed her that he personally was delighted that someone with her credentials was joining their family. (Be sure to be nice.) Henry tilted his head up and back a little. Please consider me a friend, he said. Miss Walker said nothing. Time passed slowly. The interview was ending and Henry knew it had

not gone right. The new girl seemed sad. He felt discouraged himself.

Then Miss Walker spoke to the girl. "The problem with this place," Miss Walker explained, with a chuckle in her voice, "has been that a lot of people are treated just the way mushrooms are grown: kept in the dark and piled high with manure." In a conspiratorial tone and with a twinkling smile, Miss Walker went on to explain that, with the management here, it was hard to figure out whether to be Gloria Steinem or Tinker Bell. Henry saw the new girl's spirits rising.

Then Miss Walker and Henry were alone. "I'm sorry, Henry," Miss Walker said sadly, "but it happened again. We are going to have to let you go."

Henry was upset. "But you told her all those awful things about the company management and about piling manure on the employees!" He tried to make the case for himself. "I welcomed her. I told her how much she would be part of the company family. I was the one who told her how delighted we were with her!"

"I'm truly sorry, Henry, but you just don't understand." She was right. He just didn't understand.

THE NATURE OF NONVERBAL COMMUNICATION

The causes of adjustment difficulties are sometimes mysteries. From their life experiences, individuals may be able to predict when a certain series of events will occur. For example, their best efforts at being social in large groups may be sabotaged not only by what they say but also by their actions. Yet, *exactly* what they do that makes them socially ineffective can be a mystery to them.

Before Henry Hendrickson spoke to the new employee, he thought through what he wished to say. Then he said exactly the right things to her. With great bewilderment, he found that the young women rejected him instead of being friendly toward him, and that his supervisor disapproved of instead of favored him. At other times in his life, however, Henry may have had interactions, with few or no words, that were infused with goodwill and mutual approval. The reason Henry's interactions succeeded or failed is his nonverbal communication, the voice qualities and the body and facial language that accompanied his every act.

We listen explicitly to the spoken word, but we communicate using much more than spoken language. Albert Mehrabian (1981) compared emotional communication in words to two kinds of nonverbal communication. His research indicated that only 8 percent of all feelings were transmitted by verbal messages. Vocalizations, which are voice pitch, inflections, pace, and sounds, accounted for 38 percent of the transmittal of emotional messages. Facial expressions, or the movements around the eyes, the mouth, the cheeks, and the forehead, accounted for the remaining 55 percent. Posture and other aspects of whole body communication, although not studied by Mehrabian, also contribute substantially to the emotional meanings of our messages.

Silent messages are the focus of this chapter. Such unspoken communications may be subtle, but people do notice and do react to them. In order to understand why and how others are reacting, we need to understand the effects of, for example, eye contact, lowered eyebrows, leaning forward during conversations, or sitting or leaning to one side.

Consider an excerpt from the Hunter Thompson book *Fear and Loathing in Las Vegas* (1971). Thompson wrote of the unstated tension in an angry confrontation.

> I nodded to Lucy, who was eyeing me with venom. I was clearly some
> kind of enemy, some ugly intrusion on her scene . . . and it was clear
> from the way she moved around the room, very quick and tense on her
> feet, that she was sizing me up. She was ready for violence, there was not
> much doubt about that.

(Thompson, 1971, p. 106)

As we talk about different nonverbal behaviors, we will resist the temptation to interpret each action as if it has *absolute* meaning, a meaning that applies in every situation. On the cover of the book by Julius Fast, *Body Language* (1970), an attractive woman in a short skirt leans slightly forward, with her hands resting on crossed legs, holding a cigarette. The reader is asked, What is the message? Does her body say that she's a loose woman? Does her body say that she's a manipulator? While you may think there is a sensuous message in such a posture, you can't know

What nonverbal message is this woman communicating? Do her body position and smile give an ambiguous message?

Context

unless you learn more about the **context** in which it occurs. The context refers to the larger picture of what is happening. There are three levels of contexts.

Individual level

Relationship level

*The **individual level:***   Looking only at the single person.

*The **relationship level:***   Looking at this particular person in interaction with another person.

Social-rule level

*The **social-rule level:*** Looking at these two people with other persons or groups of persons.

(LaFrance and Mayo, 1978, p. 19)

A smile is one nonverbal behavior that has been examined along these dimensions. Suppose you see a photo of a person smiling and try to judge what the smile means.

At the individual level, you might decide that the person is feeling happy. Upon widening the focus, you see there's another person in the picture; maybe the smiler is indicating liking. At the broadest level, you see a social conversation in which the woman is listening to a man. Now it may be that the woman is following the gender rule that dictates she should smile.

(LaFrance & Mayo, 1978, p. 19)

One cannot not communicate is the basic principle of nonverbal behaviors. Every effort to remain neutral, to present an impression, to disguise how one feels, sends a message. Furthermore, feeling one emotion while transmitting another often means that you are sending a complex message, one that may not be easy to understand. Suppose you are upset with a friend, but you value this friend's opinions and don't want to show how upset you are. You try to conceal your feelings. As a result, you look your friend in the eye just a little less than normal. You are quieter or occasionally are excessively friendly—both actions that carry messages of their own. Silence, for instance, conveys information about how you are reacting. Even if you precede your silence with the comment that there is nothing to be said, the actual silence adds information. Furthermore, the more your friend expects a spoken message, the more importance he or she will attribute to your silence and stillness (Poyatos, 1983). In the same sense, the more the friend expects you to express matter-of-fact, neutral feelings, the more problems he or she will have with your forced overfriendliness.

Of all the possible channels for nonverbal communication, one of the most informative and powerful is eye contact (Katz & Katz, 1983). Thus, our first point of departure into nonverbal communication is a discussion about the "windows to the soul," or how people look each other in the eyes.

EYE CONTACT

Eye contact

Initial *eye contact* is a signal of readiness to communicate. Good eye contact is a foundation for interpersonal transactions, and that foundation has some universal elements, made up of four separate momentary acts.

Looking toward the other person

A brief smile

A raising of the eyebrows

A quick head nod

In the fraction of a second during which these signals transpire, the other person learns it is his or her turn to reciprocate and to begin to relate to the originating person. Both positive and negative messages may be transmitted by eye contact (Kleinke, 1986). The command "Look me in the eye!" suggests that a person who looks away is dishonest and has something to hide. The evasion of eye contact is interpreted in our society as deceit, as shyness, or as reluctance to make contact personally and emotionally. Indeed, if lack of eye contact means the avoidance of emotional contact, prolonged eye contact may arouse strong emotions. Making eye contact with an unknown person who is attractive to you carries the messages "I like you," "I would like to meet you," or "I want you to know that you have an interesting face."

Caring and cherishing are emotions demonstrated by lovers who look deeply into each other's eyes as a sign of total attention. By looking only at the one they love, they pay less attention to other people and influences.

LOOK DEEPLY INTO MY HAND

Nonverbal communication, like all other human interactions, calls for a receiver and a sender. Much of our attention in this chapter has been directed toward the sender. The reception of nonverbal messages, however, is an emerging area of psychological study. Many messages are ambiguous, and even relatively clear messages may be interpreted in multiple ways according to the needs of the receiver.

This process of subjective interpretation of body language has led to the development of a projective personality device called the *Hand Test* (Wagner, 1962). The Hand Test consists of nine drawings of hands in varying positions and one blank card. The subject taking the test is instructed to look at each drawing and report what the hands are doing. The subject is then asked to look at the tenth blank card, imagine a hand drawn there, and state what it is doing. People who see hands hitting, slapping, punching, or poking are assumed to have hostile feelings that influence their perceptions. Similarly, people who see weak, ill, or deformed hands are believed to have feelings of personal inadequacy or depression.

The drawing shown here is not part of the Hand Test, but it can be used to illustrate the process involved. Look at the hand. How many different interpretations of what the hand is doing can *you* make?

Some forms of eye contact have highly specific meaning in subcultures or particular groups. For example, some homosexual circles have a shorthand method of making contacts with other gays. The person makes brief eye contact, lets his eyes drop quickly to the other's genital area, and then resumes eye contact. The whole event takes less than a second and is not visible to others. If the other person responds in kind, expressions of sexual orientation and interest have been exchanged without a spoken word.

The relationship and social rules influence our interpretations of eye contact. You may read brief eye contact quite differently, depending upon whether you are suspicious or open, feel threatened or self-confident, are amenable to passing contact with a stranger or find such contacts distasteful. Hugh Prather (1977) presents a way we can change the characteristic social rules that govern our eye contacts with strangers. Pretend, he advises, that you left the country for a while and are now back in your home community, except you are in the body of another person. As you walk along the street, you keep seeing people who would not recognize you in your new body, but who would in actuality be close friends of yours. Don't stop. Don't try to strike up conversations with them. Simply continue along, looking at the "close friends" you pass.

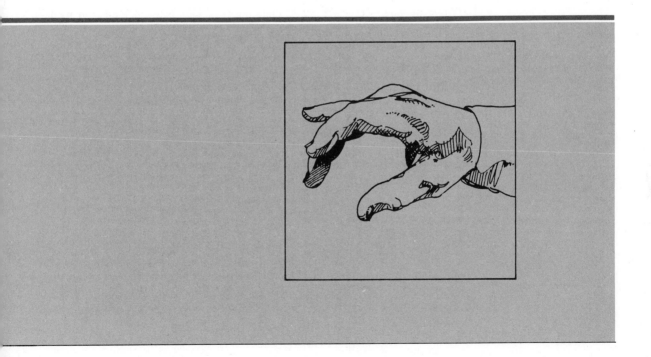

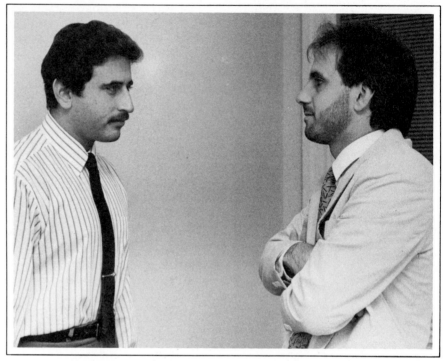

Most of us would recognize the prolonged eye contact between these two men as antagonistic. What other nonverbal clues convey this message?

When people try this exercise, it is not unusual for them to report a flood of unspoken positive feelings passing between the people they see and themselves. Strangers smile, hold comfortable eye contact, and in other ways act as if they are with a friend. Thinking of yourself as a disguised good friend promotes many subtle nonverbal messages, beyond pleasant eye contact. By thinking in this way, you modify your characteristic ways of passing strangers and looking at them, so that positive and friendly interactions occur.

Antagonistic and Restricted Eye Contact

Although prolonged eye contact is a sign of caring in the context of a loving relationship, it waves the flag of war in the context of an impersonal and hostile relationship. The visual attention becomes an angry watching, a vigilance against threat or attack. Antagonists sometimes lock themselves into staring battles. The eye contact is held fiercely, until one party cannot maintain the intensity anymore, looks away, and the other wins the battle.

Long eye contact, or gaze, is unpleasant when any negative emotion is felt. Michael Argyle and his colleagues have observed, "Most people find a steady gaze to be pleasant if they like the gazer and want to be liked by him; the same gaze will be irritating if they think the gazer has undue sexual interests or is seething with anger" (1968, p. 34). The sexual gaze, however, is partly a function of distance. That is, looking at another person walking toward you down the street is permissible if you are sufficiently far away that your eyes do not explicitly focus on any one area of the body. Once you are close enough to be seen gazing at one area, then you are perceived as rude.

Looking strangers in the eye as they pass by is perceived as an intrusion on privacy in most metropolitan communities. Streetwise citizens quickly learn the rules of looking in large cities. If you look overly long—more than glance—at a stranger who is sitting on the sidewalk, you may well be harassed with a discussion of why the world is going to end on Sunday. Eye contact is an invitation to make further contact, with consequences that are not predictable.

> In public places filled with strangers, looking away—or gaze aversion, as it is labelled by researchers—is common. People deliberately line up their bodies in public areas, such as subway stations, to avoid inadvertent eye contact with unfamiliar people. Curiously, they also play the game of trying to watch people without letting their eyes get caught. Most of us are skillful users of the "fractional glance," that momentary scanning of other people to see where they are looking.
>
> *(Coss, 1974, p. 18)*

When eye contact is restricted or blocked, as in a telephone conversation, communication often becomes more difficult. Michael Argyle and his colleagues (1968) at Oxford University studied the importance of eye contact on communication. Four visibility conditions were used.

Masks were worn that allowed the eyes to be seen.

Dark glasses were worn that hid only the eyes.

A screen was erected that hid faces but not bodies.

A full visual separation was maintained in which the other person could be heard but not seen.

The basis for assessing the communication was the extent to which the two people interrupted each other. Good communication was identified as that with few interruptions, and poor communication was defined as having many interruptions. The most interruptions in the conversation occurred when the other person was completely out of sight; the fewest interruptions occurred when the other person's eyes could be seen. Visual accessibility seems to be related directly to the quality of communication.

Heron has made the following observation:

> The most fundamental *primary* mode of interpersonal encounter is the interaction between two pairs of eyes and what is mediated by this interaction. For it is mainly here, throughout the wide ranges of social encounters, that people actually meet (in the strict sense).

(Heron, 1970, p. 171)

Gaze

Gaze

Gaze avoidance
Gaze omission

Eye contact and *gaze* are different. You can gaze at another's face without the other person actually looking back at you. For example, if you are one of thirty students looking at a teacher, the teacher may not be looking back at you individually. *Gaze avoidance* and *gaze omission* occur as well. Someone who is actively avoiding looking toward you is practicing gaze avoidance. Unintentionally not looking at another is gaze omission. In many situations, gazing is so automatic that we are distressed by its absence. Students who collaborate to look toward a lecturing instructor but to focus their eyes several feet behind the instructor's head will distress the instructor. The instructor may begin to repeat what he or she has said. The volume of his or her voice may rise. Then the pitch of his or her voice may rise. Finally, the instructor's anxiety becomes evident. Because everyone appears to be looking at the instructor, he or she cannot comprehend what is wrong. Yet the instructor knows that something is very wrong. We have similar feelings when talking to someone who has a far-off look in his or her eyes.

The power of a gaze can be strong and compelling in other situations, too. Ellsworth has found that

> . . . a direct gaze has a high probability of being noticed. For a behavior that involves no noise and little movement, it has a remarkable capacity to draw attention to itself even at a distance. . . . People often use a direct gaze to attract another person's attention in situations where noise or gesticulation are inappropriate. The fact that we expect others to be responsive to our gaze is illustrated by our exasperation when dealing with people who have learned immunity to the effects of a stare, such as waiters.

(Ellsworth, 1975, pp. 5–6, cited in Harper, Wiens & Matarazzo, 1978, p. 171)

The Eyes Have It

Up to this point, we have examined eye contact and gaze as they occur naturally in human interactions. Eye contact can be used constructively, by choice, in the interest of better communication. Four general principles may be followed.

Use gaze to make emotional contact.   When you want to communicate in a personal way, eye contact amplifies such messages—whether positive or negative.

Make small modifications in eye contact time to substantially change the quality of your interactions.   Experiment with the length of time you hold others' eyes. See if slightly longer or shorter gazes work better in achieving your interpersonal goals.

Reduce eye contact to move away from others.   Once you appreciate that eye contact does represent an involvement signal, then you may avoid gaze to minimize an unpleasant contact. Gaze avoidance always gives you an opportunity to move away from others.

Judge the context.   While this rule applies to all interactions, it is particularly important in nonverbal communication. A piercing look may be seen as interest in one situation, provocation in another situation, an invitation or a challenge in yet another. All of us use context, but not necessarily successfully. Judging the context means assessing the situation and environment before deciding how to communicate feelings and reactions.

GESTURES

Gestures

Gestures are symbolic actions; they express feelings or thoughts and serve as substitutes for verbal statements. A gesture is a nonverbal behavior in which a specific action is used to convey a particular idea. Understanding gestures is important because many gestures have multiple meanings and still others have meanings only in particular cultures or areas of a country. For example, let us look at the gesture of lightly tapping your temple with the tip of your forefinger. Desmond Morris and his colleagues (1979), who conducted research on gestures, have suggested that two strikingly different meanings may be communicated by this gesture. It may indicate either that someone is very intelligent or that he is crazy. The hand-to-brain movement symbolizes either good brain or bad brain functioning. When it represents craziness, this gesture carries very specific messages: "He's stupid. Idiot! What a fool." When indicating intelligence, the specific messages are: "He's clever. Brilliant! Very bright!" (Morris, Callette, March & O'Shaughnessy, 1978, p. 28).

Gestures are understood differently according to the country and culture in which one lives. Presented in Figure 9–1 are the meanings and derivations of four gestures that are common to the United States and four that are uncommon to the United States but common in several European countries. For example, the nose tap, indicating complicity, is rare in our culture. Thus, in the movie *The Sting*, the nose tap was a successful silent

The nose tap, an uncommon gesture in the United States, indicates complicity.

signal between Paul Newman and Robert Redford because it is uncommon in the United States.

FACIAL EXPRESSIONS

Out of the corner of your eye, you see a man watching you. As you glance to the side, his eyebrows drop closely toward his eyes and the muscles around his mouth tighten, his lips tense. The man is transmitting a negative, perhaps disapproving, message.

A woman walks into the room. As you and she notice each other, her eyes open wide and her eyebrows rise, wrinkling her forehead. Then her chin drops, leaving her mouth open. She is surprised to see you.

Facial expressions communicate much of the emotional content of our communications with others. After a century of scholarly debate

Familiar Gestures

The thumb up
Meaning: O.K.
Origin: Derived from Romans as sign of survival for fallen gladiator.

The nose thumb
Meaning: Mockery
Origin: Symbolizes putting thumb up the nose or a long, ugly nose.

The finger cross
Meaning: Protection
Origin: As the sign of the cross.

The ring
Meanings: O.K.,—good; orifice; or zero
Origin: Stands for "O" in O.K.

Unfamiliar Gestures

The chin flick
Meaning: Disinterest
Origin: A symbolic beard flick, indicating insult or boredom (length of beard grown during conversation) or a simple negative.

The fig
Meaning: Sexual comment or insult
Origin: Symbol of arousal or sexual intercourse.

The nose tap
Meaning: Complicity; be alert

The cheek screw
Meaning: Good; praise
Origin: Symbolizes "on the tooth," as in praising food; or a dimpled cheek.

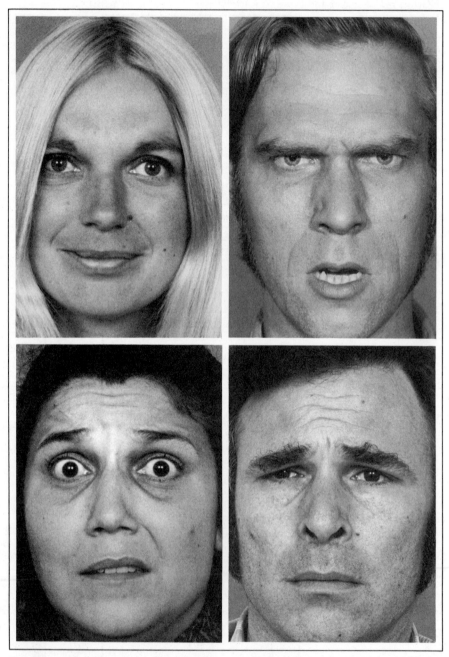

Happiness, anger, fear, and sadness are four universally recognized expressions. Everyone communicates these emotions in the same ways—even people in preliterate cultures and even blind children who have never had the chance to observe others.

about whether there are universal facial expressions of emotion, finally researchers have concluded that, in every culture, language, and race, at least six universal expressions exist (Chan, 1985; McAndrew, 1986). Happiness, sadness, surprise, fear, anger, and disgust are expressions that are always recognized, even by preliterate cultures and even when communicated by blind children who have never had the chance to observe others (Ekman, 1978).

Managing Facial Expressions

People may not want to communicate their interpersonal feelings at all times. When your employer asks you to complete an important task just as you were preparing to leave for a social engagement, you may

Not all people want to communicate their interpersonal feelings. Nonverbal leakage occurs when our attempts to conceal our emotions are unsuccessful and we manifest our true feelings in subtle, nonverbal ways. Sometimes we give our deception away because our gazes are overly fixed, our voices are higher pitched, or our muscles are tense.

Masking

Nonverbal leakage

Neutralizing
Intensifying
Deintensifying

wish to mask your reaction. *Masking* refers to maintaining an unfelt facial expression, or mask, to conceal a socially (or in this case occupationally) unacceptable feeling. When the mask does not work successfully, the result is called *nonverbal leakage.* The real feelings leak out from behind the mask and are seen. In many cases, nonverbal leakage may not be seen at all by the other person (Ekman, 1985). However, sometimes the other person does detect the deception, usually by observing an overly fixed gaze, a higher pitched voice, or tense muscles.

Masking is only one of four techniques of managing facial expressions. Masking hides an emotion with the facial expression of a different feeling. In contrast, the other three techniques are *neutralizing, intensifying,* and *deintensifying* the existing emotion.

To neutralize an emotion is to replace the true expression of a feeling with a dispassionate and unemotional facial display. A person may become poker-faced in specific situations. Skilled poker players maintain a uniformity of facial expressions, tone of voice, and body postures so that when they draw four aces in poker their reaction has no more visible impact than when they draw a pair of threes.

To intensify an emotion is to express it with even more facial reaction than one normally would show. Thus, minor pleasure is presented with an expression of ecstatic joy, and a little sadness is expressed as misery. By contrast, to deintensify is to reduce the extent of the display of feelings, so that only mild emotions are portrayed when more powerful emotions are felt. Individuals may react to threats or any emotion-eliciting event with exaggerated or minimized feelings, and their facial expressions may reflect such a choice of intensities.

Problematic Facial Expressions

The process of managing emotions through modified facial expressions can go wrong. Let's consider some of the possible difficulties resulting from presenting to others frozen, mixed, and flooded facial expressions.

Frozen affect

Frozen affect describes a relatively fixed emotional expression, caused by long-standing muscular sets. That is, a person looks somewhat bemused, or depressed, or pleased and, when not showing another reactive emotion, always presents this expression. Abraham Lincoln allegedly made the following comment to an aide about a departing visitor. "That man," Lincoln declared, "is the ugliest man I have ever seen." His aide replied, "He can't help it, Mr. President, he was born with that face." Lincoln responded, "Yes, he could help it. By the time each of us is forty, we are fully responsible for the way we look." The point is that we do form expressions, wrinkles, and muscle holding patterns that endure and communicate something of our whole life view and experiences. Indeed, the reason professional photographers are so fascinated with the faces of many elderly people is the wealth of life experiences that can be read in their expressions and faces. When a person has one emotional expression frozen in place, then the person may well be presenting an inappropriate expression in many situations and may have a problem relating to others.

Expression blends show two expressions of emotion at the same time. Such blends may arise because a person is experiencing two feelings simultaneously or as a result of an even more interesting process—a reaction to an emotion being felt. Ekman wrote, ". . . when disgust is aroused, some people may characteristically feel also afraid of being disgusted; others may feel happy and so forth" (1978, pp. 112–113). The original emotion and the secondary emotion then either blend together in a facial expression or appear one after the other in quick succession. An example of a blend is the emotional expression of smugness, which is made up of both anger and happiness. Emotional blends are troublesome to viewers, who often are confused or puzzled by them.

Flooded expressions describe excessively maintained emotions. They are emotions intensified to such an extreme that they present interpersonal difficulties. Thus, severely depressed persons typically show negative facial expressions—their faces are "flooded" by sadness—without following other rules that allow for such extreme facial expressions. The state of depressed psychiatric patients may be judged by their greeting to their doctors, for example, because there is a social ritual that must be followed. In the initial contact, the doctor's smile must be returned before the depressed feelings are facially expressed. In the absence of such a smile, the depressed patient is regarded as more seriously disturbed. The reciprocated smile need only last a fraction of a second to achieve its purpose. It is to this category of brief movements of face and body that we now turn.

Expression blends (margin note)

Flooded expressions (margin note)

MICROMOMENTARY BEHAVIORS

Micromomentary behaviors (margin note)

One reason we don't know just what is happening when we feel the impact of a nonverbal behavior is that some of these behaviors are micromomentary in nature. That is, they are often micromovements, of much less than an inch, and usually measured in millimeters (there are about twenty-five millimeters to an inch). Furthermore, these movements truly are momentary, frequently lasting only a small fraction of a second (Cacioppo, Petty, Losch & Kim, 1986). Micromomentary movements, such as the elevation and return to normal of the eyebrow, can be so rapid that they are clearly revealed only in slow motion photography. Other micromomentary movements, however, are easily observed. Let us consider four such movements (Druckman, Rozelle & Baxter, 1982).

1. *Width of eye opening.* Widely opened eyes, when the eyelids are retracted, is a behavior associated with intense feelings or the expression of surprise. The phrases "having your eyes opened" and "keep your eyes wide open" give evidence to the psychological interpretation of widened eyes. In contrast, the slight drooping of eyelids over the eyeballs often is a sign of one's distrust or distancing from another.

2. *Head angle or tilt.* A small head tilt to the side by a listener indicates his or her interest or quizzical attitude. A pronounced head tilt may be read as a sign that something is amiss in the interchange or that an element of behavioral disorder may be present. Holding one's head far to the side in a conversation is viewed as peculiar.

3. *Head position up or down.* The up and down head positions are parts of the range of movement seen in the head nod. When the head is down, with the neck less visible and eyes looking up toward the other person, the position is associated with submissiveness or depression. The head tilted up produces an impression of dominance or sometimes perceived superiority; you may be "looking down your nose" at another person when you're holding your head up.

4. *Vertical width of mouth.* By width of mouth we mean the measured distance between the top center of the upper lip and the bottom center of the lower lip in the closed mouth. A narrow width is frequently interpreted as tense, that is, a tight-lipped expression. A broad width is seen as a comfortable expression, except at its extreme, when a slack jaw is seen as a possible lack of attention or intensity.

Kinesics

One study of a psychiatric patient's micromomentary facial expressions solved a mystery (Ekman, 1985). Mary was a forty-two-year-old housewife who had attempted suicide three times. After a few weeks of psychiatric hospitalization, she convinced her doctor that she was better and she was given a weekend pass to go home. Just before she left, she confessed that she had been pretending she was well and still urgently wanted to kill herself. The mystery was why the doctor and other experts who viewed films of the interview had failed to detect her deception.

Finally, the mystery was solved after hundreds of hours were spent studying the film. Mary did indeed reveal her intentions but in micromomentary expressions.

> In a moment's pause before replying to her doctor's question about her plans for the future, we saw in slow-motion a fleeting facial expression to despair, so quick that we had missed seeing it the first few times we examined the film. . . . We also found a micro gesture. When telling the doctor how well she was handling her problems Mary sometimes showed

a fragment of a shrug—not the whole thing, just a part of it. She would
shrug with just one hand, rotating it a bit.

(Ekman, 1985, p. 17)

Momentary behaviors, such as passing facial expressions and a shrug
of the head or shoulders, have been studied scientifically. This field of
study is known as ***kinesics***, and it represents an important step in making
brief and tiny movements accessible to the observer.

Kinesics, then, is the scientific study of body motion. Ray Birdwhistle
(1970) identified the ***kine*** as the basic unit of human motion, the smallest
component of any physical action that can be described. Kines are much
like molecules; they are quite varied and fit together in complex ways
to make a distinct whole. Individual kines combine to form complicated
body movements.

Most study of nonverbal behavior looks at molar behavior—that is,
behavior that is global and composed of many parts. Birdwhistle's kines
truly are molecular, the micromomentary parts themselves. When Birdwhistle filmed body movements, he discovered that the same action repeats itself over and over. Often viewing a twenty-second film segment is
sufficient for understanding the kinesic patterns of action. The usefulness
of studying such a short behavior kine, such as an eyebrow lift and return, becomes more apparent when we realize the movement lasts for as

Kinesics

Kine

THE FINE-TUNED SALUTE

During World War II, I became at first bemused, and later intrigued, by
the repertoire of meanings which could be drawn upon by an experienced United States Army private and transmitted in accompaniment
to a hand salute. The salute, a conventionalized movement of the right
hand to the vicinity of the anterior portion of the cap or hat, could, without occasioning a court martial, be performed in a manner which could
satisfy, please, or enrage the most demanding officer. By shifts in stance,
facial expression, the velocity or duration of the movement of the salu-
tation, and even in the selection of inappropriate contexts for the act,
the soldier could dignify, ridicule, demean, seduce, insult, or promote
the recipient of the salute. By often almost imperceptible variations in
the performance of the act, he could comment upon the bravery or cowardice of his enemy or ally, could signal his attitude toward army life or
give a brief history of the virtuosity of a lady from whom he had recently
arisen. I once watched a sergeant give a 3-second, brilliant criticism of
English cooking in an elaborate inverted salute to a beef-and-kidney pie.

(Birdwhistle, 1970, pp. 79–80)

little as a few thousandths of a second. Just as any square inch of the human body contains a menagerie of mites, bacteria, and life, any second of human behavior contains a continuous stream of actions.

Kines may be seen with nearly the precision of an electron microscope. Kinesics uses a shorthand language to describe the smallest units of body motion. Symbols and letters represent the parts of the body and their positions or directions of movement. For example, the letter *H* refers to all activities of the head. When the head is nodded up and down, the movement is written 𝐇. A head shaken fully back and forth to both sides is written 𝐇̄. Eyes are indicated by two ovals. Eyes looking sideways are drawn as ∞. Kines are written for the whole body, as well. When the spine is upright, viewed in profile, it is drawn I. If the person is leaning forward, the kine for the spine is drawn as *I*. Symbols also exist for body movements showing leg positions, tense body movements, and loose movements.

When filmed segments of human behavior are transcribed using the kine symbols, a previously invisible aspect of movements becomes accessible for study. These fleeting and minute components reveal a universe of subtle and unspoken behaviors that are vital in the communication of emotions. The notations of kines have been used in dance and movement therapies to mark the progress of patients toward improved emotional expression.

FOCUS ON DEVELOPMENT

The American Adolescent Courtship Dance

Intimacy Development in the Teenage Years

When nonverbal behaviors are examined over time and in context, regular patterns of social interaction can be seen. For example, twenty-four distinct and separate steps were identified in what has been called the American adolescent courtship dance. In this "dance," or behavior sequence, each step and counterstep is taken in order for the couple to proceed from initial touch to sexual relations.

> For instance, a boy taking the girl's hand must await a counterpressure on his hand before beginning the finger intertwine. The move and countermove, ideally, must take place before he "casually" and tentatively puts his arm around her shoulders. And each of these contacts should take place before the initial kiss.

The courtship may be danced to completion in one hour or in several years, or it may never be completed. Furthermore, the identification of a person as

PSYCHOPATHOLOGY

Has the study of the kines of psychologically disturbed individuals found them to be different from the nonverbal behaviors of other people? The answer to this question is not a simple yes or no. There are differences in quantity, but not in quality. Disturbed patients do not show unique behaviors. Rather, they behave more or less in the ways everyone else does.

Consider the effects of anxiety and depression on nonverbal communication. When individuals are anxious, their body language communicates this emotion. Compared to nonanxious others, they smile less and maintain less eye contact, and they make more hand movements that do not send information. Depressed persons also maintain less eye contact and, not surprisingly, their eyes look down more often. The corners of their mouths droop more, and they move their hands less (Bull, 1983).

Schizophrenics in particular have been found to be less able than other individuals to show their feelings in meaningful nonverbal messages. Among other differences, they look at the people with whom they are talking about one-third as much as most people do. They gesture and thrust their heads toward conversational partners even much less, and they look down when they are talking much more than do most other people (Grant, 1972). Psychiatric patients in general have about ten percent lower rates of accurately reading nonverbal messages.

---

sexually slow or fast is a function of whether the person takes the steps in order, rather than actual time spent completing the dance. A fast person skips steps or prematurely rushes through steps without waiting for the expected countersignals. The person who does not respond when prompted by the partner to go to the next step is seen as slow or disinterested.

Teenagers usually develop an increasing progression through this courtship sequence. In the early adolescent years, the very earliest dance steps of hand holding and casual touch and countertouch may be daring for the teenagers' stage of social and intimacy development. As individuals enter their later adolescent years, their social experiences and information from their peers modify how they perceive the stages. An initial kiss may be risque to a twelve- or thirteen-year-old and yet minimally intimate (and not overly meaningful) to the same person six years later. The courtship progression may be danced with a single partner, either to completion or to one's stopping point; it also may be danced throughout one person's adolescence. In that case, the person acquires skill and knowledge of how much he or she wishes to dance in this nonverbal ritual.

(Birdwhistle, 1970, p. 159)

Depressed persons maintain little eye contact with others. They often look down, their mouths may droop, and they make few hand movements.

The study of incarcerated violent prisoners has drawn one specific nonverbal conclusion. That is, violent offenders have greater needs for physical distance from others than do nonviolent offenders. Several studies have supported this conclusion. These studies have asked the offenders to tell men walking toward them from different directions to stop when the men get too close. The space needed for comfort by the violent men has been found to be significantly greater than the space needed for control subjects (Kinzel, 1970). Two possible explanations of this are (1) that the greater space needs of the violent men makes them more easily threatened and therefore more violent or (2) that their violent nature has created a need for more physical distance.

A note of caution must be sounded here. While psychopathological groups may differ from others in their nonverbal behaviors, the evidence is not yet in on "normal" nonverbal actions. As we have noted, any action may be interpreted according to the individual involved, or the particular interaction, or its social meanings. Thus, we should not expect clear one-to-one relationships between most of a person's nonverbal actions and his or her personality. Rather, a more realistic goal is to understand how the individual and the social group contribute to the forces influencing nonverbal communications. Two such contributors are the next topics to be examined: gender and race.

SEX DIFFERENCES

To observe that men and women behave differently is to state the trite and obvious. Yet *just* how men and women differ is not always obvious. The nonverbal behaviors of men and women have fascinated scholars, and the study of such behaviors has revealed some of the ways each sex is socialized. These sex differences include the following:

1. Women look more at other people than do men. This pattern occurs in both speaking and listening and whether they are talking with men or women.

2. Men smile less frequently and for shorter periods than do women. Look around at men and women passing by or talking. Overall, the men will be more straight-faced and the women more smiling. Why? One likely answer is that the rearing of little girls places greater emphasis on winning social approval of others.

3. Masculine and feminine postures and gestures may be reliably differentiated. Not only can observers distinguish readily between the gestures and postures of men and women, but masculine females and feminine males may be identified in silent films.

Extensive investigations of sex differences have been conducted (for example, see Birdwhistle, 1970, and Bull, 1983). For the present, we need note only that both whole body and small gesture movements influence our judgments of masculinity and femininity. Furthermore, a variety of behaviors have been stereotyped as clearly male or female. Take the case of how we carry books.

College women carry books in decidedly different ways than do college men (see Figure 9–2). Female students at the University of Montana were found to have a 92 percent incidence of carrying their books close to the front of their bodies, with one or both arms wrapped around the books. In this same study, 95 percent of the male students carried books at the side of their bodies, supported by one hand (Jenni & Jenni, 1976). This is a typical pattern on most campuses and indicates how we may easily identify sex role by observing body posture and gestures.

FIGURE 9–2   Sex Differences in Book Carrying

Adapted from Jenni & Jenni, 1976, p. 859.

Sex role expectations are also exhibited in a behavior most of us engage in, but few of us think about: holding hands. When you walk holding hands with someone, notice whose hand is in front. In holding hands, even when the couple's fingers are intertwined, one person's hand must lead. The man's hand will be in front, in most cases. As an experiment, try reversing the position of your hands. If you're a man, hold from behind; if you're a woman, hold with your hand in front. Most people find the switched position strange, sometimes uncomfortable. Although this discomfort may be explained in part by height and hand size differences, sex roles nevertheless contribute as well.

Sex roles also determine who is to be on the right or the left when couples walk together, according to a study by Richard Borden and Gordon Homleid (1978) subtitled "Are Men Still Strong-Arming Women?" Among same-handed couples of heterosexual college students, significantly more women were found to walk on the man's preferred side (his right side if they are both right-handed) than on her preferred side. If the couple's hands or bodies touch, the effect is even more pronounced. When the couples are opposite-handed, men and women put their preferred sides together, again especially if they are touching. This pattern of preferred sides has been interpreted to reflect the social tradition of male dominance.

INTERRACIAL NONVERBAL COMMUNICATIONS

American blacks and whites have different, but sometimes overlapping, patterns of looking and listening in conversations, according to research conducted by a number of investigators. Both Kendon (1973) and LaFrance and Mayo (1976), in separate studies, found that whites look away most of the time while they are speaking and look at the speaker almost all the time while they are listening. LaFrance and Mayo found a nearly opposite pattern for blacks. While speaking, blacks look at the listener most of the time. While listening, blacks look away much of the time, maintaining only intermittent eye contact. Table 9–1 illustrates the likely outcomes of these different behaviors.

Frederick Erickson (1979) was a consultant working with a large steel company when he found that interracial job interviews frequently seemed to go wrong. When speaking with black applicants, white job interviewers had the vague uncomfortable intuition that "the black applicants don't seem to be listening." On the other hand, the black applicants said that the white interviewers kept saying the same things over and over, that the interviewers must have thought they were stupid. The young black job applicants described these conversations as tedious and demeaning. Erickson was fascinated with their perceptions, so he filmed fifty-six naturally occurring school and job interviews and twenty-six arranged conversations and looked particularly at a subsample of films between white speakers and black listeners.

The white speakers followed the pattern of explaining and reexplaining their message in increasingly concrete, simple terms until their black

TABLE 9-1 How Blacks and Whites Speak and Listen		
	White Speaker/ Black Listener	Black Speaker/ White Listener
From the point of view of the speaker	Listener is not paying attention, is sullen or frightened	Listener is insubordinate, hostile, and staring
From the point of view of the listener	Speaker is shifty eyed, nervous, or deceitful	Speaker is overbearing, insistent, and staring

listeners gave an active body signal of listening. Slight head nods were insufficient; accented head nods were required for the speaker to proceed further. The speakers felt unsure that the black listeners were understanding what was being said. On the other hand, the black listeners felt that the white speakers were talking down to them.

When the two groups' ways of making a point were compared, white speakers were found to make their points in one chunk, while black speakers would break the message down and postpone making the final point. Furthermore, black speakers expect an active listening response to a sharply falling shift in pitch—a response that white listeners almost never give to this cue. In practical terms, these differences are part of the reason white speakers overexplain and blacks feel whites are talking down to them.

Several steps may be taken to combat interracial miscommunication. Becoming aware of the nature of the problem so that a pattern of bad responses does not continue is a first step. The second step is arranging access to someone who has "bicultural competence" and can explain cultural differences. If more job interviews were conducted by people with racial and cultural backgrounds similar to those of the applicants, fewer communication problems would arise. Finally, active training in intercultural competence itself may assist interviewers in resolving just these kinds of problems (Erickson, 1979).

IMPROVING NONVERBAL COMMUNICATIONS

Influence and Persuasion

Nonverbal behaviors can lead others to listen carefully to us and believe what we say or, like Henry Hendrickson's behaviors in the orientation, lead them to listen minimally and disregard our statements. As persuaders, we are at our best when our body language says, "Listen to me. I believe in and value what I am saying, and so should you." When we act this way, our voices typically become louder, we talk more rapidly, and our gestures and expressions are more animated (Bush, 1985; Blanck, Rosenthal, Vannicelli & Lee, 1986).

The persons we are seeking to persuade are most likely to be influenced if

The persuasion effort fits well with the context of the situation;

we are at an optimal distance, not too close nor too far away;

we are perceived as having high status or expertise;

our body language indicates openness and relaxation.

Context

The importance of context is illustrated by the airport scenes in which people attempt to inform passersby about religious movements or the benefits of nuclear power. Here the persuaders have little appropriate context: airports are places where people wait for planes. The task irrelevance of such "missionaries" makes their efforts to influence unlikely to succeed. On the other hand, in a setting in which a "persuader" is believed to be knowledgeable and the subjects are open to listening, such as in classrooms or during orientations to new jobs, persuasion is more likely to occur.

Optimal distance

Optimal distance

The distance between you and others does affect the intensity of your contact and the effectiveness of your attempts to persuade. For effective individual persuasion, a distance of four to five feet works well. If one is too close, say within arm's length, the other person often will find the closeness threatening and may be resistant to any argument. In Middle East cultures, the optimal distance is different. Six to twelve inches is an optimal distance for persuasive and personal communications in many of those countries. Syrians and Turks are not uncomfortable in nose-to-nose discussions. In the United States, however, less than three to four feet is considered too close. Beyond six or eight feet, we are too far apart (except in group meetings), and the other person is not engaged; he or she is too uninvolved to be readily influenced and our impact is diluted.

Open body asymmetry

Open body asymmetry

People are influenced more by open body postures than by closed body positions, perhaps because they understand that open body positions may indicate that nothing is being hidden. In businesses, the executives and other high-status people usually assume open body positions in conversations, while low-status people close their body positions when talking to higher-up personnel.

Influence and power are associated with asymmetry as well as openness in nonverbal language. Asymmetry can be determined by drawing an imaginary line from the top of a person's head to the midpoint between his or her feet. If about equal body positions are seen on each side, the person is symmetrical. If there is a clear imbalance or a predominance to one side, then the person is asymmetrical. The new employee speaking to the company president may well sit symmetrically, both feet flat on the floor, spine straight, and hands clasped in lap. The president, however, probably will sit turned somewhat, legs crossed, relaxed, asymmetrical. If a low-status person uses open body, asymmetrical postures with a high-status supervisor, the low-status person is likely to be seen as uppity, defiant, or abrasive, regardless of the actual words he or she speaks.

Awareness of Nonverbal Behavior

When you stand in front of a three-way mirror in a clothing store or see a closed circuit TV picture of yourself, you may be startled by the images of your face and body. Each of us is accustomed to looking in a mirror in specific ways and places—usually in a bathroom or bedroom and straight on, so we see ourselves only full face and stationary. The three-way mirror and television images often startle us, and sometimes distress us, because we see ourselves in profile and in motion. "Is that really me? Does my nose truly angle that way? Do I move my head so when I walk?" we may ask.

Objective self-awareness

This experience of self has been called *objective self-awareness* by Duval and Wicklund (1972). We become *objectively* aware of how we

EXPLORATION IN WELL-BEING

The Open Body Position

In one scene in the "Star Trek" television series, Captain Kirk and Mr. Spock beam down to an alien planet, where they are greeted by the native humanoids. The natives swirl their arms so that their palms are open, their hands are forward, and their arms are apart in an unmistakable gesture of friendliness. The director of that "Star Trek" episode knew that we see the body in an open position as a universal signal of positive feeling and absence of threat.

Open body positions have been the subject of several studies, which have indicated that people trust and believe persons who present themselves with open body positions more than they trust or believe persons with closed or neutral body positions. Let us look at what we mean by open and closed body positions.

look, how we walk and stand, and how we talk when we see ourselves on closed circuit television, in a three-way mirror, on videotape, or in photographs. Objective self-awareness also occurs when we listen to ourselves on audiotape. The tape recorder plays back how we sound to others. Normally the sound of our voices is transmitted through bone to our own ears, so hearing our voice sounds transmitted through the air from a tape recorder makes our voices alien and sometimes unpleasant to us.

Chapter 3 examined how we each, in our minds, see how we come across to others. These self-images arise from the ways we understand everything we do. Some people have fairly good ideas of how they present themselves, knowing how they appear and communicate as well as they know the palms of their hands. (We should note how little we have actually studied the palms of our hands, unless we have joined a fortune-teller in carefully examining the palms for twenty or so minutes.) Other people are quite unaware of their self-presentations. When they see movies of themselves with their hair covered, walking away from the camera, for example, they are unable to recognize themselves.

Learning the effects of nonverbal communications increases objective

Closed Body Posture	Open Body Posture
Arms crossed	Arms apart
Elbows next to body	Elbows away from body
Shoulders hunched, next to head	Shoulders relaxed, away from head
Hands clenched and near body	Hands open, palms up, away from body
Knees and feet together	Legs or ankles crossed, knees apart
Legs bent with feet directly beneath knees or buttocks	Legs stretched out, with feet away from trunk

Check out for yourself the ease of making contact with others with open and closed body postures. First, assume a closed body position, tightening your muscles and closing into yourself to take up the smallest possible amount of space. Feel the sense of isolation. Try to speak to another person in this posture. Next, deliberately and slowly open your posture, stretching, reaching, loosening, moving arms, hands, legs, and feet forward and apart. Continue your conversation with the same person. You should feel better able to communicate and should feel more personal. Finally, try to observe the times your postures are open and closed with others. Experiment with opening and closing your posture, and note the resulting improvements and impairments to conversations.

In business organizations, people often communicate status through posture. Executives usually take asymmetrical open body positions, while those with less status in the company adopt closed, symmetrical positions.

self-awareness. If you are able to view your behaviors with objectivity, you may understand more clearly your impact on other people. A beginning step in acquiring such awareness is searching out objective feedback. Instead of avoiding looking at yourself on videotape or listening to yourself on audiotape, look and listen carefully; try to reconcile the images and sounds comfortably with your sense of yourself.

It's common to feel disrupted at first by this feedback. People who pay attention to the novel ways they sound or look may initially be less able to concentrate on completing other tasks, such as reading, conversing, or studying. On the other hand, developing an awareness of what you do, as others see you, gives you the opportunity to understand what triggers others' reactions to you and, over time, to take steps to draw responses that fit more closely with your goals.

How well people are aware of *others'* nonverbal cues has been a topic of systematic study. The method for such study is known as **_PONS_** (profile of nonverbal sensitivity).

PONS

Profile of Nonverbal Sensitivity

The judging of others' nonverbal cues has been investigated in a seven-year program of research developed by Robert Rosenthal and his colleagues (1979). They began with the observation that people vary widely in how accurately they are able to translate voice, body, and facial messages into understandable communications. Sensitivity to twenty different emotional messages was measured with the PONS. Subjects are exposed to 220 two-second units of a person's nonverbal behavior, some of which give only voices (with unintelligible speech), some of which show just the person's face, and others show only the body from the neck down or only the face and body to the knees. The subjects choose between alternative interpretations of each emotion portrayed. For example, after looking at a two-second film, subjects may choose "expressing jealous anger" or "talking to a lost child" as the filmed person's activity.

Who is best in nonverbal sensitivity? Of fourteen groups (totalling 4,458 people) studied, U.S. college students scored the highest; they were accurate 81 percent of the time. Psychiatric patients and alcoholics scored a low 71 percent and U.S. children scored the lowest at 67 percent. It was apparent that two seconds gave subjects more than enough time to interpret nonverbal behaviors. When the time allotted was dropped to one second, 18 percent overall accuracy was found. When it was cut to one-eighth of a second, 17 percent were accurate. Only at one-twenty-fourth of a second did accuracy fall to about 4 percent (Rosenthal et al., 1979).

Women were found to be between 2 and 4 percent more accurate than men in their nonverbal sensitivity. The accuracy of PONS performance seems to rise between the ages of eight years and twenty-five years, and then it levels off. However, people's IQ and SAT scores appear to be fully independent of their skills in reading nonverbal cues. One provocative finding was that people's ratings of their own sensitivity was unrelated to PONS results. We have no accurate sense of our skills in this area. However, spouses were found to be very good at judging subjects' nonverbal sensitivity.

The PONS has become a useful tool in the study of nonverbal awareness. It is the only set of standardized stimuli that permits testing of just how accurate any group is in reading voice, body, and facial expressions.

Using Nonverbal Knowledge

Each of us has needs for privacy in our lives. We have thoughts we prefer not to share with others. Does studying nonverbal messages invade others' privacy by reading multiple levels of their communications? Psychologists regularly encounter in others just this fear of being exposed, which often is exhibited by the people's personal discomfort and their maintenance of emotional distance. One nonverbal communications researcher describes the situation as follows:

> The assumption here is that the person trained in nonverbal communication is busy reading all kinds of deep, dark secrets, or at the very least, that he is super-capable of doing this. Thus the nervous giggle. People often become visibly uncomfortable in the face of what they perceive to be direct threat to their information preserves. Or, to put it another way, they seem to feel like the Emperor in his new clothes, right after the kid on the sidelines, unsocialized brat that he was, started pointing his finger at him . . . if everyone gets to know what he knows, sooner or later none of us will have the guts to step out in public.

(Soucie, 1979, p. 215)

In practice, the mastery of nonverbal communication is quite different. We already hear much more than the spoken word. When we look more closely at others' actions, it is certainly possible that we may make others more self-conscious for a while. However, increasing our knowledge of what is transpiring in a communication may allow us to achieve the objectives of making us and others feel happier about ourselves and more effective in our interactions. Table 9–2 summarizes how nonverbal communication can signal well-being.

TABLE 9–2   Nonverbal Communication Toward and Away from Well-Being

Toward Well-Being	Away from Well-Being
Nonverbal communication consistent with verbal communication	Nonverbal communication unknowingly inconsistent with verbal communication
Eye contact appropriate to intent and context	Excessive or insufficient eye contact for intent and context
Gestures consonant with culture and sex role	Gestures substantially dissonant with culture and sex role
Flexible and responsive facial expressions	Frozen or flooded facial expressions
Free from race-based interferences in nonverbal communication	Race-based stereotyping interferences with nonverbal communication
Postures (open or closed; symmetrical or asymmetrical) suitable to hierarchy and intent	Postures unsuitable to intent or hierarchy

SUMMARY

Communication consists of much more than the spoken word. Facial expressions, body language, and voice quality all contribute to the content of the messages we send, particularly when we are communicating emotion. To understand nonverbal communication, one must know the context, or total situation, in which the behavior occurs. There are three levels of context: the individual level, of the person alone; the relationship level, of the person interacting with another; and the social rule level, of both people interacting with other persons.

Eye contact is a silent communication that indicates interest and generates involvement. Eye contact is exhibited by four universal behaviors: looking toward the other, smiling briefly, raising the eyebrows, and a quick head nod. In the context of a caring relationship, eye contact transmits positive feelings. In a hostile interaction, eye contact transmits negative feelings. Extended eye contact intensifies an interaction, and for that reason the avoidance of gazes is a particularly frequent behavior of people in public places. In two-person interactions, a general rule is, the better the eye contact, the better the quality of the communications.

Gestures are body movements, especially of the fingers, hands, or arms, that symbolize a feeling or thought. Different cultures use quite different gestures. Thumbing the nose is a familiar gesture of mockery in the United States, but the chin flick is a predominantly European expression of lack of interest.

Much emotional content of nonverbal communication can be found in facial expressions. Six universal facial expressions exist: happiness, sadness, surprise, fear, anger, and disgust. Facial expressions also can confuse nonverbal communication. Seeking to conceal an expression is called masking. An unsuccessful mask allows nonverbal leakage of the true feelings. Neutralizing replaces an existing emotion with an unemotional front. Intensifying overexpresses the strength of the felt emotions. Deintensifying underexpresses the felt emotions. Frozen affect is a fixed emotional expression. When two or more emotions show, an expression blend is present. Flooding refers to holding an emotional expression overly long and inappropriately.

Micromomentary behaviors are small movements that last a short time. Four such movements are width of eye opening, head angle or tilt, head position up or down, and vertical width of mouth, all of which can indicate an individual's emotional state.

The scientific study of such small body motions is kinesics, which was pioneered by Ray L. Birdwhistle (1970). Kinesics studies body actions by describing their smallest component parts, called kines. The duration of a kine may be as brief as one-thousandth of a second, so a considerable number of behaviors may occur in just a few seconds. A kinesic observation of the American adolescent courtship dance reported that twenty-four separate steps must be taken, usually in order, for the courtship to proceed.

Observation of psychiatric patients has led to the conclusion that the patients differ from others in the quantity of their nonverbal behaviors. Men and women differ from each other as well, with women smiling more and looking more at their partners than men. Studies of sex differences showed that women carry their books closer to the front of their bodies than do men and walk on the dominant side of male partners. Interracial communication is sometimes impaired by the background information each group brings to their interpretations of nonverbal signals. Whites tend to look away from their listener much of the time while speaking, and they tend to look at the speaker while listening. Just the opposite patterns occur for blacks.

Efforts to influence others can be promoted by nonverbal behaviors. The behaviors that are persuasive utilize appropriate contexts, optimal distance, and open body asymmetry.

We may improve our nonverbal communications by becoming aware of our appearance to others and our self-presentations—a process that is built on the theory of objective self-awareness. The extent of people's sensitivity to the nonverbal communication of others has been assessed by the PONS, which measures the accuracy of interpretations of voice, body, and facial messages. Increasing our knowledge of our own and others' nonverbal behaviors has the potential for making clear those communications that otherwise would be implicit and invisible.

Key Terms

Context	Kine
Deintensifying	Kinesics
Expression blends	Masking
Eye contact	Micromomentary behavior
Flooded expressions	Neutralizing
Frozen affect	Nonverbal leakage
Gaze	Objective self-awareness
Gaze avoidance	Open body asymmetry
Gaze omission	Optimal distance
Gestures	PONS
Individual level	Relationship level
Intensifying	Social-rule level

Recommended Reading

Ekman, P. (1985). *Telling lies: Clues to deceit in the marketplace, politics and marriage.* New York: W.W. Norton. Yes, this book does describe how to tell lies. However, Ekman goes well beyond that and discusses what facial expressions and other forms lies take and how to detect lies.

Harper, R.G., Wiens, A.N. & Matarazzo, J.D. (1978). *Nonverbal communication: The state of the art.* New York: Wiley. Bursting with facts and studies, this book is the volume of choice for the serious researcher into nonverbal behavior.

LaFrance, M. & Mayo, C. (1978). *Moving bodies: Nonverbal communication in social relationships.* Monterey, CA: Brooks/Cole. The interested student will be able to readily comprehend nonverbal behavior applications from this book.

Morris, D. (1977). *Manwatching: A field guide to human behavior.* London: Jonathan Cape. This book has thousands of photographs and drawings illustrating nonverbal communication. It is fascinating reading. This is the kind of book you bring to your best friend to share and enjoy.

10

CHAPTER

Loving and Being Loved

His Story

When we met, it was electricity. She and I accidentally touched, and everything else faded. All other sounds and sights were far away, and we were in a little cocoon so charged with feeling that I was totally energized.

Right off the bat, we found we had a lot in common. We even liked the same music and movies. There aren't many hard-core Jimmy Buffet fans, and she knew half his songs by heart.

This was a woman I wanted to spend time with.

She very much wanted to be with me.

On our third night together, she told me not to make anything too heavy out of this, but that she loved me.

Given her cautious approach, I felt I had no choice but to say that I loved her, too. It would have been stupid to say nothing.

We talked about everything, and often slipped into a what-if world, imagining the kind of house we would live in and what our future would be like.

We agreed our favorite names for children were Karen and Scott.

We started arguing.

The arguments were about nothing, and they bothered me.

I always ended up apologizing, and that made me miserable.

I finally realized the bubble had burst and I had to get out of the relationship. We still had some good moments, but not enough.

My feelings must have been visible. I became distant.

I could not tell her, because I knew how hurt she would be.

Her Story

When we met, it was electricity. There's something about men who are physically strong but really sensitive that gets to me. I think the physical attraction was important, but I knew this was a man with a mind, too—someone I could respect.

He had the same taste for the offbeat in movies as I do. We talked about the new directors and who won the Cannes Film Festival and how we always agreed with Roger Ebert's reviews and never with Gene Siskel's reviews. And he loved Jimmy Buffet!

I thought, this is a man whose baby I would like to have.

He very much wanted to be with me.

On our third date, I knew I loved him. I didn't want to scare him off, because sometimes men think an "I love you" is a bear trap. I told him not to react too much or overinterpret how I felt, but that I loved him.

He loved me, too. I knew even before he told me. His every breath made my heart dance.

We started making plans for our lives together and even began designing our dream house.

We agreed we would name our children Karen and Scott.

We did have arguments.

They were about nothing, and they didn't mean anything.

We worked out all our arguments so they didn't drag on.

The infatuation period had passed, and we were living the normal lives of people who love each other. Some fussing went on, but we had lots of good moments.

He began acting funny.

When I asked him what was happening, he told me he was going through a tense time in school and at work.

I wanted to be as rational as I could about this, so I wrote her a letter saying we had to stop seeing each other. I didn't put a lot of details in it, because it didn't seem right to be critical in a good-bye note. I put the note in her mailbox.

I still feel a little shame at not having had the courage to tell her in person, but I'm glad I'm out of the relationship.

I don't think too much about it any more.

Then I found this brief note from him in my mailbox. It said he thought it was best for both of us if we stopped seeing each other. It was a total shock. I was devastated and couldn't stop crying for two days.

My hurt is still with me, but it has been replaced some by anger. How could I have loved a creep who would do that to me?

I keep thinking will anyone really love me? What's wrong with me?

In "His Story/Her Story," the woman's declaration of love changed how the couple defined their relationship. She became more committed. He became more cautious. She looked at events in terms of building a permanent relationship. He assumed less permanence. Because he chose to terminate the relationship, it had little lasting impact on him. Because she was committed to the relationship and surprised by his rejection, she was more affected by the ending. Their stories illustrate some of the differences between loving and being loved. It also begins for us the exploration of how romantic love influences our happiness and well-being.

Let us note that the psychological study of loving is incomplete. Instead, psychology is only beginning to understand the factors associated with the love experience from both research and clinical knowledge. This chapter examines those sources of knowledge. The difficulties and failures in loving are discussed, and possible pathways toward well-being in love relationships with others are offered.

THE SEARCH FOR LOVE

Agape

One of the universal quests is to love and be loved. Among the many experiences we call love is the religious, nonsexual love of all people. This love, or **agape,** is the caring for a stranger in need, the selfless giving to others, the universal feeling of goodwill toward other human beings (Fromm, 1956).

The love of a child by a parent, or love between brother and sister, is still another form of love. Although psychoanalysts see sexual components within such familial love, the accepted view is that it is a normal and healthy love. Such caring for a dependent child and love between brother and sister are love relationships that exist in almost every culture and society.

Romantic love

Our focus in this chapter is *romantic love.* Romantic lovers often feel closer to each other than to any other person. The couple's view of romantic love includes the sharing of intimate, personal aspects of their lives. They describe times at which they are able to adore, admire, and appreciate the other person—and, in turn, to be adored, appreciated, and valued. Artists and writers are inspired by romantic love. They often write how loving electrifies life, perhaps more than any other single experience.

Defining love is not easy. Most psychologists accept that love is learned and is based on positive feeling and emotional closeness, but no single definition is uniformly accepted. Rather, psychologists tend to describe how it develops and what form it takes (Brehm, 1985).

ROMANTIC LOVE

A Definition of Romantic Love

For this chapter, we use Zick Rubin's (1973) definition of love as consisting of three essential components: attachment, caring, and intimacy. *Attachment* is the need aspect of love, the need to be fulfilled, to be held, to be cared for, to be in emotional and physical contact, to possess another. *Caring* is loving that takes the form of altruistic giving to another, so that your well-being is dependent upon the other person's state of satisfaction and happiness. *Intimacy* is the close, private bond between two people that reaches into the most personal areas of their lives.

Attachment

Caring

Intimacy

Another way of understanding love is by looking at the common elements of and the differences between romantic love and friendship. Keith Davis (1985) has identified these characteristics and differences. The characteristics common to friendships and romantic love are enjoyment, trust, and confiding.

However, love involves more than friendship. Two sets of feelings occurring in romantic love are not present in friendship. Davis (1985) calls them a *passion cluster* and a *caring cluster* of emotions.

Passion cluster
Caring cluster

The passion cluster is composed of fascination, sexual desire, and exclusiveness. Each lover is fascinated with even small, daily ways of the other and is filled with sexual desire. (Note that desire does not always lead to sexual activity. A variety of moral or personal beliefs may redirect desire.) The exclusiveness makes this relationship a first priority, causing all other romantic loves to be set aside.

The caring aspect already has been defined as giving your utmost to the point where the other person's happiness comes before your own. Caring also means becoming a champion or advocate for the lover, staunchly defending and speaking up for him or her.

Liking and Loving

"I loved him very much," a friend explained, "but I just did not like him at all." Loving and liking are not necessarily the same. We have already considered how *love* appears to consist of attachment, caring, and intimacy. On the other hand, *like* consists of two elements: affection and respect. Affection is a general emotional closeness that comes from being in a relationship. Respect is a "cooler, more distant sort of loving" (Rubin, 1973, p. 27) that is founded on admiration of a person's accomplishments or qualities exhibited outside the relationship.

Alvin Pam and colleagues (1975) compared love relationships, dating relationships that did not involve being in love, and simple friendly relationships between members of the opposite sex. Twenty college students were studied in each category. The results confirmed the differences between liking and loving. The friendships were described as especially high on congeniality and respect. The dating relationships were high on congeniality and physical attraction. The love relationships were highest on physical attraction and attachment.

In long-term close relationships, the passion and physical attraction components evolve. They tend to take on more pronounced caring, friendship, and liking aspects. A Liking Scale and a Love Scale, which allow separation of these concepts, have been developed by Rubin (1973). Examination of these items (given in the accompanying "Exploration in Well-Being" box) will illustrate the attitudes and experiences that distinguish loving and liking.

Stages in Loving

Loving another in the most personal ways gives intimacy the opportunity to develop. Both parties need sufficient time to come to know one another. Given that time, five stages have been associated with the development of intimacy in loving: ***choice, mutuality, reciprocity, trust,*** and ***delight*** (Calderone, 1972; McCary, 1978).

Choice
Mutuality
Reciprocity
Trust
Delight

> *Choice.*   Out of the range of thousands of possible partners, you make a deliberate decision that this one person is in some way suitable for you. You seek out the time and attention of this person.

> *Mutuality.*   The other person feels the same way. Love and intimacy as we know them arise from a decision on the part of *both* individuals. You and your loved one jointly seek each other out, come to know each other better, and spend time with each other. One-sided love is a terribly painful feeling, and such love without response leads to anguish and despair.

Reciprocity. As you move closer to your partner, he or she in turn feels comfortable in moving closer to you. Each incident of sharing allows the other to share more and contributes to the foundation of the other's deeper feelings. Defensiveness and critical assessments of the other and of self begin to melt away.

Trust. As two people come to love each other, trust moves toward caring without conditions, liking without performance requirements, and cherishing without wishing either one different in any way.

Delight. Only after the choice has been mutually made and after reciprocity of positive feelings has allowed the relationship to become open and trusting can you and your partner truly delight in each other. Pleasure is found in the other person, in yourself, and in the relationship. The senses are heightened and even daily events take on the glow of beauty and joy. Shared well-being flows back and forth between you and your partner, and reaches out to comfort and please those around you as well.

Passing through these stages leads to *loving* (as opposed to falling in love, a concept we will consider shortly).

Love and trust may emerge only in small increments. We are so accustomed to performing to elicit approval from others that it is difficult for us to relinquish long-term tested ways of gaining regard. Such routinized performances end with a waiting for judgment: Does he approve?

EXPLORATION IN WELL-BEING

Personal Checklists for Love and Liking

Answer these items developed by Zick Rubin (1970) to confirm your feelings of romantic love and of liking toward the significant others in your life.

The Love Scale

1. I feel that I can confide in _____ about virtually everything.
2. I would do almost anything for _____ .
3. If I could never be with _____ , I would feel miserable.
4. If I were lonely, my first thought would be to seek _____ out.
5. One of my primary concerns is _____ 's welfare.
6. I would forgive _____ for practically anything.
7. I feel responsible for _____ 's well-being.

Does she like me? The waiting for judgment is a sign of uncertainty about the relationship and oneself. As trust grows, so does self-acceptance, and the need to have one's worth affirmed and reaffirmed diminishes (Miller & Siegel, 1972).

The person who is romantically loved develops an internal feeling of worth. "If I am loved so much by a person who is so desirable, then I am by definition a very desirable and worthwhile person." However, if a person feels unloved and unappreciated, he or she may also feel worthless and undesirable.

We feel marvelous if we see the loved person as desirable—desirable to ourselves, desirable to others. It is that social desirability, or interpersonal success, that helps make the lover's attention valuable to us. If we see our lover as having little social value, then the basis on which we judge ourselves changes. It is more meaningful to our self-esteem to have a highly desirable person loving us.

In Love and Out

In the Marilyn French novel, *The Woman's Room* (1977), one of the characters describes the perspective of falling in love. The man could do nothing wrong. He was as a god, he was wonderfully witty, and charming, and thoughtful, and she enjoyed every thing he ever did. "Whenever you are with him you're high, you're brilliant, your eyes look a little mad, but very

8. I would greatly enjoy being confided in by _____ .

9. It would be hard for me to get along with _____ .

The Liking Scale

1. I think that _____ is unusually well-adjusted.

2. I would highly recommend _____ for a responsible job.

3. In my opinion, _____ is an exceptionally mature person.

4. I have great confidence in _____ 's good judgment.

5. Most people would react favorably to _____ after a brief acquaintance.

6. I think that _____ is one of those people who quickly wins respect.

7. _____ is one of the most likable people I know.

8. _____ is the sort of person whom I myself would like to be.

9. It seems to me that it is very easy for _____ to gain admiration.

(Rubin, 1970, p. 267–268)

When two people come to love and trust each other without conditions, they experience a delight in each other, a sense of well-being, and a heightened enjoyment of life.

beautiful, you act just right" (French, 1977, p. 364). The relationship was beautiful, until . . .

> Then one day the unthinkable happens. You are sitting together at the breakfast table and you're a little hung over, and look across at beloved, beautiful, golden beloved, and beloved opens his lovely rosebud mouth showing his glistening white teeth, and beloved says something stupid. Your whole body stops midstream: your temperature drops. Beloved has never said anything stupid before . . . but that's only the start. Because he keeps on, after that, saying stupid things. And you keep turning around and looking at him strangely, and my God, do you know what, you suddenly see that he's skinny! Or flabby! Or fat! His teeth are crooked, and his toenails are dirty. You suddenly realize he farts in bed. He doesn't, he really doesn't understand Henry James.
>
> *(French, 1977, pp. 365–366)*

What happened? The infatuation had passed. The sense of "falling in love" was gone. This familiar process illustrates the difference between falling in love and loving.

Falling in love   ***Falling in love*** means that you have found another person who "fits" into your fantasy of love. Each of us carries dreams and thoughts of the perfect partner and the perfect relationship. When you meet someone who fills part of this fantasy, you are immediately, often irrationally, attracted to the person and may find yourself in love. The wondrous joy springs from the realization of the fantasy image. Your perfect lover is there, as you have always secretly hoped and dreamed. It is wonderful as long as your lover fits your fantasized image (Simmel, 1984). Erich Fromm described the exhilaration of falling in love.

> If two people who have been strangers, as all of us are, suddenly let the wall between them break down, and feel close, feel one, this moment of oneness is one of the most exhilarating, most exciting experiences in life.
>
> *(Fromm, 1956, p. 3)*

When such exhilaration arises from idealized fantasy images, this source limits the relationship. "She was always up there somewhere, high above me, like some goddess whom I had discovered and regarded as my very own. It was I, idiot that I was, who prevented her from descending to the level of other mortals" (Miller, 1962, p. 47) wrote novelist Henry Miller of his first love.

The idealizing of partners does elevate them to great heights. The person on a pedestal is not susceptible to all of the temptations, urges, and failings to which the rest of us succumb. He or she is morally superior to the lower person who has placed him or her up there. Solomon has pointed out that being put on a pedestal is more than being confined in a prison. "It is the height of a pedestal, not its diameter, that is the objection against it. Height is distance, and distance is antithetical to love. And then there is the fear of falling. When a person is so idealized, he or she cannot help but be disappointing" (Solomon, 1981, p. 192). A person at a great height and another at lower earthy levels are unequal, and love flourishes best between equals.

Merle Shain has observed that "Love often has more to do with the lover than it has to do with the beloved, and because it does there are people who prefer to fall in love with someone they hardly know. It can be more exciting to bounce love off an object than to deal with the reality of another human being" (Shain, 1974, p. 16). Alas, nobody fits forever into a fantasized image. No single personality can be identical to all the ideal and unattainable traits you carry in your mind. Differences emerge between your lover and your image, and the more you come to know your lover, the more differences emerge.

Then, presto, you're not in love. Rational reasons for the ending may all be there: He said this. She yelled. He was too controlling. She was too critical. He wasn't interested in hiking. She flirted with other men. He didn't do his share of the laundry. She spent too much time with her friends. In essence, however, the fantasy bubble burst, as it always must when we fall out of love.

The alternative to falling in love is loving—quite a different process (what has been called "standing in love"). Loving means cherishing, valuing, and wanting another for who that person truly is, not for what you want that person to be. If so much delight exists in the other that you are amazed, magnetized, and joyous, and if those feelings grow and grow as you come to know more about the other person, then you are both loving and liking your partner—and not simply falling in love.

Styles of Loving

Loving means different things to different people. For one person, loving may mean absolute fidelity and dependability. For another person, it may be the sharing of all secrets and feelings. For a third person, love may be the label for intense physical enjoyment. To help them understand the nature of love, psychologists have sought to describe the predominant styles of loving. Among the most successful of such efforts have been the works of Laswell and Laswell (1976) and Hendrick and Hendrick (1986). The Laswells and Hendricks found the following six distinct styles of loving through factor analyses of feelings and beliefs:

Friendship-based love

Friendship-based love.   Good friends who have known each other very well come to realize they love each other. People in the friendship-based style of loving assert, "It is hard to say exactly when my lover and I fell in love. Our friendship merged gradually into love over time" (Hendrick & Hendrick, 1986, p. 395).

Giving

Giving.   Support, forgiveness, unselfishness, patience are all components of the giving style of loving. Scores on a measure of the giving style of loving have been found to be mildly related to scores on the Rubin Liking Scale and to moderately overlap with scores on the Rubin Love Scale. The giving style comes close to the general concept of romantic loving. This style is captured by the statement, "I cannot be happy unless I place my lover's happiness before my own."

Possessive dependent

Possessive dependent.   In possessive dependent loving, couples pursue most activities together. The two identities tend to be merged. Jealousy and possessiveness are characteristic feelings of this style. A typical statement of possessive dependent love is, "When my lover doesn't pay attention to me, I feel sick all over."

Pragmatic

Pragmatic.   The pragmatic style of loving carefully and deliberately selects the traits of a lover, the cost–benefit ratio of a love relationship, and the arrangements of the relationship. In other words, the approach to love is rational and logical. A pragmatic lover may hold that "A main consideration in choosing a lover is how he/she reflects on my family and career."

Game playing

Game playing.   In the game playing style of loving, multiple lovers are often maintained, and personal pleasure is emphasized, with commitment, possessiveness, and exclusivity minimized. Game playing lovers say, "I believe that what my lover doesn't know about me won't hurt him/her."

Erotic

Erotic.   Love at first sight with the ideal person, physically and emotionally, is erotic loving. Sexuality, interpersonal intimacy, and physical means of pleasing the loved one are valued in this style of loving. This style fits the description that we have given of falling in love. A key erotic love statement is, "My lover and I have the right physical chemistry between us."

We don't necessarily have a single style of loving. Rather, we may demonstrate several styles of loving in our significant love relationships. Students who report they are "in love now" are higher on all styles of loving but game playing than students not presently in love (Hendrick & Hendrick, 1986). Further, at different stages in a relationship we may discover ourselves and our partners expressing quite different styles.

B-Love and D-Love

B-Love

B-love stands for being love and is defined by Maslow (1968) as healthy and nonpossessive love. B-love grows out of strength and security. It is characterized by: (1) loving others for who they are, for their being, and for what they are becoming; (2) a giving style of loving and an equitable balance, with both partners giving equally; and (3) neither partner demanding conditions or proof of love; rather, both demonstrate acceptance and comfort in the relationship.

D-Love

Each of us has needs and desires that we bring to relationships. When unmet needs turn into pressing reasons for us to seek another, then we may be experiencing what Maslow (1968) has called ***D-love***, or deficiency love. D-love has three characteristics: (1) It is an affiliation with someone else in order to correct an unhappiness, a deep gap in one's own life and self. (2) It is nonreciprocal. The needy one continually draws on the other, often desperately and insistently, and yet typically is unable to adequately return the caring. (3) It's a relationship that inevitably revolves around the deficient person's insecurities and needs as the partner responds to this

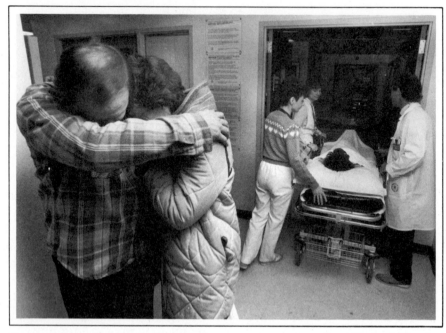

The love between these two people gives them strength, security, and comfort in a frightening situation.

internal deficiency. D-love is related to falling in love in the sense that both grow out of one's self-preoccupations.

Major differences exist between men's and women's descriptions of their capacities for love in general and for B-love particularly. Women love more deeply than do men, according to at least two studies of what men and women have said. According to Dion and Dion (1975), women report trusting their love partners more, liking their men more than their men like them, and showing more elation in the relationship. If we use B-love as our basis for assessing the self-reported quality of love, again women love better. Dietch (1978) found that, among men and women college students with about the same overall levels of psychological health, women expressed significantly higher levels of B-love.

These differences vanish if we look only at romantically oriented men. Men who have romantic attitudes toward love talk about themselves and their feelings in ways similar to women's descriptions. Men with such romantic attitudes toward love are different from nonromantic men. Among other things, these romantic men share more of themselves, disclosing highly to parents and friends (Lester, Brazill, Ellis & Guerin, 1984).

The overall finding of these studies is that women *express* more feeling, liking, elation, and B-love than men do. The cultural expectations in American society allow women to express such feelings more openly. However, expression of feelings does not necessarily correspond to experiencing of feelings, and, therefore, men and women may be more similar at the feeling level than the preceding findings indicate.

B-love has been investigated in aspects of loving other than on the basis of male–female differences. One hundred and twenty-six college students at Duke University were asked the question, "In the last three years how many romantic relationships have you had in which you felt you were really in love?" Ninety-three students said they had had one or more such relationships. These forty-nine women and forty-four men also completed a series of questionnaires about love and psychological well-being, including a questionnaire to measure B-love (Deitch, 1978).

Actualizers, that is, students high on well-being, were less likely to show resentment toward their love partners after the relationships had ended. Self-fulfillment was correlated positively with B-love in this study, but some actualizers engaged in D-love, and some people who were less fulfilled described their relationships as B-love. Nevertheless, this B-love

D-love is nonreciprocal. The needy one demands attention and affection from the other but is unable to return the same kind of caring. D-love is related to falling in love, because it too grows out of one's self-preoccupations.

scale does seem to measure something important. College students who are high on B-love are low on neuroticism and report that they feel their basic needs are being met (Lester, Doscher, Harris & Smith, 1984).

Love on a Tightrope

Your mouth is all at once dry. Your heart is beating furiously and so hard that it seems about to burst from your chest. Every nerve and muscle in your body seems energized. Rational thinking has faded away, and in its place is raging emotion, raging so that you don't know if you can stand it.

When might this description apply for you? It could apply when you are walking a tightrope stretched between two tall buildings. It could apply when you are a soldier in a unit under attack, seeing your fellow infantrymen falling wounded around you. It could refer to when you feel intense guilt, having done something awful that you hope no one will ever discover. And it could be a description of your emotional state when you are feeling wonderfully, thoroughly in love.

Intense physiological arousal at times of danger or shame or anger have much in common with the arousal experienced while in love. The emotional state is defined by both the physiological arousal and the label you attach to that arousal. Such arousal occurring in the presence of a person who is generally appropriate to love produces love, or at least attraction. Ovid advised that the best time to arouse passion in a woman is while she is watching gladiators disembowel each other in the arena, and El Cid courted his loved one, whose father he had slain, while killing her pet pigeons one at a time (Rubin, 1973).

Imagine now that you are crossing a shaky, wobbly, suspension bridge, with a drop of 230 feet below to boulders and a river. You are interviewed by an attractive person of the opposite sex while holding on to the bridge tightly and fearfully. Dutton and Aron (1974) devised this exact situation, with men being interviewed by attractive women. In the control condition of a stable, wide, safe bridge, the men were interviewed by equally attractive women. As predicted, the men were more attracted to the women on the suspension bridge; they later telephoned these women more frequently than the women they met on the stable bridge.

Disliking as well as liking can be intensified in a tightrope situation. In one study, college men running in place were exposed to an arousal condition. While running, they listened either to a tape of a humorous Steve Martin monologue or to a description of human mutilation. The same results were seen under both conditions. Compared to a control group, these men liked women they found attractive more and disliked unattractive women more (White, Fishbein & Rutstein, 1981).

However, it isn't necessary to be truly physiologically aroused for this effect to work. You only have to think you are aroused. In one study, female college students were told their heart rates rose sharply in the presence of male interviewers (in actuality, the rates hadn't risen). The males assumed rehearsed roles of pleasant and unpleasant interviewers. The female students were compared to women who were not given the incorrect heart rate information. The women who thought they were reacting found the pleasant men more pleasant and the unpleasant men more unpleasant than did the women in the control group (Walsh, Meister & Kleinke, 1977).

The lesson of these studies is that excitement generalizes. If you want to fall in love or be loved, or at least to have others more attracted to you, be around them at times that generate strong emotions. Even if these emotions are fear, anger, or despair, the attraction increases, given a starting point of some positive feelings toward you. Be with your potential love during his or her crises rather than only at quiet times. Elaine Walster and Ellen Berscheid summarized this process.

> A frightened man is a potentially romantic man. So is an angry man, a jealous man, a rejected man or a euphoric man. . . . To love passionately, a person must first be physically aroused. . . . Once he is so aroused all that remains is for him to identify this complex of feelings as passionate love, and he will have experienced authentic love. . . . Adrenalin makes the heart grow fonder.
>
> *(Walster & Berscheid, 1971, pp. 46–47)*

The Gain-Loss Effect

Gain-loss effect

> Mr. and Mrs. Doting, who have been married for 10 years, are preparing to leave their house for a cocktail party. He compliments her—"Gee, honey, you look great!" She yawns. She already knows that her husband thinks she is attractive.
>
> Mr. and Mrs. Doting arrive at the cocktail party. A male stranger begins to talk to Mrs. Doting and after a while he says, with great sincerity, that he finds her very attractive. She does not yawn. The compliment increases her liking of the stranger.
>
> This little episode is an example of what some of my students have called Aronson's Law of Marital Infidelity.
>
> *(Aronson, 1970, p. 48)*

This provocative observation by Elliot Aronson inspired a flurry of research studies on the gain–loss theory of attraction. Gain–loss theory holds that it is the *order* of the good and bad feelings someone expresses toward you that determines your attraction. If you meet a person who initially is cool and then becomes warmer, you may assume that the liking is genuine. "I am truly liked because after knowing me better he/she likes me more," is an example of gain-loss thinking. You would also value infrequent instances of liking more than the same amount of liking constantly expressed. Conversely, someone's feeling moving from warm to cold should affect you more than the consistent expression of cold feelings.

Gain-loss studies exposed college students to experimenters who acted warm throughout, cold throughout, warm and then cold, or cold and then warm. The warm behaviors consisted of smiling, directly focusing attention on the person, nodding one's head, or calling the person sincere, intellectual, and dignified. The cold behaviors were frowning, looking away, making distracting gestures, and calling the person conceited, tiresome, and immature (Aronson, 1970, 1980; Clore, Wissins & Itkin, 1975; Berschied, Brothern, & Graziano, 1976).

Research conducted by Ellen Berscheid and her colleagues (1976) showed that when the behaviors were consistently warm the subjects were less attracted to experimenters than when the warm behaviors were preceded by cold behaviors. However, this applied only when *one person* alone was warm. In comparison, when two people were interacting, there was a consistently positive evaluation. Thus, what appeared to be a revelation turned out to be inconsistent—confirmed in some research, but not uniformly found. Now the question became, under what circumstances does a gain or loss effect occur? Aronson offered the answer that the gain–loss effect fades in long-term authentically satisfying relationships. He explained, "I would suggest that the more authentic a relationship is, the less the possibility of reaching the plateau that the Dotings seem to be stuck on" (1970, p. 74). Aronson goes on to explain that, "if two people are genuinely fond of each other, they will have a more satisfying and exciting relationship over a period of time if they are able to express both positive and negative feelings than if they are completely 'nice' to each other at all times" (1980, p. 270).

BARRIERS TO LOVING RELATIONSHIPS

For every poet who has soared on clouds of love's soft joys, another has plunged to earth with sour complaints of love's pain and disillusions. One principle is clear from both experiences. Allowing oneself to love another makes one vulnerable to hurt. It's a risk.

"Courtship [is] to marriage, as a very witty prologue is to a very dull play," William Congreve (1969, p. 131) has written. The initial infatuation of romantic love typically does pass. The excitement and intensity of intimacy frequently diminish. The partners become used to each other. Both partners may attempt to please each other less frequently. Falling in love cannot be sustained, and the task of loving becomes more complex as both parties reveal all of their human fallibilities.

Breaking up may represent the best possible decision for some couples. Many individuals fail repeatedly in love relationships or get stuck in uncomfortable relationships. This section is concerned with the difficulties in love relationships: What goes wrong, and why?

Anticipatory Rejection

Anticipatory rejection

"I'll get him (or her) first" is the way *anticipatory rejection* works. The belief is that your love partner is going to reject you, sooner or later. You act upon this belief by looking for subtle signs of dissatisfaction or rejection. Once the signs are spotted (and dissatisfaction can always be found by keen observers in any relationship), then a powerful protective mechanism is triggered. Because being rejected is painful, the anticipation of rejection may lead you to move away from and then out of the relationship before your partner can reject you.

Anticipating rejection, ultimately, may cause rejection. Almost any behavior can be evoked if one thinks hard enough about it, worries hard enough about it, and looks hard enough for it. If you are worried about your loved one finding someone else, then you may maintain either an emotional distance or a grasping, clinging dependency that drives your love away. Once he or she starts moving away, your fears are confirmed; you say "Aha!" to yourself, and *you* move away faster. In the next relationship, you are even more cautious or clinging, and the pattern repeats itself.

Why do some people exhibit behavior patterns of anticipatory rejection? In some cases, the behavior grows out of a lifelong history of feeling rejected. In others, the person has been hurt recently in an adult relationship. In still others, the behavior emerges from the person's low self-concept—the belief that "I am not worthwhile enough for other persons to want me once they truly get to know how valueless I am."

Anticipatory rejection *can* be overcome by dealing with the fears and uncertainty of rejection. After all, those are the basic emotions individuals seek to avoid. Successful romantic love has been described as the reduction of uncertainty, which in turn can be achieved through the processes of good communication and reassurance so central to loving (Livingston, 1980).

I Love You and If You Really Loved Me . . .

In our opening vignette, the moment the statement "I love you" was uttered was the point at which the man and the woman assumed very different beliefs about their relationship.

The words "I love you" can be spoken in ways that are selfish, controlling, and toxic or in ways that are giving, unselfish, and nourishing. Some of the meanings of "I love you" include the following (Benson, 1974; McCary, 1978):

I want you.

I need you.

I want you to need me.

I desire you sexually.

I want you to be dependent upon me.

I want to use you.

I wish to control you.

I respect, admire, and love who you are and want to help you to continue to grow and benefit.

THE ART OF BEING REJECTED

In the book *How to Make Yourself Miserable* (1966, pp. 74, 76, 78–79), Dan Greenberg gives statements that show the speaker believes he or she is going to be rejected. For example, if you open a phone conversation by saying, "Hello. I'm awfully sorry—I guess I'm phoning at a bad time, aren't I?," you are indicating that you know the other person is unhappy with your call.

Equally effective are anticipatory rejections of appearance. "You'll have to forgive my appearance this evening." "You must always think I look this bad."

The person seeking rejection can find it everywhere.

"Tonight is the first time I've ever tried this dish, so it probably won't be any good."

"I'm afraid I made the coffee too strong."

"I'm afraid I made the coffee too weak."

"It may not taste so bad to you, but this isn't the way it's supposed to taste."

"I'm afraid this story is a little long-winded."

"I couldn't find a pair of stockings that didn't have a run in them."

"You're probably used to taller men."

"I'm probably boring you with all my problems."

Although the initial response of the person to whom you have made such statements usually will be a rapid and emphatic denial, by making persistent and sincere self-deprecating remarks you will eventually elicit the expected rejection.

The word *love* is used so freely by some people that it virtually has no meaning. Other people " . . . invest the word with such enormous meaning that they may never be able to say 'I love'. Still others consider the word such an irreversible commitment to another person that they become frightened by the enormity of the commitment and responsibilities involved" (McCary, 1978, p. 130). As a result, some people totally avoid saying the word. Among all the possible meanings of "I love you" in the preceding list, only the last definition captures the essence of B-love intimacy. When "I love you" conveys acceptance of the person as he or she is, then it reflects nonjudgmental loving.

Parallel to the manipulative use of "I love you" is the conditional use of the statement of love. Every time you say "If you really loved me, then you would . . . ," you indicate that the other person has to continue proving the extent of his or her loving and caring.

"If you really loved me" is sometimes followed by statements such as "you would not look at other men or women," "you would stay up late [or not so late]," "you would empty the garbage," "you would dress up more [or not dress up so much]," "you would be more eager to please me," "you would make love to me." These are interpersonal blackmails. The statement of love is employed in the interest of achieving some other objective, and joy and spontaneity become buried. The problem is captured in this excerpt about the word *love*.

> A word, in my ultimate speechlessness, I have uttered time and time again and now hesitate to speak at all, being, as it is, always too much to stand for what we really mean . . . And never enough.
>
> *(Blumenthal, 1987, p. 26)*

Submerging Individuality within a Love Relationship

The intimate loving of another may involve something that has been called ***the individuation–merger process*** (Levenson & Harris, 1980). In this process, one's identity is merged in part with the other person's because of the desires for unity, for completion in sexual and developmental ways, and for emotional safety. At the same time, there is a continuation (and sometimes an acceleration) of the need to individuate—to be separate and independent of the influence of others. One result of the individuation–merger process is the submersion of two separate identities into one identity. Interests and hobbies in which the partners engage are frequently only ones that both like. Friendships are sometimes made and maintained only if both partners enjoy them. Parties and sporting events and musical performances are often attended only if both wish to attend. One may not go alone to any social happening because, if he or she does, the partner is unhappy.

Individuation–merger process

EROTOMANIA: THE DE CLERAMBAULT SYNDROME

Erotomania

G.G. de Clerambault was a French psychiatrist who described the *psychose passion-alle* syndrome in 1921 (Hollender & Callahan, 1975, pp. 1574–1576). This pattern has also been called *erotomania*, delusional love, melancholic erotique, phantom lover syndrome, and the de Clerambault syndrome. The de Clerambault syndrome seems primarily to afflict women. It occurs when a woman has the delusional belief that an older and prominent man of high status loves her when he really does not. Typically, this delusion emerges in a woman without other delusions and without hallucinations, and it may persist for ten or twenty years. The intensity of this love and its extraordinary resistance to treatment by drugs, by electroshock therapies, and by psychotherapy has led to the disorder being called an insane love—thus, the label *erotomania*.

Doctors have been fascinated by this syndrome—which has appeared in less than one hundred cases in recorded medical history. At least part of their fascination arises from the frequency with which women fall in love with their doctors.

The cases of de Clerambault syndrome follow similar patterns. For example, an unattractive forty-two-year-old hospital records clerk announced to her friends and coworkers that she was going to be married shortly to the chairman of the Department of Ophthalmology—a married man who barely knew the woman and who had no plans to marry her.

In another case, a twenty-one-year-old woman became obsessed with the idea that a college classmate wanted to marry her. The young woman was rational and appropriate in conversation except when talking about this delusional lover. After two and a half years in treatment, she finally called the fantasized lover on the phone.

> The young man stated that he vaguely remembered her as a quiet unassuming young lady in his physics class, but had long since forgotten about her . . . the patient listened quite intently. After the conversation was finished, she insisted that we had not talked to him but had only gotten someone to pretend that he was her fantasized lover.
>
> *(Jordan & Howe, 1980, pp. 980–981)*

Another example is of thirty-seven-year-old woman who felt for ten years that a prominent psychiatrist was in love with her (Raskin & Sullivan, 1974). She had briefly seen the psychiatrist for advice about her marital difficulties, before her divorce. Since then, she had become convinced the psychiatrist wanted to marry her, but that he was shy and unable to leave his wife for her. Further, she believed he controlled her in order to teach her lessons about life. Ten years of psychotherapy and drug treatment had no affect on this belief in his love.

Among the few cases of male erotomania have been a man passionately obsessed with a famous popular singer, a man obsessed with a well-known attorney, and a man obsessed with the daughter of a former president of the United States. John Hinckley, Jr., who attempted to assassinate President Reagan in 1981, has also been called erotomanic. His infatuation with movie star Jodie Foster continued relentlessly over several years despite Miss Foster's lack of interest or response (Goldstein, 1986).

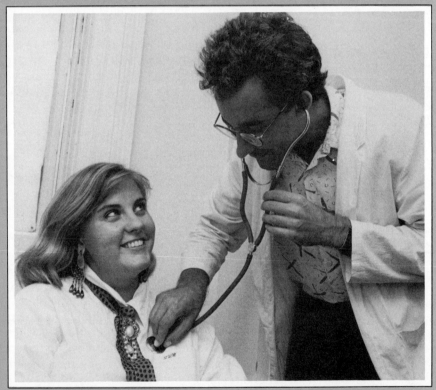

A woman afflicted with erotomania, or delusional love, believes that an older and prominent man of high status—for example, a doctor—loves her when he really does not. This delusion emerges in a woman who has no other delusions or hallucinations, and it is amazingly resistant to treatment by drugs, by electroshock therapy, and by psychotherapy. The condition may persist for ten or twenty years.

In other words, common interests are promoted. Individuation threatens the love partnership. Yet no two people, no matter how compatible, have fully identical interests, friends, and preferences. The long-run consequences of people submerging their self-interests are feelings of resentment and personal loss. In marriages where both persons' lives center around one spouses' career, such feelings may develop.

The exclusiveness resulting from the submerging of individual preferences may restrict the couple from caring for others, aside from family members. If one cares for another person outside the love partnership, a possessive partner may feel a sense of personal loss. Emotion directed toward another is seen as reducing the total amount of love in the primary relationship. Jealousy and possessiveness then intrude into both lives, as one partner's fear of losing the other makes every independent action of the other a threat. If couples deny themselves individual identities in a nearsighted commitment to each other, they both lose, and others lose as well. Fromm (1956) has called the process in which the partners allow themselves no feeling of love for others an *egotism á deux.*

The individuation–merger process does not have to have negative outcomes; it can be an opportunity to move toward more frequent states of well-being. A successful individuation within an intimate love relationship has been described as providing the potential for new levels of emotional development and growth (Gilfillan, 1985).

Too Much Invested to Quit

> "I've put a lot of time in Paul Barton and no cold-eyed, calculating viper is going to do me out of him."
>
> *(dialogue by Jane Barton in the movie* The Pleasure Seekers)

Dollar Auction game

The idea of having invested too much in a partner to quit the relationship can be related to the principle of the **Dollar Auction game,** in which players are allowed one minute to bid as high as they choose for a dollar. The highest bidder receives the dollar. It works identically to a normal auction, except that the second highest bidder is obliged to pay his or her last bid as well. It is not unusual for many of the bids to rise to more than a dollar or even much higher, to four or five dollars. The principle is that people have too much money invested to withdraw from the bidding. They are afraid of losing everything they have already committed to the auction (Teger, 1980).

In real life events, the degree of a person's commitment may increase until it becomes difficult for the person to withdraw from the situation. The process occurs when we repair an old automobile, investing amounts that would be extremely difficult to recover when selling the car. And this phenomenon appears in love relationships.

Have you ever invested so much in a project, such as repairing an old car, that you'll never be able to recover your investment? Sometimes, a person's commitment to a relationship increases to such a degree that the person has difficulty withdrawing from the relationship without suffering severe losses.

Gradually, step by step, many individuals invest more of themselves, their futures, and their feelings in a single other person. In a positive and rewarding relationship, this heavy investment can provide security, comfort, and satisfaction. However, when much of one's emotional resources are directed toward a troubled relationship with another person, one often becomes entrenched and cannot readily escape.

This personal and emotional investment is often accompanied by investments in physical possessions. It is not unusual to hear individuals in their forties and fifties tell how they would love to divorce their spouses but they just cannot afford to do so. Between dividing up the possessions, making payments on the house and cars, and covering the children's expenses, they could not afford to live apart. Nonworking women (and occasionally men) sometimes feel stuck in relationships because of their dependence on the material possessions their spouses provide. They speak of the great difficulty they anticipate in living on their own, how they are used to the comfort of their house and other current physical provisions.

George Kelling (1979) has pointed out the power of inertia in relationships. That is, a deteriorated love relationship may be sustained because the effort of taking an active step to dissolve it would be too great. Neither party is willing to take that step. The relationship may be without mutual caring and cherishing. Sexual activity and enjoyment may have diminished. Mutual joy may have become rare. However, the drive to change is not there. Rather, partners in the relationship have settled into a regular and predictable existence that is known and preferable to the uncertainties of either initiating new relationships or being alone.

LOVESICKNESS

The body reveals what words do not. This principle is dramatically illustrated in lovesickness, a physical illness promoted by hopeless, unthinkable love. In the third century B.C., Antiochus, the son of one of Alexander the Great's generals, fell impossibly and hopelessly in love with his stepmother. Determined not to show his feelings, he fell sick and resolved he should die. Doctors could not cure Antiochus nor understand the cause of his physical disorder. Finally, the famous physician Erasistratos set up a controlled observation, and he found that only when the stepmother came to see Antiochus did these startling lovesickness symptoms appear (Mesulam & Perry, 1972).

> Lo, those tell-tale signs of which Sappho sings were all there in him—stammering speech, fiery flashes, darkened vision, sudden sweats, irregular palpitations of the heart, and finally, as his soul was taken by storm, helplessness, stupor and pallor.
>
> *(Plutarch, as quoted in Mesulam & Perry, 1972, p. 547)*

The stated cure for lovesickness is to promote insight and achieve reunion with the person the patient loves. Ibn Sina, a noted tenth-century Persian physician, wrote that lovesickness is associated with an erratically fluctuating pulse. Sina went on to describe how to determine the cause of the lovesickness.

> The nature of the cure is this: let several names be pronounced, repeating them many times, and place your finger on the patients pulse. When it varies by a large fluctuation, then returns to normal, and this is repeated thereafter, and is put to the test many times, then the name of the one he loves will be known.
>
> *(Ibn Sina, as quoted in Mesulam & Perry, 1972, p. 549)*

The next step is the union of patient and loved one; this alleviates the lovesickness and restores the patient's health and vigor.

Thus, the risk of loving, at its worst, is that dissatisfaction may invade one's life. At its best, of course, loving may result in lifelong delight and growth. The fear of being hurt keeps many people at a distance they can manage. According to one observer, "the essence of romantic love is a decision, open-ended but by the same token perpetually insecure, open to reconsideration at every moment and, of course, open to rejection by one's lover at every moment too" (Solomon, 1981, p. 227).

Security or caring? That's the choice. The need for security is so great that some people select partners who are absolutely safe; they don't care

Lovesickness is a physical illness resulting from hopeless, unthinkable love. According to Plutarch, some of the tell-tale signs of lovesickness include stammering speech, hot flashes, darkened vision, sudden sweats, irregular palpitations of the heart, a sense of helplessness, stupor, and pallor. Have you ever been lovesick? What did it feel like?

enough about them to be badly hurt if the relationship doesn't work out. Fortunately, relationships don't have to be neutered and safe. Rather, many represent paths toward more frequent states of well-being.

PATHWAYS TOWARD LOVING AND WELL-BEING

Similar Partners

Opposite traits in partners were once believed to be a major factor contributing to the success of the relationship. The idea was that there should be a balance between partners' personality traits, with, for example, shy people being happiest with outgoing partners. It's not so! One review of this topic concludes as follows:

> Given how persuasive the idea is, the inability of researchers to confirm it is astonishing. . . . Perhaps we shall yet discover some ways (other than heterosexuality) in which differences breed liking. But of this much we are now sure: the "Opposites-attract" rule, if it's ever true, is of minuscule importance compared to the powerful tendency of likes to attract.

> *(Myers, 1983, p. 484)*

The reasons partners are likely to be similar are many. To begin with, we are likely to meet people similar to ourselves. Twenty-year-old college students tend not to socialize with forty-five-year-old department store clerks, who in turn do not socialize with sixty-year-old oil refinery employees. Although there are exceptions, we are less likely to become close to people who are dissimilar to us in age, social class, and education. If we have contact with such people, the contact tends to be briefer and more short-lived than our relationships with people who are similar to us.

We usually meet and become friendly with people like ourselves, and we often are most interested in spending time with such friends. If you start dating someone similar to you in terms of physical attractiveness, intelligence, education, and age, you are more likely to stay with that person than if you and your partner were different on these dimensions. In a study by Hill, Rubin, and Peplau (1976), decidedly less similarity was found in 103 couples that broke up than in couples who stayed together for two years. The lesson? The highest payoff for staying together is picking a partner very like yourself. Compatibility can be based not only on similar characteristics such as attractiveness, age, and education but also on similarity of attitudes and beliefs.

Intimacy and Vulnerability

> It's terrifying to care, of course, and the young man whom I once heard say to the girl whose hand he was holding, "Shit, I think I love you" in the ominous tones of someone declaring that he was coming down with the

We are more likely to have successful, lasting relationships with people who have similar characteristics, such as physical attractiveness, intelligence, and age, as well as share our attitudes and beliefs.

plague, probably put the fear that accompanies loving as graphically as it can be put.

(Shain, 1974, p. 5)

This observation by Merle Shain captures the feelings of vulnerability to hurt and rejection that keeps so many men and women out of intimate relationships altogether and that keeps many more men and women in nonintimate partnering. Limiting one's amount of intimacy is a common resolution, which is often adaptive but does not reflect well-being. Yet the level of intimacy many couples find for themselves is determined by the extent to which they each are emotionally prepared to expose themselves to possible hurt and to communicate their feelings to the other.

Love and intimacy have been studied by comparing happy, loving couples to couples who are having difficulties in their relationships.

Fiore and Swenson (1977) identified thirty-five married couples who had sought clinical help for an unsatisfying relationship. Each couple was then matched with a happily married couple on age, length of marriage, education, and occupation. All seventy couples were given scales tapping factors in love relationships. The dissatisfied couples *expected* more verbal expressions of affection from each other than did the satisfied couples. However, the satisfied couples were significantly higher in *actual* expressions of affection toward each other, as well as being more tolerant, being more self-disclosing, giving more moral support, and demonstrating love by giving gifts more frequently. The dissatisfied couples were higher only on the extent to which they did not express feelings. Great differences appeared between the verbal signs of love between the two groups. The dissatisfied couples did not love each other less; they simply failed to communicate feelings and concerns to each other. Thus, accurate and skilled communication is an important pathway toward well-being.

One view among scholars is that well-being includes deep and fulfilling intimacy. Modest levels of intimacy are seen as failures and are condemned as ". . . a shallow, unrewarding acquaintanceship with another person, not an honest, close bond" (McCary, 1978, p. 125). Yet the absence of closeness is not always the problem—many people know how to cope with that comfortably—rather, it is the social labelling and personal evaluation of self as failure that produces longing and dissatisfaction in the relationship.

People who choose surface involvement in relationships should not engage in self-blame. If you relate to another person cautiously and do not attain complete "oneness" with the person, and you feel badly because you "should" attain oneness, you may be engaging in a wasted effort and a frustrating process.

The zealous pursuit of loving may interfere with the ability to love. You become overly conscious about whether every social encounter will lead to true love. Engaging in the full-speed chase of loving and intimacy inevitably means that you cannot catch it. The chase does not allow the achievement of a loving relationship.

The well-being resolution is to find the optimal level of intimacy that fits who you are and where you want to be with another person. Struggling to attain intense closeness when it is neither your way nor your personal goal will be painful and difficult.

Giving

Giving of oneself is a promising path toward successful B-loving. The giving of care, affection, warmth, and joy enhances the giver. Offering these loving aspects of oneself, without requiring that the partner return anything *quid pro quo*—this for that—has been described earlier as a style

Gifts can be a very special symbol of love between two people. However, some gifts are given in order to encourage a particular response. This man may be giving this woman flowers in an attempt to make her feel obliged to him. He may become disappointed or even outraged if she is not sufficiently appreciative of the gift.

of loving closest to other romantic love concepts and highly correlated with results on the Rubin Love Scale (Laswell & Laswell, 1976).

Sheldon Kopp (1972) has observed that you can't make anyone love you. Yet many people do attempt to control their lovers, to make their lovers love them and do what they want. Such attempts include making threats about leaving the other person, stating catastrophic fears of being left, and repeatedly urging that the other person act more affectionate, loving, and reassuring. People make such efforts because they fear and anticipate rejection and feel vulnerable. Thus, the desire to *make* some other valued person love you is understandable and human. Gifts are sometimes used to achieve fulfillment of this desire.

Men and women alike engage in giving material presents, but sometimes gifts produce an obligation, making one or both partners feel that future contacts are demanded. Felt obligations interfere with trust and intimacy. Thus, giving by itself does not necessarily further love. Some people give material presents because they want to give of themselves but cannot. Other people offer gifts as a form of bribery, so that the other person feels obligated by accepting expensive, desirable presents. The giver is aware of the obligation and may be disappointed or outraged if the partner is not properly appreciative. One hears such reactions in the statements, "I gave her everything a woman could want: a lovely home, fashionable clothes, beautiful jewelry, any little thing she desired. I just don't understand why it didn't work out."

Love gifts of oneself are quite another story. One love gift you can give is to share your inner self intimately and spontaneously, demanding little in return. Erich Fromm described the benefits of the act of giving.

> In the very act of giving, I experience my strength, my wealth, my power. This experience of heightened vitality and potency fills me with joy. I experience myself as overflowing, spending, alive, hence as joyous . . . because in the act of giving lies the expression of my aliveness. . . . Giving implies to make the other person a giver also and they both share in the joy of what they have brought to life.
>
> *(Fromm, 1956, pp. 19, 21)*

The Art of Loving

Many people believe that love is something that leaps fully formed from their hearts once they have found the right partner. The task of love, then, is seen primarily as the search for the correct partner. Influenced by idealized images of the magic of love, we often expect the skies to be perpetually sunny, the flowers to pick themselves, and the course of true love to flow smoothly across calm seas. When the inevitable storms and conflicts rage, some lovers are hurt, others retreat, and still others are puzzled about what went wrong and are disillusioned with love. The reality is that, while loving another is based in part on past experiences of being loved, it is a skill as well.

Art of loving

Erich Fromm has given us the concept of the art of loving, in which one is committed to practice and master loving skills.

> This attitude—that nothing is easier than to love—has continued to be the prevalent idea about love in spite of the overwhelming evidence to the contrary. There is hardly any activity, any enterprise, which is started with such tremendous hopes and expectations, and yet, which fails so regularly, as love.
>
> . . . *love is an art,* just as living is an art; if we want to learn how to love we must proceed in the same way we have to proceed if we want to learn any other art, say music, painting, carpentry, or the art of medicine or engineering.
>
> *(Fromm, 1956, p. 4)*

Mastering the art of love calls for practicing specific skills. After all, loving often means one changes in many ways, emotionally and deliberately (Simmel, 1984). Fromm identifies *discipline, concentration, patience, sensitivity,* and *overcoming narcissism* as the key skills one must practice in order to pursue well-being in loving.

Discipline.   Acquiring the art of loving requires a disciplined, vigorous commitment of time and self. It is easy to be self-indulgent and lazy; then, loving can become peripheral in your life. Loving well entails discipline—pleasant, nonpainful discipline, but discipline nonetheless.

Concentration.   Our lack of concentration, or focused attention, is seen in the ways we simultaneously read, listen to music, smoke, drink, and carry on a conversation. To concentrate means to pay full attention to what you are doing. Concentrating in the practice of love calls for attending completely to the one person you are with and understanding that the activity in which you are engaged should be viewed as the only thing in the world that matters. When we talk with someone, our attention can be divided or lost, because we think about other things, such as past or future events or tasks we need to do. Practicing concentration means we do not allow our attention to wander.

Patience.   Continued effort is required to become proficient at any skill. One does not learn an art quickly. Rather, you learn slowly, by picking up indirect skills (such as listening well), by truly valuing the acquisition of the skills, and by patiently allowing yourself to master the art in small steps.

Sensitivity.   This skill refers to heightened awareness of feelings. It is possible to be oversensitive, reacting strongly and obsessively to every thought, whim, and feeling. However, gaining sensitivity in the service of love is learning to become aware of when things are not right, when your concentration, discipline, and patience have slipped, and when you are tense and not relating well. This heightened awareness allows you to correct the slippages and use your skills constructively.

Overcoming narcissism.   For many people, all that is important is what they experience and what they enjoy. The experiences of others are meaningful only as they relate to one's own pleasure. Narcissism is a self-centeredness, and loving requires the ability to be unselfish, to be reasonable, and to have interpersonal humility.

Fromm's five practices for the art of loving are much more than a simple prescriptive package for improving a love relationship with another. His advice applies to almost every human endeavor. Achieving such an art is ambitious and difficult for most people. In order to improve our art of loving, we must consider how much we need to practice each of the five skills. That means looking at the extent to which we take disciplined

Discipline

Concentration

Patience

Sensitivity

Overcoming narcissism

TABLE 10–1   Toward and Away from Well-Being in Loving

Toward Well-Being	Away from Well-Being
Loves *and* likes	Loves *without* liking other
Loves the other person for who he or she actually is	Falls in love with fantasized image of other
Giving style of loving	Game playing style of loving
B-Love	D-Love
Risking love	Anticipates rejection
Nonjudgmentally expresses love	Conditionally expresses love
Balance between individuation and merger in relationship	Overindividuated or excessively merged in relationship
Similar partner	Dissimilar partner
Mastery of the Fromm art of loving	Incompetence in the Fromm art of loving

approach to spending time with the other person. It means looking at the degree to which we concentrate on the other person, or how frequently we allow our attention to be fragmented. In the same sense, we must try to assess the degree of patience we show in acquiring the knowledge to become more loving. Are we able to calmly endure the discomfort and effort of mastering new behavior? Finally, we have to consider the other person's experience and be able to let go of our frequent urge to satisfy ourselves first.

These skills are acquired gradually. The skills are best built on the foundation of having selected an appropriate partner who has at least some important similar traits. Loving then becomes the wonderful process of giving of self. Table 10–1 lists traits of individuals who are moving toward well-being in their loving and traits of those individuals whose loving does not reflect well-being.

SUMMARY

Falling in love, loving, and liking are different concepts. Loving is made up of attachment, caring, and intimacy. Liking, on the other hand, primarily consists of affection and respect. Falling in love occurs when another fits your idealized, fantasy image of a perfect partner.

Love develops in five steps. A choice of the other partner is made, a mutuality of feeling develops and a decision to be together is made, a reciprocity of intimacy and caring occurs, both persons trust each other without conditions, and both take delight in each other. The more their partners are seen by others as desirable, the more the lovers will value themselves and their relationships. Six styles of loving have been identified. They are friendship, giving, possessive, pragmatic, game playing, and erotic styles. The giving style is closest to the concept of romantic love.

Abraham Maslow (1968) has described D-love as a deficiency love in which one person seeks love in order to fulfill his or her own needs. By contrast, he has defined B-love, or being love, as primarily a giving, healthy love that is not possessive or based on what the other person can give or do. B-love is a giving style of love.

Research has indicated that feelings of attraction or dislike may be intensified by general physiological arousal, or by the belief that such arousal is occurring. The changes in the warmth or coolness of one person to another have been called gain or loss effects. Although the gain–loss effect seems to occur in some circumstances, gains in liking and attraction may well be a function of honest continuing relationships.

Barriers to loving relationships include anticipatory rejection, when the fear of being rejected leads a person to preventively and defensively reject the other to avoid hurt. Some people find themselves lost as individuals within a relationship, a result of the normal individuation–merger process that occurs within couple relationships. Sometimes, persons may find that they have too much invested emotionally to be able to quit a poor relationship.

The well-being resolutions to relationship barriers include selecting partners of similar backgrounds—people who are similar tend to stay together—and finding an optimal level of intimacy. While giving of self almost always has positive results, the giving of material gifts is sometimes seen as a subtle form of bribery.

An art of loving, as described by Erich Fromm (1956), requires a deep, hard-working commitment to loving. This art demands self-discipline, concentration on what the other is doing and seeking, patience at mastering the art, sensitivity to your actions, and overcoming your own narcissism.

Key Terms

Agape	Dollar Auction game
Anticipatory rejection	Erotic
Art of loving	Erotomania
Attachment	Falling in love
B-love	Friendship-based love
Caring	Gain-loss effect
Caring cluster	Game playing
Choice	Giving
Concentration	Individuation-merger process
D-love	Intimacy
Delight	Mutuality
Discipline	Overcoming narcissism

Passion cluster	**Reciprocity**
Patience	**Romantic love**
Possessive dependent	**Sensitivity**
Pragmatic	**Trust**

Recommended Reading

Fromm, E. (1956). *The art of loving.* New York: Harper & Row. Fromm presents the nature of love and the skills in loving well from both commonsense and psychoanalytic viewpoints. He particularly considers responsibility, society, maturity, and concentration within loving relationships.

Rubin, Z. (1973). *Liking and loving.* New York: Holt, Rinehart & Winston. The social psychology of love is described in informal, sometimes chatty, but always knowledgeable and informative ways.

Shain, M. (1974). *Some men are more perfect than others.* New York: Bantam. *Also* Shain, M. (1978). *When lovers are friends.* New York: Bantam. Nobody writes with greater wisdom on romantic love than Merle Shain. These two paperbacks provide a stimulating guide to the obstacles of possessiveness, vulnerability, and personal growth in romantic love.

Solomon, R.C. (1981). *Love: Emotion, myth and metaphor.* Garden City, NJ: Anchor Press. I found it impossible to resist this mix of the wisdom of Rodney Dangerfield, playful takeoffs on Shakespeare, and perspectives of contemporary psychology on love.

CHAPTER 11

Sexual Adjustment

Anticipation

The ice penguins atop the sleigh and the ice bears skating alongside it glowed white and blue in the spotlights. All over the campus, a menagerie of sculpted ice swans, bears, rabbits, and fish burst out of the frozen water that had been sprayed over the fraternity lawns during the past week. Inside the Omega house, the band played loudly enough to rule out anything more than shouted fragments of conversation. The dancing, drinking, and mingling would have seemed festive to Peter if he hadn't been feeling so miserable. Karen held his arm as they weaved their way through the crowd. Alan, normally his roommate but sleeping in the upstairs bay this weekend, nudged him and flashed a knowing smile as they passed.

Party weekends are especially important at men's colleges located far from urban areas. Peter had never dated any townies, and this year, his senior year, the year he turned twenty-two, was the year he might no longer be a virgin. Karen was it. She was good-looking, she was fun, she was affectionate. From the time they had met last summer he had thought about inviting her to campus for this weekend. During the summer they went out a few times. Then they wrote to each other and talked on the phone. At first, they talked about classes, friends, day-to-day experiences. Then, they wrote more about each other. They each wrote that they missed the other. It is hard to be away from you, each wrote. I miss you. You are in my thoughts. I wish you were here next to me. I can't wait to touch you.

By the time Winter Carnival weekend rolled around, they were writing to each other in sexual terms. Peter wanted her more than any girl he had ever met. He thought of her constantly. She was in his mind every night.

The weekend arrived. Karen rushed into his arms and they raced to his room. Then, nothing. As fiercely as he had been aroused by the thought of her beforehand, he did not have a hint of sexual arousal. There was nothing to him. He was humiliated.

Karen had been reassuring. "It's okay, Peter. This will give us a chance to know each other first." But she was obviously disappointed.

Nothing happened Friday night. Saturday morning, they went out for coffee and doughnuts and to walk by the clock tower and the great granite rocks that erupted hard and shiny on the campus. They went back to his room at lunch time. Nothing. Now they were finally leaving the party. He normally didn't drink much, but tonight he drank. He didn't know if it would help, but he thought things could not be worse.

He was wrong. It was a time of awkward embarrassment.

Sunday, they walked back to the clock tower, where Karen's ride was to meet her. They were subdued. The exhilaration of Friday's meeting had given way to quiet distress. They held hands. They did not talk about getting together again.

Karen's ride pulled up. She put her arms around him. Then he felt a stirring. Yes, a definite stirring. More than just a stirring.

"Please stay," he exclaimed.

"I've got to go."

"Please, please, don't leave now. Can't you tell I want you?"

"They are waiting for me. I have to go."

"Stay a little longer!"

"Goodbye. It's been a really nice weekend."

Then she was in the car, and the car was pulling away, and Karen reached out and waved and blew him a kiss.

Peter leaned against the tower for a few minutes. Then he grinned, one side of his mouth pulling up in a lopsided way. He started walking back to the fraternity. Maybe it hadn't been such a bad weekend.

THE SEXUAL EXPERIENCE

The experiences of Peter and Karen highlight how intensely sexual events can affect our lives. We can be touched profoundly and deeply by our sexuality. Sometimes, it can be a source of anxiety, as it was for Peter. Other times, it is a regular but essential part of people's lives. How important it is varies greatly with individuals. In the *Republic,* Plato (1950, p. 107) wrote that there is no pleasure greater nor more intense than sexual pleasure—but also none which is more maddening and irrational. In contrast, one of the most acidic of Americans, W.C. Fields, held that "Sex is not the best thing in the world, and it's not the worst thing in the world. It's just that there is nothing quite like it."

Our task here is to examine the psychology of human sexuality. This chapter considers the range of demands, problems, and possibilities sexuality presents to us. We will look at patterns of sexual arousal and sexual problems, as well as the option of abstinence and other possible paths to sexual well-being. We do know that sexual feelings have starkly contrasting meanings for different people. That observation is the beginning point for our examination of sexual adjustment, as we consider why people have such variable understandings of sexuality in their lives.

Interpreting Sexual Meaning

The ways in which people interpret states of arousal depend on what they learn about that state, their mood, and their previous experiences. Think of people who first taste caviar or first sip an alcoholic beverage. Distaste or bemusement are as common reactions as delight to first tastings. So it is with many sexual experiences; social meaning must be attached. Gagnon and Simon put it this way:

> . . . the palpation of the breast for cancer, the gynecological examination, the insertion of tampons, mouth-to-mouth resuscitation—all involve homologous physical events. But the social situation and the actors are not defined as sexual or potentially sexual, and the introduction of a sexual element is seen as a violation of the expected social arrangement.
>
> *(Gagnon & Simon, 1973, p. 23)*

For behaviors to be sexual, sexual meanings and definitions must be attached. However, behaviors do not have to be genital in nature for them to be highly sexual; all that is needed is for the two people to mutually define the behaviors as sexual. In a scene from the Woody Allen movie *Everything You Wanted to Know about Sex,* a seductive woman looks Woody Allen in the eye, slightly flares her nostrils, and just perceptibly raises one side of her upper lip, a series of acts sufficient to bring Allen to distraction and arousal. The attribution of sexuality to states and feelings not obviously sexual extends well beyond those kinds of social cues. In

Behaviors can be highly sexual without being genital in nature. In this scene from the movie *Everything You Wanted to Know about Sex, But Were Afraid to Ask,* Woody Allen is aroused when this seductive woman slightly flares her nostrils and just perceptibly raises one side of her upper lip.

the case of some persons who have suffered injury to the spinal cord and have no pelvic feeling, the site of felt orgasmic experiences has moved to the abdomen or chest. The redefinition of arousal sources allows some people to be excited by underwear, shoes, or whips.

Sexual Interest

The circumstances that trigger sexual interest are a product of both societal beliefs and individual psychology. For example, in Japan, mixed sex nude bathing traditionally has been a matter-of-fact, ho-hum business as far as sexual interest is concerned. On the other hand, a Japanese woman flashing the bare nape of her neck is seen as a highly arousing event. Mixed sex saunas in Finland and Sweden also are not associated with sexuality. The Ute Indians are reported to make no sexual association whatever with the baring or touching of a woman's breast, in contrast to our culture, in which breasts are clearly sexualized. In the history of Western civilization, clothing and social rituals have mirrored sexual interest fads of the time.

Sexual interest is always defined in part by social values and environment. Few aspects of sexual attraction truly are universal; the culture that assigns special value to a woman's mouth, so that it must be veiled in public, often has a historical context of female mouths as erotic. The designated body areas of sexual interest in a culture reveal the roles of the sexes and the attitudes toward sex in general in that culture. In cultures uncomfortable about sex, even asking questions may be hazardous. Consider what happened to Senji Yamamoto, a Japanese university teacher and sex researcher who administered a sexual behavior inventory to his students in 1922. Not only was he dismissed from his university position, but he was later assassinated by radicals for conducting his research (Fisher & Byrne, 1981).

In the nineteenth century, the Western male's excitement at seeing a woman's ankle, like the Arab males' attitude toward viewing a woman's leg, represented sexual interest in a prudish, protected society. However, societal views and sex roles have changed, allowing more open sexual interest by both men and women. The fact that women openly sexually appraise men's bodies today reflects the growing social openness toward sex. Women's more open interest in men's bodies today has partially replaced their assessment of men as desirable because of income or status—an assessment more commonly made in the nineteenth century (Dion, 1981).

Most people learn common sources of arousal, mutually defined by adolescent peer groups and, later on, by sexual partners. Nevertheless, the potential for finding other arousal sources does exist within the minds of individuals as they come to define sexuality. Our examination of sexual experience continues with a discussion of the basic physical components of arousal.

Sexual Excitement

Vasocongestion

The body processes associated with sexual arousal have been well defined (Masters & Johnson, 1966). A *vasocongestion* occurs in both men and women. Vasocongestion is the engorgement of tissues with blood, beginning with nipple erections in all women and in at least 30 percent of men. The spongy tissues of the penis fill with blood, causing an erection. The vaginal tissues congest with blood. The vasocongestion appears as well in the form of the sex flush, a reddening of abdomen, chest, and often neck and face in about 25 percent of men and 75 percent of women.

The sex flush sometimes persists for hours. In the François Truffaut movie, *The Man Who Loved Women,* the hero has an affair with a married woman. The persistence of her sex flush after a rendezvous is so strong that they drive around the streets at high speeds with the woman leaning out of the window. She attempts to cool her face so her telltale pink cheeks would not reveal her infidelity to her husband.

Myotonia

Increased muscle tension, a state called **myotonia,** is the second sign of sexual arousal. Voluntary muscles tense in the arms, legs, and abdomen. Involuntary muscles elevate the testicles, lengthen the vagina, and tighten the buttocks.

Hyperventilation occurs, as both men and women breathe faster and deeper. The number of heart beats per minute increases dramatically, and blood pressure rises sharply. Finally, a layer of perspiration appears on the bodies of at least one-third of all men and women (Masters & Johnson, 1966).

Perception and Evaluation in Sexual Arousal

One way of organizing diverse sexual experiences is by using the cognitive model of sexual arousal developed by Susan Walen (1980). Walen suggests that two cognitive processes are present: perception and evaluation. The perceptions begin with the *detection* of a physiological happening or outside stimulation. The detection is followed by a *labelling* of the experience so that it can be categorized with other similar events. Finally, an *attribution,* or explanation is employed. For example, you may detect something happening inside you, label it as "my heart just skipped a beat," and then attribute it to the presence of a loved one (Walen, 1980, p. 87). *Evaluation* follows, which involves assigning a value to this perceived experience as good, bad, or somewhere between.

Sexual arousal cycle

The Walen model of the **sexual arousal cycle** is shown in Table 11–1. It begins with the person first perceiving the happening as sexual, next evaluating it as good, and then becoming sexually aroused. Then, the arousal itself must be detected, labelled, attributed, and evaluated positively for sexual behavior to occur. The positive evaluations of both initial arousal and sexual behavior prompt further arousal. That is, if the behavior is positively evaluated, arousal increases. If guilt or a negative evaluation follows, arousal drops.

Sexual Attractiveness

Following the popularity of the movie *10* a few years ago, a ratings phenomenon appeared in college dining halls. Male students would position themselves by the entrance and, like judges in gymnastics events, hold up cards rating the entering woman's attractiveness on a scale from 1 to 10. The women's immediate reactions were angry embarrassment and a furor

TABLE 11-1 The Sexual Arousal Cycle	
Stage	**Explanation**
1. Perception of a sexual stimulus	Sexual perceptions are culture determined and learned. People will have different perceptions of sexual stimuli.
2. Positive evaluation	If the stimulus is seen as ugly or disgusting, the cycle stops here. With a positive evaluation, it continues.
3. Arousal	Arousal is a general body state, seen in heart rate, muscle tension, and rapid breathing.
4. Perception of arousal	Males detect their sexual arousal more readily than do women, because of the obviousness of erections versus women's vaso-congestive arousal and because of cultural and sex role norms.
5. Positive evaluation	If the arousal is positively valued, the cycle continues.
6. Sexual behavior	Unless the person chooses not to, sexual activity usually follows the accurate labelling and positive valuing of sexual arousal. That is, while the person may value the arousal, he or she may anticipate a negative evaluation of sexual behavior, in which case the cycle ends.
7. Perception of behavior	The person attends to own breathing, vocalizations, or other body changes and perceives them as sexual.
8. Positive evaluation	A positive evaluation of the sexual behavior either completes the act or produces more arousal. A negative evaluation yields guilt or sexual dysfunctioning.

Adapted from Walen, 1980, pp. 89–94.

of protests to the college administrators. However, the social scientist was interested in the inconsistency of the ratings. Some men find selected physical features of women of higher sexual interest than do other men. Women, too, vary in what physical attributes of men they find exciting. But why?

One investigation considered what personality traits were associated with men who preferred large breasted women, as opposed to men who preferred smaller breasted women. In general, extroverted men indicated preferences for larger breasted women, while introverts preferred smaller breasted women (Eysenck & Wilson, 1979). Extroverts are more outgoing, sexually active, and sociable and they take more risks than introverts.

> Extroverts, having a low degree of cortical arousal, seek out experiences which strongly stimulate them and raise their arousal level to a satisfactory degree; hence they prefer women with large breasts. Introverts, on the other hand, already have a high degree of cortical arousal; they take care not to be over-stimulated, and hence prefer women with small breasts, i.e., women less likely to produce this overstimulation.

> *(Eysenck & Wilson, 1979, p. 61)*

The hypothesis that men who prefer large breasts in women are more oral, more masculine, and less conservative in values also has received research support. In the typical laboratory study, men were

One study analyzed how men characterized women with different breast sizes. The women with larger breasts were judged to be outgoing, impulsive, risk taking, and confident. The smaller breasted women were judged to be moral, competent, intelligent, and modest.

shown silhouettes of nude women, drawn so that they varied on leg, breast, and buttocks size; then, the men were asked to rate the different combinations. Types of men who were sexually interested in legs, versus those interested in breasts, and versus those interested in buttocks were generally found to be distinct. Isaac Asimov put it well in his limerick, "No Accounting for Tastes."

> There is a young fellow named Burns
> Who claims that he always discerns
> All the feminine graces
> Not so much in young faces
> As in bisected, well-rounded sterns.

(Asimov, 1976, p. 45)

In another study, Nancy Hirschberg (1980) looked at the personality characteristics of the women with different leg, breasts, and buttock dimensions. Overall, the women with larger breasts were estimated to be more extroverted (that is, more outgoing, impulsive, risk taking, and confident) than the smaller breasted women. These results are complemented by the "first impression" research that Chris Kleinke and Richard Staneski conducted with 147 male and 141 female undergraduates at Wellesley College. Kleinke and Staneski (1980) reported that, on the basis of their first impressions of color photos, the students judged smaller breasted women as more moral, competent, intelligent, and modest than larger breasted women. We should note that analogous studies on men's body types have yet to be conducted.

The research just discussed has the disadvantage of implying uniform patterns of preferences. Although the studies found significant differences statistically, some men and women fell into categories other than those noted. This research raises the issue, Is a person what his or her body is? The answer appears to be both no and yes, in that order. It is a stereotype to classify a man or woman exclusively on body type. Yet the shape of individuals' bodies does influence how others see them and how they see themselves. Further, the physical changes that occur during adolescence often produce sexual reactions in the adolescent and others that can, in turn, shape the adolescent's personality.

Fantasy

Sexual fantasies are among the primary sources of sexual arousal. Most people carry with them fantasies about acts or people that they find sexually exciting. Of all species, only humans use imagination as a source of stimulation (as far as we know). The power of sexual fantasies is strong. Sex therapist Helen Singer Kaplan has suggested "Sex is composed of friction and fantasy" (quoted in Eysenck & Wilson, 1979, p. 69). In developing a theory of sexual excitement, Robert Stoller has concluded that fantasy is the crucial piece of information about whether or not a person will be aroused by something. According to Stoller, "the essential clue lies in the detailed study of the erotic fantasy, the conscious daydreams people tell themselves . . . plus unconscious fantasy, the private idiosyncratic meaning people attach to their behavior" (1976, p. 901). This perspective is supported by the occurrence of much lower levels of fantasies during foreplay and coitus among people with low and inhibited sexual desire (Nutter & Condron, 1985).

With the publication of studies of men's and women's sexual fantasies, several consistent findings have come to light. The first is that fantasies are common among both men and women, and more sexually experienced women have significantly more fantasies than do sexually inexperienced women. The ages at which fantasies are most frequent correspond to the ages of greatest sexual capacities, with men's fantasies declining after age twenty, and women's fantasies declining after age thirty-five (Eysenck, 1976, p. 76).

Intercourse with a loved partner is the most frequent sexual fantasy for men and women. Upon further examination of fantasy content, the so-called normal sexual deviations of unusual sexual positions, multiple partners, rape, exhibitionism, and voyeurism were often found. Men's fantasies have more emphasis on specific anatomical details and processes; women's fantasies have more emphasis on feelings and relationships. Very broadly defined hostility is at the core of many sexual fantasies. Stoller believes ". . . hostility, overt or hidden, is what generates and enhances sexual excitement, and its absence leads to sexual indifference and boredom" (1976, p. 903). However, hostility was only one element in sexual fantasies reported in an investigation by Glenn Wilson.

Wilson drew up a list of the most common fantasies and looked at the extent to which ninety adults in London acknowledged having them (Eysenck & Wilson, 1979, p. 72–74). Four separate factors were found.

1. *Exploratory fantasies,* or those directed toward sexual variety. "Participating in an orgy" was an item on this factor.

2. *Intimate fantasies,* or those set in the context of a single partner and close relationship. Items on this factor included "Intercourse with a loved partner" and "Making love out of doors in a romantic setting (e.g., field of flowers, beach at night)."

3. *Impersonal fantasies,* in which no emphasis on the nature of the other person is present. Items on this factor include "Watching others have sex" and "Being excited by rubber or leather."

4. *Sadomasochistic fantasies,* in which the giving and receiving of pain is featured. Items include "Whipping or spanking someone" and "Being forced to do something."

General physiological arousal and stimulation of erotic zones influence sexual excitement as much as fantasy does. However, the fantasies we carry with us can be viewed as autobiographical scripts, with ". . . the resolution of all these elements into a happy ending, best celebrated by orgasm" (Stoller, 1976, p. 908). Sexual fantasies are not a source or symptom of disturbance. Rather, they are part of the spice of sexual life, and they serve to allow the fulfillment of felt needs through full sexual functioning.

SEXUAL BEHAVIORS AND ADJUSTMENT

Surveys of Sexual Activities

The Kinsey reports published in 1948 and 1953 signaled the beginning of an era of surveys of sexual behaviors. While many clinicians who treated sexually troubled clients had reported apparent trends, the Kinsey team initiated large-scale studies of people in general and of their sexuality in particular. H.L. Mencken's cynical comment at the time of the appearance of the Kinsey report was that all men lie when asked about sex and that academic researchers "are singularly naive and credulous creatures" (Mencken, 1969, p. 621). Since Kinsey, however, surveys of sexual behavior have increased in their sophistication and utility and have become a regular part of contemporary sex research. As a starting point, let us consider surveys and other sexual research involving college students (see Table 11–2).

In a study of students at the University of Rochester, psychiatrist Raymond Babineau and psychologist Allan Schwartz (1977) surveyed 235 undergraduate men and 215 undergraduate women. Of the men, 48 percent reported having heterosexual intercourse at least once a week. One-third of these sexually active men reported premature ejaculation at least once weekly, 13 percent reported some impotence, and 11 percent reported retarded ejaculation. Of the women, 49 percent reported having intercourse at least once a week. Approximately two-thirds of these sexually active women reported frequent intercourse without orgasm, and 24 percent described pain with intercourse.

The presence of a sexual problem by no means indicates presence of a psychological problem. Leonard Derogatis and his colleagues (1981) studied 199 men and 126 women who were treated for sexual difficulties at the Sexual Behaviors Consultation Unit of the Johns Hopkins University Hospital. Of the men suffering from impotence, 63 percent had no psychiatric disorders. Of the men with premature ejaculations, 66 percent had no psychiatric disorders. Most of the women were treated for inability to reach orgasm, and 50 percent of them were free of psychiatric disorders. Sixteen women were treated for pain with intercourse, and two

TABLE 11–2 Sexual Experiences of College Men and Women				
	197 College Men		212 College Women	
Activity	Rank	% Yes	Rank	% Yes
Female's nude breast felt by male	1	98	1	91
Male mouth contact with female's breast	2	94	2	91
Exposure to erotic materials sold openly in newsstands	3	93	17	58
Male finger penetration of vagina	4	92	3	83
Your observation of nude partner	5	91	7	78
Partner's observation of your nude body	6	91	5	80
Clitoral manipulation by male	7	90	6	79
Manipulation of penis by female	8	90	9	76
Male lying prone on female without penetration	9	87	4	83
Female mouth contact with penis	10	86	11	67
Male manipulation of vulva	11	84	8	77
Sexual intercourse, male superior	12	83	10	67
Masturbation	13	81	21	54
Clitoral manipulation to orgasm by male	14	78	19	55
Male mouth contact with vulva	15	77	12	66
Sexual intercourse, partners partially clothed	16	77	18	56
Male tongue penetration of vagina	17	76	14	66
Male tongue manipulation of clitoris	18	75	13	66
Mutual oral stimulation of genitals to orgasm	19	74	23	45
Sexual intercourse, face to face, on sides	20	73	15	60
Exposure to hard-core erotic materials	21	72	28	24
Sexual intercourse, female superior	22	71	20	45
Showering or bathing with partner	23	68	16	58
Male tongue manipulation of female genitals to orgasm	24	66	24	45
Sexual intercourse, vagina entered from rear	25	63	22	46
Hand contact with partner's anal area	26	61	25	40
Sexual intercourse, standing	27	48	27	28
Sexual intercourse, sitting	28	48	26	37
Finger penetration of partner's anus	29	39	29	19

Adapted from Cowart-Steckler, 1985, p. 50.

of them were free from a diagnosed psychiatric problem. In their study of sexual inadequacy, Masters and Johnson (1970) saw even less psychological difficulty and concluded that most of their patients were without psychological symptoms.

These figures are consistent with other studies of sexually active college men and women among whom it is common to have sexual diffi-

A sexual problem is not always an indication of a psychological problem. In fact, in a loving relationship, a sexual disorder often passes with time, practice, reaffirmation of emotional security, and mutual trust and understanding.

culties while remaining free of psychological disorders. The prevalence of sexual disorders often passes, ". . . with increased time, practice, emotional security, and the trust which develops in a consolidated relationship" (Babineau & Schwartz, 1977, p. 181).

Motives and Adjustment

The motives for engaging in sexual intercourse differ for men and women. Men tend to have pleasure and fun as their primary motives, while women tend to see intercourse as part of commitment and emotional attachment. In a study of 249 Denison University students, 64 percent of the men and 34 percent of the women identified "pleasure reasons" and being "horny" as their motives for intercourse. On the other hand, 19 percent of the men and 58 percent of the women described "emotional reasons." When these same students were asked if emotional involvement was a prerequisite for participating in sexual intercourse, 40 percent of the men and 85 percent of the women agreed this was so always or most of the time (Carroll, Volk & Hyde, 1985).

COMMITTED VERSUS CASUAL SEX

"Imagine, even as you relax as fully and completely as you can, that you are the woman in this fantasy. See, hear, and feel as completely as you can what it is to *be* this woman. You *are* this woman." One hundred University of Connecticut women students were told this by audiotape as they participated in a study conducted by Donald Mosher and Barbara White (1980). An initial fifteen-minute relaxation period was followed on the tape by ten minutes of guided imagery of a sexual invitation, ten minutes of a description of a coital contact (intercourse), and then six minutes of guided reflection about the events. In both the sexual invitation and coital contact sequences, twelve cues were inserted that identified the invitation or contact as one made in a committed relationship or one made in a casual relationship. The committed and casual sexual invitation cues given are presented in the following table.

Sexual Invitation Cues	
In a Committed Relationship	**In a Casual Relationship**
1. . . . a very special fellow, your fiance, who proposed marriage last week after a loving courtship.	1. . . . a very special fellow, an unusually attractive man who you met in one of your classes last week.
2. You know that you've come to know him well, so you can distinguish between what is really him and, your dream of him.	2. You know that you don't know him yet, so you cannot tell what is your really him and what is your dream of him.
3. After all, he is an image of the loving man who will become loving husband with who you live happily ever after.	3. After all, he is an image of the mysterious, handsome stranger who sweeps you off your feet.
4. . . . he seems hungry, greedy, and vulnerable like a baby at your breast. And you realize that it is most likely that you will have his baby at your breast someday.	4. He seems hungry, greedy, and vulnerable like a baby at your breast. And you realize that it is most unlikely that you will have his baby at your breast someday.
5. . . . you ask him to slow down. And he does, since he loves you and wants to proceed no faster than you both truly want and desire.	5. . . . you ask him to slow down. And he does, since he wants the seduction to proceed no faster than you are ready and willing to permit.

Sexual Invitation Cues (Continued)

In a Committed Relationship	In a Casual Relationship
6. You notice that there are very few words spoken between you, you know each other so well, there is really very little that needs saying.	**6.** You notice that there are very few words spoken between you, but you know each other so little, there is not really too much to say.
7. And you wonder how can this man love me so.	**7.** And you wonder how can this man intrigue me so.
8. You remember that he's your fiance and that he will still love and respect you if you do.	**8.** You remember that he is a stranger and may not really respect you if you do.
9. . . . (he) says assuringly, "I know that you're hesitant, after all we never have before, but I really love and want you now."	**9.** . . . (he) says reassuringly, "I know that you're hesitant, after all we've just met, but I really want and need you now."
10. It's as if from his experience with you, he knows exactly what you like.	**10.** It's as if from his experience with others, he knows exactly what you like.
11. And sooner or later you begin to feel reassured by the rightness of the sex by your feelings of love for him.	**11.** And sooner or later you begin to feel reassured about the rightness of the sex by the strong response of your body.
12. You hear him saying in his most masculine tone, "I want to make love to you now" . . .	**12.** You hear him saying in his most masculine tone, "I want to have sex with you now."

Adapted from Mosher & White, 1980, p. 283.

For the most part, these one hundred college women found the sequences sexually pleasurable, interesting, and arousing. The women exposed to the *committed* tape reported less sex guilt, as well as more sexual enjoyment from the imagery, than did the women exposed to the *casual* tape. Whether the women in this study had real-life sexual experience with a loved partner turned out to be more significant to their enjoyment of the imagery than did the cues hidden in the tapes. The women with more sexual experiences with loved partners reacted to the imagery with less fear, contempt, guilt, and shame than did women with limited sexual experiences with loved partners. The results of this study also contradicted the psychodynamic hypothesis that hostility is associated with sexual arousal; rather, among these women, hostility was negatively correlated with arousal.

The study of sexual activity and personal adjustment also has examined the relationship between women's sexual activity and their self-esteem. Two contrasting views have been developed: independence hypotheses and conformity hypotheses. In the first, women with high self-esteem are seen as independent of social approval needs and thus may freely choose to engage in many sexual activities (or none). In the second view, women's conformity to social norms makes them feel good about themselves (gives them high self-esteem); therefore, women with high self-esteem are neither more nor less sexually active than other people. Support for both theories has been found in different research studies, with the results arising from the social norms and values of the particular subjects studied.

Women with high self-esteem typically feel more comfortable making sexual initiatives and engaging in a variety of sexual behaviors than do women with low self-esteem. In one study of 486 single women attending Canadian birth control and pregnancy counselling centers, self-esteem was positively related to acceptance of premarital sex with affection and negatively related to acceptance of premarital sex without affection (Herold & Goodwin, 1979). The adult female's acceptance of premarital sex with affection represents a clear social norm. Furthermore, "not having met the right person" is given by both high school and college virgin women as the most common reason they have not engaged in intercourse (Herold & Goodwin, 1981).

The influence of personal beliefs on sexual activity may be seen in the case of religious practices. Frequency of church attendance has been the customary manner of assessing religious devoutness. The religiously devout have been found to differ in sexual interests and behaviors from the nondevout. They have less permissive attitudes about sex, and devout college students are less likely to engage in petting and premarital intercourse. Dating couples tend to delay intercourse if the woman is devout, while the man's devoutness appears unrelated to this decision. Devout women, like women in general, assume a gatekeeper role in sexual intimacy decisions (Fisher & Byrne, 1981).

SEXUAL MALADJUSTMENTS AND THERAPIES

A Historical Perspective

Western civilization has been described as a historically sex negative culture. Sexuality has been feared, proscribed, or criticized since the earliest days of the Judaic and Christian cultures. While early fears arose out of religion and philosophy, the eighteenth century brought with it the scientific condemnation of sexual activity. Vern Bullough and Bonnie

Bullough (1977) have written of this period, when sexuality began to be viewed not only as sinful but also as a cause of insanity.

> Starting with the observable phenomenon that orgasm in the male not only results in the ejaculation of semen but also in a general feeling of lassitude, many physicians came to feel that the rash expenditure of semen could result in growing feebleness, even insanity . . . the eighteenth-century Lausanne physician S.A.D. Tissot (1728–1797) . . . concluded that all sexual activity was potentially dangerous because it caused blood to rush to the head. Such a rush of blood, he believed, starved the nerves, making them more susceptible to damage, thereby increasing the likelihood of insanity. . . . For Tissot, the very worst kind of sexual activity was the solitary orgasm, since it could be indulged in so conveniently and at such a tender age that excess was inevitable and the resulting nerve damage irreparable.
>
> *(Bullough & Bullough, 1977, p. 59)*

Other scientific reports of the time also concluded that sexual activity led to insanity. After all, the final consequence of syphilis was insanity, and sexually active people often acquired syphilis. Furthermore, patients in mental hospitals were seen to be regularly masturbating, which was said to prove that masturbation caused mental illness.

In the nineteenth century, prudishness combined with the spirit of scientific invention to create a variety of chastity devices to prevent sexual intercourse and masturbation. Indeed, if intercourse did not potentially lead to pregnancy, then it was considered masturbation. Americans in particular became obsessed with sex and its poisonous effects. Sex manuals of the time asserted that masturbation weakened the entire nervous system and caused a wasting away of health and the loss of strength in the body (Bullough & Bullough, 1977).

Canvas and metal penis sheaths, with holes at the end for urination, were attached to belts around the waist to prevent male masturbation. Sometimes the devices included sharp points designed to cause pain in case of enlargement of the penis. (This same device, with appropriate anatomical modifications, is currently used to prevent thoroughbred stallions, rented for breeding, from masturbating against their bellies, thereby reducing the sperm count and making impregnation less likely.)

For women, the use of chastity belts to prevent sexual activity, including masturbation, goes back nearly a thousand years. The devices, typically belted around the abdomen, were padlocked metal vulva covers with a grid or holes for urination. When chastity belts failed, surgical removal of the clitoris was sometimes performed (this practice continued even into the first two decades of the twentieth century).

At the turn of the twentieth century, when Sigmund Freud made the radical proposal that sexual experiences were part of normal childhood, he was greeted with a barrage of protest. Now the majority of contemporary psychologists, and parents as well, accept the notion that at least some sexual experience occurs in childhood. However, that acceptance has not eliminated widespread fear and distress over aspects of sexuality. Thus, many children enter adolescence concerned about their sexuality.

Preadolescent anxieties intensify during adolescence. Approximately 92 percent of all adolescent boys masturbate by the time they are twenty (Downey, 1980). This introduction to erections and ejaculation typically is pleasurable, but accompanied by guilt. Boys hide during masturbation and conceal the sexual magazines they read during masturbation because of their deep-seated sense that they are doing something wrong. That sense is reinforced if the adolescent boy's actions or his masturbation aids are discovered. It is not unusual for both boys and their parents to feel shame and remorse about this common act.

Guilt over masturbation may occur as well in the adolescent girl; approximately 44 percent of girls masturbate (Story, 1985). However, the more characteristic source of guilt among girls is over their early sexual explorations. Gagnon and Simon note that, for women, "Genital localization of erotic response is a function of reactive sexual contacts with males rather than through masturbatory sexual experience" (1973, p. 63). The adolescent girl is usually in a submissive role as an object of male pursuit. If she passively allows greater privilege to the male than her internalized values can accept, the dissonant note struck between behavior and values leads the girl to feel sex guilt.

The societal condemnation of sexual activity as sinful and dehabilitating has diminished for many people. However, the experiencing of sexuality as wrong or troublesome has by no means vanished. It persists in child-rearing practices: children are punished for looking at or touching their genitals, and parents changing soiled diapers are often observed taking the infants' hands away from the genitals. It persists in the conflicting emotions many adults feel when their adolescent children begin to exhibit regular patterns of sexuality. It persists in the fierce conflicts some adults experience over their own sexuality.

At the same time that the widespread sexual prudishness and fear of the last two centuries began to dissipate, an idealization of the sexual relationship appeared. Intercourse is not only no longer considered bad, but according to current sex manuals, intercourse and orgasms are vehicles for fulfillment. Joyously satisfying intercourse and consciousness-shattering orgasms are an objective of sexuality. Part of fully becoming a person involves becoming sexual according to current theory, and this burden of sexual performance expectations has caused psychological problems for many people.

The Pursuit of the Orgasm

The mad, slapdash chase after the orgasm often means that couples develop a nearsightedness about sexuality. Only the pursuit of the orgasm stays in clear focus, resulting in what has been called the tyranny of the orgasm. Other sexual components, such as closeness to partner, pleasant excitement, sight, sound, and touch, are less in focus and less enjoyed for their own sakes.

This concentration on orgasms is also common among sexual response researchers, who consider that good sexual adjustment is characterized by the ability to have orgasms (Messersmith, 1976). Yet researchers and clinicians alike have suggested as well that more than the presence or absence of the orgasm must be considered.

For some couples, a subjective and built-in assessment of the sexual experience is based on the occurrence of the women's orgasm. If that is not present, the lovemaking is judged to have been a failure. Sometimes,

NOCTURNAL ORGASMS

Nocturnal emissions, or wet dreams, are common events in the lives of 80 to 90 percent of young adult men, and orgasms while sleeping are not uncommon among women as well. In the beginning of the nineteenth century, the term *spermatorrhea* was coined to describe the nocturnal emission. Like masturbation, this "rash expenditure of semen" (Sussman, 1976) was seen as leading to deterioration of the brain, general weakness, and physical exhaustion. The belief was that the body was a closed energy system and that loss of energy in this manner meant that energy would be unavailable for other activities. Despite the Kinsey (1954) observation that virtually all men have noctural emissions, a recent study of 104 adult males found that 28 percent of the subjects had not experienced wet dreams. Further, men who had nocturnal emissions typically felt either embarrassed or that they were abnormal (Matthews & Wells, 1983).

Women as well as men have orgasms during sleep. Henton (1976) studied the self-reports of 774 black women at a southern university and found that 174 of them, or 23 percent, reported having nocturnal orgasms and 214 reported experiencing sexual excitement during a dream. The percentages increased with age: 17 percent of freshman women versus 29.6 percent of senior women reported orgasms, and 25 percent of freshman women versus 32 percent of senior women reported sexual excitement during a dream. In another study, of 238 mostly Caucasian women at a midwestern university, 30 percent reported nocturnal orgasms (Wells, 1983). Many people are unaware that women have nocturnal orgasms, but they should not be considered unusual; they are simply one form of acceptable, frequent sexual experience.

For women, emotional closeness and deep sharing are the most valued aspects of sexual satisfaction.

there is an explicit blaming of the partner or self for the absence of the woman's orgasm. The man was too insensitive, rushed, or unskilled. The woman was too unresponsive, distracted, or cool.

However, sexual satisfaction is simply not the same as orgasm. The research on female sexual satisfaction has yielded the following findings (Jayne, 1981; Handy, Valentich, Cammaert & Gripton, 1985):

1. Up to two-thirds of women who experience sexual excitement and lubrication and who reach the plateau phase of arousal enjoy the arousal without achieving orgasm.

2. Sexual satisfaction in general is a separate dimension of female sexual arousal than orgasm, although the two are related and do overlap.

3. Emotional closeness and deep sharing within relationships are the most valued parts of women's sexual satisfaction, followed then by orgasm.

Female Orgasmic Dysfunctions

Primary orgasmic dysfunction

Secondary orgasmic dysfunction

Women who have difficulties having orgasms fall into two categories. With a ***primary orgasmic dysfunction***, the woman has never experienced an orgasm, by any means. With a ***secondary orgasmic dysfunction***, the woman's sexual history shows at least one orgasm, but she is dissatisfied with the infrequency of orgasms or the means by which they are achieved (Masters & Johnson, 1966).

The identification of female orgasm problems is a recent development. One hundred years ago, had an expert on sexual relations been approached about lack of female orgasms, he would have been puzzled, probably indicating that orgasms were proper as male, procreational behaviors. The women of the time would have been more cognizant of the issue. Rediscovered information about forty-six Victorian-era women shows that their degree of sexual responsiveness was about the same as that of present-day women (Mosher, 1980).

The nature of the female orgasm has itself been the subject of scholarly controversy. The starting psychoanalytic theory that only vaginal orgasms were true orgasms has been followed by a flood of alternate theories. The Masters and Johnson (1966) studies of the physiology of orgasms affirmed that only one kind of physiological response is present, whether due to direct stimulation of the clitoris, the vagina, or elsewhere. However, the view that only one type of orgasm occurs has been severely criticized as simplistic (Butler, 1976), and scholars have increasingly observed that contrary evidence continues to accumulate. The subjective experiences of many women have suggested that quite different feelings, regardless of physiological patterns, are associated with the different kinds of stimulation that lead to orgasms. Thus, research has attended to the different experiences of the clitoral orgasm, the deep pelvic orgasm, and the orgasm that arises from stimulation of the Graffenberg spot (the G-spot), midway along the anterior wall of the vagina. One woman reported

> In a clitoral orgasm, my teeth are bared and my brow is furrowed with "anger" lines. In this other kind of orgasm (uterine), my brow is smooth and the corners of my parted lips are drawn back, although my teeth are not bared . . . the feeling is one of "strangling in ecstasy" . . . the satisfaction is so complete that subsequent climaxes are quite impossible for at least a day.
>
> *(Singer & Singer, 1978, p. 182)*

Such reports are not definitive proof. Rather, they indicate the range of possible orgasmic experiences. It does appear that when more areas are stimulated, including genitals, breasts, and imagination (fantasy) more vasocongestion and myotonia occur. In turn, more intense orgasms result.

This phenomenon probably also occurs with males when their genitals, and nipples, and other body areas are stimulated at the same time.

The term *frigidity* has been used as a general descriptor for women's sexual problems. However, the inaccurate and stigmatizing term has been displaced by the more precise term *orgasmic dysfunction,* which describes specific behaviors (Elliott, 1985). The extent to which orgasmic dysfunction is a problem is defined jointly by the woman and her partner. As we have noted, for many women, orgasms are unnecessary for sexual satisfaction. In several studies of diverse groups, over 70 percent of women reported that sexual satisfaction was possible without orgasm (see, for example, deBruijn, 1982). Sexual satisfaction is less likely without good feelings and sexual communication between the partners. Indeed, good feelings and communication increase the likelihood of a woman's having an orgasm.

Masters and Johnson described the problem this way: "the crucial factors most often missing in the sexual value system of the nonorgasmic woman are the pleasure in, the honoring of, and the privilege to express need for the sexual experience" (1966, p. 289). In their work, Masters and Johnson seek to remove the sources of frustration and hostility in the primary relationship and replace them with a nondemanding, accepting pattern of communication.

Communication is important because it is so closely related to the development of a woman's orgasmic capacity. For most women, orgasms come about initially in the context of their relationships, and women learn about their sexual potential through their experiences with men or sometimes other women. Unfamiliarity and discomfort about "letting go" into full sexual functioning are hypothesized to be causes of late orgasmic development, along with normal variations in women's sexual functioning.

Primary orgasmic dysfunction is treated by a program that helps women to understand their own sexuality, to explore sexual areas, to learn masturbation by hand and, if needed, by vibrator, and finally to include their sexual partners in the process. Joseph LoPiccolo has been one of the pioneers in such treatment programs. LoPiccolo and Lobitz (1978) have described their treatment: First, the client is instructed to examine herself carefully with a hand mirror just after bathing. The woman then begins to do Kegel exercises and undertakes tactile exploration to get used to the feel of the genital parts. Next, she practices manual stimulation, often using erotic material as an aid to arousal. Her achievement of orgasm when alone and then with her partner's aid completes a fifteen-session treatment. LoPiccolo and Lobitz have reported that eight out of eight primary nonorgasmic women have achieved orgasms through this practice. In their much larger samples, Masters and Johnson (1966) found that 83 percent of 193 women with primary orgasmic dysfunction were successfully treated by such programs.

On the other hand, the treatment of women with secondary orgasmic dysfunctions tends to have a lower success rate. This treatment is more varied. It may include full masturbatory instruction, usually emphasizing nondemanding sexual contact, with a focus on the sensations themselves, and relationship improvement. In the Masters and Johnson (1966) work, 77 percent of 149 women with secondary dysfunctions were successfully treated. There is more evidence of psychological problems and a higher incidence of previous sexual trauma in this group. Often, resolution of incest and/or rape experience coupled with sex therapy is the best treatment approach.

EXPLORATION IN WELL-BEING

Learning to Kegel

Kegels

The muscle that surrounds the vagina and urinary bladder is called the pubococcygeus muscle. This muscle has been described as being directly related to the quality of vaginal sexual response. After urologist Arnold H. Kegel first treated a woman for loss of urine by prescribing exercises to improve pubococcygeus muscle tone, he found that intercourse unexpectedly became enjoyable and orgasmic for his patient. Subsequently, Kegel reported that one-third of all women have an underdeveloped, weak pubococcygeus muscle and, therefore, have weak vaginal muscle control and lack of sensitivity during intercourse. The exercises that have been prescribed to strengthen the muscle have been called **Kegels,** after their originator.

A Kegel is a deliberate tightening of the pubococcygeus muscle. This muscle is contracted by acting as if one is stopping in the middle of urinating. The muscle control is mastered by urinating a teaspoon at a time until the bladder is empty. Several kinds of contractions are employed, including a "contract, hold, hold, hold, extra squeeze, relax" sequence. Women who undertake this regime will Kegel twenty minutes at a sitting, between one and three times a day. Although practicing might seem tedious, simple contractions can be practiced in autos and buses on the way to work, while sitting and reading, or during any other routine activity.

If the woman persists with these exercises for a few months, her vaginal musculature is greatly strengthened. The gripping power of this muscle is measured by the perineometer, an instrument that indicates the intensity of the gripping pressure at the entry to the vagina. Although the research findings are still preliminary, successfully practicing Kegels is reported to increase sexual satisfaction and heighten orgasmic pleasure (Morokoff, 1978; Kline-Graber & Graber, 1978). One laboratory study found that women who did Kegel exercises, compared to women in control conditions, had enhanced sexual arousal. This enhancement was especially pronounced when the exercising was combined with self-generated sexual fantasies (Messe & Geer, 1985).

Many pathways to orgasmic satisfaction may be followed. Most clinicians will agree that "women should be therapeutically supported to become accepting of *their own way* to sexual satisfaction" (Lucas & Halle, 1983, p. 199).

Impotence

The erection of the penis occurs when blood from the profunda artery fills the spongy tissues and, at the same time, a small muscle (known as Houston's muscle) constricts the dorsal vein. Within three to five seconds following initial sexual excitement, full erection occurs. When an erection is not of sufficient size for intercourse to proceed, the event is labelled impotence.

Masters and Johnson (1970) have identified two distinct patterns of impotence. **Primary impotence** refers to the condition of a man who *never* has been able to maintain erections enough to engage in intercourse. **Secondary impotence** describes the condition of a man who has attained successful intercourse but who has experienced subsequent or secondary failures. Occasional impotence is common among adult men. At times of situational stress or following excessive drinking, it is not unusual for a man to experience erectile failure in a single sexual encounter. When the impotence persists and happens in a majority of attempts, then the condition acquires the status of impotence, with all of its psychological implications.

> With our society's emphasis on sexual performance, the impotent male often experiences severe humiliation and frustration. He also faces the possibility of marital difficulty; some wives respond angrily to the dysfunction, while others often report feelings of sexual and personal rejection.
>
> *(Tollison & Adams, 1979, p. 136)*

Organic impotence can be caused by physiological factors, which include too little testosterone (male sex hormone), spinal cord injuries, the effects of a variety of tranquilizing drugs, complications of diabetes, and disorders that impair blood flow to the pelvis (Reckless & Geiger, 1978). However, 90 percent of all cases of impotence are psychogenic, caused by psychological factors. If erections are present at night or in the morning, the condition is usually diagnosed as **psychogenic impotence.** Sometimes the condition may be both psychogenic and physiological. If a male experiences less rigid erections due to vascular insufficiency, he may develop performance fears and exacerbate the problem.

One more theorized type of impotence bears attention. This is the **new impotence,** which is defined as sexual impotence in response to increased sexual demands by women who feel they can assertively seek satisfaction. The new impotence has been described as resulting from

Primary impotence

Secondary impotence

Psychogenic impotence

New impotence

the strain caused by the role reversal that now allows women to initiate and dominate sexual intercourse. However, this phenomenon appears to be more a media creation than a real drop in male arousal. When male college students were exposed to guided imagery scenarios of women versus men initiating sexual contact and intercourse, no differences in arousal were found (Sirkin & Mosher, 1985). Men were neither more nor less anxious when women were the sexual initiators.

Most observers identify anxiety over the adequacy of sexual performance as the dominant cause of psychogenic impotence. In our opening story, once Peter began to worry about whether he would be able to achieve an erection, his approach to the sexual encounter changed. He did not take erections for granted and feared that he would remain soft. This anxiety, which competes with sexual arousal, is called ***performance anxiety.*** Anxiety about successful sexual performance impairs successful sexual performance.

Performance anxiety

An element of ***spectatoring*** also occurs. Detachment from the personal contact leads the man to see himself as an outside spectator, looking at the process and evaluating how well he is performing (Tollison & Adams, 1979; Masters & Johnson, 1970).

Spectatoring

Performance anxiety and spectatoring often combine. The fear prompts thoughts such as "I hope I will be able to get it up." and "Can I keep it up?" while at the same time the cognitive spectator observes, "Hmm. Only a little stirring there. Not much arousal. Looks like nothing is happening tonight."

The onset of impotence frequently begins with a single incident. When no erection is reached that first time, the man either rushes into another contact or waits a long time out of anxious concern about failing. When the next encounter occurs, the man is so concerned about being impotent, he becomes impotent. The anxiety increases in the next contact, and the cycle of anticipation of failure followed by failure accelerates, until the man is psychogenically impotent.

Several social misconceptions aid this cycle of fear and failure. Men sometimes have the following misconceptions:

> A real man can achieve an erection rapidly under any circumstance even in a casual male–female encounter.
>
> The size and firmness of the erection are necessary determinants of the female partner's satisfaction, and any deficit in either automatically causes failure in sexual intercourse.

> *(Reckless & Geiger, 1978, p. 308)*

Women sometimes have misconceptions such as the following:

> It is a man's duty to be available for sex and to give his partner orgasms in intercourse.

A man's failure to achieve an erection indicates not only a dimunition of affection for his partner but in all probability his involvement with another woman.

(Reckless & Geiger, 1978, p. 308)

Secondary impotence is an easily treatable condition. Although some clinicians believe that intensive psychotherapy is necessary, practical treatment programs as brief as one or two weeks have been developed. The best known of these is the Masters and Johnson Rapid Treatment Program. The client and his partner are brought to the St. Louis site, or another location away from their day-to-day distractions. They are given full physical examinations and, if no physical problem is found, are seen by two therapists. The treatment aims to open clear communication between the partners. Further, they are taught the psychology and physiology of sexual relations. The couple is instructed in the sensate focus techniques of touching and caressing. The breasts and genitals are specifically off limits, so that the touching is not directed toward intercourse or arousal.

Then, a "teasing" technique is used, in which gentle stroking of the penis is started and stopped so that the couple may observe the normal penis rise and fall. Again, this stroking does not lead to intercourse. The treatment next moves to penetration without thrusting, with the woman astride, and finally penetration with thrusting permitted. In a supportive and warm environment, with open communication, treatment successes occur in about three-fourths of the cases of secondary impotence and three-fifths of the cases of primary impotence (Masters & Johnson, 1970; Reckless & Geiger, 1978).

These results come from treatment of men with steady partners. With men who have changing partners as well as with men whose sexual relationships are infrequent, equally successful outcomes have been reported (Dekker, Dronkers & Staffeleu, 1985). Decreased social anxiety by itself seems to be a potent influence in lessening this sexual problem.

Premature and Retarded Ejaculation

Premature ejaculation

Premature ejaculation is when a man ejaculates quickly, before or shortly after the beginning of intercourse. This is the second most common problem (after impotence) that leads men to come for sexual treatment, and it is particularly common among young men. As a rule, the time elapsed since prior ejaculation plays a role; the greater the length of time, the more quickly ejaculation occurs. Premature ejaculation is a concern when it happens frequently, and treatment procedures are based on the development of ejaculatory control.

Some ejaculatory control develops naturally with experience and physical maturity. Men learn to recognize the signs of impending ejaculation. Before ejaculation becomes inevitable, they can reduce the level of stimulation and lessen arousal.

Treatment for premature ejaculation teaches the man or the couple to use either stop and start procedures or the squeeze technique. As the name suggests, stop and start deliberately minimizes friction prior to ejaculatory inevitability. Using the squeeze technique, the partner firmly presses the penis just below the head, which reflexively causes a reduction in arousal. Like the treatment of impotence, the treatment of most premature ejaculation cases is successful after relatively few sessions.

Retarded ejaculation
Retarded ejaculation is the inability of a man to ejaculate intravaginally, although he has had this ability in the past. This relatively infrequent problem has been reported more often in the past ten years, and sometimes it is attributed to men's overstriving to satisfy women sexually. Two possible causes of retarded ejaculation may be the man's fear of not performing adequately (as in impotence) and his hostility toward the woman (he may be unconsciously withholding orgasm in a power struggle). Lack of proper physical stimulation also has been implicated. Retarded ejaculation is readily treated, by directed masturbation leading to increasingly closer approximations of intercourse, and with the appropriate development of sexual fantasies accompanying the intercourse (Shull & Sprenkle, 1980).

Low Sexual Desire

Having a low level of sexual desire is quite different from having a problem becoming sexually excited or reaching orgasm. People with low desire are those who are rarely sexually interested but, when they are interested, are quite capable of becoming excited and climaxing. Helen Singer Kaplan (1977) reports that low desire can be be thought of as little sexual appetite.

One cause of low desire can be that the person's testosterone or estrogen-testosterone level is too low for sexual desire to occur. More frequently, people fail to feel sexual arousal because they have been victims of abuse. Women who were sexually abused as children may feel little sexual desire. For both women and men, minimal sexual interest often is associated with an intense fear of intimacy.

Desire dysfunction
Two different patterns of this *desire dysfunction* have been identified. With inhibited sexual desire, the individual occasionally feels sexually interested. In the case of phobic avoidance of sexual contact, no desire whatsover is reported.

Individuals with low sexual desire now make up the bulk of clients for many sex therapists. They often seek therapy because their spouses and they have highly discrepant sexual interest levels. Kaplan (1977, p. 8) has concluded that the conflicts underlying such low desire are "tenacious and profound," and that sex therapy is more difficult and prolonged for these patients than for people with other sexual difficulties.

SEXUAL WELL-BEING

To this point, we have considered the social meanings attributed to sex, the processes of sexual interest, arousal, and activity, and potential difficulties in sexual adjustment. Now we turn to the well-being aspects of human sexuality. The prior discussions have examined sexual behaviors

THE FETISH

Fetish

Some access to understanding sexual interest may be gained by looking at those people who have unusual special sexual desires. A *fetish* is a compulsive sexual attraction to an object not normally seen as sexually arousing. Rubber and leather fetishists are people who use these materials as sex play devices to the point that they require the use of the materials in order to become aroused or to climax. Gosselin (1981) examined thirty-eight male leather fetishists and eighty male rubber fetishists on measures of psychoticism, extroversion, and neuroticism. If these men were guilt-ridden about normal sex or otherwise maladjusted, the pathology was expected to show on the scales. Contrary to popular beliefs, no differences were found between the fetishists and the controls. This indicates that individuals can have sexual interests that depart considerably from the norm, and yet be psychologically normal according to general measures.

When fetishists are psychiatrically hospitalized, they tend to be diagnosed as suffering from severe psychological disorders. However, this diagnosis is not unique to the fetishists, because almost everyone psychiatrically hospitalized is found to have a diagnosable illness. We should note that some definitions of a fetishist would include Linus of the "Peanuts" cartoon strip, because of his ever present security blanket. For this type of fetishist, relaxation rather than arousal occurs with the use of the object (Gosselin & Wilson, 1984). Most views, though, require the response to the object to be sexual arousal before the attachment is called a fetish.

Eric Berne (1971) has observed that the fetish is not a symbol of anything sexual, but is the real thing, the true turn on. Not only is the fetish pleasurable, but, Berne has suggested, mild fetishists actually enjoy themselves more than normal people. Then, one should consider the female partner of the male fetishist.

. . . the counterfetishist, what I would like to call the fetishera. Nearly all fetishists are men. But for every man who is hung up on shoes, there is a woman ready to cater to and groove with him, and for every man who gets his thrills from hair, there is a woman who gets hers from having her

with partners. Yet sexual relations with other people are not feasible for many individuals in our society, as a result of choice or because of circumstances beyond their control. Our first topic in our consideration of sexual well-being is one significant alternative to sexual activity: celibate living.

Celibacy

Celibacy

Celibacy is the state of noninvolvement in any sexual activity. At some times in their lives, most adults find themselves in long periods of celibacy,

locks raped. Havelock Ellis has many cases of this meeting of the minds: the man who yearns to get pressed on by high heels sooner or later meets a woman who had daydreamed all her life of heel-pressing.

(Berne, 1971, p. 104)

A fetish is a compulsive sexual attraction to an object not normally considered sexually arousing. For example, leather fetishists require the use of leather as a sex play device in their sexual activities in order to be aroused or to climax.

sometimes involuntarily and sometimes by choice. Adjustment to involuntary celibacy is always more trying than adjustment to voluntary celibacy.

For some people, being celibate is seen and felt as being a failure. Samuel Johnson captured this view when he wrote, "Marriage has many pains, but celibacy has no pleasures . . . [it] is a state more gloomy than solitude: it is not retreat, but exclusion from mankind" (Evans, 1969, p. 92).

Three problem areas can arise in celibacy.

Physical needs.   Unsatisfied physical needs for sexual outlets and contacts can lead to personal discomfort. Arousal levels and desires vary greatly, from fierce, insistent longings to mild, occasional feelings of need. Martin Luther saw the physical impulse as so powerful and natural that he believed attempting celibacy was "to fall for a trick of the Devil" (Diamond & Karlen, 1980, p. 12).

Social expectations.   In many adult social groups, prolonged celibacy is a sign of peculiarity. If the group members are themselves sexually active, a celibate member can be seen as undesirable, deviant, or an outsider.

Views of self.   When the celibacy is voluntary, some persons—but not all—believe there is something personally wrong with their feelings and thinking. They ask themselves, "Why don't I want what everyone else does?" When the celibacy is involuntary, because of lack of opportunity or interested partners, people doubt their personal worth and attractiveness. The involuntary celibate often feels unloved and unlovable. The person may focus on some physical feature that he or she sees as the reason others are staying away. In any case, the involuntary abstinence prompts the person to have a sense of failing to achieve an important part of life.

The social expectation of celibacy can be positive and compelling (for example, some individuals are celibate for religious and spiritual reasons). In Eastern religions, such as Buddhism, sexual abstinence is valued as a way to heighten one's awareness and cleanse one's physical body. In the Roman Catholic tradition, celibacy has been valued as a sign of devotion to God. In both Eastern and Western religious communities, there is much social support for the celibate decision. Others share the celibate's values and beliefs. The support that is apparent in the religious communities can be found elsewhere as well. Whenever there is strong social support for the decision of voluntary abstinence, the conflicts the celibate feels about the chosen life-style are more easily resolved. On the other hand, involuntary celibacy combined with lack of social support leads the celibate to feelings of great conflict and distress that often magnify other life problems.

The fear of disease, particularly Acquired Immune Deficiency Syndrome (AIDS), has played a role in some people's decisions to become celibate. The concern about contracting the fatal disease has been sufficient to discourage many individuals—who are at high and at low risk of becoming AIDS victims—from partaking in all sexual activities. Of course, both homosexuals and heterosexuals are now wary of partners who have high levels of sexual activity with many mates.

Sometimes celibate people are simply opposed to sex. For example, in his *Religion Midici* Sir Thomas Browne wrote, "I could be content that we might procreate like trees, without conjunction, or that there were any way to perpetuate the world without this trivial and vulgar act of coition; it is the foolish act a wise man commits all his life."

This attitude was not apparent in the sexual behaviors of the 126 former nuns and priests who were surveyed by Margaret and Lauro Halstead (1978). Sixty percent of the people surveyed were former nuns, who had spent an average of 12.4 years in their religious communities; 40 percent were ex-priests who had spent an average of 18.3 years in the priesthood. Practicing full celibacy, in which masturbation was excluded, before entering the religious order was reported by 46 percent of the total group; 32 percent reported practicing full celibacy during the time in the order; and 10 percent reported practicing it after leaving the order. Masturbation was practiced by 47 percent before, 57 percent during, and 85 percent after life in the order. Intercourse was reported by 11 percent before, 15 percent during, and 82 percent after living in the religious order.

These percentages tell us not about the celibacy practices of priests and nuns who remain in their orders, but only about the practices of those who leave. To what extent were these adults able to achieve satisfactory sex lives after leaving their religious communities? The results: 48 percent of the men and 41 percent of the women reported sexual satisfaction. For the most part, this group did not stay celibate; 90 percent became sexually active. The number of people reporting sexual satisfaction in this group was strikingly similar to the number reported in control groups, despite the people's loss of personal support systems and the loneliness they often reported experiencing upon leaving the priesthood or convent. We should stress that these are the experiences of a subgroup of priests and nuns. For the majority, celibacy remains a central aspect of their religious commitment to nongential love (Goergen, 1974).

So far we have considered adjustment to celibacy. Now we move to the topic of celibacy as an option for well-being. Periods of intentional celibacy can allow a person to reassess characteristic ways of relating to others and try out new interpersonal manners, without the pressures or expectations of sex.

In her book, *The New Celibacy,* Gabrielle Brown (1980) asserted that many forms of intimacy can be best found through celibacy. Many men and women manage physically well without sex. Furthermore, a temporary vacation from sexual relations can sweeten the quality of many continuing relationships and redirect one's energies into other, more productive paths. Of the celibate man, Brown wrote

> There seems to be a kind of personal strength and charisma that celibate men manifest. A celibate man who has freely chosen to be celibate and is comfortable with it offers other people the chance to see themselves

AIDS AND SEXUAL RELATIONS

Acquired Immune Deficiency Syndrome (AIDS) has become a concern for all sexually active people, not just the intravenous (IV) drug users and promiscuous homosexual men who were the first victims of the disease. Three factors have made the fears of AIDS a prominent concern among sexually active adults.

1. The disease is considered to be inevitably fatal. Victims die as a result of increasing vulnerability to infections the body normally resists.

2. Heterosexual transmission of AIDS has been increasing. The largest numbers of AIDS victims are gay men, IV drug users, and individuals who have received blood transfusions from infected individuals. However, heterosexual and drug-free men and women have become AIDS victims as well.

3. The federal government has targeted AIDS as a serious health hazard, and the medical and scientific communities have mobilized to prevent and treat AIDS.

Not all potential victims are concerned about AIDS. One physician who specializes in immunology made the following observation:

> The majority of sexually active people are youthful and vigorous. As such they normally have little sense of their own vulnerability. Taking seriously an invisible and imperceptible threat is particularly difficult; but as with life in general, the underlying reality continues to determine the course of events—whether or not people acknowledge it.
>
> *(Robinson, 1987, p. 30)*

The underlying reality is that the more sexual partners one has, the greater the potential for one's exposure to AIDS. Thus, some dating individuals have chosen to totally abstain from sexual relationships or to severely limit the number of partners. Men and women alike have become more cautious about entering sexual relationships, and it appears that casual sexual encounters have become less frequent among many people. Women tend more to be the gatekeepers of

reflected in his eyes in other than sexual ways. It's a great gift to "see" and "be seen" without the imposition of the dominating sexual viewpoint.

(Brown, 1980, pp. 108–109)

Throughout history, celibacy has been seen as an important symbol of purity and goodness for women. In contemporary America, a residual of that symbolic perspective mixes with adult women's opportunity for sexual freedom of choice. Almost every woman goes through periods of celibacy in her adult life, a process that Brown (1980) described as having as much potential for opening up one's life as it does for closing off one's

sexual activity, and so women more than men have shown this cautiousness, although both sexes are abstaining from sex more now than in the past.

For sexually active people, a monogomous relationship with a noninfected person (who is not an IV drug user) offers safety. Because AIDS is transmitted by body fluids, many individuals are concerned about infection through the exchange of any fluids. However, some body fluids appear to be quite safe. No evidence exists that AIDS can be transmitted by the exchange of saliva or tears. The exchange of blood is clearly the highest risk situation—it's enough to make Count Dracula request blood tests before his night visits—and the introduction of semen and vaginal fluids into the blood stream, which can occur through tiny and nonobvious cuts, offers a distinct hazard.

For this reason, the use of condoms has become synonymous with safe sexual practice. Condoms are not perfect protection, against either pregnancy or AIDS. They fail sometimes, and quality control standards in factories that produce condoms permit four holes per thousand condoms—allowing a minute risk. Condom sales have soared as a result of the public's fear of AIDS infections.

A significant psychological outcome of the AIDS infection has been fear. Many individuals who have been sexually active with high-risk partners live in fear that they may be infected. People who are currently sexually active are often fearful. It is no longer unusual for a person to question a prospective sexual partner about the nature of his or her sexual history. The AIDS fear has spread even to low- and no-risk individuals. People who are not sexually active at all become fearful of acquiring AIDS from casual physical contact, which is an unlikely and often impossible source of AIDS. Individuals with no intention of becoming sexually active may worry needlessly about AIDS.

No single best means for handling fear of AIDS exists for everyone. Individuals in low- and no-risk situations may be worrying unnecessarily. Individuals in potential risk situations can change their behaviors—in terms of their sexual activity in general and the protection they seek in particular. Individuals in high-risk situations may have well-founded fears. One gay man I know has dealt with his fears by working as a volunteer in a group of AIDS patients and by seeking satisfaction and well-being from other aspects of his life. At best, then, such fears can lead to constructive actions.

Voluntary celibacy can help one to discover many other forms of intimacy. When partners take a temporary vacation from sexual relations and redirect their energies into other productive paths, they may find that the quality of their relationship improves.

options. Some women see celibacy "in a very positive way—not as a social disability but as a time for improving relationships, a time to evaluate one's sexuality and as a means for personal independence" (Brown, 1980, p. 138). If the decision to be celibate represents an angry reaction to men, little productiveness is likely to result. On the other hand, like any path chosen to help one find self and fulfillment, celibacy appears to offer the potential for substantial growth. One of the women interviewed by Brown described the effects of her celibacy.

> I decide if I like a guy without sex confusing the issue. Before, even though I was never really hung up sexually, there was always this fear that I wouldn't measure up to a man's expectations of me sexually. This was most gruesome when I wouldn't even know the man, and I'd be getting ready to be "judged" on my physical attributes by a total stranger. . . . Now, I feel in control and happy with myself and, truthfully, a lot closer to men.

> *(Brown, 1980, p. 140)*

Celibacy is not a universal answer, nor is it a coping device right for everyone. However, a celibate life, permanently or temporarily, should be viewed as a legitimate option, which can be freely and sensibly chosen. For some people whose continuing sexual experiences are unrewarding, selecting celibacy may help them to gain perspective and understand the role of sexuality in their lives.

For both those who do choose celibacy and those who maintain sexual experiences, their attitudes toward sexuality are relevant factors in their decision-making process. Our discussion on sexual well-being thus moves to the next topic: feelings and attitudes.

Attitudes

Sexuality is in part a psychological experience, which sometimes occurs in conjunction with physiological experiences. An accurate observation is that it's not what's between the legs but what's between the ears that counts. Thus, in coming to grips with our sexuality, we must consider attitudes, feelings, and beliefs. Let us examine some of these concerns. We will be drawing on the writings of sexologist Sol Gordon, who asserts that "Sexual intercourse, as an aspect of our sexuality, is greatly overrated" (1985, p. 16). What is important, then, in terms of improving our own sexuality is our attitudes. Here is a partial list of Gordon's suggestions about attitudes related to sexual well-being.

1. Give up harsh and punitive judgments about sexual thoughts, feelings, and behaviors. Feeling guilt and viewing thoughts as unacceptable are the mortal enemies of healthy sexuality. Whatever is arousing in thought or reality is okay.

   In the same sense, whatever sexual behaviors we choose are normal and acceptable, as long as they are not exploitative, they are consensual, and they are voluntary. Gordon puts it this way: "Provided sex is private, voluntary, enjoyable and does not seriously conflict with the participants' values, it does not matter how and where it takes place . . . and it does not matter who does what" (Gordon, 1985, p. 17).

2. Masturbation is healthy and, for many people, the source of their most intense orgasms. For people at all ages and in all marital situations, masturbation says nothing about satisfactions in intercourse, about one's worth, or about one's desire for others. However, guilt about masturbation can be destructive. See suggestion number 1.

3. Orgasms become less appreciated if they are our universal basis for sexual satisfaction. Don't ask partners, "Did you have one?" Sexual intimacy is closeness and physical sharing with another human being, not a function of a brief set of physical contractions. Respect, sensitivity, playfulness, adventure, and appreciation of all of the events in sexual encounters are more important.

4. Being an authentic person is the essence of being sexually attractive to another. Cosmetic elements and games fade with time, and liking ourselves, our looks, and our bodies is what makes others attracted to us. When we do feel good about both ourselves in general and our sexual beings in particular, uncanny healthy payoffs may result.

The Benefits of Intimacy

Eric Berne (1971) has described how having good sexual relationships can prevent the development of physical and mental problems. Intimacy, he has asserted, allows one to be touched and to have the health-promoting benefits of emotional and physical closeness. Berne has hypothesized that, as a result of such intimacy, a whole spectrum of psychosomatic disorders is less likely to occur.

Emotional discomfort may be prevented too, as anxiety lessens. Berne has noted that good intimacy has a health-giving closeness, which wards off free-floating anxiety. Out of intimacy comes a security that helps inoculate against anxiety attacks.

Sleeping patterns may be particularly affected. Berne has declared that "good sex is nature's sleeping pill" (1971, p. 199) and that good bedtime sex should routinely lead to a pleasant drowsiness that in turn becomes sleep. Berne concluded, "if it goes right, then in the morning it will be a cure for flat feet and dull eyes, if you remember the springy step and sparkling look of the well-cuffed couple" (1971, p. 200).

One can look beyond the absence of problems to the nature of mature sexuality, which almost always results in focusing on sex as part of the life of a fully functioning person with a comfortable acceptance of pleasure. Psychiatrist Joel Fort has described such healthy sex.

> It means a good feeling about your maleness or femaleness and about your sexual responses; an ability to respond and relate with full body and mind contact on sexual and other levels; kindness and understanding, openness, variety, and imagination with equality and mutual understanding; and free consent without exploitation.

(Fort, 1971, p. 223)

Healthy sex can be associated with general health because part of healthy sex is to accept oneself as a sexual being in a relaxed and joyous way. What most people find relaxed and joyous is long-term gratification in comfortable, genuinely pleasurable ways of sexually being with another person.

Sex as Play

One sign of your attitude toward sex is whether you are grim or playful during sexual contacts. Being grim means that you see the sexual event as serious, somber business, with a great deal at stake. Whether you perform well is important. From this viewpoint, sexual adequacy is indeed a serious question.

This attitude may be described as "sex as accomplishment." Sex manuals instruct the readers to master the technical skills necessary to be good lovers. Play is transformed into work, so that good sexual experiences absolutely require

technical know-how
rigorous practice
careful timing
proper equipment
reading and studying

(Bernard, 1971, p. 73)

On the other side of the picture is playfulness. To the extent that you feel spontaneous and able to freely say and do what comes to mind, then you are less bound. Answering the simple questions "Am I having a good time?" and "Do I laugh?" help you understand where you fall on the work–play dimension.

Harold Greenwald (1971) is a psychotherapist who has written extensively about sexuality. Greenwald tells us

to accept sex as fun, as a relaxed form of joyous play, to look at it as a form of that dreaded emotion, pleasure. . . . With the grim seriousness

Those with healthy sexual attitudes relax and enjoy themselves in playful, spontaneous sex.

characteristic of our profession—particularly those of us engaged in the study of sexual behavior—play has been one of the most neglected human activities.

(Greenwald, 1971, pp. 193–194)

Tearing of the hair and wringing of the hands may underlie much sexual activity. "Am I doing right?" "Does my partner want just that?" Anxieties, guilt, and self-doubts poison the sexual happening.

To move toward play in sex, one must realize that two distinct worlds of personal functioning are combined: self in general and self during sexual contact. The interpersonally comfortable self in general is often isolated from self during sex. That isolation can be reduced by bringing the most relaxed sense of yourself to sexuality and by not subscribing to stereotyped roles during sex.

Regenerative sexuality

Openness and nondefensiveness allow the sexual contact to be truly pleasurable. Jessie Bernard (1971) has called this openness ***regenerative sexuality.***" By this, she is referring to sexual relations that give "fresh vigor and strength" to the parties, that reinvigorate and enliven, that regenerate sexual self-confidence. Bernard has emphasized that such regeneration blooms in the soil of sexuality that offers "the gentle reassurance of warm, understanding physical contact" (1971, p. 76).

A Concluding Note on Sexual Well-Being

At times, sexual activities are discussed as if they exist apart from the people involved. However, sexual acts always occur in the context of cultural beliefs, group values, and transactions between individuals. The same behaviors that produce a bored restlessness or jittery guilt in one context, or with one person, can yield deep contentment in another context, or with another person. Each of us seeks to discover the context in which sexuality and other personal behaviors are heightened and enjoyed.

As a vehicle for communication, sexuality allows us opportunities to share poignancy, intensity, tenderness, and concern. The physical closeness both grows out of personal closeness and can help personal closeness to grow. Like all means of communication, sexuality is learned. Yet as a form of communication, sexual contact permits messages to be sent with truth and clarity that have no equivalent in speech.

One fundamental communication of sex should be pleasure. Virginia Johnson has stated

I hope you aren't underestimating the significance of pleasure—and by pleasure I don't mean fun. I mean the authentic, abiding satisfaction that makes us feel like complete human beings. . . . The way we express ourselves sexually—our most intimate way of relating to another person—reflects how we value ourselves, how we value the other person, how that person values us. It reflects all the things that mean warmth, love, affection and security to us—and which we therefore seek and cherish. It reflects, in a real way, some of the purposes and meaning of life.

(Johnson, 1974, pp. 26, 28)

If we do not cherish ourselves as full human beings, that lack of cherishing appears in our less caring sexuality. On the other hand, when our sexuality is without competitiveness and comfortably seeks pleasure

THE LANGUAGE OF SEX

People who call it necking are very bad judges of anatomy.

(Groucho Marx)

The words people use to describe the sexual experience reveal much of their underlying assumptions about the quality and nature of sex. When Albert Ellis, the developer of rational therapy, writes about "sexual adventuring," his words paint a far prettier picture than do terms such as *sexually indiscriminate* or *sexually promiscuous*. The basic Anglo-Saxon words used to describe intercourse and the genitals are also used as insults, supporting the fusion of aggression and sexual desire that analytically oriented psychologists say exists in human sexuality.

In impotence as well, the description of the nonerect penis as flaccid, limp, or soft carries negative connotations. One suggestion has been that, under such circumstances, the penis should be called "floppy," or "temporarily unemployed"—happier, more matter-of-fact descriptors. The word *impotence* itself has implications of powerlessness and weakness in personality. Calling the problem "erectile dysfunction" helps reduce the stigma (Elliott, 1985).

Sexual words need to be considered in the context in which they are used. In some cultural groups, sexually explicit words become stripped of their literal meanings and are used casually, in the way the words "you know" has become a frequent interjection in American language. In Britain, it is not unusual to hear the expression "you sod," which derives from "you sodomist." Similarly, the British use the phrase "bugger off" as a mildly vulgar equivalent to the phrase used in the United States, "buzz off." The origin of bugger is the word *buggery*, which in turn derived from the British belief that the Bulgarians' preferred mode of sexual activity was anal intercourse. As far back as two hundred years ago, the Bulgarians were called Buggers in England (rather than Bulgars, as they were called in France), and anal intercourse was labelled buggery.

A language of intimate sex exists between lovers. During sexual contacts, many people affirm the basic nature of the experience by using explicit, descriptive language. This language defines the special nature of the sexual contact as apart from other experiences, and, in some cases, the language itself is one of the cues for sexual arousal.

TABLE 11-3 Toward and Away from Sexual Well-Being	
Toward Well-Being	Away from Well-Being
Acceptance of sexuality as healthy	Sexual aversion and condemnation
Generalized sexual satisfaction and pleasure	Little sexual pleasure or nearsighted focus on orgasm
Orgasmic satisfaction	No orgasm or orgasms experienced as unsatisfactory
Comfortable levels of desire	Unsatisfactory levels of sexual desire or excitement

for another and for ourselves, it is a mature way to attain fulfillment. Table 11–3 summarizes such sexual well-being behaviors.

SUMMARY

Sexual experiences may be understood according to the meanings we learn to attach to them. In the Walen (1980) model of sexual arousal, detection of a physiological change is followed in sequence by labelling, attribution, and finally evaluation. The physical evidence of sexual arousal takes the form of vasocongestion, myotonia, hyperventilation, and, frequently, a layer of perspiration.

Surveys of college students have indicated that about half are sexually active. One-third of sexually active males describe having premature ejaculation regularly and two-thirds of sexually active females report frequently not achieving orgasm in intercourse. Such sexual dysfunctions and others, including impotence and fetishism, are unrelated to psychological disorders.

Fantasy is an important part of sexual attraction and arousal. Four types of sexual fantasies have been identified: exploratory, intimate, impersonal, and sadomasochistic fantasies.

The heritage of Victorian condemnation of sexual activities is the residual feelings of guilt we experience in normal sexual activities. Among these normal activities are masturbation; between 70 and 87 percent of all adolescent boys masturbate, and between 30 and 42 percent of adolescent girls masturbate. It is not unusual for boys and girls to feel guilt or shame about their masturbating.

Despite a heightened attention to the female orgasm in intercourse, many women report that they are sexually satisfied by emotional closeness and nonorgasmic arousal. Women with orgasmic dysfunctions have been successfully treated by learning how to understand and accept their sexuality, by learning tactile exploration, self-stimulation, and Kegel exercises, and by learning how to bring masturbatory orgasms to partner intercourse through honest and undemanding communication.

Impotence is erectile dysfunction in the male, and it most frequently arises from the psychogenic causes of performance anxiety and spectatoring. In treatment, touching and sensuality are encouraged and intercourse is made off-limits until the anxiety subsides. Premature ejaculation is treated by techniques that teach ejaculatory control. Sexual desire is more difficult to treat. This minimal interest in sex is accompanied by the full ability to function when the person is interested.

For some, absence of sexual experience, or celibacy, is their choice. The three issues for the celibate person are physical needs, social expectations, and views of self compared to others' attractiveness and sexual needs. Involuntary abstinence may cause problems, but voluntary abstinence with strong social support can give one a positive opportunity to gain perspective and understanding of oneself.

To come to grips with one's sexuality, a person should attempt to surrender harsh judgments about sexuality, to accept the option of masturbation, to be less orgasmcentric, and to attempt to be as authentic and genuine a human being in sexual contexts as in other situations. Once accomplished, these steps permit one to have a preventive intimacy with another that lessens anxiety and discomfort. Without guilt and shame, and with an open and nondefensive attitude toward sexual pleasure, sex can be playful. Sex is a vehicle for expanded communication and sharing with another that can yield deep contentment.

Key Terms

Celibacy	Primary orgasmic dysfunction
Desire dysfunction	Psychogenic impotence
Fetish	Regenerative sexuality
Kegels	Retarded ejaculation
Myotonia	Secondary impotence
New impotence	Secondary orgasmic dysfunction
Performance anxiety	Sexual arousal cycle
Premature ejaculation	Spectatoring
Primary impotence	Vasocongestion

Recommended Reading

Berne, E. (1971). *Sex in human loving.* New York: Pocket Books. When Eric Berne wrote *Games People Play,* he captivated his readers with his wit and with the commonsense truths of his observations. The same charm and truths are present in *Sex in Human Loving.* Discussing everything from sexual words and organs, to sexual games and beliefs, Berne leaves the reader with an affectionate understanding of human sexuality.

Eysenck, H.J. & Wilson, G. (1979). *The psychology of sex.* London: J.M. Dent & Sons. Hans Eysenck has served as the sharpest-biting horsefly in psychology, always quick to call attention to the scholarly vices of others and scholarly virtues of himself. However, in this book, Eysenck and Wilson have distilled the essence of current knowledge about the psychology of sex in brief, readable form.

Francoeur, R.T. (1984). *Becoming a sexual person: A brief edition*. New York: Wiley. This untextlike text is intended for human sexuality courses. The book is readable, authoritative, and a pleasant travelogue through sexual ways and living. Helpful, candid photographs are present, too.

Meyners, R. & Wooster, C. (1979). *Sexual style: Facing and making choices about sex*. New York: Harcourt, Brace, Jovanovich. The fundamental decisions people make about sexual activity, partners, and style are described. Each of the choices is accompanied by do-it-yourself exercises that help to clarify values and sexual options.

Competency and Achievement

12

CHAPTER

Work and Careers

Near most big factories there's a place where people gather after work. Sometimes it's a bar. In our neighborhood, it's the cafe, where folks get together for Mac's homemade biscuits and his cheese omelets with hot sauce. Some people eat just to fill the empty space. I guess that's why some of us drink so hard, too. It shows on our faces. Lots of hard lines and gritting and grinding our teeth. With all that hardness, Brigham stood out all the more.

He was there most mornings when the eleven to seven shift let out. You'd never know from looking at him that he'd been standing on the line for eight hours. His face was soft and unlined. A little smile played around his mouth. And Brigham was always quietly whistling to himself. Whistling with pleasure. He especially whistled that old Shaker tune. It's the one that begins, "'Tis a gift to be simple, 'tis a gift to be free, 'tis a gift to come down where you ought to be."

We didn't really know each other, but one morning I sat with him. I had left a big piece of myself back on the line, at least when I was paying attention. Half the time, I was off somewhere private and personal. "How do you manage to be so comfortable and pleased after this kind of shift?" I asked him.

Well, Brigham laughed at that question. A good laugh, the kind that rumbles deep and billows out kindly. "It's what you make of it," he told me.

Brigham said that when he first started working on the line, he felt overwhelmed. So much to do, so much to learn. But learning came with experience. At his station, the bodies came down the line every ninety seconds. Within two months, he explained, he could do the whole weld in forty seconds flat. Never longer. Then he found himself with all this time. To have fifty out of every ninety seconds to yourself, that's a lot of time, a lot, Brigham

told me. Almost nobody has that much time to themselves.

He talked about what he did with that time. At first, he would just read the newspaper or *Newsweek*. He set up a little reading stand, and marked where he was with a red marker. That felt good for a while, but then it got old. The next thing he tried was to make the welding a challenge. As each body came down the line, he would close his eyes and weld by feel. He knew how he needed to mate the body and the torch. Once he'd met that challenge, though, it didn't hold Brigham's interest for more than a month.

Finally, he explained, he found what he had been looking for. Brigham started sending his mind to other people on the line. At first, it would be just one person, across the way from him. Then he would pick out other people he liked, whether he could see them or not. He would send them his mind, in fifty-second transmissions. He sent his whole mind, he said. Everything he believed, everything he valued, everything he loved. The more he sent, the better he felt, until he was sending only a good mind, bright and clear and shining.

I told him, right, yes, that's super. And, when I could without being impolite, I scooted away. Sending other people your mind? I mean, that's about as ridiculous as ESP, maybe sillier. I didn't believe it when he told me, and I don't believe it now. I really don't.

Still, when I'm on the line, now and then a funny thing happens. I'll be at my station, not thinking of anything, and this wave of lovely warmth just kind of settles in me. I start feeling so peaceful and good, and I'm smiling before I know it. Without knowing why, I find that old Shaker tune, "'Tis a gift to be simple, 'tis a gift to be free . . ." running through my head. It doesn't mean anything, of course. But it is a funny thing.

WORK IN OUR LIVES

Ask most working adults, "How are you doing?" or "What's been happening in your life?," and the odds are good that they will talk about what has been happening at work. If we asked Brigham what he has been doing, he probably would tell us about his efforts to adjust to the boredom and repetition of working on the assembly line. His stages of adjustment are not unusual. Once he had mastered the actual task presented to him, he tried to bring more personal elements to his workplace. First he read, and then, to make the job more challenging, he tried welding with his eyes shut. Although sending your mind to other workers is hardly typical of the ways most of us come to terms with our work, Brigham's desire to make the time spent at his work a way of making positive contact with other people is. Brigham, like the rest of us, spends almost half of his waking hours on the job; he wants his job to make him and others feel good.

Feeling good at work *is* a goal for most people in Western society. In a tongue-in-cheek commentary on the joy of work, Ogden Nash penned the following rhyme:

Oh what fun to be young and healthy and alive
and privileged to do some
of the work of the world from nine to five!

(Nash, 1975, p. 6)

Yet the idea of work as pleasure is one of many recent attitudes about work in the history of humankind. Before we explore such relatively new ideas about the meaning of work, we first take a brief look at the history of work, a story that in part describes the nature of human societies.

History of Work

In human history, work probably started with the earliest primitive societies that survived by hunting and by gathering available plants and fruits. Because their food supply was so uncertain and they survived so marginally, everyone in these societies worked, even young children, and everyone did the same things. Work was a natural part of living, done continuously and universally every day.

When the first agricultural societies appeared, labor became specialized. Different workers performed different tasks, with priests, warlords, and their attendants separated from planters, herdsmen, and craftsmen by the nature of their work. As societies became more organized and better developed, there developed a negative attitude toward work. For example, at the height of the ancient Greek civilization, work was seen as degrading. Because all labor was performed by slaves—and there were

Work became specialized when the first agricultural societies appeared. Before such societies formed, everyone performed the same tasks—namely, whatever was necessary for survival.

more than enough slaves captured in the marauding and conquest of the known world to do the labor—the Greeks could afford to look down on laboring. The opinions of the slaves were not recorded (Neff, 1985).

During the Middle Ages, activity was divided into ***liberal arts*** and ***manual arts.*** By the fourteenth and fifteenth centuries, the liberal arts were devoted to intellectual and contemplative pursuits and were thought to be the highest form of human activities. The manual arts, although necessary for survival and meeting life's needs, were considered undesirable lower activities. However, this attitude changed during the Protestant Reformation. Because of the influence of Martin Luther, people began to view work as a basic necessity of Christian life. Working was seen as a sign of a commitment to making one's life meaningful and devout and thus intrinsically worthwhile. This belief in the positive value of work continues to the present day.

In the nineteenth century, Karl Marx triggered a revolution in thinking by proclaiming the world to be ***workcentric.*** He saw civilization, political societies, religion, and the arts as following (rather than leading) our labor-based economic foundations. Marx reinterpreted history by examining

Liberal arts
Manual arts

Workcentric

what workers did, how workers were treated, and how the financial resources that came from work were distributed.

At the same time, a technological revolution was taking place. The harnessing of power sources through inventions such as the steam engine led to the development of factories, places where numbers of people gathered to produce a manufactured product. Instead of working at home, or on farms, or producing individual crafts, people came to a centralized place, where the quality of their work was overseen. The industrial age had arrived and, with it, came the organized labor movement.

Industrialization also spawned a growing awareness of occupational stressors and satisfactions. No longer was the focus solely on worker productivity and product quality. What jobs meant to the psychological well-being of the workers became a consideration, and industrial psychology developed to study the question.

The Personal Meanings of Work

For most of us, work is an important part of our lives. When our work goes well, we usually feel better about ourselves. When our work is frustrating, our sense of dissatisfaction seeps into many other areas of our lives.

Work does not hold the same meaning for all people. When they find work an unpleasant and dreaded experience, employees may drink heavily on weekends and miss as many as three out of every four Monday mornings. They often resent and feel alienated from their work.

On the other hand, many people find work a rewarding and exciting activity, defining their lives in positive and fulfilling ways. Even during their leisure time, such people may think about the challenging and desirable aspects of their work. They rush eagerly to the job in the morning, voluntarily stay late, and are excited when they successfully finish a task.

Work gives meaning to life in a number of ways, but the following explores four of the more common ways (Lofquist & Dawis, 1969; Frese, 1982):

Life needs.   Work maintains a standard of living. Financial compensation from work is the only way that the overwhelming majority of the population can meet their material needs.

Interpersonal needs.   Because the law of proximity operates in friendships, we tend to be friends with people with whom we are in close proximity (contact). Work provides people with the opportunity to build friendships. Another interpersonal need that work may meet is the sense of being of genuine service to others.

Self-identity and expression.   Ask a person, "Who are you?" and there is a good chance the person will answer by stating his or her occupation, such as, "I am a teacher." Our identities are defined in part by our work. More than that, work provides us with an opportunity to express ourselves, sometimes in creative, individual, and satisfying ways. Prestige and social status are mainly determined by occupation; physicians and professors are automatically respected for their professions. Trash collectors and assembly line workers are not.

It fills the day.   To feel worthwhile, we usually need to sense that we are doing something useful. Work fills the day, promoting the feeling of time properly spent and not wasted. Jobs provide a time structure to each day, week, year, and even life.

These sources of satisfaction are most clear for white-collar and upper- and middle-status workers, but they apply to lower-level and blue-collar workers as well. However, each of the positive meanings of work just listed has potential for being interpreted negatively. People who are poorly paid often see their work as an inadequate way of meeting life needs. People who feel stuck in place at work see little opportunity for advancement and improvement. People who are substantially dissatisfied with their jobs still see work as filling the day, but they may find that what they do provides them with minimal respect and recognition. The negative meanings of work influence the relationship between work and adjustment. Work, after all, is a major means of need satisfaction. Our experiences at work reflect how satisfied we are with some of our most basic concerns.

Most of us need our work. For that reason, although machines may perform labor faster, better, and cheaper than men and women, they probably will not minimize work activities. In *Work Is Here to Stay, Alas* Sar Levitan and William Johnston (1973) concluded that most productivity gains change rather than eliminate work or improve our standard of living. People look more to other people for services that cannot be automated. As Levitan and Johnston observed, "A machine might diagnose an illness, but it could not reassure a patient" (1973, p. 15).

We genuinely need work for our well-being and emotional survival. Without meaningful work, most of us feel worthless. Levitan and Johnson have called work ". . . the fundamental effort which defines life. The drive for leisure, apart from rest and recovery, arises from the undesirability of particular and unrewarding work" (1973, p. 15). George Bernard Shaw was aware of this need for fulfilling work when he wrote that a "perpetual holiday is a good working definition of hell" (1969, p. 312).

Job Satisfaction: Interesting Work and Positive Relationships

Job satisfaction

Good pay and job security are far from enough to satisfy most workers. Americans want much more. The landmark report, *Work in America*, was issued in 1973 by the U.S. Department of Health, Education, and Welfare

(HEW). Good pay and job security ranked in importance only fifth and seventh, respectively, in this systematic survey of the experiences of over fifteen hundred workers. Interesting work was ranked first, while having enough help and equipment, having enough information, and having enough authority to get the job done were ranked second, third, and fourth, respectively. In sixth place was the opportunity to develop special abilities, and rated eighth was seeing the results of one's work.

The average workers are unhappy with significant aspects of their jobs. The same *Work in America* report observed that only 43 percent of white-collar and 23 percent of blue-collar employees would choose their same jobs if they could start all over again. Nevertheless, there are work aspects that people find deeply satisfying.

Job satisfaction was also investigated by Renwick, Lawler, and the *Psychology Today* editorial staff, who used a very different methodology. In this 1978 reader survey, twenty-three thousand readers returned a form printed in the magazine that rated satisfactions and dissatisfactions on the job. These respondents were better educated than the subjects in the HEW study, and, of course, they were volunteers who took the time to respond. Every tenth *Psychology Today* reader's response was tabulated, and it was found that, for these individuals, nothing was more important than their relationships with fellow workers and with employers.

The details of the satisfaction employees found in these relationships at work were studied. The following items (listed in order) were cited as the most important for enjoying work:

The friendliness of people I work with.

The amount of freedom I have on my job.

The respect I receive from people I work with.

The way I am treated by the people I work with.

These responses emphasized the personal satisfactions people felt about their jobs. In a separate set of interviews, the director of a bakery described that feeling of shared goodwill one gets from working with valued others.

Our bread has to taste the same way every day, but you don't have to be machines. On a good day it's beautiful to be here. We have a good time and work hard and we're laughing.

(Terkel, 1972, p. 612)

The *Psychology Today* respondents indicated that it was important to have potential for self-growth and constructive achievement at work. High importance ratings were given to the following items:

Chances to do something that makes me feel good about myself.

Chances to accomplish something worthwhile.

Most workers want their jobs to provide more than good pay and job security. In one survey, employees cited relationships with fellow workers and employers as being the most important aspect of their jobs.

Chances to learn new things.

Opportunity to develop my skills and abilities.

In fact, most respondents reported that they would continue to work even if their financial circumstances allowed them to live comfortably for the rest of their lives without having to work. When asked why, they responded that (1) they enjoyed their work, (2) a major part of their identities came from their jobs, and (3) work kept them from feeling bored. However, the study found substantial areas of dissatisfaction as well (Renwick, Lawler, the *Psychology Today* Staff, 1978, p. 54–55).

An astounding 43 percent felt they had been victims of job discrimination, because of race, sex, ethnic origin, age, or physical handicap. These respondents charged that their salaries were lower than those for other workers doing comparable work, or they were discriminated against, or, in the case of white respondents, they had not been hired because of affirmative action guidelines. Men tended to complain of reverse discrimination, and women tended to complain of being assigned extra work or less prestigious positions than other workers with similar jobs.

The HEW report relied on the results of interviews and the *Psychology Today* survey depended upon readers voluntarily completing forms and mailing them back to the editors. The more frequent approach to determining job satisfaction has been to administer standardized questionnaires such as the following one.

Try to answer these sample questions about your present or most recent job.

1. Would you recommend this job as a good one to a very close friend? Yes _____ No _____

2. Would you quit this job if you had anything else to do? Yes _____ No _____

3. Do you think you like this job more than most people like theirs? Yes _____ No _____

4. Are you enthusiastic about this job most days? Yes _____ No _____

5. Is your job like a hobby to you? Yes _____ No _____

6. Do you have to force yourself to go to work most days? Yes _____ No _____

If you answered yes to questions 1, 3, 4, and 5 and no to questions 2 and 6, you gave a strong statement of job satisfaction. The opposite answers indicate job dissatisfaction. In longer questionnaires, items such as the preceding ones have been found to be related to measures of work adjustment (Cook, Hepworth, Wall, Toby & Warr, 1982). High *job dissatisfaction* scores are significantly (and not too surprisingly) related to high rates of job turnover, to frequent thoughts of quitting, and to lower occupational prestige levels.

The kinds of job attitudes, satisfactions, and dissatisfactions we have discussed are not fixed forever. Attitudes toward work change over time, sometimes for better, sometimes for worse, and often toward the preexisting attitudes of fellow workers. This change toward workers' increasing similarity of work attitudes and beliefs is our next topic: *occupational socialization*.

Occupational Socialization

When individuals acquire the attitudes, beliefs, and values of their fellow workers, the process is known as occupational socialization. That is, individuals are molded by the occupations in which they find themselves (Frese, 1982). Although fellow workers' preexisting attitudes and traits

At the beginning of their careers, most police officers believe in the rules and regulations of police work and are altruistically dedicated to their duty. After a while, however, many officers' work experiences negate their initial idealism, and they become cynical or disillusioned.

are important, equally important to occupational socialization are the ways in which social norms are transmitted. Consider persons in the jobs of teacher, physician, or steel worker. They all learn how to think of themselves with attitudes similar to those of their fellow workers. People who feel that their work offers a socially vital service acquire this perspective in part from on-the-job socialization. So do people who come to think of their work as a dull way to earn a living.

In the case of police, the socialization process can lead to cynicism and disillusionment. Neiderhoffer (1967) observed the development of **cynicism** over time in New York City police officers; the subjects came to believe that their own needs are more important than the services they offer to the public. The police officers began their careers by believing in the rules and regulations of police work, in professionalism, and in altruistic dedication to duty. But after completing five years of service, the

Cynicism

police officers showed a pattern of "sour grapes" skepticism. Other police officers found that their work experiences reshaped their initial idealism to a bitter view of departmental favoritism and public alienation. What happens to metropolitan area police officers also happens to some degree to most other workers. A conformity effect combines with a learning process, and, to a noticeable degree, we become what we do. For that reason, working in a place where we trust others and where we feel secure is very important.

Occupational trust

Occupational Trust and Security

Think for a moment about those times in your life when you have been around people you did not trust. You probably felt uncomfortable much of the time. It's likely that you felt worried and that you deeply wished to be out of the particular situation.

Because trusting people in our immediate surroundings is crucial to our well-being wherever we may be, trust is a crucial element in our work as well. If you work where you do not trust your fellow workers or managers, it's likely that you will show general discomfort, anxiety about work tasks, and a desire to leave. Indeed, trust has consistently been associated with job satisfaction.

Trust itself comes from your perceiving coworkers and management as having good intentions and as having earned your confidence. To investigate interpersonal trust at work, the following four topics were studied (Cook & Wall, 1980):

Faith in peers, or the extent to which coworkers can be trusted to help out in work difficulties and generally relied upon.

Faith in management, or the perception of management as sincere, fair, and trying not to take advantage of workers.

Confidence in peers, or feelings that coworkers will be skilled and careful.

Confidence in management, or feelings that management is efficient, sensible, and has a good future.

The results of a series of studies showed that how old the workers were, how long they had worked at the same place, and their skill levels did not affect their ratings of these topics. However, occupational trust was significantly related to overall job satisfaction and to job motivation and involvement (Cook et al., 1982). Trusting coworkers and management allowed employees to feel secure and valued. In job environments where they saw others as able, conscientious, and having good intentions, employees developed a positive sense of occupational self-esteem.

Security and self-esteem on the job are essential, but other elements also contribute to job satisfaction. Porter (1961) has postulated five levels of needs associated with occupational satisfaction. Figure 12–1 shows these needs, from the most fundamental—feeling secure in one's position—to the highest need—feeling fulfilled and actualized in one's occupation.

These occupational needs do not apply equally to all employees. The kind of position we hold, our skill level, and our level of aspiration all influence our judgments regarding our occupational needs. Our next step, therefore, is to look at active ways to accelerate job satisfaction. *The One Minute Manager* (Blanchard & Johnson, 1983) is an example of the self-help approach to improved job satisfaction. More formal programs also exist. We now look at one program directed toward business executives.

Psychological Courses for Job Satisfaction

Executives who find their work lives unsatisfying sometimes enroll in occupation-focused psychological courses. One such course is the Menninger Foundation Executive Seminar. The Menninger Foundation in Topeka, Kansas, offers a program intended to teach executives basic mental health principles and ways of coping with stress. This one-week seminar helps many participants reexamine themselves, take a fresh look at their goals in life, and "diversify their emotional portfolios."

FIGURE 12–1   A Hierarchy of Occupational Needs

Adapted from Porter, 1961, p. 1–10.

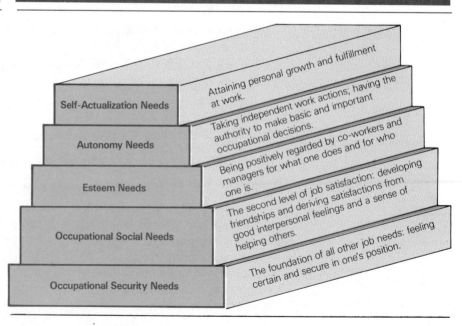

A combination of lectures and small group meetings pursue these objectives. Initially cautious, the participants eventually self-disclose and share with each other. One student reported

> The partial unmasking, and the resulting intimacy, produced a kind of group spirit or "high" comparable to that often described by teammates at the end of a winning season. . . .
>
> I, too, left Topeka on a high, convinced I had somehow been through an important and powerfully moving experience. But when I returned to my home and my office, I had difficulty explaining what I had learned. I felt I had gained some insights into human behavior, but when I tried to explain them . . . a cynical friend said it sounded like "Midwest inspirational corn."

(Rice, 1979, pp. 95, 97)

Such training programs are direct outgrowths of the training groups (**T-groups**) that developed in the 1950s. T-groups were intended to increase personal awareness and teach participants how to relate better to fellow workers. Whatever its label, the executive seminar is based on faith, not empirical results. Research has not supported sensitivity programs as vehicles for changing executives' lives, but neither has it shown such programs to be harmful. Participants in the seminars *do* believe in their worth, and organizers of such programs maintain that a week of self-examination has long-term beneficial payoffs for the participants.

In this discussion of the psychological components of work, let us not forget that straightforward talent and competence play a vital role. Yet talent and competence are not as straightforward as one might think. Are we referring to productivity? To insight? To creativity? To intelligence? One important way of defining these concepts is by looking at ***tacit knowledge,*** which is a special form of work-related intelligence.

Tacit Knowledge

You may have had a successful, self-made business manager say to you, "I'm a graduate of the college of hard knocks. Your book learning and theoretical ideas are a universe away from what it takes to make it in the business world!" Not only do executives in business often make such assertions, but so do people in a variety of other occupations. Furthermore, they may well be correct.

It's not that theories, textbooks, or even native intelligence are without worth. However, practical intelligence appears to be what makes a difference in the work world. Wagner and Sternberg (1985) have called such practical intelligence *tacit knowledge.* They have defined tacit knowledge as the ability to plan and succeed by using essential skills that are informal, useful, and rarely taught, but instead are acquired indirectly.

T-groups

Tacit knowledge

When psychologists are not studying undergraduate students in psychology, they are often studying other psychologists. So it was with Wagner and Sternberg's research. They looked first at academic psychologists and then at business managers and drew the following conclusion: Tacit knowledge was associated with success. The most successful individuals showed practical knowledge in three areas: managing themselves, managing others, and managing their careers. Furthermore, tacit knowledge was not related to results on standard intelligence tests.

Wagner and Sternberg's conclusions also serve as good guidelines for achieving work success. In the final analysis, it is what happens day in and day out that matters for most of us. The best theory is one that has meaning to real world pursuits. In studying tacit knowledge, the challenge is to look at just how skills are acquired and define exactly what they are. That process of making the unstated more available is a major part of what psychology can contribute to work satisfaction and success.

OCCUPATIONAL COSTS AND HAZARDS

Occupational stress

Occupational Stress

Job dissatisfaction carries consequences far beyond mere unhappiness. Job dissatisfaction can cause physical and psychological disorders (House, Strecher, Metzner & Robbins, 1986). An analysis of the effects of job design on mental health also drew this conclusion (Broadbent, 1985). Dissatisfied workers develop symptoms in their lives, and the people who are most dissatisfied with their jobs are likely to have the most symptoms. When Broadbent asked over a thousand British and American men how much of the time they were fed up at work, he found that the extent of their dissatisfaction was significantly correlated with their anxiety and depression as well as with the number of their somatic complaints.

Differences appeared between what caused the workers to be anxious and what caused them to be depressed. Anxiety arose much more from the work itself, and especially from paced, time-demanding, assembly-line work. Depression, on the other hand, came from interpersonal work problems. When auto factory employees wore hearing protectors and were unable to talk when they worked, they became more depressed. The pleasure of much work comes from companionship.

However, job stress may not truly lead to physical disorders. Instead, both may be products of other factors. For example, being poor, or living in grim surroundings, or feeling insecure about work may all lead to feelings of stress at work as well as to body pains, aches, and worries. Low income has a consistently great effect on mortality risk (Duleep, 1986). Determining what events actually cause which outcomes has been a challenging task for psychologists. The best information to date is that other factors are not usually the primary causes of job stress and physical disorders. Instead, work stress alone can and does directly lead to feeling bad, physically and psychologically. However, far from all of the possible problems in behavior and adjustment are explained by job stress. The correlations in research suggest significant patterns, but still do not account for much of the variability in people's reactions (Frese, 1985). It is clear that one source of variability is the kinds of occupations people have. Let us look first at the most stressful of all occupations, *paced work,* and then at comparisons of stresses and dissatisfactions in different occupations.

Paced work

Paced Work

Jackie Gleason and Charlie Chaplin, along with other comedians, made machine-paced work a target of their humor. The scenes are similar. An earnest but hapless worker strives mightily to keep up to the pace of items rushing by on the cake assembly line, for example. Eventually, the whipped cream, cherries, other toppings, and cake boxes all pile up in a glorious mess as the worker walks away, liberating himself from an impossible task. The quitting is important in this scene, because it is the sign that the worker will not give in to the tyranny of a factory that makes him an insignificant cog in an impossibly demanding environment.

Not everyone quits, nor does every worker feel oppressed in factory work. Some workers prefer and enjoy repetitive work (Cox, Thirlaway & Cox, 1983). Others find ways of mastering their discomfort in such occupations. Some workers rethink what the work means for them. They look for positive elements. A common solution is to do as Brigham did in our opening story—seek some satisfying aspect of contact with others at work. Of course, Brigham's particular method might be less common than the simple sharing of experiences and ways of mastering job problems. Finally, other workers have found psychotherapy helpful in alleviating job-related distress (Firth & Shapiro, 1986).

Not everyone suffers from paced work, but the average reaction to paced work is demonstration of substantial and negative mood changes. We now look at the *typical* employees in such a work situation. Postal work has provided an environment where reactions may be carefully studied, because in the same offices some employees run automated sorting machines while others engage in nonpaced work. An investigation compared 2,803 paced letter sorters to 2,715 other postal service employees and found great differences. The paced workers were higher on tension, depression, anger, fatigue, and confusion (Hurrell, 1985). Whether they exhibited Type A behavior patterns made no difference; the work was equally stressful for Type A and Type B individuals. However, among the male workers, more Type A's were engaged in the paced work, raising the question of a possible preselection factor.

Occupations Compared

An extensive study of stressors in varying occupations was conducted by the National Institute of Occupational Safety and Health (Caplan, Cobb, French, Van Harrison & Pinneau, 1975). Over two thousand men employed in twenty-three different jobs were selected as subjects in this study of a wide range of occupational stresses, including those known to incur high rates of peptic ulcers, high blood pressure, and other psychosomatic diseases.

Table 12–1 lists the twenty-three jobs, and their scores on selected measures of job strain. Workers in the three assembly-line jobs reported the highest degree of job dissatisfaction and machine tending and machine paced workers reported the highest work load scores, too. The lowest dissatisfaction scores were for the occupations of professor, air traffic controller at a small airport, and physician.

Let us look at stresses. The occupations in Table 12–1 are listed in order of workers' job dissatisfaction. The least satisfied were the blue-collar workers, among whom the machine tenders and continuous flow

EXPLORATION IN WELL-BEING

Job Conflict and Ambiguity

One supervisor gives you an order to do something a certain way. Then another supervisor doesn't like what you have done and gives you orders to redo the task. If you go ahead and redo it, you won't be able to complete the next assignment on time. This situation is known as role conflict, or problems created by competing demands made on a worker.

On the job, you ask your supervisor whether you can get some assistance and hire a new person. You get a vague answer that is neither yes nor no. The uncertainty you feel as a result of your supervisor's vagueness is part of role ambiguity, which is defined as the lack of clarity in description or perception of job duties.

The tension that employees feel when role conflict and role ambiguity occur has been measured by a standardized questionnaire (Kahn, Wolfe, Quinn & Smock, 1964). It poses the following questions (among others); answer them to learn how much role conflict and role ambiguity is present in your own job:

Role Conflict Questions

How frequently are you bothered at work by

Feeling that you have too little authority to carry out the responsibilities assigned to you?

monitors reported the lowest satisfaction. Three occupational stresses were especially present among the blue-collar workers: They felt that their abilities were *poorly utilized,* that they *participated minimally* in work issues, and that their jobs had *little complexity.*

Low utilization

Low utilization of abilities refers to workers not using the personal skills or abilities they acquired through academic or vocational training.

Low participation

Low participation refers to workers having little opportunity to share in the process of making decisions that will affect their work.

Low job complexity

Low job complexity describes jobs that are very uncomplicated and highly predictable and repetitive from day to day.

These factors were not job stressors for physicians, professors, or most high-status occupations. The blue-collar workers expressed the most doubt about their futures and received the least amount of social support for what they did. The physicians and professors had the fewest doubts and most social support.

In Scandinavia, the remedy for assembly-line discouragement is to

Feeling that you have too heavy a work load—one that you can't possibly finish during an ordinary workday?

Having to decide things that affect the lives of individuals you know?

Thinking that the amount of work you have to do may interfere with how well it gets done?

Feeling that your job tends to interfere with your family life?

Role Ambiguity Questions

How frequently are you bothered at work by

Being unclear on the exact scope and responsibilities of your job?

Not knowing what opportunities for advancement or promotion exist for you?

Not knowing what your immediate supervisor thinks of you and how he or she evaluates your performance?

Not being able to get information you need to carry out your job?

Scoring

In a national survey of 725 employees at all organizational levels, subjects completed the questionnaire using a five-point scale, with 1 representing "Never" and 5 representing "Nearly all the time." The survey outcome was an average score of 1.7 per item. In other words, little role conflict and role ambiguity was reported by average workers. If a person scores "Nearly all the time" on most items, the conflict and ambiguity he or she experiences at work are likely to be severe and tension producing (Kahn et. al., 1964).

Assembly-line or machine-paced workers experience more tension, depression, anger, fatigue, and confusion than do nonpaced workers.

have employees work in small teams and assemble products at their own speed. This produces a psychologically healthier work environment. Such men studied in a comparison of occupations

> . . . report more utilization of their skills and abilities, more complexity, more participation in decision making, and more of a demand for concentration (in this case a desirable aspect of the work—using one's mind). The employees in the non-machine paced work teams have significantly lower scores on boredom, anxiety, and depression.
>
> *(Caplan et al., 1975, p. 193)*

While job stress is related to the type of occupation, it can vary within a single occupation. Take the case of air traffic controllers (ATC). The

ATCs at busy airports reported quite different levels of job stress than did the ATCs at low traffic airports. The busy airport ATCs have higher rates of peptic ulcers and hypertension. Stress for these ATCs apparently derives from more conflicting job demands as well as less social support from fellow controllers, perhaps because of the larger numbers of people involved. The ATCs at quiet airports have less to do and feel part of a small, cohesive group, a situation that minimizes stress and raises job satisfaction.

TABLE 12-1 Strain Effects by Occupation*

Occupations	Job Dissatisfaction	Work Load Dissatisfaction	Somatic Complaints
Extremely high dissatisfaction			
Machine tender	167	162	137
Continuous flow monitor	160	82	85
Assembler, machine-paced	153	161	165
High dissatisfaction			
Assembler, nonmachine-paced	139	120	128
Forklift driver	136	132	108
Assembler, relief	133	151	157
Engineer	126	107	85
Tool and die maker	125	93	100
Average dissatisfaction			
Supervisor, blue-collar	115	109	111
Train dispatcher	109	119	108
Accountant	108	107	100
Electronic technician	88	97	122
Programmer	85	88	94
Scientist	85	84	77
Administrator	80	87	91
Low dissatisfaction			
Air traffic controller, large airport	79	72	134
Administrative professor	67	151	82
Delivery service courier	64	57	65
Policeman	63	81	94
Supervisor, white-collar	60	94	82
Professor	56	91	71
Air traffic controller, small airport	56	75	139
Extremely low dissatisfaction			
Family physician	50	132	74

Adapted from Caplan, Cobb, French, Van Harrison & Pinneau, 1975, p. 133.
*The average strain score was 100. Higher scores represent higher levels of strain and lower scores represent less strain.

In contrast to busy airports, which have high-stress work environments, smaller airports with less traffic allow air traffic controllers more time to become involved in a cohesive employee group. This social support from fellow workers minimizes the controllers' job-related stress and raises their job satisfaction.

The Effects of Unemployment

Work is such an important part of our lives that when people become unemployed, they often develop emotional and social adjustment problems. Sometimes problems arise from the job loss itself. Other times, the hardships associated with unemployment create difficulties. In any case, the extra time on their hands, the lessened sense of accomplishing worthwhile activities, and the loss of income substantially influence the lives of the unemployed.

The effects of unemployment were formally studied in Youngstown, Ohio, after the September, 1977, announcement that the Youngstown Sheet and Tube Company, a steel-making company, would close. Almost forty-one hundred workers were initially laid off, and more layoffs followed. One year later, 173 of the steelworkers were interviewed, and over half of these were reinterviewed two years after the layoffs. Fifty-one managers were interviewed, and over half of them reinterviewed in the follow-up (Buss & Redburn, 1983).

After two years, only 7 percent of the steelworkers and none of the managers remained unemployed. Most had been hired at nearby factories. A few had retired or been rehired by the steel company. To determine the effects of the unemployment, two-hour interviews were conducted in the homes of the steelworkers and managers, and a variety of mental health measures were gathered. The subjects reported two significant reactions.

Stunned immobility

Stunned immobility was the predominant long-term reaction. The unemployed workers not only felt depressed, but they and their families also described feeling emotional helplessness and dependency. Workers also reported feeling victimized, feeling aggressive and irritable, and using more alcoholic beverages.

Hypochondriasis

Hypochondriasis was the second reaction. The subjects reported suffering from increased body complaints of stomach upsets, headaches, and lower back pains.

Why didn't the workers have more severe reactions to unemployment? Many workers in large factory areas go through a cyclical process of being laid off, rehired, laid off again, rehired, and so on. The Youngstown studies observed of such sporadic unemployment,

> . . . it appears that brief periods of unemployment may have allowed a worker and his family to grow accustomed to the reality of a plant shut-down, perhaps in much the same way as periodic layoffs in the steel industry tend to inoculate workers against the deleterious effects of unemployment.

(Buss & Redburn, 1983, p. 73)

A final conclusion of the Youngstown studies was that few of these unemployed workers needed mental health treatment. This conclusion is in contrast to the findings of other studies, which revealed that the unemployed are more likely to seek help (Catalano, Rook & Dooley, 1986). Three factors helped to keep the effects so mild for the steelworkers. First, 95 percent of the laid-off workers were reemployed or voluntarily retired within two years of the shutdown. Second, steelworkers are among the most highly paid workers in the United States, and so they usually have adequate financial resources to draw on during layoffs. Third, the workers knew that the steel industry fluctuated, and they were emotionally and financially prepared for unemployment. Unemployment is more trying when workers are unable to find new work and especially when they are without social support.

The meaning of unemployment is underscored by messages concerning work and self-worth in the children's stories popular in our society. In the story of *The Ant and the Grasshopper*, the lazy grasshopper, who plays all summer while the industrious ant saves for the harsh winter, is taught the lesson that play doesn't pay. In the story of the *Little Red Hen*, all of the animals who refused to help in the planting, harvesting, and milling of the wheat and the baking of the bread are not allowed to eat the bread. While the intent of these stories is to teach responsibility to children, they also emphasize the principle that work is expected. People who do not work are depicted as deserving the deprivations that inevitably come to them.

These negative social attitudes add to the problems of the unem-

The majority of unemployed people profoundly miss having a job. Long-term unemployment often creates feelings of worthlessness, restlessness, or depression.

ployed. Unemployed people are often characterized as lazy. Employed observers see them as unmotivated and attribute to them a variety of negative characteristics. This common negative attitude toward the un-employed is captured in the Ogden Nash poem, "More about People."

> Anybody at leisure
> Incurs everybody's displeasure
> It seems to be very irking
> To people at work to see other people not working. . .

(Nash, 1975, p. 7)

If people are not working, it often is assumed that they are personally responsible for their unemployment. In turn, if they have a difficult time meeting expenses and other problems, they are seen as deserving such difficulties. After all, it is their own fault they are not working. Of course, some unemployed people do choose not to seek work; some make this choice because of the repeated discouragement they experienced in their job searches. However, the overwhelming majority of unemployed persons deeply and profoundly miss having a job. Unemployment by itself makes a serious adjustmental demand. Few of the long-term unemployed are able to survive without experiencing marked feelings of worthlessness, restlessness, or depression.

The Harassed Worker

When people are consistently annoyed, teased, or pressured by fellow workers or supervisors, they are being harassed. Being harassed at work has major implications for the worker's mental health; harassed people tend to become anxious, upset, and inefficient, and they often leave positions in which they would be otherwise satisfied.

Harassment at work has been described by psychiatrist Carroll Brodsky (1976) as part of his evaluation of over a thousand cases of workers who had filed claims with the California Workers' Compensation Appeals Board or with the Nevada Industrial Commission. The victims of harassment most often changed position, job assignments, or supervisors. The harassment itself is often a rejection by peers or supervisors. While good work relationships lead to job satisfaction, harassment at work makes the job a place of bitter dissatisfaction. One twenty-year-old woman wrote of her experience

> Being harassed at work makes everything hard. You can't wait to leave, you dread being there, and the job seems harder and you are less efficient at it. When I was harassed by my boss, it made every part of my life harder.

Sexual harassment
Scapegoating

Harassment takes five forms: ***sexual harassment, scapegoating, name-calling, physical abuse,*** and the selective exercise of ***work pressure*—**or "hurry-up tactics" (Brodsky, 1976).

> *Sexual harassment* occurs when coworkers or a manager makes sexually related suggestions or remarks. Usually, but not always, males make the remarks to females. Harassment behaviors include giving little pats or touching a person's bottom, making innuendos, and sexual teasing. Sexual remarks and touching are among the most frequent forms of office harassment.
>
> *Scapegoating* is the channeling of the frustration of a group toward one person. In scapegoating, the aggression is displaced, directed away from the unacceptable target, such as a supervisor, toward a person who is less of a threat and provides a comfortable escape valve.
>
> *Name-calling* is the taunting or teasing by workers who insult some characteristic of the person, the person's family, religion, race, or sex.

Coping with any work-related harassment is not easy. Many employees choose to leave their jobs rather than deal with the harassing situation. However, a worker who decides to stay on the job has two options: (1) appeal to authority, or (2) confront the harasser.

Physical abuse is actual bodily assault on a worker, an event that usually occurs after there has been mounting verbal harassment. Physical abuse often leads to the victims' quitting their jobs and feeling enraged or helpless. The working relationship ends because the victim as well as the assailant recognize that the abuse is an unacceptable solution to the work problems.

Job pressure is the insistence by a supervisor (or occasionally by coworkers) that a worker greatly increase his or her productivity. The demands are well beyond those made of comparable workers, and the insistence becomes a source of persistent tension for the worker.

Coping with harassment is never easy. Some workers follow the course of action pursued by those people interviewed by Brodsky—they quit and later file claims or suits against the company. Others take the less satisfactory action of simply quitting, but they usually carry the open wounds of their hurtful experiences for a long time. Workers who stay on the job have two courses of constructive action open to them. The first is to appeal to authority in the organization, a choice that may be effective but that may incur resentment in the workplace. Another choice is to use the methods described in the chapter on assertiveness and aggression and to assertively confront the harasser. This is not a surefire method, but, when it does work, the harassment dissipates and the victim develops a sense of dignity and personal respect.

Not all teasing and name-calling are forms of harassment. Some goes on with regularity in many workplaces as part of comfortable comradery. It becomes harassment when individuals are singled out for hostile and repeated attacks. It is not harassment if the person trusts his or her follow workers.

VOCATIONAL CHOICE

"Know thyself" is always good advice. The logical extension of this advice is that you should also be able to make important choices in your life on your own. After all, who knows you better than you do? Yet when we are making vocational decisions, our self-knowledge may be much less accurate than we would hope. We tend to be optimistic and see our vocational selves as better than we truly are.

In a study of sixty-six undergraduate business majors, the students' self-assessments were compared to experts' vocational assessments of them (Mihal & Graumenz, 1984). The two sets of assessments were alike on three abilities: to express self orally, to make prepared talks, and to write clearly. However, students consistently overestimated themselves in judging their leadership skills, initiative, motivation, ability to analyze problems, and sensitivity to others' needs.

A lesson may be drawn from this finding. Most people are not good at objectively viewing their potential career skills, because they prefer to preserve self-esteem rather than conclude they have imperfections. This desire to see career promise as unrealistically good leads us to the broad question of just how we make our vocational choices.

Trait and factor approach

The Trait and Factor Approach

In 1909, Frank Parsons wrote a book, *Choosing a Vocation*. In it, he proposed what has become the most enduring model available to career counseling, the *trait and factor (T & F) theory*. Parsons (1909) wrote that individuals go through the following steps:

1. they discover their inner *traits* or characteristics,
2. they learn about the *factors* involved in varying occupations, and
3. then they seek to *reconcile* their traits with these occupational factors.

T & F theory has been a primary force in the development of tests to measure occupational interests and attitudes (the traits) as well as to provide career information (the factors). The *Dictionary of Occupational Titles,* the *Occupational Outlook Handbook,* and the *Guide for Occupational Exploration,* all put out by the U.S. Department of Labor, offer endless and daunting lists of the factors in different occupations.

However, there are problems with trait and factor theory. To begin with, items in job descriptions can easily become outdated and are not always applicable to all geographical areas. Realistically the four thousand or more occupations listed in a handbook are not true career options. Most people decide from a narrower personal list of options.

T & F suggests only one best fit job for a person, an unlikely proposition. Furthermore, interest tests only approximate the best fit job. Most people have a story about a test that indicated that some absurdly unsuitable occupation was best for them. T & F theory also has been criticized for being static, because it focuses on one final career choice. Using the trait and factor theory alone is not an adequate approach toward making an occupational choice. However, despite its limitations, it does serve as a tool to help us think about our individual characteristics and how they can be compared with and fit to the world of work.

Vocational Choice as a Developmental Process

In 1950, the annual convention of the National Vocational Guidance Association was thrown into an uproar. Eli Ginzberg, a Columbia University economist studying work and human resources, severely chastised the counselors for not really having any theory of occupational choice (Super, 1953). Ginzberg and his colleagues (1951) subsequently constructed their own developmental theory of occupational choice. They studied the ways such choices were made by middle- and upper-class, white, college-bound males.

Ginzberg (1966) drew three conclusions: First, occupational choice is not the result of a single decision, but is the product of a series of decisions and reactions over a period of about ten years. Career choice is, therefore, a *developmental process.* Second, the decision-making process is, to a large extent, *irreversible.* That is, the further along one is in the process, the more difficult it is to change the direction of a career choice; early decisions limit later ones. Third, the entire process of career choice always ends in a *compromise* between the individual's desires and abilities and actual job opportunities.

According to Ginzberg, the development of career choice lasts from childhood until late teens, unfolding in periods and stages (see Table 12–2). Here is the process most people go through. In the *fantasy period,* which lasts until about age eleven, you think about a job in relation to your desire to be an adult. You see being a fire fighter or police officer as being grown-up rather than something to which you would be particularly suited.

From ages eleven to seventeen, you are in a *tentative period,* during which you recognize the need to choose an occupation. You begin to deal with this situation by examining the qualities that you need to possess. During the tentative period, you pass through four stages. In the *interest stage,* you try to relate occupational choices to your interests. Then comes a *capacity stage,* in which you ask, "What kind of job am I suited for?," and you begin a self-evaluation to try to determine possible careers.

The *value stage* follows; now you examine the conflicts inherent in various desires. To earn money at a part-time job means giving up your time for play. You consider the choices presented between work that is satisfying versus work that pays well. In the *transition stage,* which completes the tentative period, you feel a general calming "which reflects the end of the turmoil of early adolescence" and allows you to move on to a more realistic approach.

From around age seventeen or eighteen and on through early adulthood you are in the *realistic period,* in which you make realistic decisions

TABLE 12-2 Development Periods in Vocational Choice		
Age	**Period**	**Activities**
Before age eleven	Fantasy period	Has unrealistic thoughts, for example, wishes to become a fire fighter because of perceived excitement and glory of job
Ages eleven to seventeen	Tentative period	
	1. Interest stage	Relates jobs to emerging adult interests
	2. Capacity stage	Asks questions such as, "What can I do well?"
	3. Value stage	Weighs choices according to values and beliefs
	4. Transition stage	Approaches decision making calmly and realistically
Age seventeen through early adulthood	Realistic period	
	1. Exploration stage	Relates personal characteristics to jobs
	2. Crystallization stage	Accepts and pursues vocational aims
	3. Specification stage	Refines decisions

Adapted from Ginzberg, 1966.

about your career choices in three stages. During the *exploration stage,* you relate your personal characteristics to the opportunities in the world of work. The *crystallization stage* culminates when you have calmly accepted and are geared toward specific vocational goals. In the *specification stage,* you refine your decisions so that you can pursue your career objective.

One analysis of the Ginzberg theory concluded

> The picture that Ginzberg presents of occupational choice is like that of a complex maze, in which successive choice-points result in a progressive narrowing of the terrain that the individual is permitted to enter. Thus, an individual may wind up in an occupation that is relatively incongruent with his actual personal attributes, largely because early and irrevocable choices were made . . .

> *(Neff, 1985, p. 112)*

The Holland Theory: Vocational Choice Expresses Personality

Not all theorists feel vocational choice is unrelated to personality needs. John Holland (1985) holds that the reason an individual is interested in any particular occupation is because it fits with his or her personality. According to Holland, vocational interests are actually personality patterns, and people in specific occupational groups have similar personality types. Thus, vocational stereotypes may have much truth to them. For example, Holland would maintain that plumbers actually are handy, lawyers actually are aggressive, and accountants actually are precise.

Holland has identified six personality types and six parallel work environments. According to Holland's theory, when people are in occupational environments that match their personality types, they will be satisfied, stable, and achieve their goals. If the personality and environmental types do not match, then satisfaction, stability, and achievement are likely to be low.

Each of the Holland personality types corresponds to an occupational environment that best fits it. The **realistic type** is a person who prefers "explicit, ordered, or systematic manipulation of objects, tools, machines, animals" (Holland, 1973, p. 14). These people see themselves as mechanical and athletic; they are not at their best in educational activities or in human relations work. They prefer a *realistic environment,* which fosters technical and mechanical competency with machines and tools.

Investigative personality types prefer to make creative and systematic observations of natural and social events. They see themselves as scholarly and scientific, and they do best in *investigative environments* that value scientific abilities and scholarly achievements.

Artistic types are expressive, produce art forms (writing or acting, for example), and prefer artistic achievements. They like ambiguous, unstructured situations. *Artistic environments* foster such creative, artistic work.

Realistic type

Investigative personality type

Artistic type

According to the Holland theory, individuals choose vocations that fit their personality types. With this in mind, which of the six personality types identified by Holland do you think describes this iron worker?

Social type

Social types prefer human relations and informing or training others, and they actively dislike working with machines and tools. In *social environments,* people are engaged in helping, enlightening, or training others.

Enterprising type

Enterprising types of people engage in leadership roles and are good at persuasion. *Enterprising environments* are populated by people who manipulate products or others for economic gain or to achieve organizational goals.

Conventional type

Finally, the ***conventional type*** prefers "the explicit, ordered, systematic manipulation of data . . . organizing written and numerical data . . . operating business machines and data processing machines to attain organizational or economic goals" (Holland, 1973, p. 17). Conventional types have few artistic abilities and dislike ambiguous and unsystematized activities. *Conventional environments* demand working with data, recording or organizing information. Such environments encourage people to be both conscientious and conforming.

Figure 12–2 defines Holland's various personality types so that you may determine what type you are.

Below is an aerial view of a room in which a two-day (!) party is taking place. At this party, people with the same or similar interests have (for some reason) all gathered in the same corner of the room—as described below:

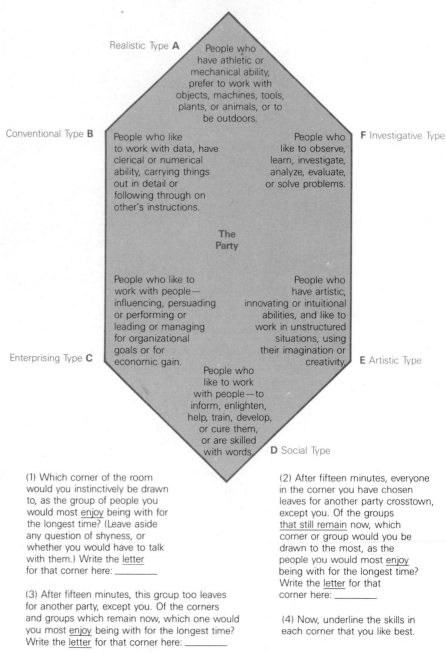

Realistic Type **A**

People who have athletic or mechanical ability, prefer to work with objects, machines, tools, plants, or animals, or to be outdoors.

Conventional Type **B**

People who like to work with data, have clerical or numerical ability, carrying things out in detail or following through on other's instructions.

F Investigative Type

People who like to observe, learn, investigate, analyze, evaluate, or solve problems.

The Party

People who like to work with people— influencing, persuading or performing or leading or managing for organizational goals or for economic gain.

Enterprising Type **C**

People who have artistic, innovating or intuitional abilities, and like to work in unstructured situations, using their imagination or creativity.

E Artistic Type

People who like to work with people—to inform, enlighten, help, train, develop, or cure them, or are skilled with words.

D Social Type

(1) Which corner of the room would you instinctively be drawn to, as the group of people you would most <u>enjoy</u> being with for the longest time? (Leave aside any question of shyness, or whether you would have to talk with them.) Write the <u>letter</u> for that corner here: _____

(2) After fifteen minutes, everyone in the corner you have chosen leaves for another party crosstown, except you. Of the groups <u>that still remain</u> now, which corner or group would you be drawn to the most, as the people you would most <u>enjoy</u> being with for the longest time? Write the <u>letter</u> for that corner here: _____

(3) After fifteen minutes, this group too leaves for another party, except you. Of the corners and groups which remain now, which one would you most <u>enjoy</u> being with for the longest time? Write the <u>letter</u> for that corner here: _____

(4) Now, underline the skills in each corner that you like best.

The Self-Directed Search

Self-directed search

The Holland approach allows a do-it-yourself approach to vocational planning. An explanation of his *self-directed search* can be found in a nine-page booklet available at most counselling centers as well as in Holland's book, *Making Vocational Choices* (1985). In Holland's self-directed search, first you list the names of occupations about which you have thought or daydreamed. Then on lists of activities in each of Holland's six categories, you indicate which ones you like and which ones you are able to do well. You then select the most appealing occupations in these categories. Finally, you rate your abilities in these areas, comparing yourself to most people your own age. The final product of the ratings is a summary code of the occupational areas of greatest, second greatest, and third greatest interest to you. You compare the summary code to codes for occupations and, *presto*, your vocational choice is indicated.

Research indicates that this direct approach is accurate, and it sometimes indicates what you already knew. Programs in which people are enrolled fit closely with the code scores they get on self-directed searches (Pichl & Clark, 1984). Even in studies where some problems occur, the accuracy rate of identifying types is high. For example, when Eberhardt and Muchinsky (1984) looked at 816 students at Iowa State University, they found that the best predictions were made for the most frequent vocational types. Thus, 59 percent of the men with investigative and enterprising codes were accurately predicted, but these were the most common types. Eighty-six percent of women with social types were correctly classified, but only because of an overprediction of social types; over two-thirds of the misses resulted from the incorrect predicting of social types.

Holland's model has generated a flood of research. The questions studied are almost always how personality types in matching or dissimilar jobs adjust to their work. The answers are consistent with the theory. In a representative study, eighty-two working adults were assessed, and the people with good occupational fits on the Holland dimensions were compared to those with poor fits. The individuals with good fits were significantly higher on standardized measures of job satisfaction and mental health (Furnham & Schaeffer, 1984). The Holland approach is part of a larger field of study concerned with the ways people fit into their work environments. We turn now to the broader question of the extent to which individuals are well-matched to their occupations.

The Person-Occupation Fit

Specific work environments are neither stressful for everyone nor comfortable for everyone. Air traffic control work and police work, to name two occupations normally perceived as demanding, are by no means demanding for all controllers or for all police officers. Although the work environment does indeed influence the worker, employees bring a wide variety of personal needs, expectations, and behaviors to their jobs. The ways in which particular jobs and particular workers fit together are defined as the ***person-occupation (P–O) fit.*** Of course, the study of persons in their surroundings considers more than just occupations and includes the full environment. However, our present concern is with employment fits.

In the chapter on physical health and illness, Type A people are described as competitive, impatient, and always striving to meet difficult time demands. By contrast, Type B people are described as more easygoing and relaxed, noncompetitive, and more ready to take things leisurely and as they come. Work environments may be divided into similar categories. Those that are extremely fast-paced, demanding, and controlling have been called ***Type A environments. Type B work environments*** are routine, moderately paced in terms of time demands, and moderately challenging (Ivanevich & Matteson, 1984). Very slow and unchallenging positions are not included at all, because they are boring and unsatisfying for either type of person (and for just about everyone else). The other extreme is omitted from P–O research, too. If the work environment is too frantic and pressured and the work load is too heavy, everybody is stressed, whatever their personalities may be.

Table 12–3 shows when the work environment fits and does not fit the person. Type A individuals, according to the table, fit best in the Type A work environment. Because they need challenge and demand in their lives, they find well-being in time-pressured, hurried jobs and do not enjoy the slower Type B environments. Of course, on the other hand, Type B individuals need the moderation of Type B work environments and are stressed in Type A settings.

The same principles that apply to the fitting of Type A and Type B individuals and settings also apply to the matching of Holland's six personality types and six occupational environments. When they match, a good P–O fit is present and occupational well-being is more likely to

Person–occupation fit

Type A environments
Type B work environments

TABLE 12–3 Person–Occupation Fit: Individual Behavior Patterns		
Work Environment	**Type A Person**	**Type B Person**
Type A work setting (challenging, fast-paced)	Good fit, feels right	Poor fit, is stressful, too demanding
Type B working setting (moderately challenging and routine)	Poor fit, provides insufficient challenge	Good fit, feels right

occur. The person has made the correct career decision. When they are diametrically opposite, the person and employer alike usually will be dissatisfied. Room exists for patterns that fall between the good match and the complete mismatch as well.

It may be that you cannot easily place yourself as Type A or Type B or one of Holland's vocational personality types, or it may be that the job you seek or have is not easily categorized. If so, you have identified the problem inherent in the P–O fit approach. Many people and occupations are just too complex to be typed. However, for those people and jobs with clear types, the model offers good guidance.

Suppose you do know what you want. Alas, wanting and getting may be decades apart, and finding a desired occupation calls for a special talent in locating jobs, a talent acquired slowly and sometimes painfully.

Job Search and Choice

Deciding on an occupation is only the first step toward getting into that occupation. One theory of occupational choice emphasizes actual job decisions and comparisons of alternative jobs. Peer Soelberg (1967) developed this *job search and choice model* after interviewing people looking for jobs. Four job search phases were found (Power & Aldag, 1985).

Phase 1: Identifying an ideal occupation. The ideal grows out of personal values that are unwritten, but influential.

Phase 2: Planning the job search. The ideal occupation is sought first by planning. This planning includes identifying entry level positions for the ideal job, career paths that lead to it, or first choices that shut as few doors as possible to the ideal job.

Phase 3: Job choice. Actual job possibilities are weighed against the ideal job criteria. The choice itself is made when one is sure of receiving an offer, when resources start to run out, and when the first job comes along that one judges "outstanding on one or more primary goals and adequate on any other primary and most secondary goals" (Power & Aldag, 1985, p. 51).

Phase 4: Decision confirmation and commitment. The choice is confirmed when one can say aloud why the job is right and be certain the position is what one assumed it to be. Commitment takes place when one announces to friends that the job is arranged. Then, once accepted, the job appears more favorable than when it was one of several possibilities.

The realities of searching for a job can be discouraging. To begin with, almost everyone hunting for work gets many more rejections than

Job search and choice model

Decision confirmation and commitment

acceptances. Nobody likes being rejected, and in the course of normal job hunting the ten or twenty or one hundred rejections a person gets may produce what Bolles (1985) calls "rejection shock": you begin to believe something is wrong with you, and you become mired in depression, apathy, or low esteem that interferes with your continued job searching. In his book, *What Color Is Your Parachute?*, Bolles offers a guide on how to successfully job hunt. He urges

1. Apply through lots of channels: register with placement services; respond to ads; ask friends, teachers, and relatives for leads; take placement and civil service tests; and apply directly to employers.

2. Invest a great deal of time in your job search (Bolles suggests thirty-five hours a week) and be truly but gently persistent. It's an important task that deserves your full attention.

3. Take the initiative! That means not only cultivating the help of everyone you know, but also thoroughly researching the organizations in which you wish to work. It's very impressive to an employer to hear from a person who cares enough about the job to have looked carefully into the company.

4. Do the basic homework on yourself, so you know exactly what your skills are and can come across as competent, sincere, and desirable in any interview. Know your skills in every possible area of work life and then relate them to building a career.

5. Find out who has genuine personnel power, arrange a face-to-face meeting with that person, and, without ever using the word *problem,* make it clear that you are capable of meeting their employment or organizational needs. That calls for doing even more homework before the interview.

As these recommendations imply, if you invest the necessary time before you start your search, you are much more likely to find the job that will fit your needs and interests.

How you approach your career and the work itself provide pathways toward or away from well-being. Table 12–4 summarizes those two pathways.

SUMMARY

Through the history of civilization, the perception of work has evolved from being seen as a taken for granted necessity, to being considered an unpleasant burden, and then to being viewed as central and vital to having a worthwhile life. Most people today need and want their jobs for reasons well beyond the provision of simple financial security. Interpersonal needs and needs for self-identity and self-expression, along with the need to structure one's day and life, are met through working.

TABLE 12-4 Work and Career Paths Toward and Away from Well-Being	
Toward Well-Being	**Away from Well-Being**
Finds work interesting, positive, and rewarding	Finds work unpleasant, dull, and unrewarding
Perceives fellow workers as friendly and respectful	Perceives fellow workers as unfriendly and not respectful
Enjoys high participation in decision making, utilization of abilities, and complexity of work	Has low participation in decision making, utilization of abilities, and complexity of work
Feels secure in employment	Feels insecure in employment or is unemployed
Perceives trust and support at work	Experiences harassment at work
Has made occupational choice and found work environment that suit personality type	Has made occupational choice and found work environment that do not suit personality type

Job satisfaction is above all a function of interesting work and good work relationships. When working relationships are good, people feel good about their work. Such relationships are a central part of occupational socialization, in which people acquire the beliefs and attitudes of fellow employees.

Trusting fellow workers and managers and having faith and confidence in them are common occupational goals. Among the contributions psychologists can make to people's achievement of occupational goals is providing courses in the psychology of seeking personal rewards at work. One of the most important attributes of successful employees is tacit knowledge, which is practiced intelligence applied to managing self, careers, and others.

Having to do unsatisfying work tasks can cause people to experience anxiety, and having unsatisfying job relationships can make people depressed. No job is reported to be more unsatisfying and anxiety producing than machine-paced assembly work; on the other hand, physicians and professors report their work to be particularly satisfying.

People may react psychologically to unemployment with both stunned immobility and hypochondriases. These and other harmful effects can be minimized in the long run if employees are in well-paid positions, are prepared for unemployment, and are reemployed within two years.

Harassment is devastating to many employees. This teasing and pressuring takes the form of sexual harassment, scapegoating, name-calling, physical abuse, or job pressures.

Most people are not good at assessing their vocational choices; they see themselves as better than they are. Among the professional approaches to assessing vocational choices are the following:

1. Trait and factor theory, which puts together individual traits (or abilities) with occupational factors needed for success.

2. The Ginzberg developmental theory, which looks at the stages of thought and decision making about careers from childhood through adulthood.

3. The Holland model, which presents six basic vocational personality types and six matched work environments.

The Holland model in particular has yielded a cornucopia of supportive research.

Once an occupational choice is made, the job still must be found, and that calls for planning the search, actually searching, and confirming the outcome. During the search, it's important not to allow rejections to be immobilizing, to gather all possible supportive resources, and to know oneself and one's target company very well.

Key Terms

Artistic type
Conventional type
Cynicism
Decision confirmation and
　commitment
Enterprising type
Hypochondriasis
Investigative personality type
Job dissatisfaction
Job satisfaction
Job search and choice model
Liberal arts
Low job complexity
Low participation
Low utilization
Manual arts
Occupational socialization
Occupational stress

Occupational trust
Paced work
Person-occupation fit
Realistic type
Role ambiguity
Role conflict
Scapegoating
Self-directed search
Sexual harassment
Social type
Stunned immobility
T-groups
Tacit knowledge
Trait and factor approach
Type A work environments
Type B work environments
Workcentric

Recommend Reading

Bolles, R.N. (1985). *What color is your parachute?* Berkeley, CA: Ten Speed Press. In the race for jobs, this book tells you where to run and what the likely payoff is for each course. The problems in getting jobs are described, and attention is directed to a careful assessment of where you want to be, what you want to do, what to say in the interview, and other step-by-step job-getting advice. It's no wonder this book has been a best-seller in annual editions for years.

Holland, J.L. (1985). *Making vocational choices: A theory of vocational personalities and work environments* (2nd ed.). Englewood Cliffs, NJ: Prentice-Hall. Intended for the scholarly reader who wants more information about the Holland system of matching personalities and jobs, this book also presents the actual instruments used in occupational self-analysis and work environment analysis.

Neff, W.S. (1985). *Work and human behavior* (3rd ed.). New York: Aldine. It's nice when one book stands above all others in a field, and Neff's book does. It is the primary compendium of psychological research and theory about work. Everything you would want to know from the scholarly point of view is here in Neff's book. All in all, this is one nifty piece of work: highly recommended!

13

The Environment

As Mervyn Highstar's voice rose in volume for the climax of his lecture, his costume and speech were being critically assessed by the dark, intense young man standing in the front. Highstar shifted the strap of his Revolutionary War colonel's uniform—a standard costume for the guides employed at the Shrines of Independence in Williamsburg—and explained how the unprecedented tradition of two centuries of continuous democracy had begun in this very chamber. Joseph Sebba continued to examine him.

Unlike most of his travels since he had left Israel to visit Europe and the United States, this tour was a problem for Joseph. Even at the beginning of the tour, when he had purchased his ticket, Joseph had been uncomfortable. In the manner of his countrymen, he liked to reach out to people and make contact. He had commented to the ticket agent that their beards looked the same. The man behind the ticket counter had looked at Joseph's chin and responded, "*I* have a beard. *You,* young man, have hair on your face."

That rebuff had discouraged Joseph, and the dark mood stayed with him. Now, as the lecture was nearly concluded, he absentmindedly listened to Highstar emphasize the history of this site. Joseph allowed his imagination to take over. Changing images flowed before his eyes. His vision unfocused, and one corner of his mouth turned upward. He was startled when Mervyn Highstar, standing directly in front of him, spoke.

"Mr. Sebba, I don't seem to have your attention."

"Yes," Joseph answered. "What?"

"You don't seem the least bit interested or impressed with the two-hundred-and-fifty-year history of Williamsburg or its contributions to two centuries of architecture in America."

"Mr. Highstar, I come from Jerusalem."

For a long moment, no one said anything. Then Highstar resumed his speech. Joseph found himself touching his beard with a satisfied smile.

THE SENSE OF SELF AS PART OF THE LARGER ENVIRONMENT

The Physical Environment

Nobody lives in a vacuum, not even astronauts. Rather, much of what we do arises from how we experience and think of the world around us. Because of his experiences as an American, Mervyn Highstar revered the environment of historical Williamsburg and was disturbed by Joseph Sebba's lack of attention. Joseph Sebba, on the other hand, considered history in the context of many centuries, not just two, because he had been raised in Jerusalem. The influences of places and time affect all of us. Ralph Waldo Emerson understood effects of the environment when he wrote, "The least change in our point of view gives the whole world a pictorial air. A man who seldom rides need only to get

into a coach and traverse his own town, to turn the street into a pup-
pet show (1969, p. 539)."

The earliest known speculations about the interaction of environment
and behavior looked at climate. About twenty-six hundred years ago, the
Greek physician Hippocrates held that climates shape national character.
European climates vary seasonally, so he thought Europeans were vigorous and alert as a result. In parts of Asia and along the Black Sea, where
temperatures are more constant, the inhabitants were described by Hippocrates as being shiftless and having little energy. Aristotle joined in the
refrain, adding that the Northern Europeans of the cold Scandanavian
climates were energetic but not particularly intelligent (Maxwell, 1983).

One thing Aristotle knew with certainty: the ideal, moderate climate
of his Greece produced the most intelligent people of the world, indeed,
the ones most fit to rule the world. A few hundred years later, when
the Roman empire was the predominant force in the Western world, the
Roman writer Vitruvius observed that the perfect, moderate climate of
Rome resulted in Romans having the most desirable physical and mental
skills. In the fourteenth century, the Arab scholar Ibn Khaldun proclaimed
that the temperate climate of the Arabian peninsula produced the most
ideal beings. Two hundred years later, the French philosopher Jean Bodin
observed that Northern Europeans were physically strong but mentally
dim and Southern Europeans were lecherous and deceitful. Of course,
France was located in the desirable middle zone of climate, yielding a
people who were "truthful, reliable, and moderate" (Maxwell, 1983, p.
52). These stereotypes were, like all stereotypes, excessively simple and
dogmatic. Yet they were founded in a belief that we can accept: the
environment in which we find ourselves has distinct demands to which
we must adapt.

Although these early speculations grew out of the belief that "we"
("we" being the nation of people whom the writer or speaker represented)
are better, brighter, and more able than all of the "theys" in other countries, there was an element of truth in the conjecture. The climate in which
people live can affect them. Current study of climate has examined as independent variables the latitude of the country, its annual duration of
sunshine, and its ambient temperature. In his review of annual rhythms
in mankind, Aschoff (1981) described positive correlations between annual sunshine and conception rates. Skeletal growth accelerates in spring
and summer. There are substantial seasonal variations in suicide and general mortality rates as well. However, the differences that exist between
individual countries can be attributed to both climate and culture. Seasonal factors appear to be increasingly overriden by cultural factors, in
part because of rising standards of living and the more common use of
central heating and air-conditioning. Industrialization and urbanization
have diminished the effects of natural, seasonal influences on behavior.

The environment in which we live affects us in many ways. Before the industrial revolution, when most people worked outdoors, temperature and climate were among the most important factors affecting people's actions. Industrialization and urbanization, however, lessened the influence of these factors on behavior.

Before the Industrial Revolution, when most people worked outdoors, temperature and climate were among the most important aspects of life. In contemporary life, where built environments constructed by people for people dominate our daily life, environments make different demands on us. Yet the demands are there, and our living, working, and studying environments call for behavioral adjustments.

Being Part of the Environment

Herbert Leff (1978) has described the sense of understanding oneself as part of a larger system. With this outlook, we move beyond self-centeredness, no longer perceiving ourselves as independent of the world around us. Instead, we develop a continuing awareness of "oneness," of becoming part of the situations and environments in which we find ourselves.

We experience this connection to our environments when we think of our ***place identities*** (Proshansky, 1978): *our* chairs, *our* favorite rooms, cities we think of as specially *ours*. It's not unusual for us to think of a common environment, such as our automobiles, as extensions of ourselves. When we scrape or come close to another car, we wince and groan, much as if

Place identities

we had scraped or nearly scraped ourselves. The reason taxiing an airplane is such an alien experience to most novice pilots is because they have so adapted to the self in automobile that the thirty-five-foot wings, the new body extensions, are too long to be comfortable for them.

Some identities are closely linked to environments. Think of what a doctor's office is like and how much your associations with physicians arise from that image. One environmental psychologist writes, "I still find it difficult to accept the idea that a doctor whose office and clinic is a storefront in a retail shopping district could be a competent physician, or that teaching children in an improvised classroom in a warehouse could be effective" (Proshansky 1978, p. 159).

Experiencing oneness with the environment means having a heightened awareness. The person who is unaware of his or her environment is half-blind. We act on the environment and respond to the environment. We create situations and we respond to situations. It is not necessary to sit back in an armchair and think profound thoughts about one's place in the world to achieve oneness. However, the more we realize that we are continuously part of our worlds, the greater potential we have to make a difference in our environments.

Our behaviors are strongly influenced by the sum of our physical and interpersonal environments. Yet it is not a one-way street. People create and modify environments, shape their worlds, and are shaped in turn. Our understanding of our environments is part of how we relate and adjust to our worlds (d'Epinay, 1986).

Our perception of this relationship between ourselves and our worlds can be applied to environmental factors that are normally background influences in our lives. Consider the water around us. Over 90 percent of the U.S. population lives within an hour's drive of a major body of water. Most cities were founded near a lake or a river, and the nearby watery environment may affect us.

> A river casts its influence over those who dwell upon its banks. . . . Rivers
> such as the Snake and the Salmon, above which eagles hang, and from
> which bears prong fish, such rivers let a clarity that is reflected in the eyes
> of the men who live nearby. The Nile, silted up and feculent, permeates
> its riverlands with a listlessness that is the precursor of fatalism. And so it
> goes.
>
> *(Selzer, 1979, p. 63)*

Valleys and hills, cities and towns, subdivisions and neighborhoods have their own special airs, atmospheres that spread out from the environment like ripples a thrown stone makes in a calm pond. Environmental psychology studies the ways in which our physical surroundings relate to our feelings and behaviors.

The Ecological Psychology of Roger Barker

Once in Brooklyn, I thought I would lose my mind. Through my error, I was taking a walk . . . everything was the same, or seemed so to me. I went to the left, to the right, I turned back, I rushed ahead, only to find the same brick houses, the same white steps in front of the same doors, the same children playing the same games. . . . At once my movements, my life, my very substance seemed to me to be illegitimate.

(Sartre, 1965, pp. 356–357)

What would be perceived as an ordinary event in one neighborhood could be seen as bizarre or threatening in another. Ecological psychology attempts to assemble the isolated fragments of an individual's actions into a larger, behavioral mosaic in order to provide a more accurate perspective on that person's behavior.

We often think everyone sees what we see. Yet our perceptions grow out of our experiences and our personal styles. Even simple objects may be reassuring or threatening, depending on who we are and the situations in which we find ourselves. Consider the quote from Sartre. What would be an ordinary event for a resident of that Brooklyn neighborhood was a striking, disorienting event for Sartre. In our opening story, what might have been an interesting but unremarkable tour of Williamsburg to a resident of Richmond was pretentious and annoying to Joseph Sebba. One behavioral research method allows us to circumvent such problems in perception.

Ecological psychology

Roger Barker and his colleagues (1978) have developed a method called ***ecological psychology,*** which observes the "stream of behavior." Other means of understanding behavior deal with small, isolated fragments of what people do. With this fragmentation, however, the greater picture of how people act and react to their worlds can be lost. Imagine a behavioral mosaic. Examining the small components of what we do is like looking only at the tiny pieces of glass or marble that a mosaic maker assembles to create the full design. While these pieces are essential, by themselves they tell little about the completed work.

In contrast to such fragmented investigations, ecological psychology assembles careful, detached observations of behavior, as recorded by neutral personnel who live in the target community. For twenty-five years, the Midwest Field Station was maintained in a Kansas town of one thousand residents to engage in just such studies. In one study, eight observers studied one day's behavior of Mary Ennis, an eight-year-old third grader. For over fourteen and a half hours, working in half-hour shifts, these eight observers recorded 969 behavior episodes in Mary's life. The following are six typical episode summaries:

> Playing on the swing with Anna
>
> Kicking tin can with Anna
>
> Chanting about can
>
> Trying to get Anna to play house
>
> Pulling Anna from swing
>
> Rolling on the grass by the dog

(Barker & Associates, 1978, p. 57)

Finally, the day of observation closed with the following report:

> 9:25 Mary settled herself on her side, wiggling a little bit. Her eyes opening and closing. She looked over once more and gave me a weak smile before she fell asleep.

(Barker & Associates, 1978, pp. 72–73)

Overall, 83 percent of Mary's behavior episodes continued until they were psychologically completed, that is, until they had an ending. Most of the endings represented Mary's positive attainment of her goals. Mary's behavior was not simple, but rather cordlike, in which two or three interconnecting strands were woven at any time. Her major modes in interaction were domination (24 percent), and nurturance or meeting others' needs (23 percent). Aggression and avoidance were infrequent behaviors. She received expressions of affection from almost everyone with whom she had contact.

Ecological psychology is significant because it calls attention to wider behavior settings. The actual environment is a complex of both physical and interpersonal events. Mary's 969 behavior episodes are not a large number of events for one day. Most college students have many more.

Ecological psychology is important for three reasons.

1. It considers broader contexts for actions and reactions, as opposed to the restricted variables that laboratory research considers.

2. It uses entirely naturalistic methods to examine behavior. By this, we mean behavior is investigated as it occurs naturally in the resident's own community, without psychologists eliciting particular actions.

3. It is not based on preexisting hypotheses. Instead, the findings on the relationships between the people and their environments come from the observed behaviors themselves.

CROWDED ENVIRONMENTS

Many psychologists have postulated that putting too many humans or animals in a limited space is harmful. This assumption was supported when John Calhoun (1962, 1966) released pregnant wild rats into a pen that should have been large enough to support many thousands of rats. Food and nesting areas were plentiful. However, the rat population in the pen leveled off at one hundred and fifty adults, far fewer than the number the space would have been expected to support. The rats fought frequently and had difficulty making nests and producing healthy offspring. The aggressive and maladaptive behaviors of these one hundred and fifty rats meant that more animals were together in the same area than they could tolerate socially.

A second study by Calhoun (1966) also demonstrated a social interaction effect. Rats were released into four connected pens. Two pens each became the home of a dominant male and a harem of eleven females. The other two pens were more crowded and without the single male plus harem arrangement; the rats in these pens behaved like the rats in the open pen in Calhoun's prior study. Under the high population density conditions, the rats did not follow normal social patterns. They became aggressive, fighting often without apparent reason. Once again,

In overcrowded conditions, rats become aggressive, violent, and socially withdrawn. People living in similarly overcrowded environments also exhibit these behaviors.

instinctive behaviors such as nest building diminished, and the rates of infant mortality and adult deaths climbed dramatically. Other effects of crowding included "predominance of homosexuality, and marked social withdrawal to the point where many individuals appear to be unaware of their associates despite their close proximity" (Calhoun, 1966, p. 54). This gloomy conclusion led one observer to suggest, "If this sounds a little like Times Square, it may not be coincidental" (Maxwell, 1983).

Crowding at Home

In general, do you have as much privacy as you want?

At home, do you have a place you consider to be your own?

At home, does it seem as if you can never be by yourself?

These questions are designed to assess feelings of privacy. Lack of privacy is part of the experience of overcrowding. Privacy is believed to allow us to develop as people, to avoid interpersonal tensions, and to contemplate our lives. Even in the most intimate attachments, people may still need to have places and time of their own. When they feel the subjective experience of being crowded, people typically say they have less privacy than they want, no place of their own, and feel they can never be by themselves (Gove & Hughes, 1983).

Territoriality

The need for privacy has been related to ***territoriality,*** which includes felt ownership of a specific household location. When couples who had been married for a certain amount of time were compared to unmarried couples who had lived together for that same amount of time, interesting differences emerged in the subjects' needs for privacy and territoriality. The unmarried couples were significantly more likely to have places to be alone within their residences; these places were interpreted as "symbols of separateness and relative freedom from togetherness" (Insel & Lindgren, 1977, p. 104). The unmarried couples sought to preserve their individual privacy and were unwilling to relinquish it as readily as married couples did.

Stimulus overload

In addition to a lack of privacy, being crowded at home produces a ***stimulus overload,*** in which the amount of contact, communications, and involvement with others is excessive. The following items assess the degree of stimulus overload:

Does it seem as if others are always making demands on you?

At home, does it seem as if you almost never have any peace and quiet?

At home, does it seem as if you are always having to do something for someone else?

When you try to do something are you almost always interrupted?

These questions were part of an extensive survey of the effects of crowding in Chicago households. Walter Gove and Michael Hughes (1983) interviewed 1,544 adults who were not living alone. The subjects lived in representative areas throughout the city. These Chicago residents were paid three dollars in return for spending an hour and a quarter talking with a researcher about their subjective experiences of crowding and about aspects of their psychological health. The typical subjects reported an average of two people for every three rooms in the household.

Crowding as measured by persons per room was associated with several reactions. When crowding was high, the individuals reported

physical withdrawal from the home

psychological withdrawal

feeling drained

poor physical health

poor mental health

less frequent sexual intercourse

poor social relationships in the home

Blacks were most reactive to crowding, Hispanics least reactive, and whites fell in the middle. People raised in the country were especially susceptible to crowding effects. Those with least power in the household, such as adult sons and daughters, had a greater likelihood of being affected. Two types of households were largely unaffected by crowding: couples only households (where others were not present), and "no kin" households (arrangements with unrelated persons living together).

Other studies of crowding have reported a *differential vulnerability,* which means that some people seem to be easily harmed by crowding and others are almost invulnerable to it. Men are decidedly more reactive to crowding effects than are women. Members of high contact cultures, such as people from Latin American countries and from Italy, are less reactive; they need less personal space and have histories of intense interpersonal stimulation. Indeed, any persons with high contact, intense stimulation, and low personal space backgrounds are likely to be immunized against harmful crowding effects (Gove & Hughes, 1983).

While some people have adverse reactions to overcrowding, others seem unaffected by it. Having a high contact, intense stimulation, and low personal space background may immunize a person against harmful crowding effects.

In one investigation of extraordinarily overcrowded living conditions in Hong Kong, ten or more people (and often two unrelated families) sharing four-hundred-square-foot living quarters were not found to suffer from psychological disorders (Mitchell, 1971). The shopkeepers of the stalls of Calcutta work in small shops, about four feet high and wide, and perhaps eight feet deep. The stalls are stacked one above the other, "so that a customer must squat to make purchases from a shop on the lower level and stretch up to deal with a shopkeeper at the second level" (Insel & Lindgren, 1977, p. 106). Yet the shopkeepers accept their spaces and do not perceive them as crowded. They do have relative privacy compared to the people sleeping nearby on the street and compared to many of their own living conditions at home.

CLOSER IS BETTER IN THE CLASSROOM

You are in the front row, center, of a class and the instructor seems to be speaking just to you. When the instructor pauses, looks at the class, and calls for questions, you feel a significant pull. You feel involved. The area in which you are sitting has been called the action zone, which includes the front rows and center area. "Action" refers to participation in the class. Teachers not only look more at students in the action zone, they also call on these students more. Students in this area volunteer more comments and questions.

Studies have randomly assigned elementary school students to seats and then moved them either to the back or to the front of the classroom. No differences were present between the students on the random assignments. However, the teachers liked the students more and rated them as more attentive if they were at the front. Students at the back of the classroom were rated less likeable and less attentive (Schwebel & Cherlin, 1972).

The same process occurs in college classes. Students in the action zone are most active and most liked by the instructor. When participation is graphed according to seating, the students at the back are least active, least called on, and rated least favorably.

Naturally, someone always must be in the back, unless there is a circular seating arrangement of only one row. Yet some students typically deliberately choose back row seating. They prefer the distance and lesser involvement. They are protected in part from requests to participate. They are able to see themselves as onlookers, a view that is particularly appealing to shy or disinterested students.

Turning to the issue of class size and teaching effectiveness, we should note research on the development of problem behavior in crowded grade school classrooms. Children are more aggressive, less involved, and more distracted in classrooms with little space or where the number of students has risen noticeably (Ahrentzen, Jue, Skorpanich & Evans, 1982).

In North American cities, crowding in general appears to intensify citizens' feelings (Creekmore, 1985). People already feeling aggressive grow even more aggressive on a crowded subway. People who are feeling good about their surroundings and basically are enjoying them may experience a heightening of those feelings at a jam-packed party. Assertive and competitive people especially flourish in densely populated cities; they perform a "psychological backflip" (Creekmore, 1985, p. 53), feeling the urban stresses as challenges and sources of potential mastery.

One universal remedy for those who suffer from crowding is access to control. The most harmful crowding effects are found in persons with no opportunity to influence their environments (MacKenzie & Goodstein, 1986). The least harm is seen in people who have control over their environments, or at least feel as if they have such control. When they feel in control, people respond to cramped living not as passive inhabitants but by feeling that they have choices about when and how they are in close contact with others.

Crowding in Prisons

Prisons sometimes are like the cages in which Calhoun's rats were packed. Between 1975 and 1985, the number of men in U.S. prisons more than doubled. As a result, prison dormitories and cells often provide less than thirty-five square feet per inmate and occasionally provide as little as thirteen square feet per inmate. (As a reference point, thirteen square feet per person means that a typical ten foot by fifteen foot college dormitory room would house eleven people.) The American Correctional Association (1966) says harm occurs at less than sixty square feet per prisoner.

Two separate elements of crowding affect prisoners: spatial density and social density. The **spatial density** is the actual amount of available physical space, usually measured in square feet per inmate. **Social density** describes the extent of a prisoner's forced contact with other people. Social density is a problem when large numbers of individuals are required to share the same areas, even if the square footage appears adequate.

A series of recent studies have found that social density is the more serious of the two conditions (Cox, Paulus & McCain, 1984). Prisoners are unharmed in single cells, even in tiny single cells, because there is no required contact with other inmates. Double cells cause more problems, multiple occupancy cells still more adjustmental stresses, and in large dormitories serious difficulties occur. Prisoners crowded into open dormitories show substantial increases in their blood pressure levels and in their complaints of being physically ill. When dormitories are partitioned into private cubicles, with separate sleeping, desk, and storage areas, these

Spatial density
Social density

problems diminish considerably. Why are single cubicles and cells so advantageous psychologically?

> Singles provide for privacy and satisfy needs for having one's own territory. Singles reduce exposure to and lack of control of unwanted levels of social stimulation or interaction. . . . In fact we have encountered inmates in state prisons who purposely violate prison regulations so that they will be placed in detention in single cells.
>
> *(Cox et al., 1984, p. 1153)*

One more way to understand crowding effects in prisons is to watch what happens as population densities rise and fall. When population density rises, disciplinary incidents, fights and deaths from fights, and

When prisons are overcrowded and do not provide inmates with sufficient personal space, incidents requiring discipline, fights, and complaints of illness may increase among the prisoners. In fact, privacy is so important to some inmates that they go as far as purposely violating prison regulations in order to be placed in single cells in detention.

complaints of illness all increase. These increases go well beyond the changes one would expect from simple changes in numbers of people. Institutions that are large and that have high spatial and social density are breeding grounds for psychological maladjustments and social tensions. Small, low-density prisons typically have few such problems.

Like residents in crowded households, not all prisoners in crowded institutions show harmful effects. The prisoners who are least susceptible to crowding effects are those who have come from crowded urban environments, those from high contact cultures, and those who voluntarily choose to live in dormitories and cells with others. Inmates often make the latter choice because it allows them to share the living space with good friends or relatives. Furthermore, there clearly is an adaptation process for some prisoners. Just as most of us adapt to cold water when swimming in a lake and to the rumble of a train when we live by the tracks, at least some people do adapt to high spatial and social density conditions. What they originally felt as an intolerable sensory overload and lack of privacy is still unpleasant, but often becomes tolerable.

ENVIRONMENTS THAT NOURISH

Think of the places where you retreat when you are feeling upset. Most of us have some special, quiet, private place, sometimes in our minds, but often in reality. We speak of retreating because we often feel that we're under attack during difficult and unpleasant times. Often, the places to which we retreat are part of natural surroundings, with few people around. Sometimes, they have symbolic meanings, and are located very high, or are insulated, or are surrounded by soothing objects, as in an aquarium or museum. Even in daily work, school, or home life, the environment molds our experiences. Surgeon Richard Selzer (1978) reminisced about the times operating rooms still had windows.

> Part of my surgical training was spent in a rural hospital in eastern Connecticut. The building was situated on the slope of a modest hill. Behind it, cows grazed in a pasture. The operating theatre occupied the fourth, the ultimate floor, wherefrom huge windows looked down upon the scene. To glance up from our work and see the lovely cattle about theirs, calmed the frenzy of the most temperamental of prima donnas. Intuition tells me that our patients had fewer wound infections and made speedier recoveries than those operated upon in the airless sealed boxes where now we strive.
>
> *(Selzer, 1978, p. 15)*

We do not know if such a positive environment actually helped the recovery rates of the surgery patients. However, for psychologically troubled persons, positive changes of environment can be dramatically helpful. Comparisons of institutional and community residences clearly support this finding.

From Institutions to the Community

Until the early nineteenth century, most citizens labelled as insane lived with relatives or in workhouses in their towns. However, around 1820, a social reform movement swept through Western society. Large, centrally run institutions, it was believed, offered close supervision, adequate food and medical care, and economy of operations. Mental patients by the hundreds and then by the thousands were gathered into institutions as the concept of the asylum took hold.

In the last twenty years, a precisely opposite movement has emerged; patients now are placed in community settings and homes. Large institutions have been identified as the frequent source of dehumanizing and

EXPLORATION IN WELL-BEING

A Place to Love, A Place to Hate

Think of two places in your city or town (or in another community you know well). The first should be a place that gives you a sense of well-being. Think of a place that you actually love, where you would make a special trip to be. It should be a place about which you have only warm and positive feelings.

Now your second task is to think of a place you hate, that brings out only negative feelings in you. It should be a place you want to avoid and about which you have thoroughly negative and unpleasant reactions.

In your mind, spend at least one-half hour in each place. Experience the places quietly, one sense at a time. Move around the places. Concentrate on tuning in to your feelings. Stop or sit down in the spot where you have the strongest reaction and make a list of your feelings. Then, make another list of the characteristics of the place.

Are the characteristics of the places totally different, or do they have any similarities? Can you draw any conclusions about how the physical characteristics of places make you feel?

(Farbstein & Kantrowitz, 1978, pp. 15–16)

Although a few environments are unpleasant for most people, our reactions to settings depend upon our experiences there and our thinking about the places. Can you assess what made you so love and so hate the places you choose? Examine your own thinking and judgments. Can you learn something about what in your environments produces such strong reactions?

impersonal treatment, which increases rather than lessens psychological maladjustments. Not everyone who is released into the community benefits. Indeed, some homeless persons who cannot care for themselves have had difficulty living independently, and concerns for their well-being have been expressed. Nevertheless, moving patients from institutional environments to positive community care has, overall, improved their adjustment and happiness.

Nowhere is this transformation more apparent than in Geel, a small town in Belgium. The most disturbed patients from all of Belgium are housed by the families of Geel. The patients socialize at some of the 143 local bars, drink coffee in the coffee shops, walk freely in the streets, and are all given a caring, paternal environment. Over thirteen hundred psychotic patients live in this town of thirty thousand. They are regularly bused to the bathhouses, where they enjoy the great pleasures of leisurely baths. While not all the patients are able to do all of these things, these seriously disordered people do find the environment provided by their family hosts to be a beneficial and positive change from institutional living (Roosens, 1979).

Vacations

For those of us who are not prisoners or patients, society has a formal system for change of environment: the vacation. Indeed, vacations are designed to move people away from their ordinary settings into environments intended to produce relaxation and pleasure. One major source of information about vacations was the *Psychology Today* survey (Rubenstein, 1980), which reported the vacation experiences of over ten thousand readers. About 28 percent of the respondents were "vacation lovers," who very much enjoyed planning and taking their vacations. These same people also enjoyed most of their other activities; 68 percent liked their work a lot or very much, and 75 percent described their lives over the prior six months as moderately or very happy.

Is change of environment an essential part of vacations? It appears so. Only 11 percent of the respondents were content to stay at home. Vacations were sufficiently important that a majority of people were willing to exchange part of their income for more free time, and 27 percent said they would take one to six months' vacation without pay if they had that choice. The importance of travel to new places was illustrated by the answers to the question, "If money and time were no object at all, which of the following vacations would come closest to being your ideal fantasy trip?" Of the eleven choices, the most popular fantasies (each selected by 30 percent of the subjects) were "spending a year in a foreign country" and "taking an ocean voyage on a luxury liner around the world" (pp. 66, 72).

Vacations aren't helpful to everyone. Eleven percent of the *Psychology Today* respondents often felt depressed after their holidays. The people who worked more than sixty-five hours a week, that is, the workaholics, felt the most discomfort with their vacations. For them, vacations frequently were sources of tension and guilt, because they found their lives revolved around their work. Nevertheless, for the great majority of people, changing environment by taking a vacation is a positive and sought after experience. Of course, the option of going on vacation is not always available. That brings us to our next topic: improving the psychological quality of our existing environment.

Enhancement and Control of the Environment

In the movie *Never Cry Wolf,* the naturalist observing wolves in the Yukon sees wolves marking their territory as canines do, by urinating around the borders. To identify his territory, the naturalist drinks twenty-six cups of tea and spends a day similarly marking his borders. This maneuver succeeded; the wolves respected his urine-marked boundaries. In human social settings, we serve the same function by personalizing our living spaces. The more of a personal imprint we put on a place, the more we feel it is ours. In university settings, such as in a dormitory, students' feelings of belonging and mastery arise in part from their making just such individual touches and markings.

In one study of forty-one double dormitory rooms occupied by male freshmen at the University of Utah, almost all rooms were decorated by the end of the term. The most popular decorations were ski posters, campus maps, calenders of campus events, abstract art, and landscape scenes. Photographs of family or girlfriends were relatively infrequent decorations (Hansen & Altman, 1976).

A significant difference was found between the rooms of students who stayed in school and those who left. Those who stayed covered about twice as much wall space as did those who left. Doing more to personalize their living spaces was seen as a sign of the students' greater commitment to that environment and perhaps as an indication of their fitting in more comfortably with their peers.

Work space as well as living space may be personalized. The office or desk with decorations, photographs, or objects that have meaning to the occupant all create more of a sense of belonging and personal territory for the worker. Barriers for emotional protection may be constructed in home and office to make a person less visible to others. Furniture arrangements that render the occupant not readily visible from the doorway, so eye contact is difficult to establish, provide such protection.

In one study of an open office environment (an office without dividing walls), desktop items of ten inches or higher were found to be

Students often personalize their dorm rooms by decorating them with photographs or other personal objects. Without these decorations, students may feel that they have less control over their environments and that their personal territories are more vulnerable to intrusion.

interpersonal barriers (Burger, 1981). People with these desktop objects were less likely to be approached by others for verbal interactions. Despite the architectural goal of promoting open communication and access, the workers in the open office space were able to make their personal accessibility or inaccessibility clear to others. Their territorial barriers provided them with privacy, which in turn allowed them to control interactions with their fellow office workers.

These considerations of dormitories and offices have looked at fairly stable environments. Yet some environments are short-lived. Environments that exist for limited points in time are known as situations and are our next subject.

SITUATIONS

Situation

The word *situation* is derived from a Latin word meaning "to place" and is defined as the temporary physical and social circumstances in which people are located. Like environments, situations describe locations outside us. A situation is meaningful only when it is a potential or actual source of experience (Carr, 1948). Most situations are not meaningful. The time you walked down the main corridor of your grade school, or the breakfast you ate yesterday, or the first person you met today probably did not constitute meaningful situations. Only being harassed in the corridor, having breakfast with friends you rarely see, or meeting a celebrity in your first personal encounter of the day would allow you to label the experiences as meaningful. Carr explains

> You are walking down the street . . . and see a crowd collecting at the next corner. You infer that something has happened, that a focus of interest has appeared, and that a more or less transient pattern of activities is forming around that focus. . . . But until you reach the scene and discover that a woman has fainted or that a taxi driver has been fighting with a passenger, you cannot define that situation . . . clearly, before you can do any defining, you must become aware that there is something to define, that there is a pattern of relationships to be explained.

> *(Carr, 1948, p. 21)*

This awareness that something is happening is the essence of a situation. One becomes aware that temporary behaviors have occurred at a physical place. In the preceding example, that street corner would be much less interesting two hours later, when nobody is present.

On the surface, the perception of a situation is self-evident. After all, on the afternoon of the Texas–Oklahoma game, the football stadium filled with yelling, stomping fans is an obviously more meaningful situation to most people than the same stadium empty later that week. Yet not all about a situation is obvious. The whole of the stadium, the teams, and the fans is greater than any of the individual parts.

Understanding situations helps us to interpret seeming inconsistencies in people's behavior. Why is a friend self-assured and comfortable at one time and at other times jittery and uncomfortable? For us to answer this question, we must understand our friend's temporary environmental circumstances and the behaviors they elicit. Let's consider a classic situation experiment.

One group of college students was shown a metal breast shield and told that soon they would have to suck on it. While these students were waiting to begin, they were given the choice of waiting alone or with others. Another group was shown a piece of candy and told they would have to suck on it soon. These subjects also were given the option of waiting with others or alone. In this experiment, many more subjects in the metal shield condition preferred to wait alone than did subjects in the candy condition (Sarnoff & Zimbardo, 1961).

In still another condition, students were told they would receive a strong electric shock shortly. In that situation, would *you* prefer to wait alone or with others? What if you were waiting for a mild shock? Subjects awaiting the strong shocks preferred to wait with others more than did people expecting the mild shocks.

Why would most people under one condition of threat prefer to wait alone while under another threat would prefer to wait in the company of others? The explanation is that the breast shield condition produced embarrassment and the strong shock condition produced anxiety. Embarrassed people prefer privacy, and frightened people prefer company. The situations themselves brought out people's preferences for either isolation or company.

Psychologists are not the only people who understand the effects of situations; artists and musicians understand them as well. Contemporary composer John Cage has written pieces in which the situation (performance) has a greater impact than the written score. His performers simultaneously play solo, in pairs, in trios, or in quartets, moving freely from one group to another and often performing from within the audience. The importance of the John Cage performances, as well as the happenings other artists have designed, is that they redefine situations. The audience members at these performances are not passive onlookers; instead, their presence helps to create the event.

It is so with all situations. People are rarely the passive onlookers they believe themselves to be. Their presence helps compose the major events in their lives, in ways they often are not aware.

When we compare what actors (people who are actually doing something) and observers judge as causes of behavior, we see that the situation is deemed a cause if you are an actor, but not if you are a judge. Outsiders looking at a person doing something—almost anything—tend to believe the action arises from the disposition of the actor. If a person is acting irritably, inlookers believe the cause is his or her grumpy nature.

The actor's viewpoint is very different. The person acting negatively tends to assign the cause to situations. If you are the person who has been seen as grumpy, you are likely to see the cause as an irritating situation; you might attribute it to having a bad day rather than to any predisposition of yours to be grumpy.

This basic finding has been generalized to many behaviors. When children are assessed in a psychiatric clinic, their problems are described as individual psychiatric disorders. However, when the same children are assessed in their schools, the evaluations are different. The children are seen more in their social roles in the schoolroom, reacting to what the teachers and other students do. Here, their misbehavior is seen more as situational (Kellam & Ensminger, 1980).

Such research findings have caused a revolution in psychological thinking. The leader of this revolution has been Walter Mischel (1984), who has denounced the acceptance of most behavior as due to global personality factors as nearsighted and wrong. Instead, he has cited situations as the primary determinants of what individuals do.

> . . . it was assumed not infrequently that one could go from a few indicators to extensive predicting and decision making about what the individual would do in new situations far removed egologically and psychologically from the original observed behavior sample. It was not unusual to predict such remote outcomes as criminal recidivism, parole violations, or psychiatric hospitalization from responses to ambiguous stimuli (such as inkblots) or from the way the individual drew a house, a tree, and a person . . . even cautious and sophisticated assessors . . . were surprised to find their own results weak, costly, and subject to risky errors.
>
> *(Mischel, 1984, p. 352)*

A quarrel erupted between those who held that the study of individual personality traits could predict behavior and those who were situationalists, believing that situations determine behavior. It was a fierce quarrel, if the word *fierce* can be applied to an argument that is conducted primarily through articles in scientific journals. The ferocity has diminished, as research findings have shown that neither position is fully accurate. Few people still hold the notion that either personality or situation is the more powerful. Rather, now psychologists emphasize a third element: ***ideation,*** or how we think about situations (Mischel, 1984).

Ideation

There is widely shared ideation, or common ways of assessing situations, in a population. People who share thinking rules for situations tend to react in similar ways. Thus, actions do not follow on a one-to-one basis from either personality predispositions or the situation, but rather from the combination of both elements plus ideation.

This discussion of situations allows us to consider the time component of the environment. After all, we all live in time as well as place, and time as part of our life environment is our next subject.

TIME AND ENVIRONMENTAL DEMANDS

Normal Rhythms

Our behaviors in response to our environments are structured in part around our concepts of time. When we think of the major places we have spent our lives, we can relate them to the passing of hours, days, weeks, years. Indeed, how we feel about ourselves in a particular setting often depends upon time-based judgments. Was this a good school *day?* Were we able to fit everything we wished into the work *week?* Was it quiet enough in the apartment building to get the seven *hours* sleep we absolutely needed? Did it seem as if he would *never* stop talking in the library? Did the one-*week* vacation at the resort seem much too short? Or much too long? Is it easy to be productive at the office in the *morning?* Are you at your best studying late at night because you are an *evening* person? "It has been observed, 'The world around us pulses in cycles great and small: we swim in a stream of time information'" (Lynch, 1972, p. 117).

Some aspects of time clarify situations. The monthly menstrual cycle sometimes serves as a guide to the emotional patterns of women. The rotation of the earth around the sun and the seasons of the year yield annual rhythms. Changes within single days arise from the daily rotation of the earth on its axis. Because the daily rotation is the shortest time cycle of which we are readily aware, it is also the one to which we tend to pay special attention.

Circadian rhythm

The term used to describe our daily variations is **circadian rhythm,** which comes from the Latin words *circa,* meaning about, and *diem* meaning day. In this period of about twenty-four hours, predictable physical rhythms appear in our respiration, urination, activity, energy, and body temperature. Consider body temperature: it falls to its lowest level during the night (at about 4 A.M.). Then it rises quickly for about seven hours (until about 11 A.M.). It continues to rise, but slowly, until 8 or 9 P.M. Then, it begins its nighttime decline.

In addition to fluctuations in body temperature, over one hundred other body functions have been found to be maintained according to circadian rhythms (White, 1987). When the circadian rhythms are disrupted, both personality and physical functioning can be affected. Airline passengers who cross multiple time zones often experience jet lag, the temporary impairment of the wake–sleep cycle and general physical and mental efficiency.

This biological clock exists in all animals. Exposure to light plays a major role in the synchronization of circadian rhythms. While it has been known for a long time that the effects of light availability in some animal species leads to dramatic behavior changes, such as hibernation, only recently have related findings emerged for human beings. In his review of this topic, White (1987) described many cases of winter depression. It appears that the lack of intense sunlight can produce a serious disorder, which disappears when spring arrives. Exposure to bright artificial lighting has proven to be an effective treatment.

Our changes throughout the day or month or year are considered to be part of our **temporal rhythms.** The word *temporal* means time-related, and such time-related rhythms profoundly influence how we think, perform, and feel. They are always important to us, which is why we are rarely impatient with people who ask us how we slept or how well we spent our day.

Temporal rhythms

Entrainment

Entrainment

Our temporal lives do not exist in isolation. Rather, we are shaped by other schedules in the environment. This process is known as **entrainment,** when our internal schedules are modified because of societal and environmental schedules. Entrainment has been explained as being much like what happens when ". . . a tuning fork is set in motion . . . and then held near another tuning fork of approximately the same frequency." The second fork vibrates, too, or ". . . is entrained (set in motion by) the first tuning fork" (McGrath, Kelly & Machatka, 1984, p. 24). Plants and animals are powerfully entrained by dark–light and warm–cold cycles. Humans are responsive as well to social and psychological factors.

Consider the time spent doing varying tasks. Some tasks are undertaken with the leisure of a sixteenth-century Indian Maharajah, not need-

EXPLORATION IN WELL-BEING

As Time Goes By

Does time pass at different speeds for different people? The answer is yes. For some individuals, time zips along rapidly, and for other people time drags with agonizing, tortoise pace slowness. You may use an exercise to check out your own experience of time passing.

Ask a companion to serve as a timekeeper, using a watch that indicates seconds. Your friend should, without telling you, choose a time interval between twenty and ninety seconds. Your task will be to judge how many seconds have passed from the moment the timekeeper says start and begins timing until the time is up and the timekeeper calls stop. Keep your eyes closed during the timing.

Few people get it exactly right, but most estimates are within ten seconds. Some estimates are far short or far long. A sixty-second time unit is sometimes judged to be as little as twenty seconds or as much as one hundred and twenty

ing to be completed at a particular time. Other tasks are undertaken with the time-intensity of a Toyko subway car stuffer, who must push every possible human into the cars in the few seconds before the doors close. In other words, pace of work is entrained or controlled by the demands of the situation.

C. Northcote Parkinson (1957) asserted in Parkinson's First Law that "work expands to fill the time allotted for it" (p. 2). Contemporary observers have rephrased the law to read, "we do what we have to do in the time we have to do it" (McGrath et al., 1984, p. 28). Whether these commonsense witticisms are true is a question that has been subjected to investigation. Using anagrams and simple performance tasks, Joseph McGrath and his colleagues essentially determined the answer to be yes. They had three central findings.

1. "The more work they [the research subjects] were given in any time period, the more they did . . . to put the matter in Parkinson's terms, the less work they were given, the less they did in any time period" (McGrath et al., 1984, p. 29). In other words, it was found that the amount of work truly did shrink or expand to fill the time allotted to it.

2. People who started off working fast, in brief time periods, continued to work fast and hard. People who were initially given lots of time started working less productively and then continued working that

seconds. The tendency to underestimate or overestimate persists even when individuals count silently one-a-thousand, two-a-thousand, and so on.

The differences in the estimates are believed to reflect people's varying experiences of the passage of time. People who considerably underestimate the passage of time sense time as passing relatively slowly. They tend to be patient. Because more is happening in their subjective time, they are thought to be less prone than other people to seek out new sensations. Persons who substantially overestimate the length of time tend to sense time as passing quickly. They are often impatient and have greater needs for stimulation and activity.

A related exercise has been applied to years as well as to seconds. Can you visualize what you will be like and what you will be doing in five years? Persons who are *time binders* see a clear continuity between what happened last year and what is likely to happen next year. They are aware of the continuous flow of time in their lives. In contrast, individuals who live primarily in the present perceive little such continuity. They experience only mild connections between yesterdays and tomorrows, which may be a mixed blessing. While they may suffer from insufficient planning in their lives, they also benefit from the freedom from excessive restrictions of past thoughts and future concerns.

Entrainment is the modification of our internal schedules by societal and environmental schedules. When we are required to punch in at work by a certain time or when we have to be in class by eight o'clock even though we could easily sleep until ten are examples of entrainment.

way, even when the amount of available time to accomplish the work was diminished.

3. The more demanding the time limit, the more time people spent directly on the task; they spent less time on irrelevant personal interactions. When people have a sense that the job has to be done and done now, they waste little time on conversation and distractions. Performance is entrained by the rigorous demands of time limits.

We tend not to be highly conscious of rhythms as primary influences on our behaviors. This phenomenon was observed in the McGrath series of studies. The effects of the time structure were largely unnoticed by the subjects, despite the effects' substantial impact on the actual behavior of the subjects.

Time and Well-Being

Not all aspects of time in our lives are hidden from us. After all, the nature of coping includes coping with time. In order to be able to deal with our environments, we need to be able to anticipate what is about to happen and to see a line that runs from what has happened to what is happening.

When we learn from the past and coordinate what we are doing now with our future plans, we have a reasonable likelihood of influencing the events of our lives. Frederick Melges has described "the capacity to bring the future into the psychological present" (1982, p. 37) as the essence of well-adjusted and integrated behavior. This anticipation of the future further provides us with a basis for making appropriate adjustments in the ways we attain our goals.

Humankind may be unique in having the ability to make extensive connections between periods of time. Understanding cause and effect relationships involves looking both backward and forward in time. Some of us have vague ideas about our futures and, often, the further away the time point, the more vague are our ideas. Nevertheless, the ability to envision the future is part of adjustment. In much the same way that sudden illness allows us to grasp the meaning of health, distortions of time allow us to comprehend the meaning of normal time. In time distortions

> . . . inner time often seems stretched out, sometimes like an eternity, and the past present and future seem mixed up in a kaleidoscopic whirl. Intermittently time seems to race ahead at an incredible rate but then suddenly comes to a standstill so that the person feels frozen in time.

> *(Melges, 1982, p. 4)*

Some people with severe psychological disorders cannot maintain an accurate sense of time. Not only are these individuals unable to plan ahead, but often they do not know the day, month, or year. They are confused about time and place. If they are depressed, they are often hopeless about the future and unable to anticipate anything beyond their immediate misery and pain.

Just as time distortions interfere with our coping, organization of time permits us to succeed in achieving many aims. This brings us to the subject of effective time management. Effective scheduling allows us to be involved in activities that otherwise we would have to omit from our lives, so that we can maintain a reasonable balance between obligations and social and recreational activities. As one optimistic social scientist has suggested, "with the help of the schedule, good time managers can go quite far in approximating a perfect equilibrium among their involvements in the various domains of their lives (Zerubavel, 1981, p. 53).

Time Management

No more perfect scheduling and ordering of activities exists than in Benedictine monasteries. Fifteen hundred years ago, St. Benedict issued rules about the precise times at which sacred study and manual labor should be undertaken. The concept of punctuality, the habit of marking hours of the day (with bells), and the invention of the mechanical clock all originated within the Benedictine monasteries (Zerubavel, 1981). As a result, in American society at least, time is often seen as an absolute reality, rather than an accepted convention.

A first issue in time management is the freeing of individuals who are captured by their time schedules to such an extent that they are unhappy and unspontaneous. When satisfying the clock seems to be a first priority, then personal choices seem to diminish. Scheduling should provide ways to meet many goals, not to become enslaved by the scheduling itself.

A second time management issue applies to the great number of people whose time is poorly organized and used. For them, efforts at organizing time have the same results as crash diets: for a few days, their efforts seem to work well, but then they slip back into ineffective patterns. To change long-established patterns of poor time use requires substantial effort and commitment. The basic steps are as follows:

1. *Record how you spend your time.* Set up a time schedule for every hour of the day for a week. Enter promptly and completely each way in which every hour is spent. Be honest. This allows to you assess factually how your time is spent.

2. *Think through what is important.* Most of us do not ever think through what is genuinely meaningful to the achievement of what we want in our day-to-day lives and in our long-range ambitions. Don't settle for something simply because it is easy to do.

3. *Establish a sensible weekly schedule.* Be realistic about the time you are willing to spend on studying or work. Plan for relaxation and routine activities.

4. *Limit studying to two-hour blocks.* Any longer, and most people become inefficient and daydream.

5. *Commit yourself to following your plan.* The nature of carrying out any important shift in personal activities is to overcome rolling momentum. That means committing yourself wholeheartedly to your new schedule.

6. *Reassess and revise your plan.* Most people who are inefficient in the use of their time are inefficient at first in reorganizing their time. You should anticipate problems. When they come up, note them. Then, take a fresh look at your plan every month or two. Revise it to eliminate the wildly optimistic goals you had at first. Fit it more closely to your own work capacities and needs for play.

These time management approaches do not eliminate entrainment. After all, we do live in a world of schedules, appointment books, clocks, and calenders. They do, however, offer us the potential to time important activities realistically and in ways that are under our control. Work and class schedules may be at odds with our circadian rhythms, but careful attention and planning can reduce our conflict with the temporal world.

TABLE 13-1 Pathways Toward and Away from Well-Being in the Environment	
Toward Well-Being	**Away from Well-Being**
Oneness with the environment	Fragmented from the environment
Ability to see broad contexts	Restricted view of behavior, isolated from context
Acknowledges need for privacy, arranges for private time	Does not feel in control of space or privacy
Successfully plans for regular vacations	Pressures of work or internal demands dominate, so there is little time off or vacation time
Good time management skills	Enslaved by time demands

Table 13–1 lists interactions with the environment that lead us toward well-being and interactions that lead us away from well-being.

SUMMARY

Environments influence people's perceptions and behaviors. From ancient Greece to contemporary life, people have seen their own climates and physical environments as superior. Whether the settings are superior or not, it is clear that environments do affect people in substantial ways.

Crowded environments increase the potential for abnormal social behaviors. Calhoun (1966) found that rats in cages with high population density become more aggressive and their mortality rates rose. Human crowding is associated with the problems of lack of privacy and stimulus overload. The consequences of these problems are people's physical and psychological withdrawal, feeling drained, and poorer social relationships. High social density in prisons breeds emotional problems.

Not everyone suffers from crowding. Members of high contact cultures and people who feel in control of their environments suffer fewer harmful effects.

Some environments are emotionally nourishing. In Geel, Belgium, living with families in their homes has been more beneficial than living in institutions for seriously disturbed psychiatric patients. For most Americans, changing environment by taking a vacation is highly valued. However, about 11 percent of people find vacations to be tension producing. People may make environments more emotionally nourishing by personalizing their living spaces and maintaining a sense of control.

Careful and detailed observation of human interaction with the environment has been carried out by Roger Barker (1978). His ecological psychology studies have assembled thousands of descriptions of people in their everyday settings and lives, so that broader contexts for behavior may be considered.

Situations are specific social and physical circumstances, limited in time. Situations are not meaningful unless they stand out from the ordinary background of environment and social relationships. Persons who are behaving in problematic ways tend to attribute the cause to the situation. Observers attribute the cause to the nature of the person. Walter Mischel (1984) has suggested that the prediction of behavior must take into account both the situation and the person's thoughts about the situation.

The experience of time structures individuals' responses to the environment. Among other time rhythms in people's lives is the circadian rhythm or the twenty-four-hour cycle of sleep and activity. The process of internal schedules becoming captured by environmental time schedules is known as entrainment. An example is the way in which work truly does expand to fit the time allotted to it. When there is little time available, people don't waste time. When much time is available, people will indulge more in personal interactions irrelevant to the task. Nevertheless, individuals can modify their own time management, particularly by recording time use, setting priorities and schedules in realistic ways, and being committed to good time management plans.

Key Terms

Circadian rhythm	**Social density**
Ecological psychology	**Spatial density**
Entrainment	**Stimulus overload**
Ideation	**Temporal rhythms**
Place identities	**Territoriality**
Situation	

Recommended Reading

Coyne, B. & Clack, R.J. (1981). *Environmental assessment and design: A new tool for the applied behavioral scientist.* New York: Praeger. Churchill is supposed to have said, "First we shape our buildings and afterwards our buildings shape us." This book tells how by presenting environmental psychology issues.

Mischel, W. (1984). Convergences and challenges in the search for consistency, *American Psychologist, 39,* 351–364. Mischel has been the leading scholar of situational influences on behavior. This sometimes slow-reading article is a guide to the evolution of Mischel's thinking and research. No better overview exists.

Priestly, J.B. (1968). *Man and time.* New York: Dell. If you are interested in time as part of the human experience, you will be fascinated by this book. Priestley explores the meaning of time throughout history, in literature, and in our daily experience. He writes in the first person, often qualifying what he writes with engaging personal statements. His experience easily becomes ours.

Psychotherapy and Well-Being

He came to see me because he was having panic attacks. When he was in shopping malls and public buildings, he would suddenly find himself frightened for no apparent reason. He would grow increasingful fearful and then run out of the building. He had been changing jobs every few months, also as a result of his growing anxiety. At the end of his second appointment, he made two things abundantly clear to me. He told me he did not want to talk about personal matters, and he let me know he had seen other therapists before coming to see me and they hadn't done him any good.

The phone call came at three in the morning. I struggled out of my sleep to answer it.

Me: "Hello."
Him: "Dr. Brodsky, I need to talk to you." His tone was urgent.
Me: (With the instant wit that has made me well-known throughout Tuscaloosa) I replied, "Huh?"
Him: "I found myself surrounded by people looking at me at the new mall today. It really bothered me."
Me: (Finally pulling myself together) I said, "It sounds like we have something to talk about. Would you like to see me first thing in the morning?"
Him: "No. I don't think so. Good-bye." He hung up.

He did not come in the following morning, nor did he show up for his next scheduled appointment, nor for any other appointment. Something was going on that he wanted me to know about but at the same time did not want me to know about. I became even more aware of his conflict when I ran into him accidentally sometime later.

The clothes dryer in my house had broken, so I went to the laundromat. My ex-client was there, loading a washing machine. As I passed by him, he simultaneously grimaced and smiled and said, "So you have come to find out what's in my dirty laundry."

I never saw him again.

Psychotherapy can have an addictive quality about it, both to the patient and to the psychotherapist. For me, what is addictive about being a psychotherapist is the profound satisfaction I feel when I'm truly helping another person who is suffering and making a meaningful difference in that person's life. When clients change their behaviors, feelings, or thinking and become more the kinds of persons they wish to be, the effect on me ranges from quiet pleasure to occasional bursts of inner exhilaration.

But it's not all exhilaration. Some clients are not so easily helped. Others can't or won't work on their problems. If my client *had* been willing to look at his psychological laundry, we could have made a difference in his life.

Psychotherapy has become an integral part of professional helping services and popular culture in America. Every medical center has its psychotherapy services. Every metropolitan telephone book has psychotherapist listings. *Cosmopolitan, Playboy,* and *The New Yorker* magazines can be counted on to have cartoons about psychotherapy. For over two million

Americans, psychotherapy is part of their lives, as they seek to cope with troubling feelings or behaviors. For many more people, psychotherapy is something they know about primarily from the media or the experiences of friends or relatives. This chapter explores the nature of psychotherapy, some of the different schools of psychotherapy, research on it, and, finally, information on how to get therapeutic help and how to help others. We start with what may have intimidated my client in the opening story but what often aids other clients: what it is like to be a client seeing a psychotherapist.

THE NATURE OF PSYCHOTHERAPY

The door closes with a solid thud. It's your first time in the psychotherapist's office. You are aware of the softness of the sounds, of the furniture that is both clinical and comfortable, and that you will be spending the next hour in this room with this person. Alone. With a person trained in psychotherapy. Working on you.

The office itself has a desk and both soft and hard chairs. You sit. You probably expect that you are going to have to immediately face up to the problems in your life, which may well be feelings of loneliness or depression or difficulties in a relationship with an important person in your life. You may never before have sat and talked about problems in this manner.

Most lives are filled with competing and multiple activities. You drive while listening to the radio and while thinking. While eating, you may be talking to someone else, or reading, or watching television. In this therapy room, you have only one task: to talk about yourself. At no other time in your life will you devote so much time—an hour a week is in truth a long time—to examining who you are and what you are doing with your life.

Psychotherapy is a concentrated, intense examination by you and your therapist together of your behaviors, thoughts, and feelings. Exactly what transpires depends on the setting, the therapists' training and personality, and you.

Three elements define psychotherapy. First, it is a verbal interchange between a troubled individual seeking assistance and another who has been trained in the helping skills called psychotherapy. Second, it is directed at changing the behavior, attitudes, or future experiences of the person seeking help. Third, it fosters the change through the personal events that occur between the client and therapist, in what has been Therapeutic alliance called the ***therapeutic alliance*** (Frieswik, Allen, Colson, Coyne, Gabbard, Horowitz & Newsom, 1986). The starting point in gaining an understanding of psychotherapy is an examination of the expectations the client brings to therapy.

Expectations

When comedian Sid Caesar began psychotherapy, he anticipated a mysterious process. He expected ". . . a man with a spade beard and piercing eyes: a magician. Instead I found a personable, soft-spoken fellow of about forty-four, very polite and with a pleasing manner" (Caesar, p. 23).

The initial meeting in psychotherapy starts with some sharing by the client. For some clients, having the opportunity to speak privately to a helper inspires them to let loose a torrent of feelings, ideas, and questions. For other clients, this initial contact is tentative. Sid Caesar's therapist began their first meeting by asking him intimate questions. When Caesar asked "What business is that of yours?," the therapist explained that it was necessary for him to know the answers to the questions in order to be of help. Caesar summarizes:

> After that first hour, I felt naked. I was not sure I wanted to go on. I could not see the value of prying into those areas of my mind that were better left unexplored. The fact is, I was scared silly. But I knew that something had to be done. Like the man with the nail in his foot, I was in real pain—and although the pain increased every time the analyst touched a sensitive spot, I knew the wound had to be probed if I was to make progress.

(Caesar, 1971, p. 24)

THE ROOTS OF PSYCHOTHERAPY

Like all healing arts, psychotherapy has its origins in ancient Greece. Antiphon, who lived in Athens from 480 to 411 B.C., is considered to be the originator of the art of talking to heal mental distress. Antiphon's methods sound startlingly contemporary. He instructed his patients to speak about their sufferings and, then, using their own words and ideas, gave them other ways to think about their concerns. This technique, in which verbal persuasion relieved pain and cured disorders, was labelled the **art of solace** (Watzlawick, 1978).

Art of solace

Rhetoric

Plato and Aristotle both used **rhetoric,** which is the way people say things and how these statements influence other people. The verbal persuasion of others was the core of Aristotle's rhetoric, suggesting that Aristotle may have been among the first psychotherapists (Glaser, 1980; Frank, 1980). Susan Glaser has described therapy as Aristolean rhetoric.

> Psychotherapy is a rhetorical process; perhaps it constitutes the most basic rhetorical act. Therapists, as certainly politicians, advertisers, or intimates, are in the business of belief and behavior change. Therapists use the spoken word to alter their clients' thoughts, feelings, and behavior in deliberate ways. . . .

(Glaser, 1980, p. 314)

One's expectation of improving may contribute to one's improving. Simply put, many people who anticipate getting better in psychotherapy do get better. Having the anticipation, by itself, sometimes spurs a person to change, to feel more effective, and to be happier. Conversely, if one enters therapy with a sense of pessimistic futility, one's likelihood of improvement is often reduced. The expectation of improvement colors the client's feelings about the therapist, about the procedures, about the length of treatment, and about the outcome. One review of all of these factors in expectation concluded that in treatment of fears and phobias expectations were especially influential but that in other treatments their degree of importance is still being determined (Garfield, 1986).

SCHOOLS OF PSYCHOTHERAPY

As many as one hundred and thirty different therapeutic approaches exist to bewilder the client who shops for therapists. Differences appear in both theories and techniques, and many, but by no means all, therapists find a single school of thought and adhere to it. "An identification with a school of therapy is likely to result in some very powerful economic, political, and social supports. After all, without a specific therapeutic orientation,

The principles of Aristotle are indeed the methods used in psychotherapy. The first principle relates to the *character of the speaker* and the extent to which the speaker is seen as an expert, as trustworthy, and as attractive. When therapists are seen as experts, they are likely to be more effective.

The second principle of rhetoric is *logical appeal.* In some psychotherapies, the treatment itself revolves around the use of reasoned arguments to correct the illogical thinking of the client. For example, the rational-emotive therapy of Albert Ellis (1973) is founded on this principle. Clients are instructed how their irrational and illogical belief systems lead to unpleasant emotional consequences.

Tension-release mechanisms are part of the third principle of rhetoric. When therapists present a hopeful expectation, or are reassuring, or use relaxation procedures, they are using such mechanisms. As clients feel less tension and anxiety, they believe that the therapy is working (as indeed it may be).

The fourth of Aristotle's rhetorical principles recommends use of *stylistic methods,* including metaphors and images. An example is when a therapist tells a client that she is a sleeping beauty, always waiting for a prince's kiss to awaken her. Such stylistic devices can make the therapy vivid and meaningful.

how would we know what journals to subscribe to or which conventions to attend?" (Goldfried, 1980, p. 996).

The major schools of therapy offer fundamentally different ways of dealing with human problems. We will consider psychoanalysis, behavior therapy, cognitive therapy, humanistic therapy, logotherapy, and, finally, the school that isn't a school, electic therapy.

Psychoanalysis

Psychoanalysis is a theory of personality as well as a set of therapeutic procedures that evolved from Sigmund Freud's early work. At first, Freud used hypnosis, but he discarded it because symptoms returned; it was only a temporary cure. Next, he tried a method called *catharsis*, in which the patient relived events that were repressed. However, this emotional release did not provide a dependable cure. Freud's next effort was the pressure technique, in which he pressed his hands on the patients' forehead, and asked questions. Having his hands on the patient's forehead seemed to get in the way of the treatment, and that too was discarded.

By 1896, Freud's early attempts had evolved into psychoanalysis as it is known today. Five essential components of psychoanalysis have been identified (Barton, 1974). They are lying down, free association, interpretation, resistance, and transference.

Catharsis

Lying down on the couch

If any one object has come to symbolize psychoanalytic treatment in the media and in the mind of the public, it is the analytic couch. In Freud's own treatment office at Berggasse 19 in Vienna, his couch was ornate, bulky, and covered with a woven fabric with a design in dark red and earth-tone colors. Lying down on the couch is important for several reasons. It relaxes the patient. It takes away the necessity for social amenities, conventions, and chitchat. It places the patient closer to the undefensive posture of sleep. It allows the less controlled, less rational, less conventional, less conscious aspects of the patient to emerge.

Free association

Free association

The rule of rules in psychoanalysis is *free association*, which instructs the patient to let go of conscious control of thoughts and allow ideas, words, feelings to flow forth without censorship, deceit, conventionality, or contemplation. When free associating, the patient feels thoughts gushing out. Free associations are the substance of the analysis. When conscious controls are relinquished, the repressed, unacceptable impulses and experiences come forward—albeit in small and sometimes disguised pieces.

Free associations provide the substance for psychoanalysis. To make free associations, patients are instructed to let go of the conscious control of their thoughts so that their ideas, words, and feelings may flow forth uninhibited.

Slips of the tongue, jokes, and dreams are subjects of free association, because they are means by which unconscious content surfaces.

Interpretation

Psychoanalysts say little to their patients, but when they do say something, it usually is an interpretation of free associations and psychological patterns. Interpretations describe underlying motives. They are intended to provide insight into why the patient feels and has symptoms. Such insight shines light onto an otherwise obscure part of the patient's self. Interpretations make a connection between what the patient does and what lies beneath the behaviors.

Psychoanalytic interpretations often correct a patient's distorted memories, as the following excerpt from the poem "Therapy . . . The Rear View Mirror" explains:

Memories grow out of memories
Like sprouts . . .
Each remembering
Is slightly distorted
From the one before
Like stories passed around a town

We become a victim
Of our own gossip . . .

That's what therapy is for . . .
To clear away debris
Around the center
To go back to the truth
However mean . . .
Or true it is . . .

(Malloy, 1977, p. 15)

Many times, patients are unable to enter the psychoanalysis sufficiently to allow the analyst to make interpretations. Such an inability is
known as resistance.

Resistance

Resistance

When patients are unwilling or unable to work on themselves or apply
their insights, they are demonstrating resistance. Patients are often frightened or embarrassed by the examination of their emotionally charged
feelings. Sometimes they feel that their underlying impulses are too unacceptable to be permitted to surface in any form. ***Resistance*** occurs when
the patient blocks thoughts or memories. It is important to recognize this
withholding because it represents a maintenance of the basic problem
in the patient's mental apparatus. Successful psychoanalysis analyzes the
resistance, so the patient learns of the blockages and how to let go of
them.

Transference

Transference

The psychoanalyst is invisible to the patient, sitting behind the patient,
out of sight. He—and it is apt to say "he" because most psychoanalysts
are men—says little, his facial expressions and postures are not visible,
and he does not engage in face-to-face social interchanges. As a result,
the patient relates to the psychoanalyst as a person (or composite of
persons) from the patient's early life. "The patient's moment-by-moment,
hour-by-hour expectation that his analyst will lose respect for him, attack,
hate, dislike, reject, lose interest in, or insist on absolute compliance
from him, smother him with commands, or make him feel guilty, is
the transference" (Barton, 1974, p. 43). The psychoanalyst interprets this
transference so that the patient can come to know the persistent ghosts
that he or she carries, ghosts that deeply influence the patient's feelings,
experiences, expectations, and relationships. Once the transference is
shattered, then the patient can live life as it is and not as a carryover
from the past.

Psychodynamic therapy

To a limited extent, the practices of lying down, free association, interpretation, resistance, and transference all appear in psychoanalysis today. They are collectively known as classical psychoanalysis. More commonly, therapists employ selected parts of psychoanalysis in psychodynamic therapy. Here, the couch and daily sessions are discarded. Free association is not a routine part of treatment. However, in psychodynamic therapy, the pursuit of insight is highly valued. Helping the patient become aware of underlying, unacceptable memories and impulses is part of the treatment. The relationship between the patient and therapist is examined, and this transference is illuminated. Resistance to therapy is another common subject.

Psychodynamic therapy also pays attention to daily experiences and problems. The conscious self and world are valued and discussed. Not all difficulties are seen as coming from excessive repression of the id. Therapy tends to be shorter than psychoanalysis, often lasting only a few weeks or months, and to be aimed at more immediate, less sweeping personality change. Finally, the therapist is far from invisible. Psychodynamic therapists not only sit face-to-face with their patients, but they also participate more actively and directively in discussions during treatment.

Behavior Therapy

Seated firmly in research on conditioning and learning, behavior therapy has several features that distinguish it from other therapies (Rimm & Masters, 1979). Behavior therapy works with clients' current observable behaviors. It assumes that if you cannot see it, hear it, or otherwise observe it, the behavior isn't available to work on. Behavior therapists are disinterested in concepts such as the unconscious. Rather, they hold that maladaptive behaviors are learned and may be equally unlearned or modified. In behavior therapy, well-defined objectives are identified, and well-specified steps are taken to achieve these objectives. Behavior therapy is a diverse and expanding field. The major methods in behavior therapy include the following:

> *Recording data.*   The behavior therapist is committed to the objective assessment of change. The therapist's first step is to identify the frequency of the behavior targeted for change. The client, or sometimes a trained observer, records the time, place, and prior conditions associated with each occurrence. Thus, if the targeted behavior is excessive eating, the client will record in a notebook each time every Dorito, Twinkie, or ice-cream cone—as well as all other food and drink—is consumed. Once base information is gathered, then a clear measure of

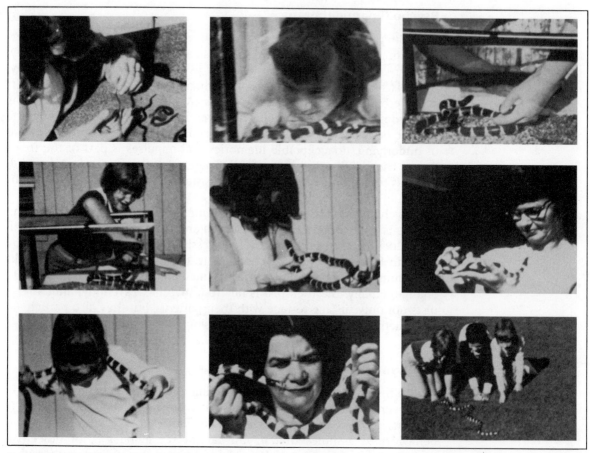

Systematic desensitization is a method for treating phobias and other fears. A client learns to relax while being confronted with a mildly anxiety-producing situation. The client's relaxation periods are gradually coupled with situations that arouse increasing levels of anxiety until the client can comfortably tolerate events that previously caused him or her to panic. A client might look at these photographs during a desensitization to a snake phobia.

success of the treatment is possible. A pleasant by-product of having clients record data is that sometimes when they learn how frequently their behavior occurs they will be motivated to change; the knowledge itself can produce change.

Contracting. The client and behavior therapist may jointly design a behavior contract, in which the consequences of specific actions are identified. A contract is actually written and signed by the client and therapist (and sometimes by witnesses). The contract identifies the goals in detail. Thus, if increased studying is the goal, the number of hours the client will spend studying per day—and where the client

Contracting

will study—will be written out. The therapist and client agree upon a positive reinforcement for accomplishment of the goal; it is essential that the payoff be truly valued by the client. The client's failure to adhere to the contract incurs a genuinely negative reinforcement. One of the most popular forms of such negative reinforcements is having the client make a check in advance to a cause that he or she finds offensive; if the client breaks the terms of the contract, the therapist sends the check to the cause. (In my case, a large check made out to the American Nazi Party would be a significant deterrent to keep me from breaking a contract.)

Systematic desensitization. In this method for treating phobias and other fears, clients are taught deep muscle relaxation. Then, clients learn to relax at the same time they are experiencing the upsetting thoughts. At first, the relaxation is paired with mildly anxiety-arousing thoughts or images, and then it is gradually paired with situations arousing greater and greater anxiety, until the client can comfortably tolerate events that previously caused him or her to panic.

Modeling. When clients observe others' behaviors—either live, filmed, or simulated—they learn new behaviors or how to change existing ones by imitating more effective actions. It is not unusual in behavior therapy for the therapist to demonstrate a needed skill, such as how to open a conversation, how to make good eye contact, or how to ask successfully for a favor. Then, the client rehearses the skill, receiving additional instruction and modeling and feedback from the therapist. This procedure is particularly effective when used in therapy directed at social skill deficits.

Other practices. The word *contingency* refers to an event or experience that reinforces a behavior—that is, that makes the behavior more likely to reoccur. **Contingency management** is the control by therapists or clients of the reinforcers that establish, shape, maintain, or eliminate behaviors. Elimination of unwanted behaviors is often achieved through aversion methods.

Aversion treatment uses unpleasant stimulation as a negative reinforcer. **Aversion methods** are designed to eliminate troublesome behaviors through direct punishment. For example, electric shock can be administered to a child molester to reduce the sexual arousal he feels when looking at slides of naked children. In other cases, the targeted behavior is paired with other unpleasant associations (Rimm & Masters, 1979).

A concluding observation needs to be made about behavior therapists themselves. At one time, the approach of behavior therapists was seen as objective and detached, and the therapists themselves were seen as cool or unfriendly. That stereotype is false. Although the underlying theory and

Systematic desensitization

Modeling

Contingency management

Aversion methods

the principles of behavior therapy are objective, behavior therapists tend to be warm, optimistic, and empathic. They share their methods with their clients, and rapport and good interpersonal contact are essential parts of their therapy (Ivey, Ivey & Simek-Downing, 1987).

Cognitive Therapy

Cognitive therapy accepts the behavioral commitment to objectivity and the scientific method, but has one fundamental difference. Cognitions, that is, thoughts, are the object of its attention. Cognitive therapy holds that what is important are not the true events in life but how one thinks about them and interprets them.

Rational-emotive therapy

The ***rational-emotive therapy*** of Albert Ellis pioneered treatment by cognitive means. Ellis (1962) asserted that irrational ideas are the bases of most emotional disturbance. He developed an A-B-C method of describing the effect of cognitions. A: At this point, an *action* occurs. Some objective facts or behaviors appear. One example Ellis gives of an action is going for an important job interview (Ellis, 1973). B: The person has a *belief* about the action. If it is a rational belief, it is supported by the facts. If it is an irrational belief, then the person is making an absolute demand. The person says he or she *should* or *must* have a particular outcome. Thus, in the case of the job interview, the person's irrational belief could be that he or she *must* get this job and it would be catastrophic to not get it. C: This is the *consequences* of the beliefs. Rational consequences are those that are appropriate to the actions or events. A rational consequence would be the person's experiencing disappointment at not getting the job, but being more determined to succeed in the next interview. Ellis described the irrational consequences as follows:

> . . . if he childishly and dictatorially believes, "it would be catastrophic if I were rejected at the job interview. I couldn't stand it! What a worm I would then prove to be! I *should* do well at this important interview!" he tends to feel anxious, self-hating, self-pitying, depressed, and enraged.

(Ellis, 1973, p. 58)

The Ellis treatment teaches the individual to dispute irrational beliefs. The individual ends up with a rational and logical understanding of actions, beliefs, and consequences.

Ellis (1962) has listed irrational ideas that cause mental disturbance and that are widely held in Western society. These irrational ideas include

> The idea that it is a dire necessity for an adult human being to be loved or approved by virtually every significant other person in his or her community.

> The idea that one should be thoroughly competent and successful in all possible respects if one is to consider oneself worthwhile.

The idea that it is awful and catastrophic when things are not the way one would very much like them to be.

The idea that human unhappiness is externally caused and that people have little or no ability to control their sorrows and disturbances.

To get a feel for rational-emotive therapy, one almost has to see Albert Ellis or his compatriates in action. They are active and, when they are teaching about irrational ideas, they may talk much more than the client. With Ellis himself, an element of showmanship is present; his gestures, phrases, and activities are colorful and dramatic. For example, Ellis uses songs to teach rational thinking and make fun of irrational thoughts. The following lyrics, to be sung to the tune of "And the Band Played On," are from his collection of rational humorous songs:

> When anything slightly goes wrong with my life,
> I'm depressed, depressed.
> Whenever I'm stricken with chickenshit strife,
> I feel most distressed.
> When life isn't fated to be consecrated,
> I can't tolerate it at all.
> When anything slightly goes wrong with my life
> I just bawl, bawl, bawl.

(Ellis, 1985, p. 2)

Since the appearance of Ellis's early work, other scholars have developed components of cognitive therapy for particular populations. For example, cognitive therapies have been developed to treat depression (Beck, 1976) and for individuals unable to handle stress in their lives (Meichenbaum & Jaremko, 1983). Although the basic commitment to reshaping thoughts and interpretations of events remains the same, these more recent cognitive therapies have one additional tie to behavioral therapy: They are committed to the measurement of change as much as to the initiation of change.

Humanistic Psychotherapy

When one looks at the history of psychology, one can see at work the principle that every strong movement produces an opposite movement. In the twentieth century, the scientific orientation of behavioral psychology was followed by an opposite movement: humanistic psychology. While behaviorism proclaimed observable behavior as the proper subject matter for psychology, humanistic psychology embraced the study of feelings. Rather than accepting measurable actions as the substance of psychology, humanistic psychology focused on identifying the subjective, unmeasurable personal world of individuals. Humanistic psychology has personal fulfillment as its goal, holding that every individual should be exploring his or her potential.

In humanistic psychotherapy, the client is seen as a fallible, mysterious, subjective human being. Humanistic psychotherapists try to be spontaneous human beings, and they talk about themselves and their life experiences. Their clients are encouraged to find their own values and identities.

Client-centered therapy

Carl Rogers's **client-centered therapy** is the most influential humanistic psychotherapy. A basic precept of this therapy is that clients determine for themselves what they seek to become. The therapist clearly recognizes his or her own values, states them when appropriate, but absolutely allows the client to be self-directed.

Rogerian therapy values feelings and aims to help make how the person acts consistent with his or her feelings. For this reason, a humanistic therapist listens with care and empathy, and he or she responds "you really feel . . ." upon becoming aware of the essence of the client's experience at the moment. During the course of treatment, a client-centered therapist might say to a client who has been suddenly rejected by an important person in her life, "You really feel helpless and hurt. It's as if a mule has kicked you in the head." This statement allows the client to let go of any ruse of not caring or to stop minimizing the loss. The full reality of the true feeling permits the client to be one person, not a fragmented being made up of compartmentalized pieces of herself.

Humanistic psychotherapists seek to help clients go beyond simple coping. The reduction of personal distress exists as a goal in all schools. However, after the client's distress has been reduced, the humanistic psychotherapist works to help the client achieve personal emancipation. As James Bugental wrote:

> The client finds a great deal more of the center of being is taken into one's self and rescued from dependence on the opinions of others. . . . There emerges a fresh vision of how life might be with most constraints relaxed.
>
> *(Bugental, 1978, pp. 9–10)*

The humanistic therapist shows genuine caring and respect, because the therapy is based on the following principles (Bugental, 1978):

Mutuality. A common bond is established, allowing both client and therapist to bring their true selves to the sessions.

Honesty. Both parties are committed to being honest and open, and the therapist avoids taking the role of blank screen.

Vital topics. Topics central to the client's future are explored, even if they are unconventional and socially questionable.

Trusting. A trusting, nonjudgmental atmosphere is established, because only such an atmosphere allows the client to weigh opportunities, feelings, and impulses as a whole person.

Humanistic psychotherapy flourished in the 1960s and 1970s and was frequently practiced by short-lived, intense groups made up of essentially healthy participants. These sensitivity groups and encounter groups were characterized by members' deep sharing, exposure of personal weaknesses, and vigorous confrontations. For the most part, such groups have vanished from sight. Mutuality, honesty, and trust have become increasingly incorporated in mainstream psychotherapeutic practice and even have become subjects of objective research. Humanistic psychotherapy has by no means been silenced; rather, it has become a quieter voice more a part of than apart from psychology. One first cousin of humanistic psychotherapy deserves separate mention: ***logotherapy.***

Logotherapy

Logotherapy

Victor Frankl is a psychotherapist who holds that the fundamental purpose of therapy is to search for meaning in life. The Frankl school of therapy is called logotherapy; it concerns itself with "making men conscious of their responsibility—since being responsible is one of the essential grounds of human existence" (Frankl, 1955, p. 29). Logotherapy explores the spiritual dimension of life by examining the specific meanings of life, existence, and values that set humans apart from animals. The fullness of the meaning of any one moment, not the feeling of pleasure or joy, is seen as the fundamental value. Frankl explained

> . . . the greatness of life can be measured by the greatness of a moment:
> the height of a mountain range is not given by the height of some valley,
> but by that of the tallest peak. In life, too, the peaks decide the meaning-
> fulness of the life, and a single moment can retroactively flood an entire
> life with meaning. Let us ask the mountain-climber who has beheld the
> alpine sunset and is so moved by the splendor of nature that he feels cold
> shudders running down his spine—let us ask him whether after such an
> experience his life can ever again seem wholly meaningless.
>
> *(Frankl, 1955, p. 50)*

This striving to understand the meaning of one's existence through therapy is called existential analysis. A successful existential analysis leaves the client fully conscious and aware of his or her responsibilities. Every situation a person faces gives that person the opportunity to act in a responsible way. When Frankl and other logotherapists work with patients, they join in the search for these values. Even suicidal patients and people dying of incurable, painful diseases, if they truly understand their uniqueness and their purposes in existence, can find content lives.

The writings of Victor Frankl blend together psychotherapy and spiritual beliefs. Emphasizing that each person is unique and that each act has the potential to be meaningful and responsible, logotherapy points the way for despairing and suffering people and for the therapists who work with them. Logotherapy swirls in a small eddy outside the main current of psychotherapies, yet it has been a source of hope in some of the most difficult treatment situations.

Eclectic Psychotherapy

If a practicing psychotherapist chosen at random were asked what school of psychotherapy he or she used, the therapist most likely would answer, "None; I am eclectic" (Wogan & Norcross, 1985). The word *eclectic* means

THE QUIET THERAPIES

Morita therapy

Naikan therapy

Psychotherapies in Japan include several methods that are special to Eastern cultures, which have been called "the quiet therapies" by David Reynolds (1980). These therapies slow down the neurotic client's pace of action and thinking. In **Morita therapy,** for example, clients are isolated in a room for a week and are not allowed to converse with anyone, to read, to write, to smoke, to listen to the radio, or to engage in any recreational activity. This isolated rest is intended to force the clients to face themselves and all of their failings without distraction. The clients' tendency to withdraw diminishes as they realize how boring withdrawal is. After one week, the clients are gradually reintroduced to being with others and working. Clients report that the result of the therapy is a fresh acceptance of responsibility for self and new appreciation for life.

In **Naikan therapy,** the week of isolation is spent in guided meditation on past experiences, particularly on how much others have done for the clients and how little the clients have done in return. From 5:30 A.M. to 9:00 P.M., the clients meditate, and eventually they recognize their self-centeredness. When the clients change their life-styles to embrace self-sacrifice, they experience a joyful burst of energy. As in Morita therapy, Naikan therapy slows down the flow of thoughts. It refocuses the mind on an acceptance of self and one's fallibilities, and it moves one toward an enlightened understanding of oneself (Reynolds, 1980).

Eclectic psychotherapy

selection from various systems or ideas, and *eclectic psychotherapy* draws on techniques from all schools. Eclectic therapists believe that they want to master all effective techniques, regardless of their theoretical origin. Wogan and Norcross found that eclectic therapists have "... a pervasive belief in a varied therapeutic arsenal" (1985, p. 66). This therapy is by no means an organized system for dealing with clients. In fact, eclectic therapists are often quite different from each other. The one thing they do have in common is their insistence on being flexible, being able to pick and choose among available therapeutic methods. Those committed to one particular system, such as psychoanalysis, see eclectic therapy as a disorganized, irresponsible approach in which therapists are not held accountable for what they do. Eclectic therapists themselves see the therapy as a way to provide the best of what is known in the interests of the client's welfare.

In Naikan therapy, participants are totally isolated for a week. During this time, they meditate about their past experiences and how much others have done for them. They eventually recognize their self-centeredness, become self-sacrificing individuals, feel a joyous burst of energy, and experience an enlightened self-understanding.

Elements Common to All Therapies

Therapists from different schools have more in common than one might think. To begin with, research has demonstrated that experienced clinicians from different therapeutic schools are more alike than are novice clinicians. Apparently, therapists discover through experience what appears to work.

ABREACTION: THE REEXPERIENCING OF TRAUMAS

Abreaction

In some psychoanalytic therapies, symptoms are seen as arising from repression of emotions associated with trauma. Through simple talking about the event, through hypnosis, or through dream interpretation, the client reexperiences the emotion. Then, the client comes to understand the emotion fully, not just intellectually, and is no longer affected in harmful ways. Clients reexperiencing war traumas or early childhood beatings through this process of *abreaction* can be as dramatic to watch as any live stage production. They scream, plead, cry, and shake uncontrollably. Behavioral therapists have been critical of this process, but rigid distinctions between the practices of behavior therapists and other clinicians are now melting away somewhat.

Individuals in psychotherapy may reexperience traumatic life events by talking about them, through hypnosis, or through dream interpretation. The clients may scream, plead, cry, and shake uncontrollably. During this process of abreaction, clients come to understand the traumatic events emotionally—not just intellectually—and are no longer harmfully affected by the memory of them.

Two common principles are present in the clinical strategies of all therapists. The first is providing new and corrective experiences. Marvin Goldfried (1980) of the State University of New York at Stony Brook has argued that having new experiences in the therapy situation serves to dispel the client's misconceptions and fears. The client has new experiences in the forms of role-playing, homework assignments, and risk taking.

The second principle is offering direct feedback to the client. The

Kenneth S. Bowers of the University of Waterloo has shared the following case study:

> I once saw a patient who had been involved in various therapies for about two years in an attempt to eliminate a persistent hair-pulling syndrome. When I saw the young woman, she was 17 years old and completely bald. By use of a hypnotic dream technique, I discovered that she had seen her older brother the last time when the latter was in the hospital just prior to (unsuccessful) brain surgery. Part of the preparation for such surgery obviously involves having one's head shaved. My patient reexperienced this last visit with her (baldheaded) brother in a highly cathartic session. Afterwards, when the patient was alerted, she had no apparent memory for the abreactive experience, stating simply that, "I must have been upset because I have tears on my cheeks."
>
> She did not again mention the incident of seeing her baldheaded brother until the next (and final) session, and did so only in the context of how psychologically unprepared she had been for her brother's death. Later in this final session, she again became upset when I asked if she had ever felt somehow responsible for the death of her brother. She reluctantly acknowledged having had this idea, and then vehemently denied that her brother's death was (literally) causing her to pull her hair. When I agreed, she became especially emotional, adding, "you're the first doctor ever to say that." Finally, as she began to calm down somewhat, I said, "Sue, do you need to pull your hair any more?" Sue: "No." Therapist: "Well, why don't you just stop." Sue: "Okay." The patient never again pulled her hair. The entire treatment took four, one-hour sessions.
>
> (Bowers, 1980, p. 182)

After the treatment ended, Bowers discovered that this woman had been conscious of her last visit to her brother and had spoken about it to other people. That is, the memory was not repressed.

The use of abreaction followed by rational discussion suggests that an eclectic drawing on both psychoanalytically oriented therapies and behavioral therapies can be helpful. The psychoanalytic attending to a client's distressing feelings is important. Furthermore, the behaviorist's direct suggestions lead to the client's gaining cognitive control over problem behavior.

therapist and client together begin paying careful attention to the client's feelings and behaviors. The result: "clients are helped to become more aware of what they are doing and not doing, thinking and not thinking, and feeling and not feeling, in various situations" (Goldfried, 1980, p. 995).

Further evidence of similarities across schools of therapy was found in a study of 319 therapists. Almost all used techniques to build relationships and almost all evaluated nonverbal behaviors as part of therapy.

However, don't think therapists are all alike. They are not! Marked differences clearly exist between the theories and techniques of different schools (Wogan & Norcross, 1985).

Nevertheless, the principles that unite therapeutic orientations also suggest a strategy for the potential client. If you are interested in locating a therapist, the therapist's school of thought may not necessarily be the most important influence on your choice. The ability of the therapist, regardless of school, may be your primary requirement.

PSYCHOTHERAPEUTIC CHANGE

Psychotherapy addresses the ways people change. Think of the Wizard of Oz as a great psychotherapist helping the Tin Man overcome his felt lack of compassion, the Scarecrow his feeling of low intelligence, and the Lion his cowardice. Sheldon Kopp (1971) said the lesson of *The Wizard of Oz* is that Dorothy and her companions needed their adventures to realize that they already were what they sought to be. He concluded

> . . . alas, there are no Wizards! And yet, as a psychotherapist, I am some-times tempted to join the Wonderful Wizard of Oz in saying, "But how can I help being a humbug, when all these people make me do things that everybody knows can't be done."

> *(Kopp, 1970, p. 98)*

Dorothy's companions did change. Clients in psychotherapy change as well. Some change simply because they are on a waiting list to begin therapy. Some change because they are ready and eager to change. Some predictably change when exposed to a treatment that has worked with others. Present-day psychotherapists have been following an increasingly well-traveled path.

We look now at therapy clients, at people who get better on their own, and, finally, at the ultimate question, does therapy work? We start by looking at who receives therapy.

Who Receives Psychotherapy?

Psychotherapy is not for everyone. Although almost everybody goes through periods when they feel demoralized, helpless, or socially isolated,

Dorothy and her companions viewed the Wizard of Oz as a sort of great psychotherapist. After their sessions with the Wizard, the Tin Man, the Scarecrow, and the Lion all realized that they already had the qualities they had been seeking. What happened? Were their transformations due to the great and magical powers of the Wizard, or were they due to something else?

only a minority of these people enter psychotherapy. About fifteen million people a year seek psychiatric or psychological help (Hunt, 1987).

In his review of client factors in psychotherapy, Garfield (1986) reported that between 23 and 42 percent of all individuals who apply for psychotherapy later refuse it. That is, over one-third of the people given definite appointments fail to come in for their treatment.

For those people who do begin therapy, about half terminate therapy quickly on their own. The typical client will attend five or six sessions before stopping. In a study of 560 mental hygiene clients, Garfield and Kurz (1952) observed that 43 percent had attended less than five sessions. In contrast, just 13 percent had twenty or more sessions. In seventeen other studies, the median number of psychotherapy interviews ranged from three to twelve (Garfield, 1986).

Who continues therapy? The answer is the same as to the question, who benefits from therapy? The better educated continue. Middle-class patients continue. Poorly educated and lower-class clients discontinue. The closer the clients are to the social class and race of the therapist, the more likely they are to continue. Clients who do continue in long-term therapy tend to be highly satisfied with what they are getting. When forty-two clients with an average of thirty treatment sessions rated their satisfaction with therapy on a five-point scale (with 1 signifying very dissatisfied and 5 signifying highly satisfied), they gave therapy a whoppingly favorable endorsement. Their mean score was 4.49, and thirty-eight of the forty-two clients were either moderately or highly satisfied (Rudy, McLemore & Gorsuch, 1985).

People who feel anxious and self-dissatisfied tend to remain in therapy. These clients are also more interested in exploring their personal problems (Garfield, 1986). One study of 287 clients at a community mental health center found that those who continued for more than three sessions had prior psychotherapy contacts and tended to be seriously disturbed. The premature terminators often had been frightened and unsure of what they wanted from therapy (Hoffman, 1985).

Most of the research on why people stop therapy has been conducted by therapists, who naturally look at the issue from the therapists' point of view. Thus, people who quit therapy are labeled as undesirable clients. An alternate explanation of the discontinuation is that psychotherapy itself is at fault. The nature of conventional treatment may need to be modified to reach people whose class, values, and verbal skills are unlike those of most therapists. Behavior therapy has highly specific goals, relatively few sessions, and directs attention to the actual behaviors that brought the client into treatment. Thus, it appears to offer a partial resolution to the discontinuation problems that plague longer-term, traditional therapies seeking to work with the person's whole life.

Spontaneous Remission

In every area of physical and psychological distress, natural healing occurs. Cuts on the skin as well as malignant cancers have been observed to be cured without medical intervention. Similarly, emotional disturbances sometimes disappear without professional help, with time acting to soothe the person and aid natural healing. When psychological disorders vanish without known professional help, the process is called ***spontaneous remis-***

Spontaneous remission

sion. Spontaneous means natural and immediate, and remission means the lessening of the symptoms.

Spontaneous remission has been a cause of controversy in psychotherapy since Hans Eysenck (1952) concluded from insurance company data that two-thirds of all neurotic disorders naturally improve over a two-year period. This high estimate was not supported by follow-up studies of patients on psychotherapy waiting lists. Rather, these studies found that the spontaneous remission rate ranged from 8 to 72 percent, depending upon the kind of disorder. Anxiety neurotics improved most by themselves. People who were phobic or obsessive-compulsive improved the least (Bergin & Lambert, 1978).

Most spontaneous remissions are not truly spontaneous. Clients who are awaiting therapy may not receive formal treatment, but they often receive advice and help from friends, clergy, physicians, or family members. Clients are often pleased with the help that friends give, and carefully selected nonprofessionals have been shown to be powerful change agents. In their review of nontherapist helpers, Lambert, Shapiro, and Bergin (1986) concluded that clients on waiting lists are frequently aided by natural helpers who may be as effective as trained professionals in relieving the clients' neurotic symptoms. In providing treatment, paraprofessionals seem to be as effective as professional helpers (Berman & Norton, 1985). These findings bring to mind the frequent advertisements that demonstrate how various makes of automobiles are faster, quieter, or otherwise better than the Mercedes-Benz. The Mercedes, like the professional helper, is seen as the benchmark by which all others are judged.

FOCUS ON DEVELOPMENT

Psychotherapies over the Life Span

The great majority of clients receiving psychotherapy are adults in individual therapy. The great majority of psychotherapists, in turn, spend their time offering individual therapy for adults. Furthermore, most theories of psychotherapy are based on individual treatment of adult clients. This chapter has reflected the focus on individual adult clients. However, psychotherapy involves more than one-to-one therapy with this client population. When treatments at different points during the span of life are examined, a variety of additional therapy methods may be noted. I will discuss therapies for three points in the life span: play therapy for young children, family therapy during the child-rearing phase in life, and reminiscence therapy for older adults.

(continued)

Play Therapy

Talking therapies may be successful if the clients are old enough to verbalize their feelings, thoughts, and problems. Many children are not able to verbalize well. Sometimes, the treatment of choice with nonverbal children is a behavioral approach, especially when the therapy is dealing with a specific problem such as bed-wetting or grinding of teeth. When treating more general problems of unhappiness or social isolation, therapists will often choose play therapy. Play therapy may be defined as the use of toys, games, or recreational activities to allow a child self-expression, a sense of competence over his or her environment, and a vehicle by which he or she can relate to an accepting adult. Successful play therapy increases the child's self-esteem and improves the child's ways of relating to adults (Axline, 1947).

Parents sometimes wonder how play can help their children. After all, parents often think, their child already has a room full of toys and has not been helped by them. One reason play therapy is effective is that outside therapy play by itself can help children's development. Play frequently practices mastery over the environment. However, therapeutic play is something more.

In play therapy, games with puppets, for example, can allow children to express feelings of rejection, guilt, or anger, and can help them work toward satisfactory resolutions of these feelings. Because therapists are not in a parenting role, therapists can be perceived as warm, nonjudgmental, accepting adults. Because the children receive positive regard and empathy from the therapists, they may think better of themselves and learn to expect more positive interactions with adults.

Family Therapy

When a child or adolescent suffers from a psychological problem, one common point of view is that the problem arises within the family and the whole family unit should be treated. Virginia Satir (1972) is a family theorist who holds that ambiguous, unclear rules of communication lead to family breakdowns and the appearance of symptoms in individual family members. If family members can express their feelings to each other, and if families have well-understood rules regarding conducting family business and making decisions, then the causes of the psychopathology diminish. Satir emphasizes the following points:

Each person needs to understand how every person in the family really feels.

In place of good communication, members of troubled families show four patterns: they placate each other, blame each other, act as impersonal computers, or distract each other from feelings and problems.

Feeling safe to express feelings is the basis for developing good communication.

Rules in the family can be assessed on the basis of how worthwhile they are and how they are made. Family business and decision making are best conducted by the entire family, with everyone present.

Satir's approach to family therapy is only one of several. For example, Minuchin (1974) developed a structural family therapy, in which the therapist actively seeks to overturn rules and structures that maintain psychopathology. Bowen (1978) described a family systems therapy, in which the therapist helps individuals differentiate themselves from fused patterns of emotional isolation. While there are substantial differences between these approaches and, indeed, vigorous arguments have arisen between their respective proponents, all focus on the family as the cause of abnormal behavior and all treat the family as a whole.

Life Review and
Reminiscence Therapy

Elderly people often discuss the important and interesting events of their lives with friends and family. This process has been called a life review (Butler, 1963) and has been interpreted as the elderly individuals' efforts to integrate their lives and give meaning and cohesion to their varying triumphs and trials. These life reviews occur as part of the last stage of adult development, Erikson's ego integrity stage, during which one assesses and then accepts the worth and meaning of one's life (White, 1984).

One day when I came with a tape recorder to visit my Aunt Edith and Uncle Louis a few years before they died, they engaged in just such a reminiscence. They spoke of growing up in small towns in Eastern Europe, sang childhood songs, and laughed and played as they recounted the memories of their youths. They had been ailing. Although their spirits had not really been depressed, their moods rose with excitement at this trip through the past. Mine did, too.

What happened between me and my aunt and uncle was individual to us, but benefits of reminiscing has led therapists to use reminiscence therapy regularly.

> When life is largely spent and the decisions made are irrevocable, it is vital to one's integrity that the past be accepted. There is no better means to do this than through sharing with others and finding that one is not alone in this dilemma. Being accepted for what one is and what one does is a very healing proposition.
>
> *(Ebersole, 1978, p. 242)*

Reminiscence therapy is used with groups of elderly persons. The clients meet for a predetermined number of sessions—eight is typical—and a leader structures their reminiscing about their lives so that everyone participates and so that both the wonderful and the dreadful events of their lives may be reviewed. In the setting of a supportive and warm group, individuals seem to gain from this process. They become less depressed. Even withdrawn, emotionally disturbed clients become alert and engrossed (Hala, 1975).

The Outcome of Treatment

To their strongest critics, psychotherapists are vain creatures who capitalize on the suffering of innocents for their personal self-interest. The essence of this view of psychotherapists as predators is captured in the Lewis Carroll poem about the little crocodile of the Nile.

> How cheerfully it seems to grin!
> How neatly spreads its claws!
> And welcomes little fishes in
> With gently-smiling Jaws!

(Carroll, 1964, p. 15)

Such critical, negative judgments of therapy also appear in sources such as Richard Stuart's book, *Trick or Treatment: How and When Psychotherapy Fails* (1970). According to Stuart, psychotherapy is based on illogical thinking, has no scientific evidence to support its existence, and indeed often *causes* mental problems rather than cures them. Stuart writes that "the patient who enters psychotherapy does so not without a distinct risk of deterioration or of simply wasting his time and money" (1970, p. 58).

The argument that psychotherapy does not work has been most often mobilized by critics of the therapies that developed from psychoanalysis. Rather than representing detached, impartial examinations, the critiques often reflect the belief that "my therapy method is better than yours." In one book examining this controversy, the authors describe the exchange of criticisms as the battlefield of a private, internal war.

> Although there are many combatants—Freudians versus cognitivists versus humanists—the principals in the war are behaviorists and nonbehaviorists. These groups have called each other names and traded high-sounding insults. But the issue was not over psychotherapy versus no psychotherapy but over brand A psychotherapy versus brand B psychotherapy.

(Smith, Glass & Miller, 1980, p. 2)

One way of resolving these differences is by using a method called meta-analysis, applied by Mary Lee Smith, Gene Glass, and Thomas Miller (1980). **Meta-analysis** is the analysis of existing research; no original data are collected. Like clerks in a secondhand shop, meta-analysts sift through materials gathered and used by other researchers, pile them in separate categories, examine the stacks carefully, and restack them again before drawing conclusions.

Meta-analysis

Smith, Glass, and Miller sorted through thousands of studies to find the ones that could be used in their meta-analysis. They located 475 controlled studies of psychotherapy effectiveness that had control groups, specific outcome measures, and statistics that could be interpreted. Psychotherapy effectiveness was judged by the size of differences in outcome between the treated groups and the control groups. The largest effects were achieved by the cognitive therapies, which actively persuade and confront clients about problematic beliefs.

When Smith and her colleagues categorized their studied therapies into six groups of basic orientations and then looked at effects, cognitive and cognitive behavioral therapies emerged at the top. Developmental and humanistic therapies were at the bottom. (See Table 14–1 for comparison of the effectiveness of the six types of psychotherapies.)

The jury was still out on the central question: What therapies worked best with what kinds of problems? To pursue this answer, Smith, Glass, and Miller divided all of the therapies into two fundamental types: verbal therapies and behavioral therapies. The verbal therapies used talking to solve problems and included psychodynamic and humanistic therapies. The behavioral therapies used principles of learning and included systematic desensitization and behavior modification.

The largest changes for both groups of therapy were associated with the treatment of problems of fear and anxiety. That is, clients who were fearful and anxious appeared to improve regardless of what method was used with them. Behavioral methods were more effective in the treatment of global adjustment problems, personality trait changes, and vocational/personal problems and in producing reductions in signs of physiological stress. Verbal methods were more effective in treating addiction problems, in modifying sociopathic behavior, and in promoting achievements in work and school. The sum differences between the verbal and behavioral therapies were judged to be unreliable.

What were the overall results? "The results show unequivocally that psychotherapy is effective" reported Smith, Glass, and Miller (1980, p. 124). They explained that the person who begins exactly at an average adjustment level before therapy is better adjusted after therapy than 80

TABLE 14-1 The Effectiveness of Six Types of Psychotherapy		
Rank	Therapy Type	Effectiveness Compared to Placebo
1 (most effective)	Cognitive	2.3 times as effective as placebo
2	Cognitive behavioral	2.2
3	Behavioral	1.6
4	Dynamic	1.4
5	Humanistic	1.1
6	Placebo	1.0
7 (least effective)	Developmental	0.75

Based on the results of the Smith, Glass, and Miller (1980) meta-analysis.

percent of similar people. In other words, almost no clients deteriorated, and the magnitude of the changes was substantial.

There were three other important findings of this meta-analysis.

1. The experience of the therapist made no difference.
2. Individual and group therapies worked equally well.
3. The clients who improved most were those with simple phobias and depression, as well as intelligent clients, female clients, and clients similar to the therapists in socioeconomic background.

This meta-analysis produced the most sweeping findings on the controversy over whether therapy helps. As Smith, Glass, and Miller concluded "[even] if only the most cautious and conservative estimate is made, the benefits of therapy remain impressive" (1980, p. 126).

Smith, Glass, and Miller hardly stand alone in their positive assessment. In their comprehensive review of psychotherapy outcomes, Lambert, Shapiro, and Bergin (1986) come to the similar conclusions that psychotherapy does result in appreciable gains for clients and, furthermore, its effects are lasting. They concluded that, for the most part, few meaningful outcome differences are present between different forms of therapy. They judged the question of comparing schools of therapy as less important than it had been, because ". . . the vast majority of therapists have become eclectic in orientation. This appears to reflect a healthy response to empirical evidence and a rejection of previous trends toward rigid alliances to schools of treatment" (1986, p. 202).

These positive conclusions fit into a pattern affectionately called by others *the dodo bird verdict*, named after the dodo bird in *Alice In Wonderland* who decided, "Everyone has won and all must have prizes." In psychotherapy, **the dodo bird verdict** is that everything works (Stiles, Shapiro & Elliot, 1986). The case against this view has been argued by Stanley Rachman and G. Terrence Wilson (1980), who believe it to be misguided, complacent, and simply inaccurate. Rachman and Wilson hold that Smith, Glass, and Miller have searched to find meaningful outcomes where none truly exist and that, in essence, some haystacks simply don't have needles. The two views do agree on one positive result, however. Both agree that behavioral therapies work well. More neutral observers, less embroiled in such squabbles, support the generally positive outlook on therapy effectiveness (see, for example, Garfield, 1983).

Dodo bird verdict

Ethical Dilemmas

"Can I tell you something absolutely between you and me?" That question from a client presents a major ethical challenge to the psychotherapist. If the psychotherapist agrees to offer full confidentiality, a problem arises if the client then says, "Tonight I am going to kill my employer and there is nothing you can do to stop me," or if the client explains that he intends to commit suicide. If the therapist calls the police, or enlists some other aid, the promise is broken.

Confidentiality

Another problem arises if **confidentiality** is not promised or implied and the therapist is later subpoenaed to appear in court. If he or she has privileged communication, the therapist will not have to testify on the witness stand. **Privileged communication** is legally guaranteed privacy so that therapists, like lawyers, cannot be forced to disclose clients' communications. In the absence of such a privilege, however, the therapist may be required to reveal possibly harmful facts about, for example, a client who is fighting for custody of a child or in another legal issue where the client's psychological well-being is a central issue.

Privileged communication

One resolution of the ethical dilemma has been the enactment of privileged communication legislation for psychotherapists. Clients' trust of the psychotherapist is crucial to successful psychotherapy. The fear that something they said in therapy could possibly be used against them has the potential to inhibit clients.

Still another resolution is the therapist's full sharing of the limits of confidentiality with the client. The therapist makes these limits explicit at the beginning of therapy so the client is aware of possible future disclosure of therapy content. The American Psychological Association's ethical guidelines on therapeutic confidentiality state that confidentiality may be broken only in cases where clear and immediate danger of physical injury to the client or another person exists. In cases when suicide, homicide, or child abuse are imminent, the psychotherapist has an obligation to call the proper authorities, even if it means telling what the client has said. While uncommon, such breaking of confidentiality reflects the primary commitment of the therapist to the protection of the client and other citizens.

Another ethical issue concerns intimate touching in the therapeutic relationship. It is an ethical violation for therapists to have sexual contact with their clients. Data on the frequency of this occurrence are difficult to obtain. The two primary sources of information are insurance company records on clients who bring legal actions against their therapists and self-reports by psychotherapists in mail surveys.

One study looked at claims made over a period of four and a half years for about thirteen thousand psychologists covered by a professional liability insurance program (Wright, 1981). Thirteen claims of sexual misconduct were made against psychologists, and almost all of the sexual conduct charges led either to the denial of the claims, the closing of the case, or token settlements. This review concluded that ". . . the dramatic and lurid stories of sex between psychologist and patient are substantially overstated" (Wright, 1981, p. 1487). However, this study hardly gives the

Therapeutic confidentiality may be broken only when there exists clear and immediate danger of physical injury to the client or another person. If a therapist's communication with a client is privileged, the therapist will not have to testify against the client in court and cannot be forced to disclose the client's communication.

whole story. By the time the 1982 to 1984 data were available, sexual malpractice lawsuits were being filed against psychologists at the rate of twenty-four per year (Cummings & Sobel, 1985). Although most suits were filed by female patients against male therapists, a new phenomenon emerged: a full one-sixth of the suits were filed by female patients against female therapists.

In a confidential mail survey of psychologists, Holroyd and Brodsky (1977) found that 5.5 percent of male psychologists and 0.6 percent of female psychologists reported sexual intercourse with clients. Pope, Keith-Spiegel, and Tabachnik (1986) surveyed 575 psychotherapists and found that 9.4 percent of the males and 2.4 percent of the females had had sexual contact with clients. Of course, these surveys do not mean that up to 10 percent of clients have sexual relations with their therapists. Because the survey covers years of practice, it is more reasonable to assume that the individual client risk is a small fraction of one percent. Furthermore, since this survey was completed, highly publicized court awards against psychotherapists who sexually exploited clients may have deterred some of these behaviors.

Nevertheless, clients in therapeutic relationships are vulnerable to such exploitation. They often become so dependent upon their therapists that their normal free choice to refuse a sexual invitation is diminished. A few therapists introduce sexual contact as a therapeutic method, making the clients' refusal even more difficult. For these reasons, the American Psychological Association and other professional organizations have identified all therapist–client sexual contact as unethical and harmful and in violation of psychologists' commitment to better the welfare of their clients.

A final cautionary note: Clients' claims of therapist sexual misconduct can grow out of problems in the therapy and may not be based on real sexual contacts. A client often becomes closely attached to a therapist. When the therapist does not respond as hoped to the client's expressions of love and passion, the rejected client occasionally files a malpractice suit. Determining whether the therapist or client is truthful is not easy; Wright (1981) reported that he found only one such unequivocal instance of a spurned client suit in his review of such cases. Cummings and Sobel (1985) stated that, of seventy-two sexual malpractice cases, only one psychotherapist has been cleared. Most of the times, the therapist *did* do it.

PSYCHOTHERAPEUTIC HELP FOR YOURSELF AND OTHERS

A Consumer's Guide to Therapy

The same principle applies in selecting a psychotherapist as in choosing any other service. You should shop around and select the provider who most closely fits your needs. The single best guide may be word-of-mouth recommendations. The best psychotherapists in any community quickly become known by reputation. If people you trust recommend a therapist, that information is more important and more meaningful to you than the specific credentials or school of thought of the therapist.

Psychiatrists are physicians holding M.D. degrees who have specialized in mental problems and abnormal behavior. They are the only therapists qualified to prescribe medication. Psychologists hold doctor of philosophy (Ph.D.) or doctor of psychology (Psy.D.) degrees and typically specialize in clinical psychology. Caseworkers hold M.S.W. degrees from schools of social work. Finally, psychoanalysts have completed a personal training analysis under extensive supervision as part of postdoctoral training to conduct psychoanalysis.

A therapist in any of the three major professions may have trained in any one of the different schools of psychotherapy. If you are interested in the therapist's approach, you should ask. This information is not usually listed in directories, and most therapists are willing to discuss with you what they believe and do. You also should look into the therapist's fee structure. Fees vary, depending on the therapist's experience and background and whether the service is offered privately or through a public agency. No therapist should mind if you inquire about the fee.

A principle of differential effectiveness is present in psychotherapy. Some therapists are more effective with some kinds of people than with others. Here's a recommended course of action: After you have sought out a therapist whose fees are satisfactory, try him or her out for three or four sessions. If you feel good about the approach and the person, then continue. If you do not like what's happening, gather up your courage and tell the therapist as clearly and directly as you can. If the therapy still does not give what you feel you need, trust yourself. Leave. Clients often leave one therapist and switch to another.

Remember, a person does not have to be a great therapist to complete training—only an adequate one. Changing therapists to find a really good one for yourself is legitimate, provided you don't become overly involved in therapist shopping and subsequently are unwilling to settle into the task of therapy.

Being honest with your therapist has great payoffs. Be honest not only about yourself but about the therapist as well. If the therapist is late, or smokes during therapy and you are annoyed by it, or has a habit of interrupting, speak out. Such candor speeds up the therapy and makes you feel better as well.

Let us turn to stopping therapy. The word used among therapists is ***termination,*** a term that probably reflects the discomfort many therapists feel when clients leave them. When you are ready to stop therapy, discuss it with the therapist. Don't simply stop going. Sometimes, making the decision to stop can lead to important therapeutic work. But if you still wish to stop, do so. It's not failing. Many clients choose to take vacations from therapy for a while.

Finally, try to bring your successes in therapy to your daily life. The greater you can generalize the ideas and behaviors, the more likely you will be pleased about your therapy.

The Art of Helping Others

We have noted that psychotherapists are not the only persons who can provide emotional aid. People frequently turn to friends, family members, pastors, and spouses for advice and counselling. When you are in the role of helper, knowing some basic guidelines for assisting friends may be helpful. These guidelines include

Acceptance. Don't be judgmental or critical of the feelings of your friends. Accept the full range of their experiences in ways that show you value them as persons.

Termination [margin note]

Listening well. Most people rush in to offer opinions before other persons have even finished explaining their problems. Let the other persons say all they need to say. Then, check with them to ensure that you have heard the essence of the problem accurately.

Deferring advice. Resist the temptation to offer advice immediately. Instead, ensure that you have a grasp of what is happening, that you have been able to demonstrate acceptance, and that you have listened well. Then you will have earned the right to give advice.

Reassurance. Emotionally upset friends benefit from reassurance that they are desirable and personally competent. If the problem seems

THE LANGUAGE OF CHANGE

Paul Watzlawick (1978) has suggested that psychotherapy change occurs in activity of the right hemisphere of the brain. The right hemisphere, Watzlawick has observed, is the source of what has been thought of as the unconscious. That is, subjective, nonverbal, intuitive functions are in the right hemisphere. The left hemisphere, by contrast, holds the use of language and more intellectual, objective functions. The right hemisphere is important in therapy because dreams, symbols, and images come from it.

Clients seeking help are usually suffering from the effects of their world view—their view not of the world as it is in reality but of the world that is in their minds. Watzlawick has targeted this world view for change and stated that this appears to be a right hemisphere function. Therefore, language that can reach the right hemisphere must be developed.

But what is right hemisphere language? Watzlawick has identified three patterns to communicate with the right hemisphere: shifts in meaning, figurative language, and paradoxes.

Shifts in Meaning

Shifts in meaning are achieved by making jokes and using phrases with multiple meanings, such as "Freudful [instead of frightful] mistakes." Once people laugh at their problems, the meanings attached to problems shift and the problems are half-solved. World views become less somber and unresolvable in the face of spontaneous laughter. Freud theorized that jokes were a communication from the unconscious to the conscious. Watzlawick maintains that jokes let us communicate the other way, to the world image of the brain's right hemisphere.

Figurative Language

Sometimes a single phrase or paragraph dramatically clarifies a person's world image, even when the logical meaning of the phrase is not immediately apparent.

(continued)

For example,

> Whoever thinks that they cannot live *without* a certain person, usually cannot live *with* him.
>
> One can do anything with bayonets, except to sit down on them.
>
> He who rides the tiger cannot dismount.
>
> Those who work do not acquire anything, and those who acquire anything do not work.
>
> If guns are outlawed, only outlaws will have guns.
>
> *(Watzlawick, 1978, p. 77)*

These ambiguities and absurdities in language speak to the right hemisphere while "circumventing or blocking the logical, critical censorship of the left hemisphere" (Watzlawick, 1978, p. 79).

Paradoxes

The critical, verbal self can be blocked (so the intuitive, symbolic self can change the person) through the use of paradoxes, or the presentation of contradictory ideas. Let us consider the paradox. In the Charles L. Harness novel, *The Rose* (1953), a street-corner barker cries out

> Tell ya what the professor's gonna do, ladies and gentlemen. He's gonna defend not just one paradox. Not just two. Not just a dozen. No, ladies and gentlemen, the professor's gonna defend *seventeen*, and all in the space of one short hour, without repeating himself, and including a brand-new one he has just thought up today: "Music owes its meaning to its ambiguity." The cost of this dazzling display . . . don't crowd there, mister . . .
>
> *(Harness, 1953, p. 12)*

Within this passage the professor discussing paradoxes on a street corner for a fee is itself a paradox.

Consider the following paradoxes:

> All truths are false.
>
> Security is dangerous.
>
> It is prohibited to prohibit anything.

In psychotherapy, giving paradoxical instructions to clients is said to set them free of lingering problems. The principle is that people rethink beliefs through the process of figuring out paradoxes. In one case study, Watzlawick, Weakland, and Fisch (1974) described a woman executive assistant who had, over many years, risen to a highly responsible position in her company. When interacting with one of her bosses, she was quite cool and condescending. In turn, he would angrily criticize her in front of other employees. The more he publicly criticized her, the more condescending she became, and the more condescending she became, the more he publicly criticized her. Finally, it reached the point where she was either going to have to resign because she could not stand it any longer, or he was going to have to fire her, because he was at the limits of his tolerance. She sought out professional help. The therapist gave her a paradoxical instruction to use the next time the boss berated her. She was told to take her boss aside after the public berating and tell him something to this effect, "I have wanted to tell you this for a long time, but I don't know how to tell you—it's a crazy thing, but when you treat me as you just did, it really turns me on; I don't know why—maybe it has something to do with my father" (1974, p. 131). She was instructed to leave immediately after saying this. At first, she was horrified by the instruction, then she was fascinated and delighted by it. She couldn't wait to try it.

When she showed up the next morning, the boss was polite and nice to her, for the first time in months. He was nice again the next day and the day after that. Relieved and puzzled, she described the events to her therapist. She hadn't said anything different. However, she had *acted* differently, so the tone of her interactions with her boss changed. Her nonobvious body language had shown that her antagonism had been replaced by positive anticipation, which in turn changed her boss's behaviors. Her preparation to act in the opposite way to her feelings (the paradox) created the change.

Reframing

Sometimes *reframing* has the same effect. *Reframing* is the presenting of alternative perspectives on behaviors. For example, consider the possible responses of a person stopped on the street by an armed man who demands money. The normal responses would be either to resist or to give in, with the former being a far riskier choice. However, by using reframing, the victim might say in a moment of courage, "I have been looking for somebody like you for a long time. You can now either take my wallet—it contains twenty dollars. Or you can earn twenty thousand by putting my wife's lover out of commission. If you are interested, come see me tomorrow and we can work out the details" (Watzlawick, 1978, p. 118).

This response reframes the situation, with the victim now offering the robber an alternative. Naturally, if the robber took the victim up on his offer, the victim would arrange to have the police waiting the next day.

In another example of reframing, students who have trouble studying are told that after so much time spent studying during the day, they can do anything *except* study for the rest of the day and night. Then their study habits show immediate improvement. This reframing escapes the hazard of all-or-nothing thinking.

The Watzlawick theories on the language of change are new, and they are not yet a part of psychotherapy research. Some therapists presently use these principles under different labels. The language of change is important because it cuts across most schools of therapy. This emerging field promises to expand our understanding of therapeutic improvement.

solvable, reassure them that events will turn out well. Most solvable problems do.

Referral.   Psychotherapists routinely refer clients to other experts when the clients have problems beyond their knowledge. When the individual you have been helping moves to a topic that seems too difficult for you to address, refer the person to professional help. Sometimes a good friend's suggesting professional counselling will be all a person needs to take that step.

A by-product of emotionally helping others can be emotional gains for yourself. Individuals who counsel others, including professionals, often gain insight into their own lives and solve their own concerns indirectly during the counselling process.

Self-Therapy

Self-therapy

Feelings, attitudes, and behaviors may improve through self-therapy as well as through professional help. **Self-therapy** is your solitary, concentrated, and regular attention to your own problems and goals, during which you deliberately pursue new experiences. While having some psychological knowledge may assist you as self-therapist, it is not required.

The instructions for self-therapy are

Set aside an appointment time at least once a week for no business other than working on yourself. Most self-therapists make more frequent appointments.

Mandate that this time is for nothing else than self-therapy. Try not to allow music, other people, food, or other distractions or activities to interrupt this time.

Give yourself homework assignments during the week, in which you try out alternate ways of relating or acting.

Use the time to do more than just think to yourself. Try writing, talking aloud, or speaking about yourself into a tape recorder. Writing or talking permits you to assess your thoughts more explicitly than does simply thinking.

Work on day-to-day feelings and problems, and set specific goals. Although you can look for profound insights, that should wait until you master your techniques for changes that are easily achieved.

Self-therapy has a history as long as psychotherapy itself. The development of psychoanalysis came about in part through Freud's own self-analysis, achieved through an intensive period of what he called "splendid isolation." Procedures for learning self-control are available; with these, you examine and modify the ways in which you are reinforcing undesirable behaviors in yourself and others.

Bibliotherapy is the branch of self-therapy that uses reading as the starting point for corrective experiences. To engage in bibliotherapy, you follow the general self-therapy instructions, but include regular reading about your particular concerns. The avalanches of popular self-help books that have tumbled onto the bookstore shelves include a few good resources for such reading. Another option in bibliotherapy is reading relevant fiction or biographies to understand problems similar to yours.

People engaged in self-therapy have the option to enter professional therapy exactly as do individuals not in self-therapy. If you see yourself as unhappy or ineffective in achieving your personal objectives, professional therapy may help. However, clearly identifying yourself as entering self-therapy defines you as engaged in problem solving, and that definition alone can mobilize your natural abilities for improvement.

Table 14–2 summarizes the behaviors that utilize psychotherapy in seeking well-being and those behaviors that hinder well-being and would benefit from therapy.

SUMMARY

Psychotherapy is defined as the interchange between a client and a trained therapist; the personal transactions and events between the two people are aimed at changing the client's behavior, attitudes, or experiences. Even before clients pass through the therapist's doorway, they bring expectations of change that may aid their improvement.

There are both differences and similarities between the major schools of psychotherapy. The differences appear between psychoanalysis, behavior therapy, humanistic psychotherapy, and logotherapy. Psychoanalysis

TABLE 14–2   Psychotherapy and Well-Being

Toward Well-Being	Away from Well-Being
Sharing of self while in psychotherapy	Closing off of self
New and corrective emotional experiences in psychotherapy	Stuck in maladaptive emotional rut
Direct feedback on behavior	No or little feedback on behavior
Seeks help when needed	Declines to seek help
Makes inquiries about who is a good helper	No inquiries
Helps others	Not emotionally available to help others
Ready for and working toward self-improvement	No or little effort at self-improvement

brings to awareness repressed, unacceptable memories and feelings. Clients recline on a couch, free associate, and have their associations interpreted by the psychoanalyst. The client's resistance to the analysis and transference of earlier relationships to the analysis are key subjects for the psychoanalyst's interpretation. Behavior therapy draws on the principles of learning to modify current maladaptive behaviors. Clients record the frequency of their behaviors, and then the therapists guide them through structured, clearly defined behavior modification procedures. Cognitive therapy assumes that how one thinks about actions influences emotional consequences, and it seeks to displace irrational beliefs with rational ones. Humanistic therapy explores feelings and seeks to move the client toward self-fulfillment. It utilizes mutuality, honesty, trust, and a focus on subjects vital to the client's life. Logotherapy considers personal responsibility in the search for meaning. Eclectic psychotherapy seeks to choose the best treatment techniques regardless of the school in which they originated. Similarities between all psychotherapies are providing new and corrective experiences for the clients and offering direct feedback.

Of all the people who apply for therapy, over one-third fail to appear for their first appointments. About one-half of the clients who begin therapy terminate quickly on their own. The average number of times a client will come is between five and six sessions. Persons who remain in therapy are described as more intelligent, better educated, middle class, more anxious, and more willing to explore psychological problems.

When people improve on their own, the process is called spontaneous remission. A great number of clients on waiting lists show such spontaneous remissions, with improvement rates from 8 to 72 percent, depending on the disorder. Often, natural helpers, such as friends, offer counsel and aid.

Critics of psychotherapy say it does not work. Meta-analysis, or the analysis of many studies, has looked at therapy outcomes and concluded that therapy works and is helpful. The average therapy client rose from the fiftieth percentile to the eightieth percentile in adjustment as a result of therapy. Cognitive behavioral therapies worked especially well according to the meta-analysis. Problems of fear and anxiety, along with simple phobias and depression, respond best to therapy.

An ethical dilemma arises in psychotherapy when a possible violation of confidentiality takes place. Therapists can reveal information learned in therapy only if there is the possibility of imminent physical harm to the client or others. Another ethical problem is sexual contact between therapist and client. Clients who are sexually approached feel less freedom to decline the invitations, but such sexual contact is an ethical violation and is an increasing source of malpractice lawsuits.

Clients seeking to begin therapy should be informed consumers. The informed client shops around, inquires by word-of-mouth, is honest with the therapist, and stops the therapy if it isn't working.

Many people with problems find that they improve by helping themselves or by helping others. When helping others, one should accept the person, listen well, defer giving advice, reassure, and refer to a professional when needed. In self-therapy, it is important to set aside private time and take actual steps to solve day-to-day problems. If reading is part of the self-therapy, it is called bibliotherapy.

Key Terms

Abreaction	**Modeling**
Art of solace	**Morita therapy**
Aversion methods	**Naikan therapy**
Bibliotherapy	**Privileged communication**
Catharsis	**Rational-emotive therapy**
Client-centered therapy	**Reframing**
Confidentiality	**Resistance**
Contingency management	**Rhetoric**
Contracting	**Self-therapy**
Dodo bird verdict	**Spontaneous remission**
Eclectic psychotherapy	**Systematic desensitization**
Free association	**Termination**
Logotherapy	**Therapeutic alliance**
Meta-analysis	**Transference**

Recommended Reading

Ivey, A.E., Ivey, M.B. & Simek-Downing, L. (1987). *Counseling and psychotherapy: Integrating skills, theory, and practice* (2nd ed.). Englewood Cliffs, NJ: Prentice-Hall. Ivey and his colleagues describe one approach to counselling and psychotherapy. Then, they present the major existing schools of therapy, giving illustrative examples of each therapy in action. The book begins with a quote from Marshall McLuhan: "Well, if you don't like that idea, I've got another . . . ." (p. xi)

Lande, N. (1976). *Mindstyles, Lifestyles: A comprehensive overview of today's life-changing philosophies.* Los Angeles: Price, Stern, Sloan. Brief synopses of nineteen different schools of therapy open this encyclopedic book of traditional, religious, and contemporary ways of changing lives and ideas.

Watzlawick, P. (1978). *The language of change: Elements of therapeutic communication.* New York: Basic Books. Watzlawick clearly describes left- and right-brain communication patterns and, with charm, wit, and delightful literary examples, tells the reader of new ways of changing world views and behavior.

15
CHAPTER

Further Pathways
to Well-Being

Their first contact was with a speaker for the society. The couple described him in terms much like the following statement:

> He was a very, very dynamic person; he just radiated when he talked. He started off normal and calm; then, he got more into it, and his eyes just glowed. It was amazing how much power his eyes had. We sat there with out eyes glued to him as he communicated this urgent message to us. . . . Because of him, we decided to accept the invitation to the weekend workshop in the country, to find out what made him so enthusiastic.

(Conway & Siegelman, 1978, p. 31)

They accepted the invitation to sit, to talk, to join in the weekend of intellectual stimulation. The atmosphere was dynamic and powerful, yet spiritual and peaceful. They found themselves in a group of warm, loving, serene people who made them feel wonderful. They wanted to be like the others. Discussing religion, philosophy, and history gave them a feeling of being truly alive. They accepted an invitation to return to meet with these people again. Ordinary life seemed dull and alien.

When the couple returned, they ran through the woods in their bare feet, danced, sang, chanted, and prayed. Encouraged by their new companions, the couple persevered until they were exhausted, hungry, barraged with new experiences. Then, something dramatic happened. They felt light-headed. Electricity rushed through their bodies. They were filled with ecstasy and awe. They had a new understanding. Everyone and everything they knew before had no meaning or value. Only this new group of people and their beliefs had meaning.

Events in their lives didn't just flow fast from there; things exploded. They felt loved, wonderfully loved—so loved they realized how much they had been missing and how very much they needed such love. The love had come from everywhere and from everyone. And when the couple talked about the society and its beliefs, the others offered even greater appreciation and caring and joy. The couple received beatific smiles and hug after hug in response to their statements about the nature of the universe and spiritual life.

Within two months, they had moved into the society's retreat in the woods. They gave their dog away to a good home. They sold their car and turned over the proceeds of the sale, along with their savings, to the leader of the society. He asked everyone to call him Kelara. Out of affection and respect, the members called him Master Kelara. The couple quit their jobs. Working in the outside world seemed irrelevant.

Working in the world of the society was relevant. Everyone pitched in to cook, clean, paint, and recruit. Especially to recruit—at shopping malls, airports, train stations, anywhere large numbers of people gathered, the couple was there.

Their parents and friends found it hard to stay in touch with them. Both of them felt they had little in common with their families, because the families just didn't understand. Friends, too. All of them were materialistic and hypocritical; they really didn't know the purpose of life. Besides, family and friends were not permitted to visit the society. The couple's phone calls and letters to their families and their friends became more and more infrequent and then stopped entirely.

Then, something happened for each of them. For him, it occurred about six months after they moved in. The Master's chief assistant had ordered him to work on the cleanup shift that week. He explained that he had been on the cleanup shift the week before and that it was too soon for him to do it again. The assistant smiled peacefully and explained, "it is the Master's will." He did work the cleanup shift, but it just didn't seem right. After that, lots of things didn't seem right.

For her, the turning point took place at the entrance to the Oakdale Mall. For two hours she had been stopping shoppers to invite them to the society's free orientation and to hand out materials. It had been a difficult day. Christmas was approaching, and the people seemed disinterested in talking to her. Finally, one man did stop. He sat down and talked to her, and he asked her if it wasn't painful to be turned down so often by so many people. Yes, she thought. It is painful. Very painful. It's like dying a thousand deaths each day as person after person refuses to acknowledge your existence.

Another year passed before they left the society. They had started to leave, changed their minds, felt more part of the group, and then less. Eventually, they ran away at night. They have resumed their presociety lives. Both of them are on good terms with their families and are working again. When asked about their time with the society, they say, "It was a heck of a way to spend two years."

The couple's motives for becoming part of the cult were much like most people's motives for participating in or undertaking other life experiences. They sought a sense of security. They felt as if they belonged with this new group. They felt worthwhile and experienced newfound self-esteem. They experienced more than just feelings of self-worth; they felt they were contributing to meaningful activities in the world. They felt as if they were fulfilling their potential as human beings.

While they were in the early, honeymoon phase, the new cult members experienced the dimensions of well-being we discussed in Chapter 1. The glow of positive affect was warm and satisfying. The negative affect that had come from the ordinary hassles of their prior lives were now memories. With their newfound spiritual partners, they were now members of a team with a mission that was profoundly satisfying. For a few months, their sense of well-being was profound and sublime.

These initial feelings passed because their choice to enter the society was not truly voluntary. Furthermore, being cut off from their families and friends troubled them.

The experiences of the new group members bring us to the topic of the general search for well-being. Every chapter has touched on this topic. In this chapter, we will consider three components of the search: choice, self-actualization, and uniqueness. To begin, we take a detailed look at the experiences of the couple in the society.

SEARCHING FOR WELL-BEING: THE CULT EXPERIENCE

Cult

A *cult* is a totalitarian group that maintains intensive control over its members and that, from a posture of moral superiority, renounces the outside world (Appel, 1983). Small religious groups are not necessarily cults. Indeed, the United States has a long history of welcoming isolated groups with idiosyncratic religious beliefs. Immigrants to the United States from Britain and other countries in the seventeenth century included members of many persecuted religious communities who were seeking freedom to worship. In the nineteenth century, religiously and politically committed groups had formed Utopian villages throughout America, in which the members could practice their beliefs together. The Shaker and Oneida communities are examples of such groups. To the present day, these types of communities have been tolerated, with the exception of those that aggressively overwhelm potential members into joining closed, authoritarian sects. This conversion process *without genuine choice* is our primary concern here. We can identify some of the processes that are associated with such conversions (Myers, 1983).

Commitment

The art of cult conversion is rooted in commitment. To inspire their commitment, potential members are not allowed to be passive spectators. They are actively brought into the group. Their identification with the group grows from an initially substantial freely chosen commitment that is made public and reaffirmed over and over through group pressure. The requests for commitment initially are made in modest ways. This is known as the foot-in-the-door phenomenon, in which small commitments are easily obtained, leaving the persons amenable to making more substantial commitments in the future. The newcomer to one of Reverend Moon's Unification Church camps, for example, is made to feel part of a generous family. The newcomer then participates in study groups, and the formerly unconditional loving he or she received from the group becomes conditional, depending on the statements of the potential member; the stronger the newcomer's statements of commitment, the more love he or she receives.

The Charismatic Leader

Typical features of a cult are its distinctive rituals worshiping a God or person, its isolation from the "evil" outside culture, and its charismatic leader (Myers, 1983). The leader energizes the cult, serves as a focus for its beliefs, and is a powerful persuader. The messiah usually presents himself as one sent to deliver the world from evil and from moral or physical destruction. Earlier in their lives, most of these "messiahs" have had emotional collapses and then looked to the cult worship as a means of achieving success in their lives. The messiah figures are influential in producing commitments from the new recruits.

Group Isolation

As members become more committed to and involved with the cult, they cut ties with their families and outside friends. This isolation within the group means they talk, play, work, eat, and interact almost exclusively with others who share the same beliefs. The members construct their own realities, because no outsiders are present to question or challenge them.

Who Joins Cults?

Willingness to make commitments to cults and accessibility to the influence of a charismatic speaker are found especially in middle-class Caucasian youths. They trust people in general more, and they don't have the streetwise skepticism of some lower-class youths. Lonely and depressed persons also are vulnerable, and the warmth and emotional support of their newfound companions makes them willing to accept the cult's ideas. Cults convert those who are least able to critically attack the cult's positions—that is, the young, the less sophisticated, and the more needy. These converts often have not yet established their own individuality. Although not psychologically disturbed in any clinical sense, they stay excessively tied to family at an age when most youths have become independent. Thus, the cult allows them a painless separation from family by providing them with another secure situation in which they can remain dependent (Levine, 1984).

Outcomes

What eventually happens to the thousands of young men and women who join cults? Virtually all of them sooner or later abandon the group. Within two years of joining, 90 percent return home and embrace the values they had rejected. Most are not harmed; however, those youths who are kidnapped and deprogrammed frequently suffer permanent psychological damage (Levine, 1984).

Can such conversions by cults be prevented? The answer appears to be yes. The way to inoculate people from being persuaded is to ensure their exposure to a diversity of ideas. If we have had mild challenges to our beliefs so we have had to rethink and defend them, we will be far more resistant to persuasion by cults and others.

The question of values always arises when assessing the desirability of any conversion efforts. Patently, not all persuasion efforts are harmful. Almost every organized group has some element of seeking to convert potential members, sometimes using methods similar to those used by cults. Consider fraternity and sorority rushes.

Fraternity and sorority members, for example, have reported that the initial "love bombing" of potential cult recruits is not unlike their own "rush" period, during which prospective pledges are lavished with warm attention and made to feel special. During the subsequent "pledge" period, new members are somewhat isolated, cut off from old friends who did not pledge. They spend time studying the history and rules of their new group, they suffer and commit time on its behalf, and they are expected to comply with all demands. Not surprisingly, the end result is usually a new member genuinely committed to the organization.

(Myers, 1983, p. 287)

It's easy to see those who agree with us as wise and those who join us in a group as enlightened. We may draw the opposite conclusions about people who leave a group to which we are committed. Such joiners and deserters can be labelled as brainwashed or tricked, particularly if they act as a result of assertive persuasion.

We return now to a fundamental issue: the question of choice. Can one make a voluntary choice to be persuaded? What roles do personal rigidity and flexibility play in individuals' making of choices?

SELF-DETERMINATION

Self-determination

The element of choice is what separates individuals who feel as if they have determined what will happen in their lives from those who feel controlled. George Eliot (1969) wrote, "The strongest principle of growth lies in human choice" (p. 103). Whether growth results or not, it seems that perceived freedom does indeed result from choice. While the issue of self-determination may be approached in many ways, this discussion looks at three aspects: (1) when choice is absent, (2) flexibility, and (3) the major theories of self-determination.

Hobson's Choice

Thomas Hobson (1544–1631) owned the largest stable in Cambridge, England, and rotated the use of his horses on a strict schedule. Whichever horse had not been ridden for the longest time was to be used next. No matter who the customer, or what the customer's preference, the horse next in line at the stable door was to be taken, or none at all would be taken. Hobson absolutely stayed with this principle. As a result of resisting pressures from the empowered gentlemen of the day, he became famous. Not only is there a street and a pub in Cambridge named after him, but his approach was incorporated in the language with the term ***Hobson's choice***—meaning, there is no choice.

Hobson's choice

Hobson's choice is what many people give themselves in important decisions and daily events alike. They act as if only one path of action is open to them. They don't think about choices. They do not engage in trying out a variety of feelings. They take the horse nearest the stable door because it is there.

Let us consider an imaginary man who has to have everything done the same way at the same time every day. He must get out of bed at the same time, wash his body in the shower in the exact same order from top to bottom, cook his eggs the same way, and take the same route to work. He counts on the rest of his day and people around him being absolutely predictable. If something causes him to act differently, he becomes distressed. He wants to know just what will be expected of him so he can respond as he always has in the past. Spontaneity and impulsiveness are alien to him. He would not walk in the rain without an umbrella, make fun of himself, order a food dish he had never heard of, or say anything unless he was certain of and prepared for the response.

We have described someone who has ordered his life to protect himself from the unexpected, including unexpected aspects of himself. While safety does exist in such an organized approach to life, it is an inflexible approach that restricts the person from having new experiences and from growing.

Flexibility in Choices

It is important to know one's options. The more choice people allow themselves in living, the more their living will be filled with intentionally chosen consequences. In other words, thoughtfully making intentional choices often leads one to a sense of feeling good about oneself. The potential for increased well-being increases when individuals have many acceptable choices at any given time. Goldiamond (1974) has called this phenomenon *constructionalism*, a term that refers to adding new behavior options. When a person truly has more choices on hand, he or she typically makes a decision that has a desirable outcome. The individuals who can only respond in anger to criticism are more limited in their potential for growth than are persons who knowingly choose from many responses. Well-being is more likely to come to persons who can just as easily respond to criticism with disarming humor, self-deprecation, reflection, or intellectual analysis.

Constructionalism

Self-Determined Behaviors

Choice involves making deliberate decisions about what ways and how to live life, a process that has been labelled *self-determination* by Edward Deci (1980; Deci & Ryan, 1985). From his studies of what intrinsically motivates people, Deci has concluded that everyone has a fundamental need to be self-determining—to choose outcomes rather than to be a pawn in others' choices.

Self-determination is separated from other motives by where it comes from. Other motivations come from felt deficiencies, or so-called tissue needs for food, water, and general physical and emotional satisfaction. Self-determination is not the result of such urges; it is not a compelled decision. Instead, it is seen as follows:

> When people are free from the intrusion of drives and emotions, they seek situations that interest them and require the use of their creativity and resourcefulness. They seek challenges that are suited to their competencies, that are neither too easy nor too difficult. When they find optimal challenges, people work to conquer them, and they do so persistently.
>
> *(Deci & Ryan, 1985, pp. 32–33)*

Self-determination takes the form of trying something new—something our hypothetical character who energetically avoided anything new never did. There are two characteristics of self-determination.

1. *A perceived internal locus of causality.* That is, the perception that the causes of events come from within you. Whether that is the true source of the causes is beside the point.

2. *A flexibility toward the external environment.* That is, flexibility in accommodating and interpreting external events and situations. What we do with others—extrinsic motivations—can be in the service of self-determination.

Self-determination begins with an awareness of potential satisfactions. Once people envision a future satisfying state, then they can make the choice or series of choices that moves them toward that state, even when they know they might experience unpleasant emotions in the short term.

> For example, people sometimes choose to explore dark rooms even if they know they will be in near panic because of their fear of darkness. . . . Going into the room will be aversive, but doing it is intended to help overcome a fear—in other words to conquer this challenge—so there will be the anticipated intrinsic reward of feeling competent and self-determining for overcoming the fear.
>
> *(Deci & Ryan, 1985, p. 233)*

From this viewpoint, which choice is made is not as important as the energizing of the behaviors—the basic get up and go feeling that prompts a person to start making choices. The opposite of self-determined behavior is automatic behavior, where little or no thought is given to behaviors and the person feels controlled by others.

As we think about how people do make self-determinations about goals and the means to attain those goals, we are brought to one of the hypothesized ultimate aims of life: to be self-actualized.

SELF-ACTUALIZATION

Maslow's Hierarchy of Needs

Abraham Maslow (1968) proposed that our needs are met in a hierarchy, or a predictable order of most basic to highest needs. These are, in order, physiological, safety, belongingness, esteem, and self-actualization needs. At the very bottom of this hierarchy are physiological needs. Until our basic physiological needs of food, water, and sleep are satisfied, we cannot address other needs. Once our physiological needs have been met, our security needs are believed to emerge. We become attentive to security from physical attack, disease, or temperature extremes. After we feel secure, then belongingness needs arise—we feel the need to belong with a spouse, coworkers, friends, and family. When we feel we belong, we begin

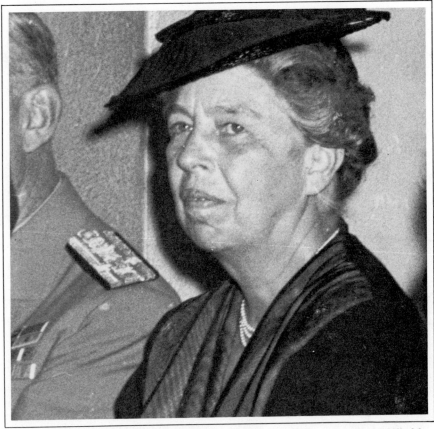

Eleanor Roosevelt was described by Maslow as a self-actualized person: She fulfilled her potential as a human being while unselfishly seeking to help others. Can you think of anyone else who fits this description?

to need to feel esteemed and we seek recognition and status. Finally, our self-actualization needs emerge. Self-actualization is the fulfillment of our human potential while we unselfishly seek to help others.

People are seen as achieving these needs in an orderly sequence. A need may be addressed only if the one below it in the hierarchy has been satisfied. Thus, people who are unsatisfied at the belongingness level, who cannot attain satisfaction from being with friends, lovers, or family, cannot deal with the next higher needs: esteem and self-actualization.

In one investigation of the Maslow hierarchy, Mathes (1981) asked fifty male and fifty female college students to evaluate their own needs according to importance to them. Five satisfiers for each level of need were paired with five of every other level (see Table 15–1). The students were asked questions such as, "If from now on, you had to choose between having no male friends [belongingness] or making no accomplishments that would live on after your death [esteem], which would you choose?"

TABLE 15-1   Needs in the Maslow Hierarchy

Physiological:	For food
	For water
	For sleep
	For elimination of wastes (urine, feces)
	For air (to breathe)
Security:	Against dying from disease
	Against dying of starvation
	Against physical attack or murder
	Against death as result of extreme heat, cold, or natural disaster
	Against mutilation or death as a result of foreign invasion
Belongingness:	With spouse or lover
	With work companions
	With female friends
	With children
	With male friends
Esteem:	From accomplishments that will live on after your death
	From high status within community and country
	From high self-esteem
	From awards and honors
	From respect from your peers
Self-actualization:	In seeking after truth
	In giving unselfish love to others
	In seeking to be a good human being
	In being just and promoting justice
	In being honest and maintaining integrity

Adapted from Mathes, 1981, p. 69.

The students were most willing to do without esteem, security, and self-actualization satisfiers. They were least willing to do without having their belongingness and their physiological needs being satisfied.

In over twenty-five independent studies, selected aspects of the Maslow theory of needs and motivation have been called into doubt. The current literature suggests that people are able to skip levels. Individuals can still love others while being in serious danger. Other people can abstain from eating to attain high levels of awareness and fulfillment.

The mixed results of the studies of the Maslow hierarchy reflect Maslow's own changing formulations. For example, Maslow originally wrote that when a person's needs are gratified at one level the person can then engage in seeking to satisfy the needs of the next level upward. However, he later became uncertain about this process. In an interview toward the end of his life, Maslow said

> I'd always assumed . . . that if you cleared away the rubbish, and the neuroses and the garbage and so on, then the person would blossom out, that he'd find his own way. I find especially with young people that it just ain't so sometimes. . . . I'm talking about people who, as nearly as I can make out, have been brought up well, in my sense, and are living in a very good situation. These are the basic need gratifications so far as safety and security is concerned. You know they have enough glory and applause and appreciation and self-respect, and yet they look out on the world and on society and say, "My God, what a shambles" and then feel hopeless, some of them.
>
> *(Frick, 1982, pp. 37–38)*

The observation that self-actualization does not always occur when expected has not deterred the substantial and persistent scholarly interest in actualization. This interest has explored two related directions: the self-actualized person and peak experiences and performances. Our next discussion investigates the self-actualized person—the individual who has satisfied all five levels of needs in Maslow's hierarchy.

The Self-Actualized Person

Self-actualized people are described as being sensitive to both their own needs and the needs of others. They are spontaneous without being irresponsible. They value their feelings and thoughts highly and, while aware of their weaknesses, they accept themselves. They show an energetic, joyful appreciation of life, marked by feelings of personal fulfillment; they show good humor, and they experience warm intimate relationships with valued others. They have actualized, or made actual, their potential as human beings.

Only a handful of truly exceptional people fit this description of

self-actualization. Maslow modified this description, adding that self-actualization can be seen as a *state*.

> . . . it is a time when a person is more open for experience, more idiosyncratic, more perfectly expressive or spontaneous, or fully functioning, more creative, more humorous, more ego-transcending, more independent of his lower needs, etc. He becomes in these episodes more truly himself, more perfectly actualizing his potentialities, closer to the core of his Being, more fully human.
>
> *(Maslow, 1968, p. 97)*

In a self-actualized person, such brief episodes are frequent and intense. These temporary states of self-actualization appear not only during emotional high points in life, but also during day-to-day existence.

Maslow's concept of self-actualization was personal to him. Because of this and because values are always difficult to factor in the psychology of adjustment, some observers have reservations about Maslow's definition. In his analysis of the values issue with respect to Maslow's definition of self-actualization, Kendler (1980) concluded

> The fault is with the manner in which Maslow chose to justify his value system. By insisting that his value system is demanded by psychological facts and is a consequence of a scientific analysis, Maslow misled himself as well as his audience.
>
> *(Kendler, 1980, p. 290)*

According to Maslow, examples of actualized people were Beethoven, Jefferson, Lincoln, and some of Maslow's own friends. Kendler noted that this selection represented a value choice.

> Suppose another psychologist, more enamored with pragmatism than Maslow, considers Henry Kissinger, Thomas Edison, Neil Simon, and Andrew Carnegie as examples of self-actualized individuals. Or perhaps, another psychologist, fascinated with the irony of life, would suggest that both Groucho Marx and W.C. Fields were fulfilled.
>
> *(Kendler, 1980, p. 290)*

In a related vein, Leonard Geller (1984) has argued that the deep expression of fulfillment and the fullest development of human powers do not necessarily emerge when basic wants are met. He points out that, after security and esteem needs are satisfied, most people don't even remotely engage in moving toward self-actualization. Instead, they "much prefer to spend their time watching television, playing golf, making love, and just having fun to develop their talents . . ." (Geller, 1984, p. 103).

Nonetheless, the potential for achieving joyous exhilaration does exist in each of us, and some people do seem to be exceptionally fulfilled, loving, effective, and spontaneous. The concept of self-actualization may be from Maslow's own value system, but it does appear that his definition reflected, in part, views broader and more commonly held than just his own.

Peak Experiences and Peak Performances

For most people, becoming an actualized self is a far-off ideal. There is good reason for this: Beethovens and Lincolns are rare. However, experiencing the temporary moments of extraordinary self-satisfaction and fulfillment we discussed is within the range of most people. These actualized states are what Maslow called **peak experiences**.

Peak experiences

> . . . think of the most wonderful experience or experiences of your life; happiest moments, ecstatic moments, moments of rapture, perhaps from being in love, or from listening to music or suddenly "being hit" by a book or a painting, or from some great creative moment. First list these. And then try to tell me how you feel in such acute moments, how you feel *differently* from the way you feel at other times, how you are at the moment a different person in some ways.
>
> (Maslow, 1968, p. 71)

People describe having several feelings and thoughts at these times of greatest fulfillment and joy. They describe feelings of unity and completeness, combined with total attention to what is happening. They see nature and objects for their own sake, and not just as humans use or need them. Their senses during peak experiences seem to be richer and more fascinating. At such moments, people forget themselves and the moment is an end to itself, with its own value. What makes it a peak, as opposed to a valley, is that the experience simply feels intrinsically good.

The experience itself is not easily put into words. Yet you may recognize a peak experience because you feel so much more peaceful or joyous than you ordinarily feel. You may recognize it when you tell others about it. People often reexperience the wonderful feelings—they relive the peak experience—in the retelling of the story.

How common are peak experiences? One answer comes from a systematic interviewing of one thousand randomly sampled adults in the San Francisco–Oakland area (Wuthnow, 1980). When asked if they ever felt in close contact with something holy or sacred, 50 percent said yes, they had, and 27 percent (of the entire sample) said the contact had had a lasting influence on their lives. When questioned as to whether they had "experienced the beauty of nature in a deeply moving way," 82 percent responded in the affirmative and 49 percent cited lasting effects. Finally, when asked if they had felt "in harmony with the universe," 39 percent said yes, and 22 percent reported lasting influences from this experience. The respondents with intense peak experiences were self-aware,

When you are having a peak experience, your senses seem keener and the world seems more fascinating. You forget yourself, and the moment becomes an end to itself. You may not be able to accurately describe a peak experience, but you probably will recognize the feeling.

self-assured, and not oriented primarily to status or materialistic posses-sions.

In another investigation of peak experiences, Marghanita Laski (1968) asked sixty-three men and women to describe their sensations of excep-tional euphoria. The circumstances that set off the peak experiences were called **triggers**. The important categories of triggers were natural scenery, sexual love, childbirth, exercise and movement, and religion. When de-scribing the peak experience, one person wrote, "Awareness of being so alive . . . you've almost touched the fringe of eternity" (1968, p. 391). An-

Triggers

other person described the experience as a "Sensation of timelessness, full of force, wonderful force, completely uplifted" (1968, p. 386).

The emotional sensation of being joyfully out of the real world was described by groups as varied as women speaking of childbirth and runners' talking about the runner's high, a point of elation after prolonged exertion. Religious peaks are frequently experienced as well, usually taking the form of a transformation or commitment to God. The following describes the typical experience of felt intensity and unity with God:

> I remember the night, and almost the very spot on the hill-top . . . I stood alone with Him who had made me, and all the beauty of the world, and love, and sorrow, and even the temptation. I did not seek Him, but felt the perfect unison of my spirit with His. The ordinary sense of things around me faded. For the moment nothing but an ineffable joy and exultation remained. . . .

> *(Laski, 1968, pp. 425–426)*

Laski described an ecstatic afterglow that follows the peak experience. This afterglow permits the person to understand the ecstasy and eventually relate it to normal living.

In every person's life, there are times when he or she is able to perform at levels far superior than any level ever before achieved. In sports, work, and many intellectual, physical, and emotional tasks, there are occasions when people's performance goes well beyond what they believed possible. This phenomenon has been called ***peak performance*** by Gayle Privette (1981).

Peak performance

Peak performance is related to peak experience. A peak experience is something *you feel*, an internal and subjective process. A peak performance is something *you do;* it is observable behavior. A person who achieves a peak performance is fulfilling a normally untapped potential. Think about the times in your life when you have been able to function in much superior ways than you ever functioned before. These may be examples of your own peak performances. Privette identified three aspects of peak performance.

Clear focus. The objects or self all at once stand out sharply from the background and are seen with great clarity, as if an improperly adjusted lens has been corrected. What you need to do is absolutely clear.

Freedom from restraints. You don't have to try very hard. Your actions occur spontaneously and effortlessly.

Self-vitality and strength. You feel naturally full of great power and strength; your senses of yourself are heightened. "One feels each part of the self moving in concert with the rest, rather like a majestic animal running with a grace unspoiled by captivity" (Privette, 1981, p. 66).

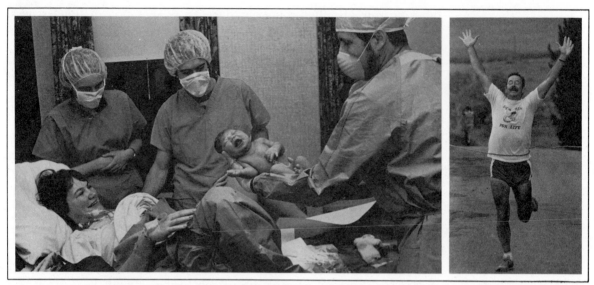

The exceptional euphoria a woman experiences after childbirth and the runner's high both have been described as examples of the ecstatic afterglow one feels after having a peak experience.

EXPLORATION IN WELL-BEING

The Minerva Experience

Minerva experience

The ***Minerva Experience*** was named by its developer, Herbert Otto (1968), after Minerva, the Roman goddess of wisdom and well-being, because the exercise makes people look at the positive emotions associated with well-being. The principle underlying the exercise is that each of us has had positive, formative experiences that contributed to our emotional development. We have forgotten many of these experiences, and Otto holds that we can improve our present functioning by recalling the genuinely good events that happened when we were growing up. Our assets become clearer when we allow ourselves to relive these times of growth and fulfillment.

To have a Minerva experience, you need to allow your mind to drift back into your past and think about happy, growthful events. Recall your most positive experiences in each of the following time periods:

Ages fifteen to twenty _____

Ages ten to fifteen _____

One way of defining peak performances is to classify them as part of the mastery of life tasks. Peak performances are frequently associated with a sense of personal competence that helps people to anticipate and succeed in most of life concerns. Danish defined personal competence as ". . . the ability to do life planning, to be self-reliant, and to seek the resources of others in coping" (1983, p. 224).

Danish has suggested that sports and fitness are means for promoting individual competence. He has pointed out that a major difference exists between **competition-motivated** players and **competence-motivated** players. The competition-motivated athletes see winning as the basic aim, and they hate to lose. In contrast, competence-motivated players focus on a sense of mastery and optimal challenge that may lead them to peak performances. Of course, competition and competence are not mutually exclusive motivators; they often overlap. However, having a sense of personal competence, whether in the absence or presence of competitiveness, seems to be a major attribute of well-being.

Competition-motivated
Competence-motivated

UNIQUENESS AND INDIVIDUATION

To this point, we have considered two major elements that influenced the couple who joined the society in the opening story. The first element was

Ages six to ten _____

Ages three to six _____

Under three years _____

Don't try to force thoughts to arise. Allow the memories to surface, and then share them with a person you trust. Let that person share his or her memories of positive experiences with you. Don't discuss traumatic incidents, even if they had later positive effects. Stay with the positive, constructive, emotional happenings. Try to associate the memories to the specific ages at which they occurred.

Recall the odors you associate with your positive experiences. Remembering odors greatly aids the recalling of the feeling part of memories. Herbert Otto has suggested that a flow of odor memories might include "The smell of the hot sun on sand, of a wet dog coming in from the rain, of the seashore and seaweeds, or bread or cookies baking, of freshly mown hay" (1968, p. 107).

As individuals participate in the Minerva experience, they find clues to their current strengths. The earlier good memories are tied to present emotional satisfactions and strengths. The Minerva experience typically leaves participants with feelings of satisfaction, achievement, energy, and excitement. Paying attention to the whole series of positive events in our lives affirms the healthy feelings within each of us.

that of self-determination. The couple's decision to join was not clearly a matter of free choice, but neither was it an automatic or controlled decision. Their decision to remain in the society, however, increasingly was based less on choice than on pressure from within the society itself.

The second element was one that fascinated the couple at the beginning of their life in the society: their newfound inner experiences. Their moments of elation and joyful exuberance fit our description of peak experiences. The moments were so pleasurable that the couple sought to experience more of them. In the early days, time spent with the other society members did feel good, did seem right, and did meet the couple's needs to belong, for esteem, and for actualization.

However, as time passed, so did the couple's feelings of elation. They discovered that they were different from other members of the society. The committed members believed and acted in ways that the couple did not enjoy nor wish to duplicate. The couple came to see and then value their own individual traits, their unique qualities that set them apart and eventually sent them parting. Our final topic in this chapter looks at that phenomenon: how we see ourselves as different and unique. Leonard Cohen wrote about this sense of uniqueness.

EXPLORATION IN WELL-BEING

Your Uniqueness

Look at the ways in which *you* are unique. You probably know that your fingerprints are different than everyone else's. Your retinal patterns and your chromosomal patterns are unique, too. Try now to consider your other unique aspects. Draw up a list of as many of your unique characteristics—characteristics that *no one* else is likely to have—as you can.

Once you have prepared this uniqueness list, draw up a second list of the ways in which you are different from *most* people around you. Use the following topic headings.

Facial features

Body features

Clothing

Language

Values

Interests

Ways of thinking

Emotional reactions

If you find these categories too general, become more detailed. Look at the wrinkles on the back of your knuckles. Look in a mirror. Study the tiny solar

I wonder if my fingerprints
Get lonely in the crowd
There are no others like them
and that should make them proud

(Cohen, quoted in Snyder & Fromkin, 1980, p. 4)

Individuation

Individuation is being aware of oneself as distinct and separate in a group. Allport wrote

. . . the outstanding characteristic of man is his individuality. . . . He is a unique creation of the forces of nature. There was never a person just like him, and there never will be again. . . . All during our waking life, and even in our dreams, we recognize and deal with people as separate, distinct, and unique individuals.

(Allport, 1961, p. 4)

Despite our frequent discomfort about our uniqueness, we all want to perceive ourselves as unique. One of the fundamental human struggles is against the social forces that try to diminish individuality. For example, a young woman I knew was acutely conscious of having a head larger

explosions around the pupils of your eyes. See the caves and valleys on the surface of your tongue. Think about the particular experiences you had while growing up that no one else could have had in just the same ways. Recall the times that made you aware of how privileged you were to be you.

The variety of unique aspects people identify about themselves can be seen in the following statements students have written:

My nose and the shape of my jaw are different than anyone else's. I have a plastic insert in my nose to keep it from collapsing.

My singing, writing, painting and past experiences are all different.

My place in the world and my relationship with God are unique.

What's unique is the way I make many different ideologies work for me at once: feminism, black politics, my mother's kitchen.

The way things taste to me, the sound of my voice, and the way I smile. The way I run. My conception of the universe.

How I kiss is different than anyone else. So is the way I squish mud between my toes.

The way I conceive of everything, life, the universe, and my imagination is unique.

My teeth and pattern of dental treatment. In fact the whole pattern of my life experiences is unique.

Nobody else has a body build just like mine, funny shaped chest and all. And there is no other graduate of Manchester Central High School here.

than average size and a crooked mouth. As long as she wore hairstyles and makeup that attempted to hide these features and make her look like everyone else, she felt that she looked bad. Once she understood that her characteristics were uniquely her, she wore teased hairstyles that exaggerated the size of her head and lipstick that made her mouth seem more prominent. Only then did she feel good about herself. She reported that others thought she looked more physically attractive, too.

The better a person adapts to his or her uniqueness, the more freedom of action that person has. Furthermore, the more comfortable a person is with his or her own uniqueness, the greater tolerance that person is likely to have of the individuality of others, according to Snyder and Fromkin (1980). In their book, *Uniqueness: The Human Pursuit of Difference,* they concluded that a heightened sense of uniqueness promotes the following:

1. A sense of responsibility for events around you. When you see yourself as separate from crowds, you are more likely to act helpfully in emergencies, taking responsibility for those in need of assistance.

All people want to perceive themselves as unique, but social forces attempt to diminish individuality. The more comfortable a person is with his or her unique personality, the more tolerant that person is likely to be of others.

2. You are more able to nurture the individual identities of those around you for whom you care and with whom you work.

3. You are more likely to be an oddball, able to come up with creative and innovative ideas.

4. You are more at peace with yourself, because you have come to accept yourself as you are.

There may be some problems with the search for uniqueness, if it is overdone. People can go beyond having a simple feeling of uniqueness to feeling vain, having an overinflated sense of their own worth, and having an exaggerated and conceited self-image. However, for most of us, understanding our uniqueness enhances our relationships with others. When we are comfortable and happy with ourselves, we can be kinder and more tolerant of those we value.

Being Rubricized

Rubrics

When people meet us for the first time, they tend to rubricize us; that is, they place us in simple categories or *rubrics*. They see us as they have seen others like us—as strong men, slight men, tall women, short women, conforming people, independent people, fraternity men, sorority women, typical yankees, typical southerners, or typical people from the Bronx. The list goes on indefinitely. Maslow called rubricizing

> A quick, easy cataloguing whose function is to make unnecessary the effort required by more careful, ideographic perceiving or thinking . . . all that has to be perceived is that one abstracted characteristic which indicates his belongingness in a class, e.g., babies, waiters, Swedes, schizophrenics, generals, nurses, etc. What is stressed in rubricizing is the category in which the person belongs, of which he is a sample, *not* the person as such.

(Maslow, 1968, p. 127)

When people place us into an overly simple category, they deny our individuality. Everyone is far richer and more complex than any single label can describe. Part of well-being is freedom from being rubricized and freedom from habitually rubricizing others. That freedom occurs when we truly see the other person. When others seek to know more about us than the obvious category within which we fit, we feel sympathetically understood and respected and we experience a sense of personal dignity.

Thomas Szasz, a psychiatrist who has been an outspoken critic of mental health practices, has claimed that psychiatric diagnoses are rubrics. Szasz (1970) has made the accusation that psychiatrists' and psychologists' diagnostic labels are forms of bad-mouthing. He has asserted that psychiatric diagnoses have a negative, destructive quality and that the labels

Does this picture confirm or negate common rubrics concerning women?

psychotic, psychopathic, and neurotic are part of the insult vocabulary of all Americans. The chief resident in psychiatry at a metropolitan hospital told me a story about the time he suggested to his supervisor that they invite Szasz to speak about depreciatory uses of psychiatric labelling. The supervisor replied, "What? Invite that paranoid schizophrenic down here?"

The phenomenon of negatively categorizing people also has been studied in prejudice research. **Prejudice** is the long-term, persistent over-categorizing of others, so that individuals are seen primarily as members of undesirable groups with negative stereotypes.

Prejudice

> And yet the prejudiced person almost always *claims* that some alleged difference is the cause of his attitude. He seems never to consider the possibility of tolerating, let alone loving, people in out-groups who are (he thinks) dull, sly, aggressive, or even smelly—not even though he may feel affection for similarly ill-favored members of his family or circle of friends.
>
> *(Allport, 1958, p. 85)*

The alternative to the closed mind of prejudice is an open mind that sees and accepts individuality. No one sees anything without drawing on some past experiences or perceptions; otherwise, nothing would be seen. Our past experiences allow us to organize and understand the world. Yet, keeping within the boundaries of those experiences, the open mind does not leap to conclusions about others.

WELL-BEING IN PERSPECTIVE

At the beginning of this book, we defined well-being generally as overall life satisfaction combined with positive affect and little negative affect. From that beginning point, we have explored the nature of adjustment and well-being within major areas of personal functioning. These areas of functioning overlap, of course. The person with high self-esteem often is likely to successfully manage the routine stressors of life. In the same vein, a person who is able to enter into and maintain friendships in positive ways will be more likely to successfully enter and maintain love and work relationships. There indeed is continuity in the lives of most individuals.

However, some sources of satisfaction and accomplishment are de-

Prejudice persistently overcategorizes others as members of undesirable groups, promoting negative stereotypes. What negative stereotypes does this photo promote?

cidedly more meaningful for us. No human being is fully and optimally functioning in every possible aspect of life, and we should not expect to be. Instead, our attainments of some successes, of some sources of self-worth and effectiveness, are significant. An old Middle Eastern saying is, "Many roads lead to Mecca." Many paths lead to positive adjustment and well-being. This chapter's discussion of the need for flexibility in making choices and the importance of determining one's own options in life has illustrated that principle. Many of the fences around our possible pathways are self-imposed and can be self-dismantled as well.

The person who expects all moments to be exuberant times of ecstatic elation will be predictably disappointed. Adjustment is not a state

THE DANCE OF FULFILLMENT

Dancing for me is like putting very small pieces of a puzzle together with intermittent moments of realizing it's not just a puzzle but another more beautiful world I'm creating.

Hooking together those puzzle pieces is really a process of accomplishing small tasks. One day, you go to the studio and realize today you can point your foot more precisely, or balance for longer, or swing your leg higher. When this happens I have a sense of progress, of I-willed-this-to-happen and a small measure of it now has come to be. It grows from there. As a part of my body responds more sensitively to commands, a sense of mastery develops. The mastery in turn allows me to make the movements my own—like notes to a song I sing with my own interpretation. I then experience a sense of my own power, exert my will, and see a result. A deep feeling of efficacy shoots me beyond what I thought I could do. And as a result my own self-concept expands and my self-esteem deepens. I exist for a moment in another more beautiful world.

What goes on in my mind is achieving competency. First, I conceive the act to perform. Second, I vividly imagine how I would like to see the act performed. Third, my fear that I haven't the talent or courage to actualize the imagined act is confronted. Fourth, I go ahead and do it despite my fears and self-doubts. My pride in overcoming the fear gives me greater confidence to perform nearer my imagined ideal.

Inevitably, I am disappointed in not achieving the ideal. At best I then accept the disparity between the actual and ideal performance. Finally, I desire to try again because each re-attempt closes further and further the gap between the actual and ideal, between the puzzle pieces and the other more beautiful worlds.

(Ann C. Freeman, 1985)

TABLE 15–2 A Summary of Further Pathways Toward Well-Being	
Toward Well-Being	**Away from Well-Being**
Self-determination	Other determined or automatic behaviors
Flexibility in life choices	Rigidity in life choices
Embraces own uniqueness	Rejects own uniqueness
Sees other as they are, and is seen by others as he or she is	Rubricizes others and is rubricized

"One day, you go to the studio and realize today you can point your foot more precisely, or balance for longer, or swing your leg higher. When this happens . . . I then experience a sense of my own power. . . . I exist for a moment in another more beautiful world."

When people reach the state of well-being, they do not experience unending happiness. Instead, although they frequently feel happy and satisfied with their lives, they nonetheless experience problematic periods. However, their adjustment allows them to manage these bad periods successfully and remain secure.

of unbroken happiness—that state occurs only in dreams and children's stories; it is not the reality of human existence. Rather, adjustment provides frequent moments of happiness, satisfaction in the achievement of goals, and the security of knowing that the in-between, problematic periods can be managed and will pass.

SUMMARY

Self-determination is an important part of well-being. Allowing oneself no choice at all, also known as Hobson's choice, is a common problem. We can increase our life choices by taking flexible approaches to adjustment and through constructionalism, or increasing our repertoire of possible behaviors.

Maslow (1968) placed self-actualization at the top of a hierarchy of needs, in which needs are addressed in a particular order. The hierarchy has physiological needs, safety needs, belongingness needs, esteem needs, and self-actualization needs. Self-actualization itself refers to achieving the fulfillment of human potential, seeking after truth, and having deep integrity and honesty. Self-actualization may be considered a product of a value system as much as a scientific phenomenon. It is considered a temporary state of being rather than a long-established trait exclusive to a few remarkable people.

Peak experiences are moments of extraordinary fulfillment and ecstatic happiness that occur at some time for most people. In contrast, peak performance is observable behavior that is much superior to ordinary functioning. When people achieve a peak performance, they report that they focus clearly on what they do, they feel free from restraints, and they feel great vitality and strength.

Every person wishes to be seen as unique and individual. The actual process of becoming an independent person is called individuation. To individuate, you must accept the ways in which you differ from everyone else and positively value those differences.

When we are not seen as individuals, we are being rubricized, or lumped into overly simple categories. Prejudice or negative sex role stereotypes arise from the squeezing of people into such rubrics. An open mind, free from jumping to quick conclusions and making closed value judgments, is the opposite of a prejudiced, rubricizing mind.

Key Terms

Competence-motivated
Competition-motivated
Constructionalism
Cult
Hobson's choice
Individuation
Maslow's hierarchy of needs
Minerva experience

Peak experience
Peak performance
Prejudice
Rubrics
Self-actualization
Self-determination
Triggers

Recommended Reading

Laski, M. (1968). *Ecstasy: A study of some secular and religious experiences.* New York: Greenwood Press. This book, just over five hundred pages long, is devoted to actual reports of wonderful, inspirational, ecstatic experiences. It is worth reading just to feel good about these people and their lovely experiences.

Maslow, A.H. (1968). *Toward a psychology of being* (2nd ed.). Princeton, NJ: Van Nostrand Insight. Peak experiences, growth motivation, and rubricizing all are discussed in this thoughtful, readable paperback. This is Maslow at his most human, provocative, and organized.

Snyder, C.R. & Fromkin, H.L. (1980). *Uniqueness: The human pursuit of difference.* New York: Plenum. Despite the cartoons throughout, this book is a serious and comprehensive presentation of uniqueness theory and research. It brings together an impressive collection of scholarly and literary sources.

Psychological Disorders

The towering obelisk of Denny Chimes not only dominates the central part of the campus at which I teach, but the area around it is one of the main thoroughfares and gathering places for the University. I was walking past Denny Chimes, absentmindedly listening to the chimes when a man tugged at my elbow and then fell in step alongside me. He was about fifty years old, his gray hair cut short and flat. He was dressed casually, but immaculately neat, and carrying a canvas sports bag.

He tugged again at my arm and asked me:

"Do you know who the three greatest men are in the history of the world?"

I don't know if anyone could determine that except by the most subjective judgments. I told him I didn't know. He then explained:

"The greatest men in the history of the world are Jesus Christ, Napoleon Bonaparte, and Everingham Marquette." He paused, then looked intently at me, and went on. "And I am all three."

At that point I withdrew into my best clinical detachment, and gave him a couple of "uh-huhs," "mm-hmms," and head nods. He was not deterred. He then wanted to know how he could alert the country about the threat of invasion from outer space. Again I told him I didn't know. He promptly began to tell me about his efforts to notify the national authorities.

He had started with the local police department. They informed him that they didn't deal with interplanetary law enforcement, and they suggested the FBI. So he called the FBI. Their spokesman pointed out that the FBI mandate limited it to investigations within the United States.

His next call was to the Central Intelligence Agency. That agency referred him to the Pentagon. At the time he stopped me, he was a regular caller to the evening duty officer at the Pentagon. He received from me what he apparently had received from the other targets of his declarations: polite skepticism and eventual disinterest. He left my side, crossed the street, and sought out someone walking the other way.

THE NATURE OF PSYCHOLOGICAL DISORDERS

Mr. Everingham Marquette presented many components of normal behavior. His emotions were calm. His tone of voice was well modulated, his demeanor earnest, and his general actions not unusual. He showed no obvious signs of disorganized thinking or bizarre behaviors, and he was not hallucinating. If one accepted the truth of his statements, he would have been seen as rational. Let us assume that this man was able to function adequately in areas unrelated to his far-fetched beliefs. He was not someone whose actions were clearly "crazy." Yet we can recognize that his words and beliefs were strange and unrealistic. How, then, do we understand what was wrong with Mr. Marquette, and with other people who are psychologically disturbed? This appendix seeks to answer that question.

You may recall in Chapter 1, I wrote of the see-saw model of adjustment, with maladjustment at one end, adjustment the balance point in the middle, and well-being at the other far point on this continuum. In this appendix, I focus on the problems that cluster around the maladjustment extreme: the problems that appear in recognizable patterns and which are of sufficient severity that they may be diagnosed as psychological disorders.

Diagnosing Mr. Marquette or indeed any individual consists of looking for a match between the individual's characteristics and categories of psychological disorder. This matching of individual and category is a basic element in science. When a butterfly is observed, the scientist will seek to classify it with similar species. The functional equivalent of diagnosis occurs with geological formations, chemical elements, all living creatures, and indeed all phenomena. One of the tasks of science is to look for what the individual case has in common, and not in common, with other subjects previously classified. So it is with psychological diagnosis. It brings order and structure to what otherwise would be a chaotic and uninterpretable array of behaviors.

Although incomplete guidelines limited to a few disorders have been in existence for over a century, the existence of a standard, comprehensive diagnostic manual for psychological disorders is relatively new. The first edition of the American Psychiatric Association's *Diagnostic and Statistic Manual* (DSM-I) was published in 1952. Two new editions, and thirty-five years later, the original concept has evolved considerably. Many concepts have been deleted, such as homosexuality, which is no longer considered a diagnosable mental disorder. Others have been modified or added, frequently as a result of research about the nature of the disorder.

The primary source in this chapter is the *Diagnostic and Statistical Manual of Mental Disorders,* Third Edition-Revised (DSM-III-R), of the American Psychiatric Association (1987). This appendix serves as an introduction to psychological disorders as defined by the DSM-III-R, rather than serving as a broader review of research or theory of psychological illness. When I give no references for a diagnostic category, it will have been drawn from the DSM-III-R. However, some cautions about the DSM-III-R are appropriate. As a start, the reader should not assume that the diagnoses are enduring truths of science, as are, for instance, the Periodic Table of Elements in chemistry. Indeed they are much closer to Robert's Rules of Order in meetings, in the sense that they are based on substantial agreement by experts on what is sensible and what works.

Each diagnosed mental disorder is not necessarily a unique and separate phenomenon, quite apart from all other disorders. Rather it is understood that some disorders overlap and that individuals may suffer from two or more disorders simultaneously. The DSM-III-R definition of a mental disorder is used in this appendix.

> . . . a clinically significant behavioral or psychological syndrome or pattern that occurs in a person and that is associated with present distress (a painful symptom) or disability . . . this syndrome or pattern must not

be merely an expectable response to a particular event, e.g., the death of a loved one. . . . Neither deviant behavior, e.g., political, religious, or social, nor conflicts that are primarily between the individual and society are mental disorders unless the deviance or conflict is a symptom of a dysfunction in the person.

(American Psychiatric Association, 1987, p xxii)

Note the words "clinically significant" at the beginning of this definition. Many idiosyncracies and peculiarities may exist in a person without a disorder being present. Behaviors are evaluated as disorders only when the individual is substantially disabled or truly emotionally distraught. Thus, neither the daily hassles discussed in Chapter 4 are part of disorders, nor are ordinary, mild worries about school, dating, or work.

Two points are important to reemphasize. The depression following loss of home and family in an earthquake is not necessarily a psycholog-

Severity of Psychosocial Stressors

Psychological disorders occur in the context of whatever else has been happening in the individual's life. Part of the assessment of psychological disorders is evaluation of the seriousness of the stressors in that person's life. The DSM-III (American Psychiatric Association, 1980) utilizes a rating scale from 1—no apparent stressor—to 7—catastrophic level of stress. The "average person" test is applied; a judgment is made of how stressful the known circumstances would be to the average person, and then a rating is made on the seven-point scale. Note that these are not ratings of the person, but rather ratings of the stressors to which the person is subjected. The term psychosocial stressors is meant to indicate that these events or situations may take place in the family, at school or at work, or involving any social circumstance which may have psychological impact. The table to the right presents the DSM-III examples of stressors.

ical disorder. Neither is anxiety about chemical weapons of war or about political candidates with whom one disagrees. Such depression and anxiety are expected reactions to crises. We consider strong, uncomfortable emotions and impairments to be disorders when they do not correspond to traumatic social events or when they are not temporary, passing concerns. With these cautions in mind, we may now consider our first category of psychological disorders: anxiety disorders.

ANXIETY DISORDERS

In the small commuter plane that flies from my university town to Atlanta, seventeen passengers are seated. Passengers sit in narrow rows on each side of the cramped cabin. The young man sitting near me was petrified as the plane rolled for take-off. He gripped tightly the side of the seat, he was

Stressor code	Severity	Adult examples	Child or adolescent examples
1	None	No apparent psychosocial stressor	No apparent psychosocial stressor
2	Minimal	Minor violation of the law; small bank loan	Vacation with family
3	Mild	Argument with neighbor; change in work hours	Change in schoolteacher; new school year
4	Moderate	New career; death of close friend; pregnancy	Chronic parental fighting; change to new school; illness of close relative; birth of sibling
5	Severe	Serious illness in self or family; major financial loss; marital separation; birth of child	Death of peer; divorce of parents; arrest; hospitalization; persistent and harsh parental discipline
6	Extreme	Death of close relative; divorce	Death of parent or sibling; repeated physical or sexual abuse
7	Catastrophic	Concentration camp experience; devastating natural disaster	Multiple family deaths

American Psychiatric Association, 1980, p. 27.

shaking, and his breath came in short gasps. It didn't take a psychologist to know that he was terrified. After the plane landed, we spoke. He explained that he had no choice about flying this day. However, he usually avoided planes, automobiles, elevators, tents, and other confined spaces as much as he could. Often he had no choice. He was afraid of dying in such situations and overwhelmed by this fear. It is likely that he was suffering from a form of anxiety disorder that is called a panic disorder with agoraphobia.

The term anxiety disorder is relatively new to the use of official diagnoses. What we recognize today as anxiety disorders were traditionally part of the larger group of neurotic disorders. However, the term neurosis has a specific meaning. It was conceptualized by Freud and his followers who referred to neurological-like symptoms stemming from anxiety over forbidden impulses or taboo memories. In Chapter 2 on theories of personality we have noted this basic psychoanalytic assumption that some impulses and memories are so unacceptable that they are repressed from awareness, and they make their way out in the form of physical symptoms.

Was Freud right? Are there in fact repressed memories and unacceptable impulses that cause these disordered behaviors? Whether the answer is yes or no has cogent implications for understanding causes and initiating research and treatment. The 1987 DSM-III-R essentially gives yes as its answer, a position taken in the face of conflicting professional opinions.

With these introductory remarks, now anxiety disorders may be addressed. Three distinct kinds of psychological disorders are grouped under this heading. They are panic disorders, phobias, and obsessive-compulsive disorders.

Panic Disorders

Recurring periods of intense fear or catastrophic apprehension are basic features of panic disorders. At least four attacks must have occurred within four weeks. Furthermore at least one of these must have been unexpected. If the precipitating situation is giving a rare public speech or the individual is otherwise the center of attention, we do not call it a panic disorder. Rather such events are more within the range of typical adjustmental crises.

Panic disorders may occur either with or without agoraphobia, which is defined as the fear of being in a place from which escape is impossible. The young man on the commuter plane suffered from agoraphobia. At its most severe, agoraphobia leads to the individual being almost completely housebound, unable to go out because of the fear of being trapped in a closed space or public place.

Phobias

One of the phobias—agoraphobia—has already been described. We now consider the phobias in general, which are intense, incapacitating fears of particular situations or objects. When the feared event is a social situation, the disorder is called social phobia:

> . . . the person is exposed to possible scrutiny by others and fears that he or she may do something or act in a way that will be humiliating or embarrassing. The social phobic fear may be circumscribed, such as fears of being unable to continue talking while speaking in public, choking on food when eating in front of others, being unable to urinate in a public restroom, or having a hand tremble when writing in the presence of others. In other cases the social phobic fears may involve most social situations, such as general fears of saying foolish things or not being able to answer questions in social situations.
>
> *(American Psychiatric Association, 1987, p. 241)*

Before we leave panic disorders and phobias, the intense nature of the anxiety and fear should be reemphasized. These are not passing moments of minor distress. You may be able to understand the severity if you imagine the greatest terror or upset you have ever experienced. Individuals with panic disorders and phobias have just such an uncontrollable fear of imminent catastrophe. What makes it a disorder is that the panic and fears arise in response to events that most people in society assess as harmless, such as being in an elevator, seeing a spider, or being in a crowd.

Obsessive-Compulsive Disorders

Obsessions are ideas or images that persist repeatedly, intrusively, and cause distress. Compulsions are repetitive and intentional behaviors designed to prevent some situation, and they often occur because of obsessive thoughts. The obsessive thought that one is dirty and evil may, for example, be followed by compulsive bathing and scrubbing of one's body as many as twenty or thirty times a day.

Obsessions and compulsions have two defining characteristics: (1) the person understands that these are excessive and irrational thoughts or actions, and (2) the person tries to deny or avoid the obsessive thoughts or compulsive acts. The compulsion may also be designed to prevent some event that is viewed with apprehension.

Obsessive thoughts and compulsive behaviors are diagnosed as a disorder when they become so intrusive that they cause serious distress, or fill much of the person's day, or interfere with work, social activities, or other routines. An example of an intrusive obsession is the repeated thought to murder a parent or child.

Highest Level of Functioning during the Past Year

One crucial piece of information about psychological disorders is the individual's most successful functioning in the recent past. Prior adjustment can indeed predict future adjustment because people in temporary psychological disarray tend to return to their characteristic states.

Adaptive functioning is assessed from three sources of information. The first source is social functioning, most particularly the quality of friendships and family relationships. The second source is occupational functioning, a term that includes not only work, but school and homemaking as well. Comfort is used to judge occupational functioning in addition to the more obvious criteria of quality and quantity of work accomplished. The third source is leisure time. High levels of leisure time functioning would reflect a wide range of and considerable depth in recreation and hobbies. Leisure time activities should be very pleasurable to reflect high adaptive levels.

Like the severity of stressors rating, a seven-point scale is used to rate high level of functioning during the past year. A rating of one indicates superior functioning. The mid-point rating of four indicates fair functioning. A rating of seven indicates gross impairment during the past year. The following table presents the DSM-III examples of highest functioning at each of the seven levels.

Levels	Adult examples	Child or adolescent examples
1. **Superior** Unusually effective functioning in social relations, occupational functioning, and use of leisure time.	Single parent living in deteriorating neighborhood takes excellent care of children and home, has warm relations with friends, and finds time for pursuit of hobby	A 12-year-old girl gets superior grades in school, is extremely popular among her peers, and excels in many sports. She does all of this with apparent ease and comfort.

Levels	Adult examples	Child or adolescent examples
2. Very good Better than average functioning in social relations, occupational functioning, and use of leisure time.	A 65-year-old retired widower does some volunteer work, often sees old friends, and pursues hobbies	An adolescent boy gets excellent grades, works part-time, has several close friends, and plays banjo in a jazz band. He admits to some distress in "keeping up with everything."
3. Good No more than slight impairment in either social or occupational functioning.	A woman with many friends functions extremely well at a difficult job, but says "the strain is too much."	An 8-year-old boy does well in school, has several friends, but bullies younger children.
4. Fair Moderate impairment in either social relations or occupational functioning, or some impairment in both.	A lawyer has trouble carrying through assignments; has several acquaintances, but hardly any close friends.	A 10-year-old does poorly in school, but has adequate peer and family relations.
5. Poor Marked impairment in either social relations or occupational functioning, or moderate impairment in both.	A man with one or two friends has trouble keeping a job for more than a few weeks.	A 14-year-old boy almost fails in school and has trouble getting along with his peers.
6. Very poor Marked impairment in both social relations and occupational functioning.	A woman is unable to do any of her housework and has violent outbursts toward family and neighbors.	A 6-year-old girl needs special help in all subjects and has virtually no peer relationships.
7. Grossly impaired Gross impairment in virtually all areas of functioning.	An elderly man needs supervision to maintain minimal personal hygiene and is usually incoherent.	A 4-year-old boy needs constant restraint to avoid hurting himself and is almost totally lacking in skills.

American Psychiatric Association, 1980, p. 27.

In Chapter 4, we discussed one further anxiety disorder: posttraumatic stress disorder (PTSD). This is the persistent reexperiencing of unusual and traumatic events that follow military combat, individual rape or assault, or natural disasters, such as floods.

SOMATOFORM DISORDERS

Throughout much of the history of organized medicine, one repeated puzzle was the apparently well patient who would display or complain of physical symptoms for which no organic cause could be detected. Some of these cases were particularly troubling to the examining physicians because the symptoms didn't make sense. An example is the person who fell to the ground in a violent seizure whenever she left her house. No environmental or chemical cause could be found, yet the patient could be seen shaking controllably on the ground. The seizure was not feigned. The patient was banging her body against the ground near her doorway, thrashing up and down in ways that seemed authentic. Eventually symptoms of this sort were understood to be caused by extraordinarily powerful psychological processes, and these symptoms were identified as being part of a category of neurosis known as somatoform disorders.

Two elements must be present for concluding that a somatoform disorder is present. First, physical symptoms must be present for which there are no known or likely organic causes. Second, a strong positive link must be present between the physical symptoms and psychological processes. We will discuss two of the somatoform disorders: conversion disorders and hypochondriasis.

Conversion Disorders

In this disorder the individual actually loses some physical capabilities or displays symptoms as a result of psychological factors being converted into body malfunctions. Among the most common physical malfunctions are blindness, paralysis, anesthesia (loss of feeling), and seizures. What are called conversion disorders today have a 3000-year history, from the ancient Greek civilization to the twentieth century, of being known as hysteria. The term hysteria is derived from the Greek word for uterus or womb; at one time the uterus was believed to wander throughout women's bodies afflicting them with this disorder. At the time of Freud's practice in Vienna, widespread denial and discomfort with sexual impulses was present, especially in women. Freud inferred that like other neurotic problems, these physical symptoms were in fact repressed sexual memories, disguised and forcing themselves into consciousness.

As the expression of sexual and aggressive impulses become more accepted, conversion disorders become less frequent in western societies.

Many psychologists and psychiatrists of my acquaintance have never seen a patient with such a condition. However, in less developed and less sophisticated countries conversion disorders are more frequent. Data gathered in India, for example, indicate that about one third of all psychiatric disorders in that country were conversion disorders.

In 1986 I had the opportunity to observe this cultural difference first-hand. While in Bangalore, I sat in during an intake interview with a 20-year-old woman with a conversion disorder. On two separate occasions she had seizures while in the bathroom, in which she fell to the floor, her left leg frozen in place, elevated above her body. No physiological cause was present. The diagnostic conclusion was that she was experiencing absolutely unacceptable sexual and hostile feelings toward a family member, and that these feelings triggered the presenting complaint.

The movie *Tommy* illustrated another such conversion disorder. Tommy was a young boy who watched his father murdered by the man living with his mother. The boy's reaction was to develop a conversion disorder in the form of becoming mute, deaf, and blind.

Hypochondriasis

The person with hypochondriasis is preoccupied with believing that he or she has a serious illness (or is preoccupied with the fear of having such an illness), in spite of the results of physical examinations to the contrary. No matter how much they are reassured by physicians or family, hypochondriacal patients remain fixed in their beliefs that they are very ill. They often fear they have cancer or are having heart attacks. Some patients interpret every cough or every mouth sore as proof that they are dying.

Hypochondriacal patients are reluctant to accept psychological treatment. Even when they are referred to mental health centers, they decline. They are so convinced that their disorders are malignant, fatal, or assuredly physical, they are insulted by suggestions they talk about their problems in psychotherapy. Instead they shop for doctors and medical centers who can affirm that they are indeed ill. This medical shopping spree is accompanied by their complaints of insensitive and incompetent physicians.

One related disorder of physical symptoms without organic causes is known as a factitious disorder. In this case the patient deliberately feigns or produces physical symptoms in order to be treated as ill or be hospitalized. The word factitious has essentially the same meaning as fictitious: made up, not real. What differentiates factitious disorders from other somatoform disorders is the *intentional* production of symptoms. Sophisticated individuals who have wide medical knowledge may deliberately induce rashes, bleeding, fevers, or complaints of pain. It is also considered a factitious disorder when the person complains of anxiety, nightmares, hallucinations, or other intentional psychological symptoms, produced so the patient will be cared for as sick.

PERSONALITY DISORDERS

When we think of the nature of personality, we include aspects of thinking, perceiving, or relating that are relatively long-standing. Passing moods are excluded from this definition in favor of enduring traits. Personality disorders are seen:

> . . . only when *personality traits* are inflexible and maladaptive and cause either significant functional impairment or subjective distress. . . .

> *(American Psychiatric Association, 1987, p. 335)*

Each of the key elements in this definition will be considered.

Inflexible and maladaptive traits. These traits endure in such a way that the person may be considered rigid and not responsive to other people and to changing events in the environment. Individuals with personality disorders go beyond normal consistency. They continue their actions even when problems arise and when the behaviors do not fit the immediate situations.

Significant functional impairment. Personality disorders diminish the ability to achieve the usual tasks of life. Work performance and interpersonal relationships suffer. These individuals are not efficient and often are not even adequate in meeting their objectives.

Subjective distress. Our criterion for a personality disorder states that significant functional impairment *or* subjective distress is present. By subjective distress, we mean that a person may be satisfactory as an employee or friend or in social relationships, but may be personally uncomfortable with problematic, privately held feelings.

If any two personality disorders stand in contrast to each other, it may well be antisocial personality disorders and schizoid personality disorders. The former is dramatic, outgoing, risk-taking. The latter is withdrawn and aloof from contact with other people. However, they have in common their limited abilities to form close bonds with others. We will now examine these two specific personality disorders in more detail.

Antisocial Personality Disorder

What accounts for the actions of a man who repeatedly steals, who assaults or harms others without the slightest twinge of conscience, who feels no attachment or loyalty to other people, and who does not find conventional punishments to be unpleasant or deterrents? Such persons have been known to us almost since the beginning of recorded human history. In the early chronicles they have been labelled as possessed or unequivocally evil. By the 19th century, however, such individuals were given the diagnosis of moral insanity. They were seen as sufficiently lacking self-control and the will to obey rules that their moral judgment was diseased.

In the twentieth century the behavior patterns acquired new names. They were called sociopathy, psychopathy, and now the current accepted diagnostic term, antisocial personality disorder. Hervey Cleckley (1964) has described such individuals as presenting a mask of sanity. On the surface they are able to appear more or less normal. Often they are charming and clever. Underneath, however, they are without guilt or remorse at their persistent antisocial acts. When they break rules and law, it is not to achieve reasonable goals. That is, the label of psychopath does not apply to the individual who steals to purchase goods he simply cannot afford. Rather the actions are impulsive and irrational. Many crimes are committed with no more thought or feeling than most of us feel killing an insect.

But why do psychopaths behave the way they do? This question has sufficiently intrigued researchers that thousands of articles, studies, and conjectures have appeared. Part of the reason for such a flood of information is sheer fascination with callous crimes and unfeeling persons. An equal part of the rationale for such interest has been the complexity of the phenomenon. Many different kinds of behaviors lead to diagnoses of antisocial personality disorders and dozens of theories have been put forth. In his book *Understanding and Treating the Psychopath,* Dennis Doren (1987) has described the four most prominent theories.

1. *Deficiency in role-playing ability.* This theory holds that psychopaths— we will refer to them here in Doren's usage as psychopaths—are unable to play or take conventional social roles. They cannot put themselves in the shoes or mind or feelings of other people. The inability to role-play means that psychopaths do not consider the effects of their behaviors on others. Although psychopaths do seem inadequate on psychological test measures related to role-playing, this theory has been criticized for being too narrow and too vague in its basic definitions.

2. *Impaired learning.* This theory holds that psychopaths are genetically predisposed from birth to be deficient in learning. These people are highly distractible and uninhibited. Their cortical functioning is typically underaroused. Thus they do not experience emotions as strongly and are not easily conditioned. Simply put, they break laws and rules because they are not fearful enough of punishment.

3. *Pathological stimulation seeking.* From this point of view, psychopaths need more stimulation than most other people. They seek out thrills, excitement, and risky situations because such events are highly stimulating. Boredom and routine are seriously unpleasant for them.

4. *Brain lesions that lead to behavior perseveration.* The word lesions here is used to describe contusions and abnormalities in one particular brain system: the limbic system. This theory holds that such lesions interfere with mechanisms that would ordinarily inhibit or disrupt behaviors. Without such inhibitions, psychopaths persevere—that is, continue inappropriately—actions that the nature of the situation should have made them cease.

This is far from an exhaustive list of theories. Doren has proposed one more approach that seeks to integrate the best of these elements. It is clear, whatever theory one accepts, that certain consistent elements are present. These are indeed individuals who are poor at role-playing,

The Three Clusters of Personality Disorders

Personality disorders are grouped in three clusters in DSM-III-R. An outline is presented here.

Cluster A: Odd and eccentric behaviors

The paranoid personality disorder: This person is characterized by pervasive and unwarranted tendencies to see others as exploiting, harming, or demeaning.

The schizoid personality disorder: These are solitary people who are indifferent to social relationships, including family relationships. By definition they are unable to have much range in either experiencing emotions or expressing emotions.

The schizotypal personality disorder: This diagnosis is reserved for individuals who are peculiar in their thinking, behavior, or appearance, but are not sufficiently peculiar to be schizophrenic. They do not relate well and show inappropriate feelings such as aloofness, silliness, or suspiciousness.

Cluster B: Emotional and unpredictable behaviors

The antisocial personality disorder: These people are irresponsible, do not conform to social norms, and perform antisocial acts, such as stealing or assaulting others.

The borderline personality disorder: The key element of this disorder is instability in moods and relationships. They are extraordinarily variable and often flamboyantly dramatic people.

they are impaired in many kinds of learning and conditioning from punishment, they do indeed seek risks, and they do not show the inhibitions that customarily discourage impulsive harmful, or aggressive acts.

Schizoid Personality Disorder

People with this disorder are passive, detached, and often without friends. They tend to be lifeless and sluggish. Other people see them as dull or as cold fish. When mild forms of this disorder are present, a lack of responsiveness may be observed. Events that would provoke elation or anger in other people have no effect on them. As two researchers in the area of psychological disorders have observed:

> They work quietly at their jobs and rarely do they attract any attention from those who would have contact with them. They tend to fade into the scenery and would prefer to live their lives undisturbed were it not

The narcissistic personality disorder: An inflated sense of one's self-importance characterizes this disorder, along with minimal empathy for the feelings of other people, and exaggerated sensitivity to how others judge them. Like other personality disorders, this type is impaired in attaining life goals and is distressed about the effects of his or her behaviors.

Cluster C: Anxious and fearful behaviors

The avoidant personality disorder: In this pattern, high levels of social discomfort are associated with both being timid and being overwhelmed by negative evaluations. Thus, as the name suggests, they actively avoid social or occupational activities that would have even a hint of criticism.

The dependent personality disorder: These submissive and dependent people continually seek advice and reassurance. They cannot take independent actions and are passive in both work and interpersonal relationships.

Obsessive-compulsive personality disorder: These people are both perfectionistic and inflexible. Nothing they do ever feels good enough to satisfy them. While true obsessions and compulsive behaviors are not present, the related traits of excessive demands on themselves and personal rigidity in goals and actions do become problematic.

The passive aggressive personality disorder: These individuals sulk, procrastinate, dawdle, or in other ways passively resist ordinary expectations in social and work settings.

for others who place certain social expectations on them. Because they experience few rewards from social interaction, schizoid personalities often turn their attention and talents to interests that do not demand interpersonal contact.

(Millon & Everly, 1985, p. 193–194)

Thus, schizoid personalities appear sometimes in jobs in which no other person is contacted, in solitary hobbies, and in private and insulated living environments.

SCHIZOPHRENIA

If any one disorder is identified in the minds of most people as serious mental illness, it is schizophrenia. After all, the largest numbers of patients residing in psychiatric hospitals are schizophrenic. The most powerful medications are used to treat persons suffering from schizophrenic disorders. Schizophrenic patients are considered to be highly resistant to the most popular and otherwise successful forms of psychotherapy. Furthermore, the term schizophrenic has been with us for over a hundred years and as Davidson and Neale (1986) point out, has gone through major evolutions in its meaning and application.

The dominant characteristic of most schizophrenic individuals is the presence of a thought disorder, in which the thinking and speech are disorganized, incoherent, or bizarre. By disorganized thought we mean fragmented ideas that are difficult to follow. Consider the following response by a schizophrenic man who I asked to subtract sevens from one hundred.

> Seven from 100 is, problem, 93. How does you get 7 from 100? I said 7 from 100 is 7 from 100. How does you get 7 from 100? (How much is 7 from 93?) You do not work it out. That's ignorance in education. 93 is 93 regardless. 7 is 7. Ignorance in education. Wheeeee. Oooooooo. 87. I don't know. 7 from 87. 80. 7 from 93 is 87, 88, 89, 90, 91, 92, that's ignorance education. I don't know why you keep asking. Nine. 1, 2, 3, 4, 5, 6. Listen. That's ignorancy. That's not to be used. That's going to the dead. You know. Ain't no sense keep on raising education to the dead. To the ignorance education. I don't like to participate in ignorancy. It's like falling dead. I don't understand how has an authority to imprison me and bother me. It's been happening since I be in confinement. I don't like to be bothered. I accept it because it meant to happen. I don't like. The mess it's going to be bothered.

These disconnected thoughts are examples of poorly organized thinking patterns. The jumping from topic to unrelated topic is known as loose associations, and is frequent in schizophrenics.

Delusions and hallucinations are common in schizophrenics as well. Delusions are defined as rigidly held beliefs that belie the reality at hand. Delusions, therefore, are fixed, false beliefs. An example of a delusional person would be the patient I saw who believed that his every act was being controlled by spies from Russia. In the morning he would feel paralyzed as part of the invisible rays sent by these skilled operatives as part of a master plan to subvert America. The more I suggested this was only in his mind, the more strongly he held it was all true.

Hallucinations are disturbances in sensory perception including the frequent sensations of feeling outside their own bodies or that everything seems unreal. Auditory hallucinations take the form of hearing voices. These voices sometimes are severely critical, at other times give instructions, and at still other times speak forbidden and unacceptable thoughts. Hallucinations may take the form of any sensory input, including taste, touch, smell, and vision. A hallucination of touch would be the reported experience of insects crawling inside the skin and biting the individual.

A final set of symptoms of schizophrenia relates to affect. In one pattern, the schizophrenic individual appears emotionless. The tone of voice is dulled, the facial expression is indifferent, and little or no animation is present in behavior or communication. In addition to this first pattern of flat affect, an alternative pattern of inappropriate affect is sometimes observed. The emotions that are exhibited simply do not fit the immediate situation. Giggling at serious moments, crying without reason, or fierce raging at innocent companions are all examples.

The DSM-III-R organizes the schizophrenias by types. The most important types are the paranoid type, the disorganized type, and the catatonic type.

Paranoid Schizophrenia

This type differs from other schizophrenics in the relative absence of incoherent thinking, loose associations, or flat or inappropriate affect. It has one clear distinguishing feature: systematic delusions or hallucinations, usually of being persecuted or being a person of grand importance.

Disorganized Schizophrenia

These schizophrenics stand in direct contrast to the paranoid schizophrenic. Where the paranoid type is relatively organized, the disorganized schizophrenic is grossly incoherent, socially inept, jumps uncontrollably from one topic from another, and may often be silly, giggling, and inventing words.

Catatonic Schizophrenia

This third distinct type is described by the DSM-III-R in this manner:

> The essential feature of this type is marked psychomotor disturbance, which may involve stupor, negativism, rigidity, excitement or posturing.

Sometimes there is rapid alternation between the extremes of excitement and stupor. Associated features include stereotypes, mannerisms, and waxy inflexibility.

(American Psychiatric Association, 1987, p. 196)

These individuals are sometimes in a frozen posture: immobile, stiff, oblivious to events and people. At other times they move and talk non-stop. With relentless agitation, they pace, shout, and are driven. Catatonic schizophrenics are rare today in the United States and Europe, but at one time in the Western world and currently in some underdeveloped countries, catatonic patients are a visible group among inpatient psychiatric populations.

Schizophrenia is not absolute or always fixed. Individuals vary in the severity and longevity of this disorder. The following excerpt illustrates a young man in transition into a newly emerging schizophrenic disorder of marked severity.

I began to see everything through a haze, as real and disorienting as a thick morning fog. There was an accompanying loss of body awareness so that as the world outside of me became less real, my own reality decreased as well. . . . [I developed] an enormous sense of persecution—really everything started to go. The world an inch out of orbit can end all life. I could not adapt; I couldn't recoup my losses; I only got worse.

(Spencer, 1979, p. 364–365)

PARANOIA

Recall the case of Everingham Marquette with whom we opened this chapter. Although only limited information was provided on Everingham, one possible diagnosis for him would be paranoia. We define paranoia as a serious psychological disorder in which a complex delusional system is present. It is always an organized and logical system, in which the individual has delusions of grand achievement and status or of being persecuted. Everingham presented both aspects, seeing himself as both Christ and Napoleon, and also seeing a threat from invaders from other planets. If Everingham were indeed suffering from the state of paranoia, he would have to be without the symptoms of schizophrenia discussed earlier; that is, he would have to be adjusted in other areas and to show no signs of the incoherence, loose thinking, disorganization of life, or hallucinations of the schizophrenias.

Paranoia takes a number of forms. You will recall in Chapter 10 a disorder called erotomania was discussed. This belief that one is loved by another person of high status also fits the delusional pattern of paranoia. Three other types have been described. The grandiose type consists of the delusion that the individual is a person of great importance. "Grandiose delusions usually take the form of the person's being convinced that he or she possesses some great, but unrecognized talent or insight, or has made some important discovery, which he or she may take to various government agencies . . ." (American Psychiatric Association, 1987, p. 200).

The jealous type of paranoid maintains the incorrect belief that his or her lover or spouse is unfaithful. This delusional individual is preoccupied with gathering evidence, accusing the lover, and restricting the movement of the lover.

The persecutory type believes in a scheme of conspiracy, spying, harrassment, or being poisoned in which he or she is the victim. The last type is the person with somatic delusion, who believes foul odors are coming from body openings, that his or her body is misfunctioning, or (inaccurately) that some body part is misshapen.

All of these delusional types may be diagnosed as paranoia only if the person's behavior is not obviously bizarre. Thus Everingham Marquette's strange behaviors, such as stopping people on the street and presenting himself as Christ and Napoleon, as well as himself, would make us consider both paranoid schizophrenia and paranoia as alternate diagnoses of his disorder.

MOOD DISORDERS

A mood disorder is a prolonged emotion of either manic and hyperactive elation or depression. We consider manic episodes first.

Manic Episodes

It is hard to forget people in manic episodes. They are balls of meteoric energy, talking, moving, thinking in such agitated or elevated states that they dominate everyone and everything around them. They can't pay attention very well to what other people are thinking because they fly from thought to thought, place to place, often distracted by passing thoughts. Sometimes they are caught up in the belief that they are invincible, invulnerable, or on a vital mission. They may write a play or opera in four hours, despite no musical knowledge or literary experience. They are often euphorically joyful, but become irritable if frustrated. They don't simply talk to a person. They carry on loudly, flamboyantly, rapidly, with a grand sense of self-importance and expansiveness. What sorts out individuals in manic episodes from active people who speak quickly? It is a difference in degree, whereby disordered persons cannot work successfully, or relate to others, or manage the ordinary aspects of their lives.

Major Depressive Episodes

Manic episodes and major depressive episodes have one common feature; they are unipolar mood disorders. That is, the person is in either a manic or a depressed state, and does not move back and forth between these emotions. Both manic and depressive behaviors may be caused by drugs. The specific diagnoses are made after the conclusion has been reached that medications or organic factors have not precipitated these maladjustments.

Major depressive episodes are characterized by deep sadness and loss of pleasure in life. If the depression endures through most of the day for at least two weeks, a major depressive episode may have occurred. These people are discouraged, feel helpless, and lose interest in their lives. Their appetites and sleeping patterns are disturbed. Sometimes they eat prodigiously and sleep all the time; more typically they lose their appetites and develop insomnia. When this disturbed behavior occurs for up to sixty days during particular periods of the year, it is considered a seasonal disorder. Such seasonal influences on behavior have been discussed in Chapter 13.

Bipolar Disorder

When both manic and depressive episodes occur in the same person, the diagnosis is a bipolar disorder; that is, both poles of emotional and behavioral reactions are experienced. The full range of symptoms of each is experienced and in some chronic forms, the person cycles rapidly from manic states to depressive states, and back, never living without one or other extreme for more than short periods.

 ## TWO CAUTIONS

As the patterns of psychological disorders are considered, two cautions are in order. First, the reader should be aware of the hazard of the medical student syndrome. When medical students study muscular deterioration, they commonly become aware of muscular pains and believe they have deteriorating muscles. When medical students study heart, kidney, or blood sugar disorders, they frequently are convinced they are suffering from heart, kidney, or blood sugar problems. So it goes for psychological disorders too. It is not unusual for psychology students to believe they are suffering from the disorder being studied.

The resolution of the medical student syndrome is to maintain a scholarly detachment. The hazard is feeling as if each disorder illuminates a pathological aspect of yourself. I suggest the alternative of being the interested and inquiring visitor to this realm of knowledge. At first, almost everyone wonders if they are phobic or suffering a personality disorder or afflicted with some other disorder. Realize it is okay to have such feelings. The realization aids in letting go of such feelings.

The second caution is that psychological diagnoses are far from descriptions of the whole person. What they do is describe particular aspects of malfunctioning. We need to remember that a person is not an anxiety disorder; rather a person may *have* an anxiety disorder. In Chapter 15 I cautioned about the hazard of rubricizing people. Rubrics vary in their power; that is, being a subscriber to *Time* magazine is a modest rubric of little labeling power. Subscribing to the newsletter of some noxious group—let us pretend it to be the Society for Vivisection of Playful Kittens—is a more compelling rubric. Carrying a psychological diagnosis as an inpatient in hospital settings is a potent rubric. The final caution thus is to be wary of such rubricizing of others, in addition to the first caution, which is to be wary of self-rubricizing.

References

American Psychiatric Association (1987). *Diagnostic and Statistical Manual of Mental Disorders* (Third Edition–Revised). DSM-III-R. Washington, D.C.: American Psychiatric Association.

American Psychiatric Association (1980). *Diagnostic and Statistical Manual of Mental Disorders* (Third Edition). Washington, D.C.: American Psychiatric Association.

Davison, Gerald C. and Neale, John M. (1986). *Abnormal Psychology: An Experimental Clinical Approach.* Fourth Edition. New York: John Wiley and Sons.

Doren, Dennis M. (1987). *Understanding and Treating the Psychopath.* New York: John Wiley and Sons.

Millon, Theodore and Everly, George S., Jr. (1985). *Personality and Its Disorders: A Biosocial Learning Approach.* New York: John Wiley and Sons.

Spencer, Scott (1979). *Endless Love.* New York: Avon.

Recommended Reading

Cleckley, H. (1964). *The Mask of Sanity.* Fourth edition. St. Louis: C. B. Mosby. Hervey Cleckley has defined the nature of psychopaths more than other single twentieth century figure. In the *Mask of Sanity,* Cleckley presents numerous case histories of remorseless and guilt-free offenders who manage to present clever and glib surface impressions. He puts to together this information in a first rate portrayal of the psychopath.

Coleman, J.C., Butcher, J.N., and Carson, R.C. (1984). *Abnormal Psychology and Modern Life.* Seventh edition. Glenview, Ill.: Scott, Foresman, and Company. This textbook is an excellent guide to the nature of psychological disorders. The historical review of abnormal behavior is comprehensive, and the discussions of different patterns of abnormality are current, clear, and cogent.

Szasz, T.S. (1961). *The Myth of Mental Illness: Foundations of a Theory of Personal Conduct.* New York: Delta. The Szaszian position is that behavior problems as mental illnesses is nonsense. Szasz asserts that problems in living are in no way similar to diseases of the body. As a result of believing that they are similar, scientific inquiry is crippled. The alternative way of interpreting symptoms is as forms of communication and part of societal game-playing.

GLOSSARY

Abreaction. The reexperiencing of emotions felt during a traumatic experience through hypnosis, dream interpretation, or talking about the event in order to fully understand the emotions and no longer be harmed by them. (Chapter 14)

Actualizing tendency. In *humanistic psychology,* an organism's movement toward the fulfillment of its potential. People striving to be the best they can; their efforts to make their potential capabilities into actual functioning. (Chapter 2)

Acute pain. Short-term intense *pain,* usually perceived as due to tissue damage or physical harm. (Chapter 5)

Adjustment. The process of dealing with the demands of our bodies, our emotions, and our environments, it can be defined as *normality, internal harmony, social competence, mastery of changing demands,* and *self-fulfillment.* See also *well-being.* (Chapter 1)

Agape. The religious, nonsexual love of all people; the universal feeling of goodwill toward others. (Chapter 10)

Aggression. An observable act, in which one person creates unpleasantness or hurt in another. Not necessarily an expression of *anger* or *hostility.* (Chapter 6)

Alarm reaction. The body's mobilization (physical or psychological) of defensive forces against any threat or attack of *stress.* The first response in the *general adaptation syndrome.* (Chapter 4)

Analgesia. An insensitivity to *pain.* (Chapter 5)

Anal stage. The second of Freud's stages of psychosexual development, in which anal sphincter control is a source of conflict; when the desire for release and satisfaction is opposed by social and parental demands for toilet training compliance. (Chapter 2)

Anger. An emotional internal state of a strong feeling of displeasure, which may or may not arise because of a situation or others' actions. (Chapter 6)

Anger management. The self-control of antagonism and *aggression* through relaxation techniques, control of hostile thoughts, and detached and alternate ways of handling *anger.* (Chapter 6)

Anorexia nervosa. Extreme undereating because of a neurotic dread of being overweight: An eating disorder. (Chapter 5)

Anticipatory mourning. A depressed emotional reaction in expectation of death; a contemporary reaction to death that has arisen from the custom of hospitalizing the dying and creating a hushed atmosphere of fearful anticipation and early condolences. (Chapter 7)

Anticipatory rejection. When one's fear of being rejected by another leads one to either reject the other defensively, in order to avoid hurt, or to adopt behaviors that incite the other to move away. (Chapter 10)

Artistic types. People who are expressive and creative, who like ambiguous, unstructured environments, and who undertake artistic achievements. One of the six personality types described by the Holland theory of vocational choice. (Chapter 12)

Art of loving. As defined by Erich Fromm, a deep, hard-working commitment to loving that practices *discipline, concentration, patience, sensitivity,* and *overcoming narcissism.* (Chapter 10)

Art of solace. One of the earliest recorded uses of verbal persuasion to relieve pain and cure disorders; instructing patients to speak about their sufferings and then using their own words to suggest other ways for them to think about their concerns. A technique originated by Antiphon in ancient Greece. (Chapter 14)

Assertiveness. Socially appropriate interpersonal behavior involving the honest and relatively straightforward expression of thoughts and feelings in a way that is considerate of others. (Chapter 6)

Assertiveness training. Treatment for *shyness, nonassertiveness,* and *passive-aggressiveness* that teaches people how to more openly express their feelings in ways that respect the rights and feeling of other people. (Chapter 6)

Assumptive world. One's expectations and interpretations of life events. *Transitions* provide one with the opportunity to reexamine assumptions and gain new perspectives. (Chapter 7)

Attachment. The need aspect of love—the need to be fulfilled, held, and cared for; the need to have emotional and physical contact with another. One of three essential components of *romantic love* as defined by Zick Rubin. (Chapter 10)

Autonomous interdependence stage. A pattern of friendship that begins when adolescence is reached and that allows friends to be both independent and at the same time to turn to each other for support and help in meeting individual needs. (Chapter 8)

Autonomy versus shame and doubt. The second psychosocial stage of development in infancy and toddlerhood described by Erik Erikson. Taking place in the first to third years of life, it is the stage when the child either successfully opposes parental demands and feels comfortable with independence or incompletely passes through the period of saying no to parents and feels ashamed and uncertain about independence. (Chapter 7)

Aversion methods. Using unpleasant stimulation (or direct punishment) as a negative reinforcer in order to eliminate a troublesome behavior, or pairing unwanted behavior with unpleasant associations in order to eliminate it. Used in behavior therapy. (Chapter 14)

Basic trust versus distrust. One of the two psychosocial stages of development in infancy and toddlerhood described by Erik Erikson. Taking place in the first year of life, it is the stage when the infant learns either that the world is a secure, nurturing, dependable place or an insecure, undependable place that should be distrusted or feared. (Chapter 7)

Basking in Reflected Glory (BIRG). When a person brags about the achievement of another in order to raise his or her own self-esteem. A form of self-evaluation maintenance. (Chapter 3)

Behaviorism. The school of psychology, developed by John B. Watson and B.F. Skinner, that scientifically observes behavior by studying the *stimulus–response* relationship and that holds behavior is learned, shaped by the environment, and not inborn. (Chapter 2)

Bibliotherapy. A form of *self-therapy* that uses reading as the starting point for self-improvement. The regular reading about one's particular problems, in self-help books and relevant fiction and biographies, in order to correct problems. (Chapter 14)

B-love. Being love, defined by Abraham Maslow as healthy and nonpossessive love that grows out of strength and security. Characterized by loving the other for who he or she truly is, by a *giving* style of loving, and by demonstrated acceptance of and comfort in the relationship without demanding proof of love or setting conditions. (Chapter 10)

Bulimia. The eating disorder of involuntary, frequent, inconspicuous binging on high-caloric food followed by shame, depression, and sometimes self-induced vomiting because of an extreme motivation to be thin. (Chapter 5)

Cancer-prone personality. The hypothesized set of emotional characteristics (such as grief, depression, anxiety, and hopelessness) that makes a person especially susceptible to cancer. (Chapter 5)

Caring. The form of love that involves altruistic giving to the other, that makes one partner's well-being dependent on the satisfaction and happiness of the other. One of three essential components of *romantic love* as defined by Zick Rubin. (Chapter 10)

Caring cluster. According to Keith Davis, the set of emotions in *romantic love* composed of lovers' altruism, putting each other's happiness before their own, and championing or advocating each other's needs and wishes. (Chapter 10)

Catharsis. The reliving of repressed events. The psychoanalytic technique of emotional release utilized by Freud in his early work. (Chapter 14)

Celibacy. The absence of sexual activity; the state of noninvolvement in any sexual experiences. (Chapter 11)

Challenge. In a *hardy personality,* the ability to successfully overcome risks and obstacles and the view that some stressful events are desirable experiences that foster growth and change. (Chapter 4)

Child abuse. A parent's (or other adult's) use of violence (ranging from slapping or beating to using a gun or knife) or the threat of violence against a child. (Chapter 6)

Choice. One of the five stages associated with the development of loving. One person's deliberate decision that another is the most suitable partner for him or her. (Chapter 10)

Chronic pain. Long-lasting *pain* that often persists not only as a result of an injury but also because of the sufferer's expression of pain and others' continuing emotional support intended to alleviate the anxiety associated with pain. (Chapter 5)

Circadian rhythm. The twenty-four-hour cycle of sleep and waking; the "biological clock" of predictable physiological fluctuations that occur each day. (Chapter 13)

Classical conditioning. The learning that occurs when a neutral stimulus (such as a light or noise) is paired with a stimulus that naturally produces some behavior. Involves an **unconditioned stimulus,** an **unconditioned response,** a **conditioned stimulus,** and a **conditioned response.** With **operant conditioning,** makes up the foundation of behavioral theory. (Chapter 2)

Client-centered therapy. The form of humanistic psychotherapy developed by Carl Rogers that allows clients to determine the direction of therapy and what they wish to accomplish, with the therapist focusing on the client's feelings. (Chapter 14)

Cognitive. A general term used to describe thought, ideas, and interpretations, rather than action. (Chapter 1)

Collective unconscious. Carl Jung's term for those inherited mental images and ideas that are common to all humanity and that, while not available to human awareness in obvious and clear forms, are released into the **conscious** through mythology, imagery, dreams, and mystical experiences. (Chapter 2)

Commitment. In a **hardy personality,** a sense of purpose in life and a belief in oneself and in one's values. (Chapter 4)

Companion animals. Pets with whom their owners have deep, intense, and positive relationships that are central to the owners' lives. Having a companion animal may improve an owner's health and morale. (Chapter 8)

Competence-motivated. When one focuses on achieving a sense of mastery and optimal challenge when performing. An attribute of

well-being that may lead to **peak performance.** (Chapter 15)

Competition-motivated. When one sees winning as the basic aim of performance. (Chapter 15)

Concentration. Paying full attention to what you are doing; attending completely to the person you are with or the activity in which you are involved. One of the skills to be practiced in order to master Fromm's **art of loving.** (Chapter 10)

Conditioned response. In **classical conditioning,** a learned response made to a **conditioned stimulus** or event that was paired with original stimulus that produced behavior. (Chapter 2)

Conditioned stimulus. In **classical conditioning,** the neutral event or stimulus (such as a bell) that is paired with an **unconditioned stimulus** to produce a **conditioned response.** (Chapter 2)

Confidentiality. The therapist's commitment not to reveal what a client discloses during therapy. Therapeutic confidentiality may be broken when legally mandated or when there is clear and immediate danger of physical injury to the client or others, according to the American Psychological Association's ethical guidelines. (Chapter 14)

Conformity. Reconciliation of individual goals with societal needs. Forced conformity is social or government pressure that requires people to surrender important aspects of themselves as individuals. Comfortable conformity reflects a healthy and productive chosen way of living. One aspect of **adjustment** and **well-being.** (Chapter 1)

Congruence. When the way people present themselves is consistent with how they feel; when people are genuine. A condition that promotes the **actualizing tendency.** (Chapter 2)

Conscious. The awareness of current thought and feelings; what one is aware of at a given instant. An aspect of Freud's theory of *psychoanalysis.* (Chapter 2)

Constructionalism. Increasing one's repertoire of possible behaviors without deleting any existing behaviors; allowing oneself many acceptable options at any given time, which increases the potential for *well-being.* (Chapter 15)

Contemplation. The second stage before change can occur during which a person thinks about what actions should be taken to achieve change. Follows the *precontemplation* phase. Chapter 1)

Context. The total situation in which behavior occurs; the overall picture of what is happening. In nonverbal communication, there are three levels of context: the *individual level,* the *relationship level,* and the *social rule level.* (Chapter 9)

Contingency management. The control, by the therapist or the client, of events and experiences that follow (and reinforce) a certain behavior in order to establish, shape, or maintain that behavior or, conversely, to eliminate an unwanted behavior. A technique of behavior therapy. (Chapter 14)

Contracting. When a client and therapist jointly draw up a contract that identifies specific behavioral goals for the client and the consequences of both the client's accomplishment of each goal and his or her failure to adhere to the contract. One of the major methods of behavior therapy. (Chapter 14)

Control. In the *hardy personality,* the belief that one can influence events and act to change things; a sense of mastery that allows one to accept and cope with *stressors.* (Chapter 4)

Conventional types. People who are good at working with data and recording or organizing information, who are ordered, systematic, and conscientious, who dislike ambiguity, and

who have little artistic ability. One of the six personality types described by the Holland theory of vocational choice. (Chapter 12)

Cooperation. The coordinated, joint behavior of two or more people aimed at achieving an end with desirable consequences for all involved; working together for a common purpose. (Chapter 8)

Cult. A totalitarian group that exerts strong continuous control over its members and renounces the outside world, assuming a posture of moral superiority. (Chapter 15)

Cutting off reflected failure. When a person distances himself or herself from unsuccessful people, institutions, or events in order to avoid being associated with something negative by others. A form of self-evaluation maintenance. (Chapter 3)

Decision confirmation and commitment. When an individual affirms aloud that a job choice is correct and appropriate (confirmation) and announces the job choice to others (commitment). The fourth job search phase of Peer Soelberg's *job search and choice model.* (Chapter 12)

Defense mechanisms. Organized and consistent patterns of responding to threat that protect one from possible hurt, failure, or rejection. A coping style or psychological device that makes threats more tolerable. (Chapter 4)

De-illusionment. Daniel Levinson's term for the midlife stage when people reexamine their values, desires, and accomplishments, reappraise their lives, and come to recognize that their long-held assumptions about themselves and their worlds are not necessarily true. (Chapter 7)

Deintensifying. Underexpressing felt emotions; displaying a mild reaction or emotion when a more powerful reaction is truly felt. A technique for managing facial expressions. (Chapter 9)

Delight. One of the five stages associated with the development of loving occurring after two people have chosen each other, reciprocated feelings, and come to **trust** one another. It is the pleasure they find in each other, themselves, and their relationship. (Chapter 10)

Denial. The exclusion from consciousness of anxiety-arousing external events. A type of **defense mechanism** related to **repression.** (Chapter 4)

Desire dysfunction. Inhibited sexual longings, when a person who is capable of becoming aroused only rarely becomes interested sexually; or the phobic avoidance of sexual contact, when a person reports never feeling sexual desire. (Chapter 11)

Despair. The dissatisfaction and unhappiness one feels when reviewing one's life and accomplishments. In Erik Erikson's model of the eight stages of life, one response to the conflict felt in old age. See also **ego integrity.** (Chapter 7)

Discipline. A vigorous commitment of time and self to routinized practice. One of the skills to be practiced in order to master Fromm's **art of loving.** (Chapter 10)

Discounting. Giving a low value to positive information about self-worth; making a negative statement that minimizes achievement out of modesty or low self-esteem. (Chapter 3)

Displacement. The channeling of threatening feelings toward nonthreatening objects or persons. Can be a maladaptive or an adaptive way of handling unacceptable thoughts or feeling (see **sublimation**). A type of **defense mechanism.** (Chapter 4)

D-love. Deficiency love, defined by Abraham Maslow as love that seeks to fulfill one's own needs and that grows out of weakness and one's self-preoccupations. Characterized by an affiliation with another in order to address one's own unhappiness with some aspect of life, nonreciprocity, and a relationship that revolves around the deficient person's needs. (Chapter 10)

Dodo bird verdict. The conclusion that all forms of psychotherapy result in appreciable and lasting gains for clients; the positive assessment of therapy effectiveness. (Chapter 14)

Dollar Auction game. A game in which players are given one minute to bid for a dollar, bids may go as high as the bidders choose, and both the highest and second highest bidders are obligated to pay their last bid at the end of the game. Based on the principle that people who have already invested money will not withdraw from the bidding because they are afraid of losing whatever they have committed to the auction. (Chapter 10)

Dualistic. The viewpoint that the body and the mind function separately. Dualistic thinkers see psychological health and physical health as altogether different and unrelated. The alternative to **holistic** thinking. (Chapter 5)

Dyadic effect. The phenomenon of disclosure begetting disclosure: When one person in a pair reveals personal information about himself or herself, the other in the pair is likely to disclose personal information. (Chapter 3)

Eclectic psychotherapy. Treatment that draws on the techniques of all schools of therapy, regardless of their theoretical origins, and chooses the therapeutic methods that best suit the client's needs. (Chapter 14)

Ecological psychology. A method for studying behavior that considers actions in the broad context of both physical and interpersonal environments, investigates behavior as it occurs naturally in the subject's own community, and is not based on any preexisting hypotheses but relies solely on the observed behaviors for its findings. Developed by Roger Barker and colleagues. (Chapter 13)

Ego. The rational and mostly *conscious* mediator between instinctive drives and the demands of the external world. The rational part of the mental structure described by Freud that also includes *id* and *superego*. (Chapter 2)

Ego defense mechanism theory. The theory that excessive emotional repression and inhibition lead to cancer. The theory of the *cancer-prone personality* that attributes the initial causes of cancer to internal psychological forces. (Chapter 5)

Ego integrity. The review of one's life and accomplishments with a sense of satisfaction. In Erik Erikson's model of the eight stages of life, one response to the conflict felt in old age. See also *despair*. (Chapter 7)

Electra complex. When a female child desires her father exclusively and sexually and competes with her mother for the father's affection, but fears punishment for the unacceptable feelings of incest. A conflict that arises during the psychosexual *phallic stage*. (Chapter 2)

Emotional arousal hypothesis. The theory that obese people are more responsive to the sight, smell, taste, and thought of food, as well as to other emotional stimuli, than are people of normal weight. (Chapter 5)

Empathic embarrassment. A way of coping with social awkwardness, chagrin, or mortification by confessing nervousness and discomfort in order to inspire onlookers to share these feelings. (Chapter 8)

Emphathic understanding. When one person accurately senses the real feelings and personal meanings of another person's communications and can relay that understanding to the other person. A condition that promotes the *actualizing tendency*. (Chapter 2)

Empathy. The ability to identify and experience another's emotions; seeing and feeling from the perspective of another. (Chapter 6)

Empty nest. The home after the last child has left, leaving the mother alone with the father, without the task of child rearing. A *life transition* in which women suffer loneliness and depression over the ending of their role as mothers. Mothers also commonly experience a sense of liberation and freedom to expand their emotional lives. (Chapter 7)

Enterprising types. People who enjoy undertaking leadership roles, who are good at persuasion, and who are skillful at manipulating objects or other people for economic gain or to achieve a goal. One of the six personality types described by the Holland theory of vocational choice. (Chapter 12)

Entrainment. The process by which one's internal time schedule is modified by societal and environmental demands; the adjustment of one's body clock to outside schedules. (Chapter 13)

Epidemiology. The study of the incidence, distribution, and control of disease in an entire population. (Chapter 5)

Erotic. One of the six styles of loving, and the style that fits the description of *falling in love*. Love that develops at first sight because the lover is perceived as being ideal, physically and emotionally; love that values sexuality, interpersonal intimacy, and physical means of pleasing the loved one. (Chapter 10)

Erotomania. The delusional belief that someone (usually older, more prominent socially, or with greater status) loves you when in fact that person has no interest in you. An obsession that primarily afflicts women who have no other delusions or hallucinations, it is resistant to treatments and may persist for one or two decades. Also known as delusional love or the de Clerambault syndrome. (Chapter 10)

Eustress. The desirable and necessary *stressors* that provide the stimulation and challenge that make life worthwhile; positive **stress.** (Chapter 4)

Exhaustion. When **resistance** to **stress** runs out, the constant wear and tear of prolonged **stressors** leads to emotional or physical collapse, serious illness, or even death. The third response to the **general adaptation syndrome.** (Chapter 4)

Expedience. Acting in a way that is immediately advantageous to one's self-interest. One of the major characteristics of the **public self.** (Chapter 3)

Experimenter effect. When researchers inadvertently structure an experiment or behave in such a way that they elicit from subjects the response that supports their hypothesis. The **self-fulfilling prophecy** in action in experimental psychology. (Chapter 3)

Expression blends. The facial expression of two emotions at the same time, because the emotions are felt simultaneously or one emotion is an immediate response to the original emotion. An example of a problematic facial expression that confuses viewers. (Chapter 9)

External locus of control. When control of one's life is perceived as being outside of oneself, as being determined by other people or outside forces. A fatalistic viewpoint, negatively related to **well-being.** (Chapter 1)

Extroversion. Being caught up in ideas and feelings directed toward events and people outside oneself. One of Jung's two descriptions of personality types; the other is **introversion.** (Chapter 2)

Eye contact. Silent communication of mutual looking at eyes that indicates interest and generates involvement; a signal indicating readiness to communicate. Associated with four universal behaviors: a look toward the other, a brief smile, a raising of the eyebrows, and a quick head nod. (Chapter 9)

Falling in love. The immediate attraction, often irrational, to someone who seems to fit your concept of the perfect partner and your fantasy of the perfect relationship; the feelings of exhilaration arising from the supposed realization of the fantasized image of love. (Chapter 10)

Fantasy. The excessive indulgence in daydreaming, wishful thinking, or fantasizing in order to escape unpleasant thoughts or feelings. A type of **defense mechanism.** (Chapter 4)

Fetish. A compulsive sexual attraction to an object, such as rubber or leather, not normally considered arousing, which the fetishist requires as a sex play device in order to become aroused or to climax. (Chapter 11)

Fight training. A course teaching couples how to fight fairly and to be assertive in verbal conflicts that respect both participants' feelings and rights; seeks to clarify and extinguish accumulated tensions within a relationship. (Chapter 6)

Flooded expressions. Emotional expressions held overly long and inappropriately; excessively maintained facial expressions of intensified emotion. An example of a problematic facial expression that presents difficulties in interpersonal communication. (Chapter 9)

Free association. When the patient releases conscious control of thoughts and allows his or her ideas and feelings to emerge without censorship or artifice. One of the five essential components of **psychoanalysis.** (Chapter 14)

Friendship-based love. Love that develops between two people who have known each other very well as good friends. One of the six styles of loving. (Chapter 10)

Friendships. Close, voluntary, and relatively enduring relationships with people central to one's life. (Chapter 8)

Frozen affect. A fixed emotional expression; a facial expression maintained continuously regardless of felt emotions. An example of a problematic facial expression. (Chapter 9)

Gain–loss effect. The theory of attraction based on changes in the warmth or coolness of one person to another. The order of feelings one person expresses toward another; when a person is initially cool and then becomes warmer toward another, or when a person is initially warm and then becomes cooler toward another, rather than when one consistently expresses liking or disliking for another. (Chapter 10)

Game playing. Love that emphasizes the individual's personal pleasure and minimizes commitment, possessiveness, and exclusivity. One of the six styles of loving, and the style that often involves having multiple lovers. (Chapter 10)

Gate control theory. An explanation of *pain* as a subjective experience, describing how mechanisms in the dorsal horns of the spine work like a gate, letting some impulses through and blocking others, depending on the number and type of impulses and the person's emotional state, background, and appraisal of the situation. (Chapter 5)

Gaze. Prolonged state of one person looking at another who may or may not return the look. (Chapter 9)

Gaze avoidance. When someone actively avoids looking toward or at another. (Chapter 9)

Gaze omission. When someone unintentionally does not look at or toward another; no intent to avoid another's gaze but the gaze is missed. (Chapter 9)

General adaptation syndrome (GAS). Identified by Hans Selye, a three-stage pattern of response to *stress,* consisting of an *alarm reaction,* a *resistance stage,* and *exhaustion.* (Chapter 4)

General life satisfaction. One's overall assessment of the felt gratification and contentment in one's life. One of three components of *well-being.* (Chapter 1)

Generativity. The renewal of oneself and the helping of the next generation. In Erik Erikson's model of the eight stages of life, a characterization of adulthood. See also *stagnation.* (Chapter 7)

Genital stage. The last of Freud's five stages of development. When full genital functioning is possible and one is capable of performing the sexual act, and when the unresolved conflicts of the *oral stage,* the *anal stage,* and the *phallic stage* surface (puberty). (Chapter 2)

Gestures. Symbolic body movements that express thoughts or feelings and substitute for or elaborate on verbal statements. (Chapter 9)

Giving. Love that supports, forgives, is patient, and is unselfish. One of the six styles of loving, and the style that comes closest to the general concept of *romantic love.* (Chapter 10)

Good theory. A clear and explicit set of statements that will withstand empirical testing. Chapter 2)

Hardy personality. One who responds to stressful events with *commitment, control,* and *challenge;* one who is less susceptible to *stressors* in life and who experiences growth from stressful events. (Chapter 4)

Hassles. The minor daily stresses in life, which may accumulate to cause distress. (Chapter 4)

Healing visualizations. Using the imaging process to fight disease by mobilizing the body's natural healing abilities; when patients visualize themselves fighting their disease in specific and understandable ways in order to serve as their own healers. (Chapter 5)

Healthy charismatics. *Type A personalities* who are more emotionally expressive (and less at risk for developing coronary heart disease) than *hostile competitives.* (Chapter 5)

High-level wellness. The lifelong product of actively preventing illness and improving physical fitness through body awareness, self-education, growth, and self-responsibility. (Chapter 5)

Hobson's choice. When no choice is allowed; when there are no alternatives. What many people give themselves when faced with making decisions, which limits their potential for growth. (Chapter 15)

Holism. The study of the whole person in the changing contexts of the person's life, environment, and motivations. According to holistic thinking, psychological health and physical health are closely related and together regulate every area of human functioning. The research approach Maslow urged psychologists to follow. (Chapters 2, 5)

Honest positives. Truly felt statements about another's likeable and desirable behaviors; genuine encouragement given to improve communication and develop good feelings in a relationship. (Chapter 8)

Hostile competitives. **Type A personalities** who are verbally competitive, potentially hostile, rapid reactors, and impatient. Type A people who are at risk for developing coronary heart disease. (Chapter 5)

Hostility. A persistent attitude, usually developed following an unpleasant experience or thought, that negatively judges another person or object. (Chapter 6)

Humanistic psychology. The school of psychology that values subjectivity, is concerned with the meaning of life, assumes that people strive to fulfill and actualize themselves, and utilizes the unique human traits of will, responsibility, and spirituality. Shaped in part by Carl Rogers, this school's tenets contrast with those of **behaviorism** and **psychoanalysis.** (Chapter 2)

Human science psychology. The school of psychology that values the perspectives of others, emphasizes qualitative, descriptive methods, and directly studies events and experiences as people observe or report them. It rejects traditional physical science methods for psychological assessments, psychotherapy, and research. (Chapter 2)

Hypochondriasis. A body complaint, such as stomach upset, headache, or back pain, arising from psychological rather than physical distress. (Chapter 12)

Id. The **unconscious** repository of primitive instinctive drives and the need for satisfaction. The primitive part of the mental structure described by Freud that also includes **ego** and **superego.** (Chapter 2)

Ideal self. The totality of the desired and fantasized selves a person wishes to be. (Chapter 3)

Ideation. How we form ideas and think about situations. The prediction of an individual's behavior that considers both the **situation** and the person's thoughts about the situation. See also **cognitive.** (Chapter 13)

Identification. The active acceptance of the point of view or position of a person who is the cause of anxiety; giving up one's own emotional stance in order to be like the person who is the **stressor.** A type of **defense mechanism.** (Chapter 4)

Identity conflict. In adolescence, when children are struggling to understand who they are and what they want to do, when they are establishing personal identities distinct from their families. According to Erik Erikson, this stage leaves the adolescent with a sense of fidelity to peers. (Chapter 7)

Identity versus role diffusion. In adolescence, the stage described by Erik Erikson when children search for personal identities and begin to wonder about what they want to do with their lives. When their search for a meaningful identity is successful, children begin to develop personal principles by which they guide their lives or commit themselves to future plans. When their search is unsuccessful, children feel lost, without meaning or purpose to their lives. (Chapter 7)

Individual level. In nonverbal communication, the *context* of the single individual. (Chapter 9)

Individuation. The process of becoming an independent person; being aware of oneself as a distinct and separate being. (Chapter 15)

Individuation–merger process. When two people partly merge their individual identities because they desire unity, emotional safety, and sexual and developmental completion, and yet seek to be separate and independent of each other. Merging promotes common interests but, if overdone, may result in feelings of resentment and personal loss. Excessive individuation threatens the relationship, but successful individuation within a relationship promotes growth. (Chapter 10)

Industry versus inferiority. In middle childhood, the stage described by Erik Erikson when children's activities revolve more around school, peers, and adult environments and less around their families; when children develop either a sense of accomplishment and competence, deriving a sense of self-worth from their activities, or feelings of worthlessness and ineptness, coming to expect that they will be unsuccessful in their endeavors. (Chapter 7)

Ingratiation. An interpersonal strategy to increase feelings of obligation and attraction for some ulterior motive; when manipulative techniques are used to manage a relationship with another person in order to achieve an individual goal. Closely related to *Machiavellianism.* (Chapter 8)

Initiative versus guilt. In early childhood, the stage described by Erik Erikson as a time when children attempt to freely explore their worlds and their capabilities on their own and ei-

ther learn to take the initiative in situations because of positive reinforcement or develop guilty feelings about themselves and their actions because their explorations are devalued. (Chapter 7)

Inner doctor. The imaginary internal physician or advisor, developed through guided imagery, who can help one to deal with everyday physical concerns by encouraging one to listen to the body's messages about how to stay healthy and deal with *stress.* (Chapter 5)

Intellectualization. Emotional detachment from discomforting events; the distant and uninvolved analysis of an anxiety-arousing event. A type of *defense mechanism* related to *rationalization.* (Chapter 4)

Intensifying. Overexpressing the strength of a felt emotion; displaying a powerful reaction when only a mild reaction is truly felt. (Chapter 9)

Internal harmony. Freedom from internal strife and comfort with personal needs and values. One of the five definitions of *adjustment.* (Chapter 1)

Internal locus of control. When one feels in control of one's destiny, in charge of one's life, and capable of making deliberate choices. Positively related to *well-being.* (Chapter 1)

Intimacy. (1) Closeness with others. In Erik Erikson's model of the eight stages of life, one of two possible resolutions to the basic conflict of young adulthood. See also *isolation.* (Chapter 7). (2) A close, private bond between two people; a couple's sharing of the most personal areas of their lives. One of three essential components of *romantic love* as defined by Zick Rubin. (Chapter 10)

Introversion. A personal emphasis on and attention to internal, subjective thoughts and feelings. One of Jung's two descriptions of personality types; the other is *extroversion.* (Chapter 2)

Investigative personality types. People who are scholarly and scientific, who enjoy making creative and systematic observations about their natural and social environments. One of the six personality types described by the Holland theory of vocational choice. (Chapter 12)

Isolation. Movement away from others. In Erik Erikson's model of the eight stages of life, one of two possible resolutions to the basic conflict of young adulthood. See also *intimacy*. (Chapter 7)

Job dissatisfaction. Employees' attitude about their work when their jobs are not interesting, do not meet their basic life and interpersonal needs, do not provide growth and advancement opportunities, and their work is not respected or recognized. Related to high job turnover rates, frequent thoughts of quitting, and lower occupational prestige. (Chapter 12)

Job satisfaction. Employees' attitude about their work when their jobs are interesting; they meet the employees' life and interpersonal needs, needs for self-identity and self-expression, and needs to be doing something worthwhile; they involve good relationships with coworkers and employers. (Chapter 12)

Job search and choice model. Peer Soelberg's theory of occupational choice that emphasizes finding a job and describes four phases in a job search: identifying the ideal job, planning the job search, choosing among actual job possibilities, and confirming the choice and committing oneself to the job. (Chapter 12)

Kegels. The deliberate tightening of the pubococcygeus muscle surrounding the vagina and bladder in order to strengthen and tone the muscle to improve urinary control, vaginal muscle control, and the quality of vaginal sexual response. Exercises named after urologist Arnold H. Kegel, who originally prescribed them. (Chapter 11)

Kine. The smallest component of a physical action; the basic descriptive unit of human movement. Identified by Ray Birdwhistle, individual kines combine to describe complicated body movements. (Chapter 9)

Kinesics. The scientific study of *nonverbal behaviors* pioneered by Ray Birdwhistle; the study of body motion through the description of *kines.* (Chapter 9)

Latency stage. When sexuality is in a state of suspension, neither appearing nor developing, and when the conflicts and impulses of the *oral stage, anal stage,* and *phallic stage* are stored in the *unconscious* (age six until puberty). One of Freud's five stages of development. (Chapter 2)

Law of effect. The law, stated by Edward Thorndike, that there is a connection between what organisms do and the consequences that follow. A basis for the *behaviorism* principle that behavior is learned. (Chapter 2)

Liberal arts. Work activity devoted to intellectual and contemplative pursuits. Thought to be the highest form of human activity in the Middle Ages. (Chapter 12)

Life events. Noteworthy happenings that have some affect on a person's life. (Chapter 7)

Life space. The parts of the environment with which one interacts. Changes to life space give one the opportunity to adjust ways of living in and interacting with physical, social, or cultural environments. (Chapter 7)

Lifestyle analysis. A way to understand the development of personality by looking at how a person's position in the family birth order and relationship to siblings and parents lead to characteristic styles of seeking attention and superiority. One of three major themes of Adlerian psychology. (Chapter 2)

Logotherapy. The Victor Frankl school of therapy that emphasizes clients' personal responsibilities and explores the meanings of life in order to help clients understand their uniqueness and their purposes for existing. (Chapter 14)

Loneliness. The state of wanting and needing more social contact; feeling negative and alienated, without attachment to community or others, and without satisfactory relationships over time. (Chapter 8)

Loss depression syndrome. The theory that a person already susceptible to hopelessness develops cancer after losing a significant person or object because the person's resistance to disease diminishes. The most common theory of the *cancer-prone personality,* and the one that attributes the initial causes of cancer to external events. (Chapter 5)

Low job complexity. When work involves doing uncomplicated, highly predictable, and repetitive tasks. An *occupational stressor* reported by blue-collar workers. (Chapter 12)

Low participation. When workers have few opportunities to share in decision-making processes on the job. An *occupational stressor* reported by blue-collar workers. (Chapter 12)

Low utilization. When jobs do not draw on the skills workers have acquired through academic and/or vocational training. An *occupational stressor* reported by blue-collar workers. (Chapter 12)

Machiavellianism. An interpersonal power strategy that uses deceit and manipulation to control others. Characterized by a relative lack of emotional involvement in interpersonal relationships and a lack of concern with conventional morality. (Chapter 8)

Maladjustment. Feelings of helplessness, misery, frustration, ineffectiveness, or having no purpose in life; arises from a distressing or burdensome life situation that seems to outweigh everything else. (Chapter 1)

Manual arts. Nonintellectual work activities necessary for meeting life's needs and survival. Considered less desirable and more lowly than *liberal arts* in the Middle Ages. (Chapter 12)

Masking. Maintaining an unfelt facial expression in order to conceal one's true feelings. A technique for managing facial expressions. (Chapter 9)

Maslow's hierarchy of needs. Abraham Maslow's proposal that human needs are met in a predictable orderly sequence, with most basic needs having to be satisfied before higher needs may be addressed. Maslow's hierarchy has physiological needs at the bottom, then safety and belongingness needs (in that order), with esteem needs next, and, finally, self-actualization needs placed highest. (Chapter 15)

Mastery of changing demands. Managing the social, technological, and environmental changes that occur throughout life in a successful manner. One of five definitions of *adjustment.* (Chapter 1)

Mental hygiene movement. The direct parent of the psychology of adjustment, founded by Clifford Beers in the early twentieth century, compared psychological adjustment to physical adjustment and promoted avoiding exposure to illness-causing environments, understanding mental health sufferers, and building strength and mental resistance. (Chapter 1)

Mentors. People who serve as guides for younger friends or colleagues, sharing the knowledge and perspectives they have gained. A role sometimes assumed by people who have successfully passed through the *renewal or resignation* stage of middle adulthood. (Chapter 7)

Meta-analysis. The study of existing research, when no original data are collected; examining, categorizing, and drawing conclusions from materials gathered and reported by other researchers. (Chapter 14)

Micromomentary behavior. Small movements, usually measurable in millimeters, that last a very short time, frequently only a fraction of a second, which can indicate the individual's emotional state. (Chapter 9)

Minerva experience. An exercise, developed by Herbert Otto and named after the Roman goddess of widsom, that helps one to recall the positive, formative experiences of growth and fulfillment that contributed to one's emotional development in order to improve present functioning. (Chapter 15)

Minimal effective response. Behavior that effectively asserts one's rights with the least effort and minimal negative emotion or consequences—ensuring that the other person's feelings are respected. (Chapter 6)

Modeling. When a therapist demonstrates a desired skill so the client may learn the more effective behavior and then provides additional instruction and feedback as the client rehearses the skill. A particularly effective procedure for correcting social skill deficits. One of the techniques of behavior therapy. (Chapter 14)

Momentary playmate stage. A preschool pattern of friendship in which young children are still quite self-centered and interested in others primarily as they relate to possessions. (Chapter 8)

Morita therapy. Treatment that first isolates clients for a week, disallowing interaction with others or recreational activities, in order to force them to think about themselves and their failings, accept responsibility for themselves, and gain a new appreciation of life and then gradually reintroduces them to outside contact. One of the "quiet therapies" of Eastern cultures that slows down the pace of and refocuses the client's thinking. (Chapter 14)

Mutable self. A changing, developing self able to adjust to changing situational demands. Flexible and open, it allows a greater range of possible satisfactions by creating options for being, thinking, and feeling. (Chapter 3)

Mutuality. When two people feel the same way about each other, seek each other out, and spend time with each other. One of the five stages associated with the development of loving. (Chapter 10)

Mutual responsibility stage. A pattern of friendship that emerges during the ages of eight to fourteen years, when children begin to base their friendships on conventional morality, mutual activities, emphathic understanding, and loyalty and commitment. (Chapter 8)

Myotonia. Increased muscle tension; in sexual arousal when voluntary muscles tense in the arms, legs, and abdomen and involuntary muscles elevate the testicles in males, lengthen the vagina in females, and tighten the buttocks in both sexes. (Chapter 11)

Naikan therapy. Treatment during which clients spend a week in isolation meditating on their past experiences with the goals of recognizing their self-centeredness, embracing self-sacrifice, and accepting and understanding themselves and their fallibilities. One of the "quiet therapies" of Eastern cultures that slows down the pace and refocuses the client's thinking. (Chapter 14)

Narcissism. Exaggerated self-esteem mixed with self-centeredness and braggadocio; simple selfishness and self-pride that puts oneself first in all circumstances. (Chapter 3)

Narrow scanners. Those who are more inclined to utilize *repression, denial,* and *projection* to protect themselves from anxiety-arousing events, thoughts, or feelings; those who use their defenses to screen and limit incoming information so that they are aware only of safe and nonthreatening data. (Chapter 4)

Negative affect. The presence of substantial feelings of unhappiness, depression, anger, frustration, or anxiety. May coexist with *positive affect.* (Chapter 1)

Negative assertions. Refusals of unreasonable requests or criticisms of another's actions in a way that shows an understanding of the other's feelings. The assertions of one's own rights; saying no when one truly wishes to say no. (Chapter 6)

Negative teasing. Badgering and tormenting another. Often appears as personal insults, aggressive remarks, or intimidation.

Negativistic personalities. People who are reluctant to accept the ideas and suggestions of others and who are resistant to and frequently disagree with others. (Chapter 8)

Neutralizing. Replacing a felt emotion with an unemotional front; being dispassionate in place of expressing one's true feelings. A technique for managing facial expressions. (Chapter 9)

New impotence. A man's inability to have intercourse because of the woman's assertive demands for satisfaction. A theorized type of impotence believed to have resulted from the strain on contemporary men caused by the newer role reversal that allows women to initiate and be dominant in sexual intercourse. (Chapter 11)

Nonassertiveness. The inability to openly express one's feelings. Closely related to *shyness.* (Chapter 6)

Nonspecificity. Hans Selye's theory that no one specific stressful event triggers unique body strain responses; rather, a series of possibly distressing events may together act as a trigger, because the same responses may arise after any one of the events. (Chapter 4)

Nonverbal leakage. Unsuccessful *masking;* when one's attempt to hide one's true feelings behind an unfelt facial expression fails and the true feelings are revealed by one's overly fixed gaze, higher pitched voice, tenseness, or other revealing behavior. (Chapter 9)

Normality. The statistical average describing the typical person. Also, the absence of incapacitating internal or social problems. One of five definitions of *adjustment.* (Chapter 1)

Obesity. Excessive overweight due to both hereditary and complex psychological factors such as an eating disorder. (Chapter 5)

Objective self-awareness. The experience of oneself as one appears to others; the nonsubjective perception of one's self-presentation—how one walks, talks, behaves—which can be obtained by studying oneself in a mirror, on audiotape or videotape, or in interactions with others. (Chapter 9)

Occupational cynicism. A negative work attitude that *occupational socialization* may promote among certain worker groups, such as the police. The loss of idealism about and belief in one's work: skepticism and bitterness. (Chapter 12)

Occupational socialization. When workers acquire the attitudes, beliefs, and values of their coworkers; when an individual is shaped by his or her occupation. (Chapter 12)

Occupational stress. When *job dissatisfaction* causes physical or psychological disorders; anxiety arising from doing unsatisfying work and/or depression arising from interpersonal problems with coworkers and employers. (Chapter 12)

Occupational trust. The feeling that develops when a worker has faith and confidence in coworkers and managers and feels secure and valued on the job; as a result the worker has good work-related self-esteem, self-confidence *job satisfaction.* (Chapter 12)

Oedipus complex. When a male child sees his father as a sexual rival for his mother's affection and develops the repressed fear that his father will castrate him because of his desire for his mother. A conflict that arises during the psychosexual *phallic stage.* (Chapter 2)

Open body asymmetry. Relaxed posture that is imbalanced, with body positions leaning more to one side of the body than the other; posture that indicates power, influence, and that nothing is being hidden. Opposite to closed body symmetry, where posture is formal or rigid and body positions are symmetrical. (Chapter 9)

Operant conditioning. When freely emitted behaviors are modified by their consequences or outcomes; when desired spontaneous behavior is rewarded. Described by B.F. Skinner. With *classical conditioning,* makes up the foundation of behavioral theory. (Chapter 2)

Opinion conformity. The process of presenting one's beliefs as similar to another's. One of the primary tactics of *ingratiation.* (Chapter 8)

Optimal distance. The most effective space between a speaker and audience for persuasive and personal communication. The distance that will allow the listener(s) to be engaged but not threatened by the speaker. Optimal distances vary from culture to culture and depending on whether the interaction is between two people or among a group. (Chapter 9)

Oral stage. One of Freud's five stages of development and the first of the psychosexual stages that also include the *anal stage* and the *phallic stage.* When pleasure and conflict center on the mouth, sucking, and oral gratification (infancy). (Chapter 2)

Overcoming narcissism. Learning to be unselfish, to be reasonable, and to have interpersonal humility rather than be self-centered. One of the skills to be practiced in order to master Fromm's *art of loving.* (Chapter 10)

Overcontrolled hostility. The denied, repressed feelings of resentment and other negative attitudes and feelings; if suddenly repressed and accumulated over time, they may explode into violence. (Chapter 6)

Paced work. Repetitive, assembly-line tasks that tend to create high levels of job-related distress among workers, including tension, depression, anger, fatigue, and confusion. (Chapter 12)

Pain. A subjective, private experience of hurt that serves as a signal of current or impending tissue damage. As much an emotional as a physical experience, it alerts one that something is wrong. (Chapter 5)

Passion cluster. According to Keith Davis, the set of emotions in *romantic love* composed of lovers' fascination with all aspects of each other, sexual desire for each other, and feelings of exclusiveness or wish to make the relationship a top priority in their lives. (Chapter 10)

Passive-aggressiveness. Intentional resistance to demands of others; obstinate and ineffective behavior masking anger, resentment, and the inability to express actual thoughts and feelings. (Chapter 6)

Patience. Allowing yourself to master a skill in small steps, making a continued effort to become proficient at a skill without expecting or seeking quick results. One of the skills to be practiced in order to master Fromm's *art of loving.* (Chapter 10)

Pattern theory. The belief that a pattern of impulses causes *pain* when it reaches the brain. When impulses are felt close together physically, with little time elapsed between each one, they create a pattern that signals pain. (Chapter 5)

Peak experiences. Temporary moments, which occur at some time in most people's lives, when extraordinary self-satisfaction, fulfillment, and happiness are felt. (Chapter 15)

Peak performance. Observable behavior that is far superior to ordinary behavior and fulfills a normally untapped potential; when one is able to perform at a much higher level than one has ever before achieved. (Chapter 15)

Performance anxiety. Fears about personal competence or adequacy, such as a man's worry that he will not be able to achieve an erection, which impairs his sexual performance. One dominant cause of **psychogenic impotence.** (Chapter 11)

PERI life events scale. Developed from the Psychiatric Epidemiology Research Interviews (PERI) rating sheet, a scale with 102 items, used to rate the stressfulness of common life events. (Chapter 4)

Personal constructs. In modern **behaviorism,** George Kelly's theory that people organize their thoughts and beliefs on the basis of how they see other people and their environment. An individual's theory about his or her personal world, shaped and modified by hypotheses and continually tested by what the person does and the consequences of the person's actions. (Chapter 2)

Personality. The stable core of who a person is; the summary of the consistent ways a person thinks, feels, and behaves. (Chapter 2)

Person–occupation (P–O) fit. The ways in which the needs, expectations, and behaviors of an individual worker matches the requirements of a particular job. (Chapter 12)

Phallic stage. One of Freud's five stages of development and the third of the psychosexual stages that also include the **oral stage** and the **anal stage.** When genitals become a source of developmental attention, gratification, and conflict; when the experience of sexuality has localized in the genitals (the fourth or fifth year of life). (Chapter 2)

Place identities. When we think of objects, locations, and environments as particularly our own, as extensions of ourselves. (Chapter 13)

Placebo effect. The expectation of improvement, associated with inert medication, physicians' attitudes, or the patient's own hopefulness, that leads to health improvement or **wellness.** (Chapter 5)

Pollyanna Principle. The common process in which pleasant events and information are sought, remembered and used far more than unpleasant events and information.

PONS (profile of nonverbal sensitivity). A method for studying how well people interpret the nonverbal cues of others. Developed by Robert Rosenthal and associates, a set of standardized stimuli that permits the testing of subjects' accuracy in reading voice, body, and facial expressions. (Chapter 9)

Positive affect. Feelings of happiness, pleasure, enjoyment, and fun. Sometimes coexists with **negative affect.** One of three components of **well-being.** (Chapter 1)

Positive assertions. The responsible expression of liking, approval, and good feelings for another that show respect for the other's feelings and rights. Unlike flattery, they indicate a real aspect or desirable behavior of the other person. (Chapter 6)

Positive Teasing. Good-intentioned joking or kidding which is relatively comfortable for both parties. Serves to reduce tension and hostility.

Possessive dependent. Love: Characterized by jealousy and possessiveness, a merging of the individuals' identities, and the joint pursuit of most activities to the near exclusion of individual action. One of the six styles of loving. (Chapter 10)

Posttraumatic stress disorder (PTSD). When emotional reaction to a **stressor** is delayed, occurring sometime after the actual experience of the stressful event. A disorder many Vietnam veterans report. (Chapter 4)

Pragmatic. Love: rational love, logical, and based on the careful and deliberate selection of a partner who meets predetermined criteria. One of the six styles of loving. (Chapter 10)

Preconscious. Thought and feelings accessible to awareness; what one can think of if one so chooses. An aspect of Freud's theory of *psychoanalysis.* (Chapter 2)

Precontemplation. The first stage before change can occur, during which a person gets ready to think about changing, deciding that something should be done. Precedes the *contemplation phase.* (Chapter 2)

Predictable transitions. Events, common throughout people's lives, for which people may prepare themselves, such as marriage, graduation, and parenthood. A kind category of *life event.* (Chapter 7)

Prejudice. The long-term, persistent overcategorizing and negative stereotyping of others as members of undesirable groups. (Chapter 15)

Premature ejaculation. The male sexual dysfunction of ejaculating quickly, either before or shortly after the beginning of intercourse. (Chapter 11)

Primary impotence. The male sexual condition of never having been able to maintain erections long enough to engage in intercourse. (Chapter 11)

Primary orgasmic dysfunction. The female sexual condition of never having experienced an orgasm. (Chapter 11)

Primary prevention. Seeking to stop illness before it develops, in contrast to secondary prevention, which treats illness when it first appears, and tertiary prevention, which treats illness after it has developed. The goal of *epidemiology.* (Chapter 5)

Private self. A person's understanding of himself or herself as he or she really is; the truly felt positive and negative aspects of self, including fears, insecurities, and inadequacies. The unfiltered core of a person's being. (Chapter 3)

Private self-consciousness. A person's awareness of what is happening within himself or herself; clearly felt states, physical and emotional. (Chapter 3)

Privileged communication. The legal guarantee that statements in therapy are private and therapists cannot be forced to disclose in court what clients have said during treatment. (Chapter 14)

Projection. A way of excluding anxiety-arousing feelings or thoughts from awareness by attributing the unacceptable feelings or thoughts to others. A type of *defense mechanism* related to *repression.* (Chapter 4)

Psychoanalysis. Theory of personality developed by Sigmund Freud that asserts that human functioning is primarily *unconscious* and irrational. Also an approach to treatment of disorders and a way of thinking about humankind that profoundly influenced twentieth-century psychology. (Chapter 2)

Psychogenic impotence. A man's inability to have intercourse because of psychological, rather than physiological, factors. (Chapter 11)

Psychogenic pain. The experience of real hurt that has no observable physical cause. (Chapter 5)

Psychological reactance. Excessive opposition to instruction on expectation; due to a situation and not a characteristic trait; this negativism is a response to threats to freedom of action or choice. (Chapter 8)

Psychosocial development. Theory of development that, through the influence of Erik Erikson, followed the Freudian theory of psychosexual development. Characterized by the initial developmental crises of trust versus mistrust, autonomy versus shame, and initiative versus guilt in relationships. This theory holds that personality continues to develop throughout the life cycle. (Chapter 2)

Public self. The image a person presents to others to evoke the socially approved view of himself or herself as competent, sincere, and likeable. (Chapter 3)

Public self-consciousness. A person's awareness and uncertainty of himself or herself in public; the discomfort or embarrassment a person feels when being observed by others or when speaking in public. (Chapter 3)

Rational-emotive therapy. Treatment of cognitions, developed by Albert Ellis, that teaches clients to dispute their irrational beliefs and rationally and logically understand their actions, beliefs, and consequences. The pioneering form of cognitive therapy. (Chapter 14)

Rationalization. An apparently logical analysis of a failure or fear; an attempt to explain away anxiety-arousing fears. A type of *defense mechanism* related to *intellectualization*. (Chapter 4)

Reaction formation. The adoption of a feeling, thought, or behavior opposite to one's actual feeling or thought. A type of *defense mechanism*. (Chapter 4)

Realistic types. People who like explicit, ordered, systematic tasks, are technically competent with machines and tools, and enjoy manipulating objects rather than working with other people. One of the six personality types described by the Holland theory of vocational choice. (Chapter 12)

Reciprocity. When two people move closer to each other, increasingly share themselves, become more intimate with each other, and let go of defensive and critical assessments of each other and themselves. One of the five stages associated with the development of loving. (Chapter 10)

Reframing. Presenting alternative perspectives on behaviors to encourage clients to rethink their actions and thoughts. A technique similar to using paradoxes (or contradictory ideas) to change a client's world view. (Chapter 14)

Regenerative sexuality. Openness and nondefensiveness in sexual contacts that reinvigorate and enliven the partners and regenerate their sexual self-confidence. A term coined by Jessie Bernard. (Chapter 11)

Regression. Behaving in a way that is appropriate only in an earlier phase of development; returning to an earlier stage of adjustment. A type of *defense mechanism.* (Chapter 4)

Relationship level. In nonverbal communication, the *context* of one person interacting with another. (Chapter 9)

Reminiscence therapy. Therapy for older adults in which they talk about their pasts and study the patterns in their lives to gain an overall perspective of their accomplishments and failures, to help them adjust to their current circumstances, and to help them become less susceptible to *despair.* (Chapter 7)

Renewal versus resignation. At the beginning of middle adulthood, the stage when people either discover a renewed commitment and purpose to their lives, or become depressed about their lives and resigned to being stuck where they are. (Chapter 7)

Repression. The exclusion from consciousness of anxiety-arousing thoughts, feelings, or memories. A type of *defense mechanism.* (Chapter 4)

Repressor. In the study of *repression,* one who usually screens upsetting thoughts or feelings from awareness. (Chapter 4)

Resistance. (**1**) Long-term adaptation and adjustment to threatened or actual *stress.* The second response in the *general adaptation syndrome.* (Chapter 4) (**2**) When a patient blocks thoughts or memories, is unwilling or unable to work on himself or herself and apply his or her insights, and does not enter into psychoanalysis enough to allow the therapist to make interpretations. One of the five essential components of *psychoanalysis.* (Chapter 14)

Retarded ejaculation. The male sexual dysfunction of being unable to ejaculate during intercourse despite previously successful intravaginal ejaculation. (Chapter 11)

Rhetoric. The way of saying something and how the statement influences listeners. Verbal persuasion; using words to alter clients' thoughts, feelings, and behaviors. Used by both Plato and Aristotle; may be considered a process in psychotherapy. (Chapter 14)

Role ambiguity. When the description of a job's duties are unclear and/or when a worker is confused about his or her job duties. (Chapter 12)

Role conflict. When competing job demands are made on a worker and the worker does not know nor is given guidelines about which demand to meet first. (Chapter 12)

Romantic love. Love between two people consisting of **attachment, caring,** and **intimacy** (according to Zick Rubin's definition); characterized by the couple's enjoyment in each other's company, mutual trust, and confidence sharing (like **friendship**); and involving a **passion cluster** and a **caring cluster** of emotions (as defined by Keith Davis). (Chapter 10)

Rubrics. Oversimplified categories of people that deny individuality and uniqueness and may spawn **prejudice.** (Chapter 15)

Scapegoating. When a group directs its feelings of frustration away from the person or people who inspire the feelings and toward a nonthreatening person who provides the group with a safe escape valve; the displacement of **aggression.** A form of harassment. (Chapter 12)

Secondary impotence. The male sexual condition of being persistently unable to have intercourse despite previous successful experiences. (Chapter 11)

Secondary orgasmic dysfunction. The female sexual condition of dissatisfaction with the frequency of orgasms experienced or the method by which they are achieved. (Chapter 11)

Selective protectiveness. In **friendships,** the identification and avoidance of overly sensitive topics and vulnerable areas; restraint from using personal information in a way that would hurt a friend. A process that fosters more closeness and sharing by guarding the disclosures already made. (Chapter 8)

Self-actualization. The state when one fulfills one's potential as a human being, has satisfied all five levels in **Maslow's hierarchy of needs** (according to Maslow), is sensitive to the needs of others as well as one's own needs, seeks truth, and has integrity. Defined on the basis of individual value systems rather than as a result of scientific analysis. (Chapter 15)

Self-concept. The totality of a person's beliefs, feelings, and perceptions about himself or herself. Consistent over time, it maximizes positive and minimizes negative views of self and evolves and changes with new experiences. (Chapter 3)

Self-determination. The feeling that one makes conscious choices in life and so controls, at least in part, what happens in one's life. An important part of **well-being.** (Chapter 15)

Self-directed search. John Holland's do-it-yourself approach to vocational planning that involves listing your desired occupations, identifying those activities in Holland's six categories of work that you like and do well, selecting the appealing occupations within Holland's categories that include your chosen activities, and then rating your abilities to do these activities compared to the abilities of others your own age. The ratings produce a summary code of the three occupational areas that are of greatest interest to you, which you compare to occupational codes to identify your ideal vocation. (Chapter 12)

Self-effacing. Making a negative or critical statement about self-achievement out of modesty. (Chapter 3)

Self-enhancing. Making a positive statement of self-achievement. (Chapter 3)

Self-fulfilling prophecy. The negative or positive influence of previous expectations on a person's self-concept and behavior. (Chapter 3)

Self-fulfillment. The realization of one's emotional, intellectual, interpersonal, and general potential for satisfaction and happiness as a human being. Includes *internal harmony, social competence,* and *mastery of changing demands.* One of five definitions of *adjustment.* See also *well-being.* (Chapter 1)

Self-interest stage. A pattern of friendship in the early school years in which children are chiefly concerned with what others can do for them personally. (Chapter 8)

Self-presentation. Showing oneself to others in a favorable light. Designed to make a friendship or relationship more valued. An aspect of ingratiation.

Self-therapy. The solitary, concentrated, and regular attention to one's own problems and the deliberate pursuit of new experiences in order to achieve one's goals. (Chapter 14)

Sensation seeking. The need for great stimulation, challenge, and diversity. Includes thrill and adventure seeking, experience seeking, disinhibition, and boredom susceptibility. (Chapter 4)

Sensitivity. A heightened awareness of feelings, learning to recognize when things are not right and you have slipped in some way. One of the skills to be practiced in order to master Fromm's *art of loving.* (Chapter 10)

Sensitizer. One who is usually alert to all possibly unpleasant thoughts or feelings and becomes upset by them. (Chapter 4)

Set point theory. The theory that all people have a biologically preset body weight determined by the number and distribution of fat cells in the body. The set point is the weight most people will maintain when they eat as they choose. (Chapter 5)

Sexual arousal cycle. According to Susan Walen's cognitive model of sexual arousal, the cycle begins with a person's perception of a sexual event, evaluation of the event as good, and ensuing sexual arousal. Then, the person must detect and label the arousal, attribute it to something, and evaluate it. Positive evaluation of arousal may lead to sexual behavior, which in turn leads to further arousal. Negative evaluation causes arousal to lessen or end. (Chapter 11)

Sexual harassment. When a coworker or manager makes sexually-related remarks, sexually teases, or inappropriately touches an employee. The most common form of on-the-job harassment. (Chapter 12)

Shaping. In *operant conditioning,* the procedure that first positively reinforces a particular freely occurring desired behavior in general and then rewards only the behavior that is closest to the final desired goal. (Chapter 2)

Shyness. A global personality characteristic, closely related to *nonassertiveness,* that is commonly exhibited by silence, inhibition, stammering, physical awkwardness, little eye contact, and a softer than usual speaking voice. (Chapter 6)

Situation. A specific social and physical circumstance limited in time; the temporary physical and social location in which one finds oneself. Meaningful only if it stands out from ordinary environments and relationships. (Chapter 13)

Social competence. The effective dealing with social environments (individuals, groups, and institutions) so that personal goals are reasonably met. One of five definitions of *adjustment.* (Chapter 1)

Social density. The extent of one's forced contact with others in a living or working environment. When a great many people are required to share the same areas, even if the *spatial density* is deemed adequate, a problem may arise because of the people's required contact with each other. (Chapter 13)

Social penetration theory. The theory that interpersonal interactions occur at different layers of the participants' personalities and that, as a relationship progresses, deeper (core) layers are penetrated and made accessible. (Chapter 8)

Social readjustment rating scale (SRRS). The 43-item scale developed by Thomas Holmes and R.H. Rahe to assess the influence of stressful life events on physical illness. (Chapter 4)

Social rule level. In nonverbal communication, the *context* of two people who have already achieved the *relationship level* interacting with others. (Chapter 9)

Social types. People who enjoy helping, training, and enlightening others, who prefer human relations work to working with machines. One of the six personality types described by the Holland theory of vocational choice. (Chapter 12)

Spatial density. The amount of physical space, usually measured in square feet, available per person in a living or working environment. (Chapter 13)

Specific receptor theory. The belief that *pain* is a sensation felt only when particular nerve endings are stimulated. A theory that was popular at the end of the nineteenth century. (Chapter 5)

Spectatoring. In a sexual encounter, a person's detachment from personal contact, leading the person to watch and evaluate his/her performance. The detachment itself often impairs sexual performance. A cause of men's *psychogenic impotence.* (Chapter 11)

Spontaneous remission. When people suffering from distress improve on their own, without professional help; the natural healing of psychological disorders. (Chapter 14)

Stagnation. Being stuck in one place with unchanging ideas and rules for living. In Erik Erikson's model of the eight stages of life, a characterization of adulthood. See also *generativity.* (Chapter 7)

Stimulus–organism–response. The theory that values the role of the organism in interpreting and reacting to the stimulus. A supplement to the *stimulus–response* theory in modern *behaviorism.* (Chapter 2)

Stimulus overload. When the amount of contact, communication, and involvement with others is excessive. A problem associated with overcrowding. (Chapter 13)

Stimulus–response. The principle of *behaviorism* that focuses scientific study of behavior on the response (behavior) of an organism to a stimulus (any object or event that makes a difference in behavior). (Chapter 2)

Stockholm Syndrome. When a victim of capture by terrorists submits to the persuasion efforts of the captors and comes to identify with the captors' views. Named after a hostage event in Stockholm, Sweden. (Chapter 4)

Strains. Our internal reactions to *stress;* our personal responses to and changes from *stressors.* (Chapter 4)

Stress. The assessment of events (internal or external) as threatening or potentially harmful and the subsequent psychological (cognitive, emotional, and behavioral) and physical responses to the threats. (Chapter 4)

Stress mediators. Psychological filters that shape the impact of *stressors.* The individual's shaping and screening system that receives and interprets stressful demands. (Chapter 4)

Stressors. External events that cause us *stress;* the outside demands for us to make adjustments. (Chapter 4)

Striving for superiority. The universal way of compensating for feelings of inferiority by developing a genuine sense of personal mastery and competence in life. One of the three major themes of Adlerian psychology. (Chapter 2)

Stunned immobility. Feelings of depression, emotional helplessness, dependency, victimization, aggression, and irritability. A long-term reaction to unemployment. (Chapter 12)

Subjective. Truth and reality as an individual personally sees and understands them; the individual's idiosyncratic ways of viewing the world. In *humanistic psychology,* the study of the subjective is primary to understanding all events and human behavior. (Chapter 2)

Sublimation. The adaptive and constructive channeling of unacceptable thoughts or feelings. A type of *defense mechanism* that is the well-being analog of *displacement.* (Chapter 4)

Supergo. The conscience, the internal moral authority that judges the rightness or wrongness of actions and thoughts. The censoring, judgmental part of the mental structure described by Freud that also includes *id* and *ego.* (Chapter 2)

Suppression. The conscious, deliberate refusal to face a real or possible threat. A type of *defense mechanism.* (Chapter 4)

Systematic desensitization. A method for treating phobias and other fears in which clients first are taught deep muscle relaxation and then learn to relax during exposure to increasingly upsetting thoughts or images until they can tolerate anxiety-arousing situations that previously made them panic. One of the major methods of behavior therapy. (Chapter 14)

Tacit knowledge. Practical intelligence; the ability to plan and successfully manage oneself, one's career, and others by using essential skills that are acquired indirectly and informally through experience. Unrelated to standardized intelligence scores. (Chapter 12)

Teachable moment. When a *transition* is an opportunity for growth; a time when a person is changing a role, behavior, environment, or other aspect of self or life and is open to new ways of living and deep, constructive change. (Chapter 7)

Temporal rhythms. The physical and psychological changes that occur through a certain time period, such as a day, month, or year; time-related bodily changes that affect how we think, feel, and perform. (Chapter 13)

Termination. The stopping of therapy; the term therapists use when treatment is ended. (Chapter 14)

Territoriality. Felt ownership of a specific location; the feeling that a certain place belongs to you. Related to the need for privacy and a place of one's own. (Chapter 13)

T-groups. Training groups, developed in the 1950s, that attempted to increase participants' personal awareness and teach them how to relate better to their coworkers and friends. The predecessors of today's executive and management seminars. (Chapter 13)

Thanatologist. One who studies death and the ways people approach death. (Chapter 7)

Therapeutic alliance. The personal bonding that occurs between the client and his or her therapist, which fosters the changes in behavior, attitude, or experience the client is seeking. (Chapter 14)

Trait and factor approach. The matching of an individual's abilities (traits) to items in a job description (occupational factors). A technique for choosing an occupation that is limited because it suggests only the approximate best fit job. (Chapter 12)

Transference. When a patient relates to the therapist as if the therapist were a person (or composite of people) from the patient's earlier life; when the patient attributes feelings, expectations, and reactions of people important in the patient's past to the therapist. One of the five essential components of *psychoanalysis.* (Chapter 14)

Transient relationships. Brief, nonrecurring, and more or less random relationships, usually with people in service occupations and for the transaction of personal or professional business. They may be nonperson relationships, relationships that focus on particular goals, relationships that involve behavior-eliciting strategies, or relationships in which one party acts as a sounding board for the other. (Chapter 8)

Transitions. Periods of change and the adjustments one makes in response to the change; balancing processes (to reestablish equilibrium after disruptive events or situations) that occur at various times throughout life. (Chapter 7)

Triggers. The circumstances that set off *peak experiences,* such as natural scenery, sexual love, childbirth, exercise, and religion. (Chapter 15)

Trust. The feeling that grows from two people's caring for each other without conditions, liking each other without performance requirements, and cherishing each other without wanting to change each other in any way. One of the five stages associated with the development of loving. (Chapter 10)

Type A behavior. Temporary, hard-driving, competitive, achievement- and/or deadline-oriented behavior that emerges in uncontrollable, stressful situations. A way of coping with a stressful environment. Not necessarily a pre-existing personality pattern. (Chapter 5)

Type A personalities. People who strive relentlessly to achieve, bind themselves with strict deadlines, and approach their worlds competitively and aggressively. Those with hard-driving lifestyles may be at risk for coronary heart disease. (Chapter 5)

Type A work environments. Extremely fast-paced, demanding, and controlling work environments, which best suit *Type A personalities.* (Chapter 12)

Type B personalities. People who are relaxed, noncompetitive, and nonhostile, with easygoing lifestyles. (Chapter 5)

Type B work environments. Routine, moderately challenging, and moderately paced (in terms of time demands) work environments, which best suit *Type B personalities.* (Chapter 12)

Ulyssean. An adventuresome and growth- and experience-seeking approach to later years in life, named after the hero of Greek literature who had grand adventures well into his seventies. (Chapter 7)

Unconditional positive regard. When a person cares about and prizes another for who that other is, regardless of what the other feels, thinks, or does; nonjudgmental affection without performance demands. A condition that promotes the *actualizing tendency.* (Chapter 2)

Unconditioned response. In *classical conditioning,* the natural, often instinctive response to an *unconditioned stimulus;* a physiological reflex or untrained action. (Chapter 2)

Unconditioned stimulus. In *classical conditioning,* the stimulus that is powerful enough to produce a behavior without any prior learning—that naturally produces a behavior. (Chapter 2)

Unconscious. The mental processes and content (unacceptable or repressed instincts, memories, feelings, and experiences) not available to awareness; what one cannot readily recall. A key aspect of Freud's theory of *psychoanalysis.* (Chapter 2)

Unexpected events. Happenings that cannot be predicted, that are nonnormative, that catch one unaware, that cause idiosyncratic responses, and that may shape adult development more than *predictable transitions.* A category of *life event.* (Chapter 7)

Universal Should List. The pattern all people have of telling themselves what they should be doing; the (unspoken) list of ideal traits and standards we each have for ourselves. (Chapter 3)

Uplifts. The minor daily positive experiences in life, which may accumulate to bring relief from *hassles* and give pleasure. (Chapter 4)

Vasocongestion. The engorgement of body tissues with blood, causing the male's penis to become erect, the female's vaginal tissues to congest with blood, and producing nipple erections and a skin flush on most women and many men. The first sign of sexual arousal. (Chapter 11)

Well-being. A subjective emotional state of *positive affect,* relatively low *negative affect,* and *general life satisfaction.* The deliberate movement toward the achievement of desired life goals and ways of being. Related to the concept of *adjustment* as *self-fulfillment.* (Chapter 1)

Wellness. The positive functioning of the whole physical person; high-level *well-being* or health well beyond the simple absence of illness. (Chapter 5)

Wife abuse. Physical violence, rape, or the threat of violence directed at a woman by her husband. Associated with verbal *nonassertiveness.* (Chapter 6)

Workcentric. The idea that all civilization—politics, culture, religion—has labor-based economic foundations. Karl Marx's reinterpretation of history as shaped by workers and their work. (Chapter 12)

Working self-concept. A self-concept that shifts subtly and temporarily, largely in response to social dynamics, without demanding major revisions to the individual's consistent view of self. (Chapter 3)

Zeitgeist. The spirit of the times; the extraordinary intellectual and social atmosphere in which people may rise above their limitations and become extraordinary. (Chapter 3)

REFERENCES

Ahrentzen, S., Jue, G.M., Skorpanich, M.A. & Evans, G.W. (1982). School environments and stress. In G.W. Evans (Ed.), *Environmental stress.* Cambridge: Cambridge University Press.

Alberti, R.E. & Emmons, M.L. (1975). *Stand up, speak out, talk back!* New York: Pocket Books.

Alberti, R.E. (Ed.). (1977). *Assertiveness: Innovations, applications, issues.* San Luis Obispo, CA: Impact.

Albrecht, G.L. & Gift, H.C. (1975). Adult socialization: Ambiguity and adult life crises. In N. Datan & L.H. Ginsberg (Eds.), *Life-span developmental psychology: Normative life crises.* New York: Academic Press.

Alden, L. & Cappe, R. (1981). Nonassertiveness: Skill deficit or selective self-evaluation. *Behavior Therapy, 12,* 107–114.

Allport, G.W. (1958). *The nature of prejudice.* New York: Doubleday Anchor.

Allport, G.W. (1961). *Pattern and growth in personality.* New York: Holt, Rinehart & Winston.

Altman, I. & Taylor, D.A. (1973). *Social penetration: The development of interpersonal relationships.* New York: Holt, Rinehart & Winston.

American Correctional Association (1966). *Manual of correctional standards.* Washington, DC: American Correctional Association.

Anderson, C.A. & Arnoult, L.R. (1985). Attributional style and everyday problems in living: Depression, loneliness, and shyness. *Social Cognition, 3,* 16–35.

Andrews, F.M. & Withey, S.B. (1976). *Social indicators of well-being: American's perceptions of life quality.* New York: Plenum.

Appel (1983). *Cults in America: Programmed for Paradise.* New York: Holt, Rinehart & Winston.

Appignanesi, R. (1979). *Freud for beginners.* London: Writers and Readers Publishing Cooperation.

Appley, M.H. & Trumball, R. (1977). On the concept of psychological stress. In A. Monet & R.S. Lazarus (Eds.), *Stress and coping, an anthology.* New York: Columbia University Press.

Argyle, M., Lalljee, M. & Cook, M. (1968). The effect of visibility on interactions in a dyad. *Human Relations, 21,* 3–17.

Aries, P. (1974). *Western attitudes toward death: From the Middle Ages to the present.* Baltimore: Johns Hopkins Press.

Aronson, E. (1970). Once we have learned to expect love, favors and praise from a person close to us, that person may become less potent than a stranger as a source of reward. *Psychology Today, 4*(3), 48–50, 74.

Aronson, E. (1980). *The social animal.* San Francisco: Freeman.

Aschoff, J. (1981). Annual rhythms in man. In J. Aschoff (Ed.), *Handbook of behavioral neurobiology* (Vol. 4). New York: Plenum.

Asimov, I. (1976). *Still more lecherous limericks.* New York: Walker & Company.

Austin-Lett, G. & Sprague, J. (1976). *Talk to yourself: Experiencing interpersonal communication.* Boston: Houghton Mifflin.

Averill, J.R. (1983). Studies on anger and aggression: Implications for theories of emotion. *American Psychologist, 38,* 1145–1160.

Axline, V. (1947). *Play therapy.* Boston: Houghton Mifflin.

Babineau, R. & Schwartz, A.J. (1977). The treatment of sexual dysfunction in a university health population. *Journal of the College Health Association, 25,* 176–181.

Bach, G.R. & Wyden, P. (1968). *The intimate enemy: How to fight fair in love and marriage.* New York: Avon.

Baltes, P.B. (Ed.) (1978). *Life-span development and behavior* (Vol. 1). New York: Academic Press.

Baltes, P.B. (1979). Life-span developmental psychology: Some converging observations on history and theory. In P.B. Baltes & O.G. Brim, Jr. (Eds.), *Life-span development and behavior* (Vol. 2). New York: Academic Press.

Bandura, A. (1977). Self-efficacy: Toward a unifying theory of behavioral change. *Psychological Review, 84,* 191–215.

Barker, R.G. & Associates. (1978). *Habitats, environments, and human behavior.* San Francisco: Jossey-Bass.

Barton, A. (1974). *Three worlds of therapy: Freud, Jung and Rogers.* Palo Alto, CA: Mayfield.

Basedow, H. (1925). *The Australian aboriginal.* Adelaide: F.W. Preece & Sons.

Bauman, K.E. & Wilken, R.R. (1976). Premarital sexual attitudes of unmarried university students. *Archives of Sexual Behaviors, 5,* 29–37.

Beck, A. (1976). *Cognitive therapy and the emotional disorders.* New York: International Universities Press.

Beers, C.W. (1907). *A mind that found itself.* Garden City, NY: Doubleday.

Bell, C., Kirkpatrick, S.W., & Rinn, R.C. (1986). Body image of anorexic, obese, and normal females. *Journal of Clinical Psychology, 42,* 431–439.

Bell, R.R. (1981). *Worlds of friendship.* Beverly Hills, CA: Sage.

Bellak, L. (1971). *The porcupine dilemma: Reflections on the human condition.* New York: The Citadel Press.

Benson, L. (1974). *Images, heroes, and self-perceptions.* New York: Prentice-Hall.

Bergin, A.E., & Lambert, M.J. (1978). The evaluation of therapeutic outcomes. In S.L. Garfield & A.E. Bergin (Eds.), *Handbook of Psychotherapy and behavior change: An Empirical analysis.* New York: Wiley.

Berman, J.S. & Norton, N.C. (1985). Does professional training make a therapist more effective? *Psychological Bulletin, 98,* 401–407.

Bernard, J. (1971). Sex as a regenerative force. In H.A. Otto (Ed.), *The new sexuality.* Palo Alto, CA: Science and Behavior Books.

Berne, E. (1971). *Sex in human loving.* New York: Pocket Books.

Berscheid, E., Brothern, T. & Graziano, W. (1976). Gain–loss theory and the "law of infidelity." *Journal of Personality and Social Psychology, 33,* 709–718.

Beyette, B. (1981, August 24). Inner health: Educating the doctor within each patient. *Los Angeles Times,* pp. V–1, 2.

Bierce, A. (1946). *The collected writings of Ambrose Bierce.* Secaseus, NJ: Citadel.

Birdwhistle, R.L. (1970). *Kinesics and context: Essays on body-motion communication.* Philadelphia: University of Pennsylvania Press.

Blackman, S. (1982). Social psychological perspectives on pain. In H.S. Friedman & M.R. DiMatteo (Eds.), *Interpersonal issues in health care.* New York: Academic Press.

Blanchard, K. & Johnson, S. (1983). *The one minute manager.* New York: The Berkley Publishing Group.

Blanck, P.D., Rosenthal, R., Vannicelli, M. & Lee, T.D. (1986). Therapists' tone of voice: Descriptive, psychometric, interactional, and competence analyses. *Journal of Social and Clinical Psychology, 4,* 154–178.

Blandford, L. (1982, August 1). Jonathan Miller meets Mozart in St. Louis. *New York Times Magazine, 131*, pp. 22–25.

Blatt, B. (1970). *Exodus from pandemonium: Human abuse and a reformation of public policy.* Boston: Allyn & Bacon.

Block, J.D. (1980). *Friendship.* New York: Macmillan.

Blumenthal, M. (1987). The word "love." *The Nation, 244* (1), 26.

Boerstler, R.W. (1986). Meditation and the dying process. *Journal of Humanistic Psychology, 26,* 104–124.

Bolles, R.N. (1982). *The basic principles of life/work planning as they apply particularly to the world of work, job hunting, and career change.* Chicago: Success Unlimited.

Bolles, R.N. (1985). *What color is your parachute.* Berkeley, CA: Ten Speed Press.

Bonaparte, M., Freud, A. & Kris, E. (Eds.). (1954). *The origins of psycho-analysis: Letters to Wilhelm Fliess, drafts, and notes: 1887–1902, by Sigmund Freud.* New York: Basic Books.

Bond, M.H., Leung, K. & Wan, K. (1982). The social impact of self-effacing attributions: The Chinese case. *The Journal of Social Psychology, 118,* 157–166.

Bordon, R.J. & Homleid, G.M. (1978). Handedness and lateral positioning in heterosexual couples: Are men still strong-arming women? *Sex Roles, 4,* 67–73.

Bowen, M. (1978). *Family therapy in clinical practice.* New York: Jason Aronsen.

Bowers, K.S. (1980). "De-controlling" cognition and cognitive control: Toward a reconciliation of cognitive and dynamic therapies. In M.J. Mahoney (Ed.), *Psychotherapy process: Current issues and future directions.* New York: Plenum.

Bradburn, N.M. (1969). *The structure of psychological well-being.* Chicago: Aldine.

Brehm, S.S. & Brehm, J.W. (1981). *Psychological reactance: A theory of freedom and control.* New York: Academic Press.

Brehm, S.S. (1985). *Intimate relationships.* New York: Random House.

Bresler, D. (1984). Mind-controlled analgesia: The inner way to pain control. In A.S. Sheikh (Ed.), *Imagination and healing* (Vol. 1). Farmingdale, NY: Baywood.

Brilliant, A. (1971). *I may not be totally perfect, but parts of me are excellent, and other brilliant thoughts.* Santa Barbara, CA: Woodbridge Press.

Broadbent, D.E. (1985). The clinical impact of job design. *British Journal of Clinical Psychology, 24,* 33–44.

Brodsky, C.M. (1976). *The harassed worker.* Lexington, MA: Lexington Books.

Brody, E.B. (1985). Patients' rights: A cultural challenge to western psychiatry. *American Journal of Psychiatry, 142,* 58–62.

Brown, B.B. (1974). The anatomy of a phenomenon: Me and BFT. *Psychology Today, 8*(3), 48–56, 74–112.

Brown, G. (1980). *The new celibacy.* New York: Ballantine.

Browne, Sir Thomas (1969). Religious Medici, II$_{ix}$. In B. Evans (Compiler), *Dictionary of quotations.* New York: Bonanza.

Bugental, J.F.T. (1967). The challenge that is man. In J.F.T. Bugental (Ed.), *Challenges of humanistic psychology.* New York: McGraw-Hill.

Bugental, J.F.T. (1978). *Psychotherapy and process: The fundamentals of an existential-humanistic approach.* Reading, MA: Addison-Wesley.

Bull, P. (1983). *Body movement and interpersonal communication.* Chichester, England: Wiley.

Bullough, V.L. & Bullough, B. (1977). *Sin, sickness and sanity: A history of sexual attitudes.* New York: New American Library.

Burger, J.M. (1981). Verbal message inhibition through nonverbal communication within an open-space office: An application of equilibrium theory to organizational contexts. Paper presented at the annual meeting of the American Psychological Association, Los Angeles.

Burgess, A.W. & Brodsky, S.L. (1981). Applying flight education principles to rape prevention. *Family and Community Health, 4,* 45–51.

Bush, D.F. (1985). Gender and nonverbal expressiveness in patient recall of health information. *Journal of Applied Communication Research, 13,* 103–117.

Buss, A.H. (1980). *Self-consciousness and social anxiety.* San Francisco: W.H. Freeman.

Buss, T.F. & Redburn, F., with J. Waldron. (1983). *Mass unemployment: Plant closings and community mental health.* Beverly Hills, CA: Sage.

Bustad, L.K. & Hines, L.M. (1983). Placement of animals with the elderly: Benefits and strategies. In A.H. Katcher & A.M. Beck (Eds.), *New perspectives on our lives with companion animals.* Philadelphia: University of Pennsylvania Press.

Butler, C.A. (1976). New data about female sexual response. *Journal of Sex and Marital Therapy, 2,* 40–46.

Butler, R.N. (1963). The life-review: An interpretation of reminiscence in the aged. *Psychiatry, 26,* 65–76.

Butler, S. (1969). *Notebooks.* Quoted in B. Evans (Compiler), *Dictionary of quotations.* New York: Bonanza.

Cacioppo, J.T., Petty, R.E., Losch, M.E. & Kim, H.S. (1986). Electromyographic activity over facial muscle regions can differentiate the valence and intensity of affective reactions. *Journal of Personality and Social Psychology, 50,* 260–268.

Caesar, S. (1971). What psychoanalysis did for me. In L. Freeman (Ed.), *Celebrities on the couch.* New York: Pocket Books.

Calderone, M.S. (1972). *Sex, love and intimacy: Whole life styles?* New York: SIECUS.

Calhoun, J.B. (1962). Population density and social pathology. *Scientific American, 206,* 139–148.

Calhoun, J.B. (1966). The role of space in animal sociology. *Journal of Social Issues, 6,* 46–58.

Calhoun, L.G., Abernathy, C.B. & Selby, J.W. (1986). The rules of bereavement: Are suicidal deaths different? *Journal of Community Psychology, 14,* 213–218.

Campbell, A., Converse, P.E. & Rodgers, W. L. (1976). *The quality of American life: Perceptions, evaluations, and satisfactions.* New York: Russell Sage Foundation.

Campbell, D.O. (1977). *Strong-Campbell interest inventory manual.* Stanford: Stanford University Press.

Caplan, R.D., Cobb, S., French, J.R.P., Van Harrison, R. & Pinneau, S.R. (1975). *Job demands and worker health* (National Institute of Occupational Safety and Health Publication No. 75-160). Washington, DC: U.S. Government Printing Office.

Carnegie, D. (1936). *How to win friends and influence people.* New York: Simon & Schuster.

Carr, L.J. (1948). *Situational analysis: An observational approach to introductory sociology.* New York: Harper & Brothers.

Carroll, H.A. (1946). *Mental hygiene: The dynamics of adjustment.* New York: Prentice-Hall.

Carroll, J.L., Volk, K.D. & Hyde, J.S. (1985). Differences between males and females in motives for engaging in sexual intercourse. *Archives of Sexual Behavior, 14,* 131–139.

Carroll, L. (1964). *Alice's adventures under ground* (A facsimile of the original Lewis Carroll manuscript). Ann Arbor, MI: University Microfilms.

Casler, L. (1973). Toward a reevaluation of love. In M. Curtin (Ed.), *Symposium on love.* New York: Behavioral Publications.

Castaneda, C. (1971). *A separate reality: Further conversations with Don Juan.* New York: Pocket Books.

Catalano, R., Rook, K. & Dooley, D. (1986). Labor markets and help-seeking:

a test of the employment security hypothesis. *Journal of Health and Social Behavior, 27,* 277–287.

Chan, D.W. (1985). Perception and judgment of facial expressions among the Chinese. *International Journal of Psychology, 20,* 681–692.

Cheek, J.M. & Buss, A.H. (1981). Shyness and sociability. *Journal of Personality and Social Psychology, 41,* 330–339.

Chelune, G.J. (1979). *Self-disclosure: Origins, patterns, and implications of openness in interpersonal relationships.* San Francisco: Jossey-Bass.

Chiriboga, D. & Gigy, L. (1975). Perceived stress across life course. In M.F. Lowenthal, M. Thurnher & D. Chiriboga and Associates (Eds.), *Four stages of life.* San Francisco: Jossey-Bass.

Christie, R. (1970). Why Machiavelli? In R. Christie & F.L. Geis (Eds.), *Studies in Machiavellianism.* New York: Academic Press.

Clore, G.L., Wiggins, N.H. & Itkin, S. (1975). Gain and loss in attraction: Attributions from nonverbal behavior. *Journal of Personality and Social Psychology, 31*(4), 706–712.

Cockerman, W.C., Leuschen, G., Kunz, G. & Spaeth, J.L. (1986). Social stratification and self-management of health. *Journal of Health and Social Behavior, 27,* 1–14.

Coleridge, S.T. (1935). *The poems of Samuel Taylor Coleridge.* London: Oxford University Press.

Congreve, W. (1969). The Old Bachelor, V_x. In B. Evans (Compiler), *Dictionary of quotations.* New York: Bonanza.

Conway, F. & Siegelman, J. (1978). *Snapping: America's epidemic of sudden personality change.* New York: Delta.

Cook, J.D., Hepworth, S.J., Wall, T.D. & Warr, P.B. (1982). *The experience of work: A compendium and review of 249 measures and their use.* New York: Academic Press.

Cook, J. & Wall, T.D. (1980). New work attitude measures of trust, organizational commitment and personal need nonfulfillment. *Journal of Occupational Psychology, 53,* 39–52.

Cooley, M.L. & Hollandsworth, J.G. (1977). A strategy for teaching verbal content of assertive responses. In R.E. Alberti (Ed.), *Assertiveness: Innovations, applications, issues.* San Luis Obispo, CA: Impact.

Coopersmith, S. (1967). *The antecedents of self-esteem.* San Francisco: W.H. Freeman.

Coss, R.C. (1974). Reflection on the evil eye. *Human Behavior, 10,* 16–22.

Cotton, N.S. (1983). The development of self-esteem and self-esteem regulation. In J.E. Mack & S.L. Ablon (Eds.), *The development and sustenance of self-esteem in childhood.* New York: International University Press.

Cousins, N. (1979). *Anatomy of an illness as perceived by the patient: Reflections of healing and regeneration.* Toronto: Bantam.

Cowart-Steckler, D. (1985). A Guttman scale of sexual experience: An update. *Journal of Sex Education and Therapy, 10,* 49–51.

Cox, T. (1978). *Stress.* London: Macmillan.

Cox, T., Thirlaway, J. & Cox, S. (1983). Repetitive work, well-being, and arousal. In H. Ursin & R. Murison (Eds.), *Biological and psychological aspects of psychosomatic disease.* Oxford: Pergamon.

Cox, V.C., Paulus, P.B. & McCain, G. (1984). Prison crowding research: The relevance for prison housing standards and a general approach regarding crowding phenomena. *American Psychologist, 39,* 1148–1160.

Creekmore, C.R. (1985). Cities won't drive you crazy. *Psychology Today, 19*(1), 46–53.

Cumming, E. & Henry, W.E. (1979). *Growing old: The process of disengagement.* New York: Arno Press.

Cummings, N.A. & Sobel, S.B. (1985). Malpractice insurance: Update on sex claims. *Psychotherapy, 22,* 186–188.

Danish, S.J. (1983). Musings about personal competence: The contributions of sport, health, and fitness. *American Journal of Community Psychology, 11,* 221–240.

Dattore, P.J., Shontz, F.C. & Coyne, L. (1980). Premorbid personality differentiation of cancer and noncancer groups: A test of the hypothesis of cancer proneness. *Journal of Consulting and Clinical Psychology, 48,* 388–394.

Davidson, L.M. & Baum, A. (1986). Chronic stress and post-traumatic stress disorders. *Journal of Consulting and Clinical Psychology, 54,* 303–308.

Davies, J. (1969). Nosce Teipsum. Quoted in B. Evans (Compiler), *Dictionary of quotations.* New York: Bonanza.

Davis, F. (1959). The cab driver and his fare: Facets of a fleeting relationship. *American Journal of Sociology, 65,* 158–165.

Davis, K.E. (1985). Near and dear: Friendship and love compared. *Psychology Today, 19*(2), 22–30.

Davis, M.S. (1973). *Intimate relationships.* New York: Free Press.

Davis, M.S. & Marsh, L. (1986). Self-love, self-control, and alexithymia: Narcissistic features of two bulimic adolescents. *American Journal of Psychotherapy, 40,* 224–232.

Deaux, K. & Farris, T. (1977). Attributing causes for one's own performance: The effects of sex norms and outcomes. *Journal of Research in Personality, 11,* 59–72.

deBruijn, G. (1982). From masturbation to orgasm with a partner: How some women bridge the gap—and why others don't. *Journal of Sex and Marital Therapy, 8,* 151–167.

Deci, E.L. (1980). *The psychology of self-determination.* Lexington, MA: Lexington Books.

Deci, E.L. & Ryan, R.M. (1985). *Intrinsic motivation and self-determination in human behavior.* New York: Plenum.

Dekker, J., Dronkers, J. & Staffeleu, J. (1985). Treatment of sexual dysfunctions in male-only groups: Predicting outcome. *Journal of Sex and Marital Therapy, 11,* 80–90.

Dembroski, T.M., MacDougall, J.M., Eliot, R.S. & Buell, J.C. (1983). Stress, emotions, behavior, and cardiovascular disease. In L. Temoshok, C. vanDyke & L.S. Zegans (Eds.), *Emotions in health and illness: Theoretical and research foundations.* New York: Grune & Stratton.

d'Epinay, C.L. (1986). Time, space and socio-cultural identity: The ethos of the proletariat, small owners, and peasants in an aged population. *Time and Society, 107*(38), 89–104.

Depue, R.A. & Monroe, S.M. (1986). Conceptualization and measurement of human disorder in life stress research: The problem of chronic disturbances. *Psychological Bulletin, 99,* 36–51.

Derogatis, L., Meyer, J.K. & King, K.M. (1981). Psychopathology in individuals with sexual dysfunction. *American Journal of Psychiatry, 138,* 757–763.

Diamond, M. & Karlen, A. (1980). *Sexual decisions.* Boston: Little, Brown & Company.

Dickens, W.J. & Perlman, D. (1981). Friendship over the life cycle. In S. Duck & R. Gilmour (Eds.), *Personal relationships: Vol. 2. Developing personal relationships.* London: Academic Press.

Dickinson, E. (1967). *Poems (1890–1896).* Gainesville, FL: Scholars' Facsimiles & Reprints.

Dictionary of Occupational Titles. (1977). U.S. Department of Labor Employment and Training Administration, 4th Ed. Washington, DC: U.S. Department of Labor.

Diener, E. (1984). Subjective well-being. *Psychological Bulletin, 95,* 542–575.

Dietch, J. (1978). Love, sex roles, and psychological health. *Journal of Personality Assessment, 42,* 626–634.

Dilley, J.W., Ochitill, H.N., Perl, M. & Volberding, P.A. (1985). Findings in psychiatric consultations with patients with Acquired Immune Deficiency Syndrome. *American Journal of Psychiatry, 142,* 82–85.

Dion, K. (1981). Physical attractiveness, sex roles and heterosexual attraction. In M. Cook (Ed.), *The bases of human sexual attraction.* New York: Academic Press.

Dion, K.K. & Dion, K.L. (1975). Correlates of romantic love. *Journal of Personality, 43,* 39–57.

Dohrenwend, B.S., Krasnoff, L. & Askenasy, A.R. (1979). Exemplification of a method for scaling life events: The PERI life events scale. *Journal of Health and Social Behavior, 19,* 205–229.

Donaldson, S. (1977). *The ill earth war.* New York: Holt, Rinehart & Winston.

Donleavy, J.P. (1975). *The unexpurgated code: A complete manual of survival and manners.* New York: Delta.

Donnerstein, E. & Donnerstein, M. (1976). Research in the control of interracial aggression. In I.N. Russell, G. Geer & E.C. O'Neal (Eds.), *Perspectives on aggression.* New York: Academic Press.

Downey, L. (1980). Intergenerational change in sex behavior: A belated look at Kinsey's males. *Archives of Sexual Behavior, 9,* 267–298.

Druckman, D., Rozelle, R.M. & Baxter, J.C. (1982). *Nonverbal communication: Survey, theory and research.* Beverly Hills: Sage.

Duleep, H.O. (1986). Measuring the effect of income on adult mortality using longitudinal administrative record data. *Journal of Human Resources, 21,* 238–251.

Dutton, P.G. & Aron, A.P. (1974). Some evidence for heightened sexual attraction under conditions of high anxiety. *Journal of Personality and Social Psychology, 30,* 510–517.

Duvall, S. & Wicklund, R. (1972). *Objective self-awareness.* New York: Academic Press.

Easterbrook, J.A. (1978). *The determinants of free will: A psychological analysis of responsible, adjustive behavior.* New York: Academic Press.

Eberhardt, B.J. & Muchinsky, P.M. (1984). Structural validation of Holland's hexagonal model: Vocational classification through the use of biodata. *Journal of Applied Psychology, 69,* 174–181.

Ebersole, P.P. (1978). A theoretical approach to the use of reminiscence. In I.M. Burnside (Ed.), *Working with the elderly: Group processes and techniques.* North Scituate, MA: Duxbury.

Eichorn, D.H., Clausen, J.A., Haan, N., Honzik, M.P. & Mussen, P.H. (Eds.). (1981). *Present and past in middle life.* New York: Academic Press.

Ekman, P. (1978). Facial expression. In A.W. Siegman & S. Feldstein (Eds.), *Nonverbal behavior and communication.* New York: Lawrence Erlbaum Associates.

Ekman, P. (1985). *Telling lies: Clues to deceit in the marketplace, politics and marriage.* New York: W.W. Norton.

Eliot, G. (1969). Daniel Deronda VI, 42. In B. Evans (Compiler), *Dictionary of quotations.* New York: Bonanza.

Elliott, M.L. (1985). The use of "impotence" and "frigidity": Why has "impotence" survived? *Journal of Sex and Marital Therapy, 11,* 51–56.

Ellis, A. (1962). *Reason and emotion in psychotherapy.* New York: Lyle Stuart.

Ellis, A. (1973). *Humanistic psychotherapy: The rational-emotive approach.* New York: The Julian Press.

Ellis, A. (1985). Rational Humorous Songs. Handout distributed at the Evolution of Psychotherapy Conference, Phoenix, Arizona, November 1985.

Emerson, R.W. (1969). Nature. In B. Evans (Compiler), *Dictionary of quotations.* New York: Bonanza.

Emmons, R.A. (1986). Personal strivings: An approach to personality and subjective well-being. *Journal of Personality and Social Psychology, 51,* 1058–1068.

Emmons, R.A. & Diener, E. (1985). Personality correlates of subjective well-being. *Personality and Social Psychology Bulletin, 11,* 89–97.

Engstrom, J. (1983, June). Starting over. *Horizon, 26,* 62–64.

Erikson, E.H. (1950). *Childhood and society.* New York: Norton.

Erikson, E.H. (1968). Life cycle. In D.L. Sills (Ed.), *The international encyclopedia of the social sciences* (Vol. 9). New York: Crowell, Collier & Macmillan.

Erikson, E.H. (1982). *The life cycle completed: A review.* New York: W.W. Norton.

Erickson, F. (1979). Talking down: Some cultural sources of mis-communication in interracial interviews. In A. Wolfgang (Ed.), *Nonverbal behavior: Applications and cultural implications.* New York: Academic Press.

Eysenck, H.J. (1952). The effects of psychotherapy: An evaluation. *Journal of Consulting Psychology, 16,* 319–324.

Eysenck, H.J. (1976). *Sex and personality.* London: Open Books.

Eysenck, H.J. & Wilson, G. (1979). *The psychology of sex.* London: Open Books.

Ezard, C.E. (1979). Facial expression, emotion, and motivation. In A. Wolfgang (Ed.), *Nonverbal behavior: Application and cultural implications.* New York: Academic Press.

Farbstein, J. & Kantrowitz, M. (1978). *People in places: Experiencing, using and changing the built environment.* Englewood Cliffs, NJ: Prentice-Hall.

Fast, J. (1970). *Body language.* New York: M. Evans.

Ferguson, T. (1980). Medical self-care: Self-responsibility for health. In A.C. Hastings, J. Fadiman & J.S. Gordon (Eds.), *Health for the whole person.* New York: Bantam.

Feshbach, N.D. (1979). Empathy training: A field study in affective education. In S. Feshbach & A. Freczek (Eds.), *Aggression and behavior change: Biological and social processes.* New York: Praeger.

Feshbach, N.D. (1983). Learning to care: A positive approach to child training and discipline. *Journal of Clinical Child Psychology, 12,* 266–271.

Fiedler, D. & Beach, L.R. (1978). On the decision to be assertive. *Journal of Consulting and Clinical Psychology, 46,* 537–546.

Fiore, A. & Swenson, C.H. (1977). Analysis of love relationships in functional and dysfunctional marriages. *Psychological Reports, 40,* 707–714.

Firth, J. & Shapiro, D. (1986). An evaluation of psychotherapy for job-related distress. *Journal of Occupational Psychology, 59,* 111–119.

Fischer, C.T. (1985). *Individualizing psychological assessment.* Monterey, CA: Brooks/Cole.

Fisher, W. & Byrne, D. (1981). Sexual background, attitudes and sexual attraction. In M. Cook (Ed.), *The bases of human sexual attraction.* New York: Academic Press.

Fitts, W.H. (1981). Issues regarding self-concept change. In M.D. Lynch, A.A. Norem-Hebeisen, & K.J. Georgen (Eds.), *Self-concept: Advances in theory and research.* Cambridge, MA: Ballinger.

Flannery, R.B., Jr. (1986). Major life events and daily hassles in predicting health status: Methodological inquiry. *Journal of Clinical Psychology, 42,* 485–487.

Ford, C.V. (1975). The Pueblo incident: Psychological response to severe stress. In I.G. Sarason & C.D. Spielberger (Eds.), *Stress and anxiety* (Vol. 2). Washington, DC: Hemisphere.

Fordyce, W.E. & Steger, J.C. (1979). Chronic pain. In O.F. Pomerleau & J.P. Brady (Eds.), *Behavioral medicine: Theory and practice.* Baltimore: Williams & Wilkins.

Forehand, R. & McMahon, R.J. (1981). *Helping the noncompliant child.* New York: Guilford.

Foreman, S.A. & Marmer, C.R. (1985). Therapist actions that address initially poor therapeutic alliances in psychotherapy. *American Journal of Psychiatry, 142,* 922–926.

Forsyth, D.R. & Strong, S.R. (1986). The scientific study of counseling and psychotherapy. *American Psychologist, 41,* 113–119.

Fort, J. (1971). Sex and health. In H.A. Otto (Ed.), *The new sexuality.* Palo Alto, CA: Science and Behavior Books.

Frank, J.D. (1961). *Persuasion and healing: A comparative study of psychotherapy.* Baltimore: The Johns Hopkins Press.

Frank, J.D. (1980). Aristotle as psychotherapist. In M.J. Mahoney (Ed.), *Psychotherapy process: Current issues and future directions.* New York: Plenum.

Frankl, V.E. (1955). *The doctor and the soul: An introduction to logotherapy.* New York: Alfred A. Knopf.

Freeman, A.C. (1987). Personal correspondence. Tuscaloosa, Alabama.

French, M. (1977). *The women's room.* New York: Jove/HBJ.

Frese, M. (1982). Occupational socialization and psychological development: An underemphasized research perspective in industrial psychology. *Journal of Occupational Psychology, 5,* 209–224.

Frese, M. (1985). Stress at work and psychosomatic complaints: A causal interpretation. *Journal of Applied Psychology, 70,* 314–328.

Freud, S. (1894). The Neuro-psychoses of defense. In J. Strachey (Ed.), *The standard edition of the complete psychological works of Sigmund Freud* (Vol. 3). London: Hogarth, 1952.

Frick, W.B. (1982). Conceptual foundations of self-actualization: A contribution to motivation therapy. *Journal of Humanistic Psychology, 22,* 33–52.

Friedman, H., Hall, J. & Harris, M. (1985). Type A behavior, nonverbal expressive style, and health. *Journal of Personality and Social Psychology, 48,* 1299–1315.

Friedman, M. & Rosenman, R.H. (1974). *Type A behavior and your heart.* New York: Knopf.

Frieswyk, S.H., Allen, J.G., Colson, D.B., Coyne, L., Gabbard, G.O., Horowitz, L. & Newsom, G. (1986). Therapeutic alliance: Its place as a process and outcome variable in dynamic psychotherapy research. *Journal of Consulting and Clinical Psychology, 54*(1), 32–38.

Frieze, I. (1980). Causes and consequence of marital rape. Paper presented at the Annual Convention of the American Psychological Association, Montreal.

Fromm, E. (1956). *The art of loving.* New York: Harper & Row.

Frost, R. (1946). *The pocket book of Robert Frost's poems.* New York: Washington Square Press.

Furnham, A. & Schaeffer, R. (1984). Person–environment fit, job satisfaction and mental health. *Journal of Occupational Psychology, 57,* 295–307.

Gagnon, J.H. & Simon, W. (1973). *Sexual conduct: The social sources of human sexuality.* Chicago: Aldine.

Galassi, J.P., DeLo, J.S., Galassi, M.D. & Bastien, S. (1974). The college self-expression scale: A measure of assertiveness. *Behavior Therapy, 5,* 165–171.

Galton, F. (1883). *Inquiries into human faculty and its development.* London: Macmillan.

Gandour, M.J. (1984). Bulimia: Clinical description, assessment, etiology, and treatment. *International Journal of Eating Disorders, 3,* 3–38.

Gardner, M.R. (1985). Hudson v. Palmer—"bright lines" but dark directions for prisoner privacy rights. *Journal of Criminal Law and Criminology, 76,* 75–115.

Garfield, S.L. (1983). Effectiveness of psychotherapy: The perennial controversy. *Professional Psychology, 14,* 35–43.

Garfield, S.L. (1986). Research on client variables in psychotherapy. In S.L. Garfield & A.E. Bergin (Eds.), *Handbook of psychotherapy and behavior change* (3rd ed.) New York: Wiley.

Garfield, S.L. & Kurz, M. (1952). Evaluation of treatment and related procedures in 1216 cases referred to a mental hygiene clinic. *Psychiatric Quarterly, 26,* 414–424.

Garner, A. (1981). *Conversationally speaking: Tested new ways to increase your personal and social effectiveness.* New York: McGraw-Hill Paperbacks.

Geller, L. (1984). Another look at self-actualization. *Journal of Humanistic Psychology, 24,* 93–106.

Gelles, R. (1979). *Family violence.* Beverly Hills, CA: Sage.

Gerber, L.A. (1982). The meanings of freedom: Thomas Mann's "Mario and the Magician." Presented at the American Psychological Association Annual Convention, Washington, DC.

Gergen, K.J. (1980). The emerging crisis in life-span developmental theory. In P.B. Baltes & O.G. Brim, Jr. (Eds.), *Life-span development and behavior* (Vol. 3). New York: Academic Press.

Gergen, K.J. (1981). The functions and foibles of negotiating self-conceptions. In M.D. Lynch, A.A. Norem-Hebeisen & K.J. Gergen (Eds.), *Self-concept: Advances in theory and research.* Cambridge, MA: Ballinger.

Gergen, K.J. (1982). From self to science: What is there to know? In J. Suls (Ed.), *The mutable self: A self-concept for social change.* Beverly Hills, CA: Sage.

Gibran, K. (1951, originally published 1923). *The prophet.* New York: Alfred A. Knopf.

Gilfillan, S.S. (1985). Adult intimate love relationships as new editions of symbiosis and the separation–individuation process. *Smith College Studies in Social Work, 55,* 183–196.

Ginzberg, E. (1966). *The development of human resources.* New York: McGraw-Hill.

Ginzberg, E. (1972). Toward a theory of occupational choice: A restatement. *Vocational Guidance Quarterly, 20,* 169–176.

Ginzberg, E., Ginsburg, J.W., Axelrad, S. & Herma, J.L. (1951). *Occupational choice.* New York: Columbia University Press.

Giorgi, A. (1970). *Psychology as a human science: A phenomenologically based approach.* New York: Harper & Row.

Glaser, S.R. (1980). Rhetoric and psychotherapy. In M.J. Mahoney (Ed.), *Psychotherapy process: Current issues and future directions.* New York: Plenum.

Gleser, G.C., Green, B.L. & Winget, C. (1981). *Prolonged psychosocial effects of disaster: A study of Buffalo Creek.* New York: Academic Press.

Goergen, D. (1974). *The sexual celibate.* New York: The Seabury Press.

Golan, N. (1981). *Passing through transitions: A guide for practitioners.* New York: Free Press.

Goldfried, M.R. (1980). Toward the delineation of therapeutic change principles. *American Psychologist, 35*(11), 991–999.

Goldiamond, I. (1974). Toward a constructional approach to social problems: Ethical and constitutional issues raised by applied behavior analysis. *Behaviorism, 2,* 1–84.

Goldman, W. (1973). *The princess bride.* New York: Ballantine.

Goldstein, R.L. (1986). Erotomania in men. *American Journal of Psychiatry, 143,* 802.

Gollwitzer, P.M., Wicklund, R.A. & Hilton, J.L. (1982). Admission of failure and symbolic self-completion: Extending Lewinian theory. *Journal of Personality and Social Psychology, 43,* 358–371.

Goodrich, F. (1956). *The diary of Anne Frank.* New York: Random House.

Goolkasian, G.A. (1986). *Confronting domestic violence: A guide for criminal justice agencies.* Washington, DC: National Institute of Justice.

Gordon, S. (1985). Before we educate anyone else about sexuality, let's come to grips with our own. *Journal of Sex Education and Therapy, 10,* 16–21.

Gosselin, C. (1981). The influence of special sexual desires. In M. Cook (Ed.), *The bases of human sexual attraction.* New York: Academic Press.

Gosselin, C. & Wilson, G. (1984). Fetishism, sadomasochism and related behaviors. In K. Howells (Ed.), *The psychology of sexual diversity.* Oxford: Basil Blackwell.

Gove, W.R. & Hughes, M. (1983). *Overcrowding in the household: An analysis of determinants and effects.* New York: Academic Press.

Grant, E.C. (1972). Non-verbal communication in the mentally ill. In R.A. Hinde (Ed.), *Non-verbal communication.* Cambridge: Cambridge University Press.

Greenburg, D. (1966). *How to make yourself miserable.* New York: Signet.

Greenwald, H. (1971). Sex as fun. In H.A. Otto (Ed.), *The new sexuality.* Palo Alto, CA: Science and Behavior Books.

Greenwood, J.W., III, & Greenwood, J.W., Jr. (1979). *Managing executive stress: A systems approach.* New York: John Wiley & Sons.

Grinspoon, L. (1964). The fallout shelter and the unacceptability of disquieting facts. In G.H. Grosser, H. Wechsler & M. Greenblatt (Eds.), *The threat of impending disaster: Contributing to the psychology of stress.* Cambridge, MA: The M.I.T. Press.

Grossarth-Maticek, R., Schmidt, P., Vetter, H. & Arndt, S. (1984). Psychotherapy research in oncology. In A. Steptoe & A. Mathews (Eds.), *Health care and human behavior.* London: Academic Press.

Grotjahn, M. (1963). A psychoanalyst passes a small stone with big troubles. In R.A. Baker (Ed.), *Psychology in the wry.* Princeton, NJ: D. Van Nostrand.

Gunther, B. (1971). Sensory awakening and sensuality. In H.A. Otto (Ed.), *The new sexuality.* Palo Alto, CA: Science and Behavior Books.

Haan, N., Honzik, M.P. & Mussen, P.A. (Eds.). (1981). *Present and past in middle life.* New York: Academic Press.

Hala, M.P. (1975). Reminiscence group therapy project. *Journal of Gerontological Nursing, 1,* 34–41.

Hall, C.S. & Lindzey, G. (1978). *Theories of personality* (3rd ed.). New York: John Wiley & Sons.

Halstead, M.M. & Halstead, L.S. (1978). A sexual intimacy survey of former nuns and priests. *Journal of Sex and Marital Therapy, 4,* 83–90.

Hamburg, D.A. (1981). An outlook on stress research and health. In Institute of Medicine, National Academy of Sciences, Committee to Study Research on Stress in Health & Disease, *Report of a study: Research on stress and human health.* Washington, DC: National Academy Press.

Hammen, C., Mayo, A., deMayo, R. & Marks, T. (1986). Initial symptom levels and the life-event–depression relationship. *Journal of Abnormal Psychology, 95,* 114–122.

Handy, L., Valentich, M., Cammaert, L.P. & Gripton, J. (1985). Feminist issues in sex therapy. *Journal of Social Work and Human Sexuality, 2*(2), 69–80.

Hansen, W.B. & Altman, I. (1976). Decorating personal places: A descriptive analysis. *Environment and Behavior, 8,* 491–504.

Hare, R.D. (1975). Anxiety, stress, and psychopathy. In I.G. Sarason & C.D. Spielberger (Eds.), *Stress and anxiety* (Vol. 2). Washington, DC: Hemisphere.

Harness, C. (1953). *The rose.* New York: Panther.

Harper, R.G., Wiens, A.N. & Matarazzo, J.D. (1978). *Nonverbal communication: The state of the art.* New York: Wiley.

Harris, P.R. (1984a). Shyness and psychological imperialism; On the dangers of ignoring the ordinary language roots of the terms we deal with. *European Journal of Social Psychology, 14,* 169–181.

Harris, P.R. (1984b). The hidden face of shyness: A message from the shy for researchers and practitioners. *Human Relations, 37,* 1079–1093.

Harvey, P.H. & Greene, P.J. (1981). Group composition: An evolutionary perspective. In H. Kellerman (Ed.), *Group cohesion: Theoretical and clinical perspectives.* New York: Grune & Stratton.

Havighurst, R.J. (1953). *Human development and education.* London: Longmans, Green.

Hawkins, R.C., II & Clement, P.F. (1984). Binge eating: Measurement problems and a conceptual model. In R.C. Hawkins II, W.J. Fremouw & P.F. Clement (Eds.), *The binge-purge syndrome: Diagnosis, treatment, and research.* New York: Springer.

Hawton, K. (1985). *Sex therapy: A practical guide.* New York: Oxford University Press.

Hayes, J.R. (1981). *The complete problem solver.* Philadelphia: The Franklin Institute Press.

Heath, D.H. (1968). *Growing up in college: Liberal education and maturity.* San Francisco: Jossey-Bass.

Heilbrun, A.B. (1984). Cognitive defenses and life stress: An information-processing analysis. *Psychological Reports, 54,* 3–17.

Heller, J. (1961). *Catch-22.* New York: Simon & Schuster.

Hendrick, C. & Hendrick, S. (1986). A theory and method of love. *Journal of Personality and Social Psychology, 50,* 392–402.

Hendricks, J. & Hendricks, C.D. (1977). *Aging in mass society: Myths and realities.* Cambridge, MA: Winthrop.

Henton, C.L. (1976). Nocturnal orgasm in college women: Its relation to dreams and anxiety associated with sexual factors. *The Journal of Genetic Psychology, 129,* 245–251.

Herold, E.S. & Goodwin, M.S. (1979). Self-esteem and sexual permissiveness. *Journal of Clinical Psychology, 35,* 908–911.

Herold, E.S. & Goodwin, M.S. (1981). Reasons given by female virgins for not having premarital intercourse. *The Journal of School Health, 51,* 496–499.

Heron, J. (1970). The phenomenology of social encounter: The gaze. *Philosophy and Phenomenology, 31,* 243–264.

Hiestand, D.L. (1971). *Changing careers after 35.* New York: Columbia University Press.

Hill, C., Rubin, Z. & Peplau, L. (1976). Breakups before marriage: The end of 103 affairs. *Journal of Social Issues, 32,* 147–168.

Hirshberg, N. (1980). Individual differences in social judgment: A multivariate approach. In M. Fishbein (Ed.), *Progress in social psychology* (Vol. 1). Hillsdale, NJ: Lawrence Erlbaum.

Hoffman, J.J. (1985). Client factors related to premature termination of psychotherapy. *Psychotherapy, 22,* 83–85.

Hokanson, J.E. (1983). *Introduction to the therapeutic process.* Reading, MA: Addison-Wesley.

Holland, B.C. & Ward, R.S. (1966). Homeostasis and psychosomatic medicine. In S. Arieti (Ed.), *American handbook of psychiatry* (Vol. 3). New York: Basic Books.

Holland, J.L. (1973). *Making vocational choices: A theory of careers.* Englewood Cliffs, NJ: Prentice-Hall.

Holland, J.L. (1985). *Making vocational choices: A theory of vocational personalities and work environments* (2nd ed.). Englewood Cliffs, NJ: Prentice-Hall.

Hollender, M.H. & Callahan, A.S., III. (1975). Erotomania or de Clérambault syndrome. *Archive of General Psychiatry, 32,* 1574–1576.

Holmes, T.H., and Rahe, R.H. (1967). The social readjustment rating scale. *Journal of Psychosomatic Research, 11,* 213–218.

Holroyd, J.C. & Brodsky, A.M. (1977). Psychologists' attitudes and practices regarding erotic and nonerotic physical contact with patients. *American Psychologist, 32,* 843–849.

Horne, R.L. & Picard, R.S. (1979). Psychosocial risk factors for lung cancer. *Psychosomatic Medicine, 41,* 503–514.

Horney, K. (1939). *The collected works of Karen Horney: Vol. 1. New ways in psychoanalysis.* New York: Norton.

Horowitz, M.J. & Solomon, G.F. (1975). A prediction of delayed stress response syndromes in Vietnam veterans. *Journal of Social Issues, 31*(4), 67–79.

House, J.S., Strecher, V., Metzner, H.L. & Robbins, C. (1986). Occupational stress and health among men and women in the Tecumseh Community Health Study. *Journal of Health and Social Behavior, 27,* 62–77.

Hovanitz, C.A. (1986). Life event stress and coping style as contributors to psychopathology. *Journal of Clinical Psychology, 42,* 34–42.

Hunt, M. (1987). Navigating the therapy maze: A consumer's guide to mental health treatment. *New York Times,* August 30, 1987, p. 28–31.

Hurrell, J.J., Jr. (1985). Machine-paced work and the Type A behaviour pattern. *Journal of Occupational Psychology, 58,* 15–25.

Huston, T.L. & Levinger, G. (1978). Interpersonal attraction and relationships. *Annual Review of Psychology, 29,* 115–156.

Huxley, L. (1963). *You are not the target.* New York: Farrar, Straus.

Iga, M. (1981). Suicide of Japanese youth. *Suicide and Life-Threatening Behavior, 11,* 17–30.

Insel, P.M. & Lindgren, H.C. (1977). Too close for comfort: Why one person's company is another's crowd. *Psychology Today, 11*(7), 100–106.

Ivanevich, J.M. & Matteson, M.T. (1984). A Type A–B person–work environment interaction model for examining occupational stress and consequences. *Human Relations, 37,* 491–513.

Ivey, A.E., Ivey, M.B. & Simek-Downing, L. (1987). *Counseling and psychotherapy: Integrating skills, theory, and practice* (2nd ed.). Englewood Cliffs, NJ: Prentice-Hall.

Jacobs, T.J. & Charles, E. (1980). Life events and the occurrence of cancer in children. *Psychosomatic Medicine, 42,* 11–23.

Jakes, J. (1972). *Mention my name in Atlantis.* New York: DAW Books.

James, W. (1890). *The principles of psychology* (Vol. 1). New York: Henry Holt & Company.

Janda, L.H. & O'Grady, K.E. (1980). Development of a sex anxiety inventory. *Journal of Consulting and Clinical Psychology, 48,* 169–175.

Janis, I.L. (1983). Stress inoculation in health care: Theory and research. In D. Meichenbaum & M.E. Jarenko (Eds.), *Stress reduction and prevention.* New York: Plenum.

Jayne, C.A. (1981). Two-dimensional model of female sexual response. *Journal of Sex and Marital Therapy, 7,* 3–30.

Jenni, D.A. & Jenni, M.A. (1976). Carrying behavior in humans: Analyses of sex differences. *Science, 194,* 859–860.

Johnson, S. (1969). Rasselas XXVI. In B. Evans (Compiler), *Dictionary of quotations.* New York: Bonanza.

Jones, E. (1953). *The life and work of Sigmund Freud: Vol. 1. The formative years and the great discoveries: 1856–1900.* New York: Basic Books.

Jones, E.E. (1964). *Integratiation: A social psychological analysis.* New York: Appleton Century Crofts.

Josten, D.M., Evans, A.M. & Love, R.R. (1986). The cancer-prevention clinic: A service program for cancer-prone families. *Journal of Psychosocial Oncology, 3,* 5–20.

Jourard, S. (1964). *The transparent self. Self-disclosure and well-being.* Princeton, NJ: D. Van Nostrand.

Jourard, S.M. (1968). *Disclosing man to himself.* Princeton, NJ: D. Van Nostrand.

Jourard, S.M. (1974). *Healthy personality: An approach from the viewpoint of humanistic psychology.* New York: Macmillan.

Kafka, F. (1936). *Metamorphosis and other stories.* Hammondsworth, England: Penguin.

Kahn, R.L., Wolfe, D.M., Quinn, R.P., Snoek, J.D. & Rosenthal, R. (1964). *Organizational stress: Studies in role conflict and ambiguity.* New York: Wiley.

Kaplan, H.S. (1977). Hypoactive sexual desire. *Journal of Sex and Marital Therapy, 3,* 3–9.

Kapleau, P. (Ed.). (1971). *The wheel of death: A collection of writings from*

Zen Buddhist and other sources on death, rebirth, dying. New York: Harper Colophon Books.

Karmel, L.J.I. (1973). The case for love. In M. Curtin (Ed.), *Symposium on love.* New York: Behavioral Publications.

Kastenbaum, R. (1975). Is death a life crisis? On the confrontation with death in theory and practice. In N. Datan & L. Ginsberg (Eds.), *Life-span developmental psychology: Normative life crises.* New York: Academic Press.

Katcher, A.H., Friedmann, E., Beck, A.M. & Lynch, J. (1983). Looking, talking, and blood pressure: The physiological consequences of interaction with the living environment. In A.H. Katcher & A.M. Beck (Eds.), *New perspectives on our lives with companion animals.* Philadelphia: University of Pennsylvania Press.

Katz, A. & Katz, U. (1983). *Foundations of nonverbal communication.* Carbondale: Southern Illinois University Press.

Kazdin, A.E. (1986). Comparative outcome studies of psychotherapy: methodological issues and strategies. *Journal of Consulting and Clinical Psychology, 54,* 95–105.

Kellam, S.G. & Ensminger, M.E. (1980). Theory and method in child psychiatric epidemiology. In F. Earls (Ed.), *Studies of children.* New York: Prodist.

Kellerman, H. (1981). The deep structures of group cohesion. In H. Kellerman (Ed.), *Group cohesion: Theoretical and clinical perspectives.* New York: Grune & Stratton.

Kelling, G.W. (1979). *Blind mazes: A study of love.* Chicago: Nelson-Hall.

Kelly, G.A. (1955). *The psychology of personal constructs* (2 vols.). New York: Norton.

Kendler, H.H. (1980). Self-fulfillment: Psychological fact or moral prescription? *Academic Psychology Bulletin, 2,* 287–295.

Kendon, A. (1973). Some functions of gaze direction in social interaction. In M. Argyle (Ed.), *Social encounters.* Chicago: Aldine.

Kenrick, D.T. & Cialdini, R.B. (1977). Romantic attraction: Misattribution versus reinforcement explanations. *Journal of Personality and Social Psychology, 35,* 381–391.

Kessler, J.W. (1982, September). The curious nature of teasing. Paper presented at the Annual Convention of the American Psychological Association, Washington, DC.

Kinsey, A.C., Pomeroy, W.B., Martin, C.E. & Gebhard, P.H. (1953). *Sexual behavior in the human female.* Philadelphia: W.B. Saunders Company.

Kinzel, A.F. (1970). Body buffer zone in violent prisoners. *American Journal of Psychiatry, 127,* 99–104.

Klausner, S.Z. (Ed.). (1968). *Why man takes chances: Studies in stress-seeking.* New York: Doubleday.

Kleinke, C. (1986). Gaze and eye contact: A research review. *Psychological Bulletin, 100,* 78–100.

Kleinke, C.L. & Staneski, R.A. (1980). First impressions of female bust size. *Journal of Social Psychology, 110,* 123–134.

Kliban, B. (1976). *Never eat anything bigger than your head and other drawings.* New York: Workman.

Kline-Graber, G. & Graber, B. (1978). Diagnosis and treatment procedures of pubococcygeal deficiencies in women. In J. LoPiccolo & L. LoPiccolo (Eds.), *Handbook of sex therapy.* New York: Plenum.

Kobasa, S.C. (1982). The hardy personality: Toward a social psychology of stress and health. In J. Suls & G. Sanders (Eds.), *Social psychology of health and illness.* Hillsdale, NJ: Erlbaum.

Kopp, S.B. (1971). *Guru: Metaphors from a psychotherapist.* Palo Alto, CA: Science and Behavior Books.

Kopp, S.B. (1972). *If you meet the Buddha on the road, kill him! The pilgrimage of psychotherapy patients.* Palo Alto, CA: Science and Behavior Books.

Krasner, L. & Houts, A.C. (1984). A study of the "value" systems of behavioral scientists. *American Psychologist, 39,* 840–850.

Krugman, M., Kirsch, I., Wickless, C., Milling, L., Golicz, H. & Toth, A. (1985). Neuro-linguistic programming treatment for anxiety: Magic or myth? *Journal of Consulting and Clinical Psychology, 53,* 526–530.

Krupnick, J.L. & Horowitz, M.J. (1981). Stress response syndromes. *Archives of General Psychiatry, 38,* 428–435.

Kruzich, T.M. (1986). The chronically mentally ill in nursing homes: Issues in policy and practice. *Health and Social Work, 11,* 5–14.

Kubler-Ross, E. (1969). *On death and dying.* Toronto: Macmillan.

Kuleshnyk, I. (1984). The Stockholm syndrome: Toward an understanding. *Social Action and the Law, 10*(2), 37–42.

Kuperminc, M. & Heimberg, R.G. (1983). Consequence probability and utility as factors in the decision to behave assertively. *Behavior Therapy, 14,* 637–646.

LaFarge, O. (1978). Spud and Cochise. In S. Robinson (Ed.), *The best of all possible worlds.* New York:

LaFrance, M. & Mayo, C. (1976). Racial differences in gaze behavior during conversation. *Journal of Personality and Social Psychology, 33,* 547–552.

LaFrance, M. & Mayo, C. (1987). *Moving bodies: Nonverbal communication in social relationships.* Monterey, CA: Brooks/Cole.

La Gaipa, J.J. (1981). Children's friendships. In S. Duck & R. Gilmour (Eds.), *Personal relationship: Vol. 2. Developing personal relationships.* London: Academic Press.

Lambert, M.J., Shapiro, D.A. & Bergin, A.E. (1986). The effectiveness of psychotherapy. In S.L. Garfield & A.E. Bergin (Eds.), *Handbook of psychotherapy and behavior change* (3rd ed.). New York: Wiley.

Laski, M. (1968). *Ecstacy: A study of some secular and religious experiences.* New York: Greenwood Press.

Laswell, T.E. & Laswell, M.E. (1976). I love you but I'm not in love with you. *Journal of Marriage and Family Counseling, 38,* 255–268.

Lazarus, R. (1969). *Patterns of adjustment and human effectiveness.* New York: McGraw-Hill.

Lazarus, R.S. (1979). Positive denial: The case for not facing reality [Interview by Daniel Coleman]. *Psychology Today, 13*(6), 44–52, 57, 60.

Leahy, P.J. (1986). The determinants of unemployment status over time. *Journal of Urban Affairs, 8,* 71–81.

Lear, E. (1978, originally published 1863). A book of nonsense. In E. Rhys (Ed.), *A book of nonsense.* New York: Everyman's Library, Dutton.

Lefcourt, H.M. (1976). *Locus of control: Current trends in theory and research.* Hillsdale, NJ: Lawrence Erlbaum Associates.

Leff, H.L. (1978). *Experience, environment, and human potentials.* New York: Oxford University Press.

LeJune, R. & Alex, N. (1974). On being mugged: The event and its aftermath. In S.L. Messinger & Associates (Eds.), *The Aldine crime and justice annual 1973.* Chicago: Aldine.

Lerner, R.M. & Ryff, C.D. (1978). Implementation of the life-span view of human development: The sample case of attachment. In P.B. Baltes (Ed.), *Life-span development and behavior* (Vol. 1). New York: Academic Press.

Lester, D., Brazill, N., Ellis, C. & Guerin, T. (1984). Correlates of romantic attitudes toward love, androgeny and self-disclosure. *Psychological Reports, 54,* 554.

Lester, D., Doscher, K., Harris, D. & Smith, D. (1984). Correlates of a healthy attitude toward loving. *Psychological Reports, 54,* 790.

Lester, D. & Wright, T. (1978). Suicide and overcontrol. *Psychological Reports, 42,* 1278.

Levenson, H. & Harris, C.N. (1980). Love and the search for identity. In K.S. Pope and Associates (Eds.), *On love and loving.* San Francisco: Jossey-Bass.

Levi, L. (1981). *Preventing work stress.* Reading, MA: Addison-Wesley.

LeVine, R.A. (1982). The self and its development in an African society: A preliminary analysis. In B. Lee (Ed.), *Psychosocial theories of the self.* New York: Plenum.

LeVine, S.V. (1984). Radical departures. *Psychology Today, 18*(8), 20–27.

Levinson, D.J., Darrow, C.N., Klein, E.B., Levinson, M.H. & McKee, B. (1978). *The seasons of a man's life.* New York: Alfred A. Knopf.

Levinson, D.J. (1986). A conception of adult development. *American Psychologist, 41,* 3–13.

Levinson, D.J. (1987). *The seasons of a woman's life.* Paper presented at the Annual Convention of the American Psychological Association, New York.

Levitan, S.A. & Johnston, W.B. (1973). *Work is here to stay, alas.* Salt Lake City: Olympus.

Levitas, G.B. (Ed.). (1965). *The world of psychoanalysis* (Vol. 1). New York: George Braziller.

Lewis, O. (1961). *Children of Sanchez: Autobiography of a Mexican family.* New York: Random House.

Lewis, P.N. & Gallois, C. (1984). Disagreements, refusal, or negative feelings: Perception of negatively assertive messages from friends and strangers. *Behavior Therapy, 15,* 353–368.

Ley, P. (1980). The psychology of obesity: Its causes, consequences, and control. In S. Rachman (Ed.), *Contributions to medical psychology* (Vol. 2). Oxford: Pergamon Press.

Lifton, R.J. (1964). Psychological effects of the atomic bomb in Hiroshima: The theme of death. In G.H. Grosser, H. Wechsler & M. Greenblatt (Eds.), *The threat of impending disaster: Contributing to the psychology of stress.* Cambridge, MA: The M.I.T. Press.

Lindner, R. (1955). *The fifty-minute hour.* New York: Bantam.

Livingston, K.R. (1980). Love as a process of reducing uncertainty-cognitive theory. In K.S. Pope and Associates (Eds.), *On love and loving.* San Francisco: Jossey-Bass.

Livson, N. (1973). Developmental dimensions of personality: A life-span formulation. In P.B. Baltes & K.W. Schaie (Eds.), *Life-span developmental psychology: Personality and socialization.* New York: Academic Press.

Lofquist, L.H. & Dawis, R.V. (1969). *Adjustment to work: A psychological view of man's problem in a work-oriented society.* New York: Appleton Century Crofts.

LoPiccolo, J. & Lobitz, W.C. (1978). The role of masturbation in the treatment of orgasmic dysfunction. In J. LoPiccolo & L. LoPiccolo (Eds.), *Handbook of sex therapy.* New York: Plenum.

Lowenthal, M.F., Thurnher, M., Chiriboga, D. & Associates. (1975). *Four stages of life: A comparative study of men and women facing transitions.* San Francisco: Jossey-Bass.

Lucas, M.J. & Halle, E. (1983). Anorgasmia. In J.K. Meyer, C.W. Schmidt, Jr. & T.N. Wise (Eds.), *Clinical management of sexual disorders* (2nd ed.). Baltimore: Williams & Wilkins.

Lumsden, D.P. (1975). Toward a systems model of stress: Feedback from an anthropological study of the impact of Ghana's Volta River Project. In I.G. Sarason & C.D. Spielberger (Eds.), *Stress and anxiety* (Vol. 2). Washington, DC: Hemisphere.

Lynch, K. (1972). *What time is this place?* Cambridge, MA: The M.I.T. Press.

Mace, D.R. (1971). Sex and marital enrichment. In H.A. Otto (Ed.), *The new sexuality.* Palo Alto, CA: Science and Behavior Books.

MacKenzie, K.L. & Goodstein, L.I. (1986). Stress and the control beliefs of prisoners: A test of three models of control-limited environments. *Journal of Applied Social Psychology, 16,* 209–228.

Mages, N.L. & Mendelsohn, G.A. (1979). Effects of cancer on patients' lives: A personological approach. In G.C. Stone, F. Cohen & N.E. Adler (Eds.), *Health psychology: A handbook.* San Francisco: Jossey-Bass.

Mahoney, M.J. & Mahoney, K. (1976). Fight fat with behavior control. *Psychology Today, 9*(12), 39–43, 91–94.

Malloy, M. (1977). *Things I meant to say when we were old.* New York: Double-day.

Markus, H. & Kunda, Z. (1986). Stability and malleability of the self-concept. *Journal of Personality and Social Psychology, 51,* 858–866.

Markus, H. & Wurf, E. (1987). The dynamic self-concept: A social psychological perspective. *Annual Review of Psychology, 38,* 299–337.

Marotz-Baden, R. & Colvin, P.L. (1986). Coping strategies: A rural–urban comparison. *Family Relations, 35,* 281–288.

Marwell, G. & Schmitt, D.R. (1975). *Cooperation: An experimental analysis.* New York: Academic Press.

Maslow, A.H. (1954). *Motivation and personality.* New York: Harper & Brothers.

Maslow, A.H. (1968). *Toward a psychology of being* (2nd ed). Princeton, NJ: D. Van Nostrand.

Masters, R. & Houston, J. (1978). *Listening to the body: The psychophysical way to health and awareness.* New York: Delta.

Masters, W.H. & Johnson, V.E. (1966). *Human sexual response.* New York: Bantam.

Masters, W.H. & Johnson, V.E. (1970). *Human sexual inadequacy.* New York: Bantam.

Masters, W.H. & Johnson, V.E. (1974). *The pleasure bond: A new look at sexuality and commitment.* Boston: Little, Brown, & Company.

Mathes, E.W. (1981). Maslow's hierarchy of needs as a guide for living. *Journal of Humanistic Psychology, 21,* 69–70.

Matlin, M.W. & Stang, D.J. (1978). *The Pollyanna principle: Selectivity in language, memory, and thought.* Cambridge, MA: Schenkman.

Matthews, B.S. & Wells, J.W. (1983). A comparative study of nocturnal emissions. *Journal of Sex Education and Therapy, 8,* 26–31.

Maxwell, R.J. (1983). *Contexts of behavior: Anthropological dimensions.* Chicago: Nelson-Hall.

McAdams, D.P., Healy, S. & Krause, S. (1984). Social motives and patterns of friendship. *Journal of Personality and Social Psychology, 43,* 829–838.

McAndrew, F.T. (1986). A cross-cultural study of recognition thresholds for facial expressions of emotion. *Journal of Cross-Cultural Psychology, 17,* 211–224.

McCary, J.L. (1978). *McCary's human sexuality.* New York: D. Van Nostrand.

McDonald, R.T. & Hilgendorf, W.A. (1986). Death imagery and death anxiety. *Journal of Clinical Psychology, 42,* 87–91.

McGrath, J.E., Kelly, J.R. & Machatka, D.E. (1984). The social psychology of time: Entrainment of behavior in social and organizational settings. In S. Oskamp (Ed.), *Applied social psychology annual 5: Applications in organizational settings.* Beverly Hills: Sage.

McLeish, J.A.B. (1976). *The Ulyssean adult: Creativity in the middle and later years.* Toronto: McGraw-Hill.

Megargee, E.I. (1971). The role of inhibition in the assessment and understanding of violence. In J.L. Singer (Ed.), *The control of aggression and violence: Cognitive and physiological factors.* New York: Academic Press.

Mehrabian, A. (1981). *Silent messages* (2nd ed.). Palo Alto, CA: Wadsworth.

Meichenbaum, D. (1974). *Cognitive behavior modification.* Morristown, NJ: General Learning Press.

Meichenbaum, D. (1985). *Stress inoculation training.* New York: Pergamon.

Meichenbaum, D. & Cameron, R. (1983). Stress inoculation training: Toward a general paradigm for training coping skills. In D. Meichenbaum & M.E. Jarenko (Eds.), *Stress reduction and prevention.* New York: Plenum.

Meichenbaum, D. & Jarenko, M.E. (Eds.). (1983). *Stress reduction and prevention.* New York: Plenum.

Meichenbaum, D., Turk, D. & Burstein, S. (1975). The nature of coping with stress. In I.G. Sarason & C.D. Spielberger (Eds.), *Stress and anxiety* (Vol. 2). Washington, DC: Hemisphere.

Melges, F.T. (1982). *Time and the inner future: A temporal approach to psychiatric disorders.* New York: John Wiley & Sons.

Melzack, R. & Wall, P. (1965). Pain mechanisms: A new theory. *Science, 50,* 971-979.

Mencken, H.L. (1969). Chrestomathy. In B. Evans (Compiler), *Dictionary of quotations.* New York: Bonanza.

Messe, M.R. & Geer, J.H. (1985). Voluntary vaginal musculature contractions as an enhancer of sexual arousal. *Archives of Sexual Behavior, 14,* 13–28.

Messersmith, C.E. (1976). Sex therapy and the marital system. In D.H. Olson (Ed.), *Treating relationships.* New York: Graphic Press.

Mesulam, M. & Perry, J. (1972). The diagnosis of love-sickness: Experimental psychophysiology without the polygraph. *Psychophysiology, 9,* 546–551.

Mihal, W.L. & Graumenz, J.L. (1984). An assessment of the accuracy of self-assessment for career decision-making. *Journal of Vocational Behavior, 25,* 245–253.

Milgram, S. (1973). Introduction. In W.H. Ittelson (Ed.), *Environment and cognition.* New York: Seminar Press.

Millay, E.St.V. (1969). Dirge without music. In B. Evans (Compiler), *Dictionary of quotations.* New York: Bonanza.

Miller, F.T., Bentz, W.K., Aponte, J.F. & Brogan, D.R. (1974). Perception of life crisis events: A comparative study of rural and urban samples. In B.S. Dohrenwend & B.P. Dohrenwend (Eds.), *Stressful life events: Their nature and effects.* New York: John Wiley & Sons.

Miller, H. (1962). *Stand still like the hummingbird.* New York: New Directions.

Miller, H.L. & Siegel, P.S. (1972). *Loving: A psychological approach.* New York: Wiley.

Miller, M.E. & Bowers, K.S. (1986). Hypnotic analgesia and stress inoculation in the reduction of pain. *Journal of Abnormal Psychology, 95,* 6–14.

Miller, M.J., Denton, G.O. & Tobacyk, J. (1986). Social interests and feelings of hopelessness among elderly persons. *Psychological Reports, 58,* 410.

Miller, M.J., Tobacyk, J.J. & Wilcox, C.T. (1985). Daily hassles and uplifts as perceived by adolescents. *Psychological Reports, 56,* 221–222.

Miller, M.J., Wilcox, C.T. & Super, B. (1984). Perceived hassles and uplifts among nursing home residents. *Psychological Report, 55,* 277–278.

Miller, R.S. (1982). Embarrassment: Situational social anxiety. Paper presented in a symposium on Recent Research in Social Anxiety: Social, Personality, and Clinical Perspectives. The Annual Convention of the American Psychological Association, Washington, DC.

Milner, J.S. & Wimberly, R.C. (1979). An inventory for the identification of child abusers. *Journal of Clinical Psychology, 35,* 95–100.

Milner, J.S. & Wimberly, R.C. (1980). Prediction and explanation of child abuse. *Journal of Clinical Psychology, 36,* 875–884.

Minuchin, S. (1974). *Families and family therapy.* Cambridge, MA: Harvard University Press.

Mischel, W. (1984). Convergences and challenges in the search for consistency. *American Psychologist, 39,* 351–364.

Mischel, W. (1986). *Introduction to personality: A new look* (4th ed.). New York: Holt, Rinehart & Winston.

Mitchell, R.E. (1971). Some implications of high density housing. *American Sociological Review, 36,* 18–29.

Morganstern, D. (1982). Toward a theory of choosing as a human function. Presidential Address, Division 32, American Psychological Association, Washington, DC.

Morokoff, P. (1978). Determinants of female orgasm. In J. LoPiccolo & L. LoPiccolo (Eds.), *Handbook of sex therapy.* New York: Plenum.

Morris, D., Callette, P., March, P. & O'Shaughnessy, M. (1979). *Gestures: Their origins and distributions.* London: Jonathan Cape.

Mosher, C.D. (1980). *The Mosher survey: Sexual attitudes of 45 Victorian women.* In J. MaHood & K. Wenburg (Eds.), New York: Arno Press.

Mosher, D.L. & White, B.B. (1980). Effects of committed or casual erotic guided imagery on females' subjective sexual arousal and emotional response. *The Journal of Sex Research, 16,* 273–299.

Myers, D.G. (1983). *Social psychology.* New York: McGraw-Hill.

Nash, O. (1975). *I wouldn't have missed it: Selected poems of Ogden Nash.* Boston: Little, Brown & Company.

Neff, W.S. (1985). *Work and human behavior.* New York: Aldine.

Niederhoffer, A. (1967). *Behind the shield: The police in urban society.* Garden City, NY: Doubleday.

Nixon, R.E. (1962). *The art of growing: A guide to psychological maturity.* New York: Random House.

Norem-Hebeisen, A.A. (1981). A maximization model of self-concept. In M.D. Lynch, A.A. Norem-Hebeisen & K.J. Gergen (Eds.), *Self-concept: Advances in theory and research.* Cambridge, MA: Ballinger.

Novaco, R. (1975). *Anger control.* Lexington, MA: Lexington Books.

Nutter, D.E. & Condron, M.K. (1985). Sexual fantasy and activity patterns of males with inhibited sexual desire and males with erectile dysfunction versus normal controls. *Journal of Sex and Marital Therapy, 11,* 91–98.

Occupational Outlook Handbook 4th Edition (1977). U.S. Department of Labor, Employment and Training Administration, 4th Ed. Washington, DC: U.S. Department of Labor.

Olson, G.A., Olson, R.D., Kastin, A.J. & Coy, D.H. (1980). The opioid neuropeptides Enkephalin and Endorphin and their hypothesized relation to pain. In W.L. Smith, H. Merskey & S.C. Gross (Eds.), *Pain: Meaning and management.* New York: SP Medical & Scientific Books.

Otto, H.A. (1968). *Group methods designed to actualize human potential: A handbook.* Chicago: Achievement Motivation Systems.

Pam, A., Plutchik, R. & Conte, H.R. (1975). Love: A psychometric approach. *Psychological Reports, 37,* 83–88.

Parkinson, C.N. (1957). *Parkinson's law.* Boston: Houghton Mifflin Company.

Parks, M.R., Stan, C.M. & Eggert, L.L. (1983). Romantic involvement and social network involvement. *Social Psychology Quarterly, 46,* 116–131.

Parlee, M.B. (1979). The friendship bond. *Psychology Today, 12* (12), 54.

Parsons, F. (1909). *Choosing a vocation.* Boston: Houghton Mifflin.

Paterson, C.R., Dickson, A.L., Layne, C.C. & Anderson, H.N. (1984). California Psychological Inventory profiles of peer-nominated assertives, unassertives, and aggressives. *Journal of Clinical Psychology, 40,* 534–538.

Patterson, M.L., Powell, J.L. & Lenihan, M.G. (1986). Touch, compliance and interpersonal affect. *Journal of Nonverbal Behavior, 10,* 41–50.

Paul, N.O. (1986). The paradoxical nature of the grief experience. *Contemporary Family Therapy, 8,* 5–91.

Peale, N.V. (1952). *The power of positive thinking.* New York: Prentice-Hall.

Pearlin, L.I. (1982). Discontinuities in the study of aging. In T.K. Hareven & K.J. Adams (Eds.), *Aging and life course transitions: An interdisciplinary perspective.* New York: Guilford.

Peck, M.S. (1978). *The road less traveled: A new psychology of love, traditional values and spiritual growth.* New York: Touchstone.

Pellegrini, R.J. (1977). Mate separation and emotional attachment in romantic love relationship: Does absence make the heart grow fonder? *Psychological Reports, 41,* 1175–1178.

Peplau, L.A. & Perlman, D. (Eds.). (1982). *Loneliness: A sourcebook of current theory, research and therapy.* New York: Wiley Interscience.

Perlman, D. & Peplau, L.A. (1982). Loneliness research: Implications for interventions. Paper prepared for a workshop on Preventive Interventions to Reduce the Harmful Consequences of Loneliness. Office of Prevention, National Institute of Mental Health, Rockville, MD.

Perls, F.S. (1969). *In and out the garbage pail.* New York: Bantam.

Peskin, H. & Livson, N. (1981). Uses of the past in adult psychological health. In D.H. Eichorn, J.A. Clausen, N. Haan, M.P. Honzik & P.A. Mussen (Eds.), *Present and past in middle life.* New York: Academic Press.

Pichl, H.A. & Clark, A.K. (1984). Congruency, achievement, and the self-directed search. *Canadian Counsellor, 18,* 79–86.

Pisano, M.D., Wall, S.M. & Foster, A. (1986). Perceptions of nonreciprocal touch in romantic relationships. *Journal of Nonverbal Behavior, 10,* 29–40.

Pitcher, S.W. & Meikle, S. (1980). The topography of assertive behavior in positive and negative situations. *Behavior Therapy, 11,* 532–547.

Plato. (1950). *The republic of Plato, translated, with an introduction by A.D. Lindsay.* New York: E.P. Dutton.

Plato (1962). *Lectures on the republic.* Edited by R. Nettelship. London: Macmillan.

Polivy, J. & Herman, C.P. (1985). Dieting and binging: A causal analysis. *American Psychologist, 40,* 193–201.

Pope, K.S. and Associates (Eds.). (1980). *On love and loving.* San Francisco: Jossey-Bass.

Pope, K.S., Keith-Spiegel, P. & Tabachnik, B.G. (1986). Sexual attraction to clients. *American Psychologist, 41,* 147–158.

Porter, L.W. (1961). A study of perceived need satisfaction in bottom and middle management jobs. *Journal of Applied Psychology, 45,* 1–10.

Power, D.J. & Aldag, R.J. (1985). Soelberg's job search and choice model: A clarification, review, and critique. *Academy of Management Review, 10,* 48–58.

Poyatos, F. (1983). *New perspectives in nonverbal communication.* Oxford: Pergamon.

Prather, H. (1977). *Notes on love and courage.* Garden City, NY: Doubleday.

Privette, G. (1981). Dynamics of peak performance. *Journal of Humanistic Psychology, 21,* 57–67.

Prochaska, J.O. (1984). *Systems of psychotherapy: A transtheoretical approach* (2nd ed.). Homewood, IL: Dorsey.

Procidano, M.E. & Heller, K. (1983). Measures of perceived social support from friends and family: Three validation studies. *American Journal of Community Psychology, 11,* 1–24.

Proshansky, H.M. (1978). The city and self-identity. *Environment and Behavior, 10,* 147–169.

Prout, M.F. & Platt, J.J. (1983). The development and maintenance of passive-aggressiveness: The behavioral approach. In R.D. Parsons & R.J. Wicks (Eds.), *Passive-aggressiveness: Theory and practice.* New York: Brunner/Mazel.

Rachman, S.J. & Wilson, G.T. (1980). *The effects of psychological therapy* (2nd ed., enlarged). New York: Pergamon.

Raskin, D.E. & Sullivan, K.E. (1974). Erotomania. *American Journal of Psychiatry, 131,* 1033–1035.

Raudsepp, E. (1980). *More creative growth games.* New York: Perigee.

Rawlins, W.K. (1983). Openness as problematic in ongoing friendships: Two conversational dilemmas. *Communications Monographs, 50,* 1–13.

Reckless, J. & Geiger, N. (1978). Impotence as a practical problem. In J. LoPiccolo & L. LoPiccolo (Eds.), *Handbook of sex therapy.* New York: Plenum.

Reese, H.W. & Smyer, M.A. (1983). The dimensionalization of life events. In E.J. Callahan & K.A. McClusky (Eds.), *Life-span developmental psychology: Nonnormative events.* New York: Academic Press.

Renwick, P.A., Lawler, E.E. & the *Psychology Today* Staff. (1978). What you really want from your job. *Psychology Today, 11*(12), 53–65, 118.

Reykowski, J. (1979). Intrinsic motivation and intrinsic inhibition of aggressive behavior. In S. Feshbach & A. Freczek (Eds.), *Aggression and behavior change: Biological and social processes.* New York: Praeger.

Reynolds, D.K. (1980). *The quiet therapies: Japanese pathways to personal growth.* Honolulu: The University Press of Hawaii.

Rice, B. (1979). Midlife encounters: The Menninger seminars for businessmen. *Psychology Today, 12*(11), 66–74, 95–99.

Richins, M.L. (1983). An analysis of consumer interaction styles in the marketplace. *Journal of Consumer Research, 10,* 73–81.

Rimm, D.C. & Masters, J.C. (1979). *Behavior therapy: Techniques and empirical findings* (2nd ed.). New York: Academic Press.

Robb, S.S. (1983). Health status correlates of pet–human association in a health-impaired population. In A.H. Katcher & A.M. Beck (Eds.), *New perspectives on our lives with companion animals.* Philadelphia: University of Pennsylvania Press.

Robinson, J.D. (1987, January 22). AIDS: Spreading the word about the dangers. *The Wall Street Journal,* p. 30.

Rodin, J. (1978). The puzzle of obesity. *Human Nature, 1*(2), 38–47.

Roe, A. (1961). The psychology of the scientist. *Science, 134,* 456–459.

Rogers, C.R. (1980). *A way of being.* Boston: Houghton Mifflin.

Rogers, D. (1979). *The adult years: An introduction to aging.* Englewood Cliffs, NJ: Prentice-Hall.

Roosens, E. (1979). *Mental patients in town life: Geel—Europe's first therapeutic community.* Beverly Hills: Sage.

Rosenbaum, A. & O'Leary, K.D. (1981). Marital violence: Characteristics of abusive couples. *Journal of Consulting and Clinical Psychology, 49,* 63–71.

Rosenberg, M. (1979). *Conceiving the self.* New York: Basic Books.

Rosenman, M.F. (1978). Liking, loving, and styles of loving. *Psychological Reports, 42,* 1243–1346.

Rosenman, R.H., Brand, R.J., Jenkins, C.D., Friedman, M., Straus, R. & Wurm, M. (1975). Coronary heart disease in the Western Collaborative Group Study: Final follow up experience of 8½ years. *Journal of the American Medical Association, 233,* 872–877.

Rosenthal, R., Hall, J.A., DiMatteo, M.R., Rogers, P.L. & Archer, D. (1979).

Sensitivity to nonverbal communication: The PONS test. Baltimore: John Hopkins University Press.

Rosenthal, R. & Jacobson, L. (1968). *Pygmalion in the classroom.* New York: Holt, Rinehart & Winston.

Rosenzweig, S. (1978). *Aggressive behavior and the Rosenzweig picture-frustration study.* New York: Praeger.

Roskies, E., Seragnian, P., Oseasohn, R., Hanley, J.A., Collu, R., Martin, N. & Smilga, C. (1986). The Montreal Type A intervention project: Major findings. *Health Psychology, 5,* 45–69.

Rotter, J.B. (1966). Generalized expectancies for internal versus external control of reinforcement. *Psychological Monographs, 81* (1, whole number 609).

Rubenstein, C. (1980). PT's survey report on how Americans view vacations. *Psychology Today, 13*(12), 62–76.

Rubenstein, C.M. & Shaver, P. (1982). The experience of loneliness. In L.A. Peplau & D. Perlman (Eds.), *Loneliness: A sourcebook of current theory, research and therapy.* New York: Wiley Interscience.

Rubin, L.B. (1976). *World of pain: Life in the working class family.* New York: Basic Books.

Rubin, Z. (1970). Measurement of romantic love. *Journal of Personality and Social Psychology, 16,* 267–268.

Rubin, Z. (1973). *Liking and loving.* New York: Holt, Rinehart & Winston.

Rudy, J.P., McLemore, C.W. & Gorsuch, R.L. (1985). Interpersonal behavior and therapeutic progress: Therapists and clients rate themselves and each other. *Psychiatry, 48,* 264–280.

Russell, D.E.H. (1982). *Rape in marriage.* New York: Collier.

Samuels, M. & Bennett, H. (1973). *The well body book.* New York: Random House & Bookworks.

Sanders, S.H. (1979). A trimodal conceptualization of clinical pain. *Perceptual and Motor Skills, 48,* 551–555.

Sarnoff, I. & Zimbardo, P.G. (1961). Anxiety, fear, and social isolation. *Journal of Abnormal and Social Psychology, 62,* 356–363.

Sartre, J.P. (1965). *Situations.* New York: George Braziller.

Satir, V. (1972). *Peoplemaking.* Palo Alto, CA: Science and Behavior Books.

Satir, V. (1978). *Too many faces.* Millbrae, CA: Celestial Arts.

Sawry, J.M. & Telford, C.W. (1963). *Dynamics of mental health: The psychology of adjustment.* Boston: Allyn & Bacon.

Scarf, M. (1980). Images that heal: A doubtful idea whose time has come. *Psychology Today, 14*(5), 32–46.

Schacter, S. (1971). *Emotion, obesity, and crime.* New York: Academic Press.

Schlossberg, N.K. (1984). *Counseling adults in transition: Linking practice with theory.* New York: Springer.

Schwartz, D. (1982, originally published 1938). All clowns are masked. Quoted by R.F. Fogelson in B. Lee (Ed.), *Psychosocial theories of the self.* New York: Plenum.

Schwartz, S. & Johnson, J.H. (1985). *Psychopathology of childhood: A clinical-experimental approach* (2nd ed.). New York: Pergamon.

Schwebel, A.I. & Cherlin, D.L. (1972). Physical and social distancing in teacher–pupil relationships. *Journal of Educational Psychology, 63,* 543–550.

Selye, H. (1976). *Stress in health and disease.* Boston: Butterworths.

Selzer, R. (1979). *Confessions of a knife.* New York: Simon & Schuster.

Shaffer, L.F. (1936). *The psychology of adjustment: An objective approach to mental hygiene.* Boston: Houghton Mifflin.

Shain, M. (1974). *Some men are more perfect than others: A book about men, and hence about women, and love and dreams.* New York: Bantam.

Shain, M. (1978). *When lovers are friends.* New York: Bantam.

Shannahoff-Khalsa, D. (1984). Rhythms and reality: The dynamics of the mind. *Psychology Today, 18*(9), 72–73.

Shaw, G.B. (1930). *Plays: XIV. Androcles and the lion; overruled; pygmalion.* New York: Wm. H. Wise.

Shaw, G.B. (1969). Parents are children. In B. Evans (Compiler), *Dictionary of quotations.* New York: Bonanza.

Sheehy, G. (1976). *Passages: Predictable crises of adult life.* New York: E.P. Dutton.

Shneidman, E.S. (1980). *Voices of death.* New York: Harper & Row.

Shull, G.R. & Sprenkle, D.H. (1980). Retarded ejaculation reconceptualization and implications for treatment. *Journal of Sex and Marital Therapy, 6,* 234–246.

Siegelman, E.Y. (1983). *Personal risk: Mastering change in love and work.* New York: Harper & Row.

Sigall, H. & Gould, R. (1977). The effects of self-esteem and evaluator demandingness on effort expenditure. *Journal of Personality and Social Psychology, 35,* 12–30.

Silk, A. (1981, October 18). The struggle of Andrew Silk: A young man confronts cancer. *The New York Times Magazine,* pp. 33–36, 92–95.

Silverstein, S. (1981). *A light in the attic.* New York: Harper & Row.

Simmel, G. (1984). *George Simmel: On women, sexuality, and love.* New Haven: Yale University Press.

Simpson, L. (1983). *People live here: Selected poems, 1949–1983.* Brockport, NY: BOA Editions, Ltd.

Singer, J. & Singer, I. (1978). Types of female orgasm. In J. LoPiccolo & L. LoPiccolo (Eds.), *Handbook of sex therapy.* New York: Plenum.

Sirkin, M.I. & Mosher, D.L. (1985). Guided imagery of female sexual assertiveness: Turn on or turn off? *Journal of Sex and Marital Therapy, 11,* 41–50.

Skinner, B.F. (1948). *Walden two.* New York: Macmillan.

Smith, M.L., Glass, G.V. & Miller, T.I. (1980). *The benefits of psychotherapy.* Baltimore: The Johns Hopkins University Press.

Smith-Rosenberg, C. (1975). The female world of love and ritual: Relations between women in nineteenth century America. *Signs, 1*(1), 1–30.

Snyder, C.R. & Fromkin, H.L. (1980). *Uniqueness: The human pursuit of difference.* New York: Plenum.

Snyder, C.R., Lassegard, M. & Ford, C.E. (1986). Distancing after group success and failure: Basking in reflected glory and cutting off reflected failure. *Journal of Personality and Social Psychology, 51,* 382–388.

Soelberg, P.O. (1967). Unprogrammed decision making. *Industrial Management Review, 8,* 19–29.

Solomon, R.C. (1981). *Love: Emotion, myth and metaphor.* Garden City, NJ: Anchor Press.

Soucie, R.M. (1979). Common misconceptions about nonverbal communication: Implications for training. In A. Wolfgang (Ed.) *Nonverbal Behavior: Application and Cultural Implications.* New York: Academic Press.

Stafford-Clark, D. (1965). *What Freud really said.* New York: Schocken Books.

Steadman, R. (1979). *Sigmund Freud.* New York: Paddington Press Ltd.

Stiles, W.B., Shapiro, D.A. & Elliot, R. (1986). Are all psychotherapies equivalent? *American Psychologist, 41,* 165–180.

Stoller, R.J. (1976). Sexual excitement. *Archives of General Psychiatry, 33,* 899–909.

Story, M.D. (1985). A comparison of university student experience with various sexual outlets. *Journal of Sex Education and Therapy, 11*(2), 35–41.

Stratton, J.G., Parker, D.A. & Snibbe, J.R. (1984). Posttraumatic stress: Study of police officers involved in shootings. *Psychological Reports, 55,* 127–131.

Strauss, M.A. (1977). Wife beating: How common and why? *Victimology: An International Journal, 2,* 443–458.

Stricker, G. (1983). Passive-aggressiveness: A condition especially suited to the psychodynamic approach. In R.D. Parsons & R.J. Wicks (Eds.), *Passive-aggressiveness: Theory and practice.* New York: Brunner/Mazel.

Striegel-Moore, R.H., Silberstein, L.R. & Rodin, J. (1986). Toward an understanding of risk factors for bulimia. *American Psychologist, 41,* 246–263.

Strupp, H.H. (1967). *An introduction to Freud and modern psychoanalysis.* Woodbury, NY: Barron's Educational Series, Inc.

Stuart, R.B. (1970). *Trick or treatment: How and when psychotherapy fails.* Champaign, IL: Research Press.

Suls, J. & Mullen, B. (1982). From the cradle to the grave: Comparison and self-evaluation across the life-span. In J. Suls (Ed.), *Psychological perspectives on the self* (Vol. 1). Hillsdale, NJ: Lawrence Erlbaum Associates.

Super, D.E. (1953). A theory of vocational development. *American Psychologist, 8,* 185–190.

Surwit, R.S. (1978). Warming thoughts for a cold winter. *Psychology Today, 12* (7), 112–115.

Sussman, N. (1976). Sex and sexuality in history. In B.J. Sadock, H.I. Kaplan & A.M. Freedman (Eds.), *The sexual experience.* Baltimore: Williams & Wilkins.

Szasz, T.S. (1970). *Ideology and insanity: Essays on the psychiatric dehumanization of man.* New York: Anchor Press.

Taylor, S.E. (1986). *Health psychology.* New York: Random House.

Teger, A.I. (1980). *Too much invested to quit.* New York: Pergamon.

Teglasi, H. & Hoffman, M.A. (1982). Causal attributions of shy subjects. *Journal of Research in Personality, 16,* 376–385.

Tennyson, A. (1872). *The poetical works.* Boston: James R. Osgood & Company.

Tesser, A. & Campbell, J. (1983). Self-definition and self-evaluation maintenance. In J. Suls & A.G. Greenwalds (Eds.), *Psychological perspectives on the self* (Vol. 2). Hillsdale, NJ: Lawrence Erlbaum Associates.

Thayer, S. (1986). History and strategies of research on social touch. *Journal of Nonverbal Behavior, 10,* 12–28.

Thomas, C.B. (1982). Stamina: The thread of human life. *Psychotherapy and Psychosomatics, 38,* 74–80.

Thompson, H. (1971). *Fear and loathing in Las Vegas.* New York: Warner.

Thoreau, H.D. (1942). *Walden, or life in the woods.* New York: Mentor.

Thurber, J. (1935). *Let your mind alone! And other more or less inspirational pieces.* New York: Grosset and Dunlap.

Tollison, C.D. & Adams, H.E. (1979). *Sexual disorders: Treatment, theory, and research.* New York: Gardner Press.

Tough, A. (1982). *Intentional changes: A fresh approach to helping people change.* Chicago: Follett.

Travis, J.W. (1977). *Wellness inventory.* Mill Valley, CA: The Wellness Resource Center.

Travis, J.W. (1981). *Wellness workbook for helping professionals.* Mill Valley, CA: Wellness Associates.

Treas, J. & Bengtson, V.L. (1982). The demography of mid- and late-life transitions. *Annals, AAPSS, 464,* 11–21.

Tucker, R.K., Weaver, R.L., Duran, R.L. & Redden, E.M. (1983). Criterion-related validity of three measures of assertiveness. *Psychological Record, 33,* 361–370.

Tucker, R.K., Weaver, R.L. & Redden, E.M. (1983). Differentiating assertiveness, aggressiveness, and shyness: A factor analysis. *Psychological Reports, 53,* 607–611.

Tunnell, G. (1984). The discrepancy between private and public selves: Public self-consciousness and its correlates. *Journal of Personality Assessment, 48,* 549–555.

Turk, D.C., Meichenbaum, D. & Genest, M. (1983). *Pain and behavioral medicine: A cognitive-behavioral perspective.* New York: Guilford.

Turkel, S. (1972). *Working.* New York: Avon.

U.S. Department of Health, Education, and Welfare, Special Task Force. (1973). *Work in America.* Cambridge, MA: The M.I.T. Press.

U.S. Department of Justice. (1983). *Report to the nation on crime and justice: The data* (NCJ-87068). Washington, DC: Bureau of Justice Statistics.

University of California, Berkeley. (1985). Laughing toward longevity. *Wellness Letter, 1*(9), 1.

Vess, J.D., Moreland, J.R. & Schwebel, A.I. (1985). A follow-up study of role functioning and the psychological environment of families of cancer patients. *Journal of Psychosocial Oncology, 3,* 1–4.

Wagner, E.E. (1962). *The Hand Test: Manual for Administration, Scoring, and Interpretation.* Akron, Ohio: Mark James Co.

Wagner, R.K. & Sternberg, R.J. (1985). Practical intelligence in real-world pursuits: The role of tacit knowledge. *Journal of Personality and Social Psychology, 49,* 436–458.

Walen, S.R. (1980). Cognitive factors in sexual behavior. *Journal of Sex and Marital Therapy, 6,* 87–100.

Walsh, N.A., Meister, L.A. & Kleinke, C.L. (1977). Interpersonal attraction and visual behavior as a function of perceived arousal and evaluation by an opposite sex person. *Journal of Social Psychology, 103,* 65–74.

Walster, E. & Berscheid, E. (1971). Adrenalin makes the heart grow fonder. *Psychology Today, 5*(1), 44–50, 62.

Watson, J.B. (1913). Psychology as the behaviorist views it. *Psychological Review, 20,* 159–170.

Watson, J.B. (1914). *Behavior: An introduction to comparative psychology.* New York: Henry Holt.

Watson, J.B. (1928). *The ways of behaviorism.* New York: Harper & Brothers.

Watzlawick, P. (1978). *The language of change: Elements of therapeutic communication.* New York: Basic Books.

Watzlawick, P., Weakland, J.H. & Fisch, R. (1974). *Change: Principles of problem formation and problem resolution.* New York: Norton.

Weiner, H. (1985). The concept of stress in the light of studies on disasters, unemployment, and loss: A critical analysis. In M.R. Zales (Ed.), *Stress in health and disease.* New York: Brunner/Mazel.

Weisman, A.D. (1972). *On dying and denying: A psychiatric study of terminality.* New York: Behavioral Publications.

Wells, B.L. (1983). Nocturnal orgasms: Females' perceptions of a "normal" sexual experience. *Journal of Sex Education and Therapy, 8,* 32–38.

West, M., Lively, W.J., Reiffer, L. & Sheldon, A. (1986). The place of attachment in the life events model of stress and illness. *Canadian Journal of Psychiatry, 31,* 202–207.

White, D.M. (1984). Changes in ego integrity status among the elderly as a function of participation in reminiscing groups. Unpublished research proposal, The University of Alabama, Tuscaloosa.

White, D.M. (1987). An investigation of the clinical features of seasonal affective disorder. Unpublished doctoral dissertation, The University of Alabama, Tuscaloosa.

White, G.L., Fishbein, S. & Rutstein, J. (1981). Passionate love and the misattribution of arousal. *Journal of Personality and Social Psychology, 41,* 56–62.

White, R.W. (1974). Strategies of adaptation: An attempt at systematic description. In G.V. Coelho, D.A. Hamburg & J.E. Adams (Eds.), *Coping and adaptation.* New York: Basic Books.

Wicklund, R.A. (1982). How society uses self-awareness. In J. Suls (Ed.), *Psychological perspectives on the self* (Vol. 1). Hillsdale, NJ: Lawrence Erlbaum Associates.

Williams, J.M. (1984). Assertiveness as a mediating variable in conformity to confederates of high and low status. *Psychological Reports, 55,* 415–418.

Wogan, M. & Norcross, J.C. (1985). Dimensions of therapeutic skills and techniques: Empirical identification, therapist correlates, and predictive utility. *Psychotherapy, 22,* 63–73.

Wolfgang, A. (1979). *Nonverbal behavior: Applications and cultural implications.* New York: Academic Press.

Wolpe, J. (1958). *Psychotherapy by reciprocal inhibition.* Stanford, CA: Stanford University Press.

Wright, R.H. (1981). Psychologists and professional liability (malpractice) insurance. *American Psychologist, 36,* 1485–1493.

Wuthnow, R. (1980). Peak experiences: Some empirical tests. In M. Bloom (Ed.), *Life-span development: Bases for preventive and interventive helping.* New York: Macmillan.

Wylie, R.C. (1979). *The self-concept* (rev. ed.): *Vol. 2: Theory and research on selected topics.* Lincoln: University of Nebraska Press.

Zee, A. (1983). Guide dogs and their owners: Assistance and friendship. In A.H. Katcher & A.M. Beck (Eds.), *New perspectives on our lives with companion animals.* Philadelphia: University of Pennsylvania Press.

Zerubavel, E. (1981). *Hidden rhythms: Schedules and calendars in social life.* Chicago: University of Chicago Press.

Zimbardo, P. (1977). *Shyness.* New York: Jove/HBJ.

Zimring, F.E. & Hawkins, G.J. (1973). *Deterrence: The legal threat in crime control.* Chicago: The University of Chicago Press.

Zuckerman, M., Eysenck, S. & Eysenck, H.J. (1978). Sensation seeking in England and America: Cross-cultural, age, and sex comparisons. *Journal of Consulting and Clinical Psychology, 46,* 139–149.

Zurcher, L.A., Jr. (1977). *The mutable self: A self-concept for social change.* Beverly Hills, CA: Sage.

Index

C